The Encyclopedia *of the*
HORSE

ELWYN HARTLEY EDWARDS

Photography by
BOB LANGRISH ✦ KIT HOUGHTON

A Dorling Kindersley Book

The Encyclopedia *of the*
HORSE

ELWYN HARTLEY EDWARDS

Photography by

BOB LANGRISH ✦ KIT HOUGHTON

A Dorling Kindersley Book

LONDON, NEW YORK, MUNICH,
MELBOURNE, DELHI

Senior Art Editor Amanda Lunn
Project Art Editor Thomas Keenes
Designers Emma Boys, Maria D'Orsi
Project Editor Antonia Cunningham
Editor Katriona John

Managing Art Editor Lynne Brown
Managing Editor Josephine Buchanan
Production Helen Creeke, Meryl Silbert

This edition revised in 2008
Editor Miezan van Zyl
DTP Designer Laragh Kedwell
Production Elizabeth Warman
Managing Art Editor Phil Ormerod
Managing Editor Sarah Larter

Produced for Dorling Kindersley by

studio cactus Ⓒ

13 SOUTHGATE STREET WINCHESTER HAMPSHIRE SO23 9DZ

First published in Great Britain in 1994
by Dorling Kindersley Limited,
80 Strand, London, WC2A ORL

This revised edition published in 2008

Copyright © 1994, 2000, 2008 Dorling Kindersley
Text copyright © 1994, 2000, 2008
Elwyn Hartley Edwards

A CIP catalogue record for this book is
available from the British Library

ISBN 978 1 4053 2148 8

Reproduced by Colourscan, Singapore
Printed and bound in China by
Toppan Printing CO (HK) LTD

Discover more at
www.dk.com

CONTENTS

Breeds are shown in *italic*

ARAB HORSES, SPAIN

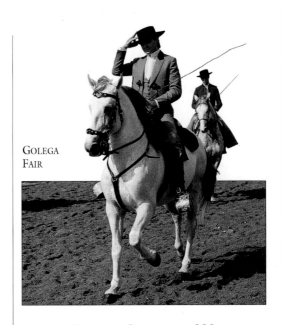

GOLEGA
FAIR

INTRODUCTION

"Man would have been a Slave had not the Horse made him a King."

THE ENCYCLOPEDIA OF THE HORSE was last updated in the Millennium year 2000. This latest revision reflects changing aspects of the horse-world since that date and provides the opportunity to examine the still-developing competitive disciplines in more depth. New material has also been included in the light of the Act of 2004, which sought to ban "hunting with dogs" in the UK. Advances made in the manufacture of horse equipment are also considered: in particular, the space-age technology employed in modern saddle production to ensure a perfect fit at every stage in the horse's physical development while still fulfilling the requirements of the rider.

Since the Millennium edition there has also been a notable extension in the range of bits available to riders over and above the conventional patterns, many of them reflecting a growing American influence. The same influence is evident in Europe in the growth of a "natural-horsemanship" lobby, although, significantly, it is less apparent in the US. These are some of the issues examined in the current edition. Otherwise, the bulk of the content adheres to the original purpose of recognizing the horse's contribution to the history of our human progression. As ever, it is offered as a tribute to the horse and an expression of gratitude and humility.

Elwyn Hartley Edwards, Chwilog

A detail from *Mares and Foals in a Landscape*, by George Stubbs (1724–1806)

HOW TO USE THIS BOOK

This book is divided into 12 historically chronological parts explaining and describing the uses to which horses have been put through the ages. They cover, in words and pictures, the development over 60 million years of the small jungle animal into the various and sophisticated breeds of the 21st century. Pages describing the history and characteristics of individual breeds are interspersed in the relevant historical section. There are also pages highlighting famous horse-and-rider partnerships or places that are significant in the horse world.

HISTORY

The development and use of the horse is traced from the early evolution of Equus to the present day.

BREEDS

The Encyclopedia illustrates over 150 individual breeds. The main image is labelled to highlight important anatomical details.

SPECIAL FEATURES

Places of interest and famous horses and their riders are highlighted and put in their historical context.

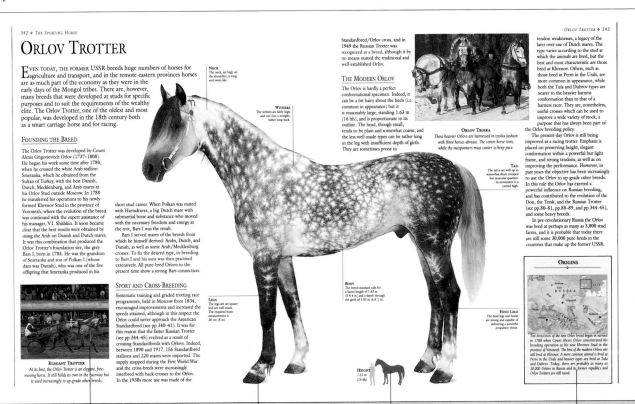

342 ◆ THE SPORTING HORSE

ORLOV TROTTER

EVEN TODAY, THE FORMER USSR breeds huge numbers of horses for agriculture and transport, and in the remote eastern provinces horses are as much part of the economy as they were in the early days of the Mongol tribes. There are, however, many breeds that were developed at studs for specific purposes and to suit the requirements of the wealthy elite. The Orlov Trotter, one of the oldest and most popular, was developed in the 18th century both as a smart carriage horse and for racing.

FOUNDING THE BREED

The Orlov Trotter was developed by Count Alexis Grigorievitch Orlov (1737–1808). He began his work some time after 1780, when he crossed the white Arab stallion Smetanka, which he obtained from the Sultan of Turkey, with the best Danish, Dutch, Mecklenburg, and Arab mares at his Orlov Stud outside Moscow. In 1788 he transferred his operations to his newly formed Khrenov Stud in the province of Voronezh, where the evolution of the breed was continued with the expert assistance of his manager, V.I. Shishkin. It soon became clear that the best results were obtained by using the Arab on Danish and Dutch mares. It was this combination that produced the Orlov Trotter's foundation sire, the grey Bars I, born in 1784. He was the grandson of Smetanka and son of Polkan I (whose dam was Danish), who was one of the five offspring that Smetanka produced in his short stud career. When Polkan was mated with Hartsdraver, a big Dutch mare with substantial bone and substance who moved with the necessary freedom and energy at the trot, Bars I was the result.

Bars I served mares of the breeds from which he himself derived: Arabs, Dutch, and Danish, as well as some Arab/Mecklenburg crosses. To fix the desired type, in-breeding to Bars I and his sons was then practised extensively. All pure-bred Orlovs to the present time show a strong Bars connection.

SPORT AND CROSS-BREEDING

Systematic training and graded trotting race programmes, held in Moscow from 1834, encouraged improvements and increased the speeds attained, although in this respect the Orlov could never approach the American Standardbred (see pp.340–41). It was for this reason that the faster Russian Trotter (see pp.344–45) evolved as a result of crossing Standardbreds with Orlovs. Indeed, between 1890 and 1917, 156 Standardbred stallions and 220 mares were imported. The supply stopped during the First World War and the cross-breds were increasingly interbred with back-crosses to the Orlov. In the 1930s more use was made of the

Standardbred/Orlov cross, and in 1949 the Russian Trotter was recognized as a breed, although it by no means ousted the traditional and well-established Orlov.

THE MODERN ORLOV

The Orlov is hardly a perfect conformational specimen. Indeed, it can be a bit hairy about the heels (i.e. common in appearance) but it is reasonably large, standing 1.63 m (16 hh), and is proportionate in its outline. The head, though small, tends to be plain and somewhat coarse, and the less well-made types can be rather long in the leg with insufficient depth of girth. They are sometimes prone to

tendon weaknesses, a legacy of the later over-use of Dutch mares. The type varies according to the stud at which the animals are bred, but the best and most characteristic are those bred at Khrenov. Others, such as those bred at Perm in the Urals, are more common in appearance, while both the Tula and Dubrov types are nearer to the heavier harness conformation than to that of a harness racer. They are, nonetheless, useful crosses which can be used to improve a wide variety of stock, a purpose that has always been part of the Orlov breeding policy.

The present-day Orlov is still being improved as a racing trotter. Emphasis is placed on preserving height, elegant conformation within a powerful but light frame, and strong tendons, as well as on improving the performance. However, in past years the objective has been increasingly to use the Orlov to up-grade other breeds. In this role the Orlov has exerted a powerful influence on Russian breeding, and has contributed to the evolution of the Don, the Tersk, and the Russian Trotter (see pp.80–81, pp.88–89, and pp.344–45), and some heavy breeds.

In pre-revolutionary Russia the Orlov was bred at perhaps as many as 3,000 stud farms, and it is probable that today there are still some 30,000 pure-breds in the countries that make up the former USSR.

ELEGANT TROTTER
At its best, the Orlov Trotter is an elegant, free-moving horse. It still holds its own in the raceway but is used increasingly to up-grade other breeds.

NECK
The neck, set high on the shoulders, is long and swan-like.

WITHERS
The withers are fairly high and run into a straight, rather long back.

ORLOV TROIKA
These heavier Orlovs are harnessed in troika fashion with three horses abreast. The centre horse trots, while the outspanners must canter to keep pace.

TAIL
The tail is set well up in somewhat short-cropped but muscular quarters. In movement it is carried high.

LEGS
The legs are set square and are well-made. The required bone measurement is 20 cm (8 in).

BODY
The breed standard calls for a barrel length of 1.61 m (5 ft 4 in) and a depth through the girth of 1.83 m (6 ft 1 in).

HIND LEGS
The hind legs and hocks are strong and capable of delivering a powerful propulsive thrust.

HEIGHT
1.63 m (16 hh)

ORIGINS

The evolution of the new Orlov breed began in earnest in 1788 when Count Alexis Orlov concentrated his breeding operation at his new Khrenov Stud in the province of Voronezh. The best of the modern Orlovs are still bred at Khrenov. A more common animal is bred at Perm in the Urals and heavier types are bred at Tula and Dubrov. Today, there are probably as many as 30,000 Orlovs in Russia and its former republics and Orlov Trotters are still raced.

THE HORSE IN CONTEXT

The smaller illustrations show the horse, or sometimes related horses, working, at rest, and in their natural environment.

BREED ILLUSTRATIONS

The main image shows an adult example of the breed. Relevant points are labelled for further information.

BREED ORIGINS

There is a map showing the country and area of origin for each horse breed. For horses developed at a particular stud or city, the stud or city alone is shown. Where two horses are shown that come from the same country, one map is used for both of them. "Types" do not have a map. Text below the map explains the breed's origins.

MAP KEY

/// Area of origin

● Major city

● City where the breed was developed

■ Stud

HEIGHT SYMBOL

The height symbol shows the height of the horse in relation to a person 1.8 m (6 ft) tall. One hand equals 10 cm (4 in).

PART ONE

THE STORY OF THE HORSE

THE STORY OF THE HORSE begins in pre-history, nearly 60 million years before the emergence of *Homo erectus*. From its small mammal beginnings, the horse, as we know it, emerged about 59 million years later. For a million years the horse herds were a source of food for the human race, their importance being recognized in the vivid cave art of Cro-Magnon Man, which is between 15,000 and 20,000 years old. Then, 5,000–6,000 years ago on the Eurasian steppes, nomadic Aryan peoples, particularly groups in those areas bordering the Black and Caspian Seas, began the process of domesticating the horse, and its development accelerated in consequence.

Cave painting of horses at Pech-Merle,
France, 20000 BC

CHARLES DARWIN (1809–82)

THE ROAD TO EQUUS

THE IDEA that animals, including humans, developed over millions of years, surviving according to their ability to adapt to the requirements of a changing environment, was first put forward in the 19th century by two British naturalists, Charles Darwin (1809–82) and Alfred Russel Wallace (1823–1913). Darwin expounded the theory of evolution, based on the "survival of the fittest", in *On the Origin of Species by Means of Natural Selection*, published in 1859. Until then the general belief was that life did not change, humans being created as humans and horses as horses – a fundamental and often inflexible stance taken by the Christian churches that depended on the account of the Creation contained in the Bible's Book of Genesis.

FINDING EOHIPPUS

Through the evidence provided by fossils, the evolution of the *equidae* can be traced from the Eocene period, some 60 million years ago, virtually to the point of their domestication in about 4000 BC. The small animal from which the modern horse has been shown to derive was called by scientists *Eohippus*, the Dawn Horse. Like everything else, it had been the subject of continual evolution. Its immediate ancestor belonged to a strain of the extinct Condylarth group, which existed about 75 million years ago and was the precursor of all hoofed creatures.

In 1867 a nearly complete skeleton of *Eohippus* was discovered in Eocene rock formations in Wyoming and it is from this and other American evidence from adjacent states that the development of the equine species can be traced. However, remains had also been found in Europe 30 years before and had been identified incorrectly as belonging to *Hyrax*, a genus of rabbit-like mammals. The animal to which they were thought to relate was called *Hyracotherium*, and this scientific title is still in current use.

The most explicit skeleton of *Eohippus* was found in 1931 in the Big Horn Basin, Wyoming, USA, and was skilfully mounted by palaeontologists at the California Institute of Technology. This reconstruction, combined with the substantive evidence offered by other remains, has to be regarded as an accurate skeletal representation of the Dawn Horse. From this evidence it has been possible for scientists to project the "probable appearance" of *Eohippus* in life.

CHARACTERISTICS

The Condylarths, from which *Eohippus* and all other hoofed animals derived, had five toes on each foot, the toes ending in very strong, thick, horny nails. Fifteen million years later the round-backed *Eohippus* was equipped with four toes on the forefeet and three behind, all terminating in thick horn. Behind the toes was a pad like that on a dog's paw. It persists in the modern horse as the "ergot", a small, horny callosity on the point of the fetlock. The broad pad, which spread the animal's weight, and the toed

THE DAWN HORSE

This is a reconstruction of Eohippus, *the Dawn Horse, from which the evolution of the horse in the New World can be traced. The average size of the animal was no bigger than a dog or a fox.*

EOCENE LANI...
The Earth and its...
something like thi...
about 60 million y...
the evolution of Eq...

the North Ameri...
development con...
starts, interposed...
scarcely perceptible...

12 ◆ THE STORY OF T...
by the central of...
indicates a g...
condition...
jungle...
st...

formation of the foot would have allowed greater ease of movement on soft soil, like that found on the floors of tropical forest and around the marshy edges of pools in that type of environment.

The eyes of *Eohippus* were set centrally in the head. This prohibited any significant degree of lateral vision, a characteristic that was only developed much later on as part of a defensive system appropriate to a far more open habitat.

Unlike the dentology to be found in the modern horse, the teeth of *Eohippus* were short-crowned, like those of pigs and monkeys. They would have been ideally suited to the consumption of soft, succulent leaves that might have been found on low-growing shrubs. Experts believe that the coat, probably similar in texture to that of a deer, would have been marked with light spots or blotches on a darker ground, thereby providing camouflage in forest surroundings and so providing defence through concealment.

These characteristics have led scientists to deduce that tropical, jungle-like surroundings were the natural environment for *Eohippus*. This assumption is supported by the fact that amongst some of its remains those of monkeys were also found.

60 MILLION YEARS AGO

The development of the equine species can be traced back to the small animal known as Eohippus, *which existed 60 million years ago. On the American continent the animal evolved in accordance with the changing environment, the stages of development culminating six million years ago, in* Pliohippus, *the single-hoofed prototype for* Equus.

The specimen restored by the California Institute of Technology stood almost 35 cm (14 in) high at the shoulder and in life would have weighed about 5.5 kg (12 lb). However, these measurements were far from being common to the species for there were numerous variations of shape and size between individuals and areas. The smallest may have been no more than 25 cm (10 in) at the shoulder, and the larger specimens were perhaps twice that size. In Europe even bigger types may have existed.

The varied versions of *Eohippus*, which spread westward and eastward over the land bridges that existed before the Glacial Age between America, Europe, and Asia, are thought to have become extinct some 35–40 million years ago, in the lower Oligocene period. The evolutionary process toward *Equus* then appears to have halted in the Old World, although pockets of strains that existed at the time may have survived until as recently as seven million years ago. On

MESOHIPPUS

The next significant development occurred in the lower and middle Oligocene period with *Mesohippus*, a recognizable enlargement of *Eohippus*, which may have stood at about 45 cm (18 in) high. The rounded back was retained, but the legs were longer in proportion and the toes on the forefeet had been reduced to three. There were the beginnings of pre-molar or incisor teeth capable of a stronger, chopping action and thus able to cope with the consumption of a greater variety of foliage.

The differences in the physical structure can be taken as adaptations reflecting a changing environment. The physical changes that occurred in *Mesohippus* point to an environment in which the jungle conditions were gradually giving way to wooded, scrub areas, probably supporting low brush and shrubs. The loss of the fourth toe, which would have caused more weight to be taken

HEIGHT
35 cm
(14 in)

HEIGHT
45 cm
(18 in)

EOHIPPUS
Eohippus *probably looked like this. It was equipped to survive in a secondary jungle-type environment as a browsing animal.*

MESOHIPPUS
Eohippus *was superseded by the larger, three-toed* Mesohippus *in the Oligocene period, 35–40 million years ago.*

FOUR-TOED
The forefeet had four toes supported by a pad.

SKULL
Short-crowned molar teeth were suited to a browsing animal.

THREE-TOED
The central toe was the most prominent.

SKULL
There are the beginnings of pre-molar, incisor teeth.

 FOUR-TOED

 THREE-TOED

BROWSERS

the three toes, also ...radual change in the ground ... As a result of the receding, wet, ... environment, the ground, though ... soft, would have been considerably firmer than previously and thus better suited to the new foot structure.

The increase in the length of leg would have produced a longer, freer movement allowing for greater speed, while the larger skull with an eye-placement further to the sides would have improved lateral vision. All these factors indicate the beginnings of a change in the defensive system, the emphasis shifting slowly away from concealment towards a mechanism based on detection and flight. While there can be no evidence to show change in the blotched coat pattern, it would not be unreasonable to assume that the stripes and blotches would have begun to fade as camouflage became less relevant.

FURTHER ADAPTATIONS

Between the end of the Oligocene period and the late, or upper, Miocene, a matter of some 15 million years, the gradual changes in climate, terrain, and vegetation continued. The jungle had given way to temperate-zone woodland and then to treeless plains and hard ground on which there would have been low growth of wiry, but nonetheless nutritious, grasses. These

environmental pressures influenced significantly the evolution of the animals leading to *Equus*, causing structural changes that increased their ability to cope with feedstuffs that would contribute to greater size and energy as well as giving them better means of escape from natural predators.

In the space of five million years or so, despite an inevitable overlap, *Mesohippus* was succeeded by *Miohippus* and then, in the lower Miocene age, by *Parahippus*, both of which were bigger and more advanced in conformation and dentology. The round, arched back that characterized the early forms of *Equus* had disappeared, and the new structure, along with even longer limbs, increased the animals' speed.

MERYCHIPPUS

In the middle and upper Miocene periods, about 25–20 million years ago, there is the important example of *Merychippus*, not yet the prototype for *Equus*, but nonetheless a most significant staging post in the progression. *Merychippus*, in general terms, measured up to and over 90 cm (36 in) at the shoulder. The animal was still three-toed but increasingly it was the central toe that bore the weight, the outside toes by then approaching the vestigial. The neck

was longer, enabling the animal to feed at ground level and raise its head higher so as to improve its range of vision. The eyes and the shape of the head were also altered so as to give an increased degree of all-round vision. Stronger, higher-crowned teeth were developed, covered in protective enamel and having a heavy cement filling to withstand the effect of the grinding action required for the ingestion of hard grasses. In addition, the animals began to complete the defence mechanism by developing the heightened senses that remain characteristic of today's naturally highly-strung horse.

Alongside the principal actors in the unfolding drama of equine evolution there existed a legion of small-part players, which were less advanced in type and destined to disappear in time according to the inexorable law of natural survival. The mammoth *Megahippus* may have survived up to the end of the Miocene period, while others, still retaining three toes, and in varied stages and forms of development were still surviving in parts of Europe and Asia up to, perhaps, seven million years ago.

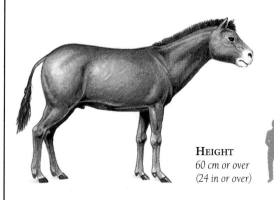

HEIGHT
60 cm or over
(24 in or over)

MIOHIPPUS
Miohippus, *a slightly more advanced form of Mesohippus in respect of feet and dentology, had evolved in the upper Oligocene period 30 million years ago.*

THREE-TOED
The outside toes still remain prominent.

SKULL
The incisor teeth are becoming more evident.

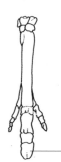

HEIGHT
90 cm
(36 in)

MERYCHIPPUS
Merychippus, *the horse of the middle and upper Miocene period, was bigger than its predecessors, and was more recognizably a horse in outline.*

THREE-TOED
Increasingly, the weight was carried on the central toe.

SKULL
The incisor teeth, suited to grazing, are now clearly defined.

THREE-TOED

BROWSERS

GRAZERS

PLIOHIPPUS

In the mid-Pleistocene period, about six million years ago, *Pliohippus*, the prototype for *Equus*, emerged. *Pliohippus* had the general proportions of the modern horse and was the first to have the powerful leg ligament controlling the single hoof. It stood about 1.22 m (48 in) at the shoulder.

The "true" horse developed from *Pliohippus* about five million years later, during the second half of the Ice Age. This horse is scientifically termed *Equus caballus*, from the word "caballine", meaning "of or belonging to horses". (The Latin *fons caballinus*, for example, relates to the fountain Hippocrene, which was fabled to have been produced by a stroke of the foot of the winged horse Pegasus: hence "fountains of inspiration" – OED.)

Pliohippus was also the source for the subgeneric group represented by zebras, domestic and wild asses, and the hemionids,

ORIGINS

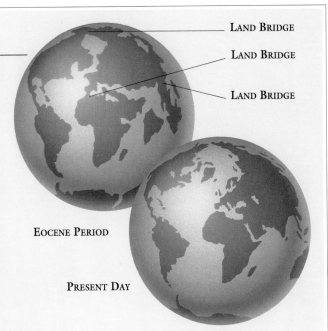

AT THE BEGINNING of the equine evolution in the Eocene period, North America, as we know it, was connected by land bridges to the mainland of Europe and Asia. That situation pertained up to the end of the final Ice Age in about 9000 BC. For perhaps a million years up to that time there were continual migrations of the species Equus to what was to become known as the Old World. However, the recession of the ice packs removed the connecting land bridges, thus isolating the American continent and leaving four related forms of Equus in the Old World. About 8,000 years ago, the horse had become extinct in America for reasons that have never been established.

LAND BRIDGE
LAND BRIDGE
LAND BRIDGE

EOCENE PERIOD

PRESENT DAY

the "half-asses" (see pp.16–17). The first true horse was in its basic structure the same as the modern horse but without the size, length of limb, and overall symmetry that are the result of centuries of artificial selection governed by man.

THE PRIMITIVE FOUNDATION

From North America *Equus caballus*, and related *equidae*, spread outwards over the existing land bridges to Asia, South America, Europe, and finally Africa. These successive migrations took place perhaps a million years ago up to about the end of the Ice Age in approximately 9000 BC. At this time the land bridge across the Bering Strait disappeared with the recession and melting of the last glacial sheet, thus isolating the American continent. Some 8,000 years ago the horse, along with the sloths and mastodons, became totally extinct there, and no explanation has been put forward to account for their disappearance. The equine species was not re-introduced into the Americas until the arrival of the Spanish conquistadores in the 16th century (see pp.216–17), when Hernán Cortés (1485–1547) landed in Mexico in 1519 with a complement of 16 horses.

Following the recession of the ice packs it is accepted that there were four related forms of *Equus*, distributed as follows: horses in Europe and Western Asia; asses and zebras in the north and south of Africa respectively; and onagers in the Middle East.

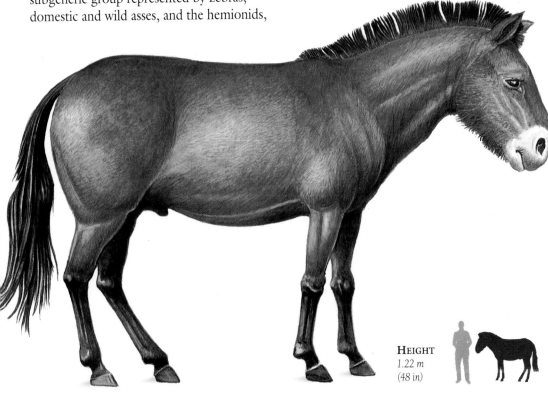

HEIGHT
1.22 m
(48 in)

PLIOHIPPUS
Pliohippus *had evolved in the lower and middle Pliocene period. This was the first single-hoofed "horse" and was the direct ancestor of* Equus.

ONE-TOED
The weight is now taken on the single, "central" toe.

SKULL
The development of the grazing teeth is now complete.

ONE-TOED

GRAZERS

FOREST HORSE

The Forest Horse, one of the founding trio of "primitive" horses, may have existed in the marshlands of Europe a million years ago.

POITEVIN

The coarse, large-footed Poitevin, hairy and heavily feathered on the lower limbs, could be regarded as the modern equivalent of the Forest Horse.

HEIGHT
*1.42–1.52 m
(14–15 hh)*

HORSE ANCESTORS

A great deal of study has been given by palaeontologists to the evolution of the horse from *Eohippus* to *Equus*, and on the whole there is general agreement on the main conclusions. Much work has also been done to establish the immediate ancestors of the domestic horse and the wild forms involved in the progression following the establishment of *Equus*. It is on this issue that acceptance of the very learned hypotheses put forward is far from being universal. Some of the difficulty and no little confusion has been caused by scientists giving different names to what, in essence, was probably the same animal, and occasionally by significantly conflicting views being expressed on particular points. Nonetheless, there is now increasing support for the theory postulating that modern horses originated from three primitive types of horse, one of which survives to this day.

Without any doubt numerous forms of *Equus* existed in the glacial and post-glacial periods, the differences being accentuated by the effects of varying environments. With the benefit of hindsight and further investigative study it now seems reasonable to attribute the foundation of the domestic horse to a) the Forest horse; b) Przewalski's Asiatic Wild Horse (see pp.18–19); and c) to the lighter and more refined Tarpan (see pp.20–21), which Professor J. Cossar Ewart of Edinburgh had called a "plateau" horse and Professor J.U. Duerst of Bern had termed a "desert" horse.

In simplistic terms it is possible to relate the existence of the present-day heavy horse breeds to the Forest Horse, allowing for some outcrossing with the coarse Asiatic Wild Horse and then later to environmental changes coupled with human intervention. The modern light horse population can be reasonably enough attributed to the Tarpan and Asiatic Wild Horse stocks, their crosses, and further subsequent derivatives.

THE FOREST HORSE

Most authorities agree that the Forest Horse (known also as *Equus caballus silvaticus*, or as the Diluvial horse, for it existed in that era) survived into post-glacial times in the probable form of *Equus caballus germanicus*. It would have stood at about 1.52 m (15 hh). It was thick-legged and heavy-bodied, weighing approximately 545 kg (1200 lb), but not as massive as the modern

ASIATIC WILD HORSE

The only surviving member of the "primitive" trio in its original form is the Asiatic Wild Horse of the Central Asian steppes, which was discovered by Colonel Nikolai Przewalski in 1879.

draught horse. It was covered in thick, coarse hair and had a heavy mane and tail, while the large, broad feet were suitable for a swamp environment. The coat colour might have been dappled and could have been made up of the red or black hairs characteristic of animals living in moist forests. Such an environment would have been provided by the forested marsh-type lands which once existed in northern Europe during successive warm (interglacial) periods. There is some evidence to suggest that a heavy type of horse, in terms of proportions if not of height, existed as long ago as the beginning of the Pleistocene period, perhaps a million years ago. Traces of a heavy, slow-moving animal that could have been a form of the Forest Horse have been found in Scandinavia and are dated as being 10,000 years old, while other findings in north-west Germany, dating from a mere 3,000 years ago, bear a marked resemblance to the massive, modern Swedish Heavy Horse and to some of the coarser heavy breeds.

THE ASIATIC WILD HORSE

The Asiatic Wild Horse is the only truly wild horse still in existence. Its scientific name is *Equus caballus przewalskii przewalskii*

Poliakov. In Mongolia it is known as the *Taki*, while the Kirghiz people call it a *Kertag*. It was discovered, or re-discovered, in the Central Asian steppes by the Russian explorer Nikolai Mikhailovitch Przewalski (1839–1888) in 1879, and was catalogued by the zoologist J.S. Poliakov in 1881.

THE TARPAN

Early evidence and information about the lighter-built Tarpan of the southern Russian steppes is extraordinarily confused and contradictory, largely because observers believed it to be a feral horse. In fact, it was a wild, primitive horse that ranged right into Eastern Europe and over the Ukrainian steppes, although by the 18th century, when it was first observed scientifically, the wild

TARPAN
The Tarpan survived in its wild form into the 19th century, when herds still ran over the Eastern European steppes. The Tarpan had a strong influence on light horse stock.

animals had mated with domestic stock. The scientific name for the Tarpan is *Equus caballus gmelini* Antonius. J.F. Gmelin was an 18th-century German-Russian scientist, and Otto Antonius, who catalogued and named the Tarpan, was a noted zoologist writing well into the 20th century.

The last wild Tarpan, a mare, died at Askania Nova (north of the Crimea, in the Ukraine) in 1880, but a "reconstituted" herd, back-bred from Tarpan-related stock, exists in a semi-wild state in the forest reserves of Popielno and Bialowieza in Poland.

THE TUNDRA HORSE

There is evidence of another wild horse, largely unconsidered by hippologists, which was called the Tundra. Horse remains have been found, along with those of mammoths, in the valley of Yana, in north-east Siberia, and sightings of groups of wild white horses in this area were reported in 1964. Scientists suggest that the smaller Yakut pony of the region could be a direct descendant of the Tundra, although the larger Yakut type is considered a derivative of the Asiatic Wild Horse. It is generally thought that the Tundra has otherwise had little or no influence on subsequent domestic stock.

TUNDRA
The Tundra is a fourth "primitive" horse but has had no influence on the subsequent equine development. Its habitat was in and beyond the Arctic Circle.

HEIGHT
1.22–1.32 m
(12–13 hh)

YAKUT
The Yakut inhabits the same area as the extinct Tundra Horse, from which it is thought to have descended. It is able to survive even in the most severe climatic conditions.

ASSES, HEMIONIDS & ZEBRAS

SOMALI WILD ASS

THE FAMILIAR grey-coated donkey or domestic ass, the two groups of wild ass (Asiatic and African), and the zebra family all belong to the genus *Equus*. However, unlike the horse, which lived in America and crossed into Asia before the disappearance of the land bridge over the North Pacific, asses and zebras originated solely in the Old World and are distinguished from the horse by specific physical characteristics. In both Egypt and Mesopotamia asses were in general use between 4000 and 3000 BC, at about the same time as the domestication of the horse was beginning in Eurasia. The Libyan tribes, for instance, living to the west of the Nile Delta, were maintaining large herds before 3400 BC, and asses were buried with their royal owners at Ur in Mesopotamia at about the same time.

THE DOMESTIC ASS

The domestic ass or donkey (*Equus asinus*) originated in North Africa, from where it has spread to almost everywhere in the habitable world. Nonetheless, it remains best suited to hot, arid countries. Its most important wild ancestor is the Nubian-Wild Ass (*Equus africanus*), which is now extinct. The name "donkey" was not used until the 18th century, and may have come from a combination of *dun*, referring to the coat colour (even though grey is the donkey's basic coloration), and *kin*, meaning small. "Jack" is the name given to the male donkey, "jennet" to the female. The average height of the common donkey is around 1.02 m (40 in) at the withers, but there are dwarf donkeys, such as those of Sicily and India, which are as small as 61 cm (24 in).

On the other hand, an Andalusian jack donkey may reach 1.52 m (15 hh). Donkeys may be black, white, or any shade of grey, and part-coloured coats are not unknown. They have a dorsal eel-stripe running down the back and a "shoulder-cross" at right angles to it over the withers. Unlike horses, donkeys have no chestnuts on their hind legs; they have five lumbar vertebrae rather than six; their ears are disproportionately long; the mane is short and upright without a forelock; and the feet are small and narrow. Their tails are tufted like a cow's, and they have flat withers that are lower than the croup. Donkeys have a gestation period of approximately 12 months (370 days), in contrast to horses, which carry their foals for a little over 11 months. Lastly, there is the animal's characteristic bray, which is quite unlike the neigh of the horse.

THE WILD ASS OF THE BIBLE
*The onager (*Equus hemionus onager*), the "wild ass" of Biblical times, is still to be found throughout the Middle East and Asia.*

HEMIONIDS

The Asiatic ass (the "wild ass" of the Bible) is often called an onager (*Equus hemionus onager*) or, in zoological terms, "hemionid", which means "half-ass". However, this term is unfortunate as it suggests an animal that is a cross between an ass and something else; it is actually meant to describe an animal that has the nature and some of the characteristics of both horse and ass, even though it has its own distinctive features as well. Probably the most notable of these features is the length of the lower leg bones, which are much longer than in any other form of *Equus*.

The sub-genus *Hemionus* is found in Western Asia, particularly Mongolia, in India, and in the Middle East. Typical of the hemionids is the Mongolian Kulan (*Equus*

JIGETAI
*The Mongolian Kulan (*Equus hemionus hemionus*), or Jigetai, as it is called locally, is found in the desert areas of Central Asia. The Kulan has some similarities with the group Asinus.*

hemionus hemionus) or *jigetai*, which means "long-eared" (there is no precise anglicized spelling). The Kulan lives in the desert areas of Central Asia. While it has some obvious similarities with the *Asinus* group, it differs from them in certain aspects: it has no shoulder stripe, although there is a dark ring around the fetlock; its ears are smaller; and its hooves are very hard, looking more like those of a horse. Its voice is also more equine than asinine. The Kulan's nostrils, perfectly adapted to the thin air of its environment, are larger than those of the horse or the domestic ass, enabling it to take in more air with each breath. Its colour varies according to the season: greyish-white in winter and a sandy red in summer, the underparts being of a lighter shade. The Kulan stands 1.22–1.32 m (12–13 hh) high.

The Tibetan sub-species Kiang (*Equus hemionus kiang*) is similar to the Kulan, but has developed characteristics suitable to its environment in the high Himalayan valleys. The Persian onager (*Equus hemionus onager*) is probably extinct in the wild state, but is preserved in zoos and reservations. It is the oldest known representative of the sub-genus, and there is ample evidence of its use by the early chariot people (see pp.32–33). The Indian onager or Ghorkar (*Equus hemionus khur*) probably still exists in the Rann of Kutch in north-west India.

THE ZEBRA FAMILY

The zebra family is distributed throughout southern Africa but only three species and a few sub-species now survive. The three

CAPE MOUNTAIN ZEBRA
The sleek Cape Mountain Zebra (Equus [hippotigris] zebra) is one of the three surviving species to be found in southern Africa. The differences between the three lie in the coat striping.

suggests, somewhat controversially perhaps, that fossil "horses" found in Los Angeles were, in fact, zebras.) Some 30,000 years ago dozens of species ranged over Europe, Africa, Asia, and North America; now the zebra family is distributed only through southern Africa and just three species survive. The Quagga, the semi-striped variety of zebra, died out in the 19th century.

GHORKAR
The very swift and enduring Indian onager or Ghorkar (Equus hemionus khur) exists in small numbers in the desert land of India's Rann of Kutch. The markings, particularly the black dorsal stripe, are very distinctive.

The most remarkable feature of this animal is its speed. R.C. Andrews, who studied the Kulan in the Gobi Desert between 1922 and 1925, reported that when pursued by a car the Kulans would set off at speeds of 56–64 km/h (35–40 mph). This is faster than their natural predators, the desert wolves, and, at 64 km/h (40 mph), faster than a Thoroughbred racehorse. One stallion averaged a speed of 48 km/h (30 mph) over 26 km (16 miles) and was only overtaken after 47 km (29 miles).

species differ in the striping of their coats as well as in other physical details. Grevy's Zebra is the largest of the group, standing at around 1.37 m (13.2 hh), and is the most handsome. It was the first to split away from the first single-hooved horse, *Pliohippus* (see pp.13–14). It is classified in the sub-genus *Dolichohippus*, while the others, which are more closely related to horses and asses, come under the sub-genus *Hippotigris*. The sleeker mountain zebra (*Equus [hippotigris] zebra*) falls into this latter grouping, along with Burchell's Zebra (*Equus [hippotigris] burchelli*), the plump little animal seen most generally in captivity.

Zebras are generally regarded as striped horses, although it is probable that early horses, up to *Equus*, had defensive striping. (One American authority, D.P. Willoughby,

GREVY'S ZEBRA
This is a splendid specimen of Grevy's Zebra. At 1.37 m (13.2 hh) these zebras are the largest of the group, and they are the most handsome.

ASIATIC WILD HORSE

BACK IN MONGOLIA
Groups of Asiatic Wild Horses bred at zoos have recently been reintroduced to their natural habitat in Mongolia.

Of THE THREE "PRIMITIVES" held to be the foundation of today's equine races, the Asiatic Wild Horse (*Equus caballus przewalskii przewalskii* Poliakov), also called Przewalski's Horse, is the only one to survive in its original form. It provides the link between the earliest types of horse and today's breeds. In prehistoric times the Asiatic Wild Horse lived on the European and Central Asian steppes east of longitude 40°, which marked the division between its habitat and that of the Tarpan (see pp.20–21). It is now preserved in a number of zoos, but selected groups have recently been returned to the wild.

DISCOVERY

There is an aura of romance and adventure about the discovery, or more accurately, the rediscovery, of the Asiatic Wild Horse. The zoologist J.S. Poliakov named the breed *Equus przewalskii* after the explorer Nikolai Mikhailovitch Przewalski, a Colonel in the army of Imperial Russia. Przewalski came across wild herds of this Mongolian horse in 1879 in the area of the Tachin Schah (the Mountains of the Yellow Horses) on the edge of the Gobi Desert. This was the area from which, six centuries earlier, Genghis Khan and the Mongol hordes had launched their violent assault upon the civilized world of the time (see pp.72–73). Przewalski was given a horse's skin obtained from local Kirghiz hunters; the Kirghiz people subsequently hunted this horse, known to them as the Taki, to the point

HEAD
The head is long and heavy with a convex profile and the eyes are set high.

MANE
The mane grows upright to a length of about 20 cm (8 in). It is very harsh and there is little or no forelock.

of extinction. Poliakov used the same skin when he made the first scientific description of this primitive equine.

Nikolai Przewalski was neither a naturalist nor a zoologist. He was an experienced military surveyor, a cartographer, and a valued agent of Czarist Russia, and was involved, like the British, in journeys of espionage in the wild, inhospitable terrain of Central Asia. The British were obsessed with the idea that Russia would attempt the invasion of India (the most important part of the British Empire) by taking a route over the Pamir Mountains and from there, on through Afghanistan. From the Caucasus mountains in the west to Tibet and China in the east, both super-powers were intent on creating a favourable power structure amongst the local rulers, while mapping the area in the interests of any future military operation.

ORIGINS

(map)
ASIA
Ulan Bator
MONGOLIA
0 800 km
0 500 miles
Hung He
Beijing
Seoul

IN PREHISTORIC TIMES *the Asiatic Wild Horse would have been found all over the European and Central Asian steppe area east of longitude 40°. By the 19th century its territory had shrunk to what is now Mongolia, with herds being noted most frequently in and around the Gobi Desert, particularly on its western edges. Colonel Nikolai Przewalski, who is credited with the discovery of the wild horse, came across herds in the area of the Tachin Schah Mountains in 1879.*

Przewalski operated in Mongolia, and later worked also in Tibet. He is almost universally credited with the discovery of the Asiatic Wild Horse, but in fact the existence of the herds had been reported many years previously. For example, the English naturalist, Col. Hamilton Smith, obtained detailed descriptions of the Wild Horse in 1814, and published his subsequent findings in a leading natural history periodical of the day, *Jardine's Naturalist's Library*.

In 1889, Russian naturalists obtained four Wild Horses at Gashun in eastern Dzungaria, on the edge of the Gobi Desert. A year later, a stallion and two mares were captured

and brought to the estate of Friedrich von Falz-Fein, a landowner at Askania Nova in the Ukraine. Within the following 12 months a large expedition was organized by Carl Hagenbach, a leading animal collector, who had been commissioned to collect specimens for the Duke of Bedford. With the help of the Kirghiz people, 17 colts and 15 fillies were captured. These horses gave zoologists the opportunity to study in detail what they soon realised was an animal with unique characteristics.

BREED CHARACTERISTICS

The Asiatic Wild Horse differs from its domestic descendant in that its chromosomes (rod-like structures that are contained in cell nuclei and are responsible for passing on hereditary characteristics) number 66 rather than 64. It also displays other particular characteristics. It is aggressive and fierce in the wild

A PRIMITIVE TEMPERAMENT
These specimens of the Asiatic Wild Horse were bred in captivity but retain much of their aggressive nature.

and is said to be migratory, moving north in the winter and returning south in the spring.

The Asiatic Wild Horse averages about 1.32 m (13 hh) in height. It is sand-dun in colour, with black legs, which are often striped like those of a zebra, and a black mane and tail. Its under-belly is cream-coloured, and there is usually a pronounced dorsal stripe, often with an accompanying cross over the shoulder. The mane is a notable "primitive" feature. It grows upright to a length of about 20 cm (8 in), unlike that of the domestic horse, which falls over one side of the neck when allowed to grow long. It also has an especially harsh texture, and there is little or no forelock. On the upper part of the tail the hairs are short, like those of a mule (see pp.330–31) or a donkey, and on the lower half they are long and coarse. The horse's head is long and heavy, with a

ZOO-BRED
Shown here are a Wild Horse mare and foal. The horses were saved from extinction by being kept in numerous zoological parks throughout Europe.

straight profile that inclines to convexity, and eyes set high, close to the ears. The colour of the hair around its eyes and muzzle is paler than the rest of the coat. The animal is straight-backed, like the onager, zebra, and the kulan (see pp.16–17), with which it often used to be confused, and it has no discernible withers. Although it obviously resembles the asinine group of *Equidae*, the Asiatic Wild Horse is essentially a member of *Equus caballus*. Its similarities to the asinine group simply denote their close proximity to a common root.

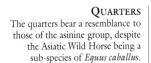

QUARTERS
The quarters bear a resemblance to those of the asinine group, despite the Asiatic Wild Horse being a sub-species of *Equus caballus*.

TAIL
The tail, like the mane, is of harsh, black hair.

LEGS
The lower legs are black, sometimes with "zebra bars".

HEIGHT
1.32 m
(13 hh)

THE TARPAN

YOUNG TARPAN

THE TARPAN (*Equus caballus gmelini* Antonius) has been a subject of confusion for over a century. This has largely been due to conflicting views put forward by eminent scientists. In fact, "tarpan" (which literally means "wild horse") was the name used, somewhat indiscriminately, by naturalists to describe both the East-European animal (now known as the Tarpan) and the Asiatic Wild Horse (see pp.18–19) – hence an understandable confusion. However, the weight of scientific opinion recognizes that the Tarpan is a true wild horse, separate from the Asiatic Wild Horse, and also one of the ancestral horse types of the post-glacial period (see pp.14–15). Indeed, the Tarpan is generally considered to be closer to the modern horse (*Equus caballus*) than is the Asiatic Wild Horse (*Equus caballus przewalskii przewalskii* Poliakov).

THE ORIGINAL TARPAN

Without question, the Tarpan, in its original, unadulterated form, had been hunted almost to extinction by the late 18th century, although Tarpans of mixed blood were numerous. This mixed stock was the result of cross-breeding between wild stallions and domesticated mares. In any event, the mares were closely related to the wild stock.

The only depiction of an original Tarpan is a drawing from life of a yearling filly by an artist called Borisow. It was published in 1841 and provided the basis for subsequent illustrations, notably those of Friedrich Specht in Brehm's *Life of Animals*, published in 1896. Borisow's picture shows a slender-legged animal, very much more refined in the head than the Asiatic Wild Horse, but with a pronounced convex profile. The overall impression is of a horse that evolved in dry, steppe-like conditions.

The Tarpan was given its scientific name, *Equus caballus gmelini* Antonius, by Helmut Otto Antonius, Director of the Schonbrunn Zoological Garden in Vienna. He named it after S.G. Gmelin, a naturalist who captured four wild specimens near Bobrowsk in Russia in 1768. Gmelin described these horses as being mouse-coloured with prominent black points and "disproportionately thick" heads, presumably referring to the pronounced convex profile of the specimen that had been drawn by Borisow. He noted that the ears were sometimes long as in the ass, and "hanging", which might mean that the animals were "lop-eared".

Helmut Otto Antonius was among the most astute and talented scientific investigators of his day. Writing in 1922, he

ARTIST'S IMPRESSION
This picture of Tarpan mares and foals by Friedrich Specht dates from the end of the 19th century. It is evidently based on the only known drawing of a Tarpan from life which was made by an artist named Borisow, and published in 1841.

made the comment that the Tarpan "was a genuine type of wild horse and, as such, of greatest importance in connection with the origin of the domestic horse". Antonius was responsible for separating out those horses that descended from the Asiatic Wild Horse and those that descended from the Tarpan. To the Asiatic Wild Horse he attributed the present-day Mongolian pony, and the ponies of Tibet, which include the characteristically large-headed ponies, such as the Spiti (see pp.202–3) and the Bhutan (both related to the Tibetan ponies). This group also includes the ponies of the Himalayan foothills and the Manipur of Assam; the ponies of Indochina and Indonesia (see pp.204–9); and the little known Japanese ponies, the Hokkaido, Kiso, and Kagoshima, the one-time wild horses of southern Kyushu (see pp.212–13).

INFLUENCE

While allowing the Asiatic Wild Horse a dominant presence in some of the steppe breeds of Eastern Europe and Western Asia, (such as the Russian Bashkir for example – see pp.200–1), Antonius considered the Tarpan influence to have extended from the Carpathian Mountains right through to Turkestan, an area which takes in the Ukraine, home to the tough Konik and Huçul horses (see pp.194–95). These horses are very closely related to the Tarpan, and in one form or another provided a base for the "noble" Trakehner horse (see pp.140–41). The area also includes the steppe-land (vitally important in terms of equine and equestrian development) around the Caspian and Black Sea, as well as Kirghizia, Kazakhstan, and western Turkestan.

From there it runs down into the Iranian plateau, the home of Persian horses of pronounced Arab type, which also have a relationship with Turkmenes and the other "desert" horses of Central Asia. Therefore, it is not too far-fetched to suggest that

HUÇUL   KONIK

TARPAN DESCENDANTS
The Tarpan influence extended over all of the Ukraine and it is thought that the Huçul and Konik ponies are both descendants of this primitive wild horse. They are the basis for the back-bred "reconstituted" Polish Tarpan herds.

the Tarpan is a far-off ancestor of the Arab (see pp.64–65). Several authorities support this theory and suggest that the Tarpan must have been the basis for the chariot horses of the eastern Mediterranean. This would also provide a connection with the Caspian stock of Iran (see pp.36–37).

Moving back into Europe there is evidence of the Tarpan influence in the evolution of the Spanish Horse, since the base stock, provided by the Sorraia ponies (see pp.106–7), is of Tarpan descent.

THE MODERN TARPAN

The modern, back-bred Tarpan has evolved by the use of selected Konik and Huçul stock, so that it resembles the original wild Tarpan. Most specimens stand at about 1.32 m (13 hh), and are mouse- or brown-dun with prominent dorsal stripes and zebra marks on the legs, which sometimes appear as stripes on the body. The coat turns white in winter, a feature of many wild animals, and is wiry in texture, like that of a deer.

The Tarpan is the perfect example of "primitive vigour". It is extremely hardy, and independent to the point of being fierce, with strength out of proportion to its size, and great qualities of endurance and stamina.

THE MODERN PRIMITIVE
The modern Tarpan is probably an accurate replica of the original wild horse. It has the curious deer-textured dun coat and the straight, asinine back. It is rarely ill, wounds heal quickly, miscarriage is unknown, and the fertility rate is higher than in domestic animals.

FOUR BASIC TYPES

THERE IS NO DOUBT about either the existence, or the ancient wild origin, of the Asiatic Wild Horse and the Tarpan (see pp.18–21). Similarly, there is ample evidence of the Forest Horse (see pp.14–15). The theory of four, further, secondary foundation lines is probably best viewed as a later extension of this tripartite theory, with the four types originating in crosses based on the initial three horses and their derivatives. The postulated existence of two pony and two horse types just before domestication, which is thought to have taken place in Eurasia, 5,000–6,000 years ago, may be seen to provide another link in the evolutionary chain and could be a possible explanation of the post-glacial development of the horse.

PROPONENTS OF THE THEORY

The theory of four post-glacial horse types was first suggested by J.G. Speed of Edinburgh, E. Skorkowski of Cracow, F. Ebhardt of Stuttgart, and the Portuguese authority R. d'Andrade, all of whom are acknowledged as leading experts in the field of equine pre-history.

Working 50 years after Ewart (see pp.14–15) and with the advantage of improved technology, the Speed group did not classify their suggested post-glacial horses as named species. They were content to refer to them as types. Nor, which would have been unthinkable, did they preclude specifically or by inference the existence of other sub-species or types alongside those delineated. Both the Asiatic Wild Horse and the Tarpan would have existed in their own recognized form as well as in combination, while the more shadowy Forest Horse was still continuing its development, as evinced by remains found in the north-west of Germany and Scandinavia.

THE PONY TYPES

The Speed group suggested that four types had evolved by the time domestication was taking place, and these would have exerted a powerful influence on subsequent domestic stock. The first of these was Pony Type 1, which became established in north-west Europe. In essence this was Ewart's Plateau or Celtic Pony, which, it is assumed, evolved from predominantly Tarpan stock. It averaged between 1.22–1.27 m (12–12.2 hh), and was brown or bay in colour.

Speed and his colleagues introduced another feature in their projection of the post-glacial horses – that of resistance to the elements. This Type 1 Pony was resistant to wet conditions and was to all intents and purposes waterproof, a characteristic of its nearest modern equivalents, the Exmoor Pony (see pp.174–75) and certain strains of Icelandic Horse (see pp.196–97).

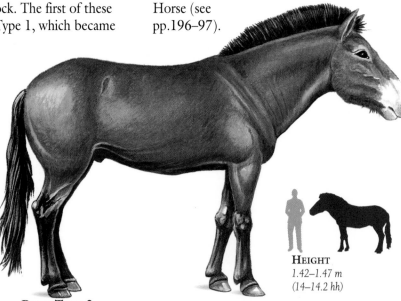

PONY TYPE 1

Pony Type 1 is thought to have lived in north-west Europe and developed a resistance to wet and cold. The modern equivalent is the Exmoor.

HEIGHT
*1.22–1.27 m
(12–12.2 hh)*

EXMOOR

PONY TYPE 2

Pony Type 2 was bigger than Type 1. It resembled the Asiatic Wild Horse, was resistant to cold, and lived in northern Eurasia. Its modern counterpart is the Highland Pony.

HEIGHT
*1.42–1.47 m
(14–14.2 hh)*

HIGHLAND PONY

Pony Type 2 was a larger specimen standing at around 1.42–1.47 m (14–14.2 hh). It inhabited northern Eurasia and was resistant to cold and frost. It was more heavily built than Type 1, coarse and heavy-headed with a convex profile. It would have trotted more easily than it galloped. It was dun-coloured, ranging into yellow, and had a pronounced "eel" or dorsal stripe. In fact, it looked very similar to the Asiatic Wild Horse. However, it did not have the same chromosome count, chromosomes being the rod-like structures that pass on hereditary characteristics. Unlike the Asiatic Wild Horse, which has 66, Type 2 had 64, like the modern domestic horse. The nearest modern equivalents to Pony Type 2 are the Highland Pony, the Norwegian Fjord, and perhaps the ancient Noriker breed of the sub-Alpine region (see pp.178–79, pp.192–93, and pp.50–51), although the Noriker was also influenced by the primitive Forest Horse.

THE HORSE TYPES

So far, Speed and his colleagues had simply refined previous theories. Now, they added a new element of vital import – the postulated existence of "desert" horses that would make possible the evolution of most of the present-day breeds and types.

Their Type 3 was indubitably a horse and, moreover, a desert horse, for by virtue of its environment it was both resistant to heat and drought. The spare frame, devoid of fatty tissue, the thin skin, and the ultra-fine coat allowed it to withstand the effects of heat and enabled it to go for long periods without water. It had an unprepossessing appearance, measuring about 1.50 m (14.3 hh), with a long, narrow, slab-sided body, long neck, and long ears. Its feet were broad and shallow, which is one way of coping with soft sand underfoot. It was goose-rumped, with the sparse mane and tail to be expected of an animal characterized by sinew and muscle and a complete absence of superfluous fat. Its habitat was Central Asia, extending westwards in pockets into Spain. Present-day breeds which resemble it most are the clay-coloured Sorraia of Portugal/Spain (see pp.106–7), which is held to have originated with Tarpan stock, and the more elegant Akhal-Teke (see pp.74–75) of the Turkmenistan desert.

The origin of Type 3 can be no more than a matter of conjecture. There is, of course, the underlying influence of the Tarpan and perhaps also, to a lesser degree, that of the Asiatic Wild Horse, through

subsequent crossings of their derivatives about which nothing is known. What is clear is that the environment was a prime influence in fixing the type and special character, albeit over huge periods of time.

Finally, there was Type 4, another horse in respect of proportions, despite being small in stature. It stood no more than 1.22 m (12 hh), and was finely boned, with none of the coarseness of Type 3. It had a refined, "quality" head, with a straight profile, which sometimes inclined towards being concave. The mane, tail, and body hair were fine and silky. The croup was flat-topped and in line with the withers, and the tail was high-set. It was native to Western Asia and like Type 3 was resistant to heat. Again, there can be no definitive explanation of its origin, but it certainly existed in that area and at that time – facts proved by both the analysis of remains and the later evidence of artefacts.

The overriding impression is of a small horse influenced by Tarpan-type stock, refined by the pressures of a dry, heat-orientated environment. It is more difficult to see any evidence of the Asiatic Wild Horse. This type is proffered, if tentatively, as a prototype Arab, and the Caspian (see pp.36–37) is seen as its nearest modern equivalent.

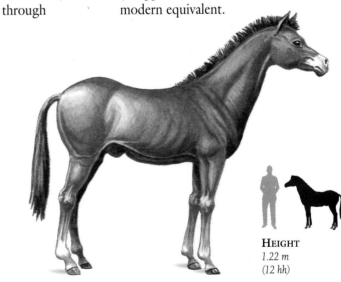

HEIGHT
*1.50 m
(14.3 hh)*

HEIGHT
*1.22 m
(12 hh)*

HORSE TYPE 3

Horse Type 3 was a desert horse resistant to heat and drought, living in Central Asia. There might have been a Tarpan influence. The Akhal-Teke is the modern equivalent.

AKHAL-TEKE

HORSE TYPE 4

Horse Type 4 was a small, fine-boned, heat-resistant desert horse. It lived in Western Asia. The influence is Tarpan and the Caspian is the modern equivalent.

CASPIAN

THE MODERN HORSE

GREGOR MENDEL

THE EVOLUTION of the horse extends over 60 million years and like that of all living creatures was governed for the greater part of that time by the process of natural selection, i.e. survival of the fittest or, more accurately, survival of those best fitted to adapt to changing circumstances. Of equal importance were the inescapable pressures exerted by the environment. Domestication of the species introduced human intervention into the natural process. From then on the evolution of the horse into the breeds and types of today was accelerated dramatically. The modern horse is the product of selective breeding supported firstly by advances in both agricultural and commercial practices, which produced quantities of nutritional foodstuffs, and secondly by continually improving methods of management.

CLASSIFICATIONS

The principal division in the modern species is between light horses, i.e. those used under saddle or as carriage horses, and the heavy agricultural breeds. The former are by far the most numerous. In the light horse section there is the sub-division between horse and pony. The word "pony" is of comparatively recent origin, deriving from the 17th-century French *poulenet*, which means a foal. Ponies are considered, perhaps arbitrarily, to be breeds and types below 1.52 m (15 hh). In reality, the difference between horses and ponies is primarily one of proportion. In the Thoroughbred horse (see pp.120–21), for instance, the distance from wither to ground exceeds the length of the body largely because of the length of the legs. In contrast, the pony is usually deeper through the body and shorter-legged in relation to its height.

A further distinction, and one that is often a source of confusion, is made between horses that are "hotbloods", "coldbloods", and "warmbloods". The Arab (see pp.64–65), and the possibly less well-developed Barb (see pp.66–67), are termed "hotbloods", along with their direct derivative, the Thoroughbred. The title indicates a unique purity of line possessed by no other breed of horses in the world. "Coldblood" is the term given to the heavy draught horses of Europe. Horses combining cold and hot blood in various percentages are called "warmbloods". Hot- and warmbloods are for the most part long in the limbs and general proportions, and narrow in the body. Conversely, the coldblood is notable for a vertically deeper chest and has shorter, thicker legs than warmblood horses of the same shoulder height. Their feet, in relation to the length of their faces, are very broad.

In the modern context, a breed refers to horses registered in a stud book. These are horses that have been bred selectively over a long enough time to ensure a consistent production of stock sharing common and defined characteristics in respect of size, conformation, action, and also possibly colour. Types are those horses that do not qualify for breed status because they lack a fixed character and are not, in consequence, entered in an accepted breed stud book. Notable examples are polo ponies, hunters, hacks, and cobs (see pp.372–73, pp.394–95, pp.404–5, and pp.410–11).

HEREDITY

A massive contribution, which added another dimension to the understanding of evolution, was made by an Austrian monk, Gregor Mendel (1822–84). He is

HEAVY HORSE
The proportions and the broad, thick structure of the heavy draught horse contrast directly with those of the Thoroughbred, and allow for the exertion of great strength at slow speeds.

LIGHT HORSE
The outline of the Thoroughbred horse is characterized by the length of the limbs and general proportions. The body is narrow and the shoulders are notably sloped.

PONY
Pony proportions are unique. The body length exceeds the height at the withers, and its depth equals the leg length. The length of the head equals the shoulder length, and the latter equals the back measurement.

POLL

FORELOCK

CHEEK
BONE

JOWLS

MUZZLE

CHIN GROOVE

THROAT

JUGULAR GROOVE

MANE | CREST

WITHERS

GIRTH | BACK

FLANK

POINT OF
CROUP

POINT OF
BUTTOCKS

ROOT OF TAIL

LOINS

CROUP

POINT OF
SHOULDER

BREAST

PECTORAL
MUSCLE

ELBOW

FOREARM

KNEE

CANNON
BONE

CORONET

HOOF

BELLY

BRISKET

CHESTNUT

TENDON

ERGOT

PASTERN

HEEL

STIFLE

QUARTERS

HOCK

SEAT OF CURB

SHANK

FETLOCK JOINT

POINTS OF THE HORSE

*The points of the horse are the external features,
which make up its conformation. No one feature
should be out of proportion with any of the others.*

responsible for the Mendelian Law
governing hereditary characteristics, which
is the basis for modern genetic science.
Briefly, each of the millions of cells making
up the body structure of a living creature
contains a pair of genes, one from each
parent. Through these genes characteristics
are passed on to the offspring, but not in
equal measure. Of the two genes, one is
dominant and one recessive. It is the
dominant gene that will prevail in the new
creature. As an example, a rudimentary
knowledge of colour genetics enables
breeders to predict the coat colour of an
unborn foal. It is known that grey, for
example, is dominant to all other colours.
The order of dominance for the other
colours is bay, brown, black, and chestnut.
Bay is thus dominant to the colours
following it, whereas chestnut is always
recessive. Therefore, while two chestnut
horses will produce a chestnut foal, a
chestnut crossed with another colour is less
likely to do so. Accepting this simple genetic
principle, it follows that it may be possible
for physical and mental characteristics, such
as jumping or racing ability for example, also
to be transmitted within a carefully
formulated bloodline.

Breeding on the basis of documented
pedigrees and performance records as well
as taking into account the proven ability of
the progeny of both parents, i.e. genotype
breeding, represents the practical application
of the genetic theory. It is central to both
the breeding of the Thoroughbred racehorse
and of Europe's competition warmbloods
(see pp.124–25).

COAT COLOURS

GREY Black skin with
a mixture of black and
white hairs

PALOMINO Golden
coat, white mane and
tail, minimum of black

BAY Reddish-brown
coat, black mane, tail,
and points

STRAWBERRY-ROAN
Chestnut coat with
white hairs

SPOTTED
This is often called
Appaloosa colouring

FLEABITTEN Brown
specks of hair flecking
an otherwise grey coat

CHESTNUT Various
shades of gold, from
pale gold to red-gold

BROWN Mixed black
and brown hairs; black
mane, tail, and legs

BLUE-ROAN Black
or brown body with
some white hair

SKEWBALD Large
white patches with any
colour except black

DAPPLE-GREY
Dark grey hairs form
rings on a grey base

LIVER-CHESTNUT
The darkest of the
chestnut shades

BLACK Black hair,
occasionally with
white marks

DUN Yellow, blue, or
mouse, depending on
diffusion of pigment

PIEBALD Usually
irregular, large areas
of black and white

PART TWO

EARLY USE

THE DOMESTICATION OF THE HORSE altered the whole concept of human life. Essentially, it conferred a hitherto inconceivable mobility on what had of necessity been a static society limited by basic considerations like the supply of constant water, for example. The use of horse-power removed the labour involved in transportation of a people's possessions, and immeasurably increased the range of available pasture. Furthermore, the horse herds, which in themselves provided the necessities of life – milk, meat, hides, and even dung for burning on fires – resulted in the development of horse cultures that had far-reaching effects upon human history.

Detail of harvest sequence in the tomb of Menna, Egypt, c.1415 BC

DOMESTICATION

FERAL STOCK

OF ALL the domestic animals, the horse was the last to be tamed. This may have been on account of its size, or maybe its unpredictable, highly-strung temperament, which would have made it difficult to catch and tame, although it was certainly hunted. The dog, the first animal to be domesticated, was tamed around or before 12000 BC, and was, as a carnivore, a natural ally in hunting. Sheep, which in certain areas were being kept in flocks by about 9000 BC, suited pastoral people who had given up the nomadic life to live in settled communities. By 7000 BC goats, pigs, and poultry were also being kept as domestic animals. Poultry was used in sacrifice and it has even been suggested that they were first domesticated for this purpose rather than for eggs and meat.

HUNTING HORSES

Before domestication the wild horse herds were a convenient source of food for primitive people in the later stages of the Ice Age, c.10000 BC. The favoured methods employed for killing horses were to drive a group of them into a natural cul-de-sac where the animals could be clubbed to death, or to drive them over a convenient cliff, which was easier.

Huge depositories of bones at sites such as Solutré and Lascaux in France, and cave drawings at Lascaux and at Santander in Spain (c.13000 BC) show that people were familiar with the nature of the horse long before it was domesticated. Essentially the paintings were used to indicate the presence of horses in the area to other nomadic hunters, although they may also have had some kind of spiritual significance.

In areas such as the river valleys of the Tigris and Euphrates in Iraq, crops were beginning to be cultivated by 9000 BC and as the agricultural lifestyle spread, so too did the practice of enclosing animals, or at least practising animal husbandry on a restricted or semi-open range. In that situation there was really no advantage in possessing a horse herd, even if one was available. The animals that the settlers already had provided food and products such as skins and milk, and were, moreover, much more tractable than horses. Cattle could work in a primitive form of draught and be used as pack animals.

HORSE DOMESTICATION

It is impossible to be precise about the date of horse domestication, but substantial evidence suggests that they were first tamed in Eurasia about 5,000–6,000 years ago, towards the end of the Neolithic period. The people primarily concerned are thought to have been nomadic Aryan tribes, speaking Indo-European languages, who moved about the steppes bordering the Caspian and Black Seas. However, it is possible that domestication was simultaneously taking place in other parts of Eurasia. By this time (4000–3000 BC), these Aryan tribes would have been used to herding animals. Initially

HORSE SLAUGHTER
Huge depositories of bones were found beneath the cliffs at Solutré, France. This 19th-century artist's impression is imaginative but far-fetched.

CAVE MESSAGE
The wall-drawing shown here is at Lascaux, France, and is probably 15,000 years old. Such drawings represent an early form of communication and probably indicate the presence of horses in the area.

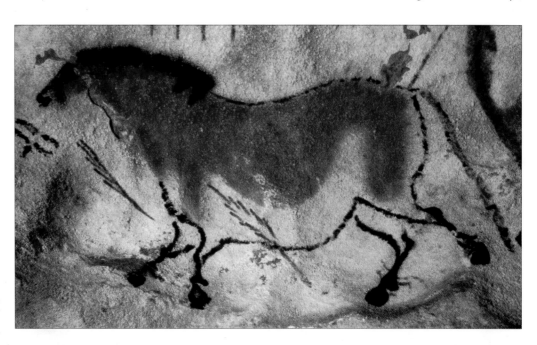

it would have meant simply following wild or semi-wild flocks of sheep, goats, or even herds of reindeer. Reindeer would have been ideal to follow for they are migratory animals, not wandering ones, their movement depending on finding the "reindeer moss" on which they feed.

It is possible that the reindeer may have been the precursor to the domestic horse. Firstly, the great reindeer herds lived in the area from the Great Wall of China to Outer Mongolia where all the horse cultures subsequently became established. The reindeer only later moved north towards the Arctic. Secondly, the reindeer herders had already grasped the concept of domestication 2,000 years before the horse was domesticated. It is known, for example, that by 5000 BC reindeer in Northern Europe were pulling sledges. Moreover, studies made in the 19th century suggest that they were also being bred and ridden.

Therefore, when horses became more numerous in the harsh steppe-lands it would have been only a short step to switch from keeping reindeer to keeping horses. Horses had more advantages. They did not follow a fixed migratory cycle and could be herded wherever the nomads wished. They were also better equipped than reindeer and other smaller animals to find food on the harsh, cold steppe, since they could dig for food lying under the snow with their hooves.

It is also interesting to note that the saddlery, for example, of reindeer people who still exist today such as the Uryanchai who live in Siberia, has not changed for thousands of years, and bears a remarkable resemblance to that used in early horse cultures. Keeping all this in mind, it is

REINDEER CULTURE
Modern reindeer in Lapland feed on a type of lichen known as "reindeer moss", which forms their staple diet. Steppe nomads were the first herders of the migratory reindeer.

ALTAI TREASURE
This highly decorative bridle was perfectly preserved when it was excavated from the Pazyryk burial mounds in the Altai Mountains of western Siberia. It is decorated with images of reindeer.

MODERN MONGOLIA
It is probable that the far-off ancestors of this modern-day Mongolian horseman were herders of reindeer before they herded and rode horses.

possible that the first steppe nomads were herders, drivers, and riders of reindeer before they kept horses.

THE PAZYRYK CONNECTION

Another possible connection between reindeer and horse domestication was provided in 1929 by the discovery of deep-frozen tombs in Pazyryk, high in the Altai Mountains in western Siberia. These tombs, excavated by Dr S.I. Rudenko, were one of the most remarkable discoveries of the 20th century. They belonged to the Scythians, one of the first and most significant of the horse peoples, and provide evidence that they had a history of horse husbandry extending back to about 3000 BC.

The contents, preserved by the ice exactly as they were 3,000 years ago on the day they were buried, included horses decorated with face-masks. Some of these transformed the head into that of a reindeer, complete with antlers. These items and others decorated with images of reindeer seem to suggest that before these fierce steppe warriors tended horses, they may have tended reindeer.

DIFFERENT THEORIES

There are authorities who find the theory of the reindeer–horse progression totally unacceptable. One school of thought believes that it was cattle and their acknowledged use in draught that provided the inspiration for the domestication of the horse.

Another suggests that onagers, which were widely used in Mesopotamia to draw chariots long before horses were employed, were the precursor. However, there were no

horses in this area until contact was made with the horse-riding, horse-herding nomads from the steppes in the north-east, who had obviously already begun to domesticate the horse. Once contact was made, it is true that the onager, a temperamentally difficult animal, was quickly replaced by the horse, which for a short period, according to the Greek geographer, Strabo, was controlled from a nose ring in the same fashion as the Sumerian onager of the third millennium BC.

STANDARD OF UR

The great Standard of Ur of the Chaldees is dated at c.2500 BC when the Sumerians were using solid-wheeled chariots drawn by onagers rather than horses. The javelin or thrusting spear seems to have been the principal weapon.

REINDEER MASK

This face-mask was worn by one of the horses interred in the Pazyryk barrows. It transformed the horse's head into that of a reindeer. Was this a backward glance at an earlier culture – a reminder of the time when a horse-people were herders of reindeer?

QUALITY HORSES

A fragment of an Egyptian relief dated c.1360 BC shows a sophisticated bitting arrangement and yoke-type harness pads. These quality horses are of Arab type.

Other authorities reject the reindeer theory on the grounds that the management of a placid migratory animal is too dissimilar to that of the more highly strung and non-migratory horse. But that is the view of learned modern scholars with little or no practical experience of animal management. The early, primitive, animal-orientated societies were intuitive in their relationships with animals and the natural world, and were remarkably adaptable. People used to the management of reindeer would have had little difficulty in making the change to the more versatile horse. The similarities between the herders of reindeer and the keepers of horses are too numerous to be merely coincidental.

THE FIRST DOMESTIC HERDS

In the first domestic horse herds, stallions would have been excluded because of their disruptive potential. Breeding would have taken place by tying out in-season females who would have attracted wild stallions to breed with them – a practice still carried out in parts of the world where feral and semi-feral stocks still exist. Young males would have provided meat, or they would have been been gelded, a practice intended to diminish their aggressive drive and ensure that they were amenable for other purposes. Fillies were more easily managed, and in time became milk producers and mothers.

HORSE-RIDING

Horse-riding may have started purely by chance: perhaps someone tending a herd of horses realized the advantage of four legs over two, and, climbing astride a quiet old mare, unknowingly became the first horse rider. Once on horseback, herding would have become much easier. A man galloping on horseback is better able to hold a herd together, heading off would-be breakaway elements, than one attempting the same task on foot. A mounted man is also able to lead the herd, so long as he has a pair of "whippers-in" to hold the

SADDLE CLOTH
This Scythian saddle cloth from Pazyryk is intricately decorated with a pattern of animals and mythical beasts. The cloth has the further macabre decoration of human scalps on the lower edge.

flanks and bring up the rear. Once a tribe learned to ride horses, and to use them to carry packs and draw sleds, mobility and speed were vastly increased and the tribe had access to a greater range of feeding grounds.

THE SPREAD OF THE HORSE

All the evidence underlines the fact that the domestic horse spread westward from the high steppe lands of Central Asia, into Central and Western Europe, then into the Caucasus and beyond, and south and east into Arabia and China.

For the next 4,000 years the horse was to be the swiftest, most efficient form of transport and communication, and the use of horses was to make possible the founding and extension of civilized life.

SCYTHIAN ART
This detail is from a felt wall-hanging found in the the frozen tombs at Pazyryk, which date from the 5th–4th century BC. The horseman has an 18th-century air about him!

CHARIOTS & HORSE PEOPLES

ASSYRIAN CHARIOT

WHETHER HORSES were first employed in wheeled vehicles or were ridden is often a matter for discussion. The answer is that it all depended on the terrain. In the flat, open country of Syria, Egypt, and the valley lands of Iraq, wheeled vehicles were more practical. The horses were too small to be ridden comfortably, but a pair harnessed to a light chariot provided transport for two or even three people. In mountainous country it was easier to ride, even though the horses were small. What is known is that wheels appeared at a very early date, long before the invention of saddles and stirrups, and were probably in use some time before general horse domestication. Solid wheels have been found in Sumerian graves excavated in the Tigris-Euphrates valley in present-day Iraq, which date from 3500 BC.

HORSE PEOPLES

During the third and second millennia BC, the nomadic peoples of the steppes had created societies based around horses, which they herded, and probably would have ridden as well. As their herds grew, so too

did their need for more extensive grazing areas. They also needed commodities, such as iron and salt, which they could only procure from more settled communities. Whatever the nomads could not gain by negotiated trade, they often obtained through violence. Their ambitions gradually increased until around 3000 BC, when the Kassites and Elamites, nomadic horse-riding peoples from what is now north-east Iran, conquered north-west Persia. At about the same period, their contemporaries, the Hittites, a nomadic, horse-riding people of mixed origin speaking an Indo-European language, entered Asia Minor (Anatolia, part of modern Turkey) on their rough, active ponies. Elsewhere, other nomadic warriors were establishing a pattern of armed migrations throughout the known world of the time.

THE FIRST CHARIOTS

The development of chariots and other wheeled vehicles marked a turning point in the association between man and horse. Chariots increased mobility in all respects, adding in particular a new dimension to warfare, enabling operations to be carried out over a broader front than would have been possible with soldiers on foot. They also allowed the use of animals too small for effective mounted action, and simplified the co-ordinated movement of large bodies of men. Importantly, the chariot made possible the exploitation of the rich valley lands of the Middle East, along the Tigris and the

METAL BITS
Metal bits made their appearance between 1300 and 1200 BC and were originally of bronze. They had previously been made from hardwood, bone, or horn.

Euphrates. At first, chariots had solid wheels, but by 2500 BC spoked wheels were widely used in Mesopotamia. The Egyptians had sophisticated war chariots by 1600 BC, and China had perfected its chariots by 1300 BC.

CHARIOT INVASIONS

With the increasingly widespread use of the chariot, Aryans travelled south out of Central Asia to overrun Persia and India, the Celts spread through Europe, and Upper Egypt was invaded and occupied from about 2000 BC by another nomadic people, the

CHARIOT ATTACK
Mastery of the chariot altered the complexion of war. Here, the Egyptian king, Sethos (Seti) I, who reigned from 1318 to 1304 BC, defeats the Libyans at Karnak.

TROOP-CARRIER
This relief in the North Palace at Nineveh depicts an Elamite troop-carrier and dates from c.645–635 BC. The vehicle was drawn by well-conditioned onagers and its wheels were multi-spoked.

Hyksos, who were not driven out until 1542 BC. It was they who introduced the wheel, the war chariot, and a new tactical concept of warfare into Egypt.

The Hittites in Asia Minor gradually extended their empire into northern Syria and conquered Babylon in 1595 BC, becoming one of Egypt's most formidable and aggressive enemies.

Conflict between the Egyptians and the Hittites continued on and off for centuries. It finally came to a close in 1286 BC when the Hittites defeated the Egyptian King Rameses I at Kadesh in Syria, with a striking force of 3,500 chariots as well as 17,000 foot soldiers. This was the greatest chariot battle of antiquity – the equivalent of the tank battles of the Second World War (and fought over much the same ground).

The Hittite chariot had a three-man crew: driver, shield-bearer, and either a javelin thrower or an archer. Horses were driven from bits acting across the lower jaw; metal bits, following on from those made of hardwood, bone, or horn, made their appearance by 1300–1200 BC. Chariot harness was adapted from the yoke that had

KADESH

The Battle of Kadesh (1286 BC), in which the Hittites defeated the Egyptian king Rameses I with a force of 3,500 chariots, is one of the earliest records of the Hittite chariot forces. The Hyksos had introduced chariot warfare to the Egyptians three centuries earlier.

been used successfully on oxen, with two horses being hitched to a central pole that passed between the two, with an outrigger hitched on each side of the pole pair.

The Hittites were also the first people to produce a horse-training manual. It was written by Kikkuli the Mittanian in about 1360 BC, and advocated the feeding of grain, lucerne, and chaffed straw in a remarkably modern way. Even more interestingly, it related feeding to systematic exercise, which was designed to maximize fitness and stamina. After 1190 BC the Hittite Empire was a spent force, but by then the chariot was widespread throughout the civilized world and was to remain so for some centuries.

LATER EMPIRES

The Hittites were succeeded by the martial empires of Babylon, Egypt, and Assyria. All these peoples practised some form of selective breeding to improve the size and performance of their horses. Assyrian art forms, dating from the 9th century BC onwards, give the most complete insight into the practices of the time, and provide a storehouse of valuable information about the empire. Assyrian art shows strong, well-conditioned, quality horses with manes and tails as extravagantly tonsured as the hair of the warriors themselves. Initially the Assyrians were chariot people, their kings and generals hunting from wheeled vehicles. Later, as the Assyrian Empire extended northwards into more mountainous country, where chariots would have been unwieldy and impractical, there is increasing evidence of the use of mounted warriors, and by the time of Tiglath-Pileser III (747–727 BC) accomplished horsemen riding spirited stallions are depicted in hundreds of bas-reliefs. Nonetheless, the chariot remained an essential means of transport throughout the world for another 700 years or more and would continue to play an important part in the armies and social structures of both Greece and Rome (see pp.38–39 and pp.44–45).

HORSE MANAGEMENT

This relief of Assyrian horses dates from c.883–859 BC. It shows a scene that can hardly have changed much in the history of mounted troops and horse management.

ASSYRIAN CAVALRY

Early Assyrian archers rode with a companion who held the horse's reins while the archer loosed his arrows. This relief is from the North West Palace of Nimrud and dates from c.865–860 BC.

THE PERSIAN EMPIRE

MITHRAS, GOD OF LIGHT

BY THE 6TH century BC the Persians had wrested supremacy from the Assyrians and were the dominant power in the East. Central to their success was the Nisean horse, the super-horse of antiquity, which had also contributed to the earlier ascendancy of both the Babylonians and the Assyrians. The Nisean horses summered in the cool, rich pastures of the foothills of north-west Iran, around Hamadan in ancient Medea, a region ideal for stock raising. Under Cyrus II the Great (c.589–529 BC), the Persian armies occupied these areas, and went on to take control of the Great Silk Road, the trade route running from the Chinese Pacific coast to Alexandria situated on the Mediterranean. By the 3rd century BC the Persian Empire stretched from Egypt to Asia Minor, and from India to the Greek Islands.

THE NISEAN HORSE

The Nisean horse proved to be the great mainstay of the Persian army of Cyrus the Great, of which the Greek historian Herodotus (c.484–430? BC) wrote: "The armoured Persian horsemen and their death-dealing chariots were invincible, no man dared face them . . . ".

The exact origins of the Nisean are not known. Both the steppe Tarpan (see pp.20–21) and the small, refined horses known as Horse Type 4 (see pp.22–23) lived in the same region. There may have also been outcrosses with the Asiatic Wild Horse (see pp.18–19). The Nisean emerged from this boiling pot of equine strains. Carefully bred, well-fed, and well-conditioned, it was bigger than any of the horses used before, and may have measured as much as 1.52 m (15 hh) or more. It was also very powerful, and required a strong bitting arrangement if it was to be controlled by the Persians, who sat on padded cloths and did not have the benefit of stirrups.

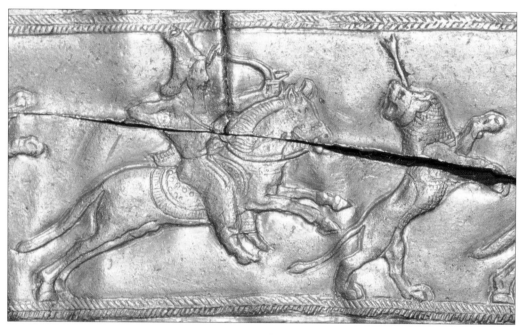

HORSE-ARCHER
This Persian gold relief of a horse-archer chasing a lion is on a scabbard from the Treasure of the Oxus, and dates from c. 5th–3rd century BC. The horse is controlled solely by the rider's legs.

THE ROLE OF THE HORSE

The possession of horses was a status symbol among the Persians, and ownership was confined to the aristocracy. Horses were used in hunting, organized racing (over courses that were 11 km [7 miles] long), and, from the 6th century BC, in an early form of polo.

CHARIOT OF GOLD
The remarkable detail of this gold model of a Persian chariot (c. 5th–4th century BC) clearly shows how a four-horse team was harnessed to a double pole by means of an extended yoke.

Horses were used as tribute: the Medean province, or satrapy, provided the Persian King with pasture for 50,000 horses, the Armenians gave him 20,000 foals a year, and the Cilicians donated one white horse each day of the year. Indeed, white horses played a prominent role in religion and connected ceremonies of tribute. Mithras, god of light and "lord of the wide pastures", was believed to drive a chariot drawn by four immortal white horses, shod with gold and fed on ambrosia. Followers of Mithras sacrificed white horses in his honour.

The horse was also vital for communication. The Persians were the first to develop a communication system that depended upon posting stations placed one day's ride apart. A similar system was operated 1,800 years later by the Mongols (see pp.72–73). However, the Mongols had the advantage of a saddle and stirrups, which would have made riding more comfortable. Since the Persians had no stirrups, trotting would have been rather uncomfortable, so the couriers would probably have cantered or galloped. They may also have used an ambling or pacing horse that used its legs in lateral rather than diagonal pairs, a motion that would have been less jolting.

PARTHIAN SHOT

An Amazon archer c. 500 BC demonstrates the "Parthian shot", made usually at the gallop over the horse's tail. The Parthians used it to effect when feigning a retreat.

MARAUDING HORSE-ARCHERS FROM SCYTHIA AND PARTHIA

For over 300 years the Persian Empire was the greatest force in the ancient world, but, like empires before and since, it had to endure some irritating thorns in its usually well-protected sides. These came in the shape of marauding nomadic horsemen who continually harassed the northern borders.

Chief amongst these were the Scythians and the Parthians, the latter deriving from a branch of the former. Both were magnificent horsemen who rarely deigned to walk more than a very short distance. They were expert horse-archers, highly successful in their own form of hit-and-run warfare, and capable of loosing clouds of arrows while riding at full gallop.

The Scythian tribes of the south Russian steppes, about whom we know so much because of the excavation of the Pazyryk tombs (see pp.30–31), never achieved a single national cohesion. But the Parthians, who gave us the term "Parthian shot", i.e. the shot over the galloping pony's tail, established a kingdom in Iran in the 3rd century BC and harried their neighbours for centuries to come. However, although they defeated the Romans at Carrhae in modern Iraq, in the 1st century AD, these nomadic warriors were more or less confined to the tactics of harassment and never achieved any sustained conquests of a lasting nature.

These martial societies were the prototypes for the Huns of Attila in the 5th century and the Mongols of Genghis Khan in the 12th century, the fierce, cruel horsemen who brought down in ruin the calm certainty of the ancient, rational world.

The reign of the Persian kings came to an end between 336 and 323 BC at the hands of the greatest hero of antiquity, Alexander of Macedon (see pp.40–41). There then emerged the two great classical civilizations of Greece and Rome, whose influence spread throughout the world and can still be felt to this day (see pp.38–39 and pp.44–45).

SCYTHIAN TOMBS

This is a detail of a colourful Persian carpet of the 5th century BC, which was discovered in the excavations of the deep-frozen Scythian tombs of Pazyryk in 1929. The tombs provided wonderfully preserved evidence of a horse culture that is thought to have extended over 3,000 years.

CASPIAN

THE CASPIAN is possibly the most fascinating of the world's ancient horse breeds. It represents a uniquely important link between the early forms of *Equus* and the hot-blooded "desert" or "plateau" horses from which the modern light horses have evolved. In almost every respect it is the incarnation of Horse Type 4, postulated by Ebhardt, Speed, Skorkowski, and d'Andrade as one of the pre-domestic sub-species of the horse (see pp.22–23). They had described what we know as the Caspian, with reasonable accuracy, half a century before these miniature horses were rediscovered by the shores of the Caspian Sea in 1965, by an American traveller, Mrs Louise L. Firouz.

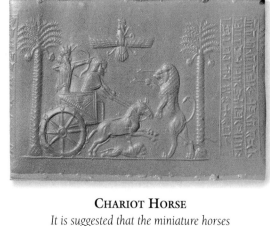

CHARIOT HORSE
It is suggested that the miniature horses depicted drawing the chariot of Darius on this cylindrical seal (c. 548–486 BC) were forebears of the modern "Caspian".

HISTORY

The discovery of the Caspian, a breed of very great antiquity, was a matter of the greatest scientific and historical importance in equine studies. There has been a great deal of scientific research done since 1965, which seems to suggest that the Caspian's antecedents were the far-off ancestors, possibly by some 3,000 years, of the Arab horse (see pp.64–65), although that supposition has yet to be established conclusively. The Caspian is certainly the oldest equine breed still in existence apart from the Asiatic Wild Horse (see pp.18–19). While a pure descent from the horses of antiquity is unlikely, this little horse is set apart from other modern breeds by several unique physical characteristics, such as a sharp difference in the shape of the scapula, a rather odd formation of the parietal bones of the head, giving a vaulted appearance to the skull, and an extra molar in the upper jaw.

Further evidence of the existence of small, quality horses of decidedly Arab appearance is provided by the many artefacts, including reliefs, from Ancient Egypt and Mesopotamia. Much later, in about 500 BC, similar miniature horses are depicted on the famous

NECK
The neck of the modern Caspian is long and gracefully arched. It gives a "length of rein" and a wither definition not usually found in pony breeds.

HEAD
The head is short with a vaulted forehead and is covered with fine, thin skin.

SHOULDERS
The shoulders are those of a quality riding "horse" and are well-sloped from relatively prominent withers. As a result the stride is long and low, endowing speed out of all proportion to the small size of the Caspian.

CANNONS
The cannons are long but the bone is considered to be dense and very strong.

BRED IN THE UK
The conformation of these Caspians has been much improved by good management and an environment that is more congenial than their original habitat.

HEIGHT
*1.02–1.22 m
(10–12 hh)*

trilingual seal of the Persian king, Darius the Great (522–486 BC). The seal shows a pair of these horses drawing the royal chariot from which Darius looses arrows at an attacking lion, which is so huge it dwarfs the horses. The Greeks also recorded the existence of a race of miniature horses in parts of ancient Medea, the area south of the Caspian Sea, and Caspian-type horse bones have also been found in Mesolithic cave remains near Kermanshah, mid-way between Baghdad and Tehran. Although the descendants of these horses have long since disappeared from the area, it seems that at some point, about 1,000 years ago, tribes from the Kermanshah region were driven out, moving themselves and their miniature horses to the northern edge of the Elborz mountains, which border the Caspian Sea.

The continuing existence of these ancient horses was not brought to world attention until 1965 when an American traveller, Mrs Louise L. Firouz, found a distinctive type of alert, quick-moving "pony", quite unlike the usual native stock, working in the narrow streets of Amol, on the shores of the Caspian Sea. She bought several of them and formed the nucleus of a stud that was subsequently established at Norouzabad. Ten years later, a stallion and seven mares were exported to the UK to form the Caspian Stud (UK). Since then Caspians have been bred as far afield as North and South America, Australia, and New Zealand.

CHARACTERISTICS

The modern Caspian is termed a "pony" on account of its size and, perhaps, also for the sake of convenience. In fact it is a horse, albeit a miniature one, with horse characteristics and proportions. Its distinctive head is short, and covered with fine, thin skin to give the "dry", thin-skinned quality usually associated with the Arab and other desert breeds. The muzzle is small and tapered, the nostrils full, and the eyes large. The Caspian's ears are very short. In the "Physical Description" given in the *International Caspian Stud Book* it is stated that the ears should not exceed 11 cm (4½ in) in length. Its feet are small and very strong, never needing to be shod even on the stoniest ground. The body is slim and narrow, making the Caspian an ideal mount for children, and its tail is set and carried high, like that of the Arab. Modern Caspians are bigger than their early ancestors, and stand between 1.02 and 1.22 m (10–12 hh) high. The principal colours are bay, grey, and chestnut, with occasional blacks and creams.

Because of the sloped shoulders and the way in which they are joined with the withers, the action is long, low, free, and fast, so that the horse appears to "float". The Caspian can keep up with larger horses at every gait except the gallop. Additionally, the little horse seems to be a natural jumper, and, though spirited, even the stallions can be handled by children. Perhaps since its ancestors were used in chariots, it naturally adapts easily to harness. The ponies that were subsequently developed outside the original environment bear little resemblance to the ones found at Amol, or to those depicted on the Seal of Darius. Selective breeding, higher management standards, and better quality food have improved the conformation immeasurably.

Essentially, however, the great value lies in the retention of genes providing a unique link with the species' primitive beginnings. The discovery of the Caspian is as fundamental to the study of equine evolution as that of the Asiatic Wild Horse and the Tarpan (see pp.20–21).

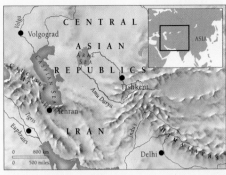

ORIGINS

THE CASPIAN BREED was discovered as recently as 1965 when the American traveller, Mrs Louise L. Firouz, observed a distinctive type of miniature horse in Amol, on the shores of the Caspian Sea. The Greeks had found such horses in the same area 2,500 years earlier. There is more evidence of the horses in the Mesolithic caves near Kermanshah, between Baghdad and Tehran. Horses from Kermanshah were moved from there about 1,000 years ago to the borders of the Caspian Sea.

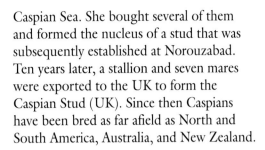

QUARTERS
The quarters are strong and proportionate with unexpected length from the hip to the point of the hock.

TAIL
The tail and mane are full and flowing. The tail is positioned high in the quarters and is carried well up when the horse is moving.

HARNESS HORSE
The modern Caspian is bold and very fast, with a long, low stride. It is a good performer in present-day scurry driving competitions.

ANCIENT GREECE

XENOPHON

BETWEEN THE 8TH and 7th centuries BC, when the first urban civilizations of Greece and Rome were established, and the 4th century AD, when the Roman Empire finally disintegrated under the onslaught of "barbaric" (i.e. non-Greek and non-Roman) horsemen, there flowered the two civilizations that more than any other were to exert a continuing influence on the affairs of mankind. They lasted for 1,000 years, and when they were gone the world entered what we call the Dark Ages. But the glories of Greece and Rome were indestructible. Elements of these classical cultures survived to provide inspiration for future generations, right up to our own times, bequeathing to the world the advantages of a rational system of order and the legacy of democratic government.

CHARIOTS TO CAVALRY

The age of Classical Greece is generally considered to have begun in 480–479 BC, after the first Persian invasions were repulsed. By this time the Greeks' association with the horse seems to have been established for about 1,500 years, since around 2000 BC. There are, for example, chariots carved on the shaft graves of the Greek Mycenaean people, which date from about 1550–1500 BC, and pictures of horses decorate vases from before that date.

One of the earliest accounts of the use of horses in battle is to be found in Homer's *Iliad*, which was probably written in about 800 BC. From it we learn that the Homeric heroes fought from two-horse chariots, from which they dismounted to fight from the ground with their swords and spears. At that time the Greeks' horses were too small to be ridden, even if the legendary heroes had ever contemplated doing so. The chariots, driven by lesser men, were withdrawn to the rear of the battle until they were required again.

However, four centuries later when the Greeks wanted to expel the Persians, they needed to employ mounted troops because Greece is a mountainous country not suited to wheeled formations. These mounted troops came from the upper classes, who were the only people who had the right to own horses, and for whom horsemanship was an essential part of their education.

THE CAVALRY COMMANDER

Although neither the Greeks nor the Romans were horsemen in the same mould as the earlier Scythians, or the later Huns or Mongols, both came to depend on horse-power to extend and support their empires. The Greeks were no better overall horsemen than their predecessors, the Assyrians and the Persians, but they left a legacy to the art of horsemanship through one of their most able generals, Xenophon (c. 430–356 BC), an eminent soldier, historian, and philosopher. His great work, a manual entitled *The Cavalry Commander*, shows how well the Greeks understood the role of the cavalry. Mounted soldiers were used to scout in advance of the main bodies of troops, and to harry the enemy at every opportunity. A principal cavalry tactic, however, was to wheel across the enemy's front throwing javelins into the massed foot formations. Although in his Indian campaigns Alexander used horsed lancers as well as javelin throwers, it was the latter that could be employed more effectively. Each soldier carried two javelins in addition to his personal weapon, the sword. When the javelins had been thrown, replacements could be obtained from a reserve of camels, which were tucked safely out of the way, or from supply chariots.

JAVELIN EXERCISE
Greek horsemen took part in javelin practice. The swift javelin attack across the enemy's front was a principal cavalry tactic.

INTO BATTLE
The decoration on this vase shows a heavily armed and armoured Hoplite (foot-soldier) about to be transported to the battlefield in his chariot.

HORSES AND THE GODS

From the earliest times horses were central to Greek life, and they occupied a special prominence in Greek mythology. Ares, the god of war, was thought to ride in a chariot drawn by the customary four white horses, symbols of the highest purity, as he preceded the rising sun. Demeter, the goddess of women, marriage, and agriculture, was depicted with the head of a black mare, and the priestesses of her temple were referred to as "foals".

Specially honoured in the prime horse-breeding area of Thessaly was the god Poseidon. As well as being god of the sea he was credited with the creation of the horse, and was believed to be "the embodiment of all horses, their god and lord". On occasion a white horse, considered to be of enormous value in Ancient Greece, was sacrificed in his honour. These horses were always drowned, in deference to Poseidon's own element, rather than being slaughtered with a knife. At Rhodes, for instance, a white horse was driven into the sea drawing a flaming chariot in a ritual to "revive the sun" after the winter months.

TEMPLE OF DEMETER
This horse head comes from a temple dedicated to the goddess Demeter. Her image was a black mare's head, and her priestesses were known as "foals".

ART OF ANTIQUITY
This extraordinary life-size bronze of horse and jockey is at the National Archaeological Museum, Athens. It is one of the most noble works of Ancient Greece.

DAY DAWNS
Helios, God of the Sun, rises from the sea at dawn in a gold chariot drawn by his winged horses. The boys, diving into the sea, represent the fading stars.

SPORTS

Chariot racing was a national sport in Greece for over 1,500 years, and the aim of every horse breeder or owner was to produce a winner at the Olympic Games. The first chariot races were for four-horse chariots, and were staged at the 25th Olympiad in 680 BC; two-horse chariot races were not introduced until 408 BC. There were races on horseback as early as 648 BC but they did not enjoy the same prestige as chariot racing until about 300 years later.

HORSE-BREEDING

Greece has never been very suitable for horse-breeding, offering little in terms of soil structure and climate. As a result, horse breeders in Ancient Greece were forced to rely upon imports. They crossed their own stock, which came mainly from Thessaly, with horses from Ferghana in the east, which gave their horses some Arabian character. To increase the size they used Scythian and Persian horses. Philip of Macedon imported 20,000 Scythian mares, and his son, Alexander, claimed a tribute of 50,000 Persian horses. Even so, it is unlikely that the Greeks' animals averaged much more than 1.47 m (14.2 hh) in height, which was not unusual for the time.

ALEXANDER & BUCEPHALUS

The partnership that created an Empire

ALEXANDER

This lively Roman bronze statuette of Alexander dates from the 2nd century AD.

ALEXANDER THE GREAT (356–323 BC), son of Philip of Macedon, was the outstanding military leader of his age, extending the Greek Empire into Egypt and east to the borders of India. He was also responsible for the civilizing spread of Greek culture throughout the world. But for all his achievements it would be unthinkable to consider him without the extraordinary horse that he rode to victory in his greatest battles.

The horse was called Bucephalus, which means "ox-head", and refers to the broad forehead and slightly concave profile characteristic of both oriental blood and a particular Thessalonian strain. Described as being "of the best Thessalonian breed", Bucephalus had a black coat and a white star on his forehead, and was big compared with his contemporaries. According to one Greek writer he also had a "wall" or blue eye. Alexander's father bought Bucephalus in 343 BC

THE BATTLE OF ISSUS

The Persian Emperor Darius flees from the Greek cavalry, led by Alexander and Bucephalus, at the Battle of Issus (333 BC). The defeat of Darius was decisive, with the Persians suffering heavy casualties.

for the equivalent of £20,000. However, when he was brought out he was so unruly that he could not be mounted. But Alexander, a precocious 12-year-old who had already seen active service, claimed he would ride him. Seeing that the horse was scared of his own shadow, as well as those of the men who tried to approach him, Alexander turned him to face the sun and leapt onto his back. After "patting and coaxing", he galloped to and fro before returning to his father. "You must look for a kingdom to match you, my son," said his father, "Macedonia is not big enough for you". From then on, Bucephalus would allow a groom to ride him bareback, but when caparisoned he let only Alexander ride him, kneeling so that he could mount more easily. Alexander rode Bucephalus for the last time in 327 BC, when he defeated the Indian King Porus at the Hydaspes River. Bucephalus was 30 years old and at the end of the day he died from his wounds. He was buried with all military honour, and the city of Bucephalia was founded by Alexander on the site.

BUST OF ALEXANDER
This bust of Alexander is usually regarded as being the most true to life. The sculptor has certainly caught something of the character of the man whose achievements altered the course of world history.

HEROIC GREECE
This heroic bronze statue of Alexander and the horse Bucephalus typifies the partnership that must have existed between the two. Horse and man were almost the same age, and both of them died when they were in their thirties.

PINDOS & SKYRIAN

G REECE HAS LITTLE to offer in terms of a natural environment suitable for horse-breeding. In Ancient Greece there were several breeds of horse, but the poor soil, sparse vegetation, and the harsh climatic conditions meant that the animals were usually rather small. In the time of the Greek historian Xenophon (430–355 BC), the Greeks had to rely on horses brought in from neighbouring areas, which they could use to improve their native breeds. They refined the quality of the indigenous ponies by introducing eastern-type horses from Ferghana, and increased the size by using Scythian stock.

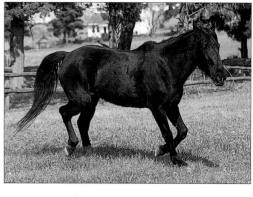

GOOD WORKER
The Pindos may not be recognizable as the horse praised by Oppian as "most noted for beauty, courage and endurance", but it is a good all-round worker.

THE PINDOS

The traditional horse-breeding areas of Ancient Greece were the lower lands of Thessaly and Epirus. For centuries this has been the habitat of the Pindos (also known as the Thessalonian). There seems to be little doubt that this breed is directly descended from the old Thessalonian, which the Greek poet Oppian (c. AD 211) recognized as the horse "most noted for beauty, courage and endurance", although it is also likely to have

HEAD
The head inclines to coarseness. The eyes appear small and mean, which would suggest that the pony is stubborn.

BODY
The body is narrow with little muscle development on the neck, although the withers are pronounced.

HEIGHT OF PINDOS
1.32 m (13 hh)

LEGS
The legs are slender with small joints. This specimen is "tied-in" below the knee. The feet are black.

PINDOS

been influenced by its absorption of the ancient Peloponnese, Arcadian, Epidaurian, and other long-forgotten strains.

Today, the sure-footed Pindos is used as a pack pony in the mountains, in light work on the small farmsteads, and in forestry, and it can also be a useful riding and driving pony. Pindos mares are often used for breeding mules (see pp.330–31).

The Pindos pony stands at about 1.32 m (13 hh). It is a tough, enduring sort, capable of surviving on minimal food supplies. The tail is set high, which indicates the presence of Horse Type 4 (see pp.22–23) in its background, but the quarters are often poor, with little second thigh. The feet are usually narrow and boxy, a characteristic condition in horses from dry, hot countries, but they

PENEIA
This sturdy Peneia pony is of the better type. It is economical to keep, since it requires only basic rations, and is capable of doing a variety of jobs. Because of selective breeding, some of the ponies may grow to 1.42 m (14 hh).

are very hard and rarely need to be shod. The Pindos is noted for its stamina, but the breed has a reputation for being stubborn.

The Peneia, from the province of Eleia in the Peloponnese, has a connection with the more numerous Pindos. It fulfils the same functions, and is also tough and economical to keep. The breed height varies greatly: the smallest animals can be as little as 1.02 m (10 hh), while the largest, perhaps as a result of selective breeding and better care, can stand at up to 1.42 m (14 hh).

THE SKYRIAN HORSE

The island of Skyros has supported ponies since ancient times, but there is no evidence to show how they got there. At one time the ponies lived wild in the mountains, and were brought in to help with the corn threshing.

The modern pony, which Skyrian breeders insist must be called the Skyrian Horse, is still a utility animal, but is also used in other ways, which include being ridden.

The Skyrian's proportions are horse-like, and the breed resembles the horses depicted in the statuary and friezes of Ancient Greece. Therefore, there may be a connection with the old Thessalonian horse. That assumption suggests an origin with Horse Type 4, while the coat and general appearance show a strong link with the earlier Tarpan (see pp.20–21).

The Skyrian breed is reputed to be good-tempered and to jump well. Its other assets include stamina and weight-carrying ability. However, it has straight shoulders and mean quarters, and is usually cow-hocked. The coat often has an eel stripe and zebra bars on the legs, indicating "primitive" ancestry, and the feet are black, as required by the breed preservation society. The usual height is 1.12 m (11 hh), but careful breeding can produce ponies of 1.22 m (12 hh) and over.

ORIGINS

THE TRADITIONAL HORSE-REARING areas of Greece were in Thessaly and Epirus. These are the habitat of the modern Pindos, which is also known as the Thessalonian. Peneia in the province of Eleia, in the Peloponnese, is home to the Peneia pony, while the Skyrian belongs to the island of Skyros in the Aegean Sea. The poor soil conditions and the hot climate ensure their ability to survive on minimal forage, but limits the size of the ponies and encourages conformational faults. Nonetheless, the formation of breed preservation societies has already done much to improve the quality and size of the Greek pony stock.

QUARTERS
The quarters are weak in appearance. The back is long and the pony seems to be "short of a rib".

HEIGHT OF SKYRIAN
1.12 m (11 hh)

HEAD
The head is now finer than it used to be. A feature is the width between the ears and across the forehead.

BODY
The body of the improved Skyrian is compact and has an acceptable forehand.

SKYRIAN

PLOUGH TEAM
Skyrian Horses are used to plough the island's impoverished soil. There is now a breed preservation society devoted to the improvement of these ponies.

THE ROMAN EMPIRE

THE ROMANS were reluctant horsemen, although chariot racing was a popular sport and horses were in general use. In a military context they preferred to put their trust in an effective naval force and the impenetrable shield-walls of their superb legions. Their cavalry, supporting foot soldiers but acting under the central command of the legion, was largely made up of foreign, mercenary horsemen. Nonetheless, they were a vigorous, practical people with a genius for rational thought and action, and they implemented far-reaching horse-breeding policies to produce horses to suit a whole variety of needs. Many of the breeds that subsequently developed in Europe were originally founded on the types that had evolved in the Roman Empire by the 3rd century AD.

HORSES FOR EVERY PURPOSE

Roman breeders produced stock for every purpose, from circus performers to pack and draught animals. Among the specialized types were *venaticus*, the hunter; *celer equus*, the race horse; *bellator equus*, the charger or war-horse; *itinerarius* and *manuus*, the draught and harness animals; and the proud and much prized "parade" horse, *cantherius*. When the conquering Caesars and their generals returned to Rome in triumph they did so either in a "triumphal" chariot drawn by as many as 10 horses, or they rode heroically on a snorting *cantherius*, which rolled "the collected fire under his nostrils" and lifted his feet in the lofty, animated trot, so well known to Xenophon (see pp.38–39). Later, this trot was part of the Renaissance Classical tradition (see pp.96–99), and in the 18th century was known as *passage*.

Understandably, since even the Romans did not use stirrups until possibly the 5th century AD, when their empire was coming to an end, the naturally ambling or pacing horse, *gradarius* or *ambulator*, was deservedly popular. The trotting horse, known as *succusator*, *concussator*, or, more tellingly, *cruciator*, was less so.

RACING AND THE CIRCUS

The chariot was the prerogative of the nobility but, as with the Greeks, chariot racing was also a national sport, arousing fierce passions in the amphitheatres of Rome. In a characteristically pragmatic way, Rome used chariot racing as a political tool; it was a means of diverting and dividing a riotous and potentially rebellious populace.

Originally there were four chariot groups distinguished by colour – green, red, blue, and

RACING QUADRIGA
In this relief of a chariot race for quadriga in the Roman arena of Campana, the winner is about to pass the winning post.

TWO-HORSE BIGA
The two-horse chariot in this bronze (c.1st–2nd centuries AD) is called a biga. The offside horse is missing but the yoke system of harnessing to a central pole is very clear.

RACING COLOURS

Roman charioteers wore protective clothing and racing colours. These figures are accompanied by horses of eastern character that would not have stood higher than 1.37 m (13.2 hh).

Following the Punic Wars (264–149 BC), Iberia became a principal centre for the breeding of cavalry remounts and more emphasis was given to mounted troops. The early legions were composed of 3,000 foot soldiers supported by 300, usually irregular, horsemen. By the 3rd century AD mounted troops, still for the most part auxiliaries,

white (for spring, summer, autumn, and winter). Each was supported by a political faction and rivalry was intense, with the day often ending in ugly street riots.

The horse, as well as being integral to the "triumphs" of victorious generals, also played a large part in the Roman circus, from which many equestrian circus acts have their origin. Gladiatorial combats on horseback, in which mounted men fought many kinds of animals from bulls to elephants, were also a popular diversion. In fact, the Greeks had also fought bulls from horseback and it is

from this Greco-Roman background that bull-fighting in Spain and Portugal derives. This may also be true of some of the American western and rodeo sports, which partly stem from an Iberian tradition.

THE ARMY

The Roman army relied heavily upon the superb foot-soldiers of the legions. However, Roman generals, though committed by training and tradition to the legions, knew there was a need for both a reliable cavalry and a supply of suitable, light draught animals to transport military provisions.

made up one-third of the army's strength. The cavalry's importance can be seen from the fact that the Roman conquest of Britain in 54 BC could only begin once the mounted division had arrived to support Julius Caesar's legions. His attempt to invade Britain a year earlier had failed because his cavalry did not arrive in time.

However, it was not until the reforms implemented by the Emperor Galliensis (AD 206–68) that the Roman cavalry was organized as a separate command structure and could be employed with maximum effect. The role of the cavalry continued to be developed under Diocletian (284–305) and Constantine (311–37), when the mounted division was divided into *clibanarii* (the light cavalry) and *catafracti* (the heavy horsemen). The latter employed the shock-

tactic of charging with lances, which they held either under their arms or with both hands.

THE FALL OF ROME

By AD 376, despite its heavy cavalry, the Empire was being besieged by Hun archers on horseback who rode with stirrups and saddles, which they used as platforms from which to let fly a deadly rain of arrows.

In 378 the Roman legions fought the Goths and the Huns at Adrianople. Steadfast to the end, they died where they stood under the onslaught of massed horsemen. This battle marked the rise of heavy cavalry in Europe and ended the invincibility of Rome. In 418 Alaric's Goths sacked the city of Rome, and in 451 Rome fought its last battle, against Attila the Hun at the Catalaunian Fields (just below Milan). Twenty years later, the Roman Empire was no more.

ROMAN CAVALRY
This tombstone depicts a 1st-century AD Thracian auxiliary of Roman cavalry, armed with a spear and broadsword. It was found in Gloucester, UK.

ARIÈGEOIS

THE MOUNTAIN PONY that lives between Rousillon and Catalonia, on the eastern edge of the Pyrenees dividing France and Spain, is sometimes called the Cheval de Mérens but is more usually known as the Ariègeois. The breed takes its name from the Ariège River that runs nearby, and although the modern world may hardly be aware of the pony's existence, there is evidence that it is very ancient. For instance, while some of the carvings and wall pictures at Niaux in the Ariège, made by Cro-Magnon man, are recognizably the Camargue horse, others, just as surely, show the Ariègeois in its winter coat, with its characteristic "beard". Julius Caesar knew this pony well enough to give an accurate description of it in his *Commentaries on the Gallic War*.

MANE
The hair of the mane and tail is thick and harsh to the touch.

COAT
The waterproof coat is always black. In winter it grows dense, and has red-brown highlights. White markings are very rare.

BACKGROUND

The Ariègeois pony almost certainly has a background of eastern blood, and it is very likely that substance was once added by being crossed with the heavy pack mares of the Roman legions. Pure-bred specimens no longer exist in the lower reaches of the Department of Ariège, for there has been much crossing of the local stock with heavy draught breeds such as the Percheron and the Breton (see pp.94–95 and pp.268–69). As a result, the progeny retains nothing more than the black colouring as a reminder of its ancient ancestry.

However, the old breed may still be found in the high valleys on the Spanish border towards Andorra. Its territory is centred on a group of relatively inaccessible

HEAD
The head is light-boned, with wide-set eyes, a flat forehead, and an expressive face. In winter the lower jaw is bearded with a heavy growth of hair.

villages – Perles, Castelet, Savignac, Vaychis, and Orgeix. (Orgeix is a familiar name to many jumping enthusiasts through one of France's greatest showjumpers, the Chevalier d'Orgeix.) The stud book was established in 1947 in order to conserve the breed, but outcrosses, in the cause of improvement, are by no means taboo, and as late as 1971 Arab blood was used as an up-grading influence.

PONIES AT TARBES
The Ariègeois is kept and selectively bred at the French National Stud at Tarbes, where teams are shown in harness. In addition, the breed is still used in its native areas. Originally a pack horse, it is also able to carry out all types of work on the upland farms.

HEIGHT
1.35–1.50 m
(13.1–14.3 hh)

FELL PONY REPLICA

The black Ariègeois ponies, seen here in their traditional mountain environment, closely resemble the Fell Ponies of the high Cumbrian Fells in north-western England.

LEGS
The legs are short, with short cannons and shanks. The joints are hard.

Curiously, there are loose parallels between the ponies of the Pyrenees and those of the British Pennines. In the Pennines, allowing for an inevitable overlap, there are Dales Ponies on one side of the mountains, and Fell Ponies on the other. Likewise, on the Spanish Marches, there are different ponies on each side – the little Pottok ponies are found in the Basque region in the west, and on the French side there is the Poney Landais whose territory extends into the plains of Chalosse near the Adour River. The geographical resemblance is most marked in the territory of the Ariègeois, where the *soulanes*, or fells, are very like the high fells of Cumbria, and the black Ariègeois ponies are almost exact replicas of the British Fell Pony (see pp.172–73).

CHARACTERISTICS

The handbook of the *Syndicat des Eleveurs de Chevaux de l'Ariège* describes the pony as standing at 1.35–1.50 m (13.1–14.3 hh), although larger animals are only likely to be found on the lower valley lands where the grazing is richer. The breed is solid black in colour, and in winter the coat has rust-brown highlights. White markings are very unusual. Its mane and tail are thick and harsh. The back is quite long, as befits a pack pony, and there is also a tendency

to cow-hocks. However, this is not unusual in mountain breeds, and does not seem to be detrimental to their sure-footedness. The Ariègeois almost always has excellent feet. It has a hardy constitution, and manages very well on poor-quality, minimal rations, without oats or any other concentrates. The breed is also impervious to severe winter conditions, and so sure-footed that it copes easily with the snow and ice on the rough mountain trails. However, it is not resistant to heat, and must have shelter from the mid-day sun in summer.

DIFFERENT USES

Ariègeois geldings work the upland farms, ploughing, harrowing, and drilling on slopes that would be impossible for a tractor or for any other horse. The pack-saddle is now less evident, but horse-drawn sleds are still used for transporting every sort of load, and the Ariègeois is no slouch as a riding pony. In the past, the breed played an important part in smuggling. As in north-eastern England up to the 19th century, smuggling was endemic along the Spanish border, and was an acceptable and established occupation. Smugglers in England's north-east used the Cleveland Bay (see pp.306–7), while in the Pyrenees the clever Ariègeois, or mules sired by Catalan jackasses out of Ariègeois mares, were employed. It is not impossible, one imagines, that contraband still finds its way over the mountains by the same means.

HOCKS
There is a tendency towards cow-hocks, as with many mountain breeds. However, this does not appear to affect the horse's ability to work.

FEET
The feet are hard and sound, and the breed is nimble and sure-footed. There is some feather on the heels.

ORIGINS

THE ARIÈGEOIS, or Cheval de Mérens, is a mountain pony from the eastern edge of the Pyrenees, between Rousillon and Catalonia. The climate in the mountains is severe, and the availability of good-quality, natural forage is limited. As a result, the ponies have developed great constitutional hardness and are entirely resistant to the most adverse weather conditions. The rough, steep mountain trails, covered with ice and snow in the winter, ensure extreme sure-footedness.

FRIESIAN

EVERYBODY HAS HEARD OF FRIESIAN CATTLE, bred in Friesland off the north coast of the Netherlands, but the Friesian horses are probably less well known, even though they inspire a fervent admiration in their native country. In fact, the black Friesian, a coldblood descended from the primitive Forest Horse (see pp.14–15), holds an important place in the equine hierarchy of Europe, and has even influenced some UK breeds such as the Fell, Dales, and Shire (see pp.172–73 and pp.288–89).

HISTORY

The Roman historian Tacitus (AD 55–120) recorded the Friesian's existence. He acknowledged its antiquity and its value as a powerful all-round utility animal, but remarked on its exceptional ugliness. It had become rather more refined by the time it carried the Friesian knights and their German neighbours to the Crusades, 1,000 years later, but it retained all its qualities of endurance, thriftiness, strength, and docility. The breed was up-graded further by the introduction of eastern blood, a result of contact made with desert horses during these campaigns, and later by crosses with the renowned Andalucian (see pp.108–9) when Spain occupied the Netherlands during the 80 Years' War (1568–1648).

The relatively small Friesian, although blessed with an impressive top line, was not in the same class as the Andalucian or the purpose-bred war-horses of Lombardy, but for centuries it was the most practical, up to weight war-horse of Europe. It was also the cheapest to keep. For the last few hundred years its versatility has been demonstrated in harness, under saddle, and in every sort of farm work. Not surprisingly, this horse was much in demand not only to improve neighbouring breeds but also as foundation stock. Marbach, the German state stud at which the Württemberger (see pp.148–49) originated, used Friesian horses in the 17th century. At the same time, the Oldenburger (see pp.308–9) was founded largely on Friesian stock from the area between the Netherlands and the River Weser.

Because of their geographical situation the Frieslanders became notable seafarers as well as farmers, and their seaborne traders, dealing in cattle, swords, cloth, and horses,

TOP LINE
The top line of the Friesian contributes to the impressive carriage.

FRIESLAND IDYLL
This powerfully built Friesian mare is a good example of the breed, and her foal displays much of her character. The Friesian is economical to keep.

FEET
The hard feet of blue horn are notably sound and well-formed. The feather on the lower limbs is characteristic of the breed.

introduced the breed to countries further afield. The Døle Gudbrandsdal of Norway (see pp.282–83) derived directly from the Friesian. The UK also owes much to the breed. The Frieslanders and their horses provided mounted auxiliaries for the Roman legions in Britain whose settlements remained long after the Romans had gone. The Friesian's influence was manifested in the Dales and Fell Ponies (see pp.172–73), and in the Old English Black from the Midlands. This former breed was used for the King's Household Cavalry during the reign of Charles II (1660–85). More importantly, it was, without dispute, the ancestor of the Shire Horse (see pp.288–89).

However, despite its eminence, the Friesian nearly became extinct during the early part of the 20th century. A stud book had been opened in 1879, but the popularity of trotting races, in which the Friesian excelled, resulted in outcrosses that increased speed at the expense of the essential type. By

THE HARRODS TEAM
This team of Friesians was kept by England's most famous department store, Harrods, for deliveries as well as for promotional purposes. On the box seat is the anchor-man of the British driving team, the Cumbrian "whip", George Bowman.

1913 only three Friesian stallions were left in Friesland. The breed was saved when vehicle and fuel shortages in the Second World War caused the Dutch farmers to return to horse-power. A new society was formed, and in 1954 this was granted the title of "Royal".

THE FRIESIAN TODAY

Today's Friesians are always black, and stand at around 1.52 m (15 hh). They are able to cope with a heavy workload, on moderate rations, without losing condition or the cheerful willingness inherent in the breed's lovable character. Friesians are used for working on the land, are driven in harness (often put to the traditional Friesian gig), and, on account of their agility and temperament, are prized as dressage horses. Furthermore, they are considered to be a useful cross with the Thoroughbred (see pp.120–21) in the breeding of competition horses. In days gone by, the funeral business made much use of them, while today they are still in demand in the circus ring. For many years Friesians were used to draw delivery vans by Harrods, the prestigious London department store.

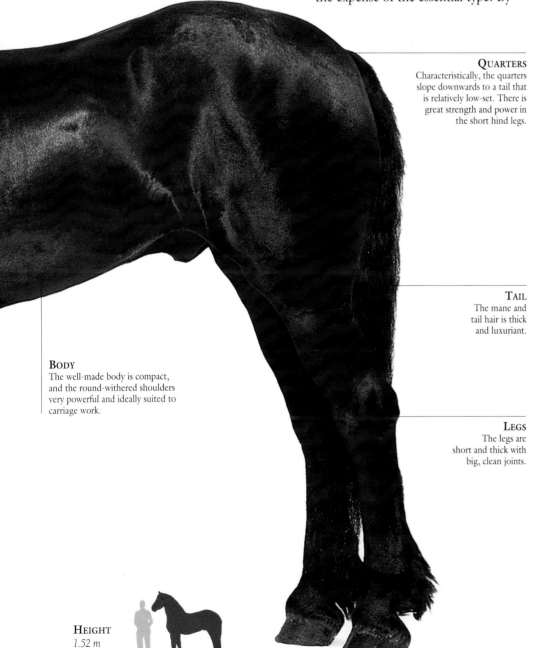

QUARTERS
Characteristically, the quarters slope downwards to a tail that is relatively low-set. There is great strength and power in the short hind legs.

TAIL
The mane and tail hair is thick and luxuriant.

BODY
The well-made body is compact, and the round-withered shoulders very powerful and ideally suited to carriage work.

LEGS
The legs are short and thick with big, clean joints.

HEIGHT
1.52 m
(15 hh)

ORIGINS

THE TRADITIONAL BREEDING area of the Friesian is the Friesland region in the north of the Netherlands. It is not bred to any great extent elsewhere but its influence has extended beyond its native shores. The Oldenburger was founded largely on Friesian blood, and in the UK the Dales and Fell Ponies and the Shire Horse also benefited at one time from a connection with the breed. The environment, combined with careful breeding, has produced a thrifty, economical horse.

NORIKER

THE NORIKER MAKES UP 50 per cent of the Austrian horse population. Like many old European breeds, it has been subject to change and improvement to meet altered circumstances and conditions. Even so, it has absorbed outcrosses without losing its essential character, and after almost 2,000 years is now a breed of fixed and clearly recognizable type, surviving in great numbers and still fulfilling a useful purpose.

EARLY HISTORY

The name Noriker is derived from the state of Noricum, a vassal province of the Roman Empire corresponding roughly to present-day Austria. It was well-served with mountain passes and the roads that were the hallmark of the Roman Empire, implying the extensive use of both draught and pack transport. Furthermore, the southern borders of Noricum were adjacent to the lands of the Venetii, a people noted as skilled horse-breeders, who had certainly occupied that area since 900 BC. These areas later became the home of the Haflinger pony (see pp.52–53), and there is, therefore, a natural connection between the two breeds.

The Noriker owes its development to Roman pragmatism. Although they were not great horsemen, the Romans were proficient at horse-breeding and established studs in every part of their huge empire for the production of purpose-bred horses. The Noriker's ancestors were probably based on the heavy war-horse produced in Juvavum (near Salzburg), which was also used in draught and under pack.

THE MIDDLE AGES

By the Middle Ages, a smallish, heavy horse, compact and sure-footed and thus suited to hard work in mountainous country, had been developed. The best were bred in the mountain region of Gross Glockner. From about 1565 the monasteries, which were often a significant factor in horse-breeding, took control of breeding, and the Noriker's characteristics were regularized

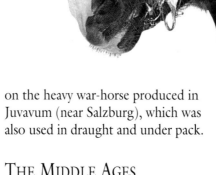

COLOUR
This is a distinctive Norik coloration – liver chestnut, with flaxen mane and tail.

WITHERS
The defined withers and good shoulders account for the trotting action.

SPOTTED NORIKER
A herd of Norikers grazes in Austrian mountain pasture. In the foreground is a spotted horse. The spotted strain of Noriker was formerly known as the Pinzgauer-Noriker after the district in which it was principally bred.

HEIGHT
1.63–1.73 m
(16–17 hh)

and improved. Under the Prince-Archbishop of Salzburg, the Salzburg Stud Book was established, new stud farms were created, and standards were laid down. Neapolitan, Burgundian, and Spanish blood increased the size, and by the 18th century a spotted coat pattern, the result of crosses with Spanish spotted strains (see pp.56–57), was evident, particularly in the Pinzgau district of Austria. This resulted in the term Pinzgauer-Noriker. However, a Pinzgauer Stud Book for this spotted strain was not opened until 1903, when it had a registration of 450 stallions and over 1,000 mares.

FORESTRY WORKER
The Noriker is adaptable, quick-moving, and very strong. It is a willing work horse and an ideal choice for timber haulage in the forest.

THE MODERN NORIKER

Today, "Noriker" includes Pinzgauer, and there are four recognized strains: Carinthian (Karntner), Steier, Tyrolean (Tiroler), and Bavarian or South German Coldblood. There are also

ORIGINS

THE NORIKER *is one of Europe's oldest breeds, taking its name from the Roman state of Noricum, which is now Austria. Early in the history of the Noriker, Juvavum (near modern Salzburg) was a noted breeding centre, and much later, in the 16th century, the Salzburg area, through its monastic houses, was the principal factor in the breed's development. The spotted Noriker of the 18th century, once known as the Pinzgauer-Noriker, was bred in the Pinzgau district around Lungau.*

QUARTERS
The quarters are strong and symmetrical with the tail well-set, but there is no heaviness. The overall outline is compact.

HIND LEGS
The hind legs are marked by strong gaskins (second thighs) and are correctly set with the hocks well let-down.

BODY
The body is distinctive for the great depth at the girth, which often exceeds the measurement from elbow to ground.

LOWER LEGS
The feet are good and sound, and the joints are large and clean.

distinct colour lines, including dappled and brindle coat patterns; black-headed dapple-grey; brown; and shades of chestnut.

Norikers must meet strict conformational breed standards, and are performance tested. They are renowned for their hardiness, hereditary soundness, and biddable temperament. The breed standards are strictly enforced, and include inspection and performance testing for stallions and mares.

BLACK FOREST HORSE
A very typical strain of Noriker, with the traditional liver-chestnut coat colour, is bred at Marbach in Württemberg, the oldest of the German state-owned studs. It is employed in forestry work and is referred to locally as the Black Forest Horse.

HAFLINGER & AVELIGNESE

THE HAFLINGER of the southern Austrian Tyrol, and the Avelignese, which is its Italian counterpart, are among the world's most attractive ponies. Although they are considered to be coldbloods, they have a strong basis of eastern blood, both breeds sharing common ancestry in the Arab foundation stallion, El Bedavi. It is also possible that their distant ancestors, horses the East Goths left behind in the Tyrolese valleys, were influenced by eastern stock. Another suggestion is that there may be a connection with an even more ancient European type or even to the old-time Alpine Heavy Horse.

SLEIGH RIDE
The Haflinger is an excellent and very reliable harness pony with great freedom of action. It carries out all types of light agricultural tasks, often on difficult ground, and can also be ridden.

THE HAFLINGER

The home of the breed is the village of Hafling in the Etschlander Mountains, and the principal stud is in Jenesien. Austria lost the district of Hafling after the First World War, and the breed was re-organized in the Austrian Tyrol; it was kept intact by some outcrosses to Huçul, Bosnian, and Konik ponies (see pp.194–95), and to smaller Noriker horses (see pp.50–51).

There is a biblical quality about the close-knit family founded by its prepotent patriarch, El Bedavi. The stallion was imported from Arabia by an Austrian commission in the 19th century. Four of the breed's five principal bloodlines can be traced to the sons, grandsons, and great-grandsons of his half-bred great-grandson, El Bedavi XXII, bred at the Austro-Hungarian stud at Radautz. The fifth line goes to 40 Willy, the great-grandson of Hafling, who was by 249 Folie, an El Bedavi XXII son. Such uniform ancestry, along with the mountain environment, has resulted in a fixed type of unmistakeable appearance.

The Haflinger is always palomino or chestnut in colour, with a flaxen mane and tail. It stands at up to 1.40 m (13.3 hh), and is strongly built, with well-made limbs, good, sloping shoulders, and the best of feet, although the back, as befits a pony used for pack purposes, is rather long. An extremely sound pony, the Haflinger has an innate ability to work on the steep mountain slopes while maintaining its long-striding, exceptionally free action.

The mountain climate contributes to the hardiness of the breed, as does the practice of raising young stock on Alpine pastures

MANE
A flaxen mane and tail is characteristic of the chestnut Haflinger.

GIRTH
The pony has depth through the girth and well-made shoulders which allow for a very long-striding walk.

LEGS
The legs are muscled but not heavy. The cannons are short and the feet are hard-wearing.

HAFLINGER

(which is known as *alpung* – "alping"), and the thinner air develops the heart and lungs. The ponies are not put to work until they are four, but it is not unknown for them to be still fit and active at 40 years of age.

A docile, frugal breed, which thrives on sparse rations, the Haflinger has a great capacity for hard work under difficult mountain conditions. The breed is used for many agricultural purposes, in draught, and under pack. In modern times it has become popular in many parts of the world as a driving and riding pony, and is often used for work in forestry and woodland. There is a notable Haflinger stud in the UK, which was founded by the Duchess of Devonshire at Chatsworth, Derbyshire. A group of Haflingers were also exported to the Indian Army studs for the purpose of breeding pack animals for use in the mountainous terrain of Jammu and Kashmir. However, on the whole, they did not adapt well to the heat of the plains where the studs are sited.

THE AVELIGNESE

The Italian version of the Haflinger is the somewhat larger Avelignese, which measures up to 1.50 m (14.3 hh). It has much the same background as the Haflinger, and the two breeds have a common ancestor in El Bedavi. Bred with great care, particularly in Bolzano and around Tuscany and Venetia, the Avelignese is another mountain horse that is used both in draught and under pack, and is invaluable on the farms where larger animals would have difficulty in working. However, unlike the Haflinger it does not bear the brand mark of Austria's native flower, the edelweiss, with the letter "H" at its centre.

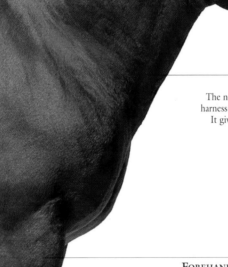

BACK
The broad, low-withered back makes the Avelignese good for pack work. It is heavier in build than the Haflinger.

HEAD
The alert, neat head reflects the Arabian influence that the Avelignese shares with its cousin, the Austrian Haflinger.

NECK
The neck is heavy and short, running into harness-type shoulders able to take a collar. It gives the impression of great strength.

FOREHAND
The chest is broad and strongly muscled, the forelegs being spaced well apart. The legs are short but not heavy.

LEGS
The legs are short with good bone and feet. There is some minimal feather on the lower legs but it is not coarse.

AVELIGNESE

ORIGINS

THE HAFLINGER *is a mountain pony that originated in the Hafling district of the Etschlander Mountains, in the southern Austrian Tyrol. The principal stud for the breed is at Jenesien. The bigger Italian version of the Haflinger is the Avelignese. This pony is bred in the mountainous areas of northern, central, and southern Italy. Both are considered coldbloods, but have a strong basis of eastern blood. The mountain climate ensures great constitutional hardiness in the horses, and both breeds can work easily on the steep mountain slopes as they are exceptionally sure-footed.*

HEIGHT OF HAFLINGER
Up to 1.40 m (13.3 hh)

HEIGHT OF AVELIGNESE
Up to 1.50 m (14.3 hh)

CHINA – BEHIND THE WALL

THE GREAT WALL OF CHINA

CHINA'S contribution to world culture is generally recognized but its significance in terms of equestrian development is less well appreciated. By nature, the Chinese were never a horse-orientated people. They were compelled to employ mounted forces, encourage the building of roads to facilitate swift means of transport, and even to embark upon breeding programmes, only because of the threat of the marauding nomads harassing their borders and usually demanding humiliating tribute to be paid for dubious assurances of non-aggression. The Great Wall, part of which had existed since the 4th century BC, was built to keep out the Asiatic Huns who were a continual threat to the stability of the Empire. It was completed to an unbroken length of 2,253 km (1,400 miles) between 259 and 210 BC.

CHINESE INNOVATIONS

The equestrian concept was not embraced in China until about the 3rd centry BC, some four centuries after the establishment of powerful cavalry armies in the Near East. But, like the Romans, the Chinese were a practical people with an ability to organize and govern – something that was never a feature of nomadic societies.

Virtually all the advances made in harnessing horses to wheeled vehicles were of Chinese origin. It was the Chinese who invented the breeching strap that passes round the lower quarters and enables the horse to exert a braking influence on the load. They were also the inventors of the breast harness and then of the horse collar, the means by which the horse can exert the most effective tractive force. As early as 1300 BC China had sophisticated wheeled vehicles, often far in advance of those used elsewhere. The Chinese were also responsible for the single horse vehicle drawn by means of lateral shafts and they introduced the practice of driving tandem, with one horse behind the other, so as to contribute to speed and performance on two-lane roadways.

Under the Ch'in (221–206 BC), who standardized the script forms and systems of weights and measures, axle widths, for instance, were classified as narrow or broad gauge, in relation to the

HORSE AND CARRIAGE
In this exquisite 17th-century painting the detail of the ornate carriage and the pony's accoutrements are shown with the utmost clarity. The Chinese were responsible for many advances in carriage and harness design of which the simple breast harness shown here is one example.

RUNNING AWAY

This rubbing taken from a Han dynasty tomb may illustrate the manner of the occupant's demise. The light-limbed, quality horses are clearly out of control.

width of the roadways. Some roads were wide enough to take three wagons abreast and in consequence there was a facility for overtaking slow-moving traffic.

THE CELESTIAL HORSES

Up to the 3rd century BC the Chinese had relied on wagon-borne infantry to repulse the attacks of the mounted nomads. Clearly, however, they were no match for swift-moving horsemen accustomed to operating effectively in the roughest terrain.

From the middle of the 2nd century BC the Chinese, under the Emperor Wu Ti (141–87 BC), pursued aggressive policies to obtain and then to breed a superior type of horse that would enable mounted troops to out-ride and out-manoeuvre the nomadic horsemen.

Following determined efforts by the Huns to penetrate deep into Chinese territory, Wu Ti sent envoys to Bactria to buy breeding stock of the Golden Horses of Samarkand. These horses were the descendants of Alexander's powerful Nisean horses (see pp.38–39). Known variously as Heavenly or Celestial Horses, these animals were also called the "blood-sweating" breed of Ili, because many of them displayed spotted coat patterns in which "blood-sweating" is a distinctive attribute. This effect is actually caused by a subcutaneous parasite, which causes minimal bleeding in warm weather. Sweat mixed with the blood produces a pink-coloured paste.

The Chinese obtained horses from around the upper Syr Darya River (Jaxartes) in Turkestan and from the Tien Shan Mountains in Ferghana, areas that have both been much concerned with horse breeding

since antiquity. The related Ili and Ferghana horses are the possible ancestors of the modern Akhal-Teke (see pp.74–75), a golden horse with a particular metallic sheen, and the closely related Turkemene, both, of course, "desert" horses with enormous powers of endurance.

DANGEROUS TRADE MISSIONS

Between 138 and 126 BC up to 10 trade missions were sent to these areas and to the western states of Aorsi, Taynan, Yueh-chi, and Parthia, horses being obtained in exchange for Chinese silks, jade, and coral. All went well until a group of envoys were put to death by the ruler of Ferghana.

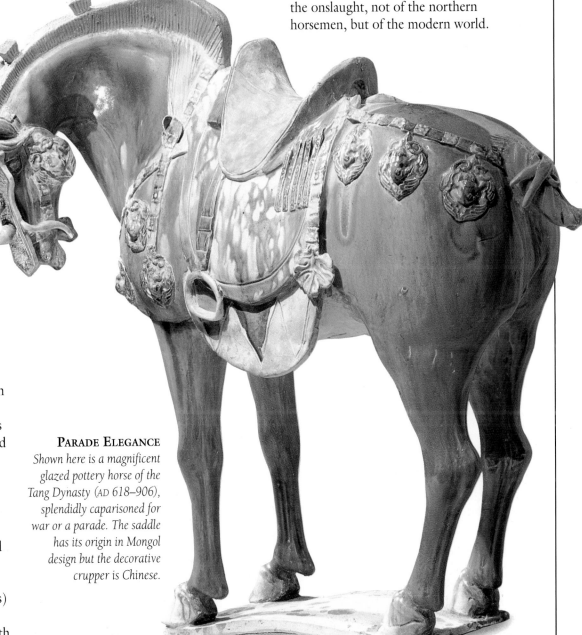

PARADE ELEGANCE

Shown here is a magnificent glazed pottery horse of the Tang Dynasty (AD 618–906), splendidly caparisoned for war or a parade. The saddle has its origin in Mongol design but the decorative crupper is Chinese.

In retaliation, Wu Ti, in 104 BC, sent an army over the 4,827 km (3,000 miles) that separated him from the source of his Heavenly Horses in order to obtain them by force. It was a costly exercise, but in the end China obtained some 3,000 breeding stock and little time was then lost in the creation of breeding studs.

By the Tang Dynasty of the 7th century stud farms for over three quarters of a million horses had been established on the northern limestone steppes.

Because of Wu Ti's incursions beyond the Wall and the formation of a sophisticated cavalry force, Chinese influence spread into Central Asia, opening up commercial trade routes in and out of China. They exerted a profound influence, which persisted right up to the fall of the Manchus in 1912 before the onslaught, not of the northern horsemen, but of the modern world.

SPOTTED HORSES

ALTAI PONY STRAIN

THE SPOTTED COAT pattern may have developed as a form of protective camouflage, and can be presumed to have first occurred in prehistoric times. The earliest evidence of the spotted colouring is provided by the remarkable cave paintings at Lascaux and Pech-Merle in France. Both show spotted mares in foal. Those at Lascaux have a base colour of red or light brown covered with dark, symmetrical spots, while those at Pech-Merle have a light tan body colour. The paintings were made in about 18000 BC, and the horses are probably the remote ancestors of present-day spotted horses. There are numerous recognized spotted coat patterns (see pp.226–27), but most spotted horses share the characteristic white sclera round the eye, similar to that of humans, mottled skin around the muzzle and genitalia, and distinctive striped feet.

HORSES IN EARLY ART

As well as cave paintings, there is pictorial evidence of spotted horses in Europe from about 1000 BC. Artefacts found in burial sites belonging to the Scythians and Celts – steppe horsemen who entered Europe in the second millennium BC – show that they were familiar with spotted horses. Finds at a burial site at Hallstatt in Austria, excavated in the 19th century, include a sword dated about 800 BC, whose scabbard is decorated with four horsemen each riding a spotted horse. An Etruscan tomb of the same date in Italy also has a picture of a spotted horse. (The Etruscans had come from Asia Minor by ship some 150 years previously.)

THE HORSES OF FERGHANA

Ferghana, an area now in the south-west of the former Soviet Union, was famous in antiquity for its superior horses. It is a

CAVE PAINTING
This cave painting, at Pech-Merle in south-west France, was painted about 20,000 BC and clearly shows the incidence of spotted coat patterns.

matter of conjecture to what extent the blood of desert-bred animals influenced the Ferghanese horses, but there was an indisputable link. Successive waves of "barbarian", nomadic steppe horsemen – Kassites, Hyksos, Acheans, and others – had had close contact with Ferghana for more than 2,000 years before the Christian era, and it was Ferghana and Ili that were the principal sources of the Heavenly or Celestial horses (see pp.54–55), so valued by the Chinese, which were as much prized for their unusual coat patterns as for their physical qualities. Rakush, the spotted war-horse of the Persian hero Rustam, was almost certainly from Ferghana, and the Persians claimed that he was the ancestor of all spotted strains – a presumptuous assertion, since Rustam did not appear on the scene until about 400 BC. The heroic exploits of Rustam and Rakush are detailed in the 11th-century epic *Shah Nameh* of Firdausi and spotted horses are frequently depicted in the magnificent

and numerous Persian and Moghul miniatures and other art forms, up to and beyond the 15th century.

SPOTTED STRAINS AND BREEDS

By the 8th century AD, tapestries and manuscripts show the presence of spotted horses all the way from Constantinople in the east to Spain in the west. Later, these dramatically marked horses appear in England, Denmark, and throughout Scandinavia with more frequency.

In the 16th century spotted horses became increasingly important and highly regarded in Austria, which like Spain was then part of the Hapsburg Empire. Large numbers of the famous Spanish horses were imported and it is mainly with this Spanish stock, combined with the genes of the earlier nomadic introductions, that Europe's spotted strains originated. Spanish horses were a predominant influence in Europe up to the end of the 18th century. Paintings by

SPOTTED BLANKET
The picture Horses Crossing a River by the Chinese artist Chao Meng-Fu (1254–1322) includes an excellent example of spotted "blanket" colouring on the horse in the centre of the painting.

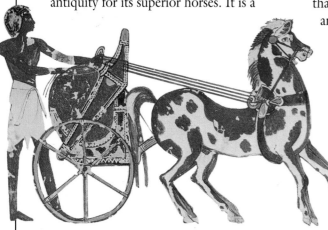

SPOTTED COMPANIONS
These spotted horses were painted in the tomb of Menna, an official of Thutmose IV, c. 1415 BC. They were probably his favourites, and for this reason were chosen to accompany him to the spirit world.

RUSTAM AND RAKUSH
The adventures of the Persian hero Rustam and his spotted war-horse Rakush are recounted in Firdausi's book Shah Nameh. *In this manuscript, which dates from 1486, Rakush is shown helping his master to kill a dragon.*

artists such as Hamilton and Ridinger include studies of the Spanish stud at Lipizza and the Spanish Riding School at Vienna (see pp.102–3), which clearly show that a powerful coloured and spotted gene was relatively common in the Spanish horses. The spotted coat pattern appeared in breeds as diverse as the Knabstrup (see pp.114–15), the Pinzgauer-Noriker (see pp.50–51), the

Gotland ponies (see pp.192–93), and in a strain of Welsh Mountain Pony (see pp.182–83). Spotted horses of great quality were also found throughout Poland.

It may be possible that there was once a spotted Arab strain, suggested by spotted horses of Arabian appearance that can be seen in early Egyptian artefacts. However, spotted or broken-coat patterns do not occur in the modern Arab, or in its derivative the Thoroughbred, although there is evidence of unusual colour patterns in imported Arab stock of the 18th century – Lord Oxford's Bloody-Shouldered

Arabian being a famous example. There is no apparent connection between this horse or his predecessors, Bloody Buttocks and Bay Bloody Buttocks, and The Tetrarch, the only known spotted Thoroughbred. Foaled in 1911, the Tetrarch represented the Herod line, founded by the Byerley Turk (see pp.120–21). He was described by Peter Willett in his book *The Thoroughbred* as "a kind of elephant grey with white and lime patches of various shapes and sizes". His brilliant daughter, Mumtaz Mahal, was not so strikingly marked, but nonetheless had a faint spotted coat pattern. There is also evidence of a coloured gene in Arab horses bred by Count Stanislas Potocki at his estate in Poland, early in the 19th century.

The Appaloosa, the American spotted breed (see pp.226–27), derives from the horses brought by the Spanish in the 16th century (see pp.216–17) and was bred along the Palouse River, from which it takes its name. Old, local names for spotted horses include *tigre* in Europe, *blagdon* in the UK and Wales (where it is still in use), and *chubarry*, a word redolent of the Romany people, with whom spotted and coloured horses are still popular.

HIGH SCHOOL
Johann Ridinger's 18th-century horseman rides a highly schooled spotted horse, which almost certainly came from one of the spotted Spanish strains that were then much in evidence.

THE BLOODY-SHOULDERED ARABIAN
Shown here is John Wootton's picture of Lord Oxford's Bloody-Shouldered Arabian, a grey with dark roan stains. It has been suggested that these markings were caused pre-natally by an accident to the horse's dam.

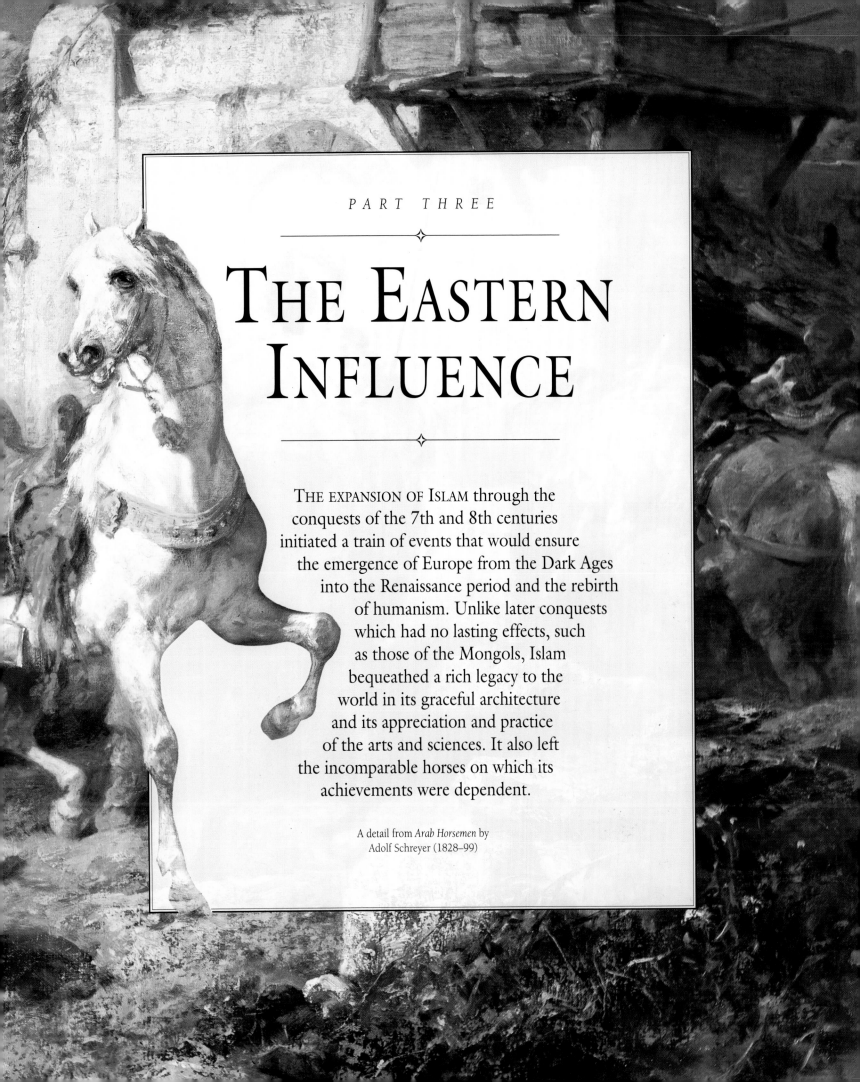

PART THREE

THE EASTERN INFLUENCE

THE EXPANSION OF ISLAM through the
conquests of the 7th and 8th centuries
initiated a train of events that would ensure
the emergence of Europe from the Dark Ages
into the Renaissance period and the rebirth
of humanism. Unlike later conquests
which had no lasting effects, such
as those of the Mongols, Islam
bequeathed a rich legacy to the
world in its graceful architecture
and its appreciation and practice
of the arts and sciences. It also left
the incomparable horses on which its
achievements were dependent.

A detail from *Arab Horsemen* by
Adolf Schreyer (1828–99)

DESERT HORSES OF THE EAST

ARAB HORSEMAN

Over the millennia a vast jigsaw of related equine strains, breeds, and types has been created. Although the horses all vary in size, conformation, colour, and character, a distinct pattern is discernible in the development of the species from the point of domestication, probably about 6,000 years ago, up to the present time. The evolution of this great variety of horses depended on three factors: the environment; human intervention in the cross-breeding of different strains; and the early existence of firmly established equine races that possessed a remarkable measure of prepotency (the ability to pass on character and type consistently). In this last respect none exceeds the influence of the eastern horses, the foundation stock for all of the world's breeds.

ANCESTRAL DESERT HORSES

These horses came from the countries of the Middle East, and extended into Central Asia. Geographical restraints, together with the powerful pressures of the desert, ensured an unequalled purity of blood, and the consequent prepotency that is the greatest weapon in the armoury of the horse breeder.

Today, these eastern ancestors are generally known as Arabian, but in England, in the formative years of the Thoroughbred during the 18th century (see pp.120–21),

they were identified, confusingly, as Syrians, Turks, and Barbs. Turks and Syrians were either identical to Arabians (see pp.64–65), or may have been strains that belonged to the same desert root. The Barb (see pp.66–67), the other wing of the eastern influence, was completely different.

THE BARB

The Barb, a North African horse introduced into Europe in quantity by the Berber horsemen of the 8th century, had little or nothing in common with the Arab in either appearance or character. Despite the inevitable crossing with Arab stock, the Barb remained genetically dominant to a massive degree. Although the Barb is not so widely recognized an influence as the Arabian, it has had a significant effect on the European and American breeds. The breed's influence was perpetuated through its most important derivative, the Spanish horse of the 16th and 17th centuries, which was considered to be the first horse of Europe well into the

TRADITIONAL SPLENDOUR
These colourful horsemen in full war regalia belong to the Fulani people of the Cameroon Republic. Their horses are Barb in appearance.

MOROCCAN BARB

In a painting of a Moroccan group by Mario Fortuny (1808–74), the horse is recognizably a Barb without any Arab blood. The Moroccan saddlery is traditional and the spur is of interest because of its length.

ARAB TYPE

This is a detail from the oil painting by J.F. Herring Senior (1795–1865). Clearly, some careless adjustment of the ornate sheet has frightened the stallion and precipitated its flight.

18th century. There is a basis of Spanish blood throughout the warmblood population of Europe, and it is there in such diverse breeds as Lipizzaners (see pp.112–13), Friesians (see pp.48–49), Frederiksborgs (see pp.114–15), Irish Draughts (see pp.396–97), Cleveland Bays (see pp.306–7), Kladrubers (see p.158), Connemaras (see pp.180–81), Highland Ponies (see pp.178–79), and Welsh Cobs (see pp.184–85). The Barb, as well as its offshoot the Spanish horse, also played its part in the evolution of the Thoroughbred (see pp.120–21), although in a secondary role to the Arabian.

THE ARAB

There are no definitive explanations for the origins of either the Barb or the Arab, but there is very strong evidence of a race of fixed and recognizable Arab character in and around the Arabian Peninsula at least 2,500 years before the Christian era. The Bedu tribes of the Arabian desert, who are indelibly associated with the Arab, trace their relationship back to around 3000 BC with the mare Baz and the stallion Hoshaba. The former was captured in the Yemen by Baz, the great-great-grandson of Noah.

The Bedu meticulously maintained the purity of the strains, and practised the careful in-breeding that fixed the most desirable

features in subsequent stock. In the absence of outside influences they created a horse that was unmistakeable in appearance, type, and movement. The harsh environment, and the rigours of nomadic life, added to its conformational and constitutional strengths, as well as to its inherent soundness and powers of endurance, which cannot be matched, except perhaps by the Barb.

It is probable that despite its ram-like profile the Nisean horse, used by the Persian armies in the 6th century BC (see pp.34–35), was influenced by the Arabian. The Bactrian horses from further to the east, near present-day Afghanistan, and the Heavenly horses that were so admired by the Chinese (see pp.54–55), may also have benefited from desert blood.

Once Arabian blood had penetrated Europe, it was used to refine and up-grade many indigenous breeds and types. It made its greatest contribution in the evolution of the English Thoroughbred. By then, eastern blood was evident in most of the native stock of Britain, Ireland, and continental Europe. Indeed, there is eastern blood in almost everything from Trakehners to Percherons, Haflingers, and French Trotters, in American breeds, and even in the small, active ponies of Indonesia.

THE THOROUGHBRED

The Thoroughbred was the end-product that arose from the import of Arab and Barb horses to England in the 18th century. This is Orlando, winner of the 1844 Derby, painted by J.F. Herring Senior.

ISLAMIC INVASIONS

BYZANTINE CAVALRY

ARAB CAVALRY

THE ISLAMIC CONQUESTS of the 7th and 8th centuries and the subsequent 700-year occupation of the Iberian peninsula were as significant in the development of civilization as the influence of Classical Greece and Rome. Islam, largely dependent upon its superlative desert-bred horses, extended its suzerainty up to the Great Wall of China, and came within an ace of enveloping Europe. There never was an occupation of so great an area which conferred so many cultural riches upon the conquered peoples, nor any conquest made from ostensibly higher motives. It was said that "from Malaysia to Morocco", Islam was "founded in the hoofprints of the Arabian horse". It would not be unreasonable to claim that the same is true of most of the world's equine races.

CAMEL MINDERS AND RIDERS

For centuries the Arab people were hardly enthusiastic horsemen, so it is necessary to understand how it was that they were able to create a large cavalry and maintain sufficient formations in the field to make possible their far-reaching conquests.

In previous centuries Arab tribesmen had filled the role of camel-minders and riders. They had served under Alexander (see pp.40–41) in those capacities, and were also used by the Romans to service baggage trains. However, in neither role could they have been regarded as being anything other than support troops for the striking force.

THE PROPHET MOHAMMED

By the 4th century AD, however, the Arab tribesmen had developed a more horse-orientated society. Nonetheless, it was not until the 6th century, with the influence of the charismatic Prophet Mohammed (570–632), that any impetus was given to the breeding and ownership of horses. This impetus provided the means for Islamic expansion, and also affected the future course of equine development. Wherever their conquests took the Muslim horsemen, their horses were inevitably brought into contact with the indigenous stock, stamping an indelible imprint upon generations of horses, which is still apparent to this day.

The Prophet Mohammed, the founder of the Islamic religion, was both a visionary and a pragmatist. He saw his mission as the unification of the tribes in a religious brotherhood dedicated to *Jihad*, the Holy War, which was to be waged not so much in the interests of material expansion, although that was not an unwelcome incentive, as for

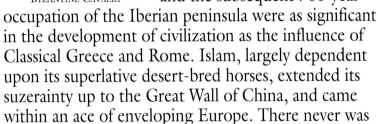

BEFORE MEDINA
In this picture from Istanbul's Topkapi Museum, the Prophet, attended by a dignitary riding a very fine ass, is shown persuading the Muslim forces to meet the Meccan pagans' attack within Medina rather than risk battle at Ohod.

19TH-CENTURY ARAB HORSES
Shown here is a painting of an Arab with two horses by François Hippolyte Lalaise (1812–84). Although it is painted in the romantic style of the 19th century, the picture is very accurate in its portrayal of detail.

WARRIORS OF ISLAM

This painting of Arab warriors in a city is by Paul Dominique Phillipoteaux. The painting is skilful, but the horses are not recognizable as Arabs, Barbs, or any other specific breed.

the valued territories of Syria, Palestine, Mesopotamia, and Armenia. By 643 they occupied all of North Africa. They had taken the Indus Valley in present-day Pakistan by 644, and by 694 were the masters of Central Asia, an area surrounded by Khorasan, Bokhara, Samarkand, and Ferghana.

The Moorish followers of the faith crossed the Strait of Gibraltar into Spain in 711, where they defeated Roderic, the last of the Visigoth kings. When they had secured the whole of the Iberian Peninsula they advanced over the Pyrenees and up into Gaul. In 732, 100 years after the death of Mohammed, they were halted and defeated at Poitiers by Charles Martel and his heavily armoured Frankish knights. Just as the Catalaunian fields was the turning point for both Rome and the Hun Empire, so this battle signalled the ultimate defeat for the Moors. They fell back into the Iberian Peninsula, and even though they occupied it for another 700 years, they never advanced any further into Europe.

the spiritual extension of Islam. It was a war for the conversion of souls that would bring all mankind to the worship of Allah as the One True God. In order to achieve his evangelizing purpose he needed an army of mounted soldiers who could make the most effective use of horses of such unique quality, and the care and management of horses was incorporated into the *Hadith*, the body of tradition concerning the Prophet. "Who feeds the horse for the triumph of religion," said the Prophet, "makes a magnificent loan to God."

In Islam, the horse is called "the supreme blessing", bringing "happiness in this world, rich booty and eternal reward". In a sense, horse care as a tenet of faith was a revival of the old Arabian religion, which had allowed the worship of the horse through the idols Ya'uk and Ya'bub.

(Conversely Islam forbids any form of idolatry, which is why there are no images to illustrate for us the Arab way of life.) Mohammed's teachings were scrupulously observed by his followers with warriors welcoming death in battle as a sure passport to the eternal joys of Paradise.

THE ISLAMIC EMPIRE

After Mohammed died in 632, the Muslim armies burst out of the desert lands of the Middle East, and in a series of conquests, led initially by the Prophet's successor Abubekr, they carried their standards east and west.

A decade later most of the Byzantine Empire had fallen to Islam and the armies of the Prophet controlled

HEAVENLY CREATURE

Al Borak (which is Arabian for The Lightning) is a mythical creature sent to earth by the Angel Gabriel. Legend describes Al Borak as having the face and voice of a man, eyes like stars, and the wings of an eagle.

ARAB

THE ARAB HORSE is regarded as the "fountainhead" of the world's breeds. Because of its genetic purity it is remarkably prepotent, consistently stamping its stock with its own powerful character and acting as an up-grading and refining influence. It has played a significant part in the evolution of almost every recognized breed, its greatest contribution being in the foundation of the Thoroughbred (see pp.120–21). Although bigger and faster than the Arab, the Thoroughbred cannot approach it in terms of stamina, soundness, intelligence, and beauty.

JANOW PODLASKI
These Arab mares are at pasture at Janow Podlaski, Poland, a stud that has become a repository for the world's finest bloodlines.

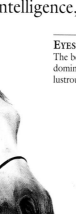

MANE
The mane and tail hair is fine and silky.

EYES
The beautiful head is dominated by the lustrous eyes.

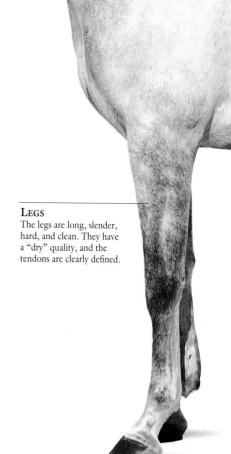

MUZZLE
The head tapers to a very small muzzle with large, flared nostrils.

LEGS
The legs are long, slender, hard, and clean. They have a "dry" quality, and the tendons are clearly defined.

LEGEND AND HISTORY

The Bedu tribes of Arabia kept few written records, but preserved horses' pedigrees by word of mouth. One of the first written accounts of the Arab was produced in about AD 786 by the Arab historian, El Kelbi, who attempted to record the history and pedigrees of the Arab horse, starting from around 3000 BC. His work, although sometimes more allegorical than factual, underlines the antiquity of this equine race.

Later, the Emir Abd-el-Kader (1808–83), in his correspondence with a Frenchman, General Daumas (1803–71), divided the history of the breed into four eras: Adam to Ishmael; Ishmael to Solomon; Solomon to the Prophet Mohammed; and then from the Prophet onwards. He also provided an explanation of the Arab's creation which, though beautiful, takes no account of the theory of evolution.

"When God wanted to create the horse, he said to the South Wind, 'I want to make a creature of you. Condense'. And the Wind condensed. The Archangel Gabriel immediately appeared and took a handful of the stuff and presented it to God, who made a brown bay, or burnt chestnut, upon saying, 'I call you Horse; I make you Arabian and I give you the chestnut colour of the ant; I have hung happiness from the forelock which hangs between your eyes; you shall be the Lord of the other animals. Men shall follow you wherever you go; you shall be as good for pursuit as for flight; riches shall be on your back and fortune shall come through your mediation.' Then He put on the horse the mark of glory and happiness, a white mark in the middle of the forehead."

The four eras proposed by Abd-el-Kader are more firmly rooted in fact. The first may not be entirely relevant, although Ishmael, the outcast son of Abraham and the first ancestor of the desert Bedu tribes, was a real person who made use of horses. After the break-up of the Bedu tribes, which followed the death of Ishmael, the story of this desert horse continues in King Solomon's reign. With total disregard for the Israelite law that forbade the keeping of horses on the grounds of idolatry, Solomon encouraged horse-breeding by keeping no fewer than 1,200 riding horses and 40,000 chariot horses in his royal stables. Finally, there is the influence of the Prophet

Mohammed (see pp.66–67) and Islam, which ensured the spread of the breed throughout the Old World.

ARAB STUDS

The 18th- and 19th-century state studs of Europe, such as Marbach in Germany, Janow Podlaski in Poland, Bábolna in Hungary, and the French studs at Pompadour, Pau, Tarbes, and Gelos, all gave impetus to the development of the Arab horse, as did some notable private studs. The Potocki family, reflecting the long Polish association with these horses, bred superb Arabians at their famous Antoniny Stud. These Arabs were to extend their influence all over the world. In the UK, Wilfrid and Anne Scawen Blunt founded the Crabbet Stud following their journeys to Arabia in 1878–79, when the degeneration

BODY GUARD STALLION
This Australian-bred Arab stallion was presented to the President of India and kept in the lines of the President's Body Guard in Delhi.

of the breed was already apparent. Later they purchased what was left of the world's most renowned collection of Arabs, which belonged to Abbas Pasha I. Crabbet horses were the foundation for the breeding of Arabs not only in the UK but also in the US, Australia, and South Africa.

CONFORMATION

The appearance of the Arab is unique among the equine races. However, it would be wrong to accept the assertion put forward by some breed enthusiasts that "there is only one true type of pure Arabian" – there are

differences of detail, nuances within an overall type. The most distinctive feature, apart from the outline, is the short, very fine, "dry" head, which has clearly visible veining. In profile, the face is notably concave, or "dished", and the forehead is convex, forming a shield shape called the *jibbah*. The muzzle is so small that it fits into a half-cupped hand, while the nostrils are very large, and can flare widely. The eyes are enormous and expressive; an accepted authority, the late R.S. Summerhays, wrote that "in appearance they must be dark and deep in colour, very soulful in the mare, in the stallion showing great alertness, with enormous challenging dignity". The ears are short and mobile, and curve inwards. The jaw bones are so generously rounded that it is possible to fit a fist between them. Another notable feature is the *mitbah*, the point where the head joins the neck. The greater the arch here, the more easily the head can be moved in all directions.

Arabs have 17 ribs, 5 lumbar vertebrae, and 16 tail bones, whereas other horses have a 18-6-18 pattern. This bone formation accounts for the distinctive shape of the back and quarters and the high tail carriage. The breed has a "floating" action, as if moving on invisible springs. Although it can be over 1.52 m (15 hh), the Arab is usually around 1.50 m (14.3 hh). However, it is always referred to as a horse, not a pony, whatever may be its height.

BODY
The body is compact, the back short and slightly concave, and the croup long and level.

TAIL
The tail is never pulled or trimmed. In movement it is carried arched and high.

HIND LEGS
The conformational failings have been largely eliminated by careful breeding since the late 19th century.

HEIGHT
1.50 m
(14.3 hh)

ORIGINS

THE ORIGIN OF THE ARAB is unclear, but there is evidence that it existed on the Arabian Peninsula around 2500 BC and was maintained there in its pure form. The Muslim conquests in the 7th century AD extended the breed's influence. During the 18th and 19th centuries it was established in the state studs of Europe, and at private studs in the UK. From there it spread to Russia, Scandinavia, the US, and the English-speaking countries, to become the major force in equine development.

BARB

THE BARB OF NORTH AFRICA is the second of the world's foundation breeds. Like its better-known neighbour, the Arab (see pp.64–65), it is a desert horse, but the two are very dissimilar in appearance and character. There is a theory that the Barb may have come from a pocket of wild horses in the fertile coastal area, which escaped the ravages of the Ice Age. If that were the case, it could be argued that it is an older breed than the Arab. However, definitive ancestry remains a vexed question, and in the absence of documentary evidence is likely to remain so.

ALGERIAN SCENE
The Barb horse is not beautiful, but it is one of the toughest and most enduring breeds in the world. This Algerian scene is typical of the area.

BARBS AND ARABS

Arab and Barb horses were probably crossed during the Muslim conquests in the 7th and 8th centuries (see pp.62–63), and the modern Barb certainly has a percentage of Arab blood. Surprisingly, however, there is little sign of the Arab's prepotency in the Barb, with its characteristically long, convex head, sloping quarters, and low-set tail; this seems to indicate a massively dominant gene in the breed. Indeed, the Barb bears some resemblance to the postulated pre-domestic Horse Type 3 (see pp.22–23), which was, it is suggested, highly resistant to heat and drought, like the Barb, and would have been just as spare and hard.

HEAD
The profile is usually straight or even convex, unlike that of the Arab. The curve of this horse's ears is not typical of the breed.

NECK
The neck is arched, and the withers are often prominent.

BARB INFLUENCE

The Berbers from North Africa formed a substantial part of the Muslim armies that invaded Spain in the 8th century, and it seems clear that their Barb horses played a major part in the development of the Spanish Horse, the modern version of which is the Andalucian (see pp.108–9). Without much doubt the Barb was also influential in the evolution of the Thoroughbred (see pp. 120–21). Horses from North Africa, variously termed

NORTH AFRICAN HORSEMEN
Berber horsemen ride in the high North African saddles that have changed little since the days of the Mameluke Turks, and they usually use the severe ring bit favoured by those warriors.

SHOULDERS
The shoulders are flat and usually rather upright.

LEGS
The legs are slender and very hard. In some horses the chest may be narrow, causing the forelegs to be set close together.

Berber, Barb, or Barbary, were imported to the Royal Studs of England from before the time of the Plantagenets. Roan Barbary, the favourite horse of Richard II (1377–99), was one of many horses of the same origin at the king's studs. Barb blood, together with that of the Spanish Jennet, itself at least a first cousin to the Barb, was certainly a predominant element in the Royal "running horses", which formed the base stock for the early Thoroughbred.

There is also enough evidence to show that Ireland's Connemara (see pp.180–81) owes a debt to Barb horses, "those swift runners that do come out of Tunnis land", as the 16th-century authority Thomas Blundeville put it. There is even more evidence showing the effect of the Barb

on French stock. The medieval Limousin, which in its time was purpose-bred as a military charger, was based largely on Barb stock brought to France by Muslim armies. The Muslims were defeated at the Battle of Poitiers in AD 732 (see pp.68–69), but after that battle Barb stock was used to upgrade the Frankish horses, which at Poitiers had been found to be far too slow to pursue the broken enemy.

The Barb may also have had something to do with the famous white horses of the Camargue (see pp.262–63), to which it bears a strong resemblance, while it is certainly possible to perceive its presence in the horse breeds and types of both North and South America. The various mustang societies of North America, whose object is the conservation of the wild horses, place much emphasis upon what they term "Spanish Barb" blood, and one organization, the Spanish Mustang Registry, defines a "primitive" Barb type which it equates with the North African Barb.

THE MODERN BARB

The modern Barb, still plentiful in Algeria, Morocco, and Tunisia, is the traditional mount of the

ORIGINS

THE BARB HORSE originated in the fertile coastal areas of North Africa, which include Morocco and the more northern parts of Algeria and Libya. It can also be found as far south in the African continent as Nigeria and Cameroon. The Barb, like the Arab and the Akhal-Teke, is a "desert" horse, fine-skinned and resistant to the heat and droughts of its natural environment. It does not have the beauty and floating movement of the Arab, but it is just as tough and enduring.

famous Spahi cavalry, which has always used Barb stallions. As a result of the Arab influence, it is usually grey, but it was originally bay or black. It stands between 1.47 m and 1.57 m (14.2–15.2 hh), and is renowned for being incredibly tough, possessed of great stamina (as well as a less than certain temper), and for having the ability to subsist on meagre rations. It is agile and very fast over short distances.

QUARTERS
This horse's quarters are rounded. More usually, the quarters slope from the croup to a low-set tail.

HIND LEGS
The hind legs are sometimes cow-hocked, but this does not prevent the Barb from being agile and remarkably sound.

FEET
As with other desert horses, the feet tend to be narrow and sometimes "boxy", but they are enormously hard-wearing.

HEIGHT
1.47–1.57 m
(14.2–15.2 hh)

A FULANI HORSE
This horse, owned by a high-ranking member of the Fulani people from the Cameroon Republic, is clearly of Barb descent. It is wearing traditional saddlery. The elaborate bridle is hand-crafted and often adorned with shells, precious stones, and even gold.

DEFENDERS OF THE FAITH

CHARLEMAGNE

THE MOORISH INVASIONS in the 7th and 8th centuries had a profound effect upon the world. The Muslim culture acted as an reinvigorating force that stretched upwards through North Africa to Spain, to touch the heart of a Europe lost in the Dark Ages, whose own cultural heritage was lying in ruins. Above all, the expansion of the Islamic Empire was to spur Christendom into a renewal of faith so powerful that it would counter, and finally break, the onrush of the Muslim armies. The defeat of the Moors at the battle of Poitiers, in AD 732, is regarded as crucial in halting the Muslims' advance into Europe. It also marked the beginning of the western concept of chivalry, in which the mounted knight represented the highest ideals of the age and became the embodiment of order, decency, and moral rectitude.

THE MOORISH HORSEMEN

That Islam had achieved so much within the space of 100 years was due to its ability to field large bodies of swiftly moving light horsemen. If Christian Europe was to have any hope of opposing the alien invasions of its borders, and thus prevent the very eclipse of Christendom, it had to create a mounted force that would be more than a match for the Moorish cavalry. It was to this task that Charles Martel, first minister to the Frankish king and known as "The Hammer of Christendom", addressed himself.

When the Moors crossed into Spain in AD 711, the Frankish kingdom of Gaul would have still been ill-equipped to offer more than a token resistance had it come under direct attack. Indeed, the power and national cohesion of Gaul had been in constant decline since the fall of Rome in the 5th century, and its mounted forces were non-existent. The last Merovingian king of Gaul had been reduced to travelling in an ox-cart, and when the Franks fought against the Goths in Italy in 539 and 552 they had done so as infantry, with only their king and his bodyguard on horseback.

MARTEL'S ARMY

Recognizing that the Moors could not be defeated without substantial cavalry support, Martel set about the reorganization of the Frankish army. He put the emphasis on heavy cavalry – the opposite of the Moorish armies. Central to the concept were large bodies of disciplined, armoured knights. These men would close ranks to form an impenetrable steel wall, which would absorb the force of the Muslim attack. Thereafter, a concerted charge by Martel's army would be able to break any concentration of lightly armed horsemen by a combination of weight and impetus.

To raise his force of mounted knights, Martel made grants of land in return for military services. This practice was to become a dominant factor in the political and social systems of the Middle Ages. Martel's way of using heavy cavalry was also

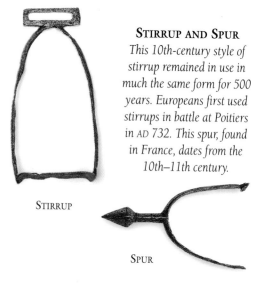

STIRRUP AND SPUR
This 10th-century style of stirrup remained in use in much the same form for 500 years. Europeans first used stirrups in battle at Poitiers in AD 732. This spur, found in France, dates from the 10th–11th century.

STIRRUP

SPUR

FORTH TO BATTLE
The fresco at the Chapel of the Templars, Cressac, depicts the battle of Brocquel in 1163. The saddle, encircling the rider for greater security, and the braced leg position, are typical of the period. If the horses portrayed here were shown in proportion to the riders, they could be no more than 1.42 m (14 hh).

1.42 m (14 hh) high, and riders who sat with short stirrups and bent knees. In this position an archer, standing in his stirrups like a polo player when he strikes the ball, could use his weapon to best effect. Such a seat also made it easier for a rider to get his weight behind a downward-slashing sword. Only rarely, if ever, did Muslim horsemen use the tactic of the concerted knee-to-knee charge.

The Frankish knights were slower, but weighed twice as much as their opponents. They operated as a compact body rather than in the loose formation of the Muslim horsemen. Riders sat with their legs thrust forwards, and braced themselves between the cantle of the saddle and the stirrup. This was one of the first occasions when the stirrup was widely used by European cavalry (see pp.92–93). In the event, repeated Moorish attacks bounced off the steel wall, and when the knights counter-attacked, the impact of the charge knocked the Moorish cavalry off its feet, although the Frankish horses were neither fast enough nor fit enough to pursue their broken enemy.

Martel's grandson, Charlemagne (742–814), continued and expanded the principle of heavy cavalry, as he drove the Moors from northern Spain and completed the unification of Central Europe. Champion of the Christian faith, and the most powerful figure in

MUSLIM VERSUS CHRISTIAN
Charlemagne, the Holy Roman Emperor, defended Christian Europe against the Muslim invaders. Here, in an illustration from Les Grandes Chroniques de France *(1375–79), he and his army face the Muslim powers, who are horribly depicted as devils beating heathen tambourines.*

Europe at that time, he founded the Holy Roman Empire in AD 800. More than anyone else, he was responsible for the romantic image of the Christian knight.

THE CRUSADES

Two hundred years after the foundation of the Holy Roman Empire, the mounted knights of Christendom were again on the offensive, with men such as El Cid (see pp.70–71) leading the *Reconquista* that would drive the Moors from the Iberian Peninsula. El Cid retook Valencia in 1094. The following year, at the synod of Clermont, Pope Urban II called on the Christian powers to join in a crusade to rid the Holy Land of the "infidel" – the Seljuk Turks, who had occupied Palestine for a quarter of a century. Geoffrey de Bouillon led the first crusade into Asia Minor in 1097, and Jerusalem fell to the Christian Knights in 1101. Thereafter, it was held, though somewhat precariously, by the order of Templars, the Knights Hospitallers, and the Teutonic Knights.

Just as participation in the *Jihad*, or Holy War, was an essential act of faith for the pious Muslim, the Crusades were, in theory, a duty for the Christian knight, which were undertaken in the service of God and one's liege lord. Thousands of men travelled eastwards, suffering the hardships of the journey as a form of pilgrimage.

CHECKMATE
This chess piece of a medieval horseman comes from the Treasure of Saint Denis Charlemagne set. It was made from ivory in central Italy, in the 11th century. The accoutrements of the knight are clearly depicted in the helm, shield, sword, chain-mail, and stirrup.

widely adopted; it encouraged the breeding of horses that were large enough to carry an armoured man, and possessed stamina and courage. The immediate need was for a cross between the slow-moving Forest-type horse of Europe and the oriental hotblood supplied by the Arab invasions. Martel's cavalry horses probably resembled coarser, much less active versions of the present-day Friesian (see pp.48–49) or perhaps even the Percheron (see pp.94–95). These horses would not have stood much above 1.52 m (15 hh).

TYPES OF CAVALRY

The battle of Poitiers in AD 732 was, among other things, a clash between sharply contrasted equestrian philosophies. The Muslim method, precursor of the light cavalry tradition, required small, tough, agile horses not more than

EMPEROR OF THE FAITH
In this 14th-century illustration by Vincent de Beauvais, Charlemagne the Great is shown holding the orb of majesty. Charlemagne, who founded the Holy Roman Empire in AD 800, championed the image of the Christian knight and expanded the principle of heavy cavalry.

EL CID & BABIECA

The spirit of the Spanish Reconquista

IN MEMORIAM
The memorial to Babieca, the steed of El Cid for 30 years, is on the former site of the monastery of San Pedro de Cardena, Burgos, Spain.

FOREMOST AMONG the heroes of Christendom was Ruy, or Rodrigo, Diaz, leader of the *Reconquista*, the movement that ended the 700-year occupation of the Iberian Peninsula by the Moors (see pp.62–63). Ruy Diaz, known by friend and foe alike as *El Cid*, the Lord, or as *El Campeador*, the Warrior, was born at Vivar near Burgos in Castile in about 1040. A ruthless, professional soldier he passed into legend as a hero, the saviour of his country. His exploits are celebrated in the 12th-century epic, *Poema del Cid*, and the later *Cronica Particular del Cid* (1512), which tell us both of the man and Babieca, the white horse on which he campaigned for 30 years. The horse was a present from El Cid's godfather, a priest known as Peyre Pringos, or "Fat Pete". Fat Pete was able to offer the young man a choice of the best colts, because Spanish religious houses, such as the Carthusians' house at Jerez de la Frontera, were traditionally concerned with the breeding of horses. The boy chose a particularly plain, immature animal, forcing the exasperated priest to exclaim "*Babieca!*" (Stupid!), by which the horse

became famous. An ideal war-horse, Babieca was what is now known as an Andalucian (see pp.108–9). Although up to weight, he was probably no more than 1.52 m (15 hh). He was responsive, agile, and full of the "*brio escondido*", the hidden metal, that gave him fire and courage. El Cid died in 1099 at Valencia, which was under siege. Aware that news of his death would lower his troops' morale and encourage the enemy, he gave his last order. In obedience to his commands, his body was secured in Babieca's saddle, his shield fastened in place, and in full armour, with his sword fixed upright in his lifeless hand, he led his silent horsemen out of the city towards the Moors' camp at midnight precisely. The knights were dressed all in white and carried white banners, and it was said that El Cid's face shone through the open visor of his helmet with an "unearthly luminence". The ghostly apparition on the pure white horse, cantering in front of the silent ranks, caused the Moors to flee, crying that El Cid had risen from the dead. The Spanish pursued them without mercy. El Cid was buried at the monastery of San Pedro de Cardena, near Burgos, although his body was later moved to Burgos Cathedral. Babieca was never ridden again. He died two years later at the age of 40.

RECONQUISTA
El Cid, the national hero of Spain, is remembered in this piece of statuary at the monastery of San Pedro de Cardena. This warlike pose typifies the philosophy of Ruy Diaz, the Warrior: "You see the horse sweating and the sword bloody, that is how one vanquishes Moors in the field".

THE LAST BATTLE

The lifeless El Cid, strapped to Babieca's saddle, led his troops out of Valencia to win his last battle against the Moors in 1099. "The battle he won, After life was done." No man ever rode Babieca again.

THE WARRIOR

This statue to El Cid (Ruy Diaz) is at Burgos, where his remains lie in the Cathedral. It commemorates and immortalizes a ruthless "freelance" who founded a Christian order of chivalry to protect the Faith and liberate Spain. His exploits against the occupying Moors earned him the adulation of his countrymen.

THE MONGOLS

MONGOL ARCHER

THE MONGOL Empire lasted from 1206 to 1405. The expansion of the empire resulted in the final and most terrible assault by nomadic barbarians on the civilized world. At its peak it was the greatest land empire in the world, and its territories stretched from Java and Korea in the east to Poland in the west. To the north it touched the Arctic Circle, while Turkey and Persia marked its southern frontiers. It was created by the most ruthlessly effective cavalry force that ever existed, the brilliantly handled "hordes" of Genghis Khan (c.1167–1227) and his successors. A fearless and inspired warrior, Genghis Khan was a cavalry commander whose genius has never been exceeded in the history of warfare.

GENGHIS KHAN

Genghis Khan, born Temujin, was a member of one of the primitive, nomadic, Mongol-speaking tribes that existed in the harsh Gobi Desert of Mongolia. He was a king at the age of 13, and by 1206 had subdued and united all the Mongol tribes. His strength was such that he had his seal engraved with one succinct sentence of supreme, unchallengeable assurance: "God in Heaven, the Kha Khan, the Power of God, on Earth".

THE BATTLEFIELD

This 16th-century miniature shows Genghis Khan on the battlefield in 1201. The bows and arrow quivers carried by the Mongol warriors were an essential part of their personal weaponry, but in close combat they used the sword, lance, and mace.

network of messengers who carried information over hundreds of routes, thousands of kilometres long, in every direction. The *Yam* was used for almost two centuries.

THE MONGOL HORDES

The Mongol armies consisted wholly of horsemen – even the siege division of 10,000 men under the Master of Artillery depended on horse power. The "hordes", a term used by the Mongols, were tightly organized formations, under the equivalent of a modern general staff system, which observed strict discipline.

The men were infinitely enduring and self-reliant. They lived off the land, without supply trains to support them. Their rations were dried meat, which was laid under the saddles or even in the seat of their trousers to soften it up, supplemented by delicacies such as butter made from mares' milk, which they kept in their clothing. They also carried dried mares' milk curds in leather bags that inflated when they forded rivers.

The Mongols rarely took off their clothes unless garments had to be replaced. Having been toughened as babies by daily dips in ice-cold water, they forsook water as a cleansing agent early in life, preferring to use

As the Mongols were not a numerous people, Ghengis Khan augmented his armies with Turkish tribesmen. His conquests were violent and almost wholly destructive. In nomad fashion he took what he wanted, and destroyed whatever was of no immediate use, including entire populations and some of the greatest cities of antiquity.

Genghis Khan administered his empire with rare and consummate skill, largely from the saddle of his horse. He created the *Yassa*, a code of remarkably just laws under which he ruled no fewer than 50 nations. He also instituted an advanced communication system known as the *Yam*. This was a

THE PERFECT WARRIOR

Genghis Khan is shown here in later life, sumptuously robed and seated on an elaborate throne. By the time of his death in 1227 the Mongol Empire extended from China to the banks of the Danube.

grease, which had the advantage of keeping out the cold. It was said that with the wind in the right direction a Mongol army could be smelt up to 30 km (20 miles) away.

Each man had up to five horses, and changed from one to another as necessary, while behind the main body there was a large herd of remounts. The presence of the herd increased the mobility of the *tumans*, which frequently travelled over 124 km (80 miles) a day. The horses also provided fresh meat, and the mares gave milk. When marching, men could be sustained by blood taken from a horse's neck, thickened over heat and then eaten like a black pudding.

Importantly, the supporting herds helped to create the impression of a vast host, an impression reinforced by tying dummies to the horses. This practice may account for the large numbers attributed to them. In fact, the largest Mongol army under Genghis Khan was no more than about 230,000 men. Initially, the horses were mainly of Mongolian pony stock, but the Mongols swiftly acquired good horses of eastern type in the course of their conquests.

TAMURLANE

Tamurlane (1370–1405), the last of the Mongol nomads and a direct descendant of Genghis Khan, was an even more ruthless warrior. To mark his victory at Isfahan, Persia, he left a pyramid of 70,000 human skulls.

TACTICS AND TRAINING

In battle, the Mongol armies had perfected a highly co-ordinated method of warfare, far superior to any practised by their adversaries. They were masters of the swift, encircling tactic called the *tulughama*. Like the hook of modern armoured divisions, this turned the enemy's flank so that the attackers could take them in the rear. Another ploy was the feigned withdrawal: the army retreated for perhaps two days then, on fresh horses, returned in less than a day so as to deliver fierce attacks on the enemy's extended lines.

The hordes trained when they were not campaigning. The highlight was the Great Hunt, which was carried out in a semi-circle over a 160-km (100-mile) front, through every sort of terrain. The game was driven before the warriors until the circle was closed, when every living creature within it was slaughtered.

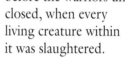

TAMURLANE

The Mongol Empire only lasted 200 years, for, as a contemporary Chinese general, Yeh-lu T'su T'su, said, "the Empire was won on horseback, but you cannot govern on horseback". The last Mongol ruler was Timur, or Tamurlane (1370–1405), who because of his limp became known as Timur-i-Leng, or Timur the Lame. He ransacked Delhi in 1398–99, but his descendants, the Moghuls, gave to India the period of her greatest splendour and cultural achievement.

AKHAL-TEKE

EQUESTRIAN HISTORY, particularly when it comes to breed origins, inevitably gives rise to obscurities, contradictions, and even mysteries. The Akhal-Teke, a desert horse that lives around oases in Turkmenistan, combines all three in generous measure. Together with the Iomud, a related type that is very similar to the horses found in the Pazyryk burial mounds (see pp.30–31), it is closely associated with the Turkmene. It is possible that the Turkmene and the Akhal-Teke are no more than variants on an ancient theme, occupying adjacent geographical positions.

HEAD
The finely-drawn head and long neck rise almost vertically from the shoulders, so that the mouth is held above the level of the withers. This is a feature peculiar to the breed.

SHOULDERS
The shoulders slope, and the withers are usually high.

ORIGINS

The origin of the Akhal-Teke is part of the mystery. In at least 1000 BC, horses bred at Ashkhabad, still a centre for the Akhal-Teke, were famed as racehorses, as they are today. Five hundred years later, the 30,000-strong Bactrian guard of King Darius of Persia (522–486 BC) were mounted on horses of this type in and around Turkmenistan. The official Russian version, which is not easily substantiated, claims that the Akhal-Teke is a pure breed. It also claims that it is as old as the Arab (see pp.64–65). Whether this is true or not, the breed approximates almost exactly to the postulated Horse Type 3 (see pp.22–23) and there is a distinct similarity to the Arab racing strain, the Munaghi. The question as to whether the Munaghi Arab

A TYPICAL EXAMPLE
This is a good and very typical specimen of the Akhal-Teke horse. It displays all the distinctive character and unique conformational features of this unusual desert breed.

influenced these desert horses of Turkmenistan is worth considering as is the opposite. What is certain is that the Akhal-Teke is unique amongst equines, just as enduring and resistant to intense heat as the Arab, and capable of covering great distances on minimal water rations.

CHARACTERISTICS

By western standards the Akhal-Teke is not a perfect specimen, a fact recognized in the breed description. Standing at about 1.57 m

ORIGINS

THE NATURAL HABITAT of the Akhal-Teke is in the oases of Turkmenistan, north of Iran and east of the Caspian Sea. The Komsomol stud farm at Ashkhabad is a major breeding centre, but the Akhal-Teke is also bred at Lugov in Kazakhstan, Gubden in Dagestan, and in a small way at the Tersk stud in the northern Caucasus. Akhal-Teke horses were also bred in the horse sections of various collective farms in Turkmenistan and are frequently crossed with other breeds.

CHEST
The chest is deep enough, but is narrow between the legs.

(15.2 hh), it is often long-backed with a tendency to be split-up behind, lacking the substantial second thigh so prized by western riders. The rib cage is also shallow but there is an unusually pronounced muscular development and the head, set on a long neck, is arresting in appearance. The skin is particularly thin and the hair is very fine, which is a characteristic of desert-bred horses. The coat colours are bay, chestnut, or dun, and they frequently have a golden metallic sheen. A peculiar feature of the breed, which is not appreciated in the West, is for the head to be carried above the level of the rider's hand. This head position is termed "above the bit", and is deemed to reduce the rider's effective control.

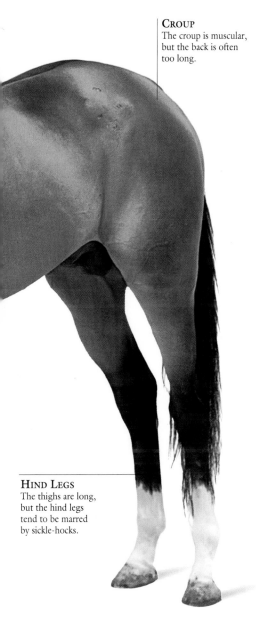

CROUP
The croup is muscular, but the back is often too long.

HIND LEGS
The thighs are long, but the hind legs tend to be marred by sickle-hocks.

WARDING OFF EVIL
A Turkmene girl shows off her Akhal-Teke horse. The ornate collar, inset with semi-precious stones, acts as a charm to ward off evil.

Racing is endemic to the Turkoman people. Until recently, they kept their charges tethered and wrapped in heavy felt both against the cold, desert nights and in the midday sun to ensure a complete absence of surplus fat. To maintain hard condition still further, they feed the horses on a high-protein, low-bulk diet. Traditionally, the feed comprises a little dry lucerne (when available), pellets of mutton fat, eggs, barley, and *quatlame*, a fried dough cake. In modern times the Akhal-Teke was "improved" for racing with outcrosses to the Thoroughbred. However, this reduced the horses' capacity to withstand intense heat. The policy has now been reversed, and breeders have returned to the pure lines.

COMPETITIVE SPORTS

The Akhal-Teke is renowned for its endurance over long distances in severe climatic conditions, even more than for its racing ability (which is not comparable to that of the Thoroughbred). The most famous test of their endurance was the ride from Ashkhabad to Moscow, made in 1935 by Akhal-Teke and Iomud horses. The

distance was 4,128 km (2,580 miles), 960 km (600 miles) of which was over desert, where water was not easily available. The horses travelled most of the way virtually without water. The journey was completed in 84 days, and the extraordinary feat has never been equalled.

In the countries that made up the former USSR, Akhal-Teke horses are used for a variety of competitive sports, such as jumping, long-distance riding, and dressage. The 1960 gold medal dressage winner in Rome, the stallion Absent, was an Akhal-Teke, and was the son of a noted high-jump specialist. It must be assumed that he was the exception proving the rule, since in order to win, he would have had to carry his head in the conventional manner, the mouth somewhat below the rider's hand.

In recent years the participation of the former Russian republics in international equestrian sport has increased, although the pattern is still far from being consistent. Inevitably, contact with foreign teams and equestrian thought and practice outside the confines imposed by the Iron Curtain concept has had its influence on the breeding of sport horses. To compete in the major disciplines with any hope of success the horses have had to meet the accepted requirements of the tests, and that has an obvious effect upon breeding policies. As a result, even the highly individual Akhal-Teke is being developed to meet new criteria and beginning to show a conformational outline closer to the pattern of the European competition horse.

AKHAL-TEKE HERD
These Akhal-Teke mares and their young are at a very well-watered oasis in Turkmenistan. The horses show a range of colours, with a metallic sheen on the coats.

HEIGHT
1.57 m
(15.2 hh)

SHAGYA ARAB & GIDRAN ARAB

HUNGARY HAS LONG been renowned for its Arab horses. Had it not been positioned geographically as the centrepiece of Europe, and subjected to successive wars, invasions, revolutions, and shifts of political frontiers that continually disrupted the long-term management of its great studs, it would have had the potential to become one of the world's greatest centres of Arab breeding. Two of the breeds derived from the pure Arab were the Shagya Arab and the Gidran Arab. Both evolved during the 19th century at Bábolna and Mezőhegyes, respectively.

HALF-BRED COMPETITION HORSES
The modern trend, spearheaded by the Mezőhegyes stud, is towards the production of a "half-bred" or warmblood horse, like these at Hortobagyi Puszta, for competitions. It is based on the Nonius and Furioso, but the Shagya and the Gidran are also used.

BÁBOLNA

Founded in 1769, Bábolna was originally an overflow establishment to Mezőhegyes, Hungary's principal stud. It followed the same policies designed to produce both quality cavalry horses and a heavier type for artillery. However, the policy changed in 1816, and the emphasis was laid firmly on pure-bred Arabs imported from an authentic

DUAL ROLE
The striking and very beautiful Shagya of Bábolna is essentially a high-quality saddle horse, but it adapts easily to working in harness.

"desert" background; pure-breds bred at the stud, the progeny of the imported stock; and part-breds, which were usually termed "Arab Race". These part-breds were the product of pure-bred Arab stallions crossed with mares carrying strains of Hungarian, Spanish, or Thoroughbred blood, but which for all that were probably Arabian in appearance.

THE SHAGYA ARAB

The Shagya Arab originated at Bábolna. It is now bred in the Czech Republic, Austria, Romania, the former Yugoslavian countries,

Poland, and Germany, as well as Hungary. The founding sire was the stallion Shagya, an Arab of the Kehilan/Siglavy strain, who was born in Syria in 1830. He was bought for Bábolna in 1836, together with seven other stallions and five mares. Shagya was big for an Arab horse, measuring 1.58 m (15.2½ hh), and was said to be a distinctive cream colour, another unusual feature. He stood at Bábolna until 1842, and sired a number of successful sons who ensured the continuation of the Shagya dynasty. Their direct descendants now stand at studs all over Europe, as well as at Bábolna.

The Shagya Arab exhibits all the characteristics of the pure Arab, and may even display more quality and type than some modern pure-breds. It rarely stands less than 1.52 m (15 hh), and usually shows more bone and substance than the fashionable pure-breds of present-day show rings. It is essentially a practical horse, used under saddle as well as driven in harness. In the past the Shagya was used as the mount for the Hungarian hussar (see pp.316–17), the *beau idéal* of the light horseman, and as such proved itself to be a swift, enduring, and very hardy cavalry horse.

THE GIDRAN ARAB

The Gidran Arab is as important a breed as any of those that originated at Mezőhegyes, and may be considered to be the Hungarian version of the Anglo-Arab. It traces back to the chestnut Arab, Gidran Senior, who was of the prominent Siglavy strain, and was imported from Arabia in 1816. He was put to a Spanish-bred mare, Arrogante, and this resulted in the birth of the stallion Gidran II, in 1820. Gidran II became the breed's

HEIGHT OF SHAGYA ARAB
1.52 m
(15 hh)

SHAGYA ARAB

foundation sire. At first he was mated with mares of a variety of different and even local breeds. Then English Thoroughbreds were increasingly introduced, followed by more Arab infusions in order to fix the type.

The modern Gidran is an upstanding horse of about 1.63 m (16 hh), and is nearly always chestnut in colour. It has a bigger frame than the Arab, but has something of the latter's fine, elegant head and high-set tail. The system of running out small herds of mares, each with its attendant stallion, ensures that the horses are tough and hardy. The correctly built Gidran Arab, with its good limbs and its ability to gallop, would not be out of place in the best of English hunting counties. It is extensively used in competitive sport, and the heavier animals make good carriage horses.

Gidran Senior was described as being "very tempestuous". This reputation has been inherited by his descendants, who are, perhaps more euphemistically, regarded as being "spirited" and "highly-couraged".

HEAD
The head of the heavier, big-framed type of Gidran lacks the Arab refinement.

NECK
The angle between head and neck allows an exceptional degree of head movement.

HEIGHT OF GIDRAN ARAB
1.63 m (16 hh)

LEGS
There is more bone and often better hind legs than in many modern show-ring Arabs.

GIDRAN ARAB

ORIGINS

THE HUNGARIAN STATE STUD of Mezőhegyes, situated in the extreme south-east of the Hungarian plain, is the oldest of the state stud farms. It was founded in 1785, and was responsible for the evolution of the Gidran Arab. The Gidran is also bred at Sütveny, and in Romania and Bulgaria. The most famous Hungarian breed, the Shagya Arab, is a product of the country's second oldest stud, Bábolna, in north-western Hungary. The Shagya is now also bred in the Czech Republic, Slovakia, Austria, Poland, Germany, and Russia and enjoys a world-wide reputation.

ANGLO-ARAB

T HE ANGLO-ARAB results from the fusion of the two pre-eminent horse breeds: the Thoroughbred (see pp.120–21), the world's greatest racehorse, and its ancestor the Arab (see pp.64–65). It originated in the UK, where the Thoroughbred was developed in the 18th and 19th centuries. Today, of course, it is bred in many other countries, especially in France, which has specialized in the production of hard, versatile Anglo-Arab horses for over 150 years. Both the UK and France recognize the cross as a composite breed, but they differ in the requirements that have to be met for entry into the respective stud books.

DRESSAGE

The best type of Anglo-Arab has the temperament, intelligence, and physique that are demanded for dressage at international level. The conformation and carriage of this Anglo-Arab horse are exemplary.

ANGLO-ARABS IN THE UK

In the UK, an Anglo-Arab is a cross between a Thoroughbred stallion and an Arab mare, or vice-versa, with their subsequent re-crossing. These two are the only strains in the pedigree and to obtain entry in the stud book a horse must be able to claim a minimum of 12½ per cent Arab blood.

The UK produces some very high-quality Anglo-Arabs, but on very minimal scale in comparison with the large, well-organized French operation. The popular practice of British breeders and others is to put an Arab stallion to a Thoroughbred mare, if the progeny are likely to be larger than either parent. The opposite combination, the mating of a Thoroughbred sire with an Arab dam, is thought to result in smaller offspring, which are of less monetary value than pure-breds of either breed.

ANGLO-ARABS IN FRANCE

The main breeding centres for the French Anglo-Arabs are at Pompadour, Tarbes, Pau, and Gelos. Although the French allow more breeding permutations, the requirement for stud book entry is still at least 25 per cent Arab blood, with only Anglo-Arab, Arab, or Thoroughbred ancestry.

The French Anglo-Arab owes its pre-eminence to the encouragement given by the long-established national studs. These have been the principal factor in horse-breeding since they were first created in the 17th century by Louis XIV's minister, Colbert. Initially they supplied the royal stables, but with the arrival of Napoleon Bonaparte at the end of the 18th century their functions began to include providing cavalry remounts for his campaigns. Central to the breeding systems employed were desert-bred Arabs, largely from Syria and Tunisia, which were crossed with native mares.

ORIGINS

THE ANGLO-ARAB HORSE *is bred throughout Europe and elsewhere, wherever there is the possibility of crossing Thoroughbreds with Arabs. France is foremost in the production of Anglo-Arabs, through the national studs of Pau, Tarbes, and Pompadour, which are all in the south-west. Horses of great merit are also bred in Hungary, at both Bábolna and Mezőhegyes, while those from the Janow Podlaski stud in Poland are world famous and prominent in international competitions.*

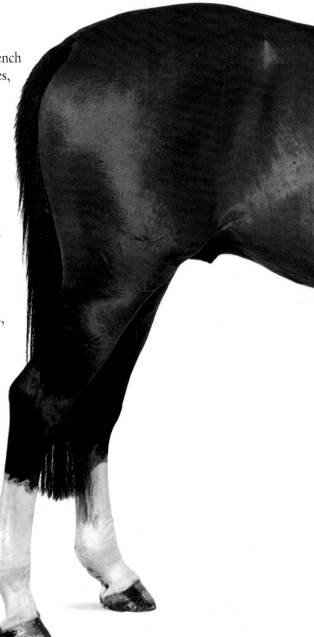

FEET
The feet are strong and exceptionally sound, and are rarely prone to disease.

BREEDING AND SELECTION

Thoroughbred blood was introduced to French horses rather imprudently in 1830, but in 1836 systematic breeding began at Pompadour in France. It was based on the use of two principal Arab stallions, Massoud and Aslan (who was described as a Turk), and three Thoroughbred foundation mares: Dair, Common Mare, and Selim Mare.

A rigorous system of selection based on performance, stamina, and conformation was built into the early breeding policies and persists to this day. Additionally, a racing programme, confined to the breed, has been evolved to provide a further means of selection according to performance. There are over 30 annual race meetings for Anglo-Arabs, as well as jumping and cross-country tests for the breed. Some of the cross-country trials take place over the formidable bank country of Pau.

In theory the crossing of the Arab with the related Thoroughbred should result in the ideal riding horse, suited to the modern competitive disciplines of showjumping, dressage, and eventing. The Thoroughbred gives size, improved scope, and a more appropriate action, while the Arab confers a level, manageable temperament, together with inherently sound limbs and constitution, intelligence, and unsurpassed qualities of endurance and stamina.

CHARACTERISTICS

The modern Anglo-Arab of French breeding may be a trifle less elegant than its British counterpart, but it is a tough, hard, enormously versatile horse, well-proven in the Olympic disciplines. The ones bred at Pompadour are, in general, larger and more muscular, but all the French stock are athletic types with pronounced jumping ability and notable correctness of action.

In appearance they tend far more towards the Thoroughbred than towards the Arab, with a straight rather than concave head profile, a longer neck (indicative of greater speed), more prominent withers, and very oblique, powerful shoulders. However, the frame is usually more solid than that of the Thoroughbred, and the croup is longer and more horizontal. Obviously, the Anglo-Arab is not as fast as the Thoroughbred, but it has far greater jumping ability. It is also well-suited to dressage, on account of both its temperament and its natural paces.

The best French Anglo-Arabs have between 25 and 45 per cent Arab blood; many of France's Olympic and international medals have been won by such Anglo-Arabs.

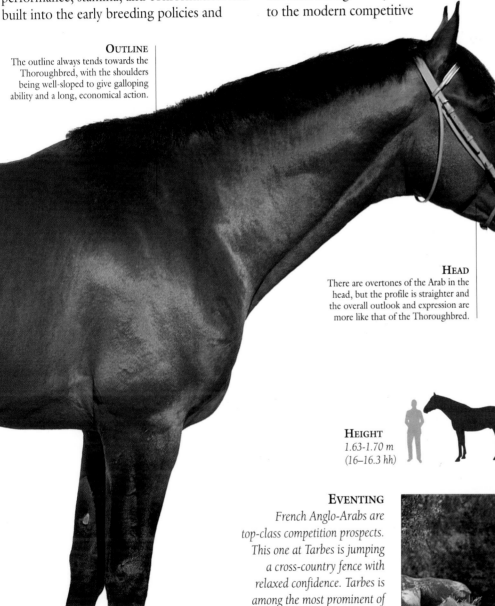

OUTLINE
The outline always tends towards the Thoroughbred, with the shoulders being well-sloped to give galloping ability and a long, economical action.

HEAD
There are overtones of the Arab in the head, but the profile is straighter and the overall outlook and expression are more like that of the Thoroughbred.

HEIGHT
1.63-1.70 m
(16–16.3 hh)

LEGS
The legs are long and slender, with well-muscled forearms, clean, short cannons, and good bone. The joints are firm, flat, well-formed, and without any puffiness. The slope of the pastern and the foot is nearly perfect.

EVENTING
French Anglo-Arabs are top-class competition prospects. This one at Tarbes is jumping a cross-country fence with relaxed confidence. Tarbes is among the most prominent of the Anglo-Arab studs.

DON

THE DON is one of the best-known of the Russian breeds. It achieved its fame as the mount of the Cossacks, those irregular bands of tribal freebooters who so effectively harried the French armies in their long retreat from Moscow in 1812. The breed evolved in the 18th and 19th centuries and was reared in herds on the pastures of the Don steppes. Its ancestors were the horses of the nomadic tribes and the early influences were those of the unprepossessing but very hardy Mongolian Nagai, the horses of northern Iran, the Persian Arabs, and the Turkmene, a desert horse closely associated with the Akhal-Teke (see pp.74–75). The Karabakh, a mountain horse from the Karabakh Mountains of Azerbaijan (see pp.82–83), is a particular influence.

HISTORY

Large numbers of these predominantly golden-dun horses were let loose on the Don steppes in the 18th century. The Don was subsequently improved and acquired greater size as a result of outcrosses to the Orlov (see pp.342–43), the Strelets Arab, which was really an Anglo-Arab (see pp.78–79), and to Thoroughbreds (see pp.120–21). No outside blood has been introduced since the beginning of the 20th century, by which time the Don had emerged as a horse of relatively fixed type. It was employed as an economical, easily kept cavalry horse, which could also be used in harness.

UKRAINIAN RIDING HORSE
This breed was developed after the Second World War, as a result of crossing Nonius, Furioso, and Gidran mares with Thoroughbred, Trakehner, and Hanoverian stallions. As with the Don, two- and three-year-olds are performance tested.

THE MODERN DON

In terms of conformational excellence, which is a subject approached realistically by Russian breeders, the Don – like so many Russian horses – is far from being an exemplary specimen. However, it is incredibly tough, can work on the shortest of rations, and is well able to live outside all year and adapt easily to every sort of climatic hardship. For these reasons it is much valued as an improver of local stock in areas where horse herds are traditional and commonplace. It has also played a significant role in some of the breeds that have evolved at the state studs, in particular the Budenny (see pp.86–87), originally a purpose-bred cavalry horse, but now produced increasingly as a specialized riding horse. The Budenny, bred at the Budenny stud where some of the best Don specimens could be found, was based on the crossing of selected Don mares with Thoroughbreds. The progeny were called Anglo-Dons, and they were carefully in-bred to produce the foundation stock for the Budenny breed.

NECK
The neck is of average length, and runs down into fairly well-defined withers.

FREEZE MARK
This horse is freeze-marked. Freeze-marking is an increasingly common method of permanent identification, which is practised worldwide.

SHOULDERS
The shoulders are noticeably short and are somewhat upright.

LEGS
The legs are usually straight, but the joints may be insufficiently large.

Russian breeders make considerable use of performance testing, and the Don, as well as being tested on the racecourse at two and three years old, is also subjected to long-distance endurance tests. As a racehorse the Don is not impressive, but it is a formidable performer over long distances. A standard test under saddle is a ride of 275 km (170 miles), which has to be covered in 24 hours.

CHARACTERISTICS

In the breed standard the Don is described as a "comparatively massive" horse, standing at between 1.60 m and 1.68 m (15.3–16.2 hh), but "massive" is probably a misnomer or a misinterpretation. A better description

QUADRIGA
The four horses are harnessed abreast to this Don-style quadriga. The outer pair of horses, which are bent to the outside by a fixed rein, canter, while the centre pair trot.

of the Don would be "substantial", at least in respect of the body, which, to meet the breed standard, should be around 1.93 m (6 ft 4 in) through the girth, with a barrel measurement of 1.65 m (5 ft 5 in). The predominant colours are chestnut and brown, often with a golden sheen, a reminder of the Turkmene and Karabakh forebears. The best Don horses are generally acceptable, although they do not always correspond to the breed standard. They are inclined to be long in the leg, and the failings of the breed, meticulously catalogued and honestly appraised, would discourage the average breeder in the West. Faults include low withers accompanied by straight, short shoulders; "calf knees" (an inward curve below the knee, considered to impinge upon the passage of the tendons); a tendency towards sickle-hocks and upright pasterns; a tail that can be set too low; and a short, constricted poll that makes flexion difficult.

Not surprisingly, as a result of these shortcomings, the movement leaves something to be desired. Indeed, it has been described as "sometimes restricted and rough". The paces are regarded as regular, but "neither elegant, elastic nor over comfortable". For all that, the Don has been about for a long time and as a practical work-horse, enduring, frugal, and equable in temperament, it has proved its worth.

CROUP
The line of the croup may be rather straight.

TAIL
The tail and mane are usually short and thin.

HIND LEGS
The second thighs may be insubstantial, and the hocks are sometimes inclined to be sickle-shaped.

BODY
The ribcage is generally wide and well sprung, and the back is straight and broad. Depth through the girth may vary between individual horses.

FEET
The pasterns tend to be upright, but the feet are usually sound, free from disease, and capable of standing up to hard wear.

HEIGHT
1.60–1.68 m
(15.3–16.2 hh)

ORIGINS

THE DON HORSE TAKES ITS NAME from its area of origin, the steppes around the Don River. The breed was raised there in herds, and benefited from this environment in terms of its hardiness, its ability to adapt and survive in climatic extremes, and its capacity for hard work on minimal rations. The breeding areas for the Don were not far from those of the Karabakh in Azerbaijan, and many Karabakh horses were loosed on the Don steppes in the 18th century, to upgrade the Don stock.

KABARDIN & KARABAKH

T HE KABARDIN AND THE KARABAKH are both mountain horses. The former is the local breed of the northern Caucasus, while the latter originated a little further south, in the Karabakh uplands, between the rivers of Araks and Kura in Azerbaijan. Therefore, the two breeds are neighbours. They are descended from the Mongolian-type steppe horse of "primitive" origin (see pp.14–15), but because of their geographical position, between the Black and Caspian Seas, they have been open to the influence of eastern stock from the bordering countries of Turkey, Iraq, Kurdistan, and Iran. However, their character results just as much from their environment as from the influence of the southern outcrosses.

MOUNTAIN HORSE
The Kabardin is held to be the finest mountain breed in the whole of the former USSR, and is capable of remarkable feats of endurance in difficult terrain and weather conditions.

THE KABARDIN

The Kabardin has been considered a breed since the 16th century. In the 17th century it became famous in the states bordering the Caucasus and further afield, and it was regarded as the finest mountain horse in the whole of the area of the former USSR. The horses have a remarkable ability to negotiate steep mountain passes, cross rivers, and go through deep snow. They also have an unerring sense of direction, which enables them to find their way in the dark and through heavy mountain mist. The breed is naturally hardy and, like many other Asian horses, is capable of great feats of endurance. During a trial held in 1935–36, following

a route round the Caucasian ridge, Kabardins covered 3,000 km (1,860 miles), in bad weather, in 37 days. This achievement has not been approached by any other breed.

The Kabardin is strongly built, with a thick-set body and short, powerful limbs. As with so many mountain horses, the hind legs are characteristically sickle-shaped. The long head is usually accompanied by a convex, Roman-nosed profile, reminiscent of the Asiatic Wild Horse (see pp.18–19). The action is energetic and fairly high, as befits a mountain horse that has to pick its way over rough ground. As a result, the Kabardin is not a fast galloper; nonetheless, the walk is even and cadenced, and the trot and canter are light and smooth. Like many other Asian horses, some Kabardins pace naturally. (It is said that the pacing gait was passed on to all horses of Mongol blood by the favourite mount of Genghis Khan.) The breed is highly regarded for its very calm and obedient temperament. It stands at around 1.52–1.57 m (15–15.2 hh), and is usually bay or black.

During the Russian Revolution in 1917 many Kabardin horses were lost. However, in the 1920s work was begun at the Kabardin-Balkar and Karachaev-Cherkess Studs to re-establish and further improve the breed. As a result, a stronger type was produced, capable of agricultural work and suitable as an army remount. The best Kabardins are bred at the Malokarachaev and Malkin studs,

ORIGINS

THE KABARDIN AND THE KARABAKH are geographical neighbours. They both evolved in a mountain environment that has developed their ability to cope sure-footedly in the steepest and most difficult terrain. The Kabardin is the breed of the northern Caucasus, the best being bred at Malokarachaev and Malkin studs. The Karabakh has its origins in the Karabakh uplands, between the rivers of Araks and Kura in Azerbaijan. Both breeds have been influenced by eastern blood from bordering countries.

BODY
The body is clearly strong enough though by no means handsome, and like most mountain horses the hind legs are sickle-shaped.

KABARDIN

HEIGHT OF KABARDIN
1.52–1.57 m (15–15.2 hh)

where they are kept at pasture on the high ground throughout the summer, and in the foothills during the winter. They are performance-tested on the racecourse when they are two years old, but are not as fast as the more specialized racing breeds. However, they are well suited for other local sporting activities.

The Kabardin horse has been improved and made bigger by heavy infusions of Persian, Arab, and Turkmene blood, and has also been crossed with the neighbouring Karabakh. Some mares have been crossed with Thoroughbreds (see pp.120–21) to produce the bigger and faster Anglo-Kabardins, the best of which carry between 25 and 75 per cent Thoroughbred blood.

THE KARABAKH

The Karabakh is a good example of a light riding horse. The breed has been heavily influenced both by the Arab horse (see pp.64–65) and by desert horses related to the Arab. The Akhal-Teke (see pp.74–75), from which the Karabakh inherits its striking coat colour, has had a particularly strong effect on the breed. The Karabakh stands at about 1.42 m (14 hh). The coat may be chestnut, bay, or dun, and it nearly always has a distinctive, well-defined, metallic sheen. Karabakh horses are performance-tested on the racecourse, and the best stock are those connected with the Akdam Stud. A similar horse, found in Azerbaijan, is the Deliboz, which should really be regarded as a strain of Karabakh.

Both the Kabardin and Karabakh seem to exemplify the qualities required of mountain horses. Horses bred for work in mountainous terrain often display a conformation in the quarters and hind legs that would be unacceptable in the usual stamp of riding horse, i.e. cow- or sickle-hocks, but which appears to be a necessary feature of the working mountain breeds.

NECK
The neck is short and upright, and the head is attractive.

HEAD
The head, as a result of outcrossing to improve the breed, is refined and well-set on an arched neck of good length.

SHOULDERS
The shoulders are upright, which seems acceptable enough in a mountain horse, but is not conducive to speed.

SHOULDERS
The shoulders have no slope by western standards, but the horse has great capability.

LEGS
The legs are slender and possibly light of bone, while the joints are small. The feet are hard wearing.

FORELEGS
The forelegs are slender but clean. The feet are sound, and the horse can be worked without shoes.

KARABAKH

HEIGHT OF KARABAKH
1.42 m
(14 hh)

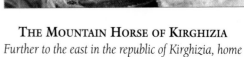

THE MOUNTAIN HORSE OF KIRGHIZIA
Further to the east in the republic of Kirghizia, home of the Ferghana horses of antiquity, the Kirghiz tribesmen perfected their own mountain horse. Since the 1950s, the Nova Khirgiz, a new, more refined breed, has been evolved.

KARABAIR

THE KARABAIR is one of the oldest and most versatile of the Central Asian horse breeds. It is found principally in Uzbekistan, an area famed in antiquity for its horses and one that is frequently mentioned in accounts of military campaigns in pre-Christian times. Geographically, Uzbekistan is positioned on a network of ancient trade routes, and certainly since the time of the Persians (see pp.34–35), around 600 BC, mounted warriors and bands of nomadic herdsmen have passed through this harsh landscape. In consequence, the local stock has been much influenced by Arabs (see pp.64–65), Turkmenes, and related desert horses from neighbouring countries.

KARABAIR HERDS
The Karabair herds alternate between the mountain pastures and grasslands on the lower foothills, according to the season. In the winter they receive supplementary feed of lucerne, hay, and some cereals.

CHARACTERISTICS

Genetically, the Karabair is the product of the crossing of southern, oriental breeds with the wider-barrelled steppe horses of "primitive" type (see pp.22–23). The result is a small, quick-moving riding horse, which stands at about 1.52 m (15 hh). The breed is coarser and less graceful than the Arab, but has many of the latter's characteristics. For the most part, however, the Karabair is without the Arab's pronouncedly "dished" profile. The face is straight, and is sometimes inclined to be Roman-nosed. The head is fine, and has the "dry" quality associated with desert horses – the noticeable absence of fleshiness, with the veins standing out under the fine skin. There is a tendency to cow- and sickle-hocks, but the limbs are exceptionally strong with ample bone below the knee; the breed standard laid down by the old USSR authority requires a measurement of 19.6 cm (7¾ in) for stallions, and 18.8 cm (7¼ in) for mares.

Constitutionally, the Karabair is a very sound horse, seldom suffering lameness, with powers of endurance beyond the norm. Moreover, it has great courage, a very necessary quality in a breed used almost exclusively in the wild game of *kokpar*, the Uzbek version of *buzkashi* (see pp.368–69). This can be a dangerous game, usually played with very few rules and resulting in numerous casualties.

QUARTERS
The quarters and hind legs of this agile, quick-moving horse are among the best to be found in the Central Asian breeds.

PLAYING KOKPAR
The Karabair is one of the toughest of the Central Asian breeds, and is much in demand for the national game of kokpar, at which it excels. It can also be used in harness.

HIND LEGS
The hind legs have considerable length from point of hip to hock, and are proportionate to the light body.

USES AND ENVIRONMENT

The Karabair is a dual-purpose horse, used both in harness and under saddle. In earlier days there appear to have been three distinct types: a spirited riding horse; a quieter, heavier ride-and-drive sort; and a longer-backed harness horse which, on account of its conformation, was also suitable for use as a pack animal. Today, the Karabair is still a dual-purpose animal, but has improved in quality and conformation. This is largely due to the breeding policies implemented by the studs at Dzhizal, near Samarkand, and at Avangard. The best specimens are to be found at these studs, and stallions there are available for the improvement of the breed.

The predominant coat colours are bay, grey, and chestnut. Dun and a dull Palomino colouring sometimes occur as well, as might be expected of a breed that is based on steppe horses. Less understandable is the occasional incidence of black and piebald horses.

The Karabairs are bred in herds that live alternately on mountain and foothill pastures. The horses are fed on lucerne and

ORIGINS

THE KARABAIR is a horse of Central Asia and is found in considerable numbers in Uzbekistan and the northern part of Tajikistan. The Dzhizak stud at Samarkand is a centre for the breed, but Karabair horses also used to be raised on many of the collective farms in the area. The geographical position of Uzbekistan, in the centre of a network of trade routes, resulted in the local stock being augmented by a variety of oriental-type horses, such as Turkmenes, Akhal-Tekes, and related breeds.

hay, and in bad weather they are even fed on cereal. It is customary for young horses to be broken at between 18 months and two years, and then to be tested on the racecourse as two- and three-year-olds.

Karabairs are raced on the Tashkent courses, and perform well in races confined to local horses. Karabair mares have been crossed with Thoroughbreds in order to produce faster horses that are suitable for competing in the international ridden disciplines. Flat racing, however, is not the forte of the pure-bred, dual-purpose Karabair, so combined competitions are organized where the horses are alternately ridden and driven in harness, a practice that gives a better indication of an individual's versatility, temperament, and stamina.

Over 50 per cent of the Uzbek people, the principal breeders of the Karabair, may still be nomadic, despite the efforts of the old USSR bureaucracy to settle them in collective farms. They live in a shrub and desert steppe country but it affords sufficient food for herds of horses, sheep, and goats. Indeed, the Central Asiatic steppe grasses offer good, nutritious feed for the horses and include some feather grass and fescue. In common with their neighbours, the Turkmene and the Kazakhs, the horse is highly regarded in Uzbek society. Among the nomadic Uzbek, the horse is looked upon as the embodiment of beauty, and, like the Arabs, the Uzbek are said to love their horses more than their women.

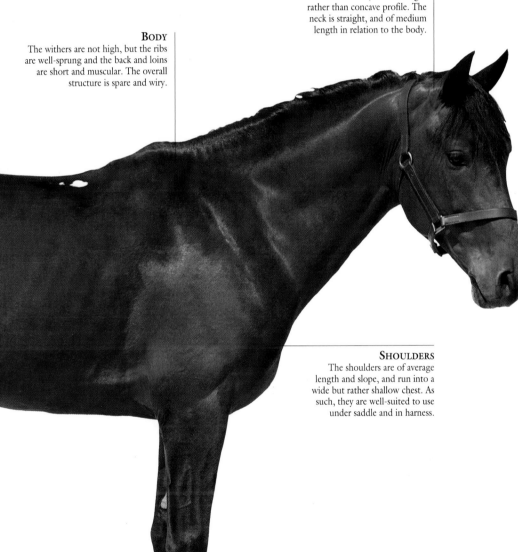

BODY
The withers are not high, but the ribs are well-sprung and the back and loins are short and muscular. The overall structure is spare and wiry.

HEAD
The head is fine, with a straight rather than concave profile. The neck is straight, and of medium length in relation to the body.

SHOULDERS
The shoulders are of average length and slope, and run into a wide but rather shallow chest. As such, they are well-suited to use under saddle and in harness.

LEGS
The legs are strong and fine, with good, hard joints and feet of exceptionally hard horn. Stallions average a bone measurement of 19.6 cm (7¾ in).

HEIGHT
1.52 m
(15 hh)

BUDENNY

T HE BUDENNY (or Budyonny) was named after Marshall Budenny,
who was one of the most famous Bolshevik cavalry commanders
of the Russian Civil War (1918–20). In essence, the Budenny is a
Russian "warmblood", created by crossing native mares
with Thoroughbred stallions. Among the Russian stud-bred
horses this breed is of particular interest, as it is a product of
the complex cross-breeding programmes that were first
instituted at the state studs after the Russian Revolution
in 1917, and which still continue. It is now bred in the
Ukraine, and in the Kazakh and Kirghiz republics, in
the southern part of the former USSR.

NECK
The neck is fairly long and straight.
It is in proportion to the light-
framed body and the fine, neat head.

SELECTIVE BREEDING

In the early 1920s preliminary selective
breeding was begun in the Rostov region,
at what later became the Budenny and First
Cavalry Army Studs. The breeders' aim was
to produce enduring cavalry horses, in order
to compensate for the enormous losses
sustained during the First World War and its
aftermath. Subsequently, horses from these
studs formed a great part of the Russian
cavalry divisions that operated throughout
the Second World War, and were retained
for some years afterwards.

HEAD
The head is intelligent
and alert, and tapers
to the muzzle.

The first step in creating this new breed
was to cross selected Don (see pp.80–81)
and Chernomor mares with Thoroughbred
stallions (see pp.120–21). The Chernomor
is a Cossack horse very similar to the Don,
but smaller, lighter, and more active. It was
originally bred around Krasnodar, north of

the Caucasus Mountains, and is descended
from the horses raised by the Zaporozhian
Cossacks, who settled on the north bank
of the Kuban River in the 18th century.
At one time, breeders used Kirghiz and
Kazakh horses (see pp.82–83 and p.201),
but the progeny either inherited the worst
conformational faults of these steppe horses
or lost their hardiness. Later, the Budenny
itself was used to improve the two breeds.

The results of the first crossings were
known as Anglo-Dons. The best of these
horses were inter-bred, and the foundation

MODERN TYPE
*The modern Budenny now carries more
Thoroughbred blood than before, to give greater
scope to the competitive performance. It is said
to jump well, and to be a good cross-country
horse with a turn of speed.*

HEIGHT
*1.63 m
(16 hh)*

stock for the Budenny was carefully selected from their offspring. Great care was taken with the brood mares, which were kept on the best pastures, housed in winter, and fed liberally. From the beginning, young stock between two and four years old were performance-tested both on the racecourse and on cavalry equitation courses.

Of the 657 mares used to create the fixed type, 359 were Anglo-Dons, 261 were Anglo-Dons crossed with Chernomors, and 37 were Anglo-Chernomors. These mares were mated with Anglo-Don stallions, and thereafter any mares with insufficiently definite Thoroughbred character were put back to Thoroughbred stallions. The breed was officially recognized in 1949.

In the early days, three types of Budenny were recognized: "Massive", "Eastern", and "Middle". Later, demand for an all-purpose competition horse led to the production of a single type, which had a greater proportion of Thoroughbred blood than earlier varieties. Modern Budenny stock has good bone, a strong build, and is distinctly Thoroughbred in appearance. They usually stand at around 1.63 m (16 hh). About 80 per cent are chestnut, and their coats have a golden sheen that is inherited

from the Don and Chernomor. The conformation is occasionally marred by offset cannon bones in the forelegs and overly straight hind legs, which result from the unsuccessful Kazakh and Kirghiz crosses, but it is generally of good riding horse type, with an elegant, high-quality head. The breed's stamina is beyond question, and it is also said to have a calm, sensible temperament.

SPORT

The Budenny is known to perform well in long-distance events and in dressage, and it has also been successful in steeplechases and cross-country competitions. It is a fast horse, although its speed is not comparable with that of the Thoroughbred.

Two-year-olds are tested for speed over a distance of 1,200 m (1,318 yd), and their average time is 1 minute 16 seconds. Three-year-olds are tested over 2.4 km (1½ miles), and average 2 minutes 38 seconds. The Gran Pardubice in former Czechoslovakia has been won by a Budenny and the entries for this gruelling steeplechase usually include some representatives of the breed.

The majority of Russian horses are renowned for their endurance – a highly prized quality throughout the Asian republics, and the Budenny is no exception. It is recorded that one stallion, Zanos, covered 309 km (192 miles) in 24 hours, resting for only 4 hours, and with a companion travelled 1,800 km (1,118 miles) in 15 days.

DRESSAGE
The Budenny is noted for its calm temperament and its regular, level paces – both important factors in the dressage horse.

BODY
The body is well-made and proportionate, with considerable depth through the girth.

LEGS
The legs are slender and straight, with neat, smallish feet and a little silky feather.

HIND LEGS
The over-straight hind legs inherited from the early Kazakh crosses have now been eliminated.

ORIGINS

A PILOT BREEDING SCHEME for the Budenny horse was begun in the Rostov region in the 1920s. Today the Budenny is bred in the southern parts of the former USSR, such as the Ukraine and the area running up to the Black Sea. It is also bred in the neighbouring Kazakh and Kirghiz republics, further to the east. An initial advantage was the availability of Don horses and the Chernomors – Cossack horses bred in the Krasnodar region along the River Kuban.

LOKAI & TERSK

THE FORMER USSR IS MADE up of large areas of forest, steppe land, and high, remote mountains where the climate is harsh and life has not changed for hundreds of years. In the early 20th century the Soviets encouraged the breeding of local horses suited to the environment and the local economy and then improved them by outcrosses and selective breeding, using performance tests as a means of evaluation. Breed standards were laid down detailing body measurements. Breeding stock is chosen from those conforming most closely to the specified standard.

THE LOKAI

The Lokai is a mountain horse bred in Tajikistan on the western edge of the Pamirs, just south of the Tien Shan range. It was developed in the 16th century by the Lokai people, a sub-tribe of the Uzbek, when they moved eastward from the shores of the Aral Sea. Initially a mix of Central Asian blood, the Lokai was more specifically improved by Iomud (Persian) blood, and by the Karabair (see pp.84–85), the main Uzbek breed and a true eastern horse with Arab and Turkmene antecedents. More recently there have been outcrosses to Tersk, Arab, and Thoroughbred stallions (see pp.64–65 and 120–21).

NECK
The neck is short and straight, and complements the Lokai's plain head and straight profile.

HEAD
The beautiful head resembles that of an Arab. The expressive face reflects the Tersk's intelligence and gentle disposition.

HEIGHT OF LOKAI
1.52 m
(15 hh)

LOKAI

ORIGINS

THE LOKAI is one of the Asian mountain horses. It is bred in Tajikistan, on the high western ridge of the Pamir mountains, and the breed was developed by the Lokai people in the 16th century. As is usual with Russian and Asian breeds, the Lokai is performance tested, and undergoes trials at the racecourses in Tashkent and Dushanbe. The Tersk horse was developed between 1921 and 1950 at the Tersk and Stavropol Studs in the northern Caucasus. It is still bred in that area today and is regarded as one of the most notable breeds produced by the Soviet horse-breeding initiative.

TOUGH ALL-ROUNDER
The Lokai is used for a variety of purposes. It provides transport over precipitous mountain country, it is raced, ridden in the game of kokpar, and it is often employed as a pack animal.

HARVESTING

Tersk horses are good competition prospects for the ridden disciplines of jumping, dressage, and cross-country, but are also quite able to take their turn in the harvest field.

The result is a lightly built, wiry, tough horse, with very hard feet. The limbs are sometimes malformed, particularly in the hocks and the splayed forefeet. Even so, the Lokai can carry a rider 80 km (50 miles) a day over mountain tracks at an average speed of 8–9.5 km/h (5–6 mph). It is raced, used under pack, and is an excellent mount for the national game of *kokpar*, the fight over the goat carcase (see *buzkashi*, pp.368–69). The herds are kept at pasture all through the year, moving up into the mountains in spring. The mares are milked in accordance with nomadic tradition.

THE TERSK

The Tersk was created between 1921 and 1950, at the Tersk and Stavropol Studs in the Northern Caucasus, when the Soviet agricultural ministry was concerned to re-establish the horse population. The new breed was planned to replace the Strelets Arabian, which had virtually disappeared in the early 1920s. Only two stallions, both silver grey, and a few mares survived. These horses were sent to Tersk in 1925 and were used as foundation stock for the new project. No attempt was made to preserve the original Strelets, since the survivors were thought to be too in-bred. However, three pure Arab stallions were introduced and a number of cross-bred mares: Arab/Don (see pp.80–81), Strelets/Kabardin, and a few cross-bred Hungarian Gidrans (see pp.76–77). The breeding of the Tersk was incredibly successful and, indeed, the breed is probably even more beautiful than its predecessor the Strelets and is highly regarded. Tersks are distinctly Arabian in appearance, and are characterized by a particularly light, elegant movement. They are good dressage prospects, having clean, defined paces; they are excellent jumpers and bold cross-country horses, and they race very successfully against Arabs. Their beauty, intelligence, and gentleness also make them popular in the great circuses, which play an important part in Russian culture.

COAT
The coat is usually grey, bay, or metallic chestnut. It is sometimes curled like that of a Bashkir.

BODY
The back is short, the trunk compact, and the ribs well-sprung. Nearly all Tersks are grey in colour, often with a silvery sheen.

TAIL
The tail is carried high, like that of an Arab. The mane and tail are usually thin and short, and the hair is very fine.

HIND LEGS
The hind legs are not exemplary, but are strong and wiry.

LEGS
The legs are clean, and in accordance with the breed standard there is 19.4 cm (7 ½ in) of bone below the knee. The feet are nicely rounded.

TERSK

HEIGHT OF TERSK
1.52 m
(15 hh)

PART FOUR

CLASSICAL RIDING

EQUESTRIAN CLASSICISM derived from the Greece
of Xenophon (430–355 BC) and his contemporaries.
However, they were not instigators of a system but
rather the inheritors of a long-standing equestrian
tradition. Later, the knights of the Middle Ages extended
the practice and principles of riding, and during the
Renaissance period it was raised to an art form
comparable to the study of the arts and sciences, which
were required accomplishments of the 16th-century
nobility. The art of riding was carried to fruition by a
succession of Masters, beginning with those of Naples and
culminating in the splendid presence of the Frenchman
François Robichon de la Guérinière. Under him riding
became a rational science, and he is acknowledged
as the "Father of Classical Equitation".

The *capriole*, an engraving by Crispin de Pas, from
Antoine de Pluvinel's *Manège Royal*, 1624

THE ARMOURED KNIGHT

CHAMFRON C. 1600–1700

By THE 16TH CENTURY the use of of gunpowder and firearms had made the heavily plate-armoured, medieval knight and his ponderous, similarly protected Great Horse an anachronism on the battlefields of Europe. Nonetheless, despite the disappearance of the knight in war, many of his riding techniques persisted, providing in part the inspiration for the growth of "school" riding. Much of the knight's equipment, such as the saddle and the long-cheeked curb bit, was passed on to the Renaissance horseman, together with the way in which he sat on his horse. Training methods and some of the movements used by the war-horse on the battlefield were also adopted and refined by gentlemen displaying their equestrian skills in the baroque riding halls of the period.

SKILLS IN BATTLE

The medieval knight practised skill-at-arms from an early age and there can be no doubt that he was a competent, even accomplished, horseman. Riding in battle required skill, since in order to leave the right hand free to carry a weapon he had to hold the reins in one hand, while carrying the shield on the forearm. This meant that he had to make effective use of his legs, both to urge the horse forward and also to reinforce the commands that he gave with the reins.

Faced with a cavalry charge, or with foot soldiers intent upon either maiming or bringing down both horse and rider, the knight relied upon his horse to be obedient and responsive to his aids, and equestrian expertise would have been at a premium.

There is very little written information about medieval horsemanship, leaving us to presume that the knightly classes were more adept with the lance, sword, and mace than with the pen. Certainly, the war-horses or

destriers (from the Latin dextrarius, meaning the right side, the side on which the squire led his master's horse) were taught to rein back. It is also very likely that they were trained to kick out backwards if they were threatened from the rear. Something like the High School levade, a half-rear movement, may have been used as a salutory deterrent, and if it could have been translated into a leap forward with the help of long, sharp spurs, it would have certainly scattered any unfortunate foot soldiers who happened to be in the way. The ability to execute the pirouette – the turn on the haunches – would also have been useful on the battlefield, facilitating the all-round use of the sword.

HIGH SCHOOL AIRS AND THE MEDIEVAL WAR HORSE

One school of thought suggests that the High School rears, leaps, and kicks, known as "airs" or "schools above the ground",

which are still demonstrated at the Spanish School (see pp.102–3) in Vienna and the Cadre Noir in Fontainbleau, are directly related to the movements practised by the medieval knight as part of his war-horse training. To what extent the knight practised these airs is debatable. It seems very unlikely that they would have been generally taught

PRIZE OF VICTORY
Prince Henry of Breslau, victor of the jousting tournament, receives a garland in this illustration from a 14th-century German manuscript.

JAVELIN CHARGE
In this detail from the Bayeux Tapestry, the Norman knights are shown attacking the shield-wall of King Harold's Housecarles at the battle of Hastings in 1066. Curiously, the knights use their spears overhand in javelin fashion, in the style of Ancient Greece and Rome.

SPEED AND STRENGTH

SPEED AND STRENGTH
The painting of the Battle of San Romano *by Paolo Uccello (1397–1475) shows how effective the huge, unwieldy lances were if delivered with momentum. Security was preserved by the bracing leg. The horse kicking out is performing a recognizable form of the classic* croupade.

TIC-TACKS

EARLY SHOES
This horse shoe design was used between 1066 and c.1550. The "tic-tacks" were thrown in front of the enemy to maim his horses.

HORSE SHOE

with any sort of precision. What is to be seen in the Winter Riding Hall at Vienna is probably best regarded as a supreme refinement of a medieval ideal that had little basis in reality. It is more likely that the High School "airs" (i.e. those incorporating the movements of *piaffe* and *passage*) were developed, if only in part, from the "parade" paces of Ancient Greece described by Xenophon, and from the more esoteric movements practised in the Byzantine circuses (see pp.100–1). It seems unlikely that towards the end of the medieval period, the overweighted horses at Agincourt would have been able to raise much more than a lumbering trot, let alone a nimble pirouette.

WAR SADDLE
This saddle design was used from the time of the early Sarmatians until the 18th century. The forward-thrust leg compelled the use of long spurs.

SPUR

SADDLE

THE MEDIEVAL SADDLE

Saddles made of stuffed pads were in use early in the history of the steppe horse peoples, although the stirrup was probably not used in Asia until the 4th century AD or in Europe until 400 years after that. The first saddles built on a wooden frame (known today as the saddle "tree") seem to have been introduced at the beginning of the Christian era by the Sarmatians, a nomadic tribe of Iranian origin. Using this saddle, the Sarmatians, alone among the steppe peoples, were able to employ heavy cavalry armed with heavy lances in the shock tactic of the charge.

Despite the lack of stirrups the deep-seated saddle offered a degree of security since the horseman could brace himself against the high cantle at the moment of impact with the enemy.

In its essentials, the boat-like shape of this early saddle remained as a principal design influence well into the Middle Ages and after and, allowing for the addition of stirrups, the saddle of the Renaissance horseman was similar in most respects. In the early years of classical riding men sat as the medieval knight had done, with a long leg thrust forward against the stirrup and the body braced against the cantle. They also used the medieval long, sharp spurs as well as the fearsome, long-cheeked curb bits that gave so much power to the hand.

In a slightly adapted, streamlined form, the medieval saddle developed into the 17th-century *selle royale*, which is still used today by the Spanish School, the Cadre Noir, and the schools in Iberia.

PERCHERON

THE PERCHERON, which originated in the Perche region in Normandy, is one of the most elegant of the heavy horses. Its principal bloodlines are dominated by Arab blood (see pp.64–65), and it has a stylish, long, free-striding action. One 19th-century expert, perhaps a little carried away, claimed that it was "an Arab influenced by climate and the agricultural work for which it has been used for centuries".

ARAB INFLUENCE

Percheron enthusiasts claim that the horse's forebears carried the Frankish knights of Charles Martel at the battle of Poitiers in AD 732, when they defeated the invading Moors. As a result, Moorish Barbs (see pp.66–67) and Arabs, with their refining qualities, became more freely available to French breeders. This influence continued when Robert, Count of Rotrou, imported eastern horses after the First Crusade in 1096–99. By 1760 the royal stud at Le Pin was making Arab sires available to Percheron breeders. Two notable Arab outcrosses were Godolphin and Gallipoly; Gallipoly sired the most famous Percheron stallion, Jean le Blanc, foaled in 1830 at Mauvres-sur-Huisne.

VERSATILITY AND POPULARITY

Over the years, the Percheron has served as a war-horse, coach horse, farm horse, gun horse, and even riding horse. Throughout its history, Percheron breeders, always sensitive to commercial demand, have switched their product to meet market requirements. For example, by the end of the 19th century they had given up the Percheron coach horse, an animal of about 1.57 m (15.2 hh), because it had been superseded by lighter and faster Cleveland and Yorkshire Coach Horse crosses (see pp.306–7), and had begun to favour a heavy draught horse. That these breeders could do so is a

HEAD
The head is pleasing, with a broad, square forehead, straight profile, and large, mobile ears. The neck is long and arched in the top line.

WITHERS
The withers are more prominent than in most heavy breeds and allow for considerable slope in the shoulders, which is reflected in the free action.

SHOULDERS
The length of the shoulders from point to withers is unusual in heavy horses: as a result the stride is long and active.

WORK HORSE
A pure-bred, Australian Percheron mare holds the unofficial world pulling record of 1545 kg (3410 lb) over the statutory 4.57 m (15 ft). The world's biggest horse was the US Percheron, Dr Le Gear, who stood at 2.13 m (21 hh).

HEIGHT
Average 1.68 m (16.2 hh)

PERCHERON ELEGANCE
*This Percheron is a particularly elegant specimen and
would be an ideal cross to produce heavyweight riding
horses. Black is a permitted
Percheron colour.*

tribute to their skill and acumen, and to the
presence of that Arab blood which had
aided the formation of diverse regional
types. With judicious cross-breeding it
was possible, because of that prepotent
blood, to produce variations on a basic
theme more surely, and within relatively
short periods of time.

The best years for breeders were between
1880 and 1920, when Percherons were
being exported to North and South America,
Australia, and South Africa. The US became
the principal market. It is estimated that in
the 1880s 5,000 stallions and about 2,500
mares were imported. By 1910 registrations
had risen to a remarkable 31,900.

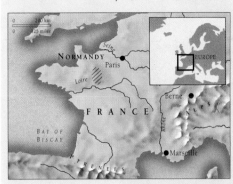

ORIGINS

*FOR CENTURIES the Percheron has been bred in the region
from which it takes its name, Le Perche in Normandy.
The fertile Normandy soil, rich in calcium, and the
nutritious pasture contributed to the character of the
breed, but the greatest credit belongs to the astute and
skilful Percheron breeders. Percherons are still bred
extensively in the US and are popular in Australia,
South Africa, South America, and the UK – even Japan
has its own Percheron society.*

The Percheron, with its eastern background,
has an advantage over many other heavy
breeds in that it adapts to different climates
more easily and is an excellent base stock
for crossing. In the bleak Falkland Islands
they are crossed with Criollo stock (see
pp.220–21) to produce tough "range"
horses, while in Australia, with an opposite
climate to the Falklands, they are out-crossed
to produce stock and competition horses.

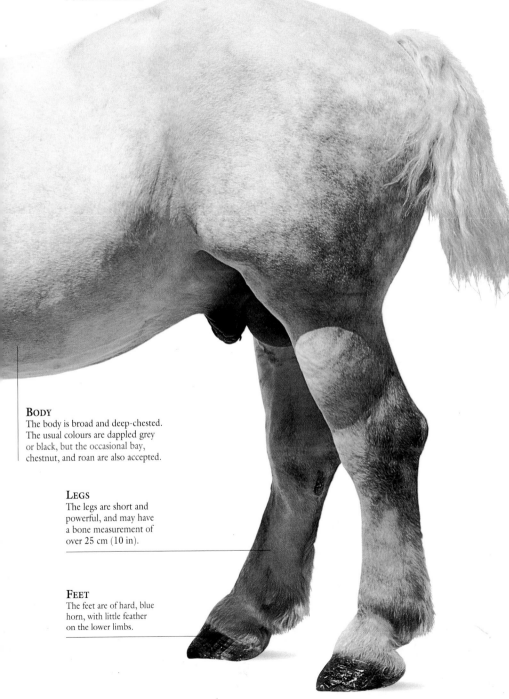

BODY
The body is broad and deep-chested.
The usual colours are dappled grey
or black, but the occasional bay,
chestnut, and roan are also accepted.

LEGS
The legs are short and
powerful, and may have
a bone measurement of
over 25 cm (10 in).

FEET
The feet are of hard, blue
horn, with little feather
on the lower limbs.

RIDING HORSE
*The Percheron, once a war-horse, can be exercised
under saddle. The leader of this group shows the old
Arab influence about the head.*

THE RENAISSANCE

FEDERICO GRISONE

THE RENAISSANCE, a term meaning "rebirth", was the period in Europe falling roughly between the 15th and 16th centuries, in which there was a huge resurgence of interest in the classical world. In the equestrian context, the return to classical learning resulted in the rediscovery of the works of the Greek general and historian, Xenophon, which were seized upon and studied with enthusiasm. Riding in the school arena, or *manège*, ultimately the splendid riding hall of the baroque period, was a necessary part of the education of the Renaissance gentleman. It was no longer practised as a training for war, but as an art form demanding the greatest dedication. This was the origin of "classical" riding, and it was centred in Naples in Italy, where a tradition of school riding had existed since the 12th century.

THE BYZANTINE INFLUENCE

In 1134, six centuries after Naples had been conquered for Byzantium (the eastern part of the Roman Empire), a riding academy was founded there based on Byzantine principles. Like the Greeks, the Romans, and the Byzantines, were familiar with movements requiring a high degree of collection, such as the *piaffe* and *passage*. However, the Byzantines had the advantage of saddle, stirrup, and the coercive curb-bit, which allowed the horse to be compressed towards its centre as it carried most of its weight over its haunches.

Between the 13th and 15th centuries, several Byzantine-influenced authors in Naples published books on management and

riding and schooling techniques. The foundations for a centre of classical riding in Naples had, therefore, already been laid when, in 1532, a Neapolitan nobleman, Federico Grisone, opened what was later acknowledged to be the first of the world's great riding schools. This school proved to have a profound influence on the evolution of academic horsemanship in Europe.

BITS AND SPURS

Grisone, who ostensibly based his ideas on the precepts of Xenophon combined with the practice of the Byzantine school, is now considered to be the first of the classical Masters. He and his near-contemporary Cesare Fiaschi, who opened a school at Ferrara in 1534, had to work, for the most

CESARE FIASCHI
Despite the use of severe bits, both Cesare Fiaschi and Federico Grisone sought to create a light, responsive mouth in a balanced, quietly submissive horse.

PARTHENON FRIEZE
These Greek horsemen of the Panathenaic procession are riding without the benefit of saddles. They sit naturally and are obviously in control of their spirited horses.

part, with the left-overs of a previous era – heavily built, common horses that possessed little or no gymnastic quality. To overcome this disadvantage, both Masters insisted on creating a light, responsive mouth by using some exceptionally severe bits, which were strong enough to gain a response from even the most insensitive war-horse.

The horse's mouth was made sensitive by first schooling the animal in a noseband (cavesson), which was fitted with studs or even spikes to make its effect more immediate. Only when the horse responded to the cavesson was control passed gradually to the bit, which was then handled gently. The required head-carriage was obtained

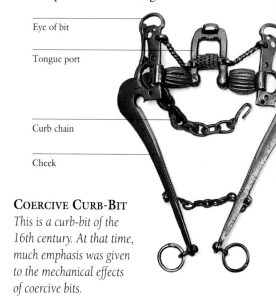

Eye of bit

Tongue port

Curb chain

Check

COERCIVE CURB-BIT
This is a curb-bit of the 16th century. At that time, much emphasis was given to the mechanical effects of coercive bits.

more by the threat of the severe curb than by its actual bearing on the mouth. Together with sharp spurs and some timely encouragement from the ground, the bit enabled the horse to be collected enough to perform the balanced movements of the *manège*, and ultimately, with the powerful application of whips and spurs, to carry out the leaps of the High School.

PERSUASION AND CORRECTION

Much emphasis was laid upon breaking resistance by "correction". Conversely, the horse was rewarded by "cherishing", which often meant no more than a temporary cessation of punishment.

Grisone's book *Gli Ordini di Cavalcare* (The Rules of Riding) contains some horrific cures for the recalcitrant equine. For example, a "nappy" horse (one who refuses to go forward) could be persuaded to mend its ways by tying flaming straw, a cat, or a live hedgehog beneath its tail. The problem might otherwise be solved by having men approach the horse from behind with a variety of inquisitorial, spiked instruments. The book, approved by Pope Julius III, was a bestseller, running into eight new editions between 1550 and 1600.

Despite these harsh methods, the early Masters obtained remarkable results and had an appreciation of balanced, rhythmic movement. Fiaschi, for example, used music as an aid in training his horses, arguing that nothing was achieved "without beat and measure".

These early efforts, together with a desire to advance academic riding, led to the use of lighter, more responsive horses. Between 1504 and 1713 Naples was under Spanish rule, and from the mid-16th century the far superior Spanish horse was increasingly employed. This noble, fiery, yet gentle horse became the cornerstone of classical equitation, and provided the foundation for the Spanish Riding School in Vienna (see pp.102–3), the greatest of the classical schools, which survives to this day to preserve the purity of the equestrian art.

THE TRAINED HORSE
A fresco from the Palazzo Ducale, Mantua, by Andrea Mantegna (1431–1506), depicts an obviously trained horse that has acquired the classical head carriage. The decorative hangers on the breastplate are forerunners of the horse brasses of a later era.

THE RATIONAL SCIENCE

WILLIAM CAVENDISH

THE LATER MASTERS of the Italian schools, although still much influenced by Byzantine practice, continued to develop the theories of their predecessors while moderating their more extreme physical methods. The most famous of these later Masters was Grisone's pupil, Giovanni Baptista Pignatelli, known as the "third man" of the Neapolitan School. He was the link between the largely mechanical Italian Schools and the more enlightened and humane systems of France. It was he who formulated the first, progressive training formula for *manège,* or school, riding and it was through one of his many distinguished pupils, Saloman La Broue, author of *La Cavalerie Françoys* (published in 1593) that by the end of the 16th century the French School, supported by royal patronage, became the predominant influence on classical equitation in Europe.

THE FRENCH COURT

Early in the 16th century the office of riding master had become a mandatory requirement of the leading courts of Europe. This was particularly true in France. The riding master was an appointment that was almost as prestigious as the great offices of state and it was usually filled by highly cultured men of aristocratic birth.

ANTOINE DE PLUVINEL

Antoine de Pluvinel de Baume (1555–1620), soldier, diplomat, and scholar, who is acknowledged as the first of the French Masters, was cast exactly in this mould. He was tutor to King Louis XIII and the author of one of the most influential books of the 17th century, *L'Instruction du Roy en l'Exercise de Monter à Cheval*, which was published posthumously in 1625 with splendid illustrations by Crispin de Pas.

Pluvinel introduced a system of gymnastic exercises designed to increase the suppleness and agility of the horse, and also largely discarded the coercive mechanics that had been commonplace in the previous century. He is generally credited with the invention of the pillars, between which the horse is taught the elements of collection and also

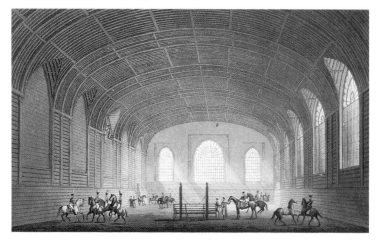

THE RIDING HOUSE AT BRIGHTON
The splendid 18th-century Riding House was designed by John Nash for the British Prince Regent (later George IV) as part of the Royal Pavilion at Brighton. The Prince Regent was a keen and gifted rider.

the *levade,* the first of the airs above the ground. It is not improbable, however, that Pignatelli, with whom the young Pluvinel worked in Naples, might also have used the pillars, which can still be seen in the Spanish Riding School and the Cadre Noir.

WILLIAM CAVENDISH

Although Britain may be considered a major contributor to the overall equine and equestrian development, it had little to do with the advancement of academic riding other than through the sole English Master, William Cavendish, Duke of Newcastle (1592–1676).

Newcastle was an incompetent cavalry commander during the English Civil War, but nonetheless ranks high among the Masters of equitation. In 1658, during his exile at Antwerp, he published in French his *Méthode et Invention Nouvelle de Dresser Les Chevaux.* He published an expanded version in 1667, when he returned to England after the Restoration in 1660. Both books received the approbation of the greatest of all the Masters, François Robichon, Sieur de la Guérinière (1688–1751). Guérinière considered Newcastle, along with La Broue, as the two equestrian authors whose work still remained valid in his own time.

BIBLE OF EQUITATION
These illustrations from Guérinière's École de Cavalerie, published in 1733, show the deep, balanced seat of the day. In both instances, the horses are light in hand and are ridden on a near-looping rein. The book encapsulates the teachings of the Master.

18TH-CENTURY CURB-BIT

This 18th-century bit is based on a pattern used by Pignatelli. The mouthpiece is fitted with a central spatula that lies on the tongue. The loose "keys" on each side of the mouthpiece encourage the horse to "mouth" the bit, relaxing the lower jaw in response to the pressure on the "bars" of the mouth.

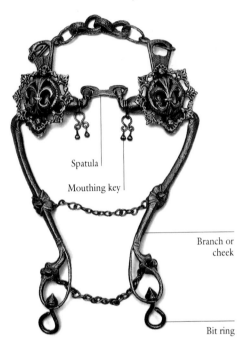

Spatula

Mouthing key

Branch or cheek

Bit ring

Cantle

Flap   Stirrup leather

Stirrup iron

CLASSICAL SEAT

This 18th-century French Selle à Piquer is very similar to the Selle Royale. Today's classical schools use the same design but the stirrup leathers are positioned further to the rear.

principles in all their purity, and even now, over 250 years later, it continues to do so and to demonstrate its art in performances all over the world.

CLASSICAL SCHOOLS

In fact, Guérinère's work is responsible for the streams of classical equitation exemplified by both the Spanish Riding School in Vienna and France's famous Cadre Noir at Saumur. Unlike the Spanish school, the Cadre Noir was a cavalry school. It was constantly developing and never lacked innovators. It combined a classical basis with other forms of competitive riding and, as it used better-bred horses such as Anglo-Arabs and Thoroughbreds, had a broader philosophy.

The third stream of classicism is in Iberia, home of the Spanish horse, which provided the foundation for equestrianism as a rational science rather than an instinctive accomplishment. It is generally less well appreciated and insufficiently recognized, but its importance in combining classical art with practical usage (managing cattle, for instance) is undeniable.

Iberia's long equestrian tradition culminated in the genius of Pedro José de Alcántara Antonio Luis de Meneses, 4th Marquis de Marialva (1713–99). Inevitably influenced by Guérinère, he is responsible for the unique quality of Iberian classicism which, like no other, manifests the ultimate lightness in hand of the balanced horse.

GUÉRINIÈRE

As equerry to Louis XIV from 1730 to 1751, Guérinère was royal riding master and director of the royal *manège* of the Tuileries. He formulated, refined, and then expanded the principles of equitation as a rational science, maintaining that "without theory all practice is aimless". He used exercises to increase suppleness and balance in a progression of systematic schooling, introducing the two-track movement "shoulder-in", the flying change of leading leg at canter, and so on. Just as importantly, he defined and taught a classical riding position that in its essentials still remains valid, whether for school or cross-country riding. His stated objectives, to make the horse calm, light, and obedient so that it was a pleasure to ride and comfortable in all its paces, remain inviolate.

In 1733 Guérinère published his book, *École de Cavalerie*. This quickly became the bible of equitation, and was embraced as

holy writ by the Spanish Riding School in Vienna (see pp.102–3), where its author was virtually canonized. Thereafter, the Spanish School devoted itself to the preservation of Guérinère's

GOAT LEAP

A horse at the Cadre Noir in France executes in-hand the capriole (the leap of the goat). The Spanish School movement differs only slightly.

THE CIRCUS

A conservatory of the equestrian art

THE SPIRIT OF THE CIRCUS
The Roman quadriga was revived in the 19th-century circus.

THE CIRCUS, with its emphasis on spectacles involving horses, played a very large part in the civilizations of Greece and Rome. For centuries horse acts were central to the circus, and there was always a strong connection with advanced horsemanship. The creation of the modern circus is credited to an English ex-Sergeant-Major, Philip Astley (1742–1814), who opened his first circus, Astley's Amphitheatre, near the present site of London's Waterloo Station. In 1769 he built a circular track fenced in with a covered stand, having found that due to centrifugal force it was easier to stand on a horse's back when it was galloping in a small circle. His arena was 13 m (42 ft) in diameter, and this has become the standard measurement for circus rings. To his horse acts Astley added tightrope artists, jugglers, acrobats, dogs, and clowns. However, the word "circus" (the Latin for circle) was not used until 1782 when Charles Hughes, a former Astley rider, opened his own Royal Circus. Circus entertainment continued to be expanded after Astley's death by his partner, the Venetian Antonio Franconi, in his huge Parisian circuses. Franconi developed all sorts of animal acts, but the *Haute École* presentations remained a fundamental, popular part of the programme. Both François Baucher (1796–1873), the genius of the French School, and the Englishman James Fillis, later Chief Instructor at the Cavalry School in St. Petersburg, demonstrated their art in the circus ring. Also included was trick riding, which has been performed for over 2,000 years and is the origin of the modern vaulting discipline. One example is "Roman riding", when the rider gallops two horses round the ring standing up with a foot on the back of each one. Circus horses fall into three main groups: the highly-schooled *Haute École* horses, usually Thoroughbred but sometimes Arab or Lipizzaner; Liberty horses, often Arab since they are not as long in the back as Thoroughbreds and take up less room in the ring; and the rosin-back or vaulting horse, often a Friesian or other heavy draught type. Whatever the horse, it must have a calm temperament, a broad, flat back, and the ability to work at a rhythmic, unbroken canter.

EQUESTRIAN ART
Haute École riding was a feature in the mammoth Parisian circuses developed by Antonio Franconi, the Venetian impresario who had been the partner of Philip Astley.

POSTER APPEAL

Circus posters were often of considerable artistic merit. The depictions of the various acts were colourful, informative, and executed with great attention to detail. Not only did they attract customers, but they also provided a valuable record of the circus equestrian repertoire.

CIRQUE OLYMPIQUE, (Exercices équestres.)

VIRTUOSITY UNLIMITED

These acts, performed by artistes of the Grand Circus Royal, London, represented the highest level of equestrian virtuosity and skill. The horses used were the traditional circus rosin-backs, which had broad backs and even paces.

TRAINING SESSION

THE SPANISH RIDING SCHOOL

VIENNA'S SPANISH RIDING School is the world's oldest riding academy. It was established in 1572 as an adjunct of the Hapsburg court, with the object of providing the nobility with an education in the equestrian arts. It is named after the Spanish horses that were used at the School's inception, and to this day Lipizzaners (see pp.112–13) are the only breed used. The Lipizzaners were founded on Spanish horses imported in 1580 to the court stud at Lipizza. They are now bred specifically for the School at the Piber Stud, near Vienna. Until 1729, when the Winter Riding Hall, the present School, was commissioned by the Emperor Charles VI, the School operated from a wooden arena next to the Imperial Palace.

HISTORY

The Winter Riding Hall was designed as part of the Hofburg Palace by Josef Emmanuel Fischer von Erlach and was completed in 1735 when the vast Austro-Hungarian Empire was at the peak of its power and influence. Alone among the numerous court schools of Europe, the Spanish Riding School survived the disintegration of the ramshackle Austro-Hungarian Empire in 1918. Today, the Austrian Republic still maintains it as a cultural institution, and it is open to the public during training sessions and for the twice-weekly gala performances. The Spanish Riding School also goes on tour from time to time to give performances in other countries throughout the world.

TRAINING

The period of training for a rider takes between four and six years before he is considered capable of riding a schooled horse. It takes another two to four years before he is considered capable of training a horse to that standard.

Every autumn eight to ten young stallions, aged three-and-a-half years old, are brought to the School from the stud in Piber. After a period spent familiarizing the young horses with their surroundings and getting them used to a regular work routine, the first year is devoted to straightforward, basic riding designed to improve their natural balance under the weight of the rider.

In the second year, referred to as the "lower" or "campaign" school, progressive gymnastic exercises are introduced, which lead to increased collection. This involves the lowering of the croup; increased engagement of the hind legs; the shortening of the base; the raising of the forehand; and the improved carriage of head and neck – in fact, the compression of the horse's powers. At the end of this stage the horse is ready to learn the advanced movements of the *Haute École*, such as the *piaffe* and the *passage*, and his aptitude for the execution of the most difficult airs – the leaps above the ground – can be assessed.

In the third and fourth years the stallions learn the advanced *Haute École* airs. These include the difficult flying changes of leg at canter, and eventually the flying change at every stride. The horses also learn to master the pirouette, the *piaffe*, and the *passage*. The *piaffe* is a lofty, highly collected trot, executed virtually on the spot. The *passage* involves the same slow, rhythmic movement as the horse majestically moves forward.

Particularly talented horses may then be selected to perform the classical school

BAROQUE PERFECTION
Riders of Vienna's Spanish Riding School perform their elegant quadrille in the magnificent Winter Riding Hall of the Hofburg Palace. At one end of the hall hangs the portrait of the School's founder, the Holy Roman Emperor Charles VI (1685–1740).

THE SCHOOL LEAPS

The School leaps are a spectacular feature of the programme. Here, the stallion prepares to execute the courbette from the levade position.

School, but by tradition one bay horse is also included. In accordance with the laws of genetics, bay Lipizzaners are produced occasionally, but they are the exceptions and are not used for breeding.

PUBLIC PERFORMANCES

For the public performances the stallions wear black bridles with gold buckles but without the customary throatlatch, and they carry the traditional white buckskin saddles – the *selle royale* of classical equitation. The riders, who are all Austrian citizens, wear snuff-coloured tailcoats, cocked hats, buckskin breeches, and high black boots. They carry long, unembellished birch switches, which are for practical use but also serve as a symbol of the rider's humility. By tradition, the riders doff their bicorn hats to salute the portrait of Charles VI, which hangs at one end of the lofty, magnificently galleried, baroque hall, as they enter and leave the school.

When the dancing white horses, under their uncannily still riders, enter the hall under the light of the glittering chandeliers, the onlooker may witness the rare beauty of "the art of riding cultivated in its purest form and brought to perfection".

leaps, which are known as the "airs above the ground". These are regarded as the highest point in the classical art and the ultimate manifestation of complete collection. They are first taught in-hand, from a lunge-rein held by the trainer. Only when the horse can perform the leaps without weight on his back does he then execute them with a rider.

In the 17th century there were seven recognized leaps, some of them amounting to no more than incomplete or perhaps preparatory movements. Today, only the three primary leaps are performed. These are the *levade*, the *courbette*, and the soaring *capriole* (the "leap of the goat", from the Italian word *capra*, meaning goat).

The *levade*, the basis for the subsequent leaps, involves the lifting of the forehand on deeply bent hind legs. The hocks are lowered to within 20–25 cm (8–10 in) of the ground, while the forelegs are held in a bent position. This attitude must then be held for a short period. *Courbette* follows on from *levade*. From the first position, the

horse is encouraged to spring forward on the hind legs, while maintaining the bent attitude of the forelegs. The ultimate extension of both movements is when the horse leaps into the *capriole*, with all four legs clear of the ground.

Only the white Lipizzaner stallions are used at the

TRADITIONAL SALUTE

A quartet of School riders lift their bicorn hats in the traditional salute as they pose before the Hofburg Palace in Vienna.

THE ART OF IBERIA

A classical tradition continued

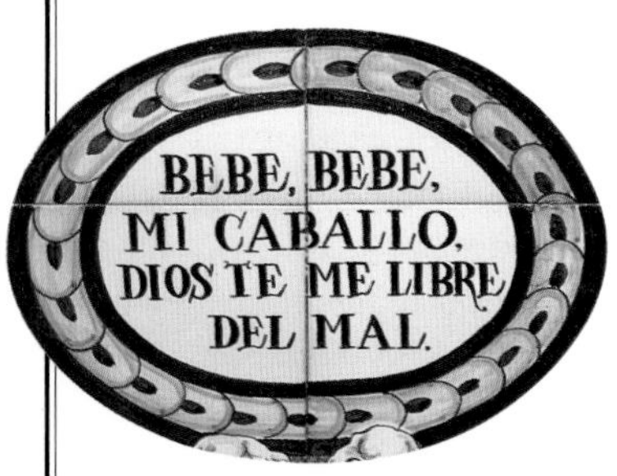

THE SPANISH HORSE was predominant in Europe for over 300 years, from the Renaissance to the early 19th century. It was, wrote William Cavendish, Duke of Newcastle and the sole English Master of the equestrian art, "... the noblest horse in the world ... and fittest of all for a king in the day of triumph". Spanish blood was used to upgrade almost every one of the known equine breeds. The Spanish Horses taken to Lipizza (Lipiça) by the Archduke Charles of Austria in 1583 were the foundation for the Lipizzaner breed, a debt acknowledged in the title of Vienna's "Spanish" Riding School, which is still, after 400 years, the world's conservatory of classical riding. Largely because of this superlative horse, there is in Spain and Portugal an even older tradition of horsemanship in which the lithe, black fighting bulls of the Peninsula have also played their part. It is recorded that Julius Caesar, a very gifted horseman, who kept a house at Jerez de la Frontera, the sherry capital of Andalucia, was the first man in Spain to fight the bull from horseback, following the manner of the bullfights that were a feature of the circuses of both Greece and Rome. Jerez, in the heartland of the Spanish horse, is today home to the Andalucian School of Equestrian Art. Naturally, the accent differs from that of the Spanish School or of France's Cadre Noire, but it remains essentially classical while displaying some of the earlier movements of classicism, like the spectacular Spanish Walk. Portugal, too, has its School of Equestrian Art that continues to reflect the artistry of the country's greatest horseman in recent times, the late Maestro Nuno Oliveira. The School uses the bay or brown Alter-Real, bred specifically as a High School horse. The classical Alter-Real survives as the result of powerful infusions of Andalucian blood from Jerez, but it retains its own characteristics, as does Portugal's Lusitano, although both breeds are indubitably of the same Spanish family.

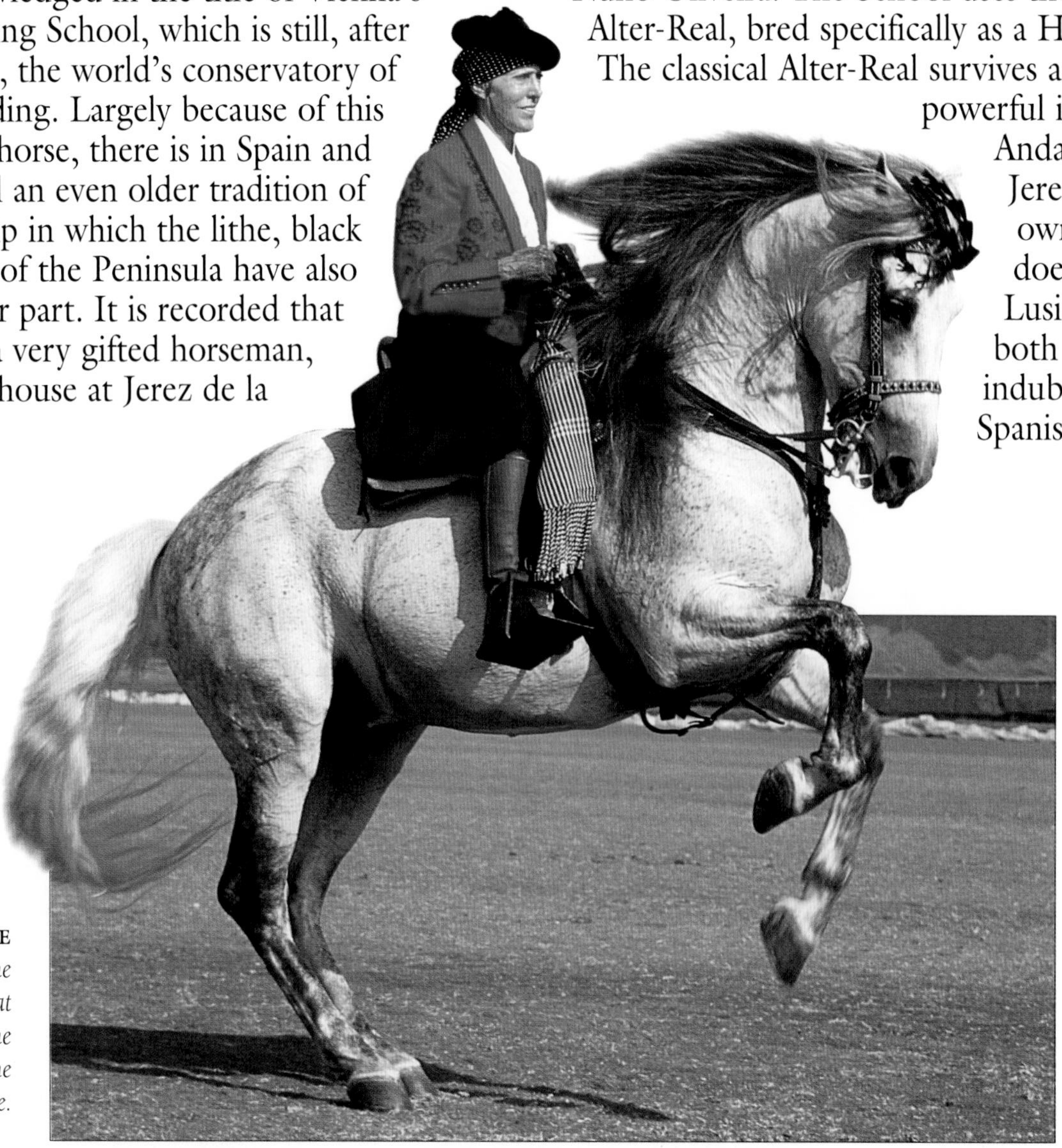

THE NOBLE HORSE

This stallion of the Andalucian School at Jerez displays all the splendour of the majestic Spanish Horse.

THE CLASSICAL ART

A stallion of the School performs the classical piaffe in-hand. The shoulders are raised, the croup lowered, and the movement epitomizes the concept of collection. The Spanish Horses have an inherited gymnastic ability and are supremely agile. Physically, these horses are particularly well-developed over the loins, with notable strength in the hocks and second thigh.

CEREMONIAL DRESS

Full dress uniform is worn by these riders of the Andalucian School, and the horses are turned out in corresponding fashion in ceremonial bridles with manes traditionally dressed.

SORRAIA

T HE SORRAIA AND THE CLOSELY RELATED GARRANOS of Iberia are
regarded as indigenous to the area, and it is probable that thousands
of years ago their forebears were the first horses to be domesticated in
Europe. Both contributed directly to the evolution of the Spanish Horse,
which became a major influence in the evolution of the equine races in
Europe and America from the 16th century onwards. That is a measure
of the importance of this ancient stock. Inevitably, the Garranos and
Sorraia ponies have been improved by human intervention; the Garranos,
which has received infusions of Arab stock, is the most affected.

INFLUENCES

Both breeds must be seen as stemming
from the same primitive stock, principally
represented by the Tarpan (see pp.20–21)
with possible traces of the Asiatic Wild
Horse (see pp.18–19). At the time of
their domestication the indigenous stock
would have been distributed over the whole
region, with groups being concentrated in
the areas that provided water, adequate
plant growth, and the best climatic
conditions. Differences in size and type
would have been related to the environment
and the dominance of particular strains.

This "primitive" Iberian stock had also
been influenced by the horses in North
Africa because of the land bridge that

existed between Spain and Africa until just
before the last Ice Age, thousands of years
ago. It provided the genetic base for the
emergence of the Iberian
horse breeds, which are
known variously as
Andalucian, Lusitano,
and Alter-Real (see
pp.108–11), but which
are really no more than
branches of the same
family tree.

The history of
Iberia – long before
its division into the
kingdoms of Leon
and Castile, Portugal,
Navarre, Aragon, and
Granada in the period between 1212 and
1402 – was a continuing saga of invasion
and occupation. Carthaginians, Vandals, and
Visigoths, together with their horses, moved
into, and sometimes through, the area that
was to become so important in terms of the
development of the equine races.

The Vandals who had settled in Andalucia
migrated to Africa, leaving what remained of
the Visigoths to be conquered by the Moors,
who were followers of Islam and came from
Algeria, Morocco, and Tunisia.

The influence of the Moors was decisive
on both the human and equine populations
of Spain. They invaded between 711 and
712 when over 25,000 men and their horses,
predominantly Barbs from North Africa (see
pp.66–67), crossed into Spain, and their
empire did not begin to decline until 1212
when its armies were defeated at Las Navas
de Tolosa by the combined forces of the
kings of Aragon and Castile. Granada, the
last Moorish state, did not fall until 1492.

ORIGINS

THE SORRAIA AND ITS NEIGHBOUR, *the related Garranos or
Minho, are indigenous to the Iberian Peninsula. The
original habitat of the Sorraia was in the plains between
the rivers of Sor and Raia (in both Portugal and Spain),
while the Garranos predominated further to the north in
the richer Portuguese valleys of Garranos do Minho and
Traz dos Montes. The Sorraia, on account of its
environment, is resistant to cold and heat and is able to
· thrive in poor soil conditions and on minimal forage.*

MINIATURE SPANISH HORSE
*The improved, modern Sorraia pony epitomizes
the Spanish Horse in miniature. The dun colouring
is typical and characteristic of its ancient origin.*

NECK
The strong neck is
uniquely Spanish in
its conformation.

LEGS
The short legs support
a robust body which is
deep and compact.

To this day, the indelible imprint of the Moorish Empire remains apparent in the art, architecture, people, and horses of Iberia.

As well as Barbs, many Arab horses (see pp.64–65) of pure desert descent entered Spain; an early Caliph of Cordoba, for example, kept no fewer than 2,000 Arab horses in his stables by the River Guadalquivir. Nonetheless, the overriding impression is that the evolution of the Iberian Horse resulted from an ongoing cross-fertilization between the indigenous stock and the Barbs of North Africa.

THE SORRAIA AND GARRANOS

It is the Sorraia Pony that represents the connection between the indigenous stock of prehistory and the present-day horses of the Peninsula. Only in comparatively recent times has its habitat been fixed as being between the rivers Sor and Raia (running through both Spain and Portugal), from which the pony's name is derived.

QUARTERS
The quarters are sloped from the croup with the tail low-set.

The habitat of the Garranos, or Minho, is in the more fertile mountain valleys of Garranos do Minho and Traz dos Montes, north of the Sor in Portugal. There is no doubt about the antiquity of the breed, but continued infusions of Arab blood made by the Portuguese Ministry of Agriculture have created a pony that, while being strong and hardy, is far removed from its primitive ancestors in appearance. It is a quality pony with a small, pretty head that – because of the Arab outcross, it has to be assumed – has a noticeably concave profile.

Although the Sorraia also betrays the improving hand of man, it still retains notable characteristics inherited from its early ancestors. Many of the ponies bear an

PRIMITIVE RED DUN
Another variation of the "primitive" dun colouring is seen in these spirited Sorraia mares and foals. The ponies are a good example of the improved type.

extraordinary resemblance to the Tarpan in conformation and in the colour and texture of the coat. As little as 50 years ago the resemblance was even closer.

The shoulder was upright, the back was straight, the tail was set low in sloping quarters, and the head was large and convex in profile.

The modern Sorraia is far more attractive, and standing between 1.22 and 1.32 m (12–13 hh) it is virtually a miniature Iberian Horse, like the Andalucian or Lusitano. As with its ancestors, it is a hardy animal, resistant to both heat and cold and able to thrive on poor soils and sparse forage. The "deer-grey" coat colour is still apparent, along with the typically primitive dun and a muddy palomino yellow. Dark points, eel stripes along the back, and frequently barred (zebra) leg markings are not unusual in the breed. The manes and tails are black and the long ears, set high on the head as in the primitive horse, are also tipped with black.

For centuries the Sorraia was used by local "cowboys" to perform a variety of light agricultural tasks. The stock then degenerated rapidly with the onset of mechanization and was only preserved through the efforts of Dr Ruy d'Andrade and his son Fernando. They kept a small Sorraia herd in the natural state, and it was this that encouraged the conservation and improvement of the breed.

THE ORIGINAL
These Mexican ponies, descendants of the first Spanish imports, are probably as close to the original Sorraia type as could possibly be found, particularly in respect of the dun colouring.

HEIGHT
1.22–1.32 m (12–13 hh)

ANDALUCIAN & LUSITANO

IN THE PATTERN of equine development the Spanish Horse occupies a position second only to that of the Arabian (see pp.64–65) and its own principal progenitor, the Barb of North Africa (see pp.66–67). For 300 years, up to the end of the 18th century, its influence on the breeds of Europe and the Americas was hugely pervasive, and such was the prepotency of "the world's most noble horse" that it persists to this day.

HARNESS CHAMPIONS
Andalucian horses are just as good in harness as under saddle. This Spanish team of Andalucians is competing at Windsor Driving Grand Prix.

TYPES OF IBERIAN HORSE

Despite its pre-eminence, much confusion exists about what constitutes a Spanish Horse, largely because of the variety of names given to what is essentially one race existing in both Spain and Portugal. Many of the names derive from the geographical area in which horses were bred and so, even allowing for regional differences and nuances of type, what is to all intents and purposes the same horse may be called: Spanish, Carthusian, Lusitano, Alter-Real, Peninsular, Zapatero, Andalucian, and so on. It would, in fact, be more satisfactory and more accurate for them all to share the common title "Iberian Horse".

MANE
The luxuriant mane and tail hair of the Andalucian is trimmed only minimally.

NECK
The short, powerful neck is carried high and contributes to the natural balance.

THE ANDALUCIAN

The name "Andalucian" is as confusing as any. Today, Andalucia embraces the area in southern Spain around Seville, Cordoba, and Granada, but for centuries *Andalus* referred to almost the whole peninsula. In fact, although other countries still use the name Andalucian, the Spanish Breeders' Association stopped using it in 1912 and replaced it with *Pura Raza Española*, meaning "the pure Spanish breed".

Modern Andalucia still remains as a centre of breeding with the Carthusian monastery of Jerez de la Frontera, founded in 1476, at its centre. This monastery was responsible for preserving the purest strain

ORIGINS

ANDALUCIAN HORSE BREEDING is still centred in the province of Andalucia in southern Spain and particularly around Jerez de la Frontera near the coast, where the purest strains were bred at the Carthusian monastery stud. The Lusitano, the Portuguese version of the Andalucian horse, is bred throughout Portugal. The environment for both these breeds is hot and dry. The horses are naturally adapted to these conditions, which contribute to the hard feet and account for the fine body hair and the distinctive mane and tail of both breeds.

HEIGHT OF ANDALUCIAN
1.57 m
(15.2 hh)

ANDALUCIAN

of Andalucian, resolutely refusing to use heavy Neapolitan outcrosses, even though this practice was supported by royal edict.

CHARACTERISTICS

The Andalucian stands no more than about 1.57 m (15.2 hh), but it is a horse of commanding presence, with lofty and

HEIGHT OF LUSITANO
1.57 m (15.2 hh)

WITHERS
The withers are rarely sharply defined but they complement the shoulders and give emphasis to the back and the loins.

spectacular paces. The facial profile is convex and the eyes are almond-shaped. It has a natural balance, and the rather sloped croup, combined with the high degree of flexion possible in the hind legs, results in the horse moving naturally in a state of collection. The breed is not built to gallop, but is extremely supple and agile. Despite being highly courageous and spirited, these horses are uniformly gentle and docile. They are still used in the bull-ring, and are particularly suited to

the *Haute École* (see pp.102–3), although their high, round action is not much appreciated in modern competitive dressage.

THE LUSITANO

The Lusitano is the Portuguese variant of the Iberian Horse. However, this has only been its official name (from *Lusitania*, the old Latin for Portugal) since 1966. The Lusitano excels in the bull-ring, which is regarded as an art-form in Portugal where the bull is not killed in the ring.

HEAD
The head is somewhat convex in profile with great width between the eyes.

The Lusitano and the Andalucian share the same genetic background and character, although there are differences of detail in conformation. For instance, the Lusitano's croup is usually more sloped, with the tail set lower in consequence, and the convexity of the head is more pronounced. All kinds of grey and bay are found in both breeds, as well as the occasional and very striking mulberry shade. In both, the mane and tail are particularly luxurious.

SHOULDERS
The shoulders are a little straight in relation to the humerus and contribute to the lofty action.

LUSITANO

LUSITANOS AT WORK
The breeding of the Lusitano horse is bound up with that of the fighting bulls. Their agility, intelligence and courage make them the ideal mounts for the campinos *who tend the herds.*

ALTER-REAL

THE ALTER-REAL has experienced a more turbulent history than any other of the Iberian breeds, and has also suffered more from ill-advised cross-breeding experiments. That it survives is due to the re-introduction of the Andalucian blood (see pp.108–9) upon which it was founded in 1748, when 300 Andalucian mares were imported from around Jerez de la Frontera in Spain. Although the Alter-Real is indubitably Iberian, it retains its individuality among the Iberian breeds and is especially suited to the *Haute École*, which was its original function. Today, the classical Alter-Real is preserved in the performances given by the Portuguese School of Equestrian Art.

NECK
The neck is muscular and fairly short, and in movement the carriage is naturally high.

THE ALTER-REAL

The Alter-Real breed takes its name from the small town of Alter do Chão, in the Portuguese province of Alentejo where it was first bred at the royal Vila de Portel stud in 1748. *Real* is Portuguese for "royal", and the purpose of the stud was to provide the royal stables at Lisbon with horses suitable for classical equitation, a pursuit followed enthusiastically by King Dom José I, as well as with quality carriage horses for court purposes. Soil and grazing conditions at Alter were conducive to the raising of top-class stock, and for many years the stud produced a particularly fine stamp of horse.

Alter and its horses were also famous because of the association with Portugal's most distinguished Master of Horse, the Marquis of Marialva (1713–99), the "Portuguese La Guérinière" (see pp.98–99).

HEAD
In profile, the head is typical of the Iberian horses.

The stud suffered during the Peninsular War of 1804–14, much of the stock being dispersed by French troops, and in 1834 it was closed by royal decree. Subsequently, attempts were made to resuscitate the Alter breed with outcrosses to Hanoverian, Norman, and English blood, and there was one experiment to "arabize" the breed. None of these crosses was successful, and the introduction of massive Arab infusions was particularly disastrous. The breed only began to improve again when new Andalucian blood was re-introduced, towards the end of

FIXED TYPE
After the vicissitudes of more than two centuries, the Alter breed is once more firmly established in its native land, and has achieved its own fixed type. In Portugal it is customary for mares living out to be fitted with bell collars.

HEIGHT
1.52–1.63 m
(15–16 hh)

the 19th century. At that time recourse was had to mares of the purest Andalucian strain, the Zapateros bred by the Zapata family.

After the dissolution of the Portuguese monarchy, at the beginning of the 20th century, the stud and the Alter breed would have disappeared entirely had it not been for the active intervention of Portugal's greatest equestrian authority, Dr. Ruy d'Andrade. He managed to save a small nucleus of the Alter-Real stock, and line-bred to just two fine stallions. In 1932 the Alter stud was handed over to the Ministry of Agriculture, and today, though small, it thrives and remains a significant part of the country's cultural heritage.

The Alter horses are trained to perform High School work, and it is claimed that the modern stock now resemble the original horses of the 18th century. The breed differs from other Iberian horses, particularly in characteristics such as the appearance of the back and the length of the pasterns and cannons. One breed expert, Signor Leather de Macedo, writing in 1971, pointed to the forearm being shorter than the cannon, and the chest is certainly particularly wide and deep – more so, apparently, than in either the Lusitano or the Andalucian. The action is extravagant with notable knee flexion, which is no detriment in a horse dedicated to the baroque principles of classicism.

The principal and accepted colours of the Alter breed are bay or brown, although de Macedo wrote of chestnut, bay, and piebald also occurring. These colours are not seen today, nor is the breed considered to be "temperamental and even violent" as it was suggested by de Macedo.

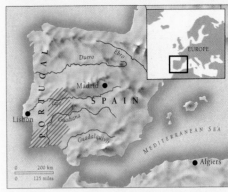

ORIGINS

THE ALTER-REAL breed of Portugal was established by the House of Braganza in 1748 to provide horses for the royal stables at Lisbon. The breed takes its name from the town of Alter do Chão in the southern province of Alentejo. This area is noted for its mineral-rich soils and for the high nutrient content of the grazing. The two factors contributed significantly to the quality of the stock. The close proximity of Spain's Andalucian breeding centres was also advantageous.

OTHER IBERIAN HORSES

Spain has a large Arab horse population, of a particular quality that is much sought after in international Arab breeding. Considerable use is also made of the Thoroughbred (see pp.120–21), with the object of producing competition stock.

The Andalucian crossed with the Arab, Anglo-Arab, or Thoroughbred, produces an elegant, free-moving horse. The stock retains the Andalucian's gentleness and some of its strength and agility but, particularly when the Thoroughbred or Anglo-Arab is used, it has more slope to the shoulder and a longer, lower action.

CROUP
The croup slopes characteristically towards a low-set tail.

HOCKS
The articulation of the powerful and well-positioned hock joints is exemplary.

THE HISPANO-ARAB
The crossing of Spanish blood with that of the Arab (or the Anglo-Arab) results in a very fine type of riding horse. It retains much of the Arabian type, particularly about the head, but combines that special refinement with the substance and the powerful back and quarters that are characteristic of the Spanish horses.

LIPIZZANER

THE LIPIZZANER is so integral to Vienna's Spanish Riding School that it would be impossible to think of one without the other. In fact, the white horses (as well as a few that are black, bay, and chestnut) are bred all over what was once the vast Austro-Hungarian Empire, not just at the Spanish School's stud at Piber in Austria. Despite the conflict in former Yugoslavia, the breed is still bred at Lipizza (Lipiça) in Slovenia where it originated, and from where, in the harsh, limestone wilderness of the Karst, it takes its name and derives much of its character.

LIPIZZANERS IN HARNESS
Lipizzaners, originally intended for carriage work as well as for riding, are still popular harness horses all over Europe. This pair was photographed at Lipizza, where the horses have been bred for 400 years.

THE STUD AT LIPIZZA

The stud at Lipizza, then part of the Austrian Empire, was founded in 1580 by the Archduke Charles II to supply a suitably grand stamp of horse to the Ducal stables at Graz and the court stables in Vienna. The fledgling Spanish Riding School (Spanish because from its outset it had used Spanish horses) had been established in Vienna eight years earlier in a wooden arena next to the Imperial Palace (see pp.102–3).

Nine Spanish stallions and 24 mares, representatives of the breed that dominated the equestrian scene well into the 18th century, were imported to Lipizza from the Iberian Peninsula. Spanish horses continued to be bought throughout the 18th century, but as the old sort became more difficult to obtain, outcrosses were also made to horses from Italy (such as the Neapolitans from Polesina and Naples), Germany and Denmark's Royal Stud at Frederiksborg. All, however, had strong Spanish connections. Finally, in the 19th century there came the powerful Arab influence through the white horse Siglavy, who joined the Lipizza stud in 1816 as a six-year-old. (Attempts have been made occasionally to introduce Thoroughbred blood, but they have never been successful.)

BLOODLINES

The six principal foundation stallions whose descendants can still be seen at the Spanish Riding School in Vienna are: Pluto, a white horse, born in 1765 of pure Spanish descent and obtained from the Royal Danish Court Stud; Conversano, a black Neapolitan, born 1767; Favory, a dun born at the Kladrub stud in 1779; Neapolitano, a bay Neapolitan from Polesina, born 1790; Siglavy, the Arab, born 1810; and Maestoso, born 1819, a white horse from the most important Hungarian stud, Mezőhegyes. Maestoso was by a Neapolitan out of a Spanish dam. Of the original 23 mare lines, 14 still exist at Piber, where the Spanish School horses have been bred since 1920, except for their stay at Hostau during the Second World War.

ORIGINS

THE ORIGINAL STUD for the Lipizzaner was in the harsh, limestone Karst at Lipizza in Slovenia, from which the horse derives much of its character. The Karst produces hard feet and strong bone, and contributes to the breed's soundness and longevity. Since 1920 the Spanish School Lipizzaners have been bred at Piber in Austria. However, Lipizzaners are bred all over what was once the Austro-Hungarian Empire, particularly in the state studs of Hungary, Romania, and former Czechoslovakia.

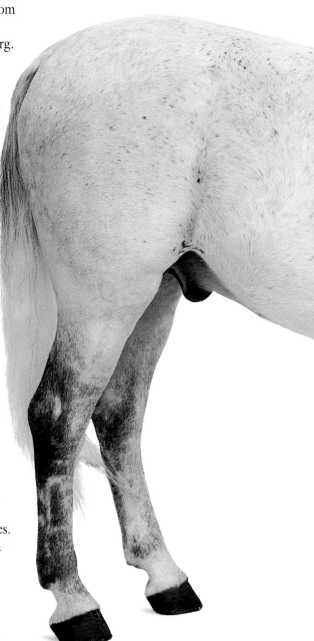

CHARACTERISTICS

It has always been the Lipizza stud's policy to breed white horses, as these were considered to be the most suitable to the dignity of the Imperial house. Even so, other colours existed until the 18th century. George Hamilton's picture of brood mares at Lipizza, painted in 1727, shows coats ranging from black, bay, dun, and cream to spectacularly spotted coats, while engravings, notably by Ridinger, depict spotted, piebald, and skewbald horses. Modern Lipizzaners bred at Piber are white, although foals are born black or brown. There are also occasional bays. Bays are not used for breeding, but traditionally one is kept at the Spanish School.

The Piber Lipizzaner is a small horse a little over 1.52 m (15 hh) but others, of the carriage type, can be as large as 1.65 m (16.1 hh). Both before and after 1920 when Piber was established, the object has been to breed virtually to the baroque pattern, producing a compact, strong-limbed horse, powerful in the quarters and neck and often retaining the ram nose of the old Spanish breed. Most important is the temperament that makes the intelligent Lipizzaner easy to teach and happy to submit to the *manège* disciplines without loss of spirit.

The rocky background of the Karst bequeathed a particular character to the Lipizzaner and, in fact, the breed only thrives in similar conditions. (At Laxenburg, where the conditions are milder, for example, the birth rate fell dramatically and there were many fatalities.) The Karst produces animals which are slow to mature but have a long life-span. Many of the Lipizzaners of Vienna perform demanding exercises when they are well over 20 years old, and some live to be over 30.

LIPIZZANERS IN EUROPE

Lipizzaners are also raised at the state studs of Hungary, Romania, and former Czechoslovakia. All maintain the six stallion lines on which the breed is founded, although Szilvasvard in Hungary, also keeps the Incitato line and its own line, the Tulipan. Variations in type do occur, however, and while all are indubitably Lipizzaner, the Piber type is by no means predominant. All Lipizzaners are ridden but many of those bred outside Piber are also used as harness horses. Some are also still used in farm work.

SHOULDERS
The shoulders are as well suited to harness as to saddle and correspond to the short neck and usually low withers.

HEAD
The head is usually neat and well-set on the neck. Sometimes an Arab influence is apparent but otherwise, the impression is usually Spanish.

HEIGHT
1.52 m
(15 hh)

LIPIZZANERS AT PIBER
Piber supplies the Lipizzaner stallions to the Spanish Riding School at Vienna. Here, brood mares and foals at Piber are being led from the stables to the pastures. The Piber mares are schooled both under saddle and as carriage horses.

LEGS
The powerful, proportionate legs, with short cannons, ample bone, and particularly hard, well-shaped feet are characteristic. The pasterns are adequately sloped.

FREDERIKSBORG & KNABSTRUP

THE FREDERIKSBORG BREED was developed at the Royal Frederiksborg Stud, founded in 1562 by King Frederik II of Denmark. Its aim was to produce military chargers that were also suitable for use in the riding school, on the parade ground, and in court ceremonies. The Knabstrup dates from the Napoleonic wars, when Spanish soldiers were stationed in Denmark. Some of their horses were spotted – a coat pattern often found in early Spanish strains.

THE FREDERIKSBORG

The foundation stock at Frederiksborg consisted of Spanish horses, brought from Iberia and from Central and Eastern Europe. Later, Neapolitan stock was imported, and in the 19th century outcrosses were made to half-bred English stallions, usually carrying Norfolk Roadster blood (see pp.122–23). Eastern horses, usually Arabs (see pp.64–65), were also used to give greater refinement.

see pp.122–23 ... see pp.64–65

STRONG DRIVING HORSE
The modern Frederiksborg is bred largely as a strong, upstanding carriage horse with a distinctive appearance and a high, showy action.

Horses from the Royal Frederiksborg Stud were, in turn, much used to improve other breeds. For example, the Danish Jutland (see pp.276–77), benefited from the Frederiksborg influence, acquiring a more vigorous action. One of the most famous exports from the Danish Court Stud was the white stallion Pluto, born in 1765. He founded the Lipizzaner line that still exists and bears his name today (see pp.112–13).

see pp.276–77 ... see pp.112–13

The original Frederiksborgs were much sought after in Europe. They were usually chestnut, and stood at a little over 1.63 m (16 hh). Elegant and spirited, they moved with a vigorous, rather high action that showed off the rider in the desirable "heroic" mould. Moreover, like their Spanish ancestors, they had the most equable of temperaments.

The popularity of the breed was its undoing. Many horses were sold abroad, including some of the foundation stock. As a result, the bloodlines that had been carefully established were so much depleted that the Royal Stud was forced to close in 1839. The Frederiksborg continued to be bred at private studs in Denmark; however, these studs increasingly tended to produce animals for use in carriages and light draught, rather than distinctive riding horses. By then, the chestnut colour was firmly established, and most specimens stood at a little over 1.63 m

IN ACTION
The attractive Frederiksborg is no speed horse but is nonetheless free and active in movement, with good head carriage.

SHOULDERS
The typical, elegant carriage shoulders complement the high head carriage and showy action. The withers are low and the back a little long.

LEGS
The legs are proportionate and have good-sized joints.

HEIGHT OF FREDERIKSBORG
1.63 m
(16 hh)

FREDERIKSBORG

(16 hh). More recently, Frederiksborg-type mares have been crossed with breeds such as the Thoroughbred (see pp.120–21) and Trakehner (see pp.140–41) to develop the Danish Warmblood (see pp.150–51). Frederiksborgs still exist in Denmark, but the old type is not much in evidence today.

THE KNABSTRUP

This breed is descended from a spotted mare of Spanish ancestry called Flaebehoppen ("Flaebe's horse"). She was bought from a Spanish officer by a butcher named Flaebe, then sold to Judge Lunn, who bred from her at his Knabstrup estate. She was noted for speed and endurance. Put to a Frederiksborg stallion in 1808, she founded a line of spotted horses. Her grandson, Mikkel, is recognized as a foundation sire.

Knabstrups are mainly white with brown or black spots on the head, body, and legs. The old type was strong with a rather coarse head. Its

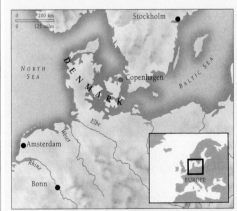

THE OLD SCHOOL
The Knabstrup of the old type was stronger and more heavily built than the horse that is more usually bred today. It was much sought after for working in the circus.

shoulders and the shortish, strong neck made it well-suited to harness work. Crossing for the spotted coat alone, regardless of conformation and constitution, as well as some in-breeding, caused the breed to deteriorate, but Knabstrups were very popular as circus horses, and were ideal for use in vaulting acts. As with the Frederiksborg, the old type is now rare; the modern Knabstrup now resembles a quality Appaloosa (see pp.226–27).

LOIN
This is a strong, broad loin without too much length in the back. The withers are not defined.

NECK
The neck is strong, very well-muscled but tending to shortness. However, the head is particularly well-set and is attractive in its outlook.

CANNONS
There is sufficient bone for the frame, the cannons are short enough, and the knees are flat and big.

KNABSTRUP

HEIGHT OF KNABSTRUP
1.57 m
(15.2 hh)

ORIGINS

200 km
125 miles

NORTH SEA

Stockholm

DENMARK

Copenhagen

BALTIC SEA

Elbe

Weser

Amsterdam

Rhine

Bonn

EUROPE

BOTH THE FREDERIKSBORG AND THE KNABSTRUP originated in Denmark; the former at the old Royal Frederiksborg Stud and the latter at the Knabstrup estate belonging to Judge Lunn. Neither have been bred in significant numbers outside Denmark, even though the Frederiksborg was exported all over Europe in the 19th century. Meanwhile the Knabstrup was much in demand for circus work – its broad back made it an excellent horse for use in vaulting acts. The Frederiksborg, however, was used to good effect on Denmark's work-horse, the Jutland, improving its action noticeably.

PART FIVE

THE GREAT STUDS

THE FIRST GREAT STUDS developed in Europe probably date from before the 12th century. They bred horses for the royal stables as well as for military purposes and reached their zenith in the architecturally magnificent establishments of the 18th and 19th centuries. Many of these studs survive in the 21st century, both as splendid examples of the architecture of the period and as important breeding centres, producing horses to fulfil the demands of sport and recreation. Not surprisingly, the valuable multi-national Thoroughbred industry has its own centres of excellence in the principal racing countries of the world. Some are national studs, but many more, including some of the most famous ones, are under private ownership.

The Festetics Stud Farm at Fenekpuszta, Lake Balaton, Hungary by Emil Adam, 1884

YEARLINGS AT TULLY, IRELAND

UK, IRISH, & US STUDS

THOROUGHBRED RACING, and in consequence Thoroughbred breeding, is carried out in most countries of the world. Foremost among the countries that have traditional Thoroughbred breeding areas, and highly developed racing industries, are the UK, Ireland, France, and the US; in all of them the majority of breeding studs are situated in or around major racing centres. Examples include Newmarket and Lambourn in England; Longchamps and Chantilly in France; the Curragh in Ireland; and the legendary Blue Grass country of Kentucky in the US. Some of the best Thoroughbred stock is also raised in Australia, New Zealand, and Italy. Increasingly, however, the major world influence is that of Dubai's ruling family, the Maktoums, which has the Dalham Hall Stud at the centre of its Newmarket operations.

ENGLAND AND IRELAND

Both England and Ireland have National Studs, although for the most part studs are in private hands. England's National Stud was gifted to the nation by the eccentric Colonel William Hall-Walker (later to become Lord Wavertree) in 1915, when he offered the Tully Stud on the Irish Curragh, and its stock, to the English Government.

Between the two world wars the most outstanding horse bred at Tully was Blandford, the sire of four Derby winners:

Trigo (foaled in1929), Blenheim (foaled in 1930), Windsor Lad (foaled in 1934), and Bahram (foaled in 1935). Other top-class horses produced at the National Stud included the classic race winners Royal Lancer (1922 St Leger); Big Game (1942 2,000 Guineas, the Oaks, and the St Leger); and Chamossaire (1945 St Leger). Tully remained as the English National Stud until 1943, when the Irish Government established its own National Stud there. The English counterpart was then moved to the Sandley Stud at Gillingham in Dorset, and

after the Second World War a further 240 hectares (600 acres) of land was leased at West Grinstead in Sussex.

The watershed in the English National Stud's history was in 1963, when its management was transferred from the Ministry of Agriculture to the Horse Race

HOME OF CHAMPIONS
England's National Stud on the old Bunbury Farm just outside Newmarket reflects the declared policy of "maintaining the British Thoroughbred at the high standard which has gained it a world-wide reputation".

SOLD AT AUCTION

Four major bloodstock sales are held during the year at the Keeneland Racetrack, Lexington, in the centre of Kentucky's Blue Grass Country. They are attended by buyers from all over the world.

Betting Levy Board. It then became a self-supporting enterprise and concentrated on the provision of stallions and stopped keeping mares. Soon afterwards the Jockey Club offered a long lease of the 200-hectare (500-acre) Bunbury Farm, Newmarket, and the present stud was built on that site.

The first two stallions to stand at Newmarket were Never Say Die and Tudor Melody. The American-bred Never Say Die had won the 1954 Derby and St Leger, and was presented to the Stud by his owner Robert Sterling Clarke. Tudor Melody was, if anything, an even more successful sire, siring the winners of 88 races in his first three seasons and heading the two-year-old sire list of 1968 and 1970. Ten years later the National Stud sires included the great Mill Reef, Grundy, and Blakeney. Mill Reef was the champion sire in England and Ireland, as well as heading the lists elsewhere in Europe. His progeny included Shirley Heights, the English and Irish Sweeps Derby winner; Acamas, winner of the French Derby; and Slip Anchor, who won the 1985 Epsom Derby.

In Ireland, the Irish National Stud Company also pursued a policy of providing top-class stallions to breeders on very favourable terms. Its stallion complement always includes important horses: stallions of the calibre of Preciptic, Vimy, Panaslipper, Miralgo, Tulyar, Eudaemon, and Sallust all stood at Tully.

KENTUCKY

Despite the effects of the 1990s recession the American bloodstock industry, centred in Kentucky, is still the largest and arguably the most influential in the world. For some 200 years the Blue Grass Country, which centres on the city of Lexington, Kentucky, has been devoted to horse-raising.

Perhaps the most opulent, resplendent, and distinguished of the Kentucky farms was Calumet. This stud was founded in 1928 by the Wrights, who made their fortune from a baking-powder called Calumet (the word is also the name for the Indian "pipe of peace"). Today it has closed, but its record is unlikely ever to be equalled. Calumet was the home of Bull Lea, five times a champion sire up to 1953 and the sire of Citation, the first "Thoroughbred millionaire", with winnings of $1,085,760. In 1948 he won the American Triple Crown. Secretariat and Seattle Slew, both Blue Grass horses, repeated that record in 1973 and 1977 respectively. Calumet Farm horses won the Kentucky Derby eight times. The Farm collected 32 titles, including "horse of the year", "best two-year-old", and "best three-year-old", and between 1932 and 1975 had won $21,863,076, a record in racing history.

HOME OF BULL LEA

A typical whiteboard building at Calumet, once the greatest of the Kentucky Blue Grass Farms and with a record of winners that is unlikely to be equalled.

KENTUCKY HEARTLAND

The pike roads of the "inner" Blue Grass surrounding Lexington are lined with some of the world's most palatial horse farms, the paddocks enclosed by miles of post and rail fencing.

THOROUGHBRED

T HE THOROUGHBRED evolved in 17th-and 18th-century England to satisfy the enthusiasm of the gentry and their kings for horse racing. The word "Thoroughbred" appeared in 1821, in Volume II of the *General Stud Book*, which contains genealogical records for British and Irish Thoroughbreds. Over the last 200 years a worldwide Thoroughbred racing industry has grown up, and the breed has emerged as the greatest single influence on the world horse population, passing on increased size, improved movement and conformation, as well as speed, courage, and mental stamina. This is due to its prepotency, the result of genetic uniformity achieved by means of carefully documented selective breeding.

A TRAINING GALLOP
Racehorses at Lambourn, one of the principal training centres in the UK, take an early morning gallop. The horses work on all-weather surfaces, and in winter they wear galloping (or exercise) sheets.

HISTORY

The evolution of the Thoroughbred is popularly attributed to the importation of three eastern horses: the Byerley Turk, the Darley Arabian, and the Godolphin Arabian, which are accepted as the three foundation sires of the breed and which were in England by the early 18th century. This view is acceptable in simplistic terms, but takes no

A UNIVERSAL SPORT
Racing, on the pattern established in the UK, is a popular sport, attracting large audiences all over the world. This picture shows racing in Jamaica.

account of the existence in England of a long-established base stock of "running horses" largely held at the royal studs. That stock, crossed with imported sires of eastern origin, was able to produce a race of horses superior in speed and power to any other.

Henry VIII, the first royal patron of horse racing (see pp.334–35), founded the Royal Paddocks at Hampton Court with horses from Spain and Italy, which were influenced by the Barb (see pp. 66–67). These horses were crossed with the native "running" stock. Principal native influences were the swift Galloways of northern

England, the ancestors of the Fell Pony (see pp.170–71), and the Irish Hobby, forerunner of the Connemara (see pp.180–81).

Later monarchs maintained a strong interest in the "running horse" studs, and a new impetus was given to racing and breeding with the Restoration of Charles II in 1660. It is against this background that the Thoroughbred racehorse evolved.

THE FOUNDING STALLIONS

Eastern horses were not used to improve speed, for in comparison with the "plaine bredde" English horses their speed was negligible. None of the founding sires ever raced, nor did more than one or two of the other imported eastern stock. The breeders who created the Thoroughbred used eastern horses because their prepotency enabled them to breed consistently true to type. It has been established that 81 per cent of Thoroughbred genes derive from 31 original ancestors, of whom the most important are the three founding stallions from whom all modern Thoroughbreds descend in the male line.

The Byerley Turk, who took part in the Battle of the Boyne in 1690 before standing at stud in Co. Durham, founded the first of the four principal bloodlines. This line starts with Herod (foaled in 1758), who was the son of Jigg, by the Byerley, and traces to horses such

QUARTERS
The quarters and the loins must be strong, to supply the power for galloping.

HIND LEGS
The hind legs are long and graceful, with the hock joints being very well formed so as to give maximum propulsive thrust.

as Tourbillon and The Tetrarch. Herod's progeny alone won over 1,000 races.

The Darley Arabian, acquired at Aleppo in 1704 and then sent to the Darley home in East Yorkshire, was wonderfully proportioned and the most striking horse of the trio. He stood at 1.52 m (15 hh), larger than most early Thoroughbreds. When mated with the mare Betty Leedes, he produced the first great racehorse, Flying Childers. This horse was, in the words of his owner, "the fleetest horse that ever raced at Newmarket or, as generally believed was ever bred in the world". His full brother, Bartlett's Childers, sired Squirt who sired Marske who, in turn, produced Eclipse, who was unbeaten on the turf. Eclipse founded the second bloodline, and some of the most influential lines of the 20th century descend from him.

The Godolphin Arabian came to England in 1728 as a teaser at Lord Godolphin's Gog Magog stud in Cambridgeshire. He fought the stallion Hobgoblin

A BLUE GRASS FOAL
This well-grown foal and its dam are at the Airdrie Stud, Kentucky – the "Horse State" of the US, which supports a huge horse industry.

for the mare Roxana, with whom he sired Lath and Cade. Cade sired Matchem, foaled in 1748, who leads the third line. The fourth line is that of Highflyer, son of Herod. Although their male lines may not have persisted, other important sires include the Curwen Bay Barb; the Unknown Arabian, sire of the breed's foundation mare Old Bald Peg, to whom millions of repeat crosses in the pedigrees of 20th-century Thoroughbreds can be traced; D'Arcy's Chestnut and White Arabians; the Leedes Arabian; the Helmsley and Lister Turks; Brownlow's Turk; and Alcock's Arabian. (These last two were responsible for the grey colour of some Thoroughbreds.) After 1770 Arabs ceased to be used in breeding, since better results were achieved with home-bred stock.

SHOULDERS
The shoulders are long and very well sloped, with prominent withers. This combination produces a long, low, economical stride.

HEAD
The head is refined and alert, with no hint of fleshiness in the jowl. It blends into a long, gracefully arched neck that, in turn, joins symmetrically with the shoulders.

BODY
The body is typically long in its proportions.

HEIGHT
1.57 m
(15.2 hh)

FORELIMBS
The forelimbs are fine, with long, muscular forearms and large, flat joints. The bone measurement below the knee is rarely less than 8 in (20 cm).

ORIGINS

THE THOROUGHBRED RACEHORSE first evolved in England during the 17th and 18th centuries, and from there it spread rapidly to Ireland. The principal areas of Thoroughbred breeding in the UK are now situated around the racing centres of Newmarket in Suffolk, Lambourn in Berkshire, and Malton in Yorkshire, but Thoroughbred horses are raised throughout the British Isles. By the beginning of the 20th century Thoroughbred breeding was being practised virtually worldwide, and it is now a multi-national industry. Horse-racing, under the rules established by the British, is carried on in the majority of the world's countries.

EUROPE

GREAT BRITAIN

IRELAND

Dublin
Amsterdam
London
Brussels
Paris

0   200 km
0   125 miles

SHALES HORSE

THE SHALES HORSE WILL NOT BE FOUND in books devoted to recording horse breeds and types, nor, in fact, is it accorded official breed status in the UK, its country of origin. Nevertheless, on the basis of recorded pedigree and purity of descent, it is more qualified than most to be regarded as a breed. Indeed, by comparison, many of the warmbloods, and some of the American horses, are not nearly so deserving of the title. For example, the horse shown here, Finmere Grey Shales, traces back through some of the greatest names in equine history to the Darley Arabian, imported to Britain in 1704 and acknowledged as one of the three foundation sires of the English Thoroughbred (see pp.120–21).

THE ROADSTER TYPE
The old Norfolk Roadster type trotted under saddle. This one, bred in Wales, is typical of the sort that played a part in the evolution of the Welsh Cob.

ORIGINS

The Shales horses are direct descendants, and the modern equivalent, of the Norfolk Trotter or Roadster. The Norfolk Roadster was the pride of 19th-century England and its prepotent blood had a great influence on the breeds of both Europe and the US. It represents an under-pinning element in the development of most of the warmblood breeds (see pp.124–25) as well as many of Europe's heavy horses. It is also at the very root of the American Standardbred harness racer (see pp.340–41).

THE NORFOLK ROADSTER

The foundation sire of the Standardbred was the 18th-century Thoroughbred stallion Messenger, a descendant of Blaze. Blaze's son, Original Shales, founded the dynasty of Norfolk Roadsters, and is responsible for the present-day Shales Horse, as well as for the high-stepping modern Hackney of the show rings (see pp.402–3).

The trotting Roadster originated from the same source of eastern blood as the Thoroughbred racehorse, and for some time during the 17th and 18th centuries the Roadster's development ran parallel with that of the Thoroughbred. The difference in the breeds' subsequent development lay in the social structures from which they sprang. The Thoroughbred was the result of the landed gentry's interest in racing and hunting. The Trotter, on the other hand, was a utilitarian horse developed largely by the agricultural community to meet their requirements for a travelling horse that could be either ridden or used in harness. For such a purpose the trot was an essential pace.

Up to the 19th century these formidable Roadsters were used more under saddle than otherwise. Their owners, in the English

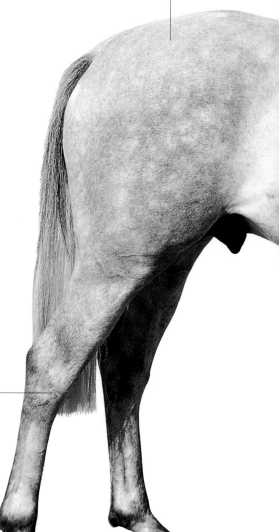

QUARTERS
The sloping quarters show length from hip to hock and prominent muscling of the second thighs.

LEGS
The hocks are clean and large. The joints are flat and well-made and the shanks are short, with a notable bone structure.

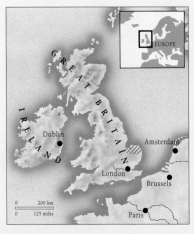

ORIGINS

THE NORFOLK ROADSTER, or Trotter, from which the Shales Horse descends, belonged to East Anglia, the area of eastern England that is comprised of the counties of Norfolk, Suffolk, Huntingdonshire, and Bedfordshire. This area had a long and robust sporting tradition supported by yeomen farmers and well-to-do tradespeople. They developed a utilitarian trotting horse that was as good under saddle as in harness and tested their horses one against the other for sport. In Norfolk, particularly, the great trotting horses of the Shales family were regarded with an admiration amounting to reverence.

sporting tradition, took great pride in the prowess of their horses, and delighted in staging matches that resulted in some extraordinary records (see pp.402–3). Remarkable as they seem now, they were nonetheless commonplace among men who thought little of riding 100 km (60 miles) or more in a day. Those early trotting Roadsters could carry a heavy man at speeds of up to 25–27 km/h (16–17 mph) over some distance and on ground that afforded far from perfect going. It was only when the roads had improved sufficiently that the emphasis shifted to the harness horse, but for many years the Roadster continued to excel in both roles.

Even when the Hackney, a harness horse also descended from the Norfolk Trotter, was firmly established, some breeders, such as Lord Ashtown in Ireland, preserved "the old riding type" at his Woodlawn Stud in Co. Cork until about 1941, while the Monson family at Walpole St Peter, in Cambridgeshire, had a Hackney strain that produced predominantly grey hunters up to the Second World War. The Monson horses of this strain, such as Monson Cadet and Monson's Walpole Shales, feature strongly in the pedigree of the stallion illustrated on these pages, Finmere Grey Shales.

THE MODERN SHALES

The modern Shales Horses have been bred by the Colquhoun family since 1922, when the mother of the present breeder, Elizabeth Colquhoun, bought a two-year-old colt by Findon Grey Shales in Devon. Findon Grey Shales had been bred by Charles Monson, and with Black Shales had stood at the Duchy of Cornwall Tor Royal Stud for some years. The colt, bred by HRH The Prince of Wales (later the Duke of Windsor), was called Royal Shales. The grand-daughter of Royal Shales out of Katinka, whose male line went back to the Thoroughbred, the Tetrarch, was a mare called Silver.

In 1950 she gave birth to Silver Shales, sire of Red Shales and grand-sire of Finmere Grey Shales.

Versatility has been the hallmark of the Shales breed, and indeed, Silver Shales was hunted, driven, and was a top-class polo pony as well. Shales horses, "quality cobs" of about 1.52 m (15 hh), are still ridden and driven in the old tradition. Blessed with the stamina of their forebears, they are hardy, extraordinarily good-tempered, and have an enviable record for producing competition stock. Outcrosses, for what is now a rare breed, are confined to the occasional Thoroughbred, a practice that was followed in the development of the Hackney well into the 19th century.

NECK
The neck is of medium length and gracefully arched with a perfect setting of the head.

SHOULDERS
There is a good slope to the shoulders and great depth through the chest.

HEAD
The intelligent, kindly head is of great quality. It is dominated by large, generous eyes and wide nostrils.

HEIGHT
1.52 m
(15 hh)

TROTTING TRADITION
This painting by John Frederick Herring depicts the Roadster Confidence bowling along at a speed of probably well over 19 km/h (12 mph). Confidence follows in the great sporting tradition of the English trotting horses that played so important a part in the formative years of the most prominent European breeds.

THE RISE OF THE WARMBLOODS

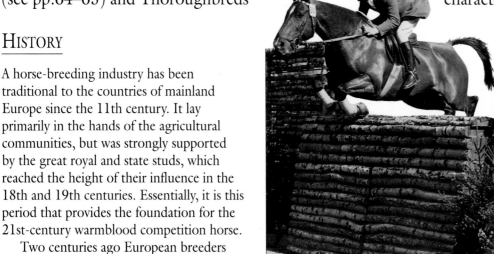

DANISH WARMBLOOD

THE 21ST-CENTURY warmblood is bred as a successful competition horse. To understand the use of the word warmblood, it is necessary to understand the terms "hotblood" and "coldblood", for the warmblood occupies the centre ground and can contain something of both "hot" and "cold". Both Arabs (see pp.64–65) and Thoroughbreds (see pp.120–21) are light riding horses of "desert" origin, and are termed "hotbloods". Sometimes in Europe they are called "fullbloods". They are the product of pure-bred stock established over a long, and carefully documented period of time without ever having been subjected to outcrosses. Heavy draught breeds, which descend from the slow-moving, primitive Forest horse and have opposing characteristics, are called "coldbloods".

HISTORY

A horse-breeding industry has been traditional to the countries of mainland Europe since the 11th century. It lay primarily in the hands of the agricultural communities, but was strongly supported by the great royal and state studs, which reached the height of their influence in the 18th and 19th centuries. Essentially, it is this period that provides the foundation for the 21st-century warmblood competition horse.

Two centuries ago European breeders were producing horses to satisfy the market demand for a general purpose agricultural horse that could take its turn as a coach horse or even as a cavalry remount. In later years a better stamp of cavalry and carriage horse was developed from that base, often by introducing English Thoroughbreds, Norfolk Roadsters (see pp.122–23), and English half-bred stallions. This was the background for the modern warmblood. In the 1960s the emphasis shifted from the heavier working horse to a lighter riding horse suitable for sport and recreation.

PRIZE WINNERS
Fritz Thiedemann, the famous German rider, and the Holsteiner Meteor, are the only partnership to have won medals at three consecutive Olympics.

THE MODERN WARMBLOOD

In the 1950s today's warmbloods would have been described as "half-", "three-quarter-", or even "seven-eighths-bred", according to the amount of Thoroughbred blood in the pedigree. A more acceptable modern definition of a warmblood might be that it is a horse representing an amalgam of bloods in which the essential element is that of the Thoroughbred horse.

GENETIC MAKE-UP
The basis of the Dutch Warmblood began with the Friesian horse, upon which both the Groningen and Gelderlander were reliant. The subsequent outcross to the Thoroughbred gave greater scope, speed, and courage, the mix being balanced by the brief introduction of associated warmbloods to give the classic warmblood breeding pattern.

FRIESIAN

GRONINGEN

In 1975 the German Warmblood Associations declared breeders should aim at producing "a noble, large-framed, correct horse with dynamic, spacious and elastic movement – well-suited to any riding purpose because of its temperament, its character and its ability to provide an easy ride".

Warmblood horses are, in almost every instance, the products of an "open" stud book. A "closed" book allows entry only to progeny of parents whose pedigrees are already in the book. The more flexible "open" book allows for the introduction of outcrosses from other breeds as and when it may seem necessary in order to achieve or reinforce a particular characteristic. Such outcrosses have to be approved by the breed society, and must be of pedigree parents already entered in their appropriate book or books.

SELECTION AND TESTING

The main feature in the breeding of warmblood horses is the meticulous attention paid to documentation and to selection against a background of mandatory performance testing in which great emphasis is placed on temperament and "rideability". With the Hanoverian, for instance, the

END PRODUCT
This international class Dutch Warmblood is competing across country in a championship three-day event. The predominant influence on a horse of this calibre is that of the Thoroughbred.

process of selection depends on four stages: 1. Foals are judged for conformation and basic action and the pedigree is subjected to careful examination. 2. Stallions must pass a licensing test which includes an assessment of action and conformation. 3. Young stallions are performance tested over a period of 100 days and then given a final test. Both the tests in stage 3 include jumping, dressage, and cross-country. 4. The progeny of the stallions are tested in competition. Mares must pass a field test, which provides evidence of character, temperament, "rideability", and performance potential.

Many modern warmblood breeds excel in jumping and dressage. They are less successful in cross-country events, which are dominated by the pure or near-Thoroughbred. From time to time, the system of breeding will result in a line that occasionally produces a specialist in one or other of the competitive disciplines, but the average product is targeted at the needs of the ordinary rider.

The principal warmbloods include horses such as the Hanoverian, Holsteiner, Trakehner, and Oldenburger, the Dutch, Danish, and Swedish Warmbloods, and the Selle Français.

GELDERLANDER

THOROUGHBRED

GRONINGEN & GELDERLANDER

THE NETHERLANDS IS NOT A LARGE COUNTRY, nor is it well-suited to raising horses, but the Dutch have made a substantial contribution to horse-breeding in Europe. For centuries, they have proved themselves to be innovatory and market-wise, breeding horses such as the Groningen and the Gelderlander for local use, and able to adjust their products to suit the demands of foreign markets. This last skill has enabled them to make use of these two old breeds as a basis for the outstanding Dutch Warmblood (see pp.128–29).

THE GRONINGEN

The Groningen, bred in the Groningen region in the north of the Netherlands, may not have had any significant export potential, but it was well-suited to the needs of the local people. The old type was based mainly on its famous neighbour, the Friesian (see pp.48–49), and almost as much on the powerful, temperate Oldenburger (see pp.308–9). By the early 19th century, it had evolved as a heavy farm horse that could carry out a variety of agricultural tasks and could also be used as a steady, very strong, but not spectacular coach horse. The early Groningen was noted for its strong quarters and ample bone, but had a restricted action. Most had upright shoulders and long backs, and tended to be round and fleshy in the joints. However, the brood mares were substantial and roomy and, when crossed with quality stallions, were capable of producing good, plain stock of considerable size and strength. These horses were, moreover, calm in temperament, easily managed, and very willing workers.

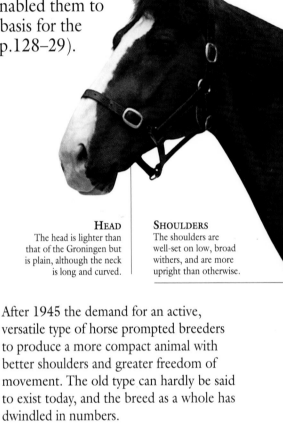

HEAD
The head is heavy and notably convex in profile. The neck is short.

HEAD
The head is lighter than that of the Groningen but is plain, although the neck is long and curved.

SHOULDERS
The shoulders are well-set on low, broad withers, and are more upright than otherwise.

After 1945 the demand for an active, versatile type of horse prompted breeders to produce a more compact animal with better shoulders and greater freedom of movement. The old type can hardly be said to exist today, and the breed as a whole has dwindled in numbers.

THE GELDERLANDER

A century ago the breeders of the Gelder province began to develop the Gelderlander, using the dull, common native mares as a

SHOWY TEAM
The chestnut Gelderlander is an impressive, high-actioned coach and carriage horse that is also increasingly successful in competition driving. It is said to be docile, but not without spirit, and is possessed of great stamina.

HEIGHT OF GELDERLANDER
1.68 m
(16.2 hh)

GELDERLANDER

base. They aimed to produce a carriage horse with presence and good action, which could be used for light agricultural work, and might also be used as a heavy stamp of riding horse. Like most European breeders, they put great emphasis on an equable temperament. The Dutch used a wide range of sires: Cleveland Bays, Roadsters, and half-breds from the UK; Arabs from Egypt; Anglo-Arabs, Nonius, and Furioso half-breds from Hungary; Oldenburgers; East Prussians from Poland; and a few Orlov and Orlov-Rastopchin Trotters from Russia. The best of the disparate progeny were interbred to obtain a fixed type. Later, more Oldenburgers and East Friesians were brought in, and in 1900 a Hackney

ORIGINS

THE GELDERLANDER *is from the Gelderland province of the Netherlands, in the area lying roughly between Apeldoorn and Arnhem. It was bred as a light agricultural horse capable of working the medium-density soils of the region, and is the product of a complex mix of bloods ranging from the Arab to the Oldenburg. The Groningen originated in the north of the Netherlands, in the Groningen province, which faces the North Sea and has its eastern boundary on the Ems. It was bred initially as a heavy farm horse and relied considerably on outcrosses with its close neighbours the Friesian and the Oldenburger.*

GRONINGEN

The Groningen is heavier than the Gelderlander and is noted for the strength of its quarters. Modern Groningens move more freely than their predecessors and are more compactly framed.

QUARTERS
The quarters are straight in the croup, and the back is still fairly long in proportion to the frame.

QUARTERS
The quarters are very strong and broad and there is good depth through the body. The back is long and the joints tend to roundness.

was used to add sparkle. Since then there have also been some infusions of Anglo-Norman blood.

The modern Gelderlander is an impressive carriage horse, with a presence enhanced by a lofty, rhythmic action (the result of good shoulders) and a tail carried high on much improved quarters. It is powerful, with short, very strong limbs carrying no feather, but is still rather plain, with a sensible rather than elegant head and a straight or slightly convex profile. Unlike the Groningen, which is bay or brown, the Gelderlander is chestnut (or occasionally grey), often with white markings on the legs and face. It stands at about 1.68 m (16.2 hh). These horses are very successful in competition driving, Gelderlander teams featuring prominently in international events. They may still be used as weight-carrying riding horses, and a few have become reliable, though not fast, showjumpers.

GRONINGEN

HEIGHT OF GRONINGEN
1.63 m
(16 hh)

DUTCH WARMBLOOD

T HE SUCCESS STORY in the history of European competition horses is that of the Dutch Warmblood, a horse of international repute that was perfected in a comparatively short space of time. In essence, the Dutch Warmblood is an outstanding example of how existing but largely redundant stock can be adapted and improved by selective breeding to fulfil a new requirement. The success of these horses might also be seen as a prime example of the results that can be obtained from positive promotion and marketing policies.

BREEDING FOR PERFECTION

Making use of the Gelderlander and the Groningen (see pp.126–27), the one having a good forehand overall and the other being especially powerful behind the saddle, Dutch breeders, as it were, put the two ends together. The resultant progeny was then refined, in line with the classic warmblood breeders' precept, by the use of the all-important Thoroughbred (see pp.120–21). The introduction of this element resulted in horses with more sloping shoulders, and thus a flatter, longer, and more economical action. It also added length to the short, thick neck inherited from the native Dutch breeds, shortened the long back typical of carriage horses, gave a different emphasis to the croup, and produced a more compact outline. Additionally, the Thoroughbred influence improved the Dutch horses' scope and speed, as well as giving them increased mental stamina and courage. At that point the product was seasoned by a return to related warmbloods such as the Oldenburger (see pp.308–9), Trakehner (see pp.140–41), and Hanoverian (see pp.144–45). This was a way of adjusting minor points of conformational detail and, in particular, it was a means of counteracting any deviation from the characteristic calm temperament that may have been caused by the Thoroughbred element.

NECK
The neck is light and of medium length. Although it is not as long and muscular as that of the Thoroughbred, it is in proportion to the shoulders.

WITHERS
The withers are reasonably defined and join easily into the neck.

HEAD
The head is sometimes plain, reflecting the background influence of the Gelderlander, but it is free of fleshiness through the jowl.

FOREARMS
The forearms are very well-muscled and the shoulders are strong with adequate slope.

COMPETITION DRIVING
With its background of coach-horse blood, the amenable and versatile Dutch Warmblood is used successfully in competition driving at international level like the Gelderlander, the traditional Dutch harness horse.

HEIGHT
1.63 m (16 hh)

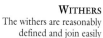

CHARACTERISTICS

The result is an athletic stamp of horse, of good riding conformation with a straight, elastic action, good limbs, and good feet – the latter not always being an outstanding feature of warmblood horses. The Dutch Warmblood stands on average something over 1.63 m (16 hh), and is usually bay or brown in colour. The temperament is even, and behavioural problems rarely arise.

The breed excels at showjumping, and several world-class international jumpers, such as Milton, a son of the famous jumping stallion Marius, are either Dutch or Dutch crosses. The Dutch horses have also made their mark in the dressage arena, largely as the result of the prominence given to the

GOOD PACES
Dutch Warmbloods perform well in dressage competitions. They have good level paces, a straight action, and an unflappable, even temperament.

breed by the English rider, Jennie Loriston-Clarke, who won a world championship bronze medal on the stallion Dutch Courage, from whom she bred extensively at her New Forest stud. Like many warmbloods, the Dutch horses are less good as cross-country rides, but this failing can be countered in part by outcrossing to Thoroughbreds.

THE SELECTION PROCESS

Horse-breeding in Holland, where horses are classed as agricultural animals and their owners benefit accordingly, is strictly controlled by the State-aided *Warmbloed Paardenstamboek Nederland*. This body pursues a rigorous selection policy based on physical assessment and performance testing. Stallions, all of which are privately owned, may not be used for breeding until they have undergone a comprehensive performance test. This test includes jumping, cross-country trials, and sometimes harness work (the Dutch also breed a warmblood carriage horse, in addition to the Gelderlander). Particular attention is paid to the reports on an individual's temperament. More than 14,000 mares may be mated each year; they are also tested, and great emphasis is placed on conformation and movement as well as temperament. Finally, the breeding value for both stallions and mares is established by monitoring the performance of their progeny – a critical feature of European warmblood breeding that finds increasing acceptance world-wide.

QUARTERS
The quarters are strongly muscled, and the hock joints are well-formed and low to the ground to give greater propulsive thrust to the action.

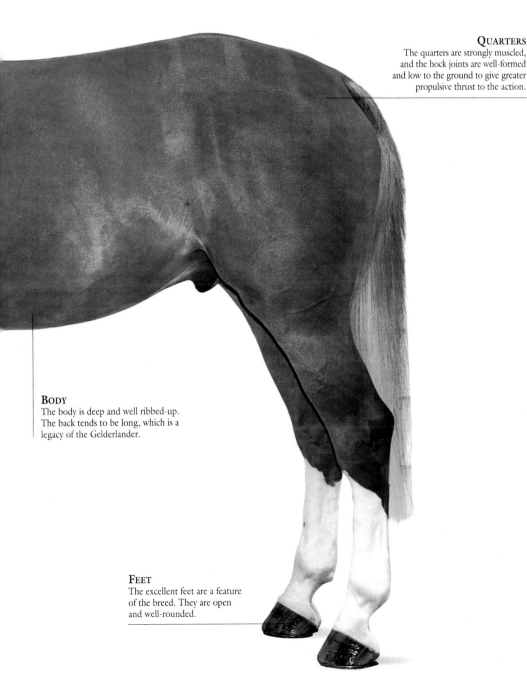

BODY
The body is deep and well ribbed-up. The back tends to be long, which is a legacy of the Gelderlander.

FEET
The excellent feet are a feature of the breed. They are open and well-rounded.

ORIGINS

THE DUTCH WARMBLOOD is a product of the Netherlands, created to fulfil the need for a competition horse. It is produced in various parts of the country, but has its beginnings with the horses of the Groningen province in the north, and those of Gelderland, the province that lies between Apeldoorn and Arnhem, near the border with Germany. The breed is used, often as an outcross, in warmblood breeding outside the Netherlands, but is bred in its pure form in its native country.

WESTERN EUROPEAN STUDS

LE LION D'ANGERS

MOST EUROPEAN countries have national studs, where horse-breeding is supported by the state. Few countries breed so great a variety of horses as France, where the range extends from heavy draught horses through Arabs (see pp.64–65), superlative French Trotters (see pp.134–35) and, increasingly, successful competition horses. Spain breeds its famous Andalucian (see pp.108–9) extensively and crosses it with Thoroughbreds (see pp.120–21) and Arabs to produce horses for all types of equestrian sports. The best known Austrian Stud is the state-owned establishment at Piber, home of the Spanish School Lipizzaners (see pp.102–3 and pp.112–13). Switzerland (home to Einsiedeln, the world's oldest stud, founded in 1064) has an enviable international competition record, but does not rank as a major horse-breeding country.

FRANCE

France has a highly organized, state-funded network of over 20 national studs. They breed for national requirements and also provide considerable encouragement to private breeders. The stud at Le Lion d'Angers in Poitou is a typical example. It has Thoroughbreds, vital for breeding competition horses; Arabs, and Anglo-Arabs (see pp.78–79), which fulfil an important role in national breeding policies; French Trotters (see pp.134–35); and the successful Selle Français (see pp.132–33). Most of the national studs also keep pony stallions, notably Connemara and Poney Français de Selle (see pp.180–81 and pp.406–7). Some also have Ariègeois horses (see pp.46–47).

The oldest establishment is Le Pin, founded in 1715 as a royal stud. It stands Trotters, Thoroughbreds, Arabs, Anglo-Arabs, Selle Français, and some Percherons (see pp.94–95), to meet the requirements of the Departments of Orne, Calvados, Eure, and Seine-Maritime. Like the other French studs, Le Pin is architecturally impressive.

The great stud of Pompadour has been running without interruption since 1872 but the history of the property goes back almost 1,000 years, when Guy de Latour built the first chateau in 1026. Later, in 1745, Louis XV acquired the property for his mistress, Madame Lenormand d'Estoiles, whom he made Marquise de Pompadour. Pompadour is the only French stud that maintains a herd

THE NATIONAL STUD
The national stud at Pau, in south-west France, together with that of nearby Tarbes, was the first to concentrate on the production of Arabs. Later on Anglo-Arabs were also bred.

of Anglo-Arab brood mares as well as a stallion centre. It is also the stud where the French Anglo-Arab originated. Today it houses over 25 Anglo-Arab stallions, as well as a few Arabs, Thoroughbreds, Trotters, and a complement of heavy horses. The stud at Tarbes in southern France is also dominated by Anglo-Arab stallions of very high quality.

SPAIN

Spain has a long equestrian tradition, and is noted for its Arab horses almost as much as for its native Andalucian. Two of its most important establishments are the army stud at Jerez de la Frontera and the stallion centre at Cordoba. Jerez de la Frontera is

MARES AND FOALS AT PIBER
The Lipizzaner stallions of Austria's Spanish Riding School are bred at Piber. They spend the summers in the Alpine pastures and join the school when they are three years old.

POMPADOUR
Pompadour has been in operation since 1872 and is architecturally as impressive as any of the great studs of France. The French Anglo-Arab evolved here and today it houses over 25 Anglo-Arab stallions.

particularly notable for being chiefly responsible for stabilizing the Andalucian type, which had been crossed with many different bloods over the years. Jerez supports Andalucian stallions and mares, Arabs, Anglo-Arabs, and Thoroughbreds. Although Spain is beginning to produce sporting horses, Andalucians and Arabs will continue to be maintained.

The stallion centre at Cordoba is noted for the magnificence of its 16th-century buildings as well as for its traditional connection with the Arab horse. It is perhaps surprising that until the 1980s it also stood 37 draught horses, mostly Breton, and over 20 jack donkeys for mule-breeding.

AUSTRIA

With the final break-up of the Austro-Hungarian Empire in 1918 and the events of the Second World War, Austria ceased to be an important horse-breeding country. Even so, it still has a unique establishment in the Federal Stud at Piber. Famous for breeding Lipizzaners, a virus epidemic led to the loss of 40 horses and 8 per cent of the expected foal crop in 1983. Piber now has an increased mare herd of about 100. In 1993, 56 foals were born, and as a result of a new veterinary centre the pregnancy return increased from 27 to 82 per cent.

Selected three-year-old stallions go to the School in Vienna, while the mares are trained for riding and more particularly for driving.

SWITZERLAND

Switzerland's main horse-breeding centres are at Einsiedeln, originally a monastery where the Einsiedler horse (see pp.136–37) has been bred since at least 1064, and the Federal Stallion Station at Avenches, where the Freiberger horse was developed from cold-blood strains. Both places use imported sires, particularly Norman and Anglo-Norman stallions. Avenches has supplied stallions for the Einsiedler mares since 1890. As well as Anglo-Normans, Avenches stands warmblood stallions and has used both Hanoverians and Swedish Warmbloods.

THE SWISS FEDERAL STUD
Swiss Warmbloods, Hanoverians, Thoroughbreds, Swedish and Selle Français horses are kept in the stable block at the Swiss Federal Stud at Avenches in a carefully planned breeding programme.

SELLE FRANÇAIS

O F THE EVER-INCREASING NUMBER of European warmbloods or "half-breds", the *Cheval de Selle Français* (French Saddle Horse) is as versatile as any and more accomplished than most. Like all warmbloods it is the result of a mixture of breeds and strains, but it differs in that there is a significant use of fast trotting stock. In the early, formative years this was supplied by the Norfolk Roadster (see pp.122–23), the greatest trotting horse of all time. The term *Cheval de Selle Français* came into use in December 1958 to describe French "half-bred" competition horses. Before then, all French riding horses, other than Thoroughbreds, Arabs, and Anglo-Arabs, were simply called *demi-sangs* or "half-breds".

CONSUMMATE SHOWJUMPER
The Selle Français is among the best of the showjumping warmbloods and is much used by the French Olympic Teams.

CREATION AND DEVELOPMENT

The development of the modern Selle Français began early in the 19th century in the horse-raising districts of Normandy, where the local and rather common Norman mares were crossed with imported English Thoroughbreds (see pp.120–21), English half-bred stallions, and some very important Norfolk Roadster lines. Indeed, at that time the English half-bred stallions would have had a pronounced Norfolk Roadster background and character.

With their usual acumen, Norman breeders were soon producing discernible types suited to the requirements of the day. They created two cross-breds: the first, the Anglo-Norman, could be divided neatly into two distinct types – a draught cob and a riding horse; the second was a fast harness horse, bred to satisfy the great interest in trotting races. In time, the harness horse split away from the mainstream to become the French Trotter (see pp.134–35).

It was the active Anglo-Norman riding horse, influenced by Norfolk Roadster blood almost as much as by that of the Thoroughbred, that was the prototype for the Selle Français. In fact, the Selle Français stud book is a continuation of the old Anglo-Norman one.

Although the two World Wars were to cause a serious depletion in the population of native Norman mares, the breeders managed to conserve some of the best stock. They were also able to make use of Thoroughbreds standing at the National Studs, to meet the new demand for a quality riding horse that would combine speed, stamina, and jumping ability.

QUARTERS
The quarters are broad and more reminiscent of the Trotter than the Thoroughbred. They are ideally suited for showjumping.

HOCKS
The strong hocks are indicative of great jumping potential.

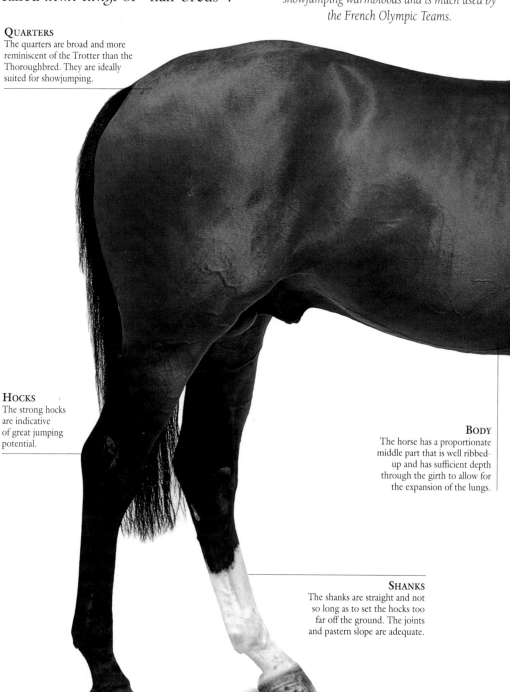

BODY
The horse has a proportionate middle part that is well ribbed-up and has sufficient depth through the girth to allow for the expansion of the lungs.

SHANKS
The shanks are straight and not so long as to set the hocks too far off the ground. The joints and pastern slope are adequate.

The great Thoroughbred sires responsible for the present-day Selle Français were notably Orange Peel, Lord Frey, and Ivanhoe. In the years after the Second World War there were also the stallions Ultimate and Furioso – Furioso being a name that occurs in the greatest half-bred lines of Central Europe (see pp.156–57). This latter-day Furioso was bought in the UK soon after the Second World War, for what would be regarded today as a derisory sum. He had no racing record of note, but he was exceptional in terms of conformation, balance, and movement. Until the 1970s, he had a brilliant stud career at Le Pin in Normandy, where he topped the sire list for 10 consecutive years, producing world-class showjumpers.

The principal area of specialization today is showjumping, although a lighter Selle Français, carrying a lot of Thoroughbred

ORIGINS

THE VERSATILE SELLE FRANÇAIS is kept at most of France's National Studs, but the breed originated in the traditional horse-raising districts of Normandy, in particular at the great stud of Le Pin in the Merlerault district, an area that is renowned for the quality of its pasture. Its prototype, a speciality of the Haras du Pin, was the active Anglo-Norman riding horse, and the Selle Français stud book is, in fact, a continuation of the old Anglo-Norman one.

SHOULDERS
The shoulders are powerful but not sufficiently sloped for great galloping ability.

BONE
The bone measurement is rarely, if ever, less than 20 cm (8 in) and the fault of small knees has been eliminated.

HEIGHT
Over 1.63 m (16 hh)

blood, is bred specifically for racing under the old appellation AQPSA (*autre que pur-sang Anglais*, i.e. horses other than Thoroughbreds). Some of these horses may compete in horse trials via the sport of cross-country racing, which remains a feature of the French equestrian scene.

CHARACTERISTICS

Most Selle Français horses are chestnut, and stand over 1.63 m (16 hh). Until the 1980s, the breed was officially split into five classifications. There were three medium-weight horses – small (1.60 m/ 15.3 hh), medium (up to 1.65 m/16.1 hh), and large (over 1.65 m/16.1 hh); and two heavyweights – small (under 1.63 m/ 16 hh), and large (over 1.63 m/16 hh). The breed is now divided into the lighter racing animal and the showjumper, although the difference is far less pronounced.

In general, 33 per cent of modern Selles Français are sired by Thoroughbreds; 20 per cent by Anglo-Arabs; 45 per cent by registered Selle Français stallions; and 2 per cent by French Trotters. Other recognized crosses are: Thoroughbred/French Trotter; Arab or Anglo-Arab/French Trotter; and Thoroughbred/Anglo-Arab, providing there is no more than 25 per cent Arab blood.

An outstanding example of Selle Français breeding is provided by the remarkable jumping stallion Galoubet. He was sired by the Selle Français Almé, out of the trotting mare Viti. Almé, a grandson of Orange Peel, was predominantly Thoroughbred but also had some Anglo-Arab blood, and Viti's pedigree contains many top-class trotting horses.

RACING TYPE
The Selle Français is bred as an all-round competition horse, but a lighter type, carrying much Thoroughbred blood, is also produced specifically for racing limited to non-Thoroughbred horses. This type performs well in jumping races.

FRENCH TROTTER

THE TROTTING TRADITION and the popularity of harness racing are firmly established throughout the US, Europe, and the countries of the former USSR. However, apart from the US, nowhere is it so deeply entrenched as it is in France. Within just over 100 years, a superlative trotting horse and a powerful supportive industry have been developed. The French Trotter is a product of Normandy, where horse-breeding has been a traditional and almost inherited skill since before the 12th century.

LEVEL BALANCE
The powerful, loose-limbed French Trotters race using the diagonal trotting gait. The long, raking action is extremely level, and the horse carries itself in virtually perfect balance.

BREEDING

After the continental trading blockade was raised, following the defeat of Napoleon Bonaparte at Waterloo in 1815, the market-wise Normandy breeders began to use their common but tough, all-purpose Norman stock as a foundation for breeding horses for general military use, both riding and light draught, and then, increasingly, to produce specialized horses of both types. Supported by the Administration of National Studs, they imported English Thoroughbreds (see pp.120–21) and, just as importantly in the context of the trotting horse, English half-bred or hunter stallions, which were then unknown in France. They also imported the incomparable Norfolk Roadster (see pp.122–23), the greatest trotter under saddle and in harness in the whole of Europe.

Chief among the early imports was the half-bred Young Rattler (foaled 1811), by the Thoroughbred Rattler, out of a mare with Norfolk Roadster connections. He is often called "the French Messenger", as his influence on the French Trotter was close to that of Messenger, the foundation sire of the American Standardbred (see pp.340–41). Young Rattler, together with other half-bred stallions and the essential contribution made by the Roadster, the Norfolk Phenomenon, improved the Norman mares in terms of conformation, movement, and scope, and prepared them for subsequent crossing with English Thoroughbreds.

Thirty years after Young Rattler, Thoroughbreds such as the Heir of Linne and Sir Quid Pigtail were making their mark. Ultimately, five important bloodlines became established: Conquerant and Normand, both sons of Young Rattler; Lavater, a horse by a Norfolk sire; and the half-breds Phaeton and Fuchsia. Fuchsia, foaled in 1883, sired 400 trotters, and over 100 of his sons were sires of winners.

In due course Standardbred blood was added to give the Trotter more speed, but it has had no effect upon the unique character of the French Trotter, which is a conventional diagonal trotter, unlike the Standardbred, which in almost every instance is a lateral pacer.

ORIGINS

THE FRENCH TROTTER is yet another product of the traditional horse-breeding skills of Normandy. The breed has benefited from the temperate climate, long growth seasons, and favourable soil conditions of the area, but the encouragement and incentive to breed is given by the powerfully supportive French trotting industry. The main breeding centres are at the national studs of Le Pin and Saint Lô. Ephrem Honel, who became the director of Saint Lô in 1836, initiated the first French trotting races.

HEIGHT
1.68 m
(16.2 hh)

In 1937, to protect the qualities of the breed, which can now beat world-class harness-racers, the *French Trotter Stud Book* was closed to non-French bred horses. Recently, however, it was partly opened to let in a few French/Standardbred crosses.

TROTTING RACES

The first trotting races for ridden horses were staged on the Champs de Mars in Paris, in 1806. The first proper raceway was built at Cherbourg in the 1830s. Today 10 per cent of all French trotting races are still for trotters under saddle. These races encourage a substantially built horse, which is able to carry a relatively heavy weight, and is perfectly balanced and extremely level in its action. These qualities have been of inestimable value in establishing the essential character of the French Trotter. The premier ridden race in France is the *Prix de Cornulier*. Like the harness equivalent, the *Prix d'Amerique*, this is staged at the leading raceway, the Hippodrome de Vincennes. It is worth FF700,000 to the winner. Very occasionally, an exceptional horse wins both races, but so far only four trotters have completed that remarkable double.

CHARACTERISTICS

Formerly the French Trotter was inclined to be raw-boned, rather coarse, and straight-shouldered. Although it is still a strong horse, retaining the powerful, sloping quarters typical of the trotting breeds, it is now much finer and closer to the Thoroughbred in appearance with good shoulders which give a long, raking action in front.

The breed averages 1.68 m (16.2 hh), the bigger horses are the best ones to ride. Predominant colours are chestnut, bay, and brown. Breeders have always sought to produce hard animals of great stamina, a quality encouraged by a programme of comparatively long-distance races at tracks such as Vincennes, which combines a downhill stretch and a punishing uphill gradient over the last 914 m (1,000 yds).

WITHERS
The withers are defined but still rounded, and are fairly flat over the top. This conformation is characteristic for trotters.

HEAD
The head is plain without being common, and is set very well on the neck.

SHOULDERS
The very strong trotting shoulders are sufficiently sloped to give the long, economical racing action.

CARRIAGE COUSINS
This team of French carriage horses is of Anglo-Norman descent. They were instrumental in the Trotter's evolution, but their action is more elevated. The natural balance of the breed is apparent.

LEGS
The legs are typically excellent, with big, flat knees, strong feet, and good bone. The quarters are exceptionally powerful.

EINSIEDLER & FREIBERGER

ALTHOUGH SWITZERLAND exported horses to France, Germany, and even England in the 19th century, and the Swiss army has maintained mounted and pack units virtually to the present day, Switzerland has usually relied heavily on imported horses. Nonetheless, horse-breeding in Switzerland can be traced back for nearly 1,000 years to the Benedictine monastery of Einsiedeln, where horses were being bred as early as AD 964. Today, however, the emphasis is on the Federal Stud at Avenches and the production of the modern Einsiedler, also called the Swiss Warmblood.

HEAD
The finely drawn head reveals the outcross to the Thoroughbred. The conformation is that of an all-round riding horse.

HEAD
The head is small, neat, and even pony-like, although the Freiberger is altogether more thick-set. The neck is short but nicely curved.

THE EINSIEDLER

The Einsiedler was founded in the 10th century on local Schwyer stock, and the first stud book was opened in 1655. However, after some unwise outcrossing to Spanish, Italian, Friesian, and Turkish stallions, a second, more comprehensive book was compiled in 1784 by Father Isidor Moser.

In the 19th century, the breed was improved by Anglo-Norman mares and a Yorkshire Coach Horse stallion, Bracken, who was imported in 1865. Later the emphasis shifted to a mix of Holsteiner/Norman crosses. Then, in the late 1960s, Swedish and Irish mares were imported to Avenches, where the breed was now being produced. The stallions used were just as varied, and included Anglo-Norman, Holsteiner, and Swedish horses, as well as some native stock.

ORIGINS

THE OLD EINSIEDLER originated in the 10th century. It was based on local stock and was first bred at the Benedictine monastery of Einsiedeln, east of Lucerne. As the Swiss Warmblood, it is now raised at the Federal Stud at Avenches (west of Berne), where the Freiberger is also bred. The Freiberger, or Franches-Montagnes, is a mountain horse that originated in the hilly Jura region on the French border, and it retains the characteristics of a mountain-bred animal that evolved as a work-horse for small upland farms. It has always been particularly popular with the Swiss Army as a pack animal.

SWISS CAVALRY TROOP HORSES
The Swiss Army has maintained mounted and animal transport units up to the present day. The Einsiedler horses are ideal cavalry troop horses.

Among the most important bloodlines were those established by the Anglo-Norman horses Ivoire (foaled in 1957), Que d'Espair (1960), and Orinate de Messil (1958). The Swedish Warmblood, Aladin (1964) had a strong influence, as did the two Holsteiners, Astral (1957) and Chevalier (1956).

The Einsiedler is a big, calm, well-made horse of about 1.68 m (16.2 hh), suitable for all sorts of riding. The breeding selection and testing is rigorous, with stallions being

CHEST
The chest is broad and deep but is sometimes inclined to be bosomy. The legs are long and slender, with good bone.

LEGS
The cannons and the hind shanks should be short. The joints should be large, flat, and hard, with no puffiness in the fetlocks.

FEET
The feet are generally well-formed and of hard horn.

EINSIEDLER

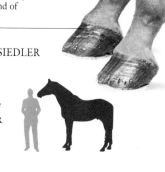

HEIGHT OF EINSIEDLER
1.68 m
(16.2 hh)

carefully selected and performance tested at the age of three and a half and then again at five. The tests include jumping, dressage, cross-country, and driving. Conformation is important, and horses are only selected if their parents have proven performance ability. Mares are tested at three years old, and cannot be registered unless their parents are registered half-breds.

Avenches continues to be catholic in its choice of stallions, and as well as the modern Einsiedler it stands Thoroughbreds, Hanoverians, Swedish horses, and Selle Français, occasionally using Trakehners as well. As a result of the breeding programme, the number of imports is decreasing.

HARNESS HORSES
The popular Freibergers are part of the complement of the Federal Stud at Avenches. They are used by the Army in pack companies, but are also very good, active horses in harness.

QUARTERS
The quarters are thick, cobby, and strongly muscled, with width between the hips. The second thighs are well-developed.

THE FREIBERGER

The Freiberger (or *Franches-Montagnes*) is a mountain-bred horse, originating in the hilly Jura region of western Switzerland. It is an active mover, naturally sure-footed, quiet, and good-natured. For generations it was the mainstay of the army pack companies, and was also ideal on small mountain farms. It stands at about 1.52 m (15 hh), and is powerfully built, with good limbs and feet.

Like the Einsiedler, it has a strong Norman background. Many Freibergers trace to one stallion, Vaillant, foaled in 1891. Vaillant was a great grandson of Leo I, a half-bred English hunter stallion with Norfolk Roadster connections, who was imported in 1865. Poulette, Vaillant's grandam on both sides, was of Thoroughbred/Anglo-Norman stock. Imprevu, an Anglo-Norman imported in 1889, produced a second important line through his great-grandson Chasseur. Other outcrosses to French, English, and Belgian horses had no lasting effect, and it was not until after the Second World War that a new bloodline emerged from Urus, another stallion with Norman blood. Since then outcrosses have been carefully monitored. Anglo-Normans are usually selected, but Arab blood has also been used.

STUD BRAND MARK
As is customary in Europe, horses at the Federal Stud, Avenches, are branded with the stud symbol, which is the Swiss cross.

FREIBERGER

HEIGHT OF FREIBERGER
*1.52 m
(15 hh)*

CENTRAL EUROPEAN STUDS

TRAKEHNERS

ALTHOUGH FRANCE may have a greater variety of equine stock, the principal force in non-Thoroughbred breeding in Europe is Germany's highly developed stud system. This dates back to the knights of the Teutonic Order who colonized East Prussia in the 13th century. Using the native Schweiken as a base, they bred military horses suited to the need of the day. Five hundred years later, in 1732, Freidrich Wilhelm I of Prussia founded the Royal Trakehner Stud Administration and the breeding of the celebrated Trakehner horse was begun. In the 1950s and 1960s, German studs successfully altered course to concentrate on the production of a "high-performance multi-purpose horse, with a good character and temperament". Today, despite the loss of Trakehnen after the Second World War, the German warmbloods are the dominant influence in performance horse breeding.

MAJOR WARMBLOOD BREEDS

The Trakehner (see pp.140–41), still the quality horse of the warmblood grouping, has been retained at many studs and is still a powerful influence in the production of quality riding horses. However, the most prominent of the German warmbloods, allowing for the Trakehner, are the Hanoverian (see pp.144–45), the Holsteiner (see pp.142–43), and the Oldenburger (see pp.308–9), all of which are now heavily infused with Thoroughbred blood (see pp.120–21).

GERMAN STUDS

The stallion station at Celle, which was founded in 1735 by George II, King of England and Elector of Hanover, is central to the breeding of the Hanoverian, which was originally based on older Holstein stock and subsequently crossed with English horses. Horses were being imported from England as early as 1770 for remount breeding, and the practice was extended as the Thoroughbred was developed. By 1790 Celle was recording pedigrees for the progeny of its stallions, and was registering mares. In this way a foundation was laid for an independent Hanoverian breed, and today, as a result, origins can be traced over 150 years to the original mares. By 1800, Celle was standing 100 stallions at 50 covering stations each year.

Celle was expanded in 1925 by the addition of another regional stud at Osnabrück-Eversburg. At that time, large numbers of Trakehners were brought to Celle and immediately became an important influence in the

CELLE STALLION STATION
This shows part of the Celle stallion station, which was founded in 1735 by George, King of England and Elector of Hanover. Celle now houses over 200 stallions.

PERFORMANCE TESTING
Young stallions at Celle are regularly assessed by an expert panel for conformation, temperament, and general suitability. Otherwise all Celle stallions are subjected to comprehensive, practical performance testing before they are selected for breeding.

WÜRTTEMBERGERS
These Württembergers are raised at the stud at Marbach. Their foundation sire was the Trakehner horse, Julmond.

16TH-CENTURY MARBACH
Marbach, founded in 1573, is the oldest of the German state-owned studs. It is noted for its Württemberger Warmbloods and is world-famous for its Arab stock.

development of the Hanoverian. Celle now houses over 200 stallions, and still keeps some Trakehners and Thoroughbreds.

The beautiful stud at Warendorf and the stud at Marbach are of equal importance. Warendorf was founded in 1826 using Trakehner stallions and became the Westphalian regional stud in 1839. In effect, modern Westphalian horses are Hanoverian, although they are still marked with the Westphalian stud's "W" brand.

Marbach in Württemberg was founded in 1573 by Ludwig von Wirtemberg, and is the oldest of the German state-owned studs. It is noted for its Württemberger Warmblood, for which the foundation sire was the Trakehner Julmond, who went to Marbach in 1960. Along with Trakehnen, which kept an Arab herd in the past, Marbach is also famous for its Arabs. Indeed, two Marbach stallions, Jasir and Hadban Enzahi (the latter standing between 1955 and 1975) had a lasting effect upon the Arab breed. They were succeeded by another Egyptian horse, the black Gharib.

After 1945 the number of German state studs was reduced; Wickrath in the Rhineland and Traventhal in Holstein, for instance, no longer exist. Warendorf has taken over from Wickrath, and in Holstein the responsibility for producing stallions is with the Holstein breeders' association at Elmshorn. The Oldenburg stallion station, although a private enterprise, comes under state supervision in accordance with the overall breeding policy.

FLYINGE

A stud of great influence in international competition is Flyinge in the Swedish province of Skåne, which in the 17th century was a part of Denmark. Flyinge was established in 1658 by Charles X of Sweden, although horse-breeding on a large scale had been carried on there from the 12th century.

FLYINGE NATIONAL STUD
Swedish Warmbloods at the National Stud of Flyinge are schooled under saddle and in harness, and are performance tested. Flyinge was first established in 1658 by Charles X of Sweden.

The stud concentrates upon the production of the Swedish Warmblood (see pp.150–51), which is based on old Swedish, Hanoverian, and Trakehner female lines. Before the Second World War Hanoverian stallions were used, but there was also the important influence of the Thoroughbred, largely through the stallion Hempelmann. After 1945 Trakehners were used increasingly; one of them, Heristal, a descendant of the famous English racehorse Hyperion, was particularly significant. Thoroughbred horses still stand at Flyinge, as do some Gotland ponies (see pp.192–93) and the Scandinavian draught breeds.

FREDERIKSBORG

The Danish Royal Stud of Frederiksborg, which was a magnificent example of baroque architecture, was created in 1532. Its product, the chestnut Frederiksborg horse (see pp.114–15), was famous in Europe as the most brilliant riding horse of its time. However, cut-backs were inevitable after the country's bankruptcy in 1813. Nonetheless, attempts were made to continue the stud and in 1840 it became a centre for Thoroughbred breeding. Unfortunately this experiment was unsuccessful, and in 1871 Frederiksborg, by then Denmark's national stud, was closed and subsequently demolished.

TRAKEHNER

T HE TRAKEHNER is as near as any to being the ideal, modern, all-round competition or riding horse. Perhaps because of the hardy base stock from which it derives, and the careful use of Arab blood at selected intervals, it seems to have been better able than most warmbloods to absorb the best Thoroughbred qualities while still retaining its own character. Its upgrading influence is evident in many of the continental sports breeds.

ORIGINS

The Trakehner originated early in the 13th century, in what used to be East Prussia. At this time, the province was colonized by the Order of Teutonic Knights, who established a horse-breeding industry, using the indigenous Schweiken pony as a base. The Schweiken, much used in farming, was a descendant of the Konik (see pp.194–95), itself a descendant of the the Tarpan (see pp.20–21), from which it inherits its natural vigour, toughness, and endurance.

In 1732, 500 years after the Order had colonized the area, Friedrich Wilhelm I of Prussia, father of Frederick the Great, founded the Royal Trakehner Stud Administration on the drained marshlands between Gumbinnen and Stalluponen in the east of his kingdom. It became the principal source of stallions for Prussia,

and renowned for producing an elegant coach horse that combined speed with stamina.

By 1787 the emphasis had switched to the production of remounts and chargers, and even at that early date an exhaustive testing system and detailed documentation of pedigrees had been introduced. This close attention to the detail of genotype breeding, supported by a series of performance tests, was to become the hallmark of warmblood production throughout mainland Europe. In its heyday during the 19th century, the stud at Trakehnen covered over 13,760 hectares (34,000 acres). It supported herds of mares that were divided by coat colour: chestnut, bay/brown, mixed colours, and black, which was a very dominant colour in the breed.

NECK
The refined head has the straight profile of the Thoroughbred and is joined to an elegantly tapered neck.

SHOULDERS
The shoulders slope very well from defined withers. The action shows great freedom at all paces.

THE CLASS HORSE
The Trakehner has an impressive competition record, and is regarded as the "class" horse among the continental warmbloods.

HEIGHT
*1.63–1.68 m
(16–16.2 hh)*

INFLUENCES

During the 19th century, English Thoroughbreds (see pp.120–21) and high-quality Arab horses (see pp.64–65) were introduced to upgrade the breed even further. Over the years, the former became predominant – by 1913, for example, 84.3 per cent of all Trakehner mares were by Thoroughbred stallions. The breed was widely used in the First World War, and was believed to be the best war-horse available. However, the Arab content always remained a powerful balancing element, to offset any deficiencies in constitution or temperament caused by the Thoroughbred. An Arab mare herd still existed in 1936, and as late as

TRAKEHNER BREEDING

Although Trakehner breeding is centred on West Germany, Trakehners are bred in many European countries from Poland to the UK.

1956–1958 the Anglo-Arabs Burnus and Marsuk were both being used at the studs at Rantzau and Birkhausen.

The greatest influence on the Trakehner breed was the English Thoroughbred Perfectionist, a son of Persimmon. Foaled in 1893, Persimmon was bred and owned by the Prince of Wales, later King Edward VII (1901–1910), and was by St Simon out of Perdita II, who in turn was by Hampton out of Hermione. Persimmon won the Epsom Derby and St Leger in 1896, and represents an important influence in the St Simon line. The blood of his son Perfectionist, along with that of Tempelhüter, the best of Perfectionist's sons, appears in nearly all modern Trakehner pedigrees. When Tempelhüter died in 1932, he had produced 54 stallions and 60 brood mares at Trakehnen. The Perfectionist/Tempelhüter line, and the Dingo line, which owed much to Tempelhüter's daughters, provide the base for the modern Trakehner.

SPORT

The Trakehner stands between 1.63 and 1.68 m (16–16.2 hh.) and has an impressive record. Trakehners dominated the 1936 German Olympic teams, which won every medal at the Berlin Games, and have continued to be successful in international competition since the Second World War.

TAIL
The tail is set high into the quarters, continuing the line of the level croup. In movement the tail is carried notably well.

BODY
The body is of medium length, strong and very well ribbed-up, with pleasantly rounded quarters. In this example the Arabian background is evident in the overall outline.

LEGS
The legs are hard with well-formed joints, short cannons, and good bone measurement below the knee. The feet are excellent and very sound.

ORIGINS

THE TRAKEHNER, based on the Schweiken, originated in the 13th century in the old province of East Prussia, in the area between Gumbinnen and Stallupönen. (This region is now in present-day Lithuania.) It was here, in the laboriously drained marshes, that the Royal Trakehnen Stud Administration was established by Frederick William I of Prussia in 1732. The breeding of Trakehners was continued in West Germany after 1945, when the horses were taken to the west to escape capture.

HOLSTEINER

THE HOLSTEINER IS THE OLDEST of the German warmbloods, and takes its name from the the Elmshorn district of Holstein, the area in which it originated. The principal breeding centre is still in this region. The Holsteiner is based on the horses that used to live in the marshes surrounding the Elbe and other neighbouring rivers. As early as 1300, the monastery of Uetersen in the Haseldorf marshes was using them at its stud, which was dedicated to breeding war-horses and horses for tournaments (tourney horses). Throughout the Middle Ages, the Kings of Denmark and the Dukes of Schleswig-Holstein greatly encouraged the breeding of such horses.

SUPREME CARRIAGE HORSE
A team of American-owned Holsteiners competes in the Stockholm Driving Championships. The traditional Holsteiner is a powerful carriage horse, perfected by selective breeding and outcrossing.

ORIGINS

The indigenous stock, in the pattern of so many of the German warmbloods, initially received a massive infusion of Spanish, eastern, and Neapolitan blood. From the 16th century through to the 18th century, Holstein horses were in demand in Denmark, Spain, Italy, France, and other European countries. They were also an increasing influence on other German warmblood breeds, and were used to improve the Westphalian and Mecklenburg stock, as well as being introduced at Celle and Dillenburg, breeding centres for the famous Hanoverians (see pp.144–45). Indeed, it was in 1680, at the royal stud of the Dukes of Holstein at Esserom, that the Holsteiner stallion Mignon was used to begin the breeding of the famous cream horses that became the pride of the Electors of Hanover and formed part of the complement of horses at London's Royal Mews (see pp.302–3) until 1920. At this time, the Holsteiner was valued as a tough, reliable carriage and coach horse, whose high, showy action, deriving from its Spanish antecedents, did not preclude its use on the land or as a heavyweight saddle horse.

BREEDING

The Holsteiner has always been very tractable in temperament, a prized characteristic fostered by very careful selective breeding. However, in 1680 it was hardly a supremely elegant horse, nor was it very fast. The conformational failures were corrected early in the 19th century by the importation of English Thoroughbreds (see pp.120–21). The coarse Roman nose began to disappear, the action became lower, and the ability to gallop was

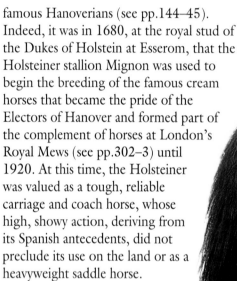

ORIGINS

THE PRINCIPAL BREEDING CENTRE for the Holsteiner, the oldest German warmblood breed, is still in the Elmshorn district of Schleswig-Holstein, the area from which it takes its name. The breed is, in fact, based on the local horses that lived in the marshlands abutting the Elbe and its tributaries. However, as breeding policies have moved further towards the production of top-class competition horses, Holsteiners have been exported in large numbers and are bred in many countries.

HEIGHT
*1.63–1.73 m
(16–17 hh)*

improved. Even more important was the introduction of Yorkshire Coach Horse stallions. These were a faster derivative of the Cleveland Bay (see pp.306–7), produced by mating Cleveland mares with half-bred Cleveland stallions. Their introduction established the Holsteiner's equable temperament and fixed a characteristically wide action that suited the relatively heavy frame. The result was a hard, handsome carriage horse that could also be employed as an artillery draught animal and as a strong riding horse, in which capacity it was in demand as a cavalry remount.

The breed was developed along these lines, chiefly at the Traventhal Stud founded by the Prussians in 1867 at Schleswig-Holstein. The stud at Traventhal no longer exists, and responsibility for the breed now lies with the Society of Breeders of the Holstein Horse in Elmshorn. The stock is subjected to the performance testing that is customary with all the European warmblood breeds (see pp.124–25).

RECENT DEVELOPMENTS

Following the Second World War, the demands of the horse market changed and German breeders responded positively, recognizing the need to produce a purpose-bred competition horse. To do so, recourse had to be made to upgrading Thoroughbred blood. The Holstein Society used more Thoroughbreds than any other society.

In a fairly short space of time, the Holsteiner became a multi-purpose riding horse of between 1.63 m and 1.73 m (16–17 hh). It was not just bred for a particular pursuit, but was suitable for all the ridden disciplines. The modern Holsteiner is lighter than before, and resembles a quality hunter with bone and substance. It has scope, is bold, and can gallop and jump. It is, in fact, the all-round competition horse, and of all the German warmbloods it is probably the best eventing prospect. As a reminder of its past, it retains a little knee action, but this is no deterrent; the movement is free and long and notably rhythmical and elastic.

One of the world's greatest showjumpers was Fritz Thiedemann's Holsteiner, Meteor. Thiedemann always favoured Holsteiners above any other breed. Other famous Holsteiners include Granat, the world champion dressage horse, and the good international eventers Albrant, Madrigal, and Ladalco.

BODY
Thoroughbred blood has lightened the heavy frame of the old Holsteiner, sometimes causing loss of type. This horse lacks depth through the girth, but this is not a general failing in the breed.

HEAD
This head inclines towards the plainer sort of Thoroughbred, but there is no longer evidence of the old Roman-nosed profile.

SHOULDERS
The shoulders are sloped, to give a longer, lower action for riding, and the withers are clearly defined.

SHOWJUMPERS
Infusions of Thoroughbred blood have resulted in a stamp of horse that is lighter than the old type. The modern Holsteiner is among the world's best showjumpers.

HANOVERIAN

THE HANOVERIAN HORSE, distinguished by its stylized "H" brandmark, is the most numerous and the best-known of the European warmbloods. The breed was established at Celle in 1735 by George II, Elector of Hanover and King of England (1727–1760), "for the benefit of our subjects". Today, over 8,000 mares a year are served by stallions of the Celle Stallion Depot.

HEAD
The head is comparatively light and of medium size.

NECK
The neck, allowing for the natural crest of a stallion, is long and fine. It runs into big, sloping shoulders topped by pronounced withers.

THE STUD AT CELLE

Even before the foundation of the stallion depot at Celle, the Hanoverian had received much royal encouragement. The white horse of Hanover graced the coat-of-arms of the Elector Ernest Augustus (1629–1698), and the famous Royal Hanoverian Creams, with their pale coffee-coloured manes and tails, were bred at Electress Sophia's instigation at the royal residence at Herrenhausen. These small coach horses were used in British royal processions from the reign of George I to that of George V (see pp.304–5).

In 1714, when George, Elector of Hanover, became George I of England, "Thoroughbreds" of the day were imported to upgrade the often unprepossessing stock, but the founding sires at Celle were 14 black Holsteiners (see pp.142–43). This breed was to be the overriding influence on horses at the depot for the next 30 years. Later, more Thoroughbred blood (see pp.120–21) was introduced. This created a lighter, more free-moving horse that was of sufficient quality to be used in carriage harness or under saddle, but was still strong enough for general farm work. From the outset all horses at Celle were registered, and by the end of the 18th century detailed pedigrees were being kept.

The stock at Celle was depleted during the Napoleonic Wars, and when the stud was re-established in 1816 there were only 30 stallions out of the 100 that had been housed there earlier. The complement was built up with more English Thoroughbred imports and with horses from Mecklenburg, the station to which the Celle stallions had been evacuated during the wars. (Interestingly, only English Thoroughbreds were used to upgrade European warmblood stock. Apart

ORIGINS

NORTH SEA

Copenhagen

EUROPE

Amsterdam • Celle

Elbe

Weser

Oder

Vistula

GERMANY

Rhine

Bonn •

Danube

Vienna •

0 ___ 200 km
0 ___ 125 miles

THE HANOVERIAN HORSE originated in the Electorate of Hanover in Germany, and is bred throughout Westphalia, where there is a stallion depot at Warendorf. The principal stallion depot is at Celle in Lower Saxony. Hanoverians are bred in considerable numbers in both North and South America, as well as in Australia. It is the best-known of the German warmbloods.

LEGS
The legs are short, with short cannons that have ample bone measurement. The joints are large and pronounced. The forearms are strongly muscled.

HEIGHT
1.60–1.68 m
(15.3–16.2 hh)

PRESENCE

The presence and correct conformation of the Hanoverian make it an ideal choice for the dressage discipline. Additionally, the action is athletic, elastic, and notably correct and true.

BACK
The back is of medium length, with particularly broad and powerful loins.

from France, and later Italy, the other countries of Europe never developed Thoroughbred stock comparable to that of the UK, Ireland, and the US.)

VARIED INFLUENCES

By the mid-19th century the increasing Thoroughbred influence (35 per cent) had resulted in a horse that was too light for agricultural use, and attempts were made to standardize the production of a heavier type by using indigenous lines within the breed.

By the time of the First World War Celle had 350 stallions, and by 1924 this number had increased to 500. To house all the horses another stud at Osnabrück-Eversburg was utilized, and the 100 stallions there were a powerful incentive to the breeding of Hanoverian horses in this region. Osnabrück-Eversburg remained operative until 1961.

QUARTERS
The tail is set well up in the quarters, and is carried high. The quarters are muscular, and there is flattening at the croup.

Between the World Wars the number of stallions available for service fluctuated, and there was some variation in type among stock bred in different areas. After the Second World War, some Trakehners (see pp.140–41) had found their way to Celle from East Prussia, and were added to the existing stock. In the 1960s determined efforts were made to adapt the Hanoverian breeding policies, in order to satisfy the new demand for high-quality riding and sport horses. The new policy's success owes much to the use of the Trakehners and Thoroughbreds that are still kept at Celle. They acted as a refining influence, lightening the still heavy-bodied Hanoverian and giving greater scope and freedom of movement.

CHARACTERISTICS

The modern Hanoverian stands between 1.60 and 1.68 m (15.3–16.2 hh), and has good conformation. It is notably correct in its action, which is athletic and elastic, and there is no longer any trace of the high knee movement that characterized the old Hanoverian carriage horse. It is claimed to be particularly equable in temperament. These horses are far more refined than their predecessors, as a result of continued outcrosses to the Thoroughbred (see pp.120–21). They are renowned as dressage performers and also as showjumpers of exceptional talent at international levels.

FEET
The modern Hanoverian has hard, well-shaped feet. The old failing of poorly made feet has been almost entirely eliminated by careful selective breeding and testing.

WESTPHALIAN

The Westphalian horse is in effect a Hanoverian, although there are sometimes differences in type. This horse, for instance, is coarser in build than usual and, though a good riding horse for the average purpose, is very much of a coaching type. Hanoverian stallions, under the name Westphalian, are used at the depot at Warendorf.

BELGIAN & BAVARIAN WARMBLOODS

THE BELGIAN WARMBLOOD is one of the more recent members of the European warmblood family and has achieved considerable success in a relatively short period of time. It is a horse that has been virtually purpose-bred for competitive dressage and showjumping, and representatives of the breed have excelled at both. The Bavarian Warmblood, not one of the most well-known of Germany's competition horses, is based on the Rottaler, one of the oldest breeds in Europe. It thus traces back to the 11th century.

BELGIAN WARMBLOOD
Belgian Warmbloods are becoming a significant force in international showjumping and are also increasingly evident in dressage competitions.

THE BELGIAN WARMBLOOD

Belgium has traditionally specialized in the production of big, powerful, heavy agricultural horses such as the Brabant (see pp.274–75). However, the emphasis has now shifted to equestrian competition and many Belgian breeders concentrate on warmblood riding horses, producing over 4,500 foals every year. The breed has a good performance record in international competition and is sold all over Europe.

The history of the breed begins in the 1950s when the lighter, cleaner-legged Belgian farm horse was crossed with the Gelderlander (see pp.126–27), to produce a heavyweight riding horse. This cross to a predominantly coldblood background was reasonably successful, producing substantial, everyday animals that were strong and reliable although neither overly talented nor

QUARTERS
The quarters are broad and strong with powerful muscling in the second thighs. The loins are also broad and the body is very compact.

BELGIAN WARMBLOOD

BELGIAN WARMBLOOD

THE BELGIAN WARMBLOOD is a fairly recent warmblood breed, and is bred all over Belgium, particularly in the traditional horse-breeding area of Brabant. It is estimated that between 4,000 and 5,000 foals are born each year. Increasingly, Belgian breeders have relied on their Dutch, French, and German neighbours for outcrosses, making use of Gelderlanders, Anglo-Arabs, and some Holsteiners, while not neglecting the essential Thoroughbred element in the genetic mix.

HEAD
The head is not unlike that of the related Selle Français. The neck, to complement the well-built body, is strong.

NECK
The long, graceful neck, and the finely drawn, quality head are strongly reminiscent of the Thoroughbred.

LEGS
The long, slender legs have joints of medium size. The feet are claimed to be very sound and not prone to disease.

BAVARIAN
WARMBLOOD

BAVARIAN WARMBLOOD

THE BAVARIAN WARMBLOOD has its origin with the Rottaler breed, raised in the fertile valley of the Rott in Bavaria, and with the horses bred at the 16th-century monastic studs in the Zweibrücken region to the east. It is a good example of breeders defining an objective and working methodically towards it. The evolution of the breed has been accomplished in carefully considered stages, designed to create a firm genetic and physical base before finally introducing the Thoroughbred.

particularly gymnastic. The Gelderlander cross was discontinued about 10 years later, once it had provided a good base for improvement. It was replaced by the Holsteiner (see pp.142–43) and the more athletic Selle Français (see pp.132–33), both of which are noted for their straight, rhythmic action.

It became increasingly apparent that if the quality, scope, and freedom of action were to be improved it would be necessary to bring in Thoroughbred blood (see pp.120–21). The Anglo-Arab (see pp.78–79), and a Dutch Warmblood cross (see pp.128–29), both sound horses with calm dispositions, were also introduced. This has produced a powerful, straight-moving horse of about 1.68 m (16.2 hh), possessed of great agility, good limbs, sound feet, and a calm temperament, well able to cope with the stress of competition. The coat can be any solid colour.

THE BAVARIAN WARMBLOOD

The Bavarian Warmblood's ancestor, the old chestnut Rottaler, was bred in the fertile valley of the Rott, an area that was noted for the excellence of its horses in the past. By the time of the Crusades in the 11th century (see pp.68–69) it was prized as a war-horse equal to the early Friesians (see pp.48–49). Later, during the 16th century, the horses were bred systematically at the monastic studs of Hornbach and Worschweiler in the Zweibrucken region. In the 18th century the stock was being upgraded by imported half-bred English stallions, Cleveland Bays (see pp.306–7), and some Norman Cobs (see pp.270–71). At the end of the 19th century Oldenburgers were used to give the Bavarian more substance and the foundation was laid for the modern competition horse.

With the introduction of Thoroughbred blood later on, the heavily built Rottaler gave way to a lighter, though still strongly built, horse averaging about 1.63 m (16 hh). The modern Bavarian ("Rottaler" was discontinued in the 1960s) is an attractive horse, with the traditional Rottaler chestnut colouring. It is deep through the girth and stands on short, strong legs with well-proportioned bone measurements. As usual, emphasis is placed on temperament and the horses undergo performance tests.

Bavarians are well-suited for dressage and jumping competitions at international level, but like many other warmbloods they are not great gallopers and in consequence are less good as cross-country horses.

HEIGHT OF
BELGIAN
WARMBLOOD
1.68 m
(16.2 hh)

HEIGHT OF
BAVARIAN
WARMBLOOLD
1.63 m
(16 hh)

RHINELANDER & WÜRTTEMBERGER

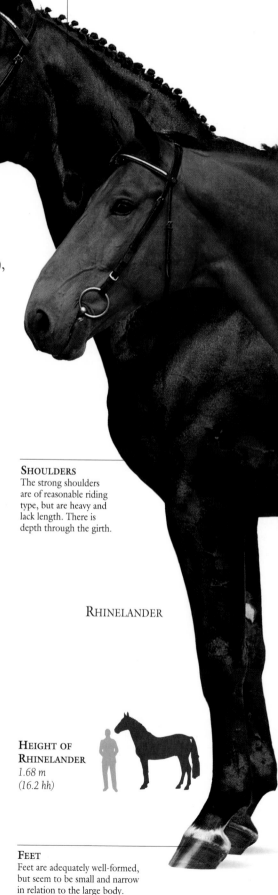

HEAD
The head is plain but pleasing in its outlook. The neck is strong but somewhat thick and short.

T HE RHINELANDER AND THE WÜRTTEMBERGER are two of the half-dozen warmblood competition horses bred in Germany. The Rhinelander is one of the most recent breeds, developed in the 1970s, while the Württemberger is one of the oldest, having been bred at the Marbach Stud since the early 19th century from stock that had been established there for over 200 years.

THE RHINELANDER

The best of the German coldblood horses was the old Rhenish-German or Rhineland heavy draught horse, based largely on the Belgian Brabant (see pp.274–75). It was once a popular workhorse in Rhineland, Westphalia, and Saxony, but with modern

MIDDLE-OF-THE-ROAD
The Rhinelander is a useful, middle-of-the-road horse, well-suited to the needs of the average rider and the growing area of leisure riding.

agricultural practice the breed became redundant and is no longer recognized in Germany. Nonetheless, the *Rhenish Stud Book* was never closed and breeders, using the lighter specimens of the old breed, moved towards creating the warmblood riding horse now called the Rhinelander.

By the 1970s there were programmes to produce a recognizable type of riding horse for the growing leisure market. Stallions from the Hanover-Westphalia area were used on

warmblood mares sired by Thoroughbreds (see pp.120–21), Trakehners (see pp.140–41), and Hanoverians (see pp.144–45), out of dams claiming a relationship with the old Rhenish breed. From this mix of bloods half-bred stallions were selected from which the modern Rhinelander has been developed.

The result is an undistinguished, but not unattractive, riding horse of about 1.68 m (16.2 hh), often chestnut in colour, which is well-suited to the needs of the club rider. The early specimens lacked bone, but that failing has now been eradicated. Breeders have concentrated on improving conformation and establishing the straight, elastic action for which the German breeds are particularly noted. As always, emphasis is given to an equable temperament. The Rhinelander may not yet be in the same class as the better-known Hanoverians and Holsteiners, but it is, nonetheless, a useful, if unpretentious, riding horse.

THE WÜRTTEMBERGER

The Marbach stud, one of the greatest of the European breeding centres, was founded in 1573. Early in its history it had established a reputation for good utility horses suitable for both riding and light harness work. These were produced by crossing the stud's various breeds, which ranged from Spanish and eastern stock to heavy horse breeds.

The Württemberger, regarded as one of Germany's classic warmbloods, evolved in the 17th century, when local mares of mixed origin were crossed with Arabs (see pp.64–65). Spanish and Barb mares and Friesian stallions were also used in the

SHOULDERS
The strong shoulders are of reasonable riding type, but are heavy and lack length. There is depth through the girth.

RHINELANDER

HEIGHT OF RHINELANDER
1.68 m
(16.2 hh)

FEET
Feet are adequately well-formed, but seem to be small and narrow in relation to the large body.

ATHLETIC

The modern Württemberger has an athletic quality and the type of conformation that allows it to compete successfully in showjumping competitions at international level.

17th century. Without losing its Arab background, the early Württemberger was indebted to Anglo-Norman blood through Faust, a horse of cob type. However, the greatest influence on the modern breed is the Trakehner stallion Julmond, who came to Marbach in 1960 and is considered to be the breed's foundation sire.

The modern Württemberger has lost some of its stockiness, but is noted as a very correctly proportioned riding horse. It is hardy, long-lived, has a quiet temperament, and is economical to keep. The action, which is energetic and true, reveals the Arab influence. It is a medium-sized horse, of good substance, standing at 1.63 m (16 hh) and upwards.

ORIGINS

THE MODERN RHINELANDER *is based on the old stock of the Rhineland, Westphalia, and Saxony, and its breeding remains centred in these regions of Germany. The Württemberg breed began its evolution some 300 years ago at the Marbach stud in Württemberg, one of Germany's oldest state-owned stud farms, which was founded in 1552, when selected Marbach Arabs, for which the stud is still famous, were mixed with local mares of mixed origin. The Württemberger is still associated with the stud, and is not bred elsewhere.*

QUARTERS

Nicely formed quarters run on from broad and muscular loins. There is good length from the hip-bone to the point of the hock.

HEIGHT OF WÜRTTEMBERGER
1.63 m (16 hh)

LEGS

Good legs, with prominent, correctly positioned hocks and flat joints, contribute to the energy of the action.

WÜRTTEMBERGER

DANISH & SWEDISH WARMBLOODS

DENMARK AND SWEDEN produce distinctive, highly successful competition horses, impressive in both conformation and overall appearance. They rely heavily on the Thoroughbred (see pp.120–21) and, as a result, resemble the very best sort of English and Irish middleweight hunter (see pp.394–95). Both countries have an ancient equestrian tradition and Sweden has the distinction of being primarily responsible for the introduction of the equestrian disciplines to the Olympic Games.

HEIGHT OF DANISH WARMBLOOD
1.68 m
(16.2 hh)

THE DANISH WARMBLOOD

In the 14th century horse-breeding in Denmark relied upon studs in Holstein, a Danish duchy until 1864. For many years the policy was to cross heavy North German mares with Spanish stallions, to produce horses like the Frederiksborg and the Holsteiner (see pp.114–15 and pp.142–43).

Nonetheless, even though it had talented riders, Denmark, like the Netherlands, did not have a national riding horse until

fairly late. Although a Danish equestrian federation existed as early as 1918, it was not until the 1960s that a stud book was opened for the Danish Sports Horse, which has since become known as the Danish Warmblood.

The basis for the new breed was the old Frederiksborg stock crossed with the Thoroughbred to produce an active riding horse that, although it retained some of the Frederiksborg's thickness and carriage character, was temperate and reasonably elegant. These half-bred mares were put to Anglo-Norman stallions (essentially Selle Français – see pp.132–33) and to Thoroughbreds, Trakehners (see pp.140–41), and the Wielkopolski (see pp.154–55), a close relation of the Trakehner. The Selle Français introduced a wiry, athletic quality and improved conformation. The Trakehner and Wielkopolski helped fix the type and contributed to their stamina, overall ability, and agreeable temperament. As usual, the Thoroughbred was the refining influence, giving a superior movement and improved quality, speed, and courage.

The mix, when carefully adjusted, produced a sound, handsome horse of Thoroughbred type but with substance, strength, and good limbs. Standing at 1.68 m (16.2 hh) the Danish Warmblood is an arresting and sometimes brilliant dressage horse and some of them are excellent cross-country prospects as well. The lack of Hanoverian blood is unusual in a European warmblood, and may account for the breed's distinctive character.

ORIGINS

EARLY HORSE-BREEDING in Denmark was largely dependent on the monastic studs of Holstein and, much later, the royal stud of Frederiksborg. The Danish Warmblood evolved largely because of the country's easy access to stock developed by its neighbours. The Swedish Warmblood also descends from imported stock, and was bred at both Stromsholm and Flyinge; the latter is the present-day centre for stallion breeding, from which horses are sent to stand at selected stations. Sweden has always paid particular attention to the choice of Thoroughbred crosses.

LIMBS
The limbs are very powerful with strongly muscled forearms, good, clean joints, short cannons, and ample bone below the knee.

FEET
Particular attention is paid to the quality, shape, and wearing properties of the feet. Uneven or diseased feet are rarely found.

DANISH WARMBLOOD

THE SWEDISH WARMBLOOD

The Swedish Warmblood was descended from horses imported in the 17th century and was originally a better-than-average cavalry horse. It was bred at the Stromsholm stud, founded in 1621, and at Flyinge, the Royal stud established in 1658 in Skåne in southern Sweden (see pp.138–39), formerly part of Denmark. Stromsholm no longer exists as a stallion depot but stallions are sent from Flyinge to stand at stations all over Sweden. The first imports, brought in from Denmark, England, France, Germany,

THE FLYINGE STUD
The breeding of the well-established Swedish Warmblood is centred on the stud at Flyinge in the province of Skåne. Flyinge was founded in 1658.

Hungary, Russia, Spain, and Turkey, were extraordinarily varied. The product was of such mixed pedigree that there could be no fixed type. Nonetheless, these horses and most particularly the Spanish and Friesian imports, as well as those of oriental ancestry, produced active, strong horses when crossed with the small, rough local mares. In the 19th and 20th centuries Arab (see pp.64–65), Thoroughbred, Hanoverian (see pp.144–45) and, very importantly, Trakehner blood was introduced into the base stock to produce big, powerful horses that were increasingly fixed in type. Flyinge was careful to use the best Thoroughbred blood available – a practice sometimes ignored in mainland Europe to the detriment of the progeny.

The modern Swedish Warmblood is a good example of riding horse conformation with easy, straight paces. It is handsome, sound, tractable, and very versatile. The best Swedish Warmbloods are well known as dressage horses of international calibre and also as showjumpers and event horses. They are also very good driving horses, and have been exported in large numbers all over Europe and to the US. The breed is performance tested, and is subject to rigorous examination before animals are accepted for breeding.

Between 1920 and 1930, an important decade in the development of the breed, the three most noticeable influences were the Hanoverians Schwabliso, Tribun, and Hamlet, and the Thoroughbred Hampelmann. After 1945, the Trakehners Heristal, Heinfried, Anno, and Polarstern had a dominant effect upon the breed. Heristal, a descendant of the great English racehorse Hyperion, produced 15 stallions and 44 mares entered in the stud book.

QUARTERS
The quarters show good muscle development with the tail set well up. The back is of medium length and the overall outline is that of a quality riding horse.

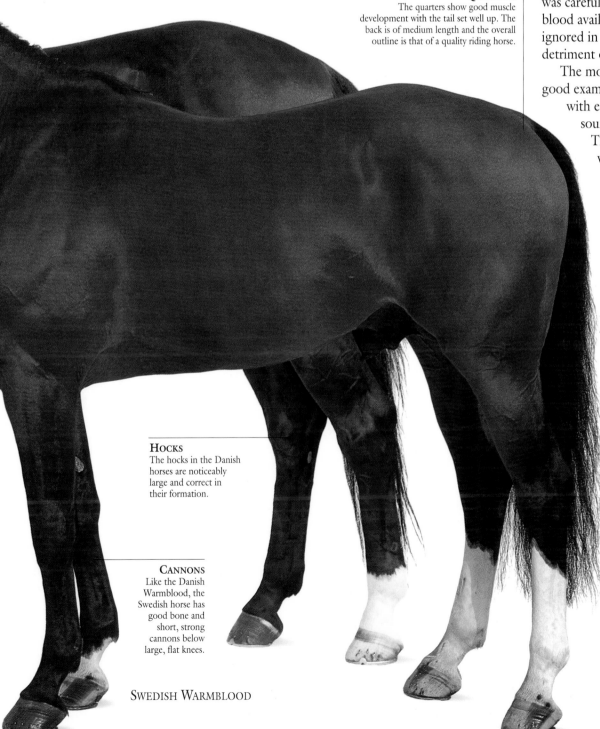

HOCKS
The hocks in the Danish horses are noticeably large and correct in their formation.

CANNONS
Like the Danish Warmblood, the Swedish horse has good bone and short, strong cannons below large, flat knees.

SWEDISH WARMBLOOD

HEIGHT OF SWEDISH WARMBLOOD
1.68 m
(16.2 hh)

EASTERN EUROPEAN STUDS

PLAQUE AT MEZŐHEGYES

THE STUDS of Eastern Europe reflect a tradition of horsemanship that began 4,000 years ago with the horse peoples of the Asian steppes. The Magyars of Hungary are the direct descendants of those peoples who, in the migration from their homeland in the Urals to their final settlement in the Caucasian basin, were in contact with both the Asiatic Wild Horse (see pp.18–19) and the Tarpan (see pp.20–21), and finally with the Arab (see pp.64–65). Their rich traditions spilled over into Bohemia and Slovakia, while to the north, Poland, closely associated with Tarpan root-stock, became the largest horse-owning nation in Europe. It was due to the Poles and Hungarians that the swift, high-spirited Arab horse became the overriding influence in the studs and breeding policies of Eastern Europe.

HUNGARY

Hungary came under Turkish rule for 150 years after the battle of Mohács in 1526. As a result, the Hungarian horse population was heavily influenced by Turkish horses of eastern origin. Nonetheless, notable breeds have since been developed based on the Anglo-Norman and the Thoroughbred (see pp.120–21), particularly at Mezőhegyes in the south-east of the Hungarian plain.

The first stud-farm in Hungary was founded on an island in the Danube in the 9th century by a tribal chief, Arpád, whose great-grandson, having embraced the Christian faith, became Stephen I, King of Hungary (997–1038).

Mezőhegyes is the oldest and one of the most important of the existing state studs. It was founded in 1785 by Joseph II (1741–90) at the instigation of Joseph Csekoniks, who established Bábolna soon afterwards. As early as 1793 it supported over 1,000 mares. It is famed for developing the Nonius, the Furioso (see pp.156–57), and the Gidran Arab (see pp.76–77), the Hungarian line of Anglo-Arabs. The emphasis is now on producing a competition horse, based on performance trial results, and for which Thoroughbreds and some proven German competition lines are used.

Bábolna, formerly the 700-year-old estate of Babunapuszta, was bought by the government from the Szapary family in 1789, almost as an overflow facility for Mezőhegyes. The decision to produce Arab-type horses was taken in 1816 when several predominantly Arab horses and some pure-breds were sent to the stud. Shagya

HUNGARY'S OLDEST STUD

A quiet interlude at Mezőhegyes, the oldest of the great 18th-century Hungarian studs. It is famed for the development of the Nonius, Gidran, and Furioso breeds.

BEAUTIFUL BÁBOLNA

Bábolna, purchased in 1789, is one of the most famous and beautiful studs in the world and its renowned Shagya horses enhance the quiet perfection of the surroundings.

(see pp.76–77), the founder of Bábolna's Shagya line, was bought from Syria in 1833 and more Syrians were imported in 1850.

Performance testing was introduced in 1869, when Bábolna was put under the control of the Hungarian ministry of agriculture. The stud's greatest period of prosperity was between the two world wars, when it had more top-quality Arabs than anywhere else in the world. The stock was almost destroyed after 1945, but Bábolna still retains its pre-eminence in Arab breeding.

The other Hungarian state studs are at Sümeg, a stallion station, and Szilvasvarad where Lipizzaners (see pp.112–13) are bred along the old classical lines.

FORMER CZECHOSLOVAKIA

Topolcianky, in the Nitra district of former Czechoslovakia, now in Slovakia, is centred on the magnificent Topolcianky Castle. It

ARABIAN CENTRE
Janow Podlaski produces some of the best Arab stock in the world. Despite Poland's turbulent history (both Russians and Germans tried to destroy the stud), it still survives as a centre of Arabian excellence.

was established in 1921 and in its time has bred various horses, such as Huçuls (see pp.194–95), Arabs, Nonius (see pp.156–57), Lipizzaners, and "English half-breds" based on the Furioso lines. The modern emphasis, as elsewhere in Europe, is now on the competition horse.

Kladrub was founded in 1597 by Emperor Rudolph II, and is one of the world's oldest studs. It enjoyed its greatest period of prosperity during the time of Charles VI in the last half of the 18th century, when it housed upwards of 1,000 horses. By introducing Lipizzaner blood, it has developed the white herd of modern Kladrubers from the old Kladruby heavy coach horse, known in earlier times as *Equus bohemicus*. A black herd is also kept at the Horse Breeding Research Station at Slatinany. English half-breds are also produced in both places.

THE KLADRUB STUD
The grey Kladruber carriage horses have been bred at the Czechoslovakian state stud at Kladrub since it was founded in 1597 by the Emperor Rudolph II. The horses were bred for the Imperial Court in Vienna. During the 18th century 1,000 horses were kept here.

POLAND

Janow Podlaski, founded in 1817, is the main Polish stud, and the worthy successor to the world-famous private studs that had so great an influence on the development of the horse throughout Europe between the 17th and 19th centuries.

In 1914 the Russians seized all the stock at Janow Podlaski. A new start was made in 1919, and a programme was set up to produce pure-bred Arabs; half-bred Arabs based on mares from the Austro-Hungarian studs at Radautz; and Anglo-Arabs, the product of English Thoroughbreds put to the half-bred mares. These horses were famous in Europe and in great demand. In 1939 the Germans nearly destroyed the stud, but by 1950 the half-bred Arabs were back at Janow and the pure-breds returned in 1960. Both pure-breds and Anglo-Arabs are produced today.

Anglo-Arabs are also bred at Walewice.

The Liski Stud, formed in 1947 in what used to be East Prussia, specializes in the old Trakehnen bloodlines (see pp.140–41).

WIELKOPOLSKI

THE WIELKOPOLSKI, ONE OF POLAND'S most important warmbloods, is a sound competition horse and, along with its close relative the Trakehner (see pp.140–41), is the warmblood with the greatest potential as an event horse. However, it is probably less appreciated than it deserves to be. This may be because Polish breeders cannot match the sales and promotions techniques of breeders in Central and Western Europe. Nonetheless, their stock and innate breeding skills are equal, and often superior to those found elsewhere in Europe.

AN ACTIVE HORSE
The powerful Wielkopolski is a very active and naturally balanced horse with good paces and an easy, amiable disposition.

THE ARAB HERITAGE

Like the Hungarians, the Poles had a tradition of horsemanship unequalled by any other European nation. Similarly, they favoured Arab or Arab-type horses to carry their renowned light cavalry and, with an intuitive breeding sense, used Arab blood to upgrade their national stock. Most Polish-bred horses are influenced by the Arab horse (see pp.64–65) in some way. Indeed, producing Arab and Arab-type horses amounts to something little short of a Polish national duty. The Wielkopolski is no exception and although it is not an Arab horse, in Poland it is inevitably much influenced by that superlative blood and retains its sound constitution.

The Arab studs in Poland, which were famous throughout Europe and produced stock of rare and distinctive quality (see pp.152–53), were created by the Polish nobility. In 1803 Prince Sanguszko was the first to import horses from the East, sending an envoy to acquire horses for his stud at Slawuta. His descendant, Count Potocki, founded the famous Antoniny Stud later in the century. Potocki, a fine horseman and a breeder of genius, produced notable strains of Arab, as well as spotted and part-coloured horses that were Arab in appearance and had the same characteristic action.

BACKGROUND

The Wielkopolski derives from the Poznan and Masuren warmblood breeds, both with Arab connections, and now officially extinct. The Poznan, a dual-purpose horse, was bred

ORIGINS

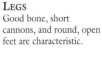

POLAND'S WIELKOPOLSKI is not the best-known of the European warmbloods, but it is one of the best. It is bred principally in central and western Poland, and derives from a combination of two older Polish warmbloods, the Poznan and the Masuren. The Poznan was originally bred near Poznan at the Posadowo, Raçot, and Gogolewo studs as an agricultural horse. The Masuren was from the Masury district and was bred mainly at Liski with stallion depots at Starogad, Kwidzyn, and Gniezno.

LEGS
Good bone, short cannons, and round, open feet are characteristic.

HEIGHT
1.68 m
(16.2 hh)

at the studs of Posadowo, Raçot, and Gogolewo, and was well-established in the 19th century. It was a good stamp of middle- to heavyweight horse, from a base provided by the hardy Konik pony (see pp.194–95), which descended from the Tarpan (see pp.20–21). It carried Arab and Thoroughbred blood (see pp.120–21), some Hanoverian (see pp.144–45), and some East Prussian Trakehner. It was used as an agricultural horse to work the medium soil of the district, but it was also a very useful riding horse.

The Masuren horse was bred in the Masury district, chiefly at Liski, which was formerly a principal remount depot, and at the state studs. Stallion depots were at Starogad, Kwidzyn, and Gniezno. The Masuren was in every way a Trakehner, with all that implies in terms of Arabian and Thoroughbred blood. Indeed, after the Second World War the nucleus of the Masuren breed was made up of stray horses, which were identified as Trakehner by the elk-antler brand and gathered together by the Polish authorities.

THE WIELKOPOLSKI

The Wielkopolski resulted as a combination of these two distinctive breeds, additional outcrosses then being made to Thoroughbreds, Arabs, and Anglo-Arabs (see pp.78–79), until differences in type had been eradicated. It is a big, quality, dual-purpose horse, which is mainly bred in central and western Poland. It is a handsome, proportionate animal, naturally balanced and noted for its good paces. It has a long, easy walk; the trot is level, straight,

QUARTERS
Strong, muscular quarters provide great propulsive thrust.

INTERNATIONAL DRESSAGE
In the world's international dressage arenas the extravagantly moving Wielkopolski enhances the performance of the test and commands attention.

HIND LEGS
The well-formed hind legs and second thighs contribute to the jumping ability and overall balance. The triangle formed by stifle, hip, and seat bone is correctly even-sided.

BODY
The body is deep and powerful, with just enough length in the back to give scope and speed. The shoulders are nicely sloped, and the neck is strong and proportionate.

HOCKS
The hock joints are clean, large, and set in the leg to allow for maximum flexion. The fetlock joints are hard and flat.

and low; and it covers a lot of ground at the canter and gallop, which is not always the case with other warmblood breeds. It stands at about 1.68 m (16.2 hh), and is found in all solid colours.

The Wielkopolski is an immensely practical horse, going as well in harness as under saddle, and is both easy and economical to keep. The heavier specimens are extremely active, powerful, and good tempered. They are quite able to carry out any job in an agricultural economy which still employs horse-power but makes little use of the heavy horse breeds. Today, however, the emphasis is upon a lighter, athletic stamp of horse that conforms to the requirements of the modern competitive disciplines without sacrificing the easily manageable temperament or the essential soundness of physique. Owing to its high percentage of Thoroughbred blood, the Wielkopolski is an excellent jumper, with the speed, mental stamina, and courage to go cross-country. It also remains a very useful light harness horse.

NONIUS & FURIOSO

THE NONIUS AND THE FURIOSO were first bred in the 19th century in Hungary, following a horse-breeding tradition that dated back 1,000 years to the settlement in the Carpathian basin of the Magyar horsemen, the descendants of the horse peoples of the Asian steppes. From then on, Hungary dominated horse-breeding in Europe, producing hardy, quality horses, greatly in demand as cavalry mounts. In the 16th century, Arab blood (see pp.64–65) was introduced. This improved and refined the native stock and the influence is still apparent.

HEIGHT OF NONIUS
1.60–1.68 m
(15.3–16.2 hh)

HEAD
The head is more refined than that of the Nonius, and inclines more to the Thoroughbred, despite the prominent ears.

MEZŐHEGYES AND BÁBOLNA

The great studs at Mezőhegyes and Bábolna, owned by the Austro-Hungarian emperors, were founded in 1785 and 1789 by the Emperor Joseph II. Successive rulers and governments encouraged the horse-breeding industry, until at the end of the 19th century Hungary had over two million horses and some of the foremost studs in the world. At its peak Mezőhegyes housed over 12,000 horses. It became the centre for the breeding of the Nonius and Furioso, while Bábolna was famed for the Shagya Arab (see pp.76–77).

THE NONIUS

Nonius Senior, the foundation sire of the Nonius breed, was foaled in Normandy, in 1810, and taken by Hungarian cavalry after Napoleon's defeat at Leipzig in 1813. It is recorded that he was by the English half-bred stallion Orion (who very probably had Norfolk Roadster blood) out of a Norman mare. Nonius stood at 1.66 m (16.1½ hh), and apparently was not a handsome horse. He was said to have a heavy

ORIGINS

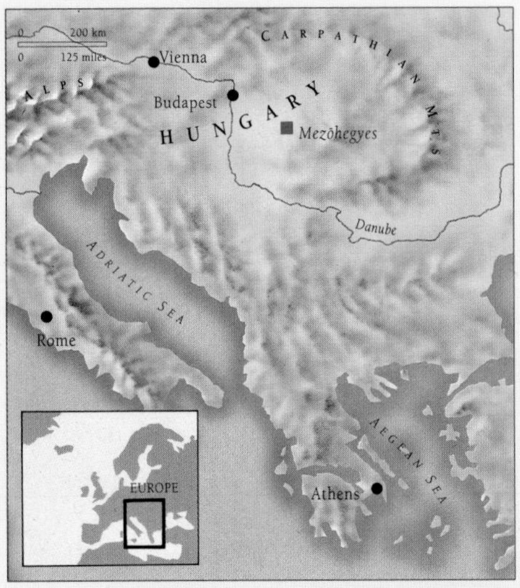

BOTH THE NONIUS AND THE FURIOSO were originally developed at the Hungarian state stud of Mezőhegyes, which is situated in the extreme south-east of the Hungarian plain. However, since 1961, Nonius breeding in Hungary has been centred in Hortobagy, while Nonius horses are also bred in Slovakia at Topolcianky. The Furioso is bred at the old stud of Apajpuszta in Hungary, between the Danube and Tisza Rivers, but is otherwise bred extensively all over Central Europe.

LEGS
Short legs, and obvious strength in the proportions, are characteristics of the older type of Nonius.

SPORTS HORSE
The Hungarian Warmblood has been developed largely at Mezőhegyes as a competition horse. The Nonius and Furioso are used as the base stock and then crossed with Thoroughbreds.

NONIUS

head with small eyes and long ears, a short neck, long back, narrow pelvis, and a low-set tail. However, he was very prolific, and his progeny far surpassed him in conformation.

At first, Nonius was crossed with all kinds of mares – Arabs, Lipizzaners (see pp.112–13), English half-breds, Spanish, and Normans. He sired 15 exceptional stallions, principally the prepotent Nonius IX. During the 1860s more Thoroughbreds were used, to eliminate the remaining physical defects, and the breed was divided into two types. The larger one became a carriage-type or light farm horse. Predominantly bay in colour, it was tough, sound, powerful, and active, with a notably economical movement and an equable nature. It stood at 1.60–1.68 m (15.3–16.2 hh). When crossed with Thoroughbred stallions, the Nonius mares produce all-round riding horses with jumping ability, and greater scope and quality than the pure Nonius. The small type, which carries more Arab blood, works very well both as a riding horse and in harness. The Nonius is long-livedbut is a late developer, not maturing until it is at least six years old.

THE FURIOSO

The Furioso, or Furioso-North Star breed, was also developed at Mezőhegyes, using Nonius mares as a base. Furioso and

TYPICAL STOCK
This is a typical Furioso mare, of good all-round riding type, with her foal at the state stud of Apajpuszta. The breed is popular throughout Europe as a reliable, even-tempered riding horse.

North Star were English Thoroughbred stallions brought to Mezőhegyes in 1841 and 1844 respectively. Furioso sired no less than 95 stallions, which were used at many of the imperial studs. North Star was a grandson of Touchstone, who won the 1834 St Leger and the 1836 and 1837 Ascot Gold Cup. His dam was a granddaughter of Waxy, the 1793 Derby winner who was himself a grandson of Eclipse, and the horse chiefly responsible for perpetuating Eclipse's illustrious line. North Star also had earlier Norfolk Roadster ancestry, but this was less important. Like Waxy, he sired many harness race winners. Later on, more Thoroughbred blood was introduced. The North Star and Furioso lines were kept distinct until 1885, when they began to be crossed. The Furioso strain has since gained the ascendancy.

The Furioso is now a first-class riding horse that stands at about 1.63 m (16 hh), and has many Thoroughbred characteristics. It is sound, hardy, and intelligent, and goes well in harness. It is also a good competition horse. The Furioso is bred all the way from Austria to Poland.

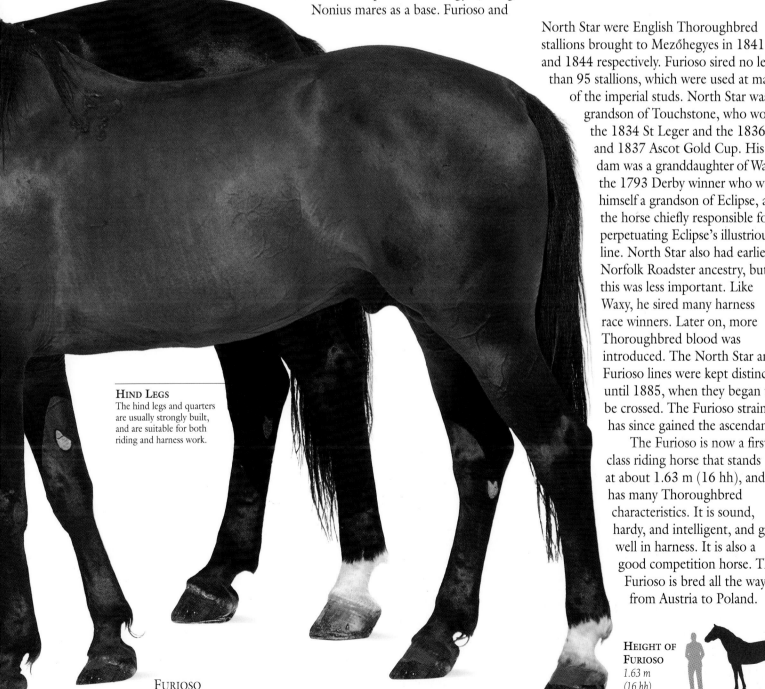

HIND LEGS
The hind legs and quarters are usually strongly built, and are suitable for both riding and harness work.

FURIOSO

HEIGHT OF FURIOSO
1.63 m
(16 hh)

CZECHOSLOVAKIAN WARMBLOOD

THE CZECHOSLOVAKIAN WARMBLOOD, which for the present is still known by this name, is a horse that has been bred primarily for modern competition. Sometimes it may be termed "Czechoslovakian Half-Bred", but essentially it is a horse produced from a reasonably judicious, if very wide-ranging, mix of the Central European breeds. The common factor in these horses, and a most important breeding objective, is that of "rideability". This horse is intended to be suitable for riders of no more than average ability, and should be easily manageable.

NECK
The neck is lean and arched gracefully, running into low, broad withers. The head shows quality.

HEIGHT
1.63–1.68 m
(16–16.2 hh)

DIVERSE INFLUENCES

The constituent elements of the Czechoslovakian Warmblood are the horses bred at the studs in Slovakia and the Czech Republic, such as Topolcianky (see pp.152–53), and more particularly those that evolved at the great stud farms in neighbouring Hungary. The Nonius and Furioso (see pp.156–57), and the Gidran (see pp.76–77), and English "half-breds" based on them, all feature in the make-up of the Czechoslovakian Warmblood, along with the influential Shagya Arab, the pride of Hungary's Bábolna Stud.

The Nonius carried Norman blood, and was also influenced, early on, by the Norfolk Roadster (see pp.122–23). The breed was continually refined by Thoroughbred blood (see pp.120–21) to produce light carriage types and then riding horses. The Furioso, developed at Mezőhegyes in Hungary, was founded on two English Thoroughbreds which were put to heavier Nonius mares. The Gidran, also originating at Mezőhegyes, can be considered as the Hungarian Anglo-

Arab, while the splendid Shagya of Bábolna, the result of 200 years of planned line-breeding, is Arab in nearly all respects, except that it rarely stands less than 1.52 m (15 hh), and has more bone and substance than the fashionable show-ring Arabs. There could hardly be a greater mix of bloods, although all, with the possible exception of the occasional Hanoverian influence, are related to a greater or lesser degree. The so-called Hungarian Warmbloods do not have such a varied background, being to all intents and purposes of Nonius breeding.

KLADRUB
The Czechoslovakian Kladruber is bred in the west of the Czech Republic, at the Kladrub state stud farm close to the German border. The breed was established in the early 18th century as powerful coach horses of majestic appearance to pull the Imperial carriages.

CHARACTERISTICS

The Czechoslovakian Warmblood resulted from this amalgam of bloods, but owing to its mixed ancestry there is no dominant type, nor is it likely that one will emerge in the near future. In most cases, however, there are discernible conformational features relating to the more prepotent elements in the background. For instance, there is a fairly clear legacy from the Arab, which may be seen in the straight line of the croup, the low, broad withers, and the set of the shoulders. The movement, however, is more like that of a light carriage horse (another contributory influence) than the floating action of the Arab. On the whole, the breed is usually strongly built, and has an acceptable, middle-of-the-road, riding horse conformation.

It would be considered as an ideal stamp of cavalry remount, and, in fact, this was the original purpose for many of them. Translated from the military to the civilian context, the Czechoslovakian Warmblood is

"RIDEABLITY"

A primary breed objective for the Czechoslovakian Warmblood is "rideability" and an even temperament. As a result of their background, the horses are generally strongly built.

essentially an attractive, reliable "riding club" horse. It has no special talent for jumping, and little cross-country ability above a good "club level", but it makes an obedient dressage ride and on the whole has paces of a fair quality. It usually stands between 1.63 and 1.68 m (16–16.2 hh), and may be any solid colour.

AN INTERESTING EXAMPLE

The horse depicted on these pages is an excellent and interesting example of Czechoslovakian Warmblood breeding. His sire was by a useful Nonius half-bred stallion of the carriage-horse stamp, out of a mare who may have been similar but whose pedigree, unfortunately, is not documented. Interestingly, the grandsire was out of a dam by a Hanoverian (see pp.144–45), which is perhaps an unexpected outcross, and her dam, in turn, came from a strong North Star-Furioso line with a further line to a Gidran. On the dam's side there are Nonius lines, with one line to a Gidran through her sire's pedigree, while on the distaff side the line is almost wholly Shagya.

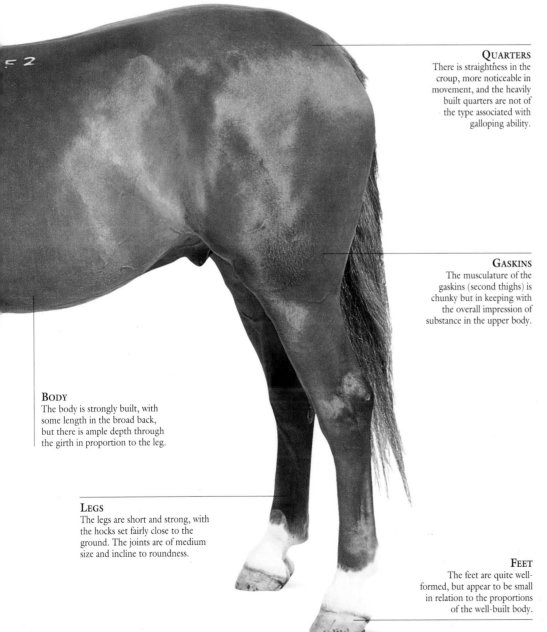

QUARTERS
There is straightness in the croup, more noticeable in movement, and the heavily built quarters are not of the type associated with galloping ability.

GASKINS
The musculature of the gaskins (second thighs) is chunky but in keeping with the overall impression of substance in the upper body.

BODY
The body is strongly built, with some length in the broad back, but there is ample depth through the girth in proportion to the leg.

LEGS
The legs are short and strong, with the hocks set fairly close to the ground. The joints are of medium size and incline to roundness.

FEET
The feet are quite well-formed, but appear to be small in relation to the proportions of the well-built body.

ORIGINS

THE CZECHOSLOVAKIAN WARMBLOOD *is a relative newcomer to the international equestrian scene, although the Topolcianky state stud, in the Nitra district, has bred warmbloods since its establishment in 1921. Much of the breeding is still centred in and around Topolcianky and also, to some extent, in the Novy Tekov state stud, where the Nonius herd was kept. Reliance is placed on the Hungarian studs of Bábolna and Mezőhegyes, the sources of the Shagya, Gidran, and Furioso blood.*

MULE COMPANY

EASTERN STUDS

EAST OF THE Suez Canal there are no studs comparable in grandeur to the long-established breeding centres of Europe, many of which were built when the Austro-Hungarian Empire was at its peak in the 18th and 19th centuries. Nonetheless, there are notable Arab studs all over the Middle East, while more are now being constructed, often on a magnificent scale, in the United Arab Emirates. Further to the east, India and Pakistan maintain army breeding and training centres to supply the large numbers of horses and mules that are still required for military use in both countries. There is a stallion station in Gujerat to encourage breeders of the local Kathiawari (see pp.162–63), and some of the old princely states of Rajasthan still have Marwari breeding studs (see pp.164–65).

ROYAL JORDANIAN STUD

Notable among the Middle Eastern studs is the Royal Jordanian Stud at Amman, founded by the late King Hussein's grandfather Abdullah, who before his accession to the Hashemite throne had fought with Lawrence of Arabia against the Turks in the First World War.

The stud began to be of international significance in 1960 when Santiago Lopez became Master of Horse and with his wife, Ursula, set about revitalizing the bloodlines. Until 1967 the 100 or so Arabs that made up the stud spent the winter at Shuna near the Dead Sea and, according to custom, returned in the summer to Hummar, just outside Amman. The war with Israel in 1967 ended the changing of summer and winter quarters, and at some risk Lopez led the horses back to Amman as hostilities began. Since then the stud has been housed in buildings designed by Ursula Lopez. They have a Spanish flavour and are notable for several original features as well as the beautiful, hand-painted tiles decorating the impressive central drinking trough.

The stud is based on seven foundation mares and seven stallions, six of the mares coming from King Abdullah's stud and the seventh from the Aduan Bedu people. The two most successful stallions were Selman, bred by the Egyptian Agricultural Organization, and Ushaahe, bred in Spain by the Duke of Veragua. The Royal Jordanian stud is also noted for housing one of the world's finest collections of eastern saddlery.

BABUGARH AND SAHARANPUR

In northern India the army stud at Babugarh, and the remount training school and depot at Saharanpur, which celebrated its bicentenary in 1979, both breed troopers (half-bred horses by

SAHARANPUR
The Indian Army Remount Training School and Depot at Saharanpur breeds good quality half-bred troopers as well as general service mules. The school, in northern India, celebrated its bicentenary in 1979.

ROYAL STUD
The Royal Jordanian Stud at Amman was founded by King Abdullah and extended significantly by the late King Hussein. It specializes in carefully selected lines of desert-bred Arabs. The stud was largely rebuilt following the war with Israel in 1967.

FRENCH STALLION AT BABUGARH
This horse is a French-bred Thoroughbred stallion that stood at the Indian Army Stud at Babugarh. The stud has also housed Breton mares for mule production, as well as some Polish mares.

enterprise, as well as the essential training facilities. Surprisingly, perhaps, the army makes little use of the breeds claimed to be indigenous to the sub-continent, the Kathiawari and Marwari. However, the Marwari is well catered for in the Jodhpur and Jaipur areas of Rajasthan, and is now often crossed with Thoroughbreds to give a bigger, scopier horse. The Kathiawari, which is used by many mounted police units, is bred on the Kathiawar peninsula, stallions being made available from the government-run Junagadh Stallion Station in Gujerat.

THOROUGHBRED BREEDING

Thoroughbred breeding is carried on everywhere there is racing, and India is no exception. There are numerous private studs near to the racing centres. In Delhi, for instance, one of the country's leading owners, Major B.P. Singh, has his Guru Hari Stud on the southern outskirts of the city. The stud carries 100 horses, stands two good-class stallions, and operates a full breeding programme as well as racing its stock extensively.

Thoroughbred sires) as well as artillery and general service mules. Babugarh has had some good French and English Thoroughbred stallions (see pp.120–21), Breton horses for mule production (see pp.268–69), and a number of Polish mares, predominantly of the old Masuren and Malapolski type (see pp.154–55).

Saharanpur, the biggest of the Indian military establishments, is primarily a training centre, but has also used similar Polish mares, as well as Argentines, Bretons, and Australian stock. Again, the stallions are English Thoroughbreds, although at one time an Anglo-Arab was used. Haflingers (see pp.52–53) were also imported to produce mules, but do not seem to have withstood the climate well. Saharanpur has also bred good competition horses and polo ponies. It is an impressive complex, extending over 810 hectares (2,000 acres), with its own dairy herd, nursery gardens, and farming

RACING STUD
Shown here is Farajullah, a Thoroughbred horse standing at the Guru Hari Stud of Major B.P. Singh at Delhi. The stud carries some 100 horses, breeding and racing its home stock with great success on the Indian race circuit.

KATHIAWAR SIRE
This Kathiawari stallion, owned by the royal family of Wankaner, Gujerat, is used on local mares in the area.

KATHIAWARI

(see pp.164–65)

T HE KATHIAWARI HORSE IS BRED principally in the Kathiawar Peninsula, an area framed by the Gulfs of Kutch and Khambat on India's north-western coast. It is also found throughout Maharashtra, Gujerat, and southern Rajasthan. Together with the Marwari (see pp.164–65), its northern neighbour in Rajasthan, and the eastern hill ponies, it is regarded as indigenous to the sub-continent.

ORIGINS AND HISTORY

The origins of the breed are not recorded, but well before the time of the Moghul Emperors (1526–1857) a native stock of mixed type existed in the provinces down the western coast as far as Maharashtra. This stock was descended from breeds such as the Kabuli and Baluchi, which came from the north and were related to the steppe and desert horses further to the west and north-west. These breeds often have curved ears and a "dry" head, like the Kathiawari, and some share its pacing ability. In the time of the Moghuls, and later under the British Raj, Arab horses (see pp.64–65) were imported from the Arabian Gulf and the Cape of South Africa. These were crossed with the native stock, itself of "eastern" origin, and therefore also played a major part in the evolution of the Kathiawari.

Traditionally, the princely houses bred these horses selectively; each specialized in its own strain, which was usually named after a foundation mare. Twenty-eight such strains are still recognized. In these noble households the horses were looked upon as favoured pets and acquired a reputation for being intelligent, docile, and affectionate. Less fortunate animals, though, are often of a more uncertain temper.

EARS
The inward-curving ears, touching at their tips, can be moved through a full 360°.

POLICE HORSE
Gujerat mounted police exclusively use Kathiawari horses for patrol work and urban policing. Easily kept, they are also not expensive to purchase.

SHOULDERS
The shoulders are strong and slope to their point from well-formed withers. The neck tapers noticeably up to the head.

LEGS
The legs are hard and sinewy, even if the bone measurement below the knee is not great.

HEIGHT
1.52 m
(15 hh)

The breed is still highly regarded in its native area. Early in the 19th century the "original Kattywar" horse was stated to be superior to all others as a cavalry mount and was used by Mahratta and British cavalry. Today it is employed by police forces throughout India. The Kathiawari Horse Breeders' Association operates a register and puts on annual breed shows. At Junagadh, the Government of Gujerat supports a stallion station and a small brood mare band, and the services of selected stallions are made available to villagers for nominal fees.

QUARTERS
The quarters have a short top line and slope downwards to the dock. The tail is set low and the hocks are held to the rear.

HOCKS
The hocks are serviceable but cow-hocks sometimes occur.

FEET
The feet are sometimes narrow and boxy, but they are hard, and lameness in the feet is a rare occurrence in the Kathiawari.

CHARACTERISTICS

In its general outline, the Kathiawari resembles the Arab. It is distinctive in appearance, and notable features include the highly mobile ears, which curve inwards to touch each other at the tips and can move easily through 360°. The curving ears are a much-prized feature, and in the past they were often cultivated by breeders to the detriment of more important points.

The best Kathiawari specimens are very attractive, especially those less than 1.52 m (15 hh). Over that height coarsening occurs and there is a loss of the essential type. These animals are of good proportions; the limbs are light of bone by western standards, but the breed is inherently sound. Like all horse breeds with a desert background, the Kathiawari is resistant to heat and can survive on minimal rations of feed and water. Less well-bred animals show signs of the degeneration typically associated with hot, dry areas and poor soil. They often have sharply sloping quarters and weak, poorly shaped hindlegs. All colours are found, except black. The most interesting colour is dun, often with a definite dorsal list and distinctive "zebra" bars on the legs. This is a primitive coat pattern, and may suggest a link with the Tarpan (see pp.20–21).

The breed has the innate ability to perform the *revaal*, which is a swift, very comfortable lateral pacing gait. This points to a connection with pacing horses from areas bordering Pakistan's north-west frontiers, such as Turkestan, Afghanistan, and the desert regions of northern Iran. Numerous manuals have been written in the vernacular about the Kathiawari and its characteristics. Almost all, however, may be classed as somewhat fanciful. For example, like the Arab tribes, the Indians place great emphasis on the significance of hair whorls and markings. The 14th-century Hindu book, the *Asva Sastra*, deals with the subject in great detail, warning against the purchase of horses displaying any one of 117 inauspicious marks, including, incongruously, "horns on the head, blue teeth, spotted testicles…",

TENT-PEGGER
Police teams almost always use Kathiawaris for the sport of tent-pegging. A Kathiawari will gallop straight, true, and fast down the pathi, *giving his rider the best chance of striking the peg cleanly.*

as well as numerous hair formations. Village breeders still consider the incidence of hair patterns to be very important, but it is a feature which has little practical relevance to the improvement of the breed.

ORIGINS

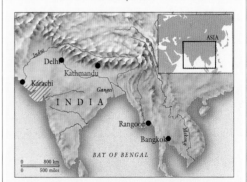

THE DRY, OFTEN ARID KATHIAWAR PENINSULA, on India's western coast, has been renowned for its horses for centuries. The Peninsula lies between the Gulfs of Kutch and Khambat, and is a part of Gujerat state. The hot climate, the shortage of water, and the dry conditions of this environment have produced a "desert-type" horse. The Kathiawari has also been influenced by importations from the Arabian Gulf to the easily accessible ports of the Peninsula between the 17th and 19th centuries.

MARWARI

FOR SEVERAL HUNDRED YEARS, horse-breeding in north-western India was centred on the state of Marwar (Jodhpur). The traditional rulers of Marwar, the Rathores, embodied the ideal of the Rajput warrior, and the Marwari horses enjoyed a reputation equal to that of their riders. Under the Moghul emperor Akbar (1542–1605), the Rajputs of this region formed an Imperial cavalry force of over 50,000 sabres (*Ek Lakh Talwaran Rathoras*). Three centuries later, during the First World War, their descendants, the lancers of Jodhpur commanded by Sir Pratap Singh, with their brothers in arms from Hyderabad and Mysore, led General Allenby's victorious advance to Haifa in 1917.

COLOUR
The range of coat colourings in the Marwari breed runs through bay, brown, and chestnut to part-coloured coat patterns. Occasionally, the palomino colouring also occurs in the breed.

ORIGINS

The earliest origin of the Marwari horse may have been in the areas to the north-west of India, on the borders of Afghanistan – in Uzbekistan and Kazakhstan, and particularly in Turkmenistan. If the breed's ancestors came from these regions, it may have a link with the Mongolian horse (see pp.198–99), as well as with the Arab-type strains that predominate in northern Iran and the steppe lands north of the Black and Caspian seas. The Marwari bears a definite resemblance to the horses of Turkmenistan (see pp.74–75) and the adjacent territories, although none of those breeds have the Marwari horse's distinctive, curving ears. When the Moghuls conquered northern India in the early 16th century, they brought Turkmene-type horses to the area now called Rajasthan, and it is extremely likely that these were used to supplement

HEAD
The head is distinctive because of the ears, but can sometimes be a little heavy.

the Rajput stock. There must also be a connection with the Kathiawari breed of Gujerat (see pp.162–63), which is the neighbour of the Marwari, and as a consequence there is the possibility of more Arab influence from that source, although the Marwari horses retain their own distinctive and recognizable character.

DESERT HORSES
The best Marwari horses are well-built, long-limbed, wiry, and muscular. Their coats are fine and silky and, like the Kathiawari breed, the horses are distinguished by their curved ears.

LEGS
The legs are hard and clean and are not disposed to disease or lameness. The feet are extraordinarily dense and hard-wearing.

HISTORY

The development of the Marwari horse was encouraged by the Rathores, the traditional rulers of Marwar, who kept the finest stallions for the use of their subjects and were carrying out a policy of strict selective breeding as early as the 12th century.

For centuries, before and after the Moghul Empire was founded in 1526, the Indian princes were almost constantly at war with their neighbours. In 1193 the Rathores lost their Kingdom of Kanauj. To regroup, they withdrew to the most inhospitable and remote areas of western India – the Great Indian and Thar deserts.

The possession of horses was vital to their existence, and, like the outcast Ishmael, the ancestor of the Arabian Bedu people (see pp.64–65), they bred horses

BODY
The body is strong and wiry, with muscular loins and depth through the girth.

HIND LEGS
The hocks and hind legs are well-set in the best type of Marwari, but in horses from the country areas there is a tendency to cow-hocks.

selectively to survive, thrive, and operate effectively in the desert environment.

This period gave rise to legends about the breed's endurance, courage, and loyalty, which have become part of the Rajput tradition. The most famous is the story of Chetak, who is commemorated in the altar at Haldi Ghati, the Chetak Chabutra, and in statuary and paintings.

Chetak was the mount of Maharana Pratap of Mewar, and at the battle of Haldi Ghati in 1576 the pair attacked the commander of Akbar's forces, Raja Man Singh, in the howdah of his war-elephant. In a stupendous leap, the equivalent of the High School *capriole*, Chetak enabled his rider to strike at Man Singh with his lance. The thrust missed but the attack was pressed home with Chetak striking the elephant's head with his forefeet. In the *mêlée*, however, Chetak's fetlock was slashed off at the joint. Hotly pursued, Chetak galloped on three legs, ensuring his master's escape by a last enormous leap over the gorge at Haldi Ghati, where this remarkable horse died, his head in the arms of his master.

Today, there is a Chetak Horse Society, and a Horse Fair held at Haldi Ghati. Two aircraft are named after Chetak, as well as a popular make of motor scooter.

By the 1930s, however, the breed had deteriorated and was saved only by the intervention of the Maharaja Umaid Singhji, a work continued

KATHIAWARI HORSE
The Kathiawari breed is related to the Marwari. It is similar to the Marwari in most respects, though it is possibly a little smaller. There is an Arab influence in this Kathiawari.

energetically by his grandson, the present Maharaja Gaj Singh II. A Marwar Horse and Cattle Show is held annually, and there is an active Marwari breeders' association.

CHARACTERISTICS

The best examples of the modern Marwari stand at about 1.50 m (14.3 hh) and are very elegant. This breed is strong, wiry, and well-muscled, with long limbs and very hard feet that rarely need to be shod except in the stoniest areas. The Marwari often has the natural pacing gait, known as *revaal*, which is a feature of many Asian strains, and the tradition of "High School" leaps, far older than that of Europe, is still retained, with performances given at fairs and events.

As with the Kathiawari, great importance is attached to the position of hair whorls on the horse's body. There is also a particular way of determining the correct proportions of the Marwari, based on the width of a finger, which is said to equal five grains of barley. For instance, the length of the face, from the poll to the upper lip, may vary between 28 and 40 fingers, and four times the length of the face is equal to the length from the poll to the dock.

HEIGHT
*1.50 m
(14.3 hh)*

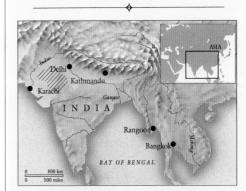

ORIGINS

THE ORIGINS OF THE Marwari horse may lie in the lands around Afghanistan, but since well before the Middle Ages the traditional home of the breed has been in Rajasthan, particularly in the state of Marwar (Jodhpur). The rulers of this state, the princely family of Rathore, were already practising selective breeding in the 12th century. The desert conditions and the extremes of climate have produced a tough horse that is resistant to heat and drought and has an enviable reputation in Rajasthan.

INDIAN HALF-BRED

T HE BREEDING OF HALF-BREDS, by crossing Thoroughbreds with other breeds, is well-established on the sub-continent. Half-breds in India are produced mainly by the Indian army studs, which are responsible for supplying troop horses to cavalry units and sometimes also to mounted formations in the police force. These horses are also bred at private establishments, and many are sold at the various horse fairs that are held in northern and western India. Some of the animals bred at the Indian studs have been successfully sold abroad, to the United Arab Emirates and other states bordering the Arabian Gulf.

HORSE LINES

Polo ponies, many of them good-quality half-bred types, are stabled in open horse lines at Delhi during the polo season. This takes place in the winter and is when the principal tournaments are contested.

FOREIGN INFLUENCES

During the 19th century Indian cavalry at first made use of predominantly Arab-type horses, then later switched to the bigger Australian Waler (see pp.292–93), which was generally regarded as the world's finest cavalry horse. Today, there is little, if any, sign of the Arab horse, although at one time, in the years immediately following the First World War, races for Arabs were staged at the principal Indian racecourses, especially in western India at Bombay, Poona (Pune), and Bangalore. Similarly, the importation of Australian horses has long since ceased. Therefore, in the absence of any indigenous horse breeds other than the Kathiawari (see pp.162–63) and its neighbour the Marwari (see pp.164–65), India has formulated a horse-breeding policy that is dependent on imported stock, particularly the English Thoroughbred (see pp.120–21).

Thoroughbred horses can adapt to the Indian climate more easily than, for instance, warmblood breeds, and when crossed with carefully selected mares they produce troop horses that are well-suited to the country. One example was the stallion Thomas Jefferson, imported from the UK, who was used successfully at Babugarh and Saharanpur (see pp.160–61) for several years. Following the partition of the sub-continent between India and Pakistan in 1947, India kept eight British and four French Thoroughbreds, and these horses provided the base for future breeding.

ORIGINS

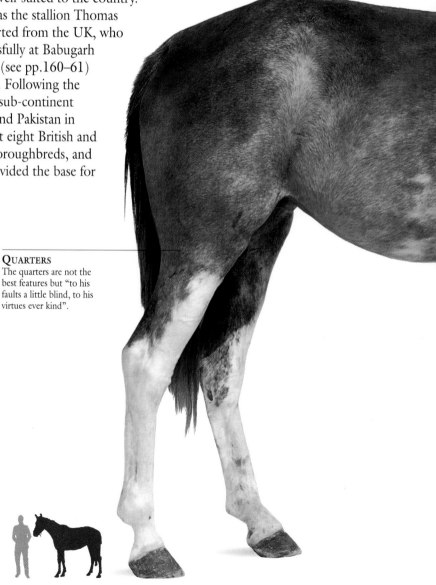

INDIAN HALF-BREDS ARE BRED ALL OVER INDIA, although the climate is not ideal for horse-breeding. The best come from the army remount depot at Saharanpur and from army studs such as Babugarh. They are the products of Thoroughbred crosses with country-bred mares, or, in military breeding establishments, with imported stock, some of it from Poland and Australia. Thoroughbreds are available at the major racing centres at Bombay, Bangalore, Madras, Calcutta, and Delhi.

QUARTERS
The quarters are not the best features but "to his faults a little blind, to his virtues ever kind".

HEIGHT
1.57 m
(15.2 hh)

The army's breeding policy was further developed, in order to produce mules, troop horses, and high-quality competition horses. Some fine Polish mares, of the Masuren (see pp.154–55) and Malapolski types, were used. These were good riding horses and typically Polish in character, with well-made shoulders and limbs, and many of them would have carried a significant percentage of Thoroughbred and Arab blood.

Argentine mares have also played a part, as well as the active French Bretons (see pp.268–69), which were used to produce mules. At one time, Bretons at the Saharanpur horse depot were mated with the old Anglo-Arab horse Mystère, who had an excellent breeding record, to produce some substantial, upstanding carriage horses. Haflingers (see pp.52–53) have been used for mule production, but in general they adapt to the climate less satisfactorily.

THE MODERN HALF-BRED

India is not an ideal country for breeding and raising horses, and there is always the possibility of stock degenerating as a result of the harsh climate, deficiencies of natural

ARMY HALF-BREDS
These are excellent examples of the best type of half-bred produced at the military stud farms. They stand at about 1.57 m (15.2 hh).

minerals in the soil, food shortages, and so on. Nonetheless, the modern Indian half-bred is a much improved horse, and although it sometimes varies a little in type, some specimens are very good indeed. Half-breds are, naturally, medium-sized animals of a hard, wiry sort. They have ample bone, as well as legs and feet that will stand up to continual work on hard ground. In addition, they are both hardy and enduring.

The high standard of horses produced at the army studs undoubtedly results from management of an equally high order. At Saharanpur, for instance, the young horses run in and out of the paddocks at liberty. They are well-fed on carefully balanced rations, and are not broken in until they are four-year-olds. The training period lasts for nine months, and progress is carefully checked each month.

The Indian Army still maintains a significant number of mounted units as well as animal transport companies, while police forces continue to support mounted branches in the towns and cities as well as in the more remote country areas. These purposes are fulfilled by the product of the army studs, but a percentage of the horses find their way to civilian riding clubs in the cities. Increasingly, too, as India and its horsemen became more involved in competitive sports at home and abroad, excellent, tough half- and three-quarter-bred horses are produced for the recognized competitive disciplines.

TOP LINE
The quarters fall away, but the back and withers are reasonably well-formed.

HEAD
This is an acceptable head. There is a suggestion of the curved Kathiawari ears.

FOREHAND
The legs are slender and the neck quite well-formed, although the shoulders are upright and the chest lacks width.

COUNTRY-BRED
This is a country-bred pony of a type common throughout India. Its conformation leaves much to be desired but such ponies are capable of working hard on a very basic ration.

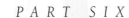

PART SIX

THE INFLUENCE OF THE PONY

INDIGENOUS PONY BREEDS occur throughout Europe, Scandinavia, and Asia, and the better known and more selectively developed are exported to countries that have no native pony population. Essentially, the pony, more so than the horse breeds (with the possible exception of the Arab), is a product of its early environment despite subsequent refinement through human intervention. Its size and proportions apart, the pony has a unique character, and a constitutional strength, that has no counterpart in the horse breeds. In modern times, pony-breeding, for all types of children's competition and for driving, is one of the major equine industries.

A detail from *The Frisky Pony* by
Sir Alfred J. Munnings

NINE BRITISH BREEDS

HIGHLAND PONY

THE NINE NATIVE pony breeds of the UK are often referred to as the Mountain and Moorland breeds, because their original habitats were the wild, sparsely populated moorlands and mountainous areas of Britain. Nowadays there are no longer any truly feral stocks, but many ponies are still kept by their owners in their original, formative environments. All nine breeds are also bred at studs in the UK, as well as elsewhere in the world. The breeds that have survived to the present day are the Exmoor, Dartmoor, New Forest, Welsh, Fell, Dales, Highland, Shetland, and Connemara (see pp.172–85). They represent a unique equine grouping, each breed retaining its own character and appearance while sharing a constitutional strength, hardiness, and innate sagacity that are derived from their environment.

EARLIEST ANCESTORS

Exactly what comprised the primitive ancestry of these ponies is beyond precise definition, but it is possible to perceive a pattern of development. The earliest types of horse – the Asiatic Wild Horse, the Tarpan, and the Forest Horse – as well as the later hypothetical sub-types, Pony Types 1 and 2 and Horse Types 3 and 4 (see pp.22–23), had evolved long before the British Isles separated from Europe during the Ice Age. The last land bridge, which joined Britain and the Scilly Isles, broke down in the Old Stone Age, around 15000 BC, and from that point no further additions to the British equine population could be made for about 14,000 years, an adequate period of time for the development of a fixed character. It is not unreasonable to assume that following that land division the equine population would have consisted of Type 1, and Type 1 crossed with Type 4, as well as some heavier

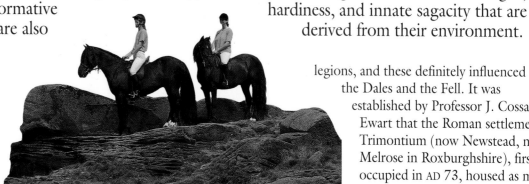
DALES
Today, this sure-footed breed is ideal for pony-trekking over rough country. In the 19th century, Dales ponies carried lead ore from moorland mines to the ports at the mouth of the Tyne. They were also used in coal mines and as pack ponies.

specimens from Type 2, or Type 1 crossed with Type 2. The presence of any element of Horse Types 3 and 4, animals resistant to heat and unsuited to the cold, is unlikely.

IMPORTED HORSES

It was not until the Bronze Age (c.1000 BC), when ships were being built that were big and strong enough to transport cattle and horses, that any other types of horse were seen in Britain. For example, there is evidence of horses being brought to Britain from Scandinavia, and it is almost certain that the Shetland came from there. The Shetland's diminutive stature was fixed by both the pressure and the isolation of its habitat, which also precluded the possibility of outcrosses. The Dales, Fell, and Highland ponies, on the other hand, would all have benefited from stock brought in by Scandinavian marauders, both during the Bronze Age and later. In Roman times, Friesian horses (see pp.48–49) were imported by the Frieslanders, the auxiliary horsemen employed as flank-guards to the legions, and these definitely influenced both the Dales and the Fell. It was established by Professor J. Cossar Ewart that the Roman settlement at Trimontium (now Newstead, near Melrose in Roxburghshire), first occupied in AD 73, housed as many as 1,000 horses. The remains of six principal equine types were found there: a horse resembling a Tarpan, which Ewart named the Celtic pony; two types similar to the Exmoor, one eastern in character, and the other a heavier specimen like the Forest Horse; a Shetland-like type; a bigger type like an Arab; and some larger, heavy horses with coarse heads, probably of Forest Horse derivation. This was the melting pot from which, in the course of less than 2,000 years, the Mountain and Moorland ponies emerged. After the Romans left, the next significant outcrosses to oriental blood were made possible around the 13th century, by the Phoenicians, who sold eastern horses along their western trade routes.

DARTMOOR
The action of the Dartmoor Pony is notable for its lack of lift at the knees. As a result, the breed's movement is long, low, and economical – typical hack or riding horse action.

FELL
The swift Fell Pony is the modern equivalent of the extinct Scottish Galloway. This Fell mare has a well-grown foal with noticeably good limbs. It has the typical breadth across the forehead.

such as those for the Connemara, Highland, Fell, Dartmoor, and Exmoor, have not been running for much more than 60–70 years.

What is left are nine breeds that have been "improved" over the centuries, but which, nonetheless, retain special qualities that result from environmental influences and a long period of geographical isolation from mainland Europe. The environment governs the size and character of each breed, and also influences movement. In addition, the sparseness of naturally available feed ensures a remarkably efficient nutrient conversion. Isolation results in the retention of the hardiness, prepotency, and the strong constitution of their primitive forebears. This natural vigour is not nearly so evident in later breeds that have been invented by humans for a particular purpose.

CONNEMARA
The Connemara's original habitat, on the west coast of Ireland, accounts for its exceptional hardiness. It is a brilliant riding pony and a superb jumper.

EXTINCT PONIES

In the past there were more British pony breeds than the nine that are recognized today. These included the Lincolnshire Fen ponies – rough, unprepossessing specimens, suited to the wet, inhospitable environment of the Fenlands; the enduring Goonhilly of Cornwall; the swift Irish Hobby; and the Scottish Galloway, which was famous as the mount of the Border raiders. These ponies became extinct either because there was no further use for them in a changing society, or because they were absorbed by more fashionable strains. The Fen Pony, for example, went into swift decline following the Fen drainage schemes carried out by Dutch engineers in the 17th century, while the Galloway began to be absorbed into the Fell Pony a century later. Once, too, in the 17th century there was a Lincolnshire Trotter, which was used as a coach horse, and during the same period there was also a Devonshire Pack Horse.

BREEDING AND STUD BOOKS

Even before the Roman occupation of Britain, selective breeding and outcrossing were an accepted way of improving stock and fixing type, and there is no doubt that before the establishment of stud books Britain's pony stock was already being "improved" or "modernized" to accord with a prevailing demand and circumstance. Only the Exmoor and the Shetland, which lived in more isolated regions than the other pony breeds, may be exceptions.

Today, the breed societies maintain stud books and ensure that all the stock that is entered is pure-bred. However, none of these societies is yet 100 years old, and some,

NEW FOREST SALES
The sales of New Forest ponies have been held at Beaulieu Road since 1941. Previously they were held at Martinstown Fair, Dorset, and then at Ringwood, Lyndhurst and Brockenhurst in the New Forest.

WELSH COB
During the 19th century Welsh Cobs were used almost as much under saddle as in harness. This picture, painted by Edward Tolley in 1887, portrays an excellent representative of the breed.

FELL & DALES

THESE TWO BREEDS ORIGINATED IN THE NORTH OF ENGLAND, on either side of the Pennine hills. The heartland of the Fell Pony encompasses the northern and western edges of the Pennines, along with the moorlands of Westmorland and Cumberland. The neighbouring, and related, Dales Pony belongs to the eastern side of the country, and is found in North Yorkshire, Northumberland, and Durham. In fact, both breeds are branches descended from the same root, though they developed slightly differently according to the uses made of them, with the Fell evolving as a smaller and lighter animal than the Dales.

SHEPHERDS' PONY
Dales ponies can be used for all sorts of work on the farm. They can draw a harrow, go in harness, or be used under saddle by shepherds.

FOUNDATION BREEDS

There can be little doubt that the black, cold-blooded Friesian (see pp.48–49), a descendant of Europe's primitive Forest Horse, was an early ancestor of these breeds. The greatest influence, however, is that of the strong, swift Galloways, and it remains particularly evident in the modern Fell Pony.

GALLOWAY STOCK
The modern Fell derives in part from the swift Galloway of the 19th century, and is probably very similar in appearance to its forebear.

The Galloway was the mount of the border raiders, and then of the Scottish drovers who brought their cattle into England. It was bred between Nithsdale and the Mull of Galloway, and though extinct since the 19th century, the sterling qualities it bequeathed to British stock are still evident. The Galloway stood at 1.32–1.42 m (13–14 hh), was hardy and sure-footed, had great stamina, and was very fast. It was probably among the native stock which, when used with the eastern sires of the 17th and 18th centuries, gave rise to the English Thoroughbred (see pp.120–21). The most famous of the early Fell foundation

HEIGHT OF FELL
Up to 1.42 m (14 hh)

QUARTERS
The quarters and the second thighs are strongly muscled.

WITHERS
The withers are not fine, but the shoulders are laid-back and sloped, ensuring a smart, not over-high action. The body is deep, round-ribbed, and well-coupled.

HOCKS
The hocks are set low, and are powerfully flexed when the pony moves. Fell ponies never have sickle- or cow-hocks.

FEET
The feet are round and well-formed, open at the heels, with hard, blue horn. The heels carry fine feather.

FELL

stallions was the 18th-century Lingcropper, who was probably a Galloway. He was found during the Jacobite rising of 1745 "cropping the ling" (eating the heather) at Stainmore, Westmorland, still carrying his saddle.

THE FELL PONY

In its homeland, the Fell Pony is often referred to as the Brough Hill Pony because of its association with the Brough Hill Fair.

It was traditionally used as a pack pony, like its neighbour the Dales. Moreover, the Fell was, and still is, a tremendous trotter that was used as much under saddle as in harness. Today, it is much sought after in its own right for both riding and driving, and in addition it is an excellent cross to produce horses of competition potential. Through the Wilson ponies (see pp.402–3), it was also a foundation breed for the modern Hackney Pony. The Fell does not exceed 1.42 m (14 hh) in height. The breed colours are black, brown, and bay, preferably with no white markings apart from an occasional star. Grey is allowed, but is not often found.

THE DALES PONY

The Dales Pony, from the upper Dales in northern England, is larger and heavier than the Fell. It provided power in the lead mines of Allendale and Alston Moor, working underground and carrying lead ore to the Tyne seaports. The ponies were also used in coal mines, on farms, and in pack trains. They were, and are, able to bear loads out of proportion to their size; the average weight that they had to carry was 100 kg (2 cwt). The old Dales was a great trotter in harness or under saddle, and could cover 1.6 km (1 mile) in three minutes while carrying considerable weight. To heighten trotting ability Welsh Cob blood (see pp.184–85), in particular that of the trotting stallion Comet, was introduced in the 19th century. The Dales was also crossed with Clydesdales (see pp.286–87), although this was not a success. Indeed, by 1917 the breed was regarded as being two-thirds Clydesdale.

The modern Dales Pony, in which the Clydesdale influence is no longer apparent, has excellent bone and limbs, and hard, blue feet. It is a brilliant harness pony, and is also used for riding, particularly for trekking. The breed combines courage and stamina with a calm temperament.

HEAD
The head is fairly small and finely chiselled in outline. It is broad across the forehead, and tapers to the muzzle.

SHOULDERS
The shoulders are heavier than those of the Fell, laid-back, and very deep.

HEAD
Although larger than the Fell's, the head is neat, wide between the eyes with small ears.

BODY
There is good depth at the girth, and the ribs are well-sprung. The Dales has a short back and very strong, broad loins. The overall outline should be compact.

LOWER LEGS
The cannons are short and flat, with not less than 20 cm (8 in) of bone. The lower legs carry abundant, fine, silky feather. The feet are excellent.

DALES

HEIGHT OF DALES
1.47 m (14.2 hh)

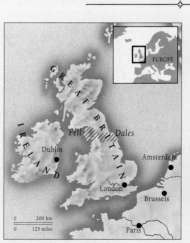

ORIGINS

FELL AND DALES ponies are bred in various parts of the UK, but their traditional breeding areas are in the northern counties of England. The Fell Pony is said to belong to the northern edges of the Pennines and the high moorlands of Cumbria to the west. The genetically related Dales Pony is from the eastern Pennines – Durham, Northumberland, and North Yorkshire. The steep, rocky terrain and harsh climate have made the ponies sure-footed and hardy. They are economical to keep, and, like all moorland stock accustomed to forage on minimal plant growth of low nutrient value, are efficient convertors of food into energy.

EUROPE

GREAT BRITAIN

IRELAND

Fell · Dales

Dublin

Amsterdam

London

Brussels

Paris

0   200 km
0   125 miles

DARTMOOR & EXMOOR

THE WILD MOORLANDS OF SOUTH-WESTERN ENGLAND are home to two very different breeds of pony. The beautiful Dartmoor has been subjected to numerous outcrosses during its history. Its environment was easily accessible by land and sea, and many different breeds were brought in and so influenced the native ponies. In contrast, the Exmoor, which is the oldest of the British Mountain and Moorland ponies, has remained pure since prehistoric times, as the remoteness of its habitat ensured the breed's immunity from influence by alien blood.

ELEGANCE
Shown here are a Dartmoor mare and foal. The Dartmoor is considered to be one of the most elegant riding ponies in the world. It also jumps well.

THE DARTMOOR PONY

Up to the end of the 19th century, the Dartmoor ponies were crossed with a great variety of outside blood. The moor ponies of the day may not have been attractive, but equestrian authorities commented favourably on their jumping ability and good shoulders. At the height of the Industrial Revolution, Shetland stallions (see pp.178–79) were turned out on the moor to produce pit ponies, and as a result the tough Dartmoor of good riding type almost disappeared. After that disastrous experiment, though, the breed was saved by the introduction of Welsh Mountain Ponies (see pp.182–83), a Fell (see pp.172–73), and the polo pony stallion Lord Polo.

The greatest influence on the Dartmoor's development was The Leat, a stallion by the Arab, Dwarka (foaled in 1922), bred by the remarkable Miss Sylvia Calmady-Hamlyn, Honorary Secretary of the Dartmoor Pony Society for 32 years. The Leat's daughter,

HEAD
The head is small and refined, well-set on the neck with no fleshiness through the jowl. The ears are small and alert.

HEAD
The forehead is wide, with prominent, wide-set eyes. Other features are the mealy muzzle and wide nostrils. The ears are short.

HEIGHT OF DARTMOOR
1.27 m
(12.2 hh)

LOWER LEGS
The lower legs have short cannons with sufficient bone, flat joints, and perfectly sloping pasterns.

DARTMOOR

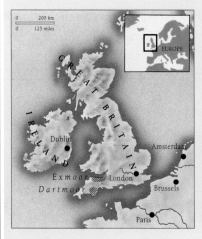

ORIGINS

THE DARTMOOR AND EXMOOR *ponies have their natural habitat on the wild moorlands in the south-west of England. The Exmoor, though not as numerous as in previous times, still lives and breeds on the moor; few are bred away from their natural environment. There are still ponies on Dartmoor, but most are scrub stock. The popular Dartmoor is bred extensively at studs in the UK and mainland Europe. Unlike the Dartmoor, the Exmoor has changed little over the centuries and over that period of time has, with its double coat, hooded eyes, and long nasal passages, developed an effective weather-proofing system.*

Juliet IV, mated with the Welsh Mountain Pony Dinarth Spark, produced Jude, the most famous Dartmoor stallion of all.

During the Second World War when the moor was used as a training area, the breed was again close to extinction, and only two males and 12 females were offered for registration between 1941 and 1943. Miraculously, the Dartmoor was saved again by the efforts of a few dedicated breeders. In the 1920s there were three distinct herds on the moor, but most of today's Dartmoors are bred on private studs throughout the UK.

This chequered history, and this mixture of disparate bloods, have produced one of the most elegant riding ponies in the world.

Together with the Welsh, the Dartmoor has dominated the riding pony classes and has contributed significantly to the development of the British Riding Pony (see pp.406–7). It is very popular in Europe, and in Belgium the ponies are even raced. It jumps as well as its forebears, but now with more scope, and it can be successfully crossed with the Thoroughbred and the Arab. The second cross with the Thoroughbred produces a top cross-country horse or hunter.

The height of the modern Dartmoor is limited to 1.27 m (12.2 hh). No colours are barred, other than skewbald or piebald, but bay, black, and brown are preferred. The action, on account of the good shoulders, is notable among the pony breeds. It is low, long, and economical – "typical hack or riding action", as the breed standard states.

THE EXMOOR PONY

The Exmoor's principal ancestor is believed to be Pony Type 1 (see pp.22–23). Like that primeval pony, the Exmoor has a distinctive jaw formation, and the beginnings of a seventh molar, which are found in no other equine. Other characteristic features include the unique hooded "toad" eye, the "ice" tail, which has a thick, fan-like growth of short hair at the top, and the virtually double-textured coat.

MOOR PONIES
The strong, independent Exmoor Pony is well able to cope with the difficulties and hazards of its stark environment.

SHOULDERS
The shoulders are laid-back, and the shoulder blades are close at the withers.

BODY
The body is compact and deep at the girth, with a level back and breadth over the loins. The ribs are long and well spaced.

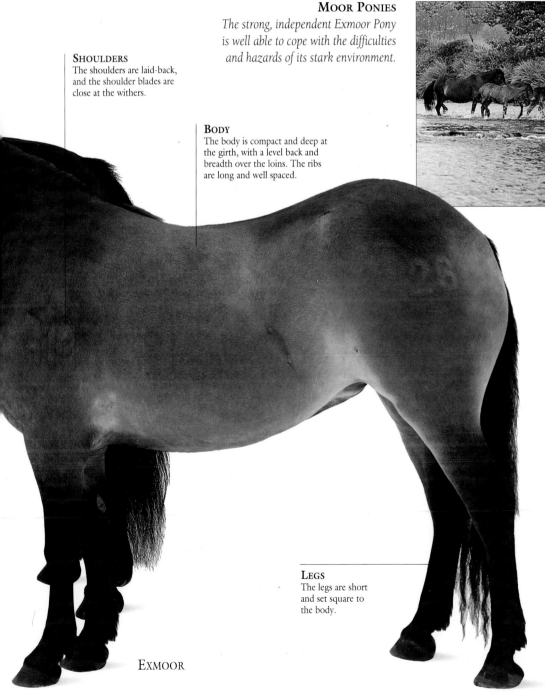

EXMOOR

LEGS
The legs are short and set square to the body.

In the Bronze Age, the Exmoor was used to pull chariots. Thereafter, it became a saddle horse, and it is capable of carrying a man hunting. Between the World Wars, it was used as a child's pony and although in that role its popularity has waned, if properly schooled it is a grand, tough pony for a keen child or a small adult. As harness ponies the Exmoors can be easily matched, and they have great stamina. They also make valuable base stock for the breeding of bigger horses.

There are still herds on Exmoor, whose purity is jealously guarded by breeders and by the Exmoor Pony Society. Small numbers are bred away from the moor, but they tend to lose type outside their natural habitat. The coat is bay, brown, or dun, with black points and a mealy colouring on the muzzle, round the eyes, and on the inside of the flanks. There are no white markings. The height for stallions and geldings is 1.30 m (12.3 hh), and for mares 1.27 m (12.2 hh).

HEIGHT OF EXMOOR
*1.27–1.30 m
(12.2–12.3 hh)*

NEW FOREST PONY

NONE OF THE BRITISH NATIVE BREEDS has a genetic background as varied as that of the New Forest Pony, but then none belongs to so accessible a habitat. Before the Norman Conquest in AD 1066, when Winchester in the west was England's capital city, the New Forest, in south-west Hampshire, was passed through by anyone travelling in that direction. This provided many opportunities for the ponies to mate with domestic stock, either animals passing through the forest or horses kept locally. Nevertheless, the environment did produce a distinctive type.

FOREST STOCK
This mare and foal are in their natural habitat. The New Forest stock still lacks fixed type, and there is some variation in the height.

HISTORY

We know from the Forest Law of Canute, proclaimed in Winchester in 1016, that there were ponies in the forest at that time. After the Norman Conquest, William Rufus (1087–1100) made the New Forest a royal hunting ground, preserving the deer and also consolidating the Rights of Common Pasture for those occupying forest land.

The first recorded attempt to up-grade the stock was made in 1208, when 18 Welsh mares were introduced. However, the most distinguished outside influence on the New Forest Ponies was that of the Thoroughbred, Marske, even though the long-term effect of his stay in the forest area may be debatable. Marske came to the forest in 1765, after the dispersal of the studs belonging to HRH The Duke of Cumberland. Like all the Thoroughbreds of the time he would not have stood more than 1.47 m (14.2 hh). He had no success on the racecourse, but he was the sire of Eclipse, arguably the greatest racehorse of all time. Eclipse established his

HEAD
The head is sometimes rather horse-like.

reputation in his first racing season in 1769, and Marske was immediately rescued from obscurity to stand at stud in Yorkshire.

The people living in the forest may have practised some form of selective breeding in the following years, but by the 19th century the stock had degenerated to a point where it was necessary to take positive action. In 1852 Queen Victoria lent the Arab stallion Zorah, but in four years he covered only 112 selected mares. The deterioration of the

TRAFFIC-PROOF
The New Forest Ponies have no fear of traffic. Many frequent the verges of the roads, in the hope of being fed by tourists, a practice to be discouraged.

HEIGHT
1.22–1.47 m
(12.2–14 hh)

New Forest Ponies continued as a result of in-breeding within the herds. A stallion premium scheme was set up, and in 1889 Queen Victoria lent two more stallions, the Arab Abeyan and the Barb Yirrassan. They had more influence, particularly through a son of Abeyan out of a Welsh mare.

IMPROVING THE STOCK

Degeneration would probably have occurred again had it not been for the intervention of Lord Arthur Cecil and Lord Lucas. In order to correct the Forester's lack of substance, bone, and hardiness, Cecil brought in huge amounts of native blood, using ponies from the Isle of Rùm (Black Galloways) and other Highlands (see pp.178–79), Dales, Fells, Dartmoors, Exmoors, and Welsh (see pp.172–75 and pp.182–85). Lucas added the famous Welsh Starlight blood through his Picket ponies, and also used Dartmoors, Exmoors, and Fells. He even introduced a

FOREST FEED
Water, marsh, and bog are features of the New Forest. The terrain provides a sufficient, if not plentiful, diet of coarse grasses together with bramble and gorse tips.

Basuto Pony (see pp.208–9) that he had brought back from South Africa, although no discernible influence can be attributed to it.

MODERN FOUNDATION SIRES

The *éminence grise* of the breed was the polo pony Field Marshall. He stood in the New Forest in 1918–19, and appears significantly in the lines of the famous Brookside ponies. After the Second World War there emerged a group of

five stallions that are recognized as being the founding sires of the modern breed. These horses, found in the pedigrees of the best modern Foresters, are Danny Denny, with a line to Dyoll Starlight; Goodenough, out of a Welsh type dam reputedly by Field Marshall; Brooming Slipon, a chestnut by Telegraph Rocketer out of Judy XV; Brookside David, descended from Field Marshall; and Knightwood Spitfire, by Brookside Spitfire out of Weirs Topsy, whose sire was the black Highland, Clansman, from whom all dun strains in the Foresters are thought to descend.

CHARACTERISTICS

It is possible to detect some of the various contributing elements in the New Forest; for instance, the heads can still be rather horse-like. There remains a definite variation in height: forest-bred ponies may be as small as 1.22–1.27 m (12–12.2 hh), but the stud-bred Forester can reach 1.47 m (14.2 hh). Nonetheless, the environmental influence is apparent. While conformational weaknesses are still evident in the forest-bred ponies, they are largely offset by very good riding shoulders. The Forester is naturally sure-footed. It has a longer stride than most other native ponies, and is notable for the easy smoothness of its canter, a characteristic encouraged by the terrain of the forest and not nearly so apparent in the other native British breeds. The breed society, which produced its own stud book in 1960, is the New Forest Breeding and Cattle Society. It permits any coat colour except piebald, skewbald, and blue-eyed cream.

QUARTERS
The quarters and hind legs are symmetrical, and the tail is set high.

LEGS
The legs are slender but strong, and the action is long, low, and free.

ORIGINS

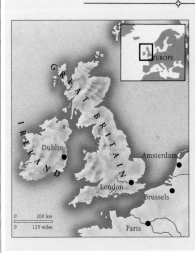

THE VERSATILE AND POPULAR New Forest Pony is bred at studs throughout the UK and mainland Europe. Its original habitat is the New Forest in south-west Hampshire. This tract of land was the royal hunting ground of England's Norman kings in the 11th century. Herds of ponies, which are the property of the Commoners, still live in the forest, and are subject to the inevitable influence of a natural environment. Unhappily, they are also affected by modern pressures on the environment, which result in a reduction of the available grazing areas and a deterioration in the quantity and quality of the feed supporting them.

SHETLAND & HIGHLAND

THE FAR NORTH OF THE BRITISH ISLES is home to two ancient pony breeds, the Shetland and the Highland. The Shetland Pony, which is thought to have existed since the Bronze Age, evolved on the Shetland Islands, about 160 km (100 miles) off the north coast of Scotland. The Highland Pony comes from northern Scotland and the Western Isles. It has prehistoric origins, but throughout its history there have been many outside influences on the native stock.

HEAD
The head is fine and tapered, very broad across the forehead, and short between the eyes and the muzzle.

COLOUR
The dun colour is an attractive feature. It is always accompanied by black points and usually by a list, or dorsal stripe.

THE SHETLAND PONY

The Shetland is the smallest of the British breeds, averaging only 1.02 m (40 in) at the wither. (The Shetland is always measured in inches rather than hands, although the metric measurement is now increasingly used.) The basic coat colour is black; other common colours are brown and chestnut, and grey, skewbald, and piebald also occur.

The breed's origins are not known, but there was probably a connection between ponies of Tundra type (see p.23) and the

ponies were employed as pack and harness animals, and could also be ridden by full-grown men. They were exported for use in harness and as children's ponies, in circuses, and as attractions in public parks or in the grounds of great houses. Following the Act of 1847 that prohibited the use of women and children in coal-mines there was a huge demand for Shetlands as pit ponies, and for that purpose a heavier,

MANE
The mane, like the tail, is very thick, to provide protection against the weather.

SHOULDERS
The shoulders are powerful, and there is a good slope to them.

IN THE WILD
These Shetlands are in their natural environment. Coat colours that occur in the island stock include black, piebald, skewbald, chestnut, and grey.

Scandinavian stock. In the 2nd and 3rd centuries AD there would have been some eastern influence, through ponies from Celtic settlements. Later came the Vikings, who imported their own ponies. Carved stones on Bressay and Burra, dated to about the end of the 9th century, show men riding light-boned, active ponies that, compared with the human figures, could not have exceeded 1.02 m (40 in) in height.

In proportion to its size, the diminutive Shetland is among the most powerful equines in the world. On the islands the

coarser animal was developed alongside the existing type. The breed is now consistent in type, and has excellent proportions.

The Shetland Pony has been exported all over the world. The US, Canada, and Europe have large populations, and operate their own stud books, and there are probably more Shetlands in the Netherlands than in any other country. In North America the breed has been crossed with the Hackney Pony (see pp.402–3) to create the smart American Shetland (see pp.244–45), and with the Appaloosa (see pp.226–27) to

SHETLAND

produce the Pony of the Americas (see pp.242–43). In Argentina the Shetland was used as the base for the pygmy Falabella.

THE HIGHLAND PONY

It has been suggested that the ponies living in northern Scotland after the Ice Age were derived from Pony Type 2 (see p.22), which resembled the Asiatic Wild Horse, possibly crossed with Pony Type 1, which was similar to the Exmoor. Archaeological evidence shows that horses were imported from Scandinavia during the Bronze Age, and later from Iceland. Around 1535 the size and quality of the breed was improved by French horses, which would have included ancestors of the Percheron. Spanish horses, such as those imported by the Chief of Clanranald to improve the Uist ponies, were used in the 17th and 18th centuries. A Norfolk Roadster-type Hackney was brought to

the Isles in 1870, and had a particular influence on the Arran ponies, and the odd Dales and Fell were also used.

The addition of eastern blood had the greatest impact of all. The Duke of Atholl, whose stock became a cornerstone of the breed, used eastern horses in the 16th century, and the Calgary strain, evolved by J.H. Monroe-Mackenzie on Mull, was based on the Arab horse, Syrian. The Macneils of Barra also used Arabs (see pp.64–65), and bred small, light, fast, Arab-type ponies.

On the crofts, the Highland was used in draught, under pack, and was also ridden. It was easy to keep, strong, healthy, and sure-footed. In the hills the ponies were ridden; they also carried game panniers, and deer carcases weighing up to 114 kg (252 lb). This last task says a lot for their unflappable nature, as few horses will calmly carry a dead animal. The modern Highland is an ideal family pony; although not fast, it is safe and a willing jumper. It is also popular in pony-trekking, because of its size and docility.

Until recently there were two types: one bred on the Western Isles, and a heavier one bred on the mainland. This difference has now disappeared. The breed has a height limit of 1.47 m (14.2 hh). In the 19th century the ponies, especially on the islands, were about a hand smaller; the present size may have resulted from crossing with Clydesdales (see pp.286–87), to produce strong animals for forestry work. The coat colours, include grey, brown, black, the "primitive" dun with an eel stripe and often zebra-barred legs, and the striking dark, or "bloodstone", chestnut, with a silver mane and tail.

PONIES OF THE WESTERN ISLES
The Isle of Rùm is renowned for its distinctive strain of Highland pony. This group includes dun ponies with the typical black points.

QUARTERS
The quarters are well-formed and run into broad loins and a short, fairly wide back.

HIGHLAND

HEIGHT OF SHETLAND
1.02 m
(40 in)

HIND LEGS
The tail is set high in the quarters, and the hind legs are correct in their proportions.

HEIGHT OF HIGHLAND
Up to 1.47 m
(14.2 hh)

ORIGINS

THE ORIGINAL HABITAT of the Shetland Pony was the Shetland Islands. However, today, the US, Canada, and several European countries have large numbers of Shetlands, with the Netherlands having the most. The small stature of the ponies accords with the inhospitable environment and the frugal keep it affords, their small body surface resulting in a commensurately lower level of heat loss. The Highland Pony is the all-purpose horse of the Scottish Highlands and Islands, in particular of the Western Isles. Ponies are now bred extensively over the border in England, and there is a strong enclave in the south-west of the UK.

CONNEMARA

THE CONNEMARA PONY, Ireland's only indigenous breed, originated in Connemara on the west coast. Before the arrival of Celtic raiders and traders in the 5th and 6th centuries BC, these ponies were similar to the ponies that now inhabit Shetland, Norway, and Iceland. An eastern-type influence was introduced by the Celts, who maintained links with other Celtic tribes in mainland Europe, including the Brigantes tribe in Spain. In the 16th century, when Galway City was an important trading centre, rich merchants reinforced the Spanish element by importing the best horses from Iberia (see pp.108–9).

NATURAL ENVIRONMENT
These Connemara Ponies are living wild in their native habitat, on the rough moorlands and coastal areas of Galway in western Ireland.

HISTORY

The Connemara has long been famous for the "easiness" of its gaits – "easiness" in this context refering to a pacing or ambling gait. The existence of such a gait underlines the link between the Irish Hobby (the Connemara of the 16th and 17th centuries) and the ambling Spanish Jennet, which was held in high esteem throughout Europe.

"Arab" blood (more likely to have been Barb – see pp.66–67) was brought into Connemara by various landowners during the 19th century. However, by the end of the century the Connemara had deteriorated in quality because of the impoverishment of the farming communities. In an attempt to redress this problem, Welsh Cob stallions (see pp.184–85) were introduced under government horse-breeding schemes, and in 1897 a Royal Commission, headed by Professor J. Cossar Ewart of Edinburgh, was set up to examine horse-breeding in Ireland.

This Commission marked the emergence of the modern Connemara. The comments of those giving evidence to the Commission, as well as the opinions expressed by Ewart himself, are worthy of note. The latter described the old dun type of Connemara pony as " strong and hardy as mules . . . fertile and free from disease" and "capable of living where all but wild ponies would starve". Samuel Usher Roberts CB declared in his evidence that the Connemara ponies were "without exception the best animals I ever knew . . . an extremely hardy, wiry class of pony showing a great deal of the Barb or Arab blood". A leading expert, Lord Arthur Cecil, commented in 1900 on the good riding shoulders and "marked natural proclivity for jumping", which are still the hallmarks of the modern Connemara. Thoroughbred, Roadster, and Hackney blood were introduced (see pp.120–23 and pp.402–3) on the advice of the commission. However, the

QUARTERS
The quarters are well-formed with the tail set high. There is great strength in the broad loins.

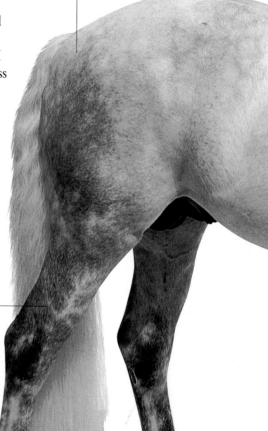

HIND LEGS
Pronounced second thighs and well-placed, strong hocks give galloping and jumping ability.

(see pp.108–9)

ORIGINS

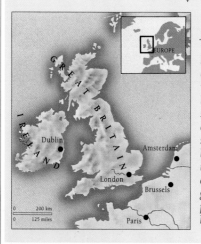

THE CONNEMARA PONY takes its name from the part of Ireland that lies to the west of Loughs Corrib and Mask, an area bounded by Galway Bay to the south and facing the Atlantic Ocean to the west. It is a wild, empty land of bogs, lakes, and mountains, and the ponies subsist on rough herbage in conditions of some severity. However, there are several compensatory factors, such as a long season of plant growth, and a soil that is thin but rich in phosphates and other minerals that are necessary for growth. This environment has produced ponies that are remarkable for their hardiness, strength, and endurance.

Connemara Pony Breeders' Society was not established until 1923, and a stud book was only set up in 1926. The English Connemara Pony Society was formed in 1947, and now has its own stud book. There are also Connemara Societies in the US, Australia, Sweden, Denmark, Holland, and France.

FOUNDATION SIRES

Two great influences on the Connemara are acknowledged to be the stallions Rebel and Golden Gleam, foaled in 1922 and 1932 respectively. However, the most memorable and the most colourful influence is probably the grey stallion Cannon Ball, sired by Dynamite out of a native mare and grandson of the Welsh Cob, Prince Llewellyn. Born in 1904, Cannon Ball was the first stallion to be recorded in the 1926 stud book. He won the Farmers' Race at Oughterard 16 years running. A local story has it that he was fed half a barrel of oats the night before the race – a practice that speaks volumes for his constitution and digestion. He worked in harness throughout his life and was known to trot home from market while his owner, Harry Toole, slept off the effects of a bout of heavy drinking in the bottom of the cart. Cannon Ball's death was marked by a traditional Irish wake that lasted the whole night through, before he was laid to rest in his field at dawn.

LATER INFLUENCES

Later, important influences included the stallion Carna Dun (1948–73), who was by the Thoroughbred Little Heaven (the sire of Ireland's famous international show jumper, the pony Dundrum), and the Irish Draught, Mayboy. More Arab blood was introduced through Clonkeehan Auratum (1954–76), who was by the pure-bred Arab, Naseel, one of the founders of the British Riding Pony (see pp.406–7). In the 1953 stud book there was another stallion of Welsh origin, named Dynamite (after Cannon Ball's sire), another Irish Draught, Skibbereen, and a grey Thoroughbred, Winter, who was by Manna out of Snowstorm. At one time there was a less desirable Clydesdale influence.

BREED CHARACTERISTICS

From this amalgam the Connemara has emerged as a brilliant performance pony. When crossed with Thoroughbeds or Arabs, it produces the best type of cross-country horse, which retains all the hardiness and constitutional soundness derived from the Connemara's wild environment. Without exception these ponies are all of real riding type and quality, but of course can still be used in harness. They are also suitable for adults, as they stand up to 1.47 m (14.2 hh). Many have as much as 17.5–20 cm (7–8 in) of bone below the knee, and most of them are excellent jumpers. Colours include grey, black, bay, brown, and a hard, primitive dun. Occasionally roans and chestnuts appear.

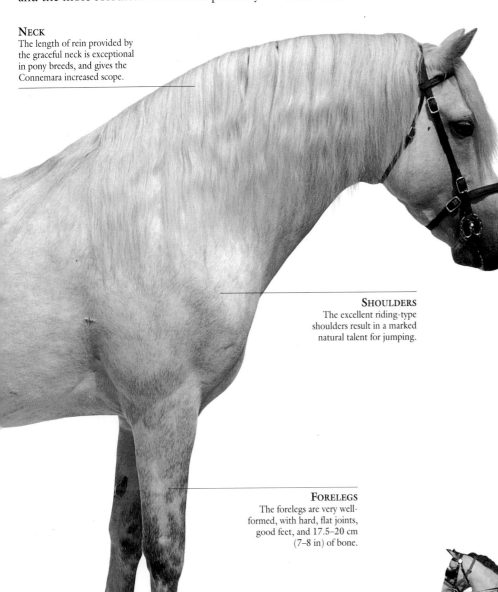

NECK
The length of rein provided by the graceful neck is exceptional in pony breeds, and gives the Connemara increased scope.

SHOULDERS
The excellent riding-type shoulders result in a marked natural talent for jumping.

FORELEGS
The forelegs are very well-formed, with hard, flat joints, good feet, and 17.5–20 cm (7–8 in) of bone.

HEIGHT
Up to 1.47 m (14.2 hh)

HARNESS PONY
Connemaras are just as bold and onward-going in harness as under saddle. The traditional dun colour is associated with exceptional hardiness.

WELSH SECTIONS A & B

THE WELSH MOUNTAIN PONY is considered by many people to be the most beautiful of the British native ponies. It occupies Section A of the *Welsh Pony and Cob Stud Book*, and with a height limit of 1.22 m (12 hh) it is the smallest of the four Welsh breeds. It is the foundation for the other three types, and derives from the original prehistoric British stock. Section B of the stud book is devoted to the Welsh Pony of Riding Type, which should not exceed 1.37 m (13.2 hh).

STALLIONS
It is said of the Welsh that they have "fire in the belly", and stallions can become aggressive if they feel that their territory is being threatened.

THE WELSH MOUNTAIN PONY

Before the establishment of the stud book in 1902, marking the break between the "old breed" and the "improved" modern ponies of strictly fixed type, the Welsh Mountain Pony was influenced by a variety of different breeds. The first improving blood came from the eastern horses introduced by the Romans. In the 18th and 19th centuries Arabs (see pp.64–65), Thoroughbreds (see pp.120–21), and

HEAD
The head has a unique beauty. The eye is large and bold, and the ears are small and pointed.

QUARTERS
The quarters are long and fine with the tail well set-on. They are never goose-rumped.

HEIGHT OF SECTION A
Up to 1.22 m (12 hh)

NATURAL COAT COLOURS
The range of colours in the Welsh breeds is wide. Greys are the most common, but palominos, bays, chestnuts, and roans all abound.

Hackneys of the old Roadster type (see pp.402–3) were also introduced. Two outside influences, particularly in the north, were a small 18th-century Thoroughbred named Merlin, descended from the Darley Arabian, who was run out on the Ruabon hills, and later a stallion called Apricot, by a "Barb-Arab" out of a Welsh mare, who was out on the hills of Merioneth. Merlin's influence was such that a pony in Wales is still called a "merlin".

BODY
The breed should have a "bread basket", or depth through the girth, and a well-ribbed middle.

LEGS
The slender, elegant legs have short cannons and flat, well-formed joints. The bone is dense and sufficient for the frame.

WELSH SECTION A

Since 1902, however, the refined and distinct appearance of the Mountain Pony has been the result of careful selection within the breed itself, although the "founding father" of the modern breed, the legendary Dyoll Starlight, may have carried Arab blood through his dam Moonlight. She was described by her owner, Howard Meuric Lloyd, as a "miniature Arab" and was believed to be a descendant of the Crawshay Bailey Arab, who was turned out on the Brecon Beacons in the 1850s. Starlight's sire, Glassallt, was a very good specimen of the "old breed", with excellent limbs and great strength over the loins. He was black, but both his sire, Flower of Wales, and his son, Starlight, were grey. Through Starlight's influence, grey remains the most common colour.

The modern Welsh Mountain Pony is distinctive in appearance and notable for its uniquely powerful action, its intelligence, and its in-bred constitutional hardiness, a legacy of the harsh environment that formed its character. It is a superb riding pony, and is also exceptional in harness. Exported all over the world, it is one of the finest foundations for horse breeding, passing on the invaluable qualities of bone, substance, and constitutional soundness. Along with the Section B pony, it is much used in the breeding of the Riding Pony (see pp.406–7).

THE WELSH PONY SECTION B

Originally the Welsh Pony Section B was a cross between the Mountain Pony and the smaller Cob (see pp.184–85). However, the modern, refined, longer-striding Section B of the show ring and competitive sport is founded largely on three stallions, two of which were descended from the later Section A patriarch, Coed Coch Glyndwr. The "Abraham" of Section B, a description used by the Welsh breeds' authority, Dr Wynne Davies, was Tan-y-Bwlch Berwyn. He was by a Barb (with pronounced Arab characteristics) called Sahara foaled in 1908, and his dam was a Section A mare by Dyoll Starlight's famous son Bleddfa Shooting Star. The second founding sire was Criban Victor, the archetypal Section B combining both substance and quality. He was by Criban Winston, a son of Coed Coch Glyndwr. The third sire is Solway Master Bronze, the latter's son out of Criban Biddy Bronze. On retirement in 1974, Solway Master Bronze had sired 541 foals.

The Section A pony has remained true to Welsh type, but whether that is so of the Section B is a subject for controversy. At times the latter may have inclined too much towards the Riding Pony type, but the best examples have all the attributes of the Mountain Pony and are talented, versatile performers, both under saddle and in harness. Both types of Welsh pony can be crossed to produce larger animals, which inherit much of the sound constitution, and some of the pony sagacity, that are the hallmarks of the Welsh breeds.

HEAD
The head is essentially the same as that of the Mountain Pony. In this instance the eye and profile show clear Arab influence.

SHOULDERS
The shoulders are long and sloping, giving the pony a superlative action. The withers are moderately fine, and the long curved neck is carried well.

OUTLINE
The flowing outline is symmetrical and balanced in its proportions. It is full of quality and pony character.

FORELIMBS
The forelimbs are exemplary, with long, muscled forearms, well-developed knees, short cannon bones, perfectly sloped pasterns, and good feet.

WELSH SECTION B

HEIGHT OF SECTION B
Up to 1.37 m
(13.2 hh)

ORIGINS

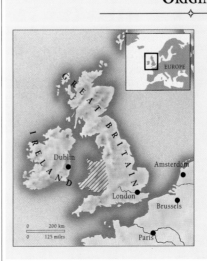

THE WELSH PONIES *belong firmly to the Principality of Wales. For centuries they have been bred on the hills and uplands. Their unique character and action, if now much refined, derive from the rough terrain and the severe climate of their habitat. The constitution and the extraordinary feed-conversion ability comes from the consumption of the sparse, reedy grasses and mosses that were the ponies' principal diet. Such is the popularity of the Welsh breeds that today they are bred in huge numbers all over the world. In their native country they remain a unique feature in rural life.*

WELSH SECTIONS C & D

THERE ARE TWO SECTIONS for the Cobs in the *Welsh Pony and Cob Society Stud Book*. The Section C pony, described as the Welsh Pony of Cob Type, is the smaller of the two, with a height limit of 1.37 m (13.2 hh), while Section D encompasses cobs above that height, with no upper limit being imposed. In fact, many present-day Section D Cobs are 1.52 m (15 hh) and more – a reflection of the market demand.

HISTORY

Both types of Cob evolved from crosses of the Welsh Mountain Pony (see pp.182–83), first with the horses brought by the Romans when they settled in Wales, and later with Spanish horses. In the 12th century Giraldus Cambrensis, Archdeacon of Brecon, wrote that there were in mid-Wales "most excellent studs . . . deriving their origin from some

NECK
The neck is gracefully arched, and the stallions have a significant crest. There is no fleshiness through the jowl.

HEAD
The head is a larger replica of that of the Mountain Pony.

BODY
The body is compact and deep through the girth. The short, strong loins facilitate the powerful action.

LEGS
Short, muscular legs, good bone, and free action from the shoulder are hallmarks of the Cobs in both Sections.

HEIGHT OF SECTION C
Up to 1.37 m (13.2 hh)

WELSH SECTION C

fine Spanish horses". These horses, crossed with mountain mares, produced the Powys horse, which was the principal remount for English hh armies from the end of the 12th century onwards. The old Welsh Cart Horse may also have come from this source. Modern Cobs are virtual replicas, in a larger size, of the Mountain Pony, although they owe much to the later influence of the Norfolk Trotter or Roadster (see pp.122–23), the Yorkshire Coach Horse (see pp.306–7), and the early Hackney of Roadster type.

FOUNDATION SIRES

The four stallions that appear most often in the WPCS Stud Book are: Trotting Comet, foaled in 1840; True Briton (foaled in 1830); Cymro Llwyd (foaled in 1850); and Alonzo the Brave (foaled in 1866). Trotting Comet was out of a famous Cardiganshire trotting mare, and his sire was the blind black horse, Flyer. Flyer was by a Welsh Cart Horse, out of a Norfolk trotting mare. True Briton was sired by Ruler, a Yorkshire Coach Horse, and his dam was reputed to be an Arab mare named Douse. Cymro Llwyd was by the Crawshay Bailey Arab, whom the ironmaster Crawshay Bailey kept on the Brecon Beacons, and was out of a trotting mare. A palomino or dun horse, he was the ancestor of many cream, dun, and palomino Cobs. His most famous recent descendant was Llanarth Braint. Alonzo the Brave, who stood at all of 1.63 m (16 hh), came from old Hackney stock, whose ancestry can be traced to the Darley Arabian (see pp.120–21) through Shales Original and Norfolk Shales (see pp.122–23).

UTILITY AND SPORT

For centuries Welsh Cobs were an integral part of Welsh life, and were used for farm and harness work. A good trade in Cobs developed with the army, where they were used to haul guns and equipment

WELSH PART-BRED
The Welsh Part-Bred is gaining recognition as a potential top-class competition horse. The most usual cross with the Cob is the Thoroughbred.

and were ridden by mounted infantry. They were also in great demand with the big city dairies, bakeries, and other companies.

Before stallion licensing was introduced in 1918, a form of "performance testing" was practised, in which breeding stock was selected on the basis of trotting matches. A favourite route was the 56 km (35 miles) uphill from Cardiff to Dowlais, which the best could cover in under three hours.

The modern Welsh Cobs are courageous harness horses, sure-footed hunters, and natural jumpers. They are economical to keep, easily managed, and very sound. The cross with the Thoroughbred, the basis for the Welsh part-bred, produces a competition horse for riding and driving that is superior to many in terms of courage, versatility, and soundness of limbs and constitution. The Section C Cobs often result from Section D/Welsh Mountain crosses.

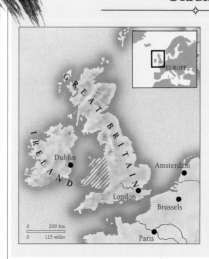

BODY
The "middle piece" of the Cob is deep, short-coupled, and well ribbed-up. There is great strength in the back and loins.

QUARTERS
The strong quarters, and the powerful flexion of the hocks, generate the spectacular Cob action.

FEET
The feet are always well-shaped, and the horn is usually particularly dense. Some silky feather occurs on the heels.

WELSH SECTION D

HEIGHT OF SECTION D
Up to 1.52 m (15 hh)

ORIGINS

LIKE THE WELSH MOUNTAIN PONY and the Welsh Pony of riding type, Sections A and B respectively in the stud book, the two Cob sections, C and D, originate in Wales and are bred from Anglesey in the north to the Gower Peninsula in the South. Without doubt, however, the traditional heartland of the Welsh Cobs is in mid-Wales, in the old county of Cardiganshire, now called Ceredigion, and it remains so to this day. It was in mid-Wales, too, that the 12th-century Powys Cob evolved. The Crawshay Bailey Arab, however, which plays a large part in the evolution of the Welsh breeds, was put out on the Brecon Beacons.

Dublin

Amsterdam

London

Brussels

Paris

EUROPE

GREAT BRITAIN

IRELAND

0   200 km
0   125 miles

EUROPEAN PONIES

POTTOK

THROUGHOUT mainland Europe and Scandinavia there are ponies of ancient origin. The majority are still working, agricultural animals, which play an important part in the rural economy, while those in mountainous areas are usefully employed as pack animals. However, increasingly, ponies of riding quality are being bred to meet the recreational requirements of young people. France, for instance, is developing its own riding pony, the Poney Français de Selle (see pp.406–7), and even the little-known Spanish breed, the Asturçon, is proving itself to be a suitable mount for children. Interestingly, the underlying influence on these European ponies is that of the two founding "primitive" horses, the Asiatic Wild Horse and, more noticeably, the Tarpan (see pp.18–21).

THE PRIMITIVE CONNECTION

The most prominent descendants of the Tarpan, which once roamed the steppe and forest lands in huge herds, are the Konik, Huçul, and Bosnian ponies (see pp.194–95), and the Swedish Gotland (see pp.192–93). They display something of the "primitive" character, particularly in the colour of the coat and sometimes in its deer-like texture. However, Arab influence (see pp.64–65) is also evident in the Huçul and the Gotland, both of which have received infusions of eastern blood since the late 19th century.

Both the indigenous ponies of Norway, the striking Fjord, in former times often called the Westland, and the Northlands, a pony close to the famous Icelandic pony (see pp.196–97), are also of "primitive" origin, although they have been much refined. The former clearly has a strong connection with the Asiatic Wild Horse, while the Northlands would seem to have been influenced by the Tarpan as well.

The Icelandic pony is unique in that it has not been subject to any infusion of outside blood for 800 years. Like the people of Iceland it came to the island from Norway in the 9th century. Later settlers introduced ponies of the Shetland type (see pp.178–79) from the Western Islands, and so the modern pony is of mixed origin, though underpinned by the Asiatic Wild Horse and probably the Tarpan. Some experts think

ICELANDIC

Icelandic ponies have been bred pure for more than 800 years, during which time there has been no outcrossing. They came to Iceland from Norway in the 9th century.

FJORD

Norway's Fjord, an enormously popular pony in both Scandinavia and Europe, is held to have a strong connection with the Asiatic Wild Horse, to which it bears some resemblance.

that there could also be a Yakut connection, although there is no firm evidence to support this theory.

Although ponies are not much in evidence in Italy, Spain, and Portugal, the Iberian ponies are of special interest. The Sorraia and Garrano (see pp.106–7) have a common root in the Tarpan with overtones of the Asiatic Wild Horse, and descend from the first indigenous stock to be domesticated in Europe. This stock later contributed in its formative stage to the Spanish Horse, which exerted so great an influence on the horses of both Europe and the Americas. The modern Garrano has been substantially improved by introducing Arab blood, and to a lesser degree this may be true of the Sorraia.

The Asturçon is the third Iberian pony. It comes from northern Spain, and was ridden by the Asturian horsemen who formed part

of the Roman auxiliary cavalry. The pony, like those early horsemen, is Celtic, and has close similarities to the ponies of Dartmoor and Exmoor (see pp.174–75). In the early 20th century thousands ran virtually wild in the mountains, but there are now only about 200 animals registered in the stud book. However, the recently formed Spanish Pony Club is now encouraging their use as riding ponies, and it was an Asturçon that won the Spanish Championships for ponies standing up to 1.37 m (13.2 hh).

The Bardigiano (see pp.190–91), a breed from the northern Appenine Mountains, also resembles the Exmoor. Finally, there are the ponies of Greece: the Pindos, Skyrian, and Peneia (see pp.42–43). Their primary influence may be the Tarpan developing into Horse Type 4 (see pp.22–23).

GERMANY, AUSTRIA, AND FRANCE

Germany is famous for its warmbloods, but has no pony breeds of note. There is the Dülmen, a pony of mixed origins, which resembles the British New Forest, although

NORTHLANDS

The Northlands may have its origins in both the Asiatic Wild Horse and the Tarpan. In its native Norway it is, like the Fjord, called a "horse".

DÜLMEN

The Dülmen ponies have run out on Westphalia's Meerfelder Bruch since the early 1300s. The last existing herd on the Meerfelder Bruch is owned by the Duke of Croy.

there is no link between the two. It runs semi-wild on the estate of the Dukes of Croy in the Meerfelder Bruch, Westphalia, and fulfils no practical purpose except that of ornament. The other German pony was the Senner of the Teutoburg Forest. It had the reputation for being incredibly hardy, but for all that it is now regarded as extinct. It is suggested that both of these breeds may have contributed to the early Hanoverian horses (see pp.144–45).

A far more important breed is Austria's attractive and versatile Haflinger (see pp.52–53). This may be a descendant of the Forest Horse (see pp.14–15), and certainly has Noriker connections (see pp.50–51), although the foundation sires are Arabs.

France has no pony tradition. The Camargue really has to be classed as a horse, and both the Landais and the Pottok (see pp.188–89) were classed until comparatively recently as semi-wild. Both, however, are now much improved by outside crosses, notably Arabs and Welsh Section B riding ponies (see pp.182–83).

LANDAIS & POTTOK

THE THREE PONY BREEDS considered to be natives of France are the Ariègeois (see pp.46–47), the Landais, and the Pottok. The Landais lives in the wooded region of the Landes in south-west France, which is possibly the biggest forest in Europe. A larger version of the pony used to exist on the Chalosse plain near the Adour River, at the foot of the Pyrenees, and yet another, which was often called the Barthais, lived on the Adour's marshlands. The Pottok, the pony of the Basque region, is found in the mountainous provinces of Labourd, Basse-Navarre, and Soule, on the border with Spain. Both the Pottok and the Landais are ancient breeds, descended from primitive equine types.

LANDAIS PONIES AT PAU
Landais ponies, in the past described as semi-wild, are now kept at the National Stud at Pau. Today's Landais ponies are the result of a much improved selective breeding programme.

THE LANDAIS

The Landais pony used to be semi-wild. It is likely that it could be descended from the primitive steppe Tarpan, which was probably a mixture between Pony Type 1 of north-west Europe, and the prototype Arab, Horse Type 4 (see pp.22–23).

Arab blood (see pp.64–65) was widely introduced at the end of the 19th century, and again in 1913, when there were about 2,000 ponies in the Landes area. After the Second World War the breed came near to extinction, with perhaps no more than 150 animals in existence. So few ponies remained that in-breeding became an urgent

HEAD
The head is neat and attractive with some Arab character.

SHOULDERS
The shoulders are much improved in the modern pony, and the withers are more prominent.

problem. Breeders remedied this situation by outcrossing the stock with Welsh Section B stallions (see pp.182–83), strongly supported again by infusions of Arab blood.

The modern Landais stands at 1.19–1.35 m (11.3–13.1 hh). Grey, once the dominant colour in the forest type, is now rarely seen, and the usual colours are bay, brown, chestnut, and black. The Landais is a refined animal. The neat pony head shows Arab character, and has also retained the small, pointed Welsh ears. The tail is carried high. A well-made riding pony, the Landais has lightly built limbs, a good length of rein, and sloped shoulders. It is hardy, frugal, adapts easily to heat and cold, and is docile and intelligent.

The formation of pony clubs in the early 1970s encouraged the breeding of the Landais and its use as a children's pony. It has also played a part as base stock in the

ORIGINS

THE LANDAIS AND THE POTTOK, two of the indigenous ponies of France, are native to the south of the country. The Landais inhabited the forest regions of the Landes region as well as the more fertile Chalosse plain. Its neighbour the Pottok, on the other hand, is a mountain pony of the Pyrenean Pays Basque, and is found principally in the provinces of Labourd, Basse-Navarre, and Soule. Like all mountain horses, it has developed an inherent sure-footedness and agility over rough ground. Both ponies are descended from primitive stock and until recent times were considered to be wild or semi-wild.

HEIGHT OF LANDAIS
1.19–1.35 m (11.3–13.1 hh)

BONE
The breed standard stipulates a constant 17–18 cm (6½–7 in) bone measurement.

LANDAIS

production of the Poney Français de Selle, the French Riding Pony (see pp.406–7). This new pony, which breeders hope will come to rival its British counterpart, is a careful amalgam of native and French Pony mares crossed with Arab, Connemara (see pp.180–81), New Forest (see pp.176–77), and Welsh stallions.

THE POTTOK

The Pottok is usually described as being wild or semi-wild, although it is perhaps less so today, now that official bodies, the National Pottok Association and the *Direction des Haras*, are responsible for its development. This breed's antecedents are probably even closer to the primitive horses than those of the Landais, and once more crosses have been made to selected Arab and Welsh Section B stallions.

There are three types of modern Pottok: the Standard Pottok, the Double Pottok, and the Piebald Pottok. The first and last types vary in height from 1.14–1.32 m (11.1–13 hh), while the Double stands at 1.30–1.47 m (12.3–14.2 hh). The Pottok ponies are less refined than their neighbour the Landais. They have a straight profile with a characteristic slight concavity between the eyes. The limbs and feet are good, but the neck is short, the shoulders are straight, and the back is long. The predominant coat colours for the Standard Pottok and the Double Pottok are chestnut, brown, and bay. The Piebald Pottoks are unusual in that their coats may be not only black and white (the accepted piebald colouring) but also chestnut, white, and black, or chestnut and white.

Smuggling was a way of life in the Basque country, as it was in the Ariègeois pony's homeland in the eastern Pyrenees, and right up to the Second World War (and perhaps later) the Pottok was the Basque smuggler's pack pony. Having now acquired a veneer of respectability, it is used as a child's pony and in harness. Like the Landais, it was used in the creation of the Poney Français de Selle (French Riding Pony – see pp.406–7).

BODY
The body tends to be long in the back. The shoulders are straight.

HEAD
The profile is straight, but there is a slight concavity between the widely-spaced eyes.

HEIGHT OF POTTOK
1.14–1.47 m (11.1–14.2 hh)

HIND LEGS
The hind legs are well-muscled. The thick, coarse tail is set high in the quarters.

LEGS
The legs are fine and small, and the round feet are well-made and very hard.

POTTOK

SMUGGLER'S PONY
In the Basque country of the Pyrenees, the little Pottok pony played a useful part in the pre-Second World War economy as a pack pony carrying contraband over the steep mountain trails.

BARDIGIANO

ALTHOUGH ITALY HAS PRODUCED some of the world's greatest Thoroughbreds (see pp.120–21), largely through Federico Tesio's Dormello Stud on the shores of Lake Maggiore, and has had a profound influence on Thoroughbred breeding in general, it has no indigenous breeds of any great note. Indeed, in antiquity, Italy had no native horse or pony breeds, and stock had to be brought into the country from Spain, Persia (Iran), and probably from Noricum, a vassal province of the Roman Empire corresponding to modern Austria. It is from this last source that the most attractive but least known of Italian breeds, the Bardigiano, derives.

TRUE PONY
This is a good stamp of Bardigiano stallion standing at the stud at Crema, near Milan. Selective breeding has both preserved and improved these very attractive ponies. The head of the Bardigiano is notable for its true pony character.

INFLUENCES

Noricum was the home of an ancient breed of horses that was known to the Romans as the *Abellinum*. This former breed is represented today by the striking Haflinger pony of the Austrian Tyrol (see pp.52–53) and its closely related Italian neighbour, the Avelignese, which is bred in the mountainous areas of northern, central, and southern Italy, particularly in Tuscany and Venetia and around Bolzano.

There can be little doubt that the Bardigiano, which inhabits the northern Appenine region of Italy, has a pronounced connection with the Avelignese as well as owing something to the heavier Italian mountain strains. Both the Haflinger and the Avelignese share a common ancestry in the Arab stallion El Bedavi, and trace back to that horse's half-bred great-grandson

133 El Bedavi XXII, bred at the Austro-Hungarian stud of Radautz, and to his son the influential 249 Folie. That influence remains apparent in the Bardigiano, which is noticeably eastern in appearance, particularly in respect of the neat head, tapered muzzle, and slightly dished profile.

However, there are further, even more interesting resemblances to other breeds that make the Bardigiano particularly notable. It has a similarity to the obscure Asturçon pony (see pp.106–7), which lives in the mountainous regions of northern Spain – an area which, in relative terms, is not so far removed from the habitat of the Bardigiano. It also resembles quite closely the oldest of the British native breeds, the Exmoor pony (see pp.174–75). Therefore, it is not unreasonable to suppose that all three breeds have some common root in Celtic pony stock, with the Asturçon and the Bardigiano

QUARTERS
The quarters are muscled and rounded and the heavy, thick tail is well-set. The second thighs are pronounced and the hocks are clean.

NATURAL ENVIRONMENT
This group of Bardigiano ponies is on the island of Corsica, a mountainous environment not dissimilar to that of the northern Appenine range, which is considered to be the principal breeding area. The ponies are well-grown and in excellent condition.

representing isolated pockets of strains that existed in Europe prior to the Ice Age (c.10000 BC) and have survived in their distinctive form into the present day.

CHARACTERISTICS

Like the Avelignese and the Haflinger, the Bardigiano is a working mountain pony, physically equipped for use on rough, steep terrain at high altitudes. It is hardy, easily kept, quick-moving, and innately sure-footed in difficult mountain conditions. It is also strongly built with sufficient length in the back for it to be able to carry a pack saddle.

The shoulders tend to be upright by riding standards, but in consequence are ideally suited to light draught work.

The head is especially interesting because it exemplifies the true pony character. It is small, never approaching coarseness, there is wonderful breadth across the forehead, and the ears are short, mobile, and constantly pricked. The wide nostrils and the long nasal passages, allowing air to be warmed before inhalation, are typical of the descendants of the primitive Pony Type 1 (see pp.22–23), which was resistant to both cold and wet. The Bardigiano rarely exceeds 1.32 m (13 hh). The trio of related mountain ponies

AN ANCIENT BREED
The Bardigiano stock has similarities to the little-known Asturçon ponies of northern Spain, and in more than one respect resembles the oldest pony breed in the UK, the Exmoor. Possibly all three may share a common root stock.

formed by the Haflinger, Avelignese, and Bardigiano are among the most interesting in the world and are probably the most versatile. In comparison with the others, the Bardigiano is hardly known outside its traditional breeding areas. Nonetheless, it is the equal of its relatives in terms of conformation and movement, and has particular features that are just as distinctive.

HEAD
The head has true pony character, with a broad forehead and small, neat ears.

BODY
There is depth through the strongly-built body and the broad chest, the latter allowing ample room for large lungs.

SHOULDERS
The withers are fairly well-defined, but the shoulders tend to be short and upright by riding standards.

LEGS
The legs are short and usually sufficiently muscled, while the joints are well-pronounced and the bone measurement adequate.

HEIGHT
Up to 1.32 m (13 hh)

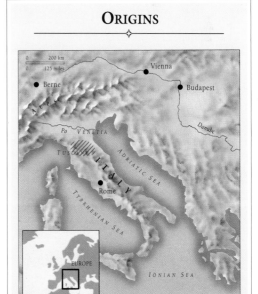

ORIGINS

ITALY'S ATTRACTIVE BARDIGIANO may have its origin in the Avelignese breeding areas in Venetia and in the mountainous part of Tuscany to the south. However, the modern Bardigiano is associated principally with the highlands of the northern Appenines, which lie between Venetia and Tuscany and are therefore geographically accessible to both regions. The mountain environment and work on the rough, steep terrain contribute significantly to the breed's character and physique.

GOTLAND & FJORD

T HE GOTLAND PONY, also known as the Skogsruss, is native to Sweden. It is the most ancient of the Scandinavian breeds, and is still mainly primitive in character. The breed's original habitat was Gotland, an island off the Swedish coast, where it has probably existed since the Stone Age. The Fjord, sometimes called the Westland (Vestfjord), is indigenous to Norway, but is found in variant types throughout Scandinavia and beyond. It is bred principally in Norway, where a strict breeding policy has been practised since the beginning of the 20th century.

ISLAND STOCK

Some of Sweden's Gotland ponies still live on Gotland Island, but they are now bred all over Scandinavia as riding and trotting ponies.

THE GOTLAND PONY

The Gotland resembles the Huçul and Konik of Poland (see pp.194–95), and like them is believed to have descended from the Tarpan (see pp.20–21). Crosses to eastern blood were made in the 19th century and possibly later, and for some years the ponies have been bred selectively. The stallions that had the greatest influence on the breed were

HEIGHT OF GOTLAND
1.22–1.27 m
(12–12.2 hh)

BODY
The quarters are heavily muscled, and the body is short and compact, with a deep barrel. The dun colour and dorsal list are characteristic of the breed.

NECK
The neck is short, and usually runs down to a long back and unimpressive quarters. The frame is light and narrow.

ORIGINS

THE ANCIENT SWEDISH GOTLAND or Skogsruss Pony was, at one time, confined in a semi-feral state on Gotland Island in the Baltic Sea, and may have been there since the Stone Age. Today, it is bred on the Swedish mainland and elsewhere in Scandinavia. Its neighbour, the Fjord Pony, is also found throughout Scandinavia, but is bred principally in Norway, and is considered to be indigenous to that country. The lesser-known Northlands is also indigenous to Norway. The Gotland and Northlands are not much known outside their native countries, but the Fjord is increasingly popular throughout Europe.

Olle, a Syrian Arab/Gotland cross who introduced the yellow dun coat colour, and the Arab, Khedivan, who is responsible for the grey coloration. At one time the ponies were semi-wild, and lived on Gotland and in the forest of Löjsta on the Swedish mainland. Today they are bred all over Sweden and throughout Scandinavia, as well as on Gotland.

The Gotland was once used for general farm work, but it is now kept principally as a riding pony; it is said to excel at jumping and in trotting races. The walk and trot are fast, but the gallop is laboured and restricted.

These ponies have a rather light, narrow build, with sloping quarters and a low-set tail. In general, the hind legs are poorly made, but the feet are good and hard. There is no doubting the breed's endurance and hardy constitution. The Gotland stands at 1.22–1.27 m (12–12.2 hh), and there is a variety of coat colours including brown, dun, black, chestnut, grey, and some palomino.

GOTLAND

THE FJORD PONY

Of all the modern equine breeds the Fjord bears the most striking resemblance to the Asiatic Wild Horse of the Ice Age (see pp.18–19). It retains much of its ancestor's primitive vigour, as well as the uniform dun coat colour. The latter is accompanied by an eel stripe running from the forelock to the tip of the tail, and sometimes by zebra bars on the legs. The mane and tail are usually lighter in colour, and can be almost silver.

A notable feature is the coarse, erect mane, which is characteristic of primitive equines. Were it left alone the mane would grow as long as that of any other breed, but by ancient tradition it is hogged (clipped) so that the black hairs at the centre stand above the rest. It is cut in a crescent shape from poll to withers, giving a pronounced crest to the neck.

VARIED USES

Fjord Ponies are used for a wide range of agricultural work, including hay-making and ploughing. On remote mountain farms they are often employed instead of tractors. They are also ridden.

Horses with their manes hogged in this way appear on the runestone carvings of the Vikings, which may still be seen in Norway. The Fjord was the Viking horse, and was used in the popular sport of horse-fighting, when horses were pitted against each other, and sometimes fought to the death.

The Highland Pony (see pp.178–79) resembles the Fjord in both conformation and colouring. This is a result of the close connection between Scandinavia and the Western Isles of Scotland. The first Norse raiders to reach the Western Isles came from Hordaland in Norway, the chief habitat of the Fjord. As late as 1890, two Norwegian stallions were brought to the Hebrides to upgrade the stock there, and the incidence of ponies with silver manes and tails is often attributed to their influence.

The modern Fjord of the best type stands at 1.32–1.42 m (13–14 hh). It is compact and strongly muscled, and has short limbs with plenty of bone. The head is wide, with small ears, and is of pony type. Despite the overall similarity to the Asiatic Wild Horse, there is no sign of the primitive, convex profile in modern stock.

In Norway the Fjord is used for ploughing, as a pack pony, in harness, and under saddle. It is sound and hardy, and can operate on a modest diet. Fjords have been successful in European driving competitions, and their stamina and courage are an asset in long-distance riding.

CHEST
The chest is broad and deep, with the forelegs being set wide apart. The shoulders are heavy and strong, and the withers are flat and round.

LEGS
The legs are short, with short cannons and flat, dense bone. Some feather occurs on the heels. The feet are open and hard.

FJORD

HEIGHT OF FJORD
1.32–1.42 m (13–14 hh)

NORTHLANDS
The Northlands Pony of Norway is popular as a riding and harness pony. The breed was much improved by the extensive use of the selected stallion Rimfakse in the late 1940s.

HUÇUL & KONIK

ALTHOUGH THE BRITISH native ponies are by far the most dominant group in Europe, there is a huge pony population that stretches all the way from the Mediterranean to Scandinavia. In many instances, these ponies remain integral to the rural economies of much of Central and Eastern Europe. Like the British ponies, those on mainland Europe have been improved both in the natural course of evolution and as a result of human influence. Nonetheless, despite this process, some European breeds reflect close genetic links to the primitive horses of pre-history. Three of the most ancient and closely related are the Huçul, the Konik, and the Bosnian, the native mountain pony of former Yugoslavia.

THE HUÇUL

The Huçul, a native of the Carpathian Mountains, is held to be directly descended from the primitive Tarpan (see pp.20–21), and at least one authority thinks it should be described as the Forest Tarpan. It is also suggested that there have been infusions of eastern blood. Moreover, the head shape and the yellow-dun colouring provide visual evidence of another genetic presence, that of the Asiatic Wild Horse (see pp.18–19).

For centuries the Huçul was used as a pack pony, and was renowned for carrying heavy loads over difficult mountain paths often covered in snow and ice. Most of the modern ponies are used in harness, although they can also be ridden, and they are still indispensable on the highland farms of southern Poland.

ORIGINS

THE BALKAN GROUP OF PONIES comprises the Huçul, the Konik, and the Bosnian. These ponies are widespread from the Adriatic coast to the Black Sea. The Huçul is a native of the Carpathian Mountains, but is bred all over Central Europe. It was bred selectively at the Luczyna stud in the 19th century, and then at Siary, near Gorlice, in Poland. The Konik is also Polish. It is bred selectively at Popielno and the state stud at Jezewice. The Bosnian is the most numerous breed and is found throughout former Yugoslavia. The principal centre of selective breeding, in former years, was at the Borike Stud in Bosnia.

HEIGHT OF HUÇUL
1.24–1.35 m
(12.1–13.1 hh)

HUÇUL PONIES
The Huçul is native to the Carpathians, but is also bred throughout Central Europe. The breed is thought to descend from primitive Tarpan stock.

BODY
The body is short and compact, with upright shoulders and low withers. Dun is the most usual colour, but piebald and skewbald are also common.

The Huçul has a short, compact appearance, and is often somewhat over-topped, with the sickle-hocks that occur so frequently in mountain breeds. The pony stands between 1.24 m and 1.35 m (12.1–13.1 hh). It is strong and willing, with a docile nature. There are said to be three types of Huçul, although these are very mixed.

THE KONIK

The word *Konik* means "pony" or "little horse". This breed is widespread throughout Poland, and in rural areas it is still integral to the agricultural economy. It also descends from the Tarpan, and retains much of its ancestor's characteristics and looks. In fact, the "re-constituted" Tarpan herd that runs wild at Popielno, where the Konik is bred selectively, has been built on Konik stock. The pony is also bred at the state stud at Jezewice, and by many small farmers.

The Konik stands at 1.32 m (13 hh). Many animals have the typical Tarpan colouring – mouse-dun with a black dorsal stripe. This attractive pony has a kind temperament, works willingly on minimal rations, and has the Tarpan's robust constitution; however, like the Huçul, it is prone to sickle-hocks.

ANOTHER TARPAN DESCENDANT

The Bosnian, a pony similar to the Huçul, is also thought to have developed from the Tarpan crossed with the Asiatic Wild Horse. The horses bred in Thessaly by the Ancient Greeks (see pp.38–39) may also have been among its ancestors. Eastern blood, introduced by the Turks, had a refining influence, but too much of it resulted in a weak-limbed pony that was too light to be practical. Thereafter, breeders returned to the old lines exhibiting strong Tarpan character.

Three stallions, active during the 1940s, had a particular impact. Misco, a small pony of distinctive type, had the greatest influence. Barut and Agan were heavier, and more like the Asiatic Wild Horse. Up to the outbreak of civil war in former Yugoslavia, much attention was paid to stallion selection. All stallions undergo a test in which they carry a 100-kg (2-cwt) pack over 16 km (10 miles) of difficult mountain country. This distance has been covered in as little as 1 hr 11 mins.

The improved pony retains Tarpan character. It stands at 1.32–1.47 m (13–14.2 hh). Dun is a predominant colour, but browns, blacks, and chestnuts also occur.

HEAD
The head is in proportion to the overall frame. The neck is short and strong.

SHOULDERS
The rather upright shoulders, and the low withers, make the Konik well-suited to harness work.

BODY
The body is strong, broad-backed, and deep at the girth. The coat colour is usually one of the shades of dun.

TAIL
The tail is set high in improved Huçul stock. The mane and tail hair is thick and coarse.

FORELEGS
The forelegs are strong, and well-placed in relation to the shoulders.

THE BOSNIAN PONY
The Bosnian, like the Huçul and the Konik, is of Tarpan origin. It is much used for pack transport in remote, mountainous regions, and elsewhere it is used for all sorts of agricultural work.

HEIGHT OF KONIK
1.32 m (13 hh)

ICELANDIC

THE ICELANDIC HORSE is one of the most famous features of this land of ice and fire that lies in the inhospitable North Atlantic. A strong and affectionate respect for the horse, amounting almost to reverence, persists to this day among the Icelandic people, in whose life and folklore it has occupied a central place for over 1,000 years. The ratio of horses to people is extraordinarily high, and the Icelandic Horse is used for every sort of work in a land of glaciers, rivers, lava fields, and stony desert, where roads are not much in evidence. The breed's use in sport is just as important, and competitive events such as horse shows and races are frequent and well organized.

WORKING ROLE
The Icelandic Horse is used for every sort of work on the island, and can carry grown men for long periods without being distressed.

HISTORY AND LEGEND

The Norse settlement of this volcanic island took place between c. AD 860 and 935, the settlers bringing their horses with them in open boats. The first immigrants are said to have been two Norwegian chieftains, Ingolfur and Leifur, and they were followed by people from the Norse colonies in the Western Isles of Scotland, in Ireland, and on the Isle of Man. The foundation stock for the Icelandic Horse was, therefore, drawn from all of these regions.

For the hippologist, the most fascinating feature of the Icelandic horse culture is the extreme genetic purity of the equine population. There have been no infusions of outside blood for over 800 years. Once,

ORIGINS

ICELAND LIES IN THE MIDDLE OF the North Atlantic, just south of the Arctic Circle, and has supported the Icelandic Horses for over 1,000 years. No attempt has been made to outcross the native stock for 900 years, and this factor, combined with the severity of the climate and the absence of abundant foodstuffs, has contributed to the breed's unique character. Icelandic Horses are also bred outside Iceland, but whether the essential type can be maintained has yet to be proved.

MANE
Chestnut Icelandic Horses usually have either white or flaxen manes and tails.

HEAD
The head is plain and rather heavy in proportion to the body, revealing a "primitive" connection. The horse is thick through the jowl.

about 900 years ago, an attempt was made to introduce eastern blood to the Icelandic Horses. This failed disastrously, resulting in a long-lasting degeneration in the stock, and as a result, in AD 930 the Althing, the world's oldest parliament, passed laws prohibiting the importation of foreign horses into the country.

In the early days of the Norse settlement the horse was worshipped as a deity and a symbol of fertility, and a white horse was slaughtered ceremonially at sacrificial feasts. The medieval *Sagas* are full of myths and heroic legends in which the horses play prominent roles. Numerous episodes describing the bloody horse-fights between stallions (which were used as a basis for breeding selection as well as being an exciting spectacle) occur in the literature and written records of Iceland's Commonwealth period (AD 930–1262).

SHOULDERS
The shoulders are upright, and contribute to the elevated action displayed at gaits such as the *tölt*.

LEGS
The legs are short and strong, although the hind legs appear light. The cannons are short, and there is a good slope to the pasterns. The feet are sound.

BREED TYPES

Experts can discern four types of Icelandic Horse. There are, for instance, animals that were originally intended specifically for pack and draught. These are distinct in terms of conformation from the best-quality saddle horses, which are carefully bred to improve the ability to perform the five gaits for which the Icelandic Horse is well-known. Additionally, there were herds bred solely for their meat, for long a staple diet for Icelanders in a land where it would be impossible to winter out beef cattle. The best-known type is the Faxafloi, bred in the south west, the area that receives the heaviest rainfall. It is very like the Exmoor (see pp.174–75), the most ancient of the British native breeds. There are no fewer than 15 basic colour types and combinations of Icelandic, including piebald and skewbald. Some studs breed to a favoured coat colour. In the south

EXCEPTIONAL QUALITY
These two Icelandic horses are exceptionally good examples. They represent the very best type, and their heads show unusual refinement.

of the island, for instance, the Kirkjubaer Stud concentrates on a distinctive chestnut, much more red than palomino, with a near-white mane and tail. The range of colours is a matter of pride among Icelanders, and includes chestnut, usually with white or flaxen manes and tails, bay, black, grey, shades of dun, palomino, and albino.

Selective breeding on a practical scale began in the most famous breeding area, Skagafjörður in northern Iceland, in 1879. Breeding programmes are based principally on the quality of the five gaits peculiar to the Icelandic Horse. The five characteristic gaits are the walk (*fetgangur*), which is mostly used by pack animals; the trot (*brokk*), used when crossing rough country; the fast gallop (*stökk*); and the two gaits of antiquity – the pace (*skeið*), and the *tölt*, which in the US is called the rack. Pacing is a fast, smooth lateral gait. In pacing races, the horse changes to the *skeið* after a 50 m (55 yd) gallop. The *tölt* is a four-beat running walk, which is used for traversing broken ground. In this gait the horse is capable of explosive acceleration.

RACING AND HORSE SHOWS

Despite increased mechanization and improvements to roads, horses still feature in Icelandic life, particularly in horse shows and

race meetings. The first race meeting of modern times was held at Akureyri in northern Iceland in 1874, and today weekend meetings are held in different parts of the country from April to June, the biggest being that at Reykjavík on Whit Monday. Flat races are run at the gallop over distances of 1500, 800, 400, 350, and 300 m (1 mile, 880, 440, 380, and 330 yds), while races for pacing horses under saddle are over 250 m (270 yds). There are also some steeplechase races.

Horse show classes are for four-gaited horses (walk, trot, gallop, and pace) and for five-gaited horses, which are also required to show the *tölt*.

The National Association of Riding Clubs, which is made up of over 40 riding clubs, together with the Agricultural Society of Iceland organizes regular meetings, which include show classes of all types, racing, and classes for breeding stallions.

CHARACTERISTICS

Although the Icelandic Horse stands at no more than 1.37 m (13.2 hh), and may be as small as 1.30 m (12.3 hh), Icelanders never refer to it as a pony. Though small, it is an enormously muscular animal. The head is heavy, and the body is compact. This breed is possessed of great agility and is also very sure-footed. It can and does carry grown men at speed without tiring. The Icelandic is, moreover, economical and easy to keep. Horses that are kept in semi-wild conditions, and there are still some of them, are rarely given anything to supplement their diet of grass, although they are occasionally fed the highly nutritional herrings with which the Icelandic seas abound.

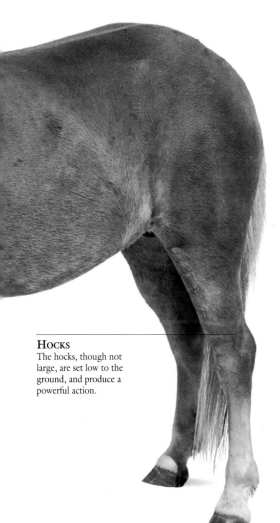

HOCKS
The hocks, though not large, are set low to the ground, and produce a powerful action.

HEIGHT
1.30–1.37 m
(12.3–13.2 hh)

LONG, FREE ACTION
The action of this grey Icelandic Horse is free, long, and very active, with conspicuous and powerful engagement of the hind leg.

ASIA & THE EAST

ZASKARI PONY, LADAKH

ASIA IS THE WORLD'S largest continent, extending from the Arctic Circle to the Equator, and has corresponding extremes of climate and terrain. Its pony breeds are numerous and complex, but in the whole vast area one factor emerges as being common to almost all. It is the pervasive influence of Mongolia, the centre of equine evolution and the home of the Asiatic Wild Horse (*Equus caballus przewalskii przewalskii* Poliakov), the last wild, primitive horse (see pp.18–19). The influence of the Asiatic Wild Horse has been passed on to many eastern ponies, through its direct descendant, the Mongolian Pony. A distinctive, if unprepossessing animal, the Mongolian Pony occupies a most important place among the Asian horse breeds because of its powerful influence on them. The breed's primitive genetic background endows it with stamina, endurance, and a far greater degree of hardiness than most other horses except the Arab.

THE MONGOLIAN PONY

Outer Mongolia still has the largest number of horses per head of population in the world, but, despite the common root, some variation in type occurs as a result of differing climatic and natural conditions. A small strain of pony, about 1.24 m (12.1 hh), predominates south of the Gobi Desert, while a bigger type is bred in the western part of Mongolia. In central areas there are cross-breds with some Don and Trotter blood (see pp.80–81 and pp.344–45). These horses are bigger and faster, but they lack the true Mongolian

STEPPE HERD
The horse herds in Mongolia are just as much a part of life today as they were in the past. Among this herd on the Orkhon steppes the traditional dun colouring remains predominant.

Pony's stamina and tenacious ability to survive on minimal feed in the hard climatic conditions. The pony is quite capable of travelling 80–95 km (50–60 miles) a day, and 190 km (120 miles) is not uncommon even on very rough ground. Horse racing is a part of the Mongol lifestyle, and races are run over proportionate distances, usually of 30–65 km (20–40 miles).

MONGOLIAN-INFLUENCED PONIES

The huge number of animals, combined with the inherited "primitive vigour" that results in exceptional prepotency, is responsible for the widespread influence of the Mongolian Pony. This influence extends northwards almost as far as the Siberian uplands, and west to the Urals and Kazakhstan. In the west, there is also a critical cross-fertilization with desert stock from the northern frontiers of Iran, Iraq, and Kurdestan. The ponies of the Altai Mountains in Mongolia certainly carry Mongolian blood, and so do the Kirghiz and the Kazakh (see pp.82–83 and pp.200–1). To the east there is still more evidence of a Mongolian presence. Mongol stock may have reached the Punjab and northern Rajasthan to play some part in the evolution of the Marwari (see pp.164–65). It may have also influenced the Kathiawari (see pp.162–63) further south in Gujerat, which occasionally reveals its primitive connection in dun-coloured horses with dark barring on the lower limbs and a dorsal eel stripe. However, both breeds are predominantly influenced by Arab horses (see pp.64–65)

GOBI DESERT
The Gobi Desert was the homeland of Genghis Khan and the Mongols. These modern herdsmen are supervising a herd of camels, an essential means of transport in desert areas. They are mounted on small, typical Mongolian Ponies.

or their derivatives. There is no doubt about the close ties of the Tibetan Pony which, in common with many of the Himalayan hill ponies, is also dun-coloured. The Spiti (see pp.202–3), the more refined Zaskari on the Tibetan borders, and the ponies of Bhutan, all show unmistakable Mongolian character. Although they may appear to be of degenerate stock, these small ponies, like their progenitor, are incredibly enduring and hardy, and well able to carry loads out of proportion to their size.

Even further to the east, the Chinese ponies are clearly of Mongolian origin. Like the Mongolian Ponies, they are often raced at organized meetings, and are surprisingly fast. In recent years China maintained a cavalry division mounted on these ponies on its northern border with the old USSR. The Japanese Hokkaido, Kiso, and Kagoshima ponies (see pp.212–13), and the Shan or Burma Pony, are also Mongolian derivatives.

MONGOLIAN MEETS ARAB

The connection is continued with the Shan or Burma Pony and in the Manipuri of Assam. In the latter, however, there is visual

THE SPITI
In the Himalayas, tough, sure-footed ponies such as the Spiti are the only means of transport in the mountainous terrain.

KAZAKH HUNTER
This present-day Kazakh tribesman is practising the sport of his forebears with his hunting eagle. A desert fox hangs from his saddle.

evidence of upgrading by infusions of Arab blood, an understandable practice since these ponies were the first on which the British administrators and military of the 19th century played polo, a game they learnt from the Manipuri people. They would certainly have sought to improve the native stock and they had access to Arab horses, which

though expensive, were to be found among the administrators and planters of Bengal. Until relatively recently, Indonesia was a land full of ponies, which were vital to the economy of the islands. The Mongolian influence on these ponies is recognized by the respected authority Daphne Machin-Goodall. The ponies provide an indisputable example of the "primitive" Mongolian blood meeting that of the desert Arab, for at an early date the Dutch colonists imported Arab-related horses from the Cape in South Africa to improve the stock. The colonists later established a stud at Minankababau in central Sumatra, where they stood Arab stallions to further upgrade the indigenous pony strains. The Sandalwood Ponies (see pp.206–7) show the greatest Arab influence, having pronounced Arab character about the head, and the fine, silky coat of the desert horse. They are spirited and fast, and are much used for racing. Other Indonesian pony breeds resemble the Mongolian more closely than the Arab. Both the Sandalwood and the Timor Ponies (see pp.204–5) were once exported to Australia, which, of necessity, has had to rely upon imports to establish its own horse stock.

BASHKIR

THE BASHKIR is one of northern Eurasia's steppe and mountain breeds; similar breeds are the Kazakh and its sub-types the Adaev and the Dzhabe, and the Buryat of Siberia. All of these horses survive and even flourish in extreme climatic conditions, living in herds all year round as they have done since before the horse was domesticated. Indeed, horses were probably first domesticated in and around the areas that form the natural habitat of these ponies, lands that extend from the steppes bordering the Black and Caspian Seas in the south, to both sides of the Ural Mountains in the north.

BASHKIR HERDS

The Bashkir, or Bashkirsky, pony evolved in Bashkiria, around the southern foothills of the Urals, at some point in pre-history. It attracted attention during the 19th century on account of its remarkable qualities and the important place that it occupied in the local economy. Breeding centres were set up in 1845 to improve the stock for agricultural purposes, for work in harness and under saddle, and to increase the productivity of the herds in terms of the yield of meat, milk, and other products for which the Bashkir had traditionally been kept.

Despite the harshness of their lives, the Bashkir mares are famous for their milk yield. An average mare will give upwards of 1,500 litres (330 gallons) during a seven- to eight-month lactation period, and the best may produce as much as 2,700 litres (550 gallons). Much of the milk is used in dairy products, but a significant percentage is employed in making *kummis*, the fiery "hooch" of the steppes, which the former Soviet authorities hastened to extol as having valuable dietetic and medicinal properties.

The Bashkir can be used as a mountain pack-pony, under saddle, and in draught. Their endurance is legendary: a Bashkir *troika* is claimed to be able to cover 120–140 km (75–85 miles) a day in the snow. Equally, the breed is almost unimaginably hardy, and the herds are well able to live out in deep snow and blizzard conditions at temperatures which in winter fall to between –30 and –40°C.

CHARACTERISTICS

Two types of Bashkir pony have been developed – the mountain type, which is suitable for riding, and the rather heavier steppe variety. The Bashkir, which stands at 1.32–1.42 m (13–14 hh), is a wide-bodied, short-legged, stocky animal, with substantial

AMERICAN VERSION
The American Bashkir "Curly" is claimed to have links with the steppe Bashkirs of the Urals. It has the same curly coat, but otherwise the resemblance is not close.

QUARTERS
The best specimens are well-built with broad quarters, but they are often slightly cow-hocked.

UNIVERSAL PROVIDER
The Bashkir herds are very important to the steppe economy. They provide fresh meat and other products, and the mares are milked, as shown here. The ponies are also used for transport and agricultural purposes.

LEGS
The legs are generally short and set four-square on the wide body. Bone is adequate in proportion to the size.

bone below the knee; some ponies may have an extraordinary 20 cm (8 in). The neck is short, strong, and fleshy, and the head is often described as "massive". Particular features of the breed are the thick, curly coat and the luxurious growth of mane and tail. Combings from the hair can be woven to make blankets and garments, and American sources claim that such cloth can be used without ill effect by those usually allergic to horses – a condition, one imagines, not much found in steppe society.

THE AMERICAN BASHKIR

This indomitable universal provider, for all its sterling attributes, can hardly be cast in the romantic role of "mystery horse", yet it is at the centre of a fascinating hippological puzzle (or, perhaps, a colossal leg-pull). The

mystery lies in the fact that there are about 1,100 registered Bashkirs (possibly a refined form of the Russian pony) in the north-western states of the US.

The Americans claim that the horses, known in the US as Bashkir Curlies, were first noticed in the Mustang herds during the early 1800s, and the suggestion is that they arrived on the continent with their owners thousands of years ago, across the land bridge that is now the Bering Strait. That would, of course, have been perfectly possible; in fact, the Native American peoples may have come to North America in that way. However, this theory takes no account

of the fact that the land bridges connecting the North American continent to Europe and Asia were swept away during the Ice Age, and that, for reasons unknown, the horse became extinct in the Americas some eight to ten thousand years ago. It was not reintroduced there until the arrival of the Spanish conquistadores (see pp.216–17) in the 16th century.

ORIGINS

THE BASHKIR, OR BASHKIRSKY, comes from Bashkiria in the southern foothills of the Ural Mountains, close to the steppes of Kirghizia and Kazakhstan, where it has lived from time immemorial. It is naturally hardy and resistant to wet and cold, and the Bashkir herds live out all year round, often in conditions of deep snow and with temperatures as much as 30–40°C below freezing. Mountain-bred Bashkirs are lighter and smaller than those bred on the steppe.

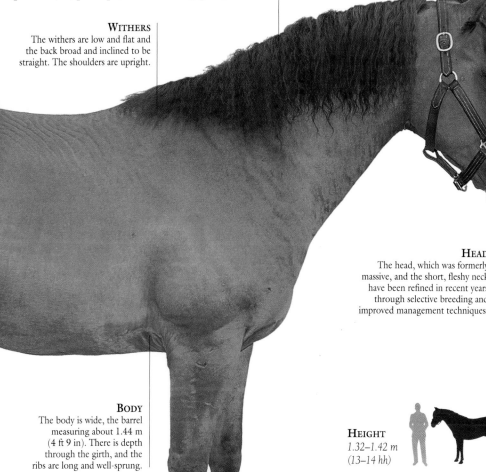

WITHERS
The withers are low and flat and the back broad and inclined to be straight. The shoulders are upright.

MANE
The mane and tail are exceptionally thick. The thick, curly winter coat is a feature peculiar to the breed.

HEAD
The head, which was formerly massive, and the short, fleshy neck have been refined in recent years through selective breeding and improved management techniques.

BODY
The body is wide, the barrel measuring about 1.44 m (4 ft 9 in). There is depth through the girth, and the ribs are long and well-sprung.

HEIGHT
1.32–1.42 m
(13–14 hh)

FEET
The feet are sound and hard in the tradition of the steppe and mountain horse. The pasterns are inclined to be upright.

KAZAKH

The Bashkir's neighbour, the Kazakh, is also kept on the steppe in large herds, largely for meat. However, the Kazakh people also have a tradition of racing and other horse sports that provides a powerful incentive for keeping and improving their stock.

INDIAN COUNTRY-BRED

IN THEORY, THE TERM "INDIAN COUNTRY-BRED" means no more than "bred in India". However, "country-bred" is also used in the looser sense to describe a variety of animals of mixed breeding, from a very acceptable stamp of horse to an under-sized degenerate specimen that hauls a grossly over-loaded cart in the bazaars of the great cities or is driven loose in a pack train along the *katcha* (rough) track bordering the Grand Trunk Road. The Indian horse population is diverse and extensive, but it is not without discernible patterns as well as some breeds and strains of particular interest and merit.

OUTSIDE INFLUENCES
The influence of Tibet is evident in the man's clothing and the prayer wheel, but the saddle design of this Spiti pony in East Ladakh is Mongolian.

EARLY HISTORY

The remains of prehistoric horses have been found in the foothills of the Siwaliks, in northern India, and it is possible that there were horses and ponies here long before they made their way to Europe. What effect they may have had no-one can tell; however, it is possible to trace a number of major influences that have played a part in the creation of the equine population of the subcontinent. For centuries there was a constant flow of horses from the north through the passes of the Hindu Kush into the Punjab. From there they spread into northern India and Rajasthan and continued southwards. They also came over the trade routes from Kandahar in Afghanistan, through Quetta, and crossed the Indus at Sukkur, making their way into Rajasthan and Gujerat. Another route was from Baluchistan by way of Hyderabad and Karachi. Many of these were steppe horses of oriental origin – Persians, Turkmenes, and Arab strains, Shirazi from southern Persia, Jaf, and Tchenarani, as well as Kabuli ponies from Afghanistan and the robust,

iron-legged Baluchis. Early in the 19th century there was a regular trade in Arabs from the Arabian Gulf to the ports of Bombay and Veraval in Kathiawar, which gave an additional supporting element to the mix, and increased the size of the subsequent progeny when crossed with pony stock of mixed type.

RECENT INFLUENCES

From this influx of predominantly eastern horses, some of which would have had at least a sprinkling of Mongolian blood, there emerged the strong horses of the Punjab, noted particularly for the quality and substance of the mares; the Kathiawari and Marwari horses of Gujerat and Rajasthan (see pp.162–65); and the Deccanis of central and southern India, which provided the cavalry for the Duke of Wellington's successful campaigns of the 18th century. They were also just as highly regarded and extensively used by his enemies.

The huge imports of Walers from New South Wales in Australia (see pp.292–93) had their inevitable and often beneficial

QUARTERS
The quarters have a wiry quality, though the hind legs do not have strong second thighs. The tail is low-set.

FEET
The feet are often upright and boxy, but are surprisingly hard-wearing.

THE TONGA
Tonga carts are used in every Indian city. They are drawn by uncomplaining ponies, and are often grossly overloaded with passengers or goods. Nonetheless, they provide a basic, cheap form of transport.

HEIGHT
*1.42–1.52 m
(14–15 hh)*

effect on the country-bred pony. After the First World War Thoroughbreds (see pp.120–21) were introduced and became central to the breeding policy of the Army Remount Department. Selected Punjab mares were crossed with Arabs (see pp.64–65), and the resultant fillies were put to English Thoroughbreds. This breeding policy was practised up to the time of partition between India and Pakistan in 1947. In the northern hill states the brooding presence of the hardy, vigorous Mongolian horse still persists. In the mountains of Chitral, Hunza, Nagar, Gilgit, and Kashmir, people do not walk. They ride one or other of the hill pony strains, all of

them having the Mongolian connection. The Mongolian has also stamped the breeds along India's northern frontier states, the Tibetan (Nanfan), the Bhutia, Spiti, and then, further to the east, the Burma ponies of the Shan Hills, and the remarkable Manipuris which were responsible for polo being played in India and then subsequently in almost every country of the world.

The hill ponies are used as pack animals and are also ridden, while in the states on the north-west frontier the locals play polo regularly, frequently, and usually violently, for the rules of the English Hurlingham Club are not acknowledged there. All these horses and ponies, their crosses and derivatives, make up the wonderfully varied spectrum of the Indian country-bred. The emphasis, however, is on the north of the Indian subcontinent,

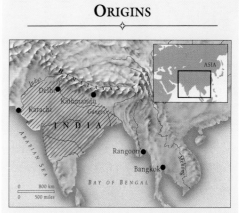

ORIGINS

THE INDIAN COUNTRY-BRED *is of infinitely mixed ancestry, and is to be found all over the subcontinent. India is generally poor horse-raising country, and many country-bred ponies reflect the poor soil condition and lack of nutritious feed in their lack of size, substance, or bone, and in some weak conformational features. Nonetheless, the ponies are willing workers, enduring, and very tough. They are naturally economical to keep and can work on modest rations.*

NECK
The long neck runs into clearly defined withers.

HEAD
The head is usually plain and exhibits no special features.

BODY
The body often lacks depth, with the ribs being insufficiently sprung. The chest is often narrow.

POLO-BRED
Polo is the national game of Manipur, and is played in every village. The Manipuri pony is wiry, nimble, and surprisingly fast, but small in size, so riders must use shortened mallets.

particularly with the people of the north-west, who have a cultural connection with the tribes of Central Asia and the Middle East and whose brethren extend beyond the Afghanistan frontier.

Elsewhere, an equestrian tradition is much less in evidence. Indeed, the ordinary Indian villager, as well as the millions who have left the countryside to join the teeming populations of the cities, have little or no contact with the horse. Once in a lifetime, on the occasion of his wedding, an Indian peasant, whether villager or town-dweller, may bestride a horse for the journey to the house of his intended bride. The horse, and those who ride him in ceremonial procession, is seen as the image of power and majesty, and for a brief moment the humble villager, dressed in bright finery, assumes the heroic mould that is otherwise the prerogative of the great and noble.

For the greater part of India, climatic conditions are unsuited to horse-breeding. Much of the country is semi-tropical and the heat and the humidity prohibit the effective use of the horse in draught. For that purpose, water buffalo and cattle are more suitable and are better able to withstand the climatic conditions. The demands made on cultivated land leave nothing for the grazing of horses. Indian horses are fed on what hay is available, which is often of poor quality, on cut grasses of variable nutritional content, on the chaff left after threshing, and occasionally on barley.

SUMBA & TIMOR

INDONESIA IS MADE UP OF A CHAIN OF SOME 300 ISLANDS, the largest of which is Sumatra. Most of the islands support small, primitive-type ponies such as the Sumba and the closely related Sumbawa, but there are others that have been improved by Arab blood introduced by the Dutch colonists in the 17th century. Although all the Indonesian ponies were originally imported to the islands, there is little doubt that they derive from the Mongolian (see pp.198–99), which spread both eastwards and southwards from the Indian hill states and neighbouring Tibet to reach the Indonesian islands through Thailand and, perhaps, China. The primitive influence is most evident in the Sumba/Sumbawa ponies.

WEIGHT-CARRIERS
The extraordinarily tough Sumbawa ponies are quite able to carry weight out of all proportion to their diminutive size. The dun colour of this pony is typical of Indonesian stock.

THE SUMBA AND SUMBAWA

The Sumba and Sumbawa ponies are in every respect identical, but originate in the different islands from which they take their names. They are found all over Indonesia, particularly on Sumatra. It is impossible to say when the ponies first came to Indonesia, or for what reason. In the early days they might have come from Indian or Chinese sources. Later, both the Dutch and Portuguese brought in many ponies.

The ponies are small, about 1.27 m (12.2 hh), and very primitive in appearance. The head is large in comparison with the body, the profile being either straight or convex, and there is a close resemblance to the Mongolian horse and its progenitors, the Asiatic Wild Horse and the Tarpan (see pp.18–21). The resemblance is reinforced by the predominantly dun coat-colour. This is usually accompanied by a pronounced dorsal stripe, a dark mane and tail, and either black or zebra-striped lower limbs. These ponies

are not dissimilar to the Chinese pony, with which they share common ancestry, but on the whole the conformation is better and the Sumba/Sumbawa stock are more agile.

The ponies are exceptionally hardy, as they need to be in a country where grazing is poor, and in which nourishing, body-building feed is minimal. Unusually, for

HEIGHT OF SUMBA
1.27 m
(12.2 hh)

COLOUR
The dun colouring, usually accompanied by a dorsal stripe, is typical of the horse.

BODY
The body's conformation is not perfect but the back is strong.

HEAD
The head is common and of the Mongolian type. It is set on a short neck.

THROWING THE LANCE
The game of throwing the lance is played with great enthusiasm on Sumba, using the small but surprisingly fast and agile Sumba ponies. The ponies are ridden in traditional bitless bridles.

SUMBA

ponies of close primitive descent, which can be fierce and aggressive, the Sumbas are exceptionally co-operative and willing.

The ponies are ridden by grown men, mostly without saddles, and are controlled by bridles of plaited leather with just a noseband and no bit. These bridles are identical to those used in Central Asia 4,000 years ago by horse-people like the Scythians, and they are not dissimilar to the *bosal* and hackamore, the nosepieces that are still used in California, Mexico, and South America.

The Sumba and Sumbawa ponies are used as pack animals, and can carry loads well out of proportion to their size. They are also notable for their speed and agility when playing the local sport where two sides ride against each other throwing lances. The game ends when one side has no more riders to be struck by the opponents' lances.

The most prized Sumba ponies are those selected to dance. These ponies are carefully chosen for the elegance and lightness of their movement and their natural agility. With bells attached to their knees they dance to the rhythm of tom-toms, the owner directing the movement and beating time

TIMOR PONY
The ponies of Timor are hardy and versatile. They have been exported to Australia and are considered to be good riding ponies.

while holding the pony on a loose lunge rein attached to the bridle. A small boy usually rides the pony as it dances, sitting with great suppleness. The horse dancing tradition is very old, and interestingly, is also to be found in some of the remoter areas of Central Asia. Such performances can also be seen in India's Kathiawar Peninsula and at the horse fairs held in Rajasthan.

THE TIMOR

On Timor, a Portuguese colony in the 16th century before it came under Dutch influence in the 17th, horses were important and the number of horses per head of population was very high. At one time the ratio was estimated to be one horse to six people, while the ratio in Laos was 1:110 and in Malaysia only 1:200.

Horses, and possibly the toe-stirrup as well, were probably introduced to Timor from India. The Portuguese and then the Dutch were responsible for encouraging the use of horses for pack, transport, and riding. Writing in 1943, Stuart St Clair, ("Timor: A Key to the Indies", *National Geographic*) reported that men, women, and children went everywhere on horseback. Certainly, the local "cowboys" used the ponies for working with cattle and used a rope lasso, as in the American West.

Apart from the encouragement of Dutch and Portuguese traders, the large number of horses on Timor can be linked to its huge savannahs, which provide good grazing. However, even with that, the ponies are small and rarely exceed 1.22 m (12 hh).

Australia, whose northern coast faces Timor, imported its first Timor pony in 1803. Thereafter the Timors were instrumental in improving the stamina and toughness of much of the Australian stock.

HEIGHT OF TIMOR
Up to 1.22 m (12 hh)

HEAD
The mane and tail are full and the coat is fine. The head is common and the neck is noticeably short.

BODY
The body is straight-backed with upright shoulders. The tail is set high.

TIMOR

ORIGINS
◆

THE SUMBAWA AND SUMBA ponies of Indonesia are virtually identical. They take their names from the islands of Sumbawa and Sumba which lie between Java and Timor, but they are to be found all over the archipelago, particularly in Sumatra. The small Timor pony inhabits the island of that name which is separated from northernmost Australia by the Timor Sea. Because the Timor Pony is integral to the island's economy the equine population is necessarily large, but the extensive savannahs provide a good growth of various wiry grasses that are capable of sustaining the numbers involved.

SANDALWOOD & BATAK

THE SANDALWOOD PONY was originally developed on the islands of Sumba and Sumbawa, while the Batak has been selectively bred at studs on Sumatra since the days of the Dutch colonists. Both ponies owe much to the Arab stallions (see pp.64–65) that were imported by the Dutch to improve the Indonesian breeds. Selected mares were sent to stallions standing at the studs on Sumatra, and the young stock was then dispersed to other islands to help upgrade the stock there. The Sandalwood and the Batak are refined, quality animals with little trace of the Mongolian character so apparent in the other Indonesian ponies.

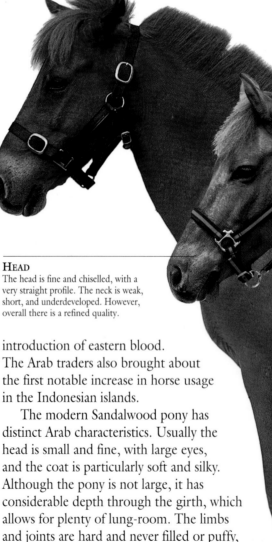

ARAB INFLUENCE
Some of the Sandalwood stock are well-made ponies. The influence of the Arab, in this instance, is evident in the tail carriage and in the head, although the latter is heavy.

THE SANDALWOOD

The Sandalwood pony is named after the type of wood that is one of the principal exports of Sumba and Sumbawa. In fact, the breed itself has contributed significantly to the economy of the islands. Together with shipments of sandalwood, many ponies were exported to Australia, where they were considered to be good children's ponies. Sandalwoods were also sold to Thailand, where they were highly regarded as racing ponies. The breed is raced extensively in

HEIGHT OF SANDALWOOD
Up to 1.35 m (13.1 hh)

EAR MARKS
Indonesian ponies are often ear-marked in intricate fashion as a way of identifying ownership, just as sheep are ear-nicked in the Western world.

Indonesia, often over distances of 4–5 km (2½–3 miles). In these events the ponies are usually ridden bareback, in the traditional bitless bridle (see pp.198–99). In Malaysia, the Sandalwood has been crossed with Thoroughbreds (see pp.120–21) in order to produce bigger, faster horses. Some of these cross-breds were used for racing in other Southeast Asian countries, such as Thailand and Cambodia.

The Sandalwood pony, like the Batak, has been much influenced by Arab blood, and probably for a long time before Indonesia came under Dutch rule. Horses were introduced to Southeast Asia from India, probably during the first three centuries of the Christian era. However, it was Arab traders, several centuries later, who were largely responsible for the

HEAD
The head is fine and chiselled, with a very straight profile. The neck is weak, short, and underdeveloped. However, overall there is a refined quality.

introduction of eastern blood. The Arab traders also brought about the first notable increase in horse usage in the Indonesian islands.

The modern Sandalwood pony has distinct Arab characteristics. Usually the head is small and fine, with large eyes, and the coat is particularly soft and silky. Although the pony is not large, it has considerable depth through the girth, which allows for plenty of lung-room. The limbs and joints are hard and never filled or puffy, while the feet are naturally tough and never need to be shod. This breed is the biggest of the Indonesian ponies, and may measure as much as 1.35 m (13.1 hh). Because it has better shoulders than the more primitive Indonesian breeds, the Sandalwood is fast and very active. It resembles the good-quality ponies that were bred at the stud at Padang Mengabes (see pp.208–9), which was founded by the Dutch colonists.

SANDALWOOD

FEET
The horn of the feet is unusually tough and hard. It is a particular feature of the breed.

THE BATAK

The Batak pony is native to central Sumatra. The people of this area are as dependent on horses as the inhabitants of Timor, the island to the east of Sumba and the closest to the Australian coast, which has the highest proportion of horses to people in the whole of Southeast Asia. One of the greatest authorities on the region, William Marsden (*The History of Sumatra*, 1966), says of the Batak people that they consider horse flesh "their most exquisite meat and for this purpose feed them upon grain, and pay great attention to their keep". Marsden also reports the popularity of horse-racing among these tribes, and their obsessive interest in gambling. Indeed, at one time any Batak gambler who lost more than he could pay could be sold into slavery, unless his creditor was generous enough to let him repay the debt by slaughtering a horse for a public feast. Another authority, the Austrian Edwin Loeb (*Sumatra: Its History and People*, 1935), describes horse sacrifices made by the Toba, a Batak tribe. Loeb regarded this practice as being related to a Hindu form of sacrifice, and wrote about it in some detail. The Toba have a trinity of gods to whom horse sacrifice is made, and each clan keeps three sacred horses, each dedicated to one of the gods. The horses are "unviolable and non-alienable", being allowed to graze and wander where they will. When a sacred horse grows old he is sacrificed, then eaten, and a young horse appointed in his place.

Today, the Batak is a working pony, and is widely used for riding. It also performs an important function as the core of Indonesian horse breeding, and is instrumental in upgrading poorer stock on the other islands. It is a handsome pony, with definite Arab character and good proportions, and stands at up to 1.32 m (13 hh), although some are smaller. The Batak has a reputation for being docile and good-natured, but it is also spirited and agile. Like all the Indonesian stock, the Batak is economical to feed and easily managed. There is a wide range of coat colours in both the Sandalwood and the Batak, and no one colour predominates.

The Batak was sometimes referred to as the Deli pony, after the port from which large numbers of animals were once exported to Singapore. Another pony, presumably a Batak strain, was to be found in northern Sumatra. It was called the Gayoe, and was more heavily built than the Batak. Less Arab in character, it lacked the Batak's speed and spirited nature. In its original form it may no longer exist in large numbers, most of the Gayoe stock having been assimilated with the lighter, more active Batak.

RIDING PONIES
Sandalwood ponies can also show traces of their Mongolian ancestry, particularly in the head and the set of the neck. They are noted as good riding ponies.

RUMP
This is an excessively high "goose rump". The pony also has a long, narrow back and slack loins.

TAIL
The tail and mane hair is fine rather than coarse, and is sometimes somewhat sparse. The tail is set well up and in movement is carried high.

LEGS
The legs are slender and the ponies lack bone. The hocks are set high on long shanks, and there is little development in the gaskin.

BATAK

HEIGHT OF BATAK
Up to 1.32 m (13 hh)

ORIGINS

THE INDONESIAN *equine population was much influenced by the Dutch colonists of the Dutch East Indies, who imported stock from both India and the Cape. The Sandalwood, one of the principal pony breeds, is important. It was originally developed on the islands of Sumba and Sumbawa, and resembles the quality ponies bred by the Dutch at Padang Mengabes in neighbouring Sumatra, which may well have had an influence in its development. The Batak, with which there may also be a connection, is native to Central Sumatra, while the old Gayoe strain was found in the north of the island.*

JAVA & PADANG

THE DUTCH established a factory at Bantam on Java as early as 1598, and in 1619 they set up the eastern headquarters of the Dutch East India Company close by, on the site of the modern city of Jakarta. Arab and Barb horses, probably brought in by Arab traders in earlier days and then supplemented by the Dutch, were certainly on the island in the 17th century and would have had an effect on the Java stock. Equally, the selectively bred stock developed at Padang Mengabes in neighbouring Sumatra could have had some influence in improving the conformation of the local ponies.

TRANSPORT SYSTEM
A principal use for Java ponies is for drawing taxi carts (called sados) in the towns. These carts provide a remarkably effective system of transport and delivery, carrying not only passengers but also all sorts of commodities.

THE JAVA

The Arab influence (see pp.64–65) is not very apparent in the appearance of the Java pony, although the Java has inherited both the Arab's stamina and its resistance to heat. The less visually attractive Barb (see pp.66–67) also played a major role in its development, further adding to the desert character and contributing significantly to the Java pony's incredible toughness.

The Java, at 1.27 m (12.2 hh) or so, is a little larger than most of the island ponies, with the exception of the Batak and Sandalwood (see pp.206–7), and more strongly built. It is not unprepossessing but it is by no means of exemplary conformation

JAVA

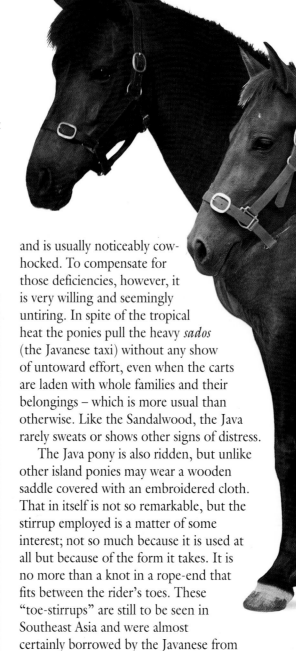

HEIGHT OF JAVA
1.27 m (12.2 hh)

LEGS
The legs and joints are underdeveloped and give no impression of strength, even though the Java is a tireless worker.

CANNONS
The Padang ponies have better conformation than other Sumatran breeds but are long in the cannons and light of bone.

FEET
The feet are hard and quite well-formed but the pasterns appear to be weak.

ORIGINS

PONIES ARE SPREAD over the whole Indonesian archipelago and most of them share a common root. There are differences in detail in the stock according to the island the ponies inhabit. The Java pony is numerous and is fairly distinctive. The more refined Padang is a type upgraded from the local stock of central Sumatra and takes its name from Padang Mengabes where the Dutch founded a stud. The tropical heat and the generally sparse, mineral-deficient grazing both have an influence on the character, lack of bone, and light conformation of the ponies.

and is usually noticeably cow-hocked. To compensate for those deficiencies, however, it is very willing and seemingly untiring. In spite of the tropical heat the ponies pull the heavy *sados* (the Javanese taxi) without any show of untoward effort, even when the carts are laden with whole families and their belongings – which is more usual than otherwise. Like the Sandalwood, the Java rarely sweats or shows other signs of distress.

The Java pony is also ridden, but unlike other island ponies may wear a wooden saddle covered with an embroidered cloth. That in itself is not so remarkable, but the stirrup employed is a matter of some interest; not so much because it is used at all but because of the form it takes. It is no more than a knot in a rope-end that fits between the rider's toes. These "toe-stirrups" are still to be seen in Southeast Asia and were almost certainly borrowed by the Javanese from their close neighbours on the small island of Timor. They may have been introduced into

Timor by Indian travellers and traders well before the arrival of the Portuguese in the 16th century. Surprisingly, the toe-stirrup was not generally adopted on the islands of Sumba and Sumbawa, which lie between Java and Timor. These toe-stirrups are of significance because it is possible that they were the prototype for the larger foot stirrup made from metal or wood.

EXPORTS FROM JAVA

The Javanese Arab and Barb population was to influence the evolution of other horses and ponies, apart from those in Indonesia. In 1653 Arabs and Barbs from Java were exported to South Africa, where they were the original founders of the Cape Horse. (Thoroughbred infusions were made between 1770 and 1790. This resulted in the Basuto pony of Lesotho, which can be dated from about 1830.) The Cape Horse

was subsequently introduced into India in some numbers during the 19th century, and as the first horse to be introduced into Australia it also played an important part in the evolution of the Australian Waler (see pp.292–93). The first imported horses, the descendants of the Arabs and Barbs that had

PADANG
The Padang ponies, upgraded from local ponies, show the refining influence of the improving Arab on the Mongolian root stock.

been sent to the Cape from Java in the previous century, landed in Sydney Cove on 26 January 1788.

THE PADANG

The Padang pony of Sumatra is no more than a type developed from the Batak strains. It was bred selectively by the Dutch at Padang Mengabes on the south coast of the island, and was upgraded with Arab blood. It is a lightly built pony of some quality and spirit and is said to make a good, free-going riding pony. Without doubt, it has had an improving influence on a number of Indonesian ponies, including the Java pony. Like the Java, it is strong and persevering out of proportion to its size and does not sweat noticeably even when working hard in considerable heat.

The predecessors of the ponies bred at Padang Mengabes may have been a little-known strain called the Preanger, which was no more than a cross between local mares and imported Arabs or Barbs. However, it would have provided a sound genetic base for a further outcross to the Arabs.

In a country like Indonesia, which lacks the climatic and ground conditions necessary for the raising of well-grown equine stock, there is no doubt that the only possible outcrosses that could be calculated to improve the native ponies are the Arab and the Barb. Furthermore, without regular infusions of outside blood it would be difficult to prevent the stock degenerating.

HEIGHT OF PADANG
1.27 m
(12.2 hh)

QUARTERS
The quarters are adequately well-formed and, although short in the croup, are without the customary goose rump.

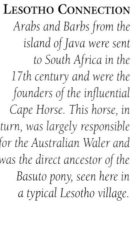

PADANG

LESOTHO CONNECTION
Arabs and Barbs from the island of Java were sent to South Africa in the 17th century and were the founders of the influential Cape Horse. This horse, in turn, was largely responsible for the Australian Waler and was the direct ancestor of the Basuto pony, seen here in a typical Lesotho village.

AUSTRALIAN PONY

HORSES ARE NOT INDIGENOUS TO AUSTRALIA and so, of necessity, the early Australians had to rely upon imported horses and ponies to help them exploit the vast potential of their new country. Horses and ponies were brought into Australia with each new arrival of immigrants, and ponies from nearby Indonesian islands were also acquired. By 1920 a type of Australian Pony had emerged and within 10 years the Australian Pony Stud Book Society had been formed. The breeding of an Australian Pony is much encouraged by a wide range of classes at the big major shows and by a large and enthusiastic membership of the Pony Club, managed on the same lines as its parent body in England.

WELSH INHERITANCE
The Australian Pony retains the ability of the Welsh breeds to perform most creditably in harness while inheriting much of the Welsh sagacity and spirit.

EARLY IMPORTS

The first elements in the evolution of the Australian Pony were the small, very hardy ponies from Timor, the Indonesian island off Australia's northern coast (see pp.204–5), which were increasingly imported after 1803. It is probable that other Indonesian ponies, such as those from the islands of Sumba and Sumbawa, including the more refined Sandalwood pony (see pp.206–7), would also have been imported. These ponies had connections through the Mongolian Pony to the early primitive horses, the Asiatic Wild Horse and the Tarpan (see pp.18–21), with subsequent infusions of "desert" blood resulting from the Arab and Barb influence in the islands. Horses were also imported into Australia from South Africa, the first arriving in 1788. All these ponies and horses would have been used to both heat and cold and resistant to the effects of the climate.

This was the background that provided a base stock equipped in all respects to cope with the climatic conditions and feed availability of the habitat. It was, therefore, ideal stock with which to cross imported ponies from the northern hemisphere that were not by nature accustomed to such circumstances.

Early in the 19th century, Arab horses (see pp.64–65) were being brought in from India, most of them being shipped from Calcutta, which is geographically the most convenient of the Indian ports. Obviously, these horses were just as accustomed to the tropical conditions as the ponies of Indonesia. They were, however, bigger, better made, freer in their movement, and far more versatile. Moreover, the Arab is infinitely prepotent, stamping its stock indelibly with its special character and quality and thus upgrading anything with which it is crossed.

PONIES FROM THE UK

At the same time, however, Australians were looking to the native pony breeds of "the old country". Both the Exmoor and the Shetland (see pp.174–75 and pp.178–79) were imported, as well as the New Forest, the Highland, and the Irish Connemara (see pp.180–81). Hackneys (see pp.402–3), which at that date would have been of pronounced Roadster type,

HIND LEGS
The conformation of the hind legs is exemplary and virtually the same as that of the Welsh Pony (Section B). There is notable length between hip and hock joint.

NATIVE TYPE
The Australian Pony may vary in height between 1.22 and 1.42 m (12–14 hh) and there is still some variation in type. In general the ponies incline more towards the British native ponies than otherwise, with some excellent specimens of pronounced Welsh Pony (Section B) type.

HEIGHT
1.22–1.42 m
(12–14 hh)

were also acquired. However, the greatest contribution was made by the Welsh Mountain Pony (see pp.182–83). From this melting-pot of breeds emerged the Australian Pony, as a breed in its own right. Its prime influences were increasingly Welsh and Arab with, perhaps, an occasional input of Thoroughbred blood. The foundation sire is recognized as the Welsh Mountain Pony Dyoll Greylight, son of the patriarch Dyoll Starlight, "the most beautiful pony in the whole world", whose dam, Moonlight, was described as a "miniature Arab". Dyoll Greylight was exported to Australia in 1911 for the then enormous price of 1,000 guineas. In Australia he is regarded with the same veneration as his sire and shares with him the accolade of "the most beautiful pony in the world". Dyoll Greylight was bought by Mr Antony Hordern, whose

daughter gave £21,000 for the stallion Coed Coch Bari when Coed Coch, the greatest of the Welsh studs, was dispersed in 1978. Bari traced to Starlight through his sire Salsbri and his grand-sire, the world famous Coed Coch Madog. Many other exports were made to Australia in the 1960s and 1970s, but the Starlight blood remains predominant in those ponies, as it does in the Australian Pony. Australia still keeps large numbers of the British native breeds, particularly Welsh ponies, all of which are of the best quality and have their own breed societies and stud books. For many years Australia was the most important market for British ponies and at one time was also a big importer of the best Clydesdale strains (see pp.286–87).

ORIGINS

THE FIRST HORSES were imported into Australia in the 18th century, but the evolution of the Australian Pony is almost wholly attributed to the 19th- and 20th-century imports of British native ponies, particularly the Welsh Mountain. Encouraged by the enthusiasm of Australians for equestrian sports and by some of the biggest horse shows in the world, the Australian Pony is now bred in Victoria, New South Wales, the coastal areas of Queensland, and also parts of Western Australia.

CHARACTERISTICS

The Australian breeders have, nonetheless, created a show pony distinguished by its own special qualities. The height may still vary between 1.22 m and 1.42 m (12–14 hh) but the pony has more in common with the British native than with the highly refined Riding Pony (see pp.406–7). It has substance, excellent bone with short cannons, and the splendid feet of its Welsh ancestors. As a result of the Arab and Thoroughbred influence, the action is distinctive. The forehand conformation, and the set and slope of the shoulders, resemble that of a much larger horse, so the stride is exceptionally smooth and long, providing a delightful ride for children and smaller adults.

TOP LINE
The flowing top line and the well-formed withers, back, and trunk are characteristic of the finest type of riding pony.

HEAD
The head retains pony character. It is neat, dominated by large eyes, and is beautifully tapered to the muzzle.

SHOULDERS
The shoulders and forelegs are difficult to fault. They contribute materially to the pony's long stride and the smooth, straight, and level paces.

PONY CLUBS
Pony Club mounted games are pursued with as much enthusiasm by Australia's Pony Club members as by their UK counterparts.

HOKKAIDO, KISO & KAGOSHIMA

THE FIRST HORSES brought to Japan probably came with Central Asiatic peoples, who arrived from Korea in the 3rd century AD. Their burial mounds contain *haniwa*, or terracotta figures, which include models of horses as well as of humans. Kublai Khan, grandson of Genghis Khan, also tried to invade Japan from Korea, in 1274 and 1281. The invasions were frustrated by storms, but may well have provided Mongolian ponies to supplement the Japanese stock.

BREEDS

The Hokkaido, the Kiso, and the Kagoshima are neither distinctive nor very numerous. All three are obviously descended from the ponies of Mongolia, China, and Korea. It is likely that the Hokkaido, which used to be known as the Dosanko, came from north-east China. The Kiso (from the mountainous Kiso-Sanmyaku, due west of Tokyo) and the Kagoshima probably came from Korea. Until recently, the latter was considered to

KISO
The Kiso ponies live in the mountainous central region of Kiso-Sanmyaku and at one time were commonly used in agriculture.

BODY
The pony has low, flat withers, upright shoulders, a short neck, and a head betraying its Mongolian antecedents.

FOREHAND
The forehand is heavy and unbalanced by the large head, but the legs are well-made.

HEAD
The head is undistinguished and dull in its expression. It shows evidence of the Mongolian pony background in the Japanese stock.

LEGS
The legs are light and slender with some fine feathering at the heels. The feet are of surprisingly good shape.

KISO

be a wild horse, and it was given the generic name "Kyushu". All of these ponies stand at about 1.32 m (13 hh).

HORSE-RIDING IN JAPAN

The Japanese have never been outstanding horsemen, although Yoshifuru Akiyama, a French-trained cavalryman, scored a surprising victory over the Cossacks in the Russo-Japanese War of 1904–5, and one Japanese rider, Captain Nishi, won the gold medal in showjumping at the 1932 Olympic Games. Nonetheless, for centuries horses have played a major part in Japanese history.

In early Japan, mounted warriors were part of the aristocracy. During the Japanese medieval period, civil and military officials were commanded to ride and to practise the use of arms. The Japanese had an equivalent

ORIGINS

MUCH OF JAPAN'S HORSE-RAISING *country is mountainous with soil and natural herbage of poor quality. In consequence the size of the ponies is limited. The best area is on the northern island of Hokkaido, where there is still open land capable of providing sufficient grazing, and a lower density of population. The breeding area for the Kiso is around the mountainous Kiso-Sanmyaku in the very centre of the country, due west of Tokyo, while the habitat of the Kagoshima is the southernmost island of Kyushu, where until relatively recent times the breed was regarded as being wild stock.*

HEIGHT OF HOKKAIDO
1.32 m (13 hh)

of the European chivalric ideal, in the symbol of the "trinity of the horse, the warrior, and the flower". As Kenrick records in *Horses in Japan* (1964), the prime accomplishments of the *samurai* knight were "his skill in horsemanship and archery, fencing and ju-jitsu" – the *bujutsu*, or military arts.

Travelling civilian dignitaries sat on wide wooden saddles like pack saddles, which were covered with cloaks and bedding. The "horseman" sat cross-legged, or with his legs resting either side of the horse's neck. Civilians rarely took hold of the reins – that was the prerogative of the fighting man – so the horse was led by footmen. The Japanese also developed equestrian sports

HOKKAIDO
The open ground on Hokkaido is capable of supporting an equine population. The ponies are still used in farming, haulage, and under pack.

HEIGHT OF KISO
1.32 m
(13 hh)

based on Central Asian and Chinese games, and for centuries there was a Japanese circus whose principal feature was trick riding.

At the end of the 19th century, bigger, faster horses were imported, and European riding became popular. Today, most riders use Thoroughbred-type horses, and adopt

the European style. However, the old sport of *yabusame*, in which *samurai* on galloping horses fire arrows at a target, has survived as a Shinto ritual.

OTHER USES

Until the 1930s, horses were widely used in farming, for haulage, and under pack, while the cavalry rode horses that were crosses, or second crosses, with native ponies. A few ponies still work on farms, particularly in mountain areas. In Hokkaido they are used to pull sleds, and until recently some were employed in small coal mines.

The early Japanese, copying the Chinese, sacrificed horses in order to propitiate their gods. According to Kenrick (1964), "Within living memory, the country custom was observed of hanging the heads of horses at the entrances of farmhouses. The horse possessed the qualities of an agricultural god, and his head acted as a charm".

KAGOSHIMA

HEIGHT OF KAGOSHIMA
1.32 m
(13 hh)

HOKKAIDO

FEET
All the Japanese ponies appear to have hard, nicely rounded feet, frequently of bluish horn.

KAGOSHIMA
The Kagoshima lives in the south of Kyushu island. It is descended from the ponies of Mongolia, China, and Korea and until recently was considered to be wild.

PART SEVEN

THE AMERICAS

THE HISTORY OF THE MODERN HORSE in the New World begins just over four centuries ago, when it was re-introduced by the early Spanish conquistadores. But in that short space of time, minimal in the context of the overall equine development, the horse population of the Americas has become the largest in the world, the most varied, and arguably the most colourful. North America has one of the greatest Thoroughbred bloodstock industries. It also has its own long-established "all-American" breeds, which may now be described as indigenous and which, for the most part, are based on the early Spanish imports. These include a unique grouping of gaited horses that preserve a tradition once cherished in Europe but now lost to the Old World.

A buffalo hunt, 19th century. A lithograph from Catlin's
North American Collection

THE CONQUISTADORES

SPANIARDS IN PERU

THE ERA of exploration culminating in the conquest of the Americas was spearheaded by the Spanish and Portuguese in the 15th and 16th centuries. Under Prince Henry "the Navigator", a Portuguese fleet pushed on from the coast of Africa in 1458 with the object of seeking trade routes to the east. On the same quest, Bartholomew Diaz rounded the Cape of Good Hope in 1488 and in 1497 Vasco da Gama reached India. America was discovered unexpectedly by Christopher Colombus in 1492. By then America was ripe for discovery, exploration, and, inevitably, the exploitation of its peoples. The horse had been extinct for 8,000 years, but within 400 years there were over 25 million horses in America, a third of the human population.

CHRISTOPHER COLUMBUS

Christopher Columbus made four voyages to the New World. On his first expedition he landed in the Bahamas and the West Indies, where he left 30 horses on the island of Hispaniola (now Haiti). Within 10 years studs had been set up on the larger islands, and within 20 years there was a large horse population in the West Indies. He later sailed to South America and the Gulf of Mexico.

THE CONQUISTADORES

Exploration had received impetus once the 700-year-old Moorish occupation of the Iberian Peninsula ended in 1492. This left

INDIAN ALLIES
On at least one expedition into Mexico, the Spaniards were helped by Indians who acted in support of the horsemen. The feathered headbands of the Aztecs indicated prowess in battle.

a nucleus of skilful, experienced professional soldiers without employment. Spurred on by tales of fabulous wealth and the rich pickings that were said to be had in the New World, these mercenary adventurers came to be known as *conquistadores* (the Spanish word for conquerors), and formed the hard core of the Spanish conquests of Mexico and South America in the 16th century. By the early years of the 17th century the Spaniards had established horse-raising establishments around Santa Fé in the American south-west, and from these settlements horses spread north and east.

On the whole, the conquistadores were unsavoury characters, and the atrocities they committed against the native people, overtly

CONQUEST
This strangely disjointed battle scene shows the conquest of Mexico. It has the Aztec army being bombarded by artillery, while Cortés and his horsemen advance towards the Aztec chieftains.

in the name of God but more generally in a spirit of avarice, were marked by a disregard for human values that was callous even by the standards of their time. The two men responsible for crushing two of the great American civilizations were Hernán Cortés (1485–1547), who arrived in 1519 and crushed the Aztec nation in his conquest of Mexico, and Francisco Pizzaro (1475–1541), who arrived in 1531 and conquered the Inca people of Peru with incredible savagery.

TERRIFYING HORSES

Cortés landed in Mexico in 1519 with a force of only 600 Spanish infantry, 250 Indians, and the 16 horses that were to reinstate the equine species on

CONQUEST
This strangely disjointed battle scene shows the conquest of Mexico. It has the Aztec army being bombarded by artillery, while Cortés and his horsemen advance towards the Aztec chieftains.

FEAR OF THE HORSE
In the Historia de las Indias, *by Diego Duran, Hernán Cortés has been depicted in a more familiar role. He was to claim that "next to God, we owed the victory to the horses".*

PAYING TRIBUTE *(LEFT)*
In this picture, Hernán Cortés, supported by a heavily armed escort (and a peculiarly dwarf pony), receives the gift of a necklace from the conquered Indians. Cortés often relied upon the support of friendly tribes to supplement his force of Europeans, employing them in the conquest of the Aztecs.

the American mainland. He claimed that "next to God, we owed the victory to the horses", for they struck terror into the natives, who naturally had never seen the like of these armoured beasts before. It is likely that it was the Spanish infantry, attacking with their terrible, short, sharp swords, that did most of the damage, but the psychological effect of even a dozen armoured horsemen charging together into the Indian flanks was clearly enormous.

The 16 horses taken by Cortés were well-documented: 11 stallions, two of which were part-coloured or spotted, and five mares. They were mostly of the renowned Cordoba strain, to which Cortés' own horse, El Morzillo ("The Black One") belonged.

EL MORZILLO

Cortés rode El Morzillo on his expedition in Honduras in 1524. It was the worst sort of country for cavalry, through tropical forest and over rough terrain. El Morzillo damaged a foot so severely that he was unable to continue. Cortés left the horse in the care of friendly Indians and promised to return for him, but was never able to do so. The superstitious Indians, greatly fearful of this strange animal and in awe of the white men, did their best. They housed the horse in a temple and had garlanded maidens served him choice fruits and dishes of chicken. El Morzillo, appreciating neither his deification nor his diet, had no

alternative but to die. The Indians, terrified of reprisals, and with naive inspiration, created a statue of him, and placed it on one of the many islands in the lake. In time, it came to be worshipped as Tziunchan, the God of Thunder and Lightning. It remained there until 1697, when more Spanish armies entered into Yucatan, followed by missionary priests greedy for converts. Two Franciscans, Fathers Orbieta and Fuensalida, discovered the statue of the god Tziunchan, and the former, "filled with the spirit of the Lord and carried off with furious zeal for the honour of God", seized a rock and broke the idol into pieces. But by then the horses of El Morzillo's breed had ensured the success of the Spanish conquests.

THE QUEST FOR GOLD
Frederic Remington's evocative painting shows Coronado's expedition of 1540, when the Spaniards marched through the deserts of Arizona, New Mexico, and Texas in search of the legendary (and fictional) Seven Cities of Gold.

MUSTANG & GALICENO

Both the Mustang and the Galiceno pony of Mexico descend from Spanish stock introduced to the American continent by the conquistadores in the 16th century. Mustang is a corruption of *mesteña*, meaning a group or herd of horses, and is used to refer to the wild or semi-wild horses that used to roam in great numbers in the western states. The Galiceno, originating in Galicia in north-west Spain, was introduced into the US during the 1950s and was officially recognized as a breed in 1958.

LITTLE HORSES
The popular Galiceno of Mexico is regarded as a pony, but although no more than 14.2 m (14 hh) it has the character and movement of a small horse.

MUSTANG

THE MUSTANG

Descended from the Spanish horses brought to America by the conquistadores (see pp.216–17), the Mustang population is now much reduced but some still survive in wild horse refuges in the western states. At the beginning of the 20th century there were an estimated one million wild horses. However, organized killing to supply pet food and meat for human consumption had reduced the number so drastically by 1970 that the Mustang was protected by law as an

FOREHAND
The forehand is not impressive because of the short neck and long cannons, but the top line is acceptable.

endangered species. Anxious to conserve the wild horse heritage, enthusiasts formed a variety of societies to preserve, improve, and promote Mustang stock.

The first Mustang support group was the Spanish Mustang Registry, founded by a Mustang breeder, Robert Brislawn, in 1957. It aimed to preserve the purest possible strains of early Spanish horses of both Barb and Andalucian type. Then in the 1960s the American Mustang Association was formed to preserve and promote the Mustang through registration and an intelligent breeding programme. A third organization, the Spanish Barb Breeders' Association, was formed in 1972 with the aim of restoring the true Spanish Barb horse. It set up a breed standard based on documented descriptions made between the 15th and 18th centuries and encouraged highly selective breeding. All these societies

ROUND UP
The modern way of rounding up wild horse stock in Nevada, for inspection or other purposes, is from a helicopter rather than on a horse.

HEIGHT OF MUSTANG
About 1.42 m (14 hh)

seek to preserve strains, or related strains, of horses that have in effect been lost in the Old World and now survive in environments that have been instrumental in fixing their original character. There are also numerous welfare groups such as the International Society for the Protection of the Mustang and Burros, the Wild Horse Organized Assistance, the National Mustang Group, and the National Wild Horse Association, which between them are involved in legislative activities, research work, and practical work in the field.

There can be no overall description of the Mustang, since in the vast area involved even the least adulterated strains will vary according to the perception of those attempting selective breeding. Nonetheless, the Mustang breeder Robert Brislawn was definite about the type

of horse he wanted to preserve in Wyoming. He looked for a small horse of about 1.42 m (14 hh), short in the back, low in the withers, with a low, sloping croup, and weighing about 360 kg (800 lb). In fact, after a study of skeletal remains, Brislawn believed that the horse, which he called a "primitive Barb" ("primitive" meaning early in the context of the American horse population), should have 17 ribs and 5 lumbar vertebrae like the Arab horse, rather than the 18 ribs, 6 vertebrae structure of other breeds. Coats range from roan or *grulla* (slate-blue to mouse-brown) to dun and buckskin

ORIGINS

THE MUSTANG *is the descendant of Spanish horses that formed feral herds after the Spanish conquests in the 16th century. They are the wild horses of the US and are to be found in large numbers in the western states. The Galiceno pony belongs to Mexico, taking its name from the Spanish province of Galicia where it was first developed. It was introduced to the US in the 1950s and is now bred there, as well as in Mexico. It is a popular mount for young riders.*

(dark cream). Mane, tail, and lower limbs are black, ears are small and rimmed with black hair, and the head is small and neat.

HEAD
The head is neat with an alert expression, but it does not show pony character.

PLEASURE SADDLE
This is a light, Mexican-type pleasure saddle. The tree, including the roping horn, is built in contrasting woods and the leather parts are skilfully engraved. Buckles, studs, and stirrups are heavily decorated.

GALICENO

HEIGHT OF GALICENO
1.42 m (14 hh)

THE GALICENO

The Galiceno pony of Mexico is another example of the Spanish legacy. It takes its name from its place of origin, Galicia, an area famed for its smooth-gaited horses, which were distinguished by a swift, running walk. That natural gait, so much prized in 16th-century Europe, is retained by the modern Galiceno, which, though not standing much more than 1.42 m (14 hh) and referred to as a pony is, in fact, a small horse in both character and proportion. The breed derives from some of the earliest horses brought by the Spanish from Hispaniola (also known as the island of Haiti) in the 16th century and is probably much influenced by the hardy Sorraia and Garranos (see pp.106–7) of the Iberian peninsula. They have certainly inherited their tough constitution and are said to be tractable, intelligent, and versatile. They are naturally quick, responsive, and agile and are popular for ranch work and competition. In Mexico the Galiceno is still used as an everyday riding horse and is also worked in harness.

CRIOLLO & PERUVIAN PASO

BOTH THE ARGENTINIAN CRIOLLO and the Peruvian Paso are of early Spanish descent. The first significant importation of horses to Argentina was made in 1535 when Pedro de Mendoza, the founder of Buenos Aires, brought 100 Spanish horses to Rio de la Plata. Five years later the settlement was sacked by the indigenous Charros and the horses ran loose. Within 50 years they had bred so freely that some herds were over 20,000 strong. The first horses in Peru were imported in 1531–32 by Francisco Pizarro, and the Peruvian Paso evolved from these animals.

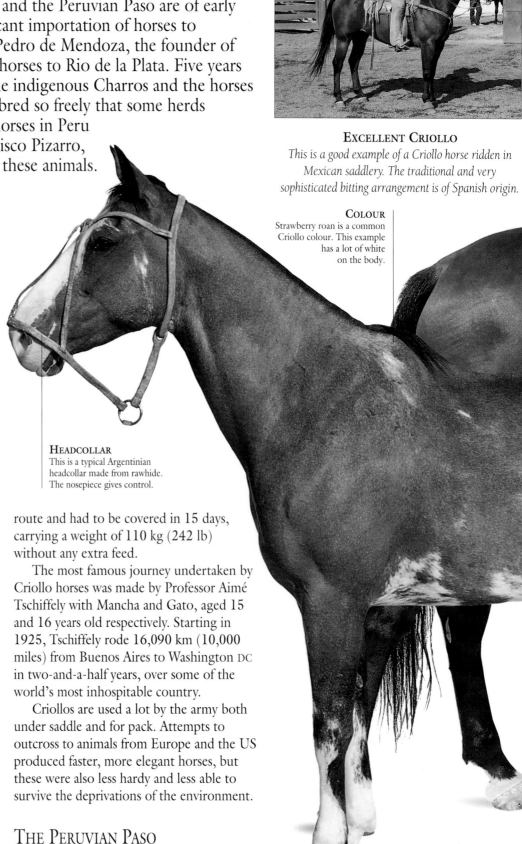

EXCELLENT CRIOLLO
This is a good example of a Criollo horse ridden in Mexican saddlery. The traditional and very sophisticated bitting arrangement is of Spanish origin.

COLOUR
Strawberry roan is a common Criollo colour. This example has a lot of white on the body.

HEADCOLLAR
This is a typical Argentinian headcollar made from rawhide. The nosepiece gives control.

THE CRIOLLO

The word *Criollo* literally means "of Spanish origin", and is a generic term covering a variety of related South American horses, including the *Crioulo Braziliero*, from Brazil, and the tough *Llanero* cattle horse from Venezuela, which, allowing for regional differences, is not dissimilar to the Argentine Criollo with which it shares a common background.

The Argentine Criollo descends from early Andalucian stock (see pp.108–9) in which Barb blood was predominant. In addition, there is a strong element of Sorraia blood (see pp.106–7) and also probably that of the Asturçon. The Criollo is generally a shade of dun, although there are also blue and strawberry roans, chestnut, skewbald, piebald, and the prized *grulla* or *gateado* colouring, a brown or mouse-dun shade.

A stockily built animal, the Criollo stands between 1.42 and 1.52 m (14–15 hh). The neck is short and thick, and the head profile is distinctively convex. While most modern Criollos move in the conventional diagonal trot, a number still retain the old lateral ambling gait of the Spanish horses.

The breed is among the toughest, soundest, and most enduring horses in the world, and is capable of carrying heavy weights over long distances and very difficult terrain. Severe climatic conditions, inadequate feed, and an almost constant shortage of water ensure an unrivalled constitutional hardness and an ability to survive in near-impossible circumstances.

A breed society was formed in 1918, and began rigorous endurance tests as a means of selection. Marches covered huge distances; one of them was over a 756-km (470-mile)

route and had to be covered in 15 days, carrying a weight of 110 kg (242 lb) without any extra feed.

The most famous journey undertaken by Criollo horses was made by Professor Aimé Tschiffely with Mancha and Gato, aged 15 and 16 years old respectively. Starting in 1925, Tschiffely rode 16,090 km (10,000 miles) from Buenos Aires to Washington DC in two-and-a-half years, over some of the world's most inhospitable country.

Criollos are used a lot by the army both under saddle and for pack. Attempts to outcross to animals from Europe and the US produced faster, more elegant horses, but these were also less hardy and less able to survive the deprivations of the environment.

THE PERUVIAN PASO

The Paso, or Peruvian Stepping Horse, is the most prominent of the Peruvian breeds. It was developed over 300 years by

HEIGHT OF CRIOLLO
1.42–1.52 m
(14–15 hh)

incredibly skilful and highly selective breeding, and is thought to be made up of three quarters Barb blood (see pp.66–67) and one quarter Andalucian. It is also noted for its natural, entirely unique, lateral gait. This gait, although similar to the rack of the American Saddlebred, or the running walk of the Tennessee Walking Horse and the Missouri Fox Trotter, is marked by a characteristically energetic, round, dishing action of the forelegs, supported by a

powerful movement of the hind legs overstepping the prints of the forefeet. The quarters are noticeably lowered and the back is held straight and rigid. The Paso can maintain a steady 18 km/h (11 mph) for long periods over rough mountain

HEIGHT OF PERUVIAN PASO
1.42–1.52 m (14–15 hh)

ORIGINS
◇

THE CRIOLLO *originated in Argentina with the 100 Spanish horses brought to Rio de la Plata by Pedro de Mendoza in 1535. Since then, the breed has spread throughout South America. The Paso is a Peruvian breed descended from the horses first introduced to Peru by Francisco Pizarro, in 1531. It is also bred in Colombia and the US.*

country, and can reach a top speed of 21 km/h (13 mph) without discomfort to the rider. Indeed, the action is said to be so smooth that a rider can carry a full glass of water without spilling it. The hind legs and hind pasterns are very long and the joints unusually flexible, both factors which contribute to the smoothness of the gait. Like all Criollo-based stock, the Paso also has excellent bone and feet, as well as a huge heart and lungs in relation to its size. It usually stands between 1.42 and 1.52 m (14–15 hh), and all colours occur.

The Paso Fino, originally from Puerto Rico, is a gaited breed related to the Peruvian Paso. It has a virtually four-beat gait, divided into *paso fino*; *paso corto*, in which more ground is covered with each step; and *paso largo*, the fast, extended gait.

NECK
The neck is short and upright but well-muscled.

CHEST
The muscle structure of the chest is notable.

FORELEGS
The relation of forelegs and shoulders gives a naturally rolling, elevated action.

PASO FINO
This is an American-bred Paso Fino, a direct derivative of the Peruvian Paso from the same Spanish root. The Paso Fino is very popular in the US.

PERUVIAN PASO

CRIOLLO

THE AMERICAN INDIAN

FULL WAR REGALIA

HORSES WERE reintroduced into America by the Spanish conquistadores (see pp.216–17). As early as 1579 there were wild horse herds in northern central Mexico, and these quickly spread northwards. By the early part of the 17th century the Spanish had developed horse-raising settlements in the south-west, and the equine species was once more firmly established on the continent in which it had first developed. As a result, a new era of equestrian nomadism was born as the Indian people of the Great Plains acquired horses, by trade, theft, or by capturing feral stock. Within the space of 200 years horses had completely altered the character of Indian life, and had transformed the tribes into the very last of the world's "horse people".

THE FIRST INDIAN HORSEMEN

The horse culture period of the Plains Indians is placed between about 1540 and 1880, but for most tribes it began much later. Certainly, the Pueblo Indians of Mexico, living in an area where horses were easily available, were mounted by 1582, but many of the northern tribes, such as the powerful Blackfoot, did not have horses in significant numbers until around 1730, while the Dakota Indians still depended upon canoes until as late as 1766. For the Indian tribes the buffalo herds were vital to their way of life. They provided meat throughout the year, as well as by-products such as hides, which were used for clothing, rugs, ropes, and the covering of the *tepi* or wigwam. The use of horses made buffalo hunting much easier and more productive than when it was attempted on foot. The possession of horses also conferred a new mobility: it shortened the time taken to move camp, liberated the Indian women from the labour involved in transporting possessions, and made travelling easier for the older and less active members of the tribe.

INDIAN HORSES

By 1874, when the incursions of the white settlers and the policies of the US Government had ensured the demise of America's "horse people", it was estimated that 120,000 Plains Indians owned 160,000 horses. Tribes such as the Nez Percé, the renowned breeders of the Appaloosa (see pp.226–27), had as many as 12,000 animals, while the Cayuse and Umatilla had a ratio of

BUFFALO HUNTER
For the Plains Indians the buffalo provided food, clothing, and the means for constructing shelters. Without horses, hunting was hardly possible.

11.7 horses to one person. A wealthy Blackfoot often owned as many as 40 horses, and even the poorest members of the tribe had 5 or 6 animals. An average family, to be comfortable, needed 12 horses to fulfil the primary requirements of hunting, warfare, and moving camp.

Ten types of horse were recognized by the Blackfoot, a tribe well-documented by European observers. There was the buffalo horse or war-horse; a winter hunting horse; a riding horse for journeys; a *travois* horse; a pack horse, and one to drag the *tepi* poles; a racehorse; a stallion; a brood mare; and a steady lead mare for the grazing herds. The buffalo horses and racing horses received special attention, and the racehorses were often more than a match for the white men's horses, even though the latter were usually bigger. Writing about the Indian pony in 1867, Colonel de Trobriand of the US Cavalry had this to say: "The Indian pony without stopping can cover a distance of from 60 to 80 miles [96–128 km] between sunrise and sunset, whilst most of our horses

THE RAIDING PARTY
As shown here, in Charles M. Russell's picture Stolen Horses, *horses were essential to life on the plains, and they would be acquired by any means possible.*

are tired out at the end of 30 or 40 miles [48–64 km]." Because of in-breeding, severe climatic changes, and hard work, an Indian pony suffered in respect of both size and quality, but it never lost its hereditary tough constitution. Moreover, it was never corn-fed but subsisted on the range feed of hard, wiry grasses. In winter, however, the diet of buffalo horses and war-horses was supplemented with the inner bark of the cottonwood tree.

To the American Indian riding was an essential skill, accomplished with the most basic equipment. A simple bridle could be made from a length of rope looped round the lower jaw, while the pad saddle, apart from the addition of stirrups, was an almost exact replica of that used by early Scythian horsemen. Ingeniously made wood-framed saddles, such as the famous type known as the "prairie chicken snare", were used by women and the older members of the tribe. Selective breeding and castration were practised, and geldings were universally employed for racing and hunting.

A nearly parallel development in the use of horses took place in South America, and the results can be seen today in the Spanish-style ranching enterprises employing the South American Indian cowboys (*gauchos*). However, the South American Indians never became as advanced a horse people as their northern cousins. Nor were they breeders of horses; instead they preferred to raid Spanish settlements as the need arose.

THE ASIAN CONNECTION

The horse culture of the native American was uncannily close to that of the nomadic tribes of Asia. Indeed, the similarities between them are too numerous to be coincidental and suggest a positive, and quite possible, connection between the steppe people and those of the Great Plains. The shamanistic beliefs of the Ural-Altaic people of Siberia, for example, are almost identical to those held by the American Indian, the medicine-man being the counterpart of the Asian shaman, or priest.

Nonetheless, there was a fundamental difference between the nomadic horse peoples of the Old and New Worlds. In Eurasia, the wealth of the steppe people lay in cattle, sheep, and goats, as well as in the horse herds. Conversely, that of the Plains Indian came to lie solely in horses, since they played such a vital part in buffalo hunting. The Eurasian nomad was essentially a herdsman, while the native American was a hunter on horseback who never achieved the advanced social structures of the steppe tribes. At

WOLF ATTACK
Wild horses will form a protective circle against predators such as these prairie wolves, and kick out with their heels to discourage their attackers. This picture, Flying Hoofs, is by Charles M. Russell.

no time would it have been possible for the Indian tribes to mount large-scale offensive operations, far less to create empires such as those of the Huns and the Mongols.

In the end the horse culture period left no legacy to modern America, unless it was that the presence of mounted Plains Indians blocked the northward expansion of the Spanish Empire in the New World. Otherwise, nothing remains but a legend, and one which for the most part is grievously misrepresented.

TRAVOIS
The travois *carried the Indians' belongings, or it could be used to transport the sick or old. It is virtually a replica of that which originated in Eurasia.*

BRAVE AND HIS PONY
Frederic Remington's realistic picture of an Indian brave was painted in 1888, at Fort Reno in Indian Territory. The Indian ponies were often coarse in appearance, but they were incredibly tough and surprisingly fast and enduring.

PALOMINO & PINTO

COLOURED HORSES occur all over the world, and the spotted, part-coloured, gold, and Albino coats are all of ancient origin. Many coloured types exist in North and South America, and are promoted through various societies. The American coloured types derive from the Spanish imports in the 16th century, when there were numerous part-coloured and spotted strains amongst Spanish stock. Many of those strains have disappeared, but coloured horses are still much in evidence worldwide.

MANE
The mane and tail are white. A maximum of 15 per cent darker hair is permissible in both.

THE PALOMINO

The Palomino, with its striking golden coat and flaxen mane and tail, is found in many countries, but it is bred more extensively in North America than anywhere else. However, even there it cannot be granted true breed status because of the variations in size and appearance. Like the Pinto, it is a colour type rather than a breed. The golden coat is not the result of a "Palomino" gene, and it can, in theory, occur in any breed or strain where the spotted gene has been bred out. So it is possible, for instance, though most unlikely, for there to be a Palomino Thoroughbred as a result of colour crossing. The Palomino colouring is found in many breeds and types, particularly in the Quarter Horse (see pp.230–31).

Most Palomino horses are registered with the Palomino Horse Association Inc. The Association defines ideal features in its "breed standard". The height may be 1.45–1.63 m (14.1–16 hh), but the colour requirement is specific. The skin may be either dark or of a golden colour. The coat colour must be no more than three shades lighter or darker than a newly minted gold coin, with no smudges. The mane and tail should be white, with not more than 15 per cent of darker hairs in either. The eyes must be dark or hazel; horses of Pinto, Albino, or Appaloosa parentage, which may have pink, blue, or wall eyes, are ineligible. White facial markings are limited to a blaze, snip, or star, and on the legs white hair must not extend above the knees and hocks. To qualify for entry in the breeding register, stallions and mares should have one parent in the register, and the other must be Quarter Horse, Arab, or Thoroughbred (see pp.64–65 and pp.120–21). Crossings that produce Palominos may include Albino, but the favoured cross, which produces the richest colour, is considered to be Palomino crossed with chestnut.

The origin of the name Palomino is unclear. At least one

PLEASURE HORSE
Palominos are much favoured as "parade" horses, but since the colour can be found in all types of animal no specific use can be assigned. This excellent example, for instance, would do well in any sphere.

PALOMINO

HEIGHT OF PALOMINO
1.45–1.63 m (14.1–16 hh)

COLOURFUL DUO

This pair of constrastingly coloured Paints exhibit interesting and attractive coat patterns. They are both good types with pleasingly correct conformation.

source traces it to the Spanish *palomilla*, one meaning of which is "a cream-coloured horse with white mane and tail" (D.P. Willoughby, *Empire of Equus*). Others link it to a golden grape of a similar name, or to the Spanish word for dove, *paloma*.

THE PINTO

The name Pinto comes from the Spanish *pintado* ("painted"), and in the US this has become "paint". At one time the word "calico" was also used. In Europe horses with coats of two colours, other than the spotted breeds, are called part- or odd-coloured.

The British distinguish between coats with patches of black and white, known as "piebald", and those with patches of white and any other colour, known as "skewbald". ("Bald" is the old English term for a white-faced horse.) In the US, more precise definitions are favoured (see below).

There are two societies for part-coloured horses. The Pinto Horse Association of America maintains a large register for horses, ponies, and miniature horses. Entries are divided into stock type, of mainly Quarter Horse breeding; hunter type, descended largely from Thoroughbreds; pleasure type, with Arab or Morgan background; and saddle type, with Saddlebred, Hackney, or Tennessee Walking Horse blood. Similar classifications exist for ponies. The American Paint Horse Association registers stock-type horses with bloodlines from Thoroughbreds, Quarter Horses, and Paints. The criteria for entry concern bloodlines rather than colour. Most Paints are Pintos, but not every Pinto is a Paint because of the breed restriction.

Pinto coat patterns fall into two types: Tobiano and Overo. In the Tobiano the coat is white, with large patches of solid colour. The legs are usually white, and white crosses the back or rump. Overo is a coloured coat with splashes of white, which almost never cross the back. Among the 19th-century Sioux and Crow Indians Pintos were valued for both their colour and their hardiness. Registered modern Pintos are usually well-made, even though they are of no fixed type.

COLOUR
This very well-made Tobiano has exceptionally defined and attractive markings including two colours in the mane and tail hair.

HEIGHT OF PINTO
Horses – 1.52–1.63 m (15–16 hh)
Ponies – up to 1.52 m (15 hh)

PINTO

ORIGINS

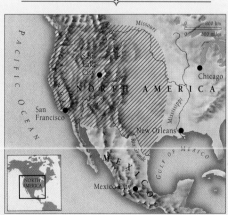

THE AMERICAN PALOMINO AND PINTO *are bred extensively all over the western states of the US, but gold or part-coloured coats are not a prerogative of American breeds and coloured horses and ponies occur in almost every horse-raising country of the world. The Palomino and part-coloured horses came to America with the Spanish in the 16th century, and the golden Palomino colouring is now found in many American breeds, in particular the Quarter Horse. Similarly, "Paint" colouring can often be found in horses that have predominantly Quarter Horse or other breeding.*

APPALOOSA

THE APPALOOSA IS AN AMERICAN SPOTTED BREED, which was developed by the Nez Percé Indians in the mid-18th century from the horses that were introduced by the Spanish conquistadores (see pp.216–17). The Nez Percé inhabited the lands in the north-east corner of Oregon, the south-east corner of Washington, and the bordering Idaho country. Their principal horse-breeding areas, providing good keep in both summer and winter, were in and around the sheltered valleys of the Snake, Clearwater, and Palouse rivers. The word "Appaloosa" is a corruption of "Palouse", the name of the river.

APPALOOSA EYES
The white sclera of the eye is characteristic, as is the distinctive mottled skin occurring round the muzzle of the Appaloosa.

HISTORY

Among the first horses that the Spanish adventurers introduced to the Americas in the 16th century were a number that carried spotted genes. Through the agency of the Plains Indians, these and other horses spread northwards from Mexico, and they came to form the foundation stock of the Nez Percé tribe in the north-eastern states of the US. The Nez Percé were the most skilful horse-breeders among the Indian peoples, and by the mid-1700s they practised a strict selective breeding policy. This included gelding male horses that were below their required standard, and disposing of unsuitable females through trade with other tribes.

Although colour and ornamentation were important considerations, as they were for all Indian tribes, the Nez Percé required, above all, hardy, practical work horses, which were suitable for both war and hunting. By 1806, when they are mentioned specifically in the journal kept by the Lewis and Clarke expedition, the quality of the Nez Percé horses was widely recognized.

The Appaloosa breed was virtually wiped out 70 years later, when the US was seizing tribal lands and moving the Indians to reservations. Under their leader, Chief Joseph, the Nez Percé retaliated, and conducted a fighting retreat over some of the most mountainous country in the West. Finally they tried to seek sanctuary over the border in Canada. After a march of about 2,100 km (1,300 miles), they were brought to bay and forced to surrender in the Bear Paw Mountains of Montana, just short of the border they thought they had crossed. Their wealth was confiscated, and their herds were slaughtered.

REVIVAL OF THE BREED

In 1938, on the basis of a few surviving descendants of the Nez Percé horses, the breed underwent a revival, and the

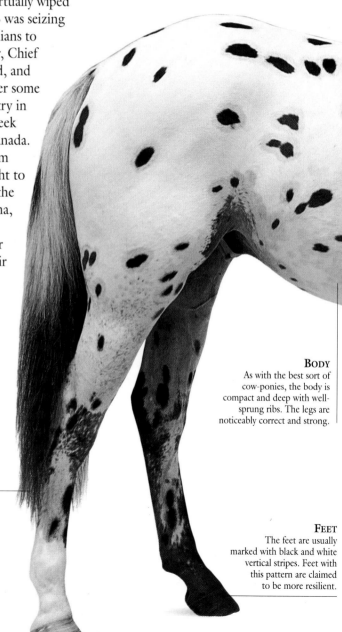

BODY
As with the best sort of cow-ponies, the body is compact and deep with well-sprung ribs. The legs are noticeably correct and strong.

FEET
The feet are usually marked with black and white vertical stripes. Feet with this pattern are claimed to be more resilient.

BLANKET PATTERN
The spotted blanket coat is one of the five recognized colourings of the Appaloosa breed. There should also be vertically striped hooves and mottled genitalia.

TAIL
The hair of the tail and mane is usually wispy, fine, and sparse. This feature was encouraged to avoid entanglement with thorny scrub.

HEIGHT
1.47–1.57 m
(14.2–15.2 hh)

Appaloosa Horse Club was formed in Moscow, Idaho. In less than 50 years the Appaloosa breed registry was the third largest in the world and had over 400,000 registered horses. In the UK the very active British Appaloosa Society (affiliated to the Appaloosa Horse Club) operates a grading register, with the declared aim of producing a stud book in the future.

The modern Appaloosa usually stands at 1.47–1.57 m (14.2–15.2 hh). In the US it is used as a stock and pleasure horse, as well as for racing, jumping, and western and long-distance riding. There is some divergence in type, particularly in the US where there has been much outcrossing to the Quarter Horse (see pp.230–31). The best specimens look like well bred cow ponies – compact, with very strong, correct limbs. The breed is claimed to be innately hardy, very willing, and to have a very tractable temperament.

COAT PATTERNS

There are five principal coat patterns that are recognized in the breed. They are: Leopard, characterized by a white area over all or part of the body, and dark, egg-shaped spots within the white area; Snowflake, in

NECK
The length of neck is proportionate to the body. The withers are clearly defined and the slope of the shoulder ensures long, free action.

CAYUSE INDIAN PONIES
The Cayuse Indian Pony of the American West was developed by the Cayuse tribe and was derived from a Spanish Mustang strain. It was noted for its stamina and speed and was frequently found to be superior to the horses of the US Cavalry.

which white spotting occurs all over the body but is usually concentrated over the hips; Blanket, where the coat colour over the hips can be either white or spotted; Marbleized, where there is a mottled pattern all over the body; and Frost, which consists of white specks on a dark background.

In addition to the coat pattern, the Appaloosa has other characteristics that are also passed faithfully from one generation to the next. The mane and tail are sparse and wispy (it is said that this is to prevent them from being caught up in thorny scrub); the sclera, the area of the eye surrounding the iris, is white, as it is in humans; the skin is noticeably mottled on the muzzle and around the genitalia; and the feet are marked with vertical black and white stripes. The feet are very sound and said to be more resilient than those of other breeds, and to contribute to the Appaloosa's powers of endurance.

In the US there is the Pony of the Americas (see pp.242–43), a "breed" that was developed from an Appaloosa/Shetland cross and which displays all the Appaloosa coat patterns. The Colorado Ranger Horse is another American spotted horse based on Arab and Barb foundation sires and is eligible for registration with the Appaloosa Horse Club. However, Appaloosas are not always eligible for entry in the Colorado Ranger's book.

THE AMERICAN COWBOY

MEXICAN VAQUERO

THE SPANISH SETTLERS brought both horses and a tradition of cattle ranching to the New World, and established the earliest cattle ranges in Argentina and Mexico. Initially, their principal product was not meat but leather. By the 19th century, however, the pressures of the increasing population in Europe and North America had shifted the emphasis to the production of beef in quantity. As a result, cattle ranching spread rapidly into the western US. An industry on this scale involved large numbers of horses, mostly wild Mustangs (see pp.218–19), which had to be trained in cattle herding. The cowboys had to be tough, resourceful men, who were capable of coping with the hardships and deprivations of the long cattle trails through harsh country.

THE COWBOY LEGEND

Around these horsemen grew the legend of the American West. Created by a handful of writers, and assiduously cultivated by the Hollywood movies, this became one of the great phenomena of the 20th century. The reality was less romantic. Life was unremittingly hard and not at all heroic. It demanded not only special skills but also a whole range of practical equipment to meet the needs of a big, empty country, where a man on foot stood little chance of survival.

HERDING CATTLE

The principal requirement was the horse itself. In the early days, cowboys' horses barely differed from the Indian ponies, and stood no more than 1.42 m (14 hh) or so. After the Civil War (1861–65) and the introduction of heavier cattle, stronger horses evolved, including the supreme cattle horse, the Quarter Horse (see pp.230–31).

Many of the horses were wild Mustangs, and most were broken in rough and ready fashion by professional "bronc-busters". The élite of the cow ponies was the cutting horse, whose job it was to "cut", or separate, a designated steer from the rest of the herd. Equally prized was the roping horse, which, having placed the rider in the best position to throw his rope at a steer, would brace itself against the struggling animal and keep the rope taut, even when the rider had dismounted. There was also the "night-horse". This horse was chosen for its steadiness and ability to work in the dark, needing to be exceptionally sure-footed in the event of a night-time stampede.

The cowboy (called variously "*vaquero*", "cowpuncher", "cow-hand", or "buckaroo", according to the part of the country in which he worked) rode geldings, which were considered to be more reliable than mares. The preferred gaits were the lope, which was a relaxed loose-rein canter, and the jog, also executed on a loose rein. The cowboy, who rode with long stirrups and did not rise to the trot, could cover about 8 km (5 miles) in an hour at a steady jog, while at the lope he could ride at 9.5–13 km/h (6–8 mph).

EQUIPMENT

When the Spanish came to the Americas, they brought not only horses, but also the methods of schooling and riding that had been developed on the Iberian Peninsula

PRACTICAL DRESS
This picture shows a Montana trail boss in the 1880s. His clothing and equipment are strictly utilitarian, from his wide-brimmed Stetson to the loose-rowelled spur on his heel. Similarly, his horse would have been chosen for practical reasons.

MODERN-DAY COWBOYS
The herds of white-faced Hereford cattle that are traditional to the New Mexico ranges are still moved today by horses and cowboys.

AT WORK
This picture, painted by Charles Russell in 1904, shows cowboys roping a steer. Interesting details include the carefully drawn brand marks.

THE WESTERN SADDLE

The saddle was essentially a work platform designed to carry the cowboy and all his gear. It was broad and could weigh between 18 and 23 kg (40–50 lb). A heavy, folded blanket placed underneath prevented galling, and could be used as a bed-roll for the rider.

HORN
The rope is tied around the saddle horn.

STIRRUPS
The heavy *trapaderos* fitted round the wide tread stirrup give protection to the foot in rough country.

during the 700 years of Moorish occupation (see pp.62–63). They also had an overriding influence on the type of saddles and bridles used by the cowboys for work and training.

The western saddle varied from one part of the country to another, but all derived from the saddle of the conquistadores (see pp.216–17), inherited by the Mexican *vaquero*, the West's first cowboy. The horn at the front acted as a post to which the lariat, or rope, could be tied when a steer was roped. Until the horn appeared in the early 19th century, when roping techniques were being developed, the end of the lariat was secured to the horse's tail, a practice that had significant drawbacks. Texan and

Californian lariats vary in that the former is a 9–12 m (30–40 ft) manila rope called a "riata" or "lasso", while the Californian type is a 18–20 m (60–65 ft) rawhide rope, which is thrown in a big loop.

Western saddles were fitted with broad leather fenders, which protected the rider's legs from being chafed or soaked in sweat, rather than the narrow stirrup leathers of the European pattern. The stirrups were large, and made from wood covered in rawhide, instead of metal which would have been cold for the rider's feet in bad weather conditions.

DRESSED FOR WORK

Clothing was equally specialized and practical, even if it was sometimes heavily decorated in silver. The broad-brimmed hat, which was called a Stetson after its principal manufacturer, John Batterson Stetson, gave protection against sun, wind, rain, or snow. It could also be used to scoop water, or to wave at a wandering steer. A Jewish tailor from New York, Levi Strauss, was the inventor of the low-hipped, narrow-legged denim trousers that are still called "Levis".

Cowboys paid considerable sums of money for their boots. Made to measure, these half-length boots were built from the softest leather, and often elaborately tooled. Most importantly, they had high, forward-sloping heels that could be dug into the ground when holding a roped calf. Spurs, too, were often highly ornamented. They

were heavy, and were fitted with large loose rowels which jangled as the owner rode round nervous cattle and gave them warning of his presence. Stout leather chaps were an essential piece of protective clothing in Texan country, which was full of strong, sharp, thorny scrub. In California, where the range was more open, sheepskin chaps were often worn in cold winter weather. Even the cotton bandana tied around the cowboy's neck was practical. It could be used to filter water, as a mask against the dust, or, if necessary, it could be made into a bandage.

THE VERSATILE STETSON
The Stetson, named after its maker John Batterson Stetson, fulfilled a variety of purposes, even serving as a useful water scoop.

QUARTER HORSE

T HE AMERICAN QUARTER RUNNING HORSE, sometimes described in more grandiose terms as the Famous and Celebrated Colonial Quarter Pather, was first bred very early in the 17th century, in Virginia and the other settlements on the east coast. A highly distinctive type, it is the oldest all-American breed, although the Morgan Horse, which did not come into being until the late 18th century, is the oldest documented American breed. *The Morgan Horse and Register* was first published in 1894, whereas the American Quarter Horse Association was not formed until 1940–41.

"COW SENSE"
Speed, balance, and agility, as well as an uncanny instinct for the job, make the Quarter Horse the finest cow pony in the world.

ORIGINS

The early settlers in the New World inherited the horses that had been introduced by the Spanish explorers (see pp.216–17). By that time, the stock was a mixture of Spanish horses (Andalucian in modern parlance – see pp.108–9); the Barb; and the Arab (see pp.64–67), which had been established on the Iberian Peninsula during the long Islamic occupation (see pp.62–63). These horses represented a base stock of very great potential, and when they were crossed with horses imported from England they laid the foundation for the uniquely built American Quarter Horse.

The first significant importation of English horses to Virginia was a cargo of 17 stallions and mares, which arrived in 1611. These horses were of the native "running horse" stock that provided the base element for the English Thoroughbred (see pp.120–21), which did not evolve until the 17th century. It has been suggested that these running horses would have had strong connections with the now extinct Galloways, the swift ponies that were raised in northern Britain between Nithsdale and the Mull of Galloway (see pp.172–73), and also with the Irish Hobby, a breed of pony found in Connemara in the west of Ireland in the 16th and 17th centuries (see pp.180–81).

The Quarter Horse evolved from this amalgam of bloods as a compact, chunky horse standing about 1.52 m (15 hh) high, with massive and enormously muscled quarters. The American authority, David P. Willoughby, likens the Quarter Horse to "a strongly-built sprinter standing between a slender distance runner and a powerfully-muscled shot-putter or weight-lifter".

HEAD
The head is neat, but distinctively shorter and wider than that of the Thoroughbred. The muzzle is small.

LASSO
The lasso, or lariat, is an integral part of the cowboy's working equipment. The Texan version is made of manila rope, and may be up to 9–12 m (30–40 ft) in length.

WORKING AND RACING

These horses were used for many purposes, including work on the farm; rounding up cattle; hauling goods and lumber; drawing the carriage on Sundays; and being ridden. They were also frugal horses, demanding little in the way of food.

Versatile though it was, the most prized characteristic of this horse, created by the sport-loving English settlers, was the ability to sprint over short distances from an explosive standing start. The horses were raced over half-kilometre (quarter-mile)

KNEES
The knees must be big, broad, and flat. Like the other joints, they should be hard, with no sign of puffiness.

stretches cut through the scrub, over similar distances on paths among the plantations, or even in the village street. For this reason the horse became known as the "Quarter Horse" or "quarter-miler".

The power and muscular conformation of the Quarter Horse were ideally suited to this form of racing. By 1656 Quarter Horse racing in Virginia was established and popular, and the breed was becoming recognized as the supreme short-distance racer. Later, when the Thoroughbred was introduced to the US, oval tracks were constructed and distance racing was introduced. As a result, the popularity of the quarter-mile sprints declined and within a short time these races were abandoned in the eastern states. (However, Quarter Horse

racing is once again a popular sport in the US.) The Quarter Horse then shifted to the west, where its speed, balance, and agility made it the perfect cow pony. It moved at such high speed that people said that it could "turn on a dime and toss you back nine cents change" from a flat-out gallop.

The breed excels as a trail-riding mount, and also in the traditional rodeo classes (see pp.380–81). Recently there has been an incredible revival in Quarter Horse racing, with prize-money often exceeding that available in Thoroughbred racing. As a result, the Quarter Horse seems to have gained more Thoroughbred blood and lost some of the old "bulldog" character. The Quarter Horse register, the largest in the world, now has an entry of millions.

ORIGINS

THE QUARTER HORSE IS CLAIMED to be the oldest North American breed. The ancestors of the modern Quarter Horse were being bred in Virginia by the early 17th century. Today the horse is bred in many countries, including the UK, but the largest Quarter Horse population outside the US is to be found in Australia. Although the horse originated in the eastern states of the US, it was quickly appreciated in the western states because of its ability as a cow pony.

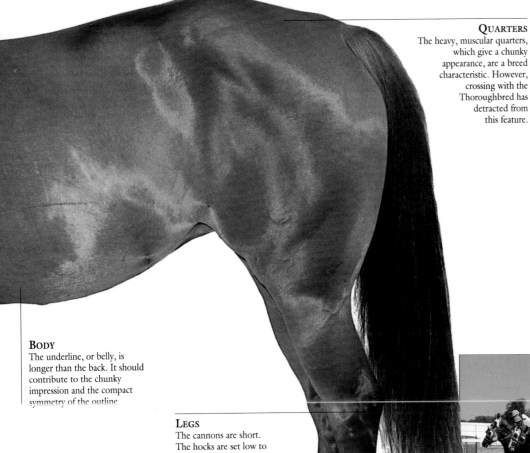

QUARTERS
The heavy, muscular quarters, which give a chunky appearance, are a breed characteristic. However, crossing with the Thoroughbred has detracted from this feature.

BODY
The underline, or belly, is longer than the back. It should contribute to the chunky impression and the compact symmetry of the outline.

LEGS
The cannons are short. The hocks are set low to the ground and have a high degree of flexion.

HEIGHT
1.52–1.60 m
(15–15.3 hh)

QUARTER HORSE FAMILIES

There are 12 principal Quarter Horse families, at the root of which are the breed's two most notable foundation sires – Janus and Sir Archy. Janus, an imported English horse who died in 1780, was responsible, through his son of the same name, for the great Printer line, which is one of the most influential. Sir Archy, the son of the first English Derby winner, Diomed, was also concerned with the beginnings of the American Saddlebred (see pp.234–35). The Shiloh, Old Billy, Steel Dust, and Cold Deck families trace to him, and two of the best and most influential of the 20th-century sires, Joe Bailey and Peter McCue, are his descendants.

QUARTER HORSE RACING
Quarter Horse racing is still growing in popularity in the US, and the prize-money is often more than in Thoroughbred racing. Racing has encouraged an increased use of the Thoroughbred outcross.

MORGAN

THE MORGAN HORSE, the first documented American breed, owes its existence to one phenomenal horse of unprecedented potency – the stallion Justin Morgan. He was as remarkable a horse as any in the recorded history of the equine species, but his origins are not totally clear and are a subject of conjecture among horse experts. Morgan Horses contributed significantly to the development of both the American Saddlebred (see pp.234–35) and the Standardbred (see pp.340–41).

JUSTIN MORGAN

The Cinderella story of the little, dark bay horse, who weighed 360 kg (800 lb) and stood no more than 1.42 m (14 hh), begins in about 1795, when a two-year-old colt was given to Justin Morgan, an impoverished music master, school master, or innkeeper (depending on your source) in part payment of a debt. The colt's date of birth is usually given as 1793, but the Morgan Horse Club accepts 1789. However, it is generally agreed that the horse was foaled at West Springfield, Massachusetts. Originally called Figure, the horse was only called Justin Morgan after his owner died. Thereafter, he belonged to a number of different owners. He died in 1821, when he was 32 years old.

Figure was first rented to one Robert Evans, who discovered that he could out-run and out-haul anything else in the area. From then on the horse was used incredibly hard in the plough, at woodland clearance, and in all sorts of draught. His last owner used him to haul a muck spreader, even denying him the comfort of stabling in the harsh north-eastern winters. Justin Morgan competed in hauling contests of great severity throughout his life and was continually raced under saddle and in harness. He was never beaten.

As a result, the little horse was much in demand as a sire, invariably stamping his progeny with his special character and appearance. Together with his three most famous sons, Sherman, Woodbury, and Bullrush, to whom all present-day Morgan Horses are traced, Justin Morgan created what is regarded as the first American breed.

The present-day Morgan stands between 1.45–1.57 m (14.1–15.2 hh), larger than his illustrious forebear, and undoubtedly shows greater refinement while still retaining the distinctive body conformation and characteristic carriage.

THE ORIGINS OF JUSTIN MORGAN

The question that cannot be answered with any certainty concerns the breeding of Justin Morgan himself. Some authorities suggest that his dam was by the imported stallion Wildair. He was a Thoroughbred,

SPORT
Morgans are very versatile. They figure in both ridden and harness classes, and are used for driving, western and pleasure riding, and trail riding. At one time, the Morgan horse was the chosen mount of the US army.

HEAD
The head is of medium size, and tapers to the muzzle. The profile is usually straight. The ears are pointed and set well apart.

SHOULDERS
The shoulders slope from well-defined withers, and are built for strength rather than speed. The chest is broad, and the action straight and free.

LEGS
The legs are slender, but there is sufficient bone. The joints are hard and well-formed, and will stand up to all work.

FEET
When trimmed naturally, the feet are round and medium-sized, but here the feet are long to enhance the action. The pasterns are not unduly sloped.

although this term was not then in general use, and Nearco and Nasrullah, two of the greatest racehorses of the 20th century, were descended from him on the female side. Wildair belonged to the same owner as the Thoroughbred True Briton, who is often claimed as Justin Morgan's sire. True Briton, a good racehorse, would have resembled the Arab or Barb far more closely than today's Thoroughbred does. However, there is no proof that True Briton sired Justin Morgan. Another faction claims his sire was a Friesian stallion in the Springfield area at that time.

A third theory claims that Justin Morgan was by a Welsh Cob. The 20th-century authority Anthony Dent supports this view, stating that "there can be little doubt that Figure was essentially a Welsh Cob with a touch of either Thoroughbred or Arabian blood". It is certainly true that there was, and is, a strong Welsh colony in Vermont, and a strong conformational likeness between the Morgan and the Welsh Cob.

THE INFLUENCE OF THE MORGAN

The Morgan influence can be seen in the Standardbred and Saddlebred, and also in the characteristics of the Tennessee Walking Horse (see pp.238–39). The Standardbred was influenced through Justin Morgan's grandson Black Hawk, and through Black Hawk's son Ethan Allen. In 1853 Ethan Allen was the first horse to break the 2½ minute mile, trotting it in the old, heavy country sulky, in 2 minutes 25½ seconds. The stallion George Wilkes, head of the Standardbred principal line that ends with

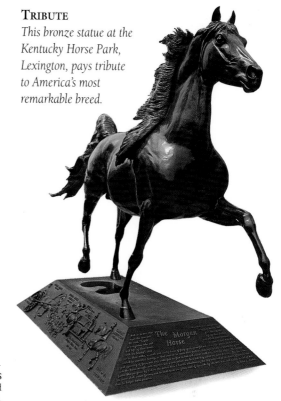

TRIBUTE
This bronze statue at the Kentucky Horse Park, Lexington, pays tribute to America's most remarkable breed.

Hambletonian, was out of a Morgan mare called Dolly Spanker. Two other foundation sires, Cabell's Lexington and Coleman's Eureka, were also by Morgan stallions, as were many record-breaking Standardbreds. The Saddlebred was influenced in its early stages by Peavine 85, a great-grandson of Ethan Allen. A prolific stallion, he was foaled in 1863 and was the most prominent sire of Saddlebred brood mares.

It can be said that the Morgan provided an important under-pinning influence in the evolution of American horse breeds.

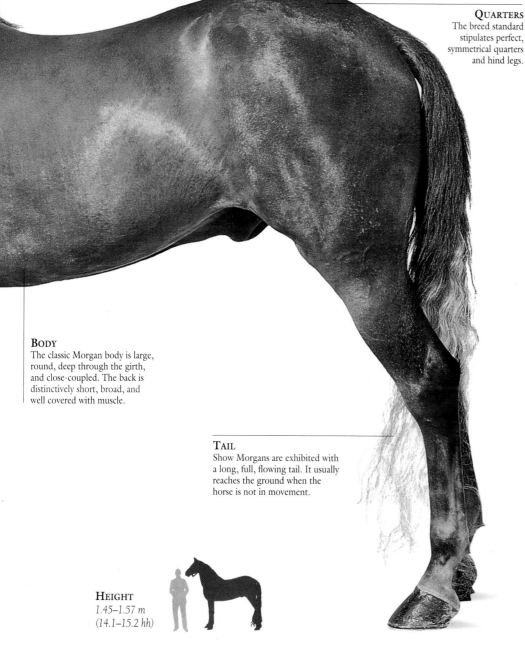

QUARTERS
The breed standard stipulates perfect, symmetrical quarters and hind legs.

BODY
The classic Morgan body is large, round, deep through the girth, and close-coupled. The back is distinctively short, broad, and well covered with muscle.

TAIL
Show Morgans are exhibited with a long, full, flowing tail. It usually reaches the ground when the horse is not in movement.

HEIGHT
1.45–1.57 m
(14.1–15.2 hh)

ORIGINS

THE FOUNDING SIRE FIGURE, later called Justin Morgan, is believed to have been born at West Springfield, Massachusetts. A statue of America's most famous horse stands at the University of Vermont Morgan Horse Farm. The Morgan has widely influenced American breeds, especially the Standardbred, the Saddlebred, and the Tennessee Walking Horse. Today there are a number of Morgan Horse farms in the southern states of the US and a breed society in the UK.

AMERICAN SADDLEBRED

BOTH TROTTING HORSES and the highly prized ambling and pacing horses went out of fashion in England in the 17th century as a result of the establishment of Thoroughbred racing (see pp.334–35). Many of these discarded strains found their way to America and in a short space of time founded "American" breeds in which these gaits were preserved, refined, and adapted to meet the needs of the colonists. The American Saddlebred is based upon two of these early American pacers, the Canadian Pacer and the Narragansett Pacer.

EARLY PACERS

The Canadian Pacer and the Narragansett Pacer had the smooth, comfortable gaits of their English forbears, and provided the foundation for not only the American Saddlebred but also the Standardbred (see pp.340–41) and the less well-known Tennessee Walking Horse (see pp.238–39). The Canadian Pacer came from France and was descended from ambling horses imported from Britain in the Middle Ages, while the Narragansett was developed in New England, in particular by the plantation owners around Narragansett Bay, Rhode Island. Both breeds became extinct; the latter largely because of its great popularity with sugar-cane planters in the West Indies, where it was exported in such large numbers that the stock was virtually sold out by the end of the 18th century.

THE SADDLEBRED

The Saddlebred, like many of the American breeds, began as an essentially practical animal, albeit one that was created to satisfy both the aesthetic requirements and the day-to-day needs of the southern aristocracy.

It evolved during the 19th century in the southern states, particularly around Kentucky, and was initially known as the Kentucky Saddler. Standing at 1.63 m (16 hh) or more, it was the result of selective breeding based on the Canadian and Narragansett Pacers; the Morgan Horse (see pp.232–33), which by then was

HEAD
The head is neat and fine with no fleshiness through the jowl.

NECK
The neck is long and elegant, its juncture with the withers ensuring a distinctively high carriage in movement.

SHOULDERS
The position of the shoulder blades allows notably free action.

BRILLIANT ACTION
The heavily shod feet and the nicked, high-set tail contribute to the breed's artificial show-ring image, but the action remains undeniably brilliant.

LEGS
The legs are long and very slender, and are often light of bone beneath the knee. The pasterns are usually long, giving a comfortable, "springy" ride.

HEIGHT
1.63 m
(16 hh)

well-established in Vermont; and the Thoroughbred (see pp.120–21). The result was an elegant utility horse. In the early days it would have been used in the plough, carried a man in comfort throughout a long day over rough terrain, and could have doubled up as a smart carriage horse to go to church on Sundays.

A MULTI-PURPOSE HORSE

The modern Saddlebred is perhaps best known as a show-ring animal exhibited under saddle. However, it is also a fine harness horse. In many respects it is not dissimilar from the British Hackney (see pp.402–3), although it has a far more pronounced riding wither, a long, elegant,

acutely curved neck, and greater refinement about the head. The ability to move in the specialized high-stepping action is the legacy of the old pacers and amblers; while the speed, courage, and beauty of form derive from the Thoroughbred.

SCHOOLING AIDS
Schooling tackle designed to impose the required carriage, as well as blinkers, are used in the training of the American Saddlebred horse.

With its feet trimmed normally, rather than for the show ring, the Saddlebred is also used extensively for pleasure and trail riding; it can cut cattle, jump well, follow hounds, or compete in dressage. It is claimed that despite having a "natural fire" it is a very docile and co-operative horse.

IN THE SHOW RING

The modern Saddlebred is shown in the show ring both under saddle and in harness. In the saddle division, it is shown in either three- or five-gaited classes. Three-gaited horses are shown at walk, trot, and canter, each gait being performed in a slow, collected manner with high action. Three-gaited horses are shown with a hogged mane and trimmed tail. The five-gaited horse, the supreme Saddlebred, is shown with a full mane and tail. As well as the first three gaits, it performs the slow gait, a prancing, four-beat motion with a moment of deliberate suspension preceding each footfall, and the rack, the full-speed "flashy, four-beat gait free from any lateral movement or pacing".

The breed suffers possibly from its show-ring image, which to many horse people appears unacceptably artificial because of the nicked tails, the long, heavily shod feet, and the use of training "aids".

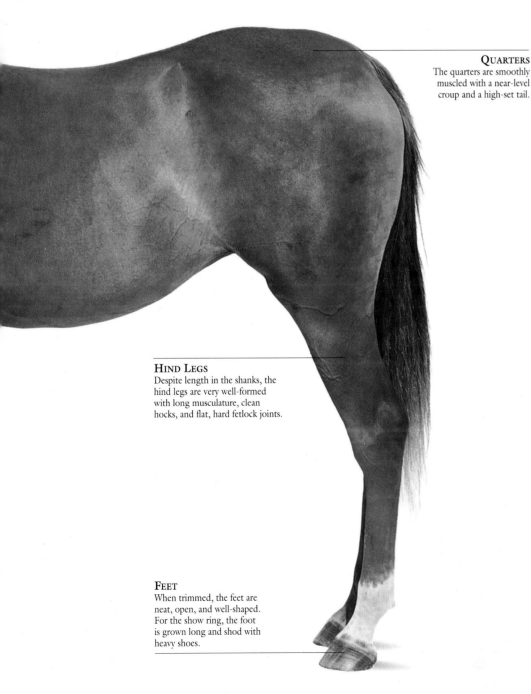

QUARTERS
The quarters are smoothly muscled with a near-level croup and a high-set tail.

HIND LEGS
Despite length in the shanks, the hind legs are very well-formed with long musculature, clean hocks, and flat, hard fetlock joints.

FEET
When trimmed, the feet are neat, open, and well-shaped. For the show ring, the foot is grown long and shod with heavy shoes.

ORIGINS

THE ANCESTOR OF THE AMERICAN SADDLEBRED was the Narragansett Pacer, developed in New England, in the area of Narragansett Bay, Rhode Island. Its descendant, the Saddlebred, came from the American South and was initially called the Kentucky Saddler. The principal breeding area is still in Kentucky's Blue Grass country, around Lexington. The breeding of the Saddlebred is encouraged by a diversity of show-ring classes, and the horse has an enthusiastic following.

MISSOURI FOX TROTTER

THE MISSOURI FOX TROTTER, one of the oldest and possibly least-known of the American breeds, completes the trio of gaited horses. It was beginning to be established as early as 1820, when the settlers moving westwards across the Mississippi from the hills and plantations of Kentucky, Tennessee, and Virginia made their homes in the Ozark Hills of Missouri. Clearly, they were a sporting people, and they took with them Thoroughbred horses as well as Morgans and Arabs (see pp.120–21, pp.232–33, and pp.64–65). The mares were bred to the fastest sires available and a number of famous families developed, most of which were called after the founding stallion. A stud book was opened in 1948, and within 30 years contained over 15,000 registrations.

A SPECIALIST GAIT
The fox trot gait has a sliding action. The back remains level and the rider does not feel the effects of the movement.

FOUNDING FAMILIES

One of the earliest and most prominent families was the Brimmer, which was descended from a racehorse of that name, who traced to the imported Thoroughbred, Jolly Roger. The Brimmer horses were bred by Moses Locke Alsup, whose family had settled in the Ozark Hills before the Civil War (1861–65). The Kissees were another family famous for its horses. They established the Diamond and Fox strains, while William Dunn, using good Morgan horses from Illinois and Kentucky, to which was added a Thoroughbred cross, produced Old Skip, who became a prepotent sire. Later, two great Saddlebred sires

HEAD
The neat, clean head has pointed, well-shaped ears and a tapered muzzle.

(see pp.234–35) were used to improve the breed: Chief, who was from the founding Denmark strain, and Cotham Dare, a prolific sire of Trotters in Douglas, Wright, and Ozark counties. Some infusions of Tennessee Walker blood (see pp.238–39) were also introduced to the breed.

CHEST
The chest is wide and deep, the relatively low action coming from sloped and particularly strong shoulders that have rounded withers.

THE FOX TROT

Originally, horses such as the Brimmers, the Colddecks, and the Copper Bottoms were bred to race, as well as to be all-round utility horses. However, Puritan religious intolerance soon put a stop to what was regarded as a frivolous and thus sinful pastime. As a result, the Ozark horsemen concentrated their efforts on the production of a new type of horse suited specifically to their conditions and needs.

What was wanted was a strong, enduring horse with a smooth action that would take it long distances over rough ground with a minimum of fatigue to itself and its rider.

FEET
Good feet, able to stand up to varied going, are a necessary feature of the sure-footed Missouri Fox Trotter.

ORIGINS

THE MISSOURI FOX TROTTER is in the tradition of the southern states of the US, and was bred as a smooth-gaited riding horse that would be comfortable to ride for long distances over rough ground. It originated with the settlers from Kentucky, Tennessee, and Virginia who made their home in the Ozark Hills of Missouri. It is still a horse entirely suited to the rough and varied Ozark country, where it is the ideal trail riding mount, but is also shown in riding classes in the southern states.

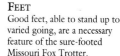

As a result of fixing a type through skilful in-breeding and adding Saddlebred blood, a very smooth-moving horse evolved, which employed a unique, characteristic gait that proved ideal. The gait, called the fox trot, is a broken gait that ensures great sure-footedness. In simple terms the horse performs an active walk in front while trotting behind, the hind feet stepping down and sliding over the track of the forefeet. The sliding action, which must be entirely straight, reduces concussion in the lower limbs and reduces movement in the back very considerably, allowing it to remain peculiarly level. As a result, the rider is able to sit undisturbed in the saddle without feeling the effects of the action. The fox trot can be maintained over long distances at between 8–12 km/h (5–8 mph), and over short stretches speeds of 16 km/h (10 mph) can be reached. The gait is accompanied by an up-and-down movement of the head, similar to that of the Walking Horse, while the slightly elevated tail bobs rhythmically.

The other gaits are the four-time walk, performed with the hind feet distinctly overstriding the front track, and the canter, which is between the low, fast, long-rein lope of the cow pony and the high, slow gait of the Tennessee Walker or Saddlebred. Unlike the last two horses, the Fox Trotter is not a high-stepper and no artificial

PLEASURE RIDING
The Missouri Fox Trotter, ridden in western gear, is ideal for pleasure riding purposes. It is a comfortable and sure-footed horse.

appliances such as false tails or tail sets, the latter giving a high upright carriage to the tail, are allowed. Similarly, excessive weighting of the feet with specially designed shoes is forbidden at shows, and if any horse is seen to have sores round the coronet or legs, indicating the use of chains, they will suffer immediate disqualification. In show classes 40 per cent is awarded for the fox trot and 20 per cent each for the walk, canter, and general conformation. Unlike the Saddlebred and the Tennesee Walking Horse, the Missouri Fox Trotter is usually ridden in western gear.

CHARACTERISTICS

The Fox Trotter stands between 1.42 and 1.63 m (14–16 hh). The predominant coloration is chestnut in all shades, usually with white markings, although any colour is accepted. The Fox Trotter has to have a back of reasonable length to perform the fox trot gait, but is otherwise a fairly compact, well-made horse though somewhat plain in appearance. All horse shows in the Ozark area will feature classes for the breed but for most owners, whether adults or children, the Fox Trotter, with its easy gait and reassuring sure-footedness, is an ideal and very reliable trail riding horse, which is economical to keep.

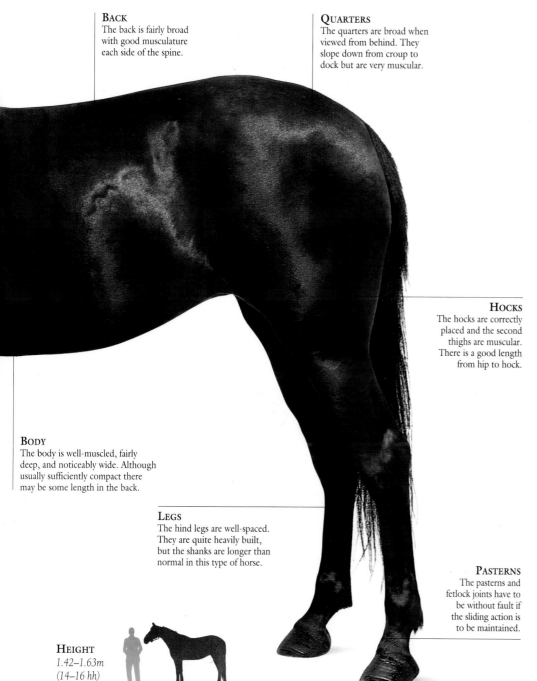

BACK
The back is fairly broad with good musculature each side of the spine.

QUARTERS
The quarters are broad when viewed from behind. They slope down from croup to dock but are very muscular.

HOCKS
The hocks are correctly placed and the second thighs are muscular. There is a good length from hip to hock.

BODY
The body is well-muscled, fairly deep, and noticeably wide. Although usually sufficiently compact there may be some length in the back.

LEGS
The hind legs are well-spaced. They are quite heavily built, but the shanks are longer than normal in this type of horse.

PASTERNS
The pasterns and fetlock joints have to be without fault if the sliding action is to be maintained.

HEIGHT
1.42–1.63m (14–16 hh)

TENNESSEE WALKING HORSE

THE TENNESSEE WALKING HORSE, also called the Tennessee Walker, plays a major role in the unique American gaited horse tradition, and its development runs parallel to that of the American Saddlebred (see pp.234–35). The Tennessee Walking Horse Breeders' Association was formed in 1935 at Lewisburg, Tennessee, and the breed was officially recognized in 1947 by the US Department of Agriculture. Such is the enthusiasm for this remarkable horse that classes at the annual Walking Horse Show held at Shelbyville, Tennessee, attract more entries than any other American horse show.

COAT COLOUR
Part-coloured coat patterns occur within the Tennessee Walker breed, as well as the more frequent shades of black and chestnut.

HISTORY

The Tennessee Walking Horse evolved in the state of Tennessee in the mid-19th century, after the first pioneers had crossed the Appalachian Mountains to establish outposts in Kentucky, Tennessee, and Missouri. In time, the richest of those early settlers set about breeding a stylish horse that would complement their lifestyle as well as serving a practical purpose.

The settlers aimed to create a horse of endurance and stamina, which would be able to carry its owner for long hours while he was overseeing work on the land. Although great speed was not required, the horse did need to be able to cover long distances reasonably fast. In the early days the horses were known as Southern Plantation Walking Horses or Tennessee Pacers, or more familiarly as Walkers or "Turn-Row" horses; they earned this last name because they could turn easily between plantation rows without damaging young plants.

Like all the American gaited breeds, the Walking Horse is descended from the old Narragansett Pacer (see p.234), with additional input from the Thoroughbred (see pp.120–21), Standardbred (see pp.340–41), Morgan (see pp.232–33), and Saddlebred (see pp.234–35). The Standardbred stallion Black Allan, and his son Roan Allan, are recognized as the breed's foundation sires. Black Allan, by Allendorf, was descended from a line of Standardbred trotters (not pacers), and was out of a Morgan mare named Maggie Marshall. He was a failure as a harness racer because of his peculiar walking pace, but he transmitted this feature faithfully to his descendants, and it became their most prized characteristic. In 1903, when he was brought to Tennessee, he was crossed with the existing Tennessee Pacers to create the foundation stock for the modern Walker. Subsequently, refinement and quality were provided largely by a Saddlebred stallion called Giovanni. This horse was brought from Kentucky in 1914 to stand at Wartrace, Tennessee, the town that is regarded as the birthplace of the Walking Horse.

THE MODERN WALKER

The Tennessee Walking Horse is a larger-boned horse than the Saddlebred. It is deep-bodied and short-coupled, with a head that tends to be rather plain. It carries its head

ORIGINS

THE WALKING HORSE EVOLVED IN the state of Tennessee in the mid-19th century with the entry of the first pioneers into the territory. Its development was influenced by the needs of a plantation economy and the lifestyle of the society that had created that environment. Breeding the Tennessee Walker is still focused on the state, with the Tennessee Walking Horse Breeders' Association's headquarters at Lewisburg and the annual Show at Shelbyville.

HIND LEGS
The hind legs are powerful and, when ridden, the horse brings them well under the body in a long, gliding motion.

much lower than does the Saddlebred, and the horse moves with a far less elevated action. The breed stands between 1.52 m and 1.63 m (15–16 hh). Predominant colours are black and all shades of chestnut, sometimes with prominent white markings.

Today, the Tennessee Walking Horse is primarily a show and pleasure horse. It also has a reputation as the most reassuring of horses for the novice or nervous rider. Its attractions are highlighted by the Tennessee Walking Horse Breeders' Association, an organization that was formed in Lewisburg, Tennessee in 1935, and promotes the breed with the sales pitch "Ride one today and you'll own one tomorrow". The Tennessee Walker's reputation has been earned on two counts: its most amiable disposition, and the famous running walk, a wonderfully soft, gliding gait that is described as being "bounce-free" and entirely relaxing. Both give great comfort and encouragement to reluctant or nervous riders.

HEAD
The head is fairly large, plain, and unremarkable. In action, it is nodded in time to the movement of the body.

LEGS
The legs are clean and hard. The feet are usually grown long and fitted with shoes that encourage the lift in the action.

HEIGHT
1.52–1.63 m
(15–16 hh)

BOUNCE-FREE
"Ride one today and you'll own one tomorrow". The soft, gliding gait of the Walker is "bounce-free" and gives the rider a comforting feeling of security. The head nods conspicuously in time with the movement of the body.

CHARACTERISTIC GAITS

The Tennessee Walking Horse has three gaits: the flat walk, the running walk, which is the predominant feature, and the rolling, "rocking-chair" canter, a smooth, collected movement in which the head nods in a distinctive fashion. Both of the walks are in four-time, with the horse's head nodding conspicuously in time with the movement and the hind legs over-tracking the imprints of the forefeet. They are described in the breed standard as being "a basic, loose, four-cornered lick", a 1-2-3-4 beat with the horse's feet hitting the ground separately at regular intervals (left fore, right rear, right front, and then left rear). The gaits are believed to be inherited, and it is certain that they cannot be taught successfully to any other breed.

In the running walk, horses can maintain a speed of between 9–14 km/h (6–9 mph) for a considerable time, while over short distances the Walker can approach 24 km/h (15 mph). However, speed is not an important criterion; the Breed Association states that "a good running walk should never allow proper form to be sacrificed for excessive speed". In this gait, the front foot strikes the ground just before the opposite diagonal hind foot, and the hind feet overstep by anything between 15 and 38 cm (6–15 in). The result is a remarkably smooth gliding motion, which is accompanied by swinging ears as well as the characteristic nodding head movement, and, at top speed, clicking teeth!

KENTUCKY HORSE PARK

The American tribute to the horse

SADDLEBRED
Shown here is the life-size bronze of Supreme Sultan, at the Kentucky Horse Park.

KENTUCKY, the horse state of the US, has the greatest concentration of Thoroughbred horse farms in the world around its capital, Lexington, as well as many farms for Standardbreds (see pp.340–41) and Saddlebreds (see pp.234–35). The Kentucky Horse Park is set near Lexington, in 405 hectares (1,000 acres) of rolling Blue Grass country wooded with oaks and sycamores. Opened in 1978, it hosted the World Three-Day Event Championship the same year. The architecture, quietly blending old with new, is typical of the region. There is the whiteboard Big Barn, which accommodates over 50 horses and a sale ring; a Hall of Champions, where some of America's greatest horses are stabled; the magnificent museum, with its exhibits displayed on an ingenious spiralling ramp; the American Saddle Horse Museum, its entrance marked by the life-size bronze of one of the greatest Saddlebreds, Supreme Sultan, who is buried by the wrought-iron entrance gates; the Breeds Barn, which houses over 40 horse and pony breeds; and the Draft Barn, where the big Belgian horses, a feature of the Park, are stabled. There is a racecourse, a cross-country course, polo grounds, schooling arenas, a huge covered school, and stabling for hundreds of horses. Hubert Heseltine's statue of Man o' War dominates this "tribute to the Horse". This famous horse, also known as Big Red, is buried in the park with one of America's greatest jockeys, Isaac Burns Murphy (1861–96), who won 628 races out of 1,412, and had a reputation for never betting, gambling, or breaking a contract. He and Big Red are fitting guardians to Kentucky's temple of the horse.

DRAFT BARN
The Belgian Brabants are kept in the Draft Horse Barn. They draw tour charabancs, and also do general draught work.

MAN O' WAR (RIGHT)
Man o' War, or Big Red, was a legend in his lifetime. He was odds-on favourite in all his 21 races, and was only beaten once, as a two-year-old. When he died in 1947, over 1,000 people went to his funeral.

MULES
The Park is famed for its powerful, distinctively coloured mammoth mules, bred from Belgian mares.

MAN O' WAR

COLORADO RANGER HORSE & PONY OF THE AMERICAS

ALTHOUGH AMERICAN HORSES are noted for the variety of their coat patterns, there are only three spotted horse breeds – the Appaloosa (see pp.226–27), the Colorado Ranger Horse, and the Pony of the Americas. The Appaloosa probably influenced the Colorado Ranger, and certainly played a part in the creation of the Pony of the Americas. However, colour is not a prerequisite for entry into the *Colorado Ranger Stud Book*; that is governed by the possession of a pedigree tracing to the required foundation bloodlines.

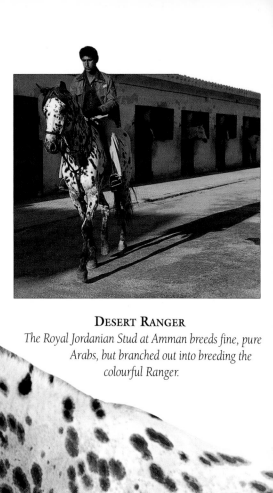

DESERT RANGER
The Royal Jordanian Stud at Amman breeds fine, pure Arabs, but branched out into breeding the colourful Ranger.

COLORADO RANGER HORSE

The history of Colorado Rangerbred Horses, i.e. Colorado horses bred under open range conditions, began not in the US but in Constantinople, when General Ulysses S. Grant was on a visit to Sultan Abdul Hamid of Turkey in 1878. As a token of regard, the Sultan presented Grant with two horses: a grey, pure Siglavy-Gidran Arab, foaled in the desert in 1873, named Leopard, and a pure blue-grey Barb, foaled in 1874 called Linden Tree.

At first the two were used by Randolph Huntington in Virginia as the foundation sires for a breed of light harness horses that he proposed to call Americo-Arab. Then, as old horses, they spent a season at the Colby ranch in Nebraska siring stock from the native mares, some of them spotted or coloured. These horses quickly attracted the attention of the Western breeders on account of their overall excellence as well as their attractive colours. A.C. Whipple, of Kit Carson County, Colorado, obtained an outstanding band of mares from the Colby ranch, all of which had been sired by either Leopard or Linden Tree, and he chose a white stallion with black ears, called Tony, to head the herd. Tony was "double bred" to Leopard, i.e. Leopard was the grandsire on both sides of the pedigree, and the Whipples carried on an extensive line-breeding programme using this horse and his sons.

OUTLINE
The outline suggests a combination of strength and athleticism. The short legs are a notable feature.

However, the Colorado Ranger breed was essentially the creation of one man, Mike Ruby of the big Lazy J Bar Ranch. He bought Patches, a son of Tony, and then the Barb, Max (a son of Waldron Leopard of the original line), and used them as the foundation sires for the new breed, which, increasingly, exhibited a lot of unusual colourings. The horses were named Colorado Rangers in 1934, at the instigation of the Colorado State University, and Mike Ruby was President of the Colorado Ranger Horse Association until his death in 1942.

The Rangers were bred as superlative working horses, hard as iron and possessed of great stamina. They have a particular refinement as a result of the Arab/Barb foundation, and some of their colour could be inherited from the Barb, via the Spanish horses brought to the Americas in the 16th century, for which the Barb was responsible. The Ranger is, nonetheless, a compact horse

HEIGHT OF COLORADO RANGER HORSE
1.57 m
(15.2 hh)

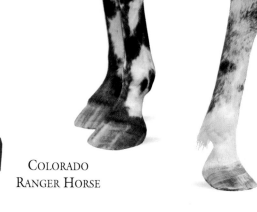

COLORADO RANGER HORSE

with powerful limbs and quarters. The average height is 1.57 m (15.2 hh), and most have a patterned coat. A Ranger can, indeed, also be registered as an Appaloosa, but an Appaloosa cannot be registered as a Ranger.

PONY OF THE AMERICAS

The Pony of the Americas is an officially recognized American breed with its own stud book and registry. Like the Ranger, it is the result of the efforts of one man: Leslie Boomhower of Mason City, Iowa. His object was to produce a conformationally correct riding pony, attractively marked, which would be suitable for children in every sort of activity whether ridden in western or English tack. Furthermore, Boomhower wanted a product that was

HELPING HAND
The Pony of the Americas is smart and colourful, and an all-American product. It is also the perfect choice for this young disabled rider.

indubitably American, as opposed to the customary British imports. He founded the Pony of Americas Club in 1956. The breed's foundation stallion, Black Hand, foaled in 1954, was the product of a Shetland stallion and an Appaloosa mare. Later there were outcrosses to Arabs and Quarter Horses, and the breed standard calls for a pony that

has the appearance of a miniature Quarter Horse/Arab cross, with Appaloosa colouring and some of that breed's features. (There is little evidence now of the early Shetland blood.) Within 15 years registrations had reached 12,500, and they have continued to grow ever since.

Today's ponies vary between 1.17 and 1.37 m (11.2–13.2 hh), and are all inspected before full registration to ensure that they meet the breed specifications. Emphasis is given to substance, refinement, and a stylish, straight, balanced action marked by a notable engagement of the hocks under the body.

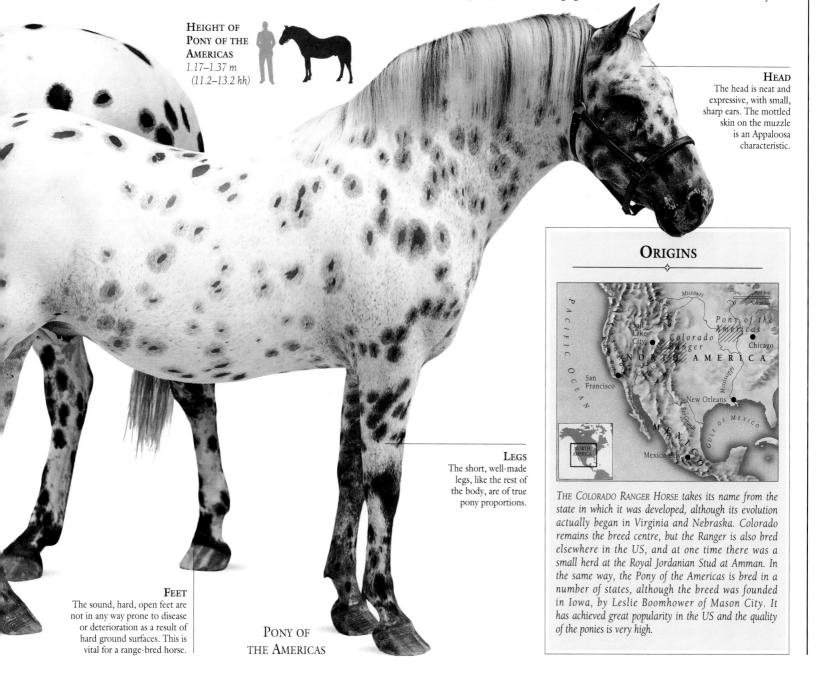

HEIGHT OF PONY OF THE AMERICAS
1.17–1.37 m
(11.2–13.2 hh)

HEAD
The head is neat and expressive, with small, sharp ears. The mottled skin on the muzzle is an Appaloosa characteristic.

LEGS
The short, well-made legs, like the rest of the body, are of true pony proportions.

FEET
The sound, hard, open feet are not in any way prone to disease or deterioration as a result of hard ground surfaces. This is vital for a range-bred horse.

PONY OF THE AMERICAS

ORIGINS

THE COLORADO RANGER HORSE *takes its name from the state in which it was developed, although its evolution actually began in Virginia and Nebraska. Colorado remains the breed centre, but the Ranger is also bred elsewhere in the US, and at one time there was a small herd at the Royal Jordanian Stud at Amman. In the same way, the Pony of the Americas is bred in a number of states, although the breed was founded in Iowa, by Leslie Boomhower of Mason City. It has achieved great popularity in the US and the quality of the ponies is very high.*

FALABELLA & AMERICAN SHETLAND

SMALL HORSES ARE USUALLY THE PRODUCT of a severe natural environment, where the harsh climatic conditions combined with the low availability of feed has contributed to their small stature. However, with a knowledge of genetics, it is also possible to breed specifically for size – either miniatures or, equally, very large horses. At various periods in equine history miniature horses have been bred as pets and for curiosity value. Today, the Falabella is the best-known miniature. It is always claimed to be a miniature "horse", on account of its proportions and character, and not a pony. Miniatures outside the Falabella breed are now bred increasingly, particularly in the US.

EQUINE PYGMY
The woolly Falabella looks like an even smaller version of the Shetland Pony, which stands at 1.02 m (40 in), but it has better limbs than most Shetlands. The Falabella stands at no more than 76 cm (30 in).

THE FALABELLA

The Falabella evolved from a selective breeding policy perfected by the Falabella family at their Recreo de Roca Ranch, outside Buenos Aires, Argentina. To obtain these dwarf horses they crossed the smallest Shetlands (see pp.178–79) available with a very small Thoroughbred stallion (see pp.120–21). They then subsequently down-bred by mating the smallest animals with each other and fixing the dwarf character by intensive in-breeding.

One of the smallest "miniatures" ever bred was a mare called Sugar Dumpling who belonged to Smith McCoy of Roderfield, West Virginia, USA. The horse was only 51 cm (20 in) high, and weighed just

13.5 kg (30 lb). The aim of breeders is to produce a near-perfect equine specimen in miniature, but the practice of in-breeding to reduce size often results in a lack of conformational vigour. The best Falabella and miniature horse stock often retain the better points of the Shetland, but otherwise many of these equine dwarfs are disproportionate, with large, heavy heads, weak quarters, and sometimes misshapen lower limbs. However, they are said to be good-tempered and friendly when kept as pets. Coat patterns vary but attractively

spotted animals are not unusual. The preferred height of the Falabella is about 76 cm (30 in) at the withers.

THE AMERICAN SHETLAND

The US has a substantial pony population as a result of imports of some established European breeds, in particular the Mountain and Moorland ponies native to the UK (see pp.170–85). Apart from these breeds there are, or were, no ponies of a comparable standard that might be termed native to the country. American breeders, however, have a genius for adaptation and a strong entrepreneurial instinct, so within about 50 years of the first importation of 75 Shetland ponies, two different

WITHERS
The flat withers, upright shoulders, and small size make the Falabella unsuitable for riding.

HIND LEGS
The hind legs in this instance are acceptable to the overall frame. Usually they are weak.

SHOULDERS
The excessively straight shoulders limit the practical use of the breed.

HEIGHT OF FALABELLA
76 cm (30 in)

FALABELLA

THE FALABELLA is still the best known "miniature" horse, although types of miniature horse, usually based on the Shetland, are widely found throughout the world, particularly in the US. The Falabella was originally developed by the Falabella family just outside Buenos Aires, Argentina. The small size is brought about by in-breeding closely.

Shetland-based breeds emerged: the Pony of the Americas (see pp.242–43) and the numerous and very popular American Shetland.

The original Shetland, for all its small size and relatively restricted use, has been successfully exported worldwide for over 100 years. Indeed, today there are probably more Shetlands in the Netherlands than in the UK. It is the most popular pony in the US, where there are over 50,000 of them. The first 75 Shetlands were imported in 1885 by a man called Eli Elliot, and an American Shetland Pony Club was formed three years later. Thereafter, the movement towards an improved pony gathered momentum. Today, the modern American Shetland bears little resemblance to the original, tough, island pony that can thrive in severe weather conditions on minimal subsistence.

The "new breed" is essentially a smart harness pony, and was created by selecting the finer types of Island Shetland and then crossing them with Hackney Ponies (see pp.402–3). Outcrosses were then made to Arabs (see pp.64–65) and small

AMERICAN SHETLAND
An American Shetland competes in a "roadster" class, in which a more natural gait is required. Harness classes call for a higher action.

Thoroughbreds to produce what is a relatively distinctive type, with an eastern overtone to a predominantly Hackney outline. It also has the pronounced Hackney character and brilliant, high-stepping action. The thick, woolly coat of the Shetland has gone, although the mane and tail retain some of its luxuriance. The limbs are longer and finer, and the height

limit is 1.17 m (11.2 hh), a hand higher than the average for the original Shetland Island Pony.

It is claimed that the pony still has much of the traditional hardiness and robust condition. This is perhaps questionable, but there is no doubt about the pony's versatility. It is shown in harness classes to four-wheeled buggies, and is expected to move as well as a Hackney Pony; it competes drawing two-wheeled vehicles in Roadster classes (the equivalent of the British driving classes), in which a different set of criteria apply; and it races in lightweight harness sulkies. It is also expected to go well under saddle in either western or English tack. The "hunter" type competes over a small jumping course, while others, with weighted shoes, long toes, and set-up tails, are show-ring ponies.

Prices for top-class ponies are stunningly high by British Shetland standards. Thirty years ago, when demand reached a peak, five- and six-figure sums were being paid for breeding stock and stallion syndication.

TAIL
The luxurious growth of the mane and tail recalls the Shetland ancestry.

WITHERS
The withers, unusually prominent for a pony, contribute to the slope of the shoulders.

HEAD
The head and ears are long, and the profile is usually straight. There is a noticeable lack of pony character.

HIND LEGS
The length of the hind legs has been much increased by outcrosses to Hackney Ponies, Arabs, and small Thoroughbreds.

GIRTH
There is good depth in the body, although the slender limbs are too long in proportion.

HEIGHT OF AMERICAN SHETLAND
Up to 1.16 m (46 in)

AMERICAN SHETLAND

THE BREEDING OF THE AMERICAN SHETLAND was centred originally on the state of Indiana, following the large imports of ponies from the Scottish Shetland Islands that began in 1885. An American Shetland Pony Club was formed in 1888, and since then the breeding of the "new-look" Shetland has extended to most parts of the country. The American pony, unlike its Scottish antecedent, is not the product of its environment but has resulted entirely from selective breeding.

CHINCOTEAGUE

T HE ISLANDS OF CHINCOTEAGUE (a Native American name meaning "Beautiful Land across the Waters") and Assateague, off the coast of Virginia, USA, represent one of the last remaining habitats for "wild" equine stock. Over 200 ponies, called Chincoteague ponies, live on Assateague, the larger of the two islands, which is now a national park and has an important wild-fowl population conserved by the Federal Fish and Wildlife Service. Until the fierce storms of 1933 Assateague was connected to the mainland, but it is now separated from it and the neighbouring island of Chincoteague by a narrow strip of water.

CONSERVATION
The ponies, some of which now display pinto colouring, share the Assateague National Park with a variety of sea birds.

ORIGINS AND CHARACTERISTICS

The Chincoteague ponies probably derive from stock that strayed or was abandoned by colonists in the 17th century. They would therefore have an earlier Spanish or North African connection. The story of a ship carrying Moorish horses of, presumably, Barb/Spanish origin, from North Africa to Peru, which was supposedly wrecked off the coast in the 16th century, is less credible, and lacks supporting evidence. Like all the other convenient shipwrecks that feature in the evolution of so many breeds, it should be regarded with some suspicion.

It was not until the 1920s, when the Chincoteague Fire Department (the unlikely body which is responsible for the management of the islands) took an interest in the island stock, that the existence of

these feral ponies became generally known. At that time the island stock exhibited all the signs of degeneration. The growth was stunted, and there were the conformational defects and even distortions associated with uncontrolled in-breeding. Limbs, for instance, were misshapen, forelegs were offset from the knee, and hind legs were more often than not sickle- and cow-hocked. Chests, in particular, were exceptionally narrow, exemplifying the horseman's description of "both legs coming out of the same hole". Inevitably, the quality of the bone was poor and the animals lacked substance. In particular, the heads were large and coarse and out of proportion to the weak body structure. The characteristics of the ponies inclined more towards those of stunted horses, even though the average height was not more than about 1.22 m (12 hh). Pony quality, especially in respect of the heads, was not much in evidence, and even today that remains true to a degree.

As an additional deterrent to growth, feed on the sandy, salt-laden marshlands was limited and of poor quality. On the other hand, such a habitat ensured the survival of none but the toughest, hardest, and most adaptable, and those with a high degree of resistance to the rigours of the climate.

Since the 1920s, positive and not unsuccessful efforts have been made to improve the stock. At one time Shetland and Welsh Pony blood (see pp.178–83) was introduced. Both these breeds were compatible with the island stock and acted

ORIGINS

THE CHINCOTEAGUE PONIES live in the small, low-lying and marshy islands of Chincoteague and Assateague, off the coast of Virginia, to which the latter was connected until the fierce storms of 1933. Although the sandy, salt-laden marshlands provide only the poorest feed, the ponies are tough and highly resistant to extremes of climate. Nonetheless, such a habitat can also produce degeneration of bone, substance, and overall structure. There are about 200 ponies on the islands.

COLOUR
Pinto blood has improved the stock, as shown in the colours.

FOREHAND
The forehand is weak but an improvement on past conformation.

LEGS
The cannons are long and most of the ponies are light of bone with poorly developed joints.

SALT AND WATER
A group of wild ponies grazes the salty scrub that forms a large part of their diet on the wastes of Assateague Island, off Virginia.

SALT AND WATER
A group of wild ponies grazes the salty scrub that forms a large part of their diet on the wastes of Assateague Island, off Virginia.

to up-grade the ponies. Less understandable, but now far more noticeable, was the use of the Pinto (see pp.224–25), even though it and the island ponies might have shared some common ancestry in the distant past. The Pinto outcross has produced much part-coloured stock, although other coat colours are also found. It may have also contributed to the still "horsey" appearance of the head.

ISLAND LIFE

The Chincoteague Volunteer Fire Department continues to be concerned with the ponies' welfare. Each year it holds two Pony Penning Days, which are held on the last Thursday and Friday of July. On these occasions the men of the Fire Department round up the ponies on Assateague and swim them over the channel to the adjacent island of Chincoteague. Once there, they are

QUARTERS
The quarters are better but the hind legs are still weak.

driven into holding pens where the yearlings are auctioned. The proceeds of the sale are put towards the costs of managing the herd.

However, there have been conflicts of interest between the Fire Department and another well-meaning conservation group, the Federal Fish and Wildlife Service, introduced to Assateague in 1943 with the object of protecting and encouraging the islands' wildfowl population. In an effort to prevent their "government-built pools" from being disturbed and trampled by the ponies, the FFWS fenced them off and thus restricted the ponies' movement to a small, low-lying and marshy part of the 3,600-hectare (9,000-acre) island. This not only reduced the amount of grazing that was available to the ponies, but, just as importantly, it prevented them from reaching the sea where for centuries they had gone to avoid the onslaught of the summer mosquitos. Largely as a result of the enclosures, a number of ponies could not return inland and were trapped by high water, and carried out to sea when an Atlantic storm blew up unexpectedly in 1962.

MISTY OF CHINCOTEAGUE

The ponies were brought to the attention of a wider public by the publication in 1947 of the children's book called *Misty of Chincoteague*. It was written by Marguerite Henry, who had purchased a week-old Chincoteague foal on a visit to the pony sales in the previous year. In 1961 the Chincoteague ponies received wider publicity and gained an even more enhanced reputation when 20th Century Fox made

the film *Misty*, which was based on Marguerite Henry's book. There is little doubt that the interest generated by the book and then the film was responsible for the subsequent popularity of the pony and gave positive encouragement to the improvement of the stock.

Today, the Chincoteague has a sizeable, if perhaps largely uncritical, following, and is claimed to be a good child's pony if it is properly handled. Interestingly, the Chincoteague, along with the Mustang of the western states (see pp.218–19), is an example of what can be achieved once public interest has been focussed on a particular problem. The ponies also have the distinction of being the only indigenous "pony" group in the US.

SABLE ISLAND
Along with the Chincoteague stock the 300 or so ponies on Sable Island, which are descended from French stock, are among the last of the world's wild equine population. Sable Island is virtually a sand bank off Nova Scotia, Canada.

HEIGHT
1.22 m
(12 hh)

PART EIGHT

THE WORKING HORSE

ALL HORSES MAY BE SAID to work in some capacity, but a loose distinction can be drawn between those used for recreation and those employed directly in commerce, industry, and agriculture. The world economy certainly depended upon the use and exploitation of horse-power until the end of the 19th century and well into the first part of the 20th century. Today, there are still parts of Eastern Europe where the horse remains an essential element of rural life, and in some eastern republics of the former USSR the horse herds support an economy that has hardly changed for thousands of years. In fact, the working horse was still in everyday use only 50 years before the first man walked on the moon.

A Waggon and Travellers on a Country Road in Winter
by John Frederick Herring Jnr. (1815–1907)

THE HORSE IN INDUSTRY

THE PERIOD between 1789 and 1832 marked a fundamental change in British society, which had an effect on the whole framework of international trade. It was the Industrial Revolution, in which machines took over work that had for centuries been done by hand. Nonetheless, the new industrial age was dependent almost entirely on the efforts of hundreds of thousands of horses. Even when the railways brought to an end the magnificent era of the road coach, the horse remained an essential element. In fact, the railways, servicing the burgeoning manufacturing industry, were a positive incentive to a huge increase in the employment of horses and, in consequence, to the commercial breeding of heavy draught animals.

THE RAILWAYS

For well over a century the railway companies were the biggest employers and owners of horses in the UK. In the 1890s mainline companies kept stables of up to 600 horses in London alone, where the total horse population was estimated at over 300,000. In 1928 the London, Midland and Scottish Company (LMS) still owned 9,681 horses and 10 years later it still had over 8,500.

Horses moved goods and raw materials, coal to feed the furnaces, and foodstuffs for the city dwellers to and from the railheads, while more and more people used the railways, and required the services of vehicles such as station cabs, brakes, and omnibuses. Heavy horses were used in the goods yards and to shunt rolling stock. They were cheaper than steam engines, more convenient, and more efficient. The last shunting horse in Europe was stationed at Newmarket, the headquarters of the British racing industry. It moved horse-boxes in the sidings (the transportation of horses by rail, rather than road, then being the rule rather than the exception) and it was not retired until 1967, barely a year before the last steam engine was withdrawn from the railways.

Most railway horses worked in cartage and delivery. Teams of Shires (see pp.288–89) were used for heavy transport; "vanners", often of Irish Draught type (see pp.396–97), for lighter goods; and Hackney-type cobs or

RAIL DELIVERIES
This South Western Railways delivery cart was operated by Chaplins, one of the largest private carrier companies in the UK.

the ubiquitous Welsh Cob (see pp.184–85) for the express parcel delivery service, carried at a swift trot at 19 km/h (12 mph). These services were continued into the 1960s.

HORSE-DRAWN TRAINS

Although George Stephenson (1781–1848) opened the first steam railway in 1825, when his *Locomotion 1* pulled a train of wagons with passengers on the 33-km (20-mile) railway between Darlington and Stockton,

horses hauled freight and passenger coaches over short and medium distances both before and after that date. The first horse-drawn train, connecting Wandsworth with Croydon, was the Surrey Iron Railway, which started operating in 1803. One similar branch line in Northern Ireland, which terminated at Fintona Station, used horse-drawn coaches up to 1957.

A delightfully Ruritanian horse-drawn railway connected the city of Linz in upper Austria with Budweis in Bohemia (now in the Czech Republic). It was the principal means of carrying salt – previously carried by humans or pack ponies – to Bohemia, and it also transported passengers in some style. It was opened on 21 July 1832 by the Emperor Franz I who, with his Empress, journeyed from Urfahr to St Magdela in a state landau fitted with flanged iron wheels. The total length of the track was 200 km (124 miles), and in its heyday the line carried 159,000 passengers annually and 100,000 tonnes of freight. It operated for 40 years, closing in 1872.

MINING AND PACK TRANSPORT

The main source of power for the Industrial Revolution and the supporting railways was coal. At the pitheads, horses turned the

THE SHUNTER
Horses were used extensively in the railway goods yards and for shunting work. In this painting by William Francis Freelove (1846–1920), cattle trucks are being moved in the sidings by a single horse. The last shunting horse in Europe did not retire until 1967.

windlass of the hoist, moved or operated other heavy machinery, and hauled coal wagons. Thousands of ponies worked and lived underground from the 19th century until 1994, when the last ones were retired from the Ellington colliery, Northumberland.

Until the 19th century the UK also had a network of pack trails. In Europe and other areas where there was mountainous terrain and few proper roads, greater use was made of pack transport right into the 20th century.

PIT PONIES

Thousands of ponies, which were stabled underground during their working lives, worked in the British coal industry up to 1994. They were an essential force in the operation of the hundreds of pits that powered the Industrial Revolution.

LUMBER HAULAGE

Large numbers of horses were required in the American lumber industry. In this Californian forest railway eight-horse teams were needed to cope with the steep gradients.

INDUSTRY IN THE US

American industry was similarly dependent on horse-power and used thousands of horses in its cities. There is no record of horse-drawn railways in the US, but tracks were laid in the big lumber camps to ease the movement of the big and very heavy logs. Teams of six or eight horses were needed to haul lumber up steep inclines, and there is some evidence of mules also being used. Mules were favoured throughout the US, particularly in the southern states, but pack mules were never a feature of the economy. The extensive use of mules and of a generally lighter stamp of horse, as the 19th-century American economy swiftly expanded, was partly due to the lack of the heavy horse types found in Europe, although the Dutch were importing heavy draught breeds into their New Amsterdam colony by the end of the 18th century. The machinery used on the

prairies (see pp.256–57) had to be drawn by teams of 30 or more, which by European standards were nearly all of light vanner type.

The US and Canada lead the world in the use of horses in pharmaceutical research, and many farms are maintained for that purpose in both countries. Ontario, for example, has over 100 farms where urine is collected from pregnant mares to produce oestrogen for birth-control pills and medicines to relieve the effects of menopause.

HARD-WORKING DONKEYS

In the labour-intensive society of India, donkeys take the place of mechanical diggers and heavy machinery to move soil and rubble during road-building operations. Otherwise, donkey trains are used to transport all sorts of commodities.

COAL CART

CITY DRAUGHT

In the UK, the rapid growth of urban population following the Industrial Revolution of the 19th century demanded a corresponding increase in horses kept to service the everyday needs of the cities. The same applied to the conurbations of mainland Europe, even though the spread of urbanization was less rapid. American cities relied on huge numbers of horses until the early years of the 20th century. Both in the UK and the US horse-drawn milk and bakery carts survived until after the Second World War, while breweries in London still continue to make deliveries by horse-drawn drays. By the 1890s the horse populations of cities such as London and New York were large enough to pose serious health and pollution problems, which were only solved by the introduction of the automobile.

DIFFERENT USES

Mail and goods deliveries were made by horse, and carriage horses, whether privately owned or hired from the jobmasters' yards, formed a large part of the horse population. London, alone, burned five million tonnes of coal a year, all of it delivered by horse-drawn vehicles. London also employed the peculiarly named "vestry" horses, the municipal cart horses operated by the vestries (parochial boards) to clear the city refuse, and these had their counterparts in all the great cities. Horses serviced the Fire Brigades; the "black masters" conveyed the dead to their last resting place in ornate hearses; there were thousands of trade carts drawn by both donkeys and horses; and huge numbers were required to service passenger transport. In the 1890s, for instance, London had 11,300 cabs, requiring twice that number of horses in order to be operated effectively.

In 1900 it was estimated that American cities had between three and five million horses. New York City had 150,000–175,000 horses in 1880, and a town such as Milwaukee, with a population of 350,000, had 12,500. Adding to the congestion in the city streets were the carts bringing in enormous supplies of fodder each day. That was all converted to excrement, and its presence and removal created major difficulties and health hazards in urban areas. Milwaukee's 12,500 horses produced 133 tonnes of manure a day. In Rochester, New York, 15,000 horses produced, in a year, "enough manure . . . to make a pile 175 ft high, covering an acre of ground and breeding 16 billion flies" (J.A. Tarr, *American Heritage XXII*, 1971). In dry weather the air was filled with "powdered horse manure that settled on the passerby and had to be wiped from eyes and lips". In wet weather cesspools of manure and urine accumulated in the streets.

FIRE!

There was no aspect of life in 19th-century London in which the horse did not play a part. The London Fire Brigade employed many hundreds of horses, mostly of the light vanner type.

THE FUNERAL HORSE

The 19th-century, Victorian funeral hearse was drawn by black horses, often Friesians, which were suitably plumed and caparisoned in the ornate trappings of mourning.

Many horses working in the cities, especially those belonging to small traders and cab proprietors, were worn-out cast-offs that were cruelly treated and often literally worked to death. Largely as a result of the efforts of Richard "Humanity" Martin, founder of the Society for the Prevention of Cruelty to Animals (later the "Royal" Society), the British Parliament passed an act in 1822 to prevent ill-treatment of animals.

Most city horses, if they did not die in harness on the streets, ended their lives at the knacker's yard, and in death contrived still to be of service. Horse disposal companies vied for the carcases, which were methodically processed. Bones were ground for fertilizer, after the grease had been extracted to make candles and leather dressings. Other bones went to make buttons; skin and hoofs were

OMNIBUSES AND TRAMS

For some 70 years, up to the advent of the electric tram (in the 1880s) and then the trolleybus and the petrol-driven vehicle, public transport was provided by horse-drawn omnibuses and later by horse-trams running on rails. Omnibus horses, which were always mares, had a working life expectation of about four years, the same as horses employed in heavy freight haulage. Tram horses lasted a good year less because of the greater weight involved and because dirt clogging the tram rails made it more difficult to start the vehicle.

The first coach/omnibus service was run in Paris as early as 1662 by Blaise Pascal. It was, however, short-lived and it was not until 1828 that a regular passenger service, also in Paris, was set up by Stanislaus Baudry. His early omnibuses were run in Nantes where his terminus was outside the premises of a Monsieur Omnes, who inspired the name for the new form of public transport.

The French service was copied by George Shillibear, who set up a service between Paddington Green and the Bank in London in 1829. Shillibear soon became bankrupt, but his omnibus service flourished and for years the vehicles were known as "Shillibears".

In 1839, 10 years

SHORT-LIVED TRAM HORSES
This is a 19th-century, single-horse tram in Berlin. The work was so hard that tram-horses were worn out well before the end of the four-year working life allowed for heavy freight horses.

after Shillibear's first 'bus, 62 'buses were operating in London. By 1850 the number had increased to 1,300 and 40 years later there were 2,210. The service then employed 11,000 men and twice that number of horses. The French, who had been active in the initiation of Shillibear's service, retained an interest in the omnibus and the leading company in London, *Compagnie Générale des Omnibus de Londres*, did not anglicize its title to the London General Omnibus Company until 1862, when it was by far the largest company operating horse-drawn buses in the whole of Europe.

A HARD LIFE
Only too often were overloaded horses beaten unmercifully in the city streets, causing no concern to onlookers. This illustration appeared in the American Harper's Weekly in 1866.

made into glue; manes and tails were used to upholster furniture and to make fishing lines and violin bows; hides were for the manufacture of all sorts of leather goods. In the UK and the US, the meat went to cats and dogs. Even the shoes were removed to make a new set – nothing was wasted.

TRAFFIC JAM
In 1850, Ludgate Circus, London, could produce traffic jams to equal the present-day city, with no traffic lights or pedestrian crossings to make life easier. By the 1890s central London was even more congested.

CANAL HORSES

A SYSTEM OF waterways was common to a number of European countries in the 18th century, but the British network of canals, which developed as a result of the Industrial Revolution, was by far the most comprehensive. Both freight and passengers were carried in the canal barges, which were drawn by horses called "boaters", or sometimes by mules or even donkeys. In spite of the development of the railways in the early 19th century, barges held their own throughout the century. Indeed, there were even a few still at work in the 1950s. There never was a breed or specific type of barge horse. They were usually a strong vanner type (a light draught horse, often of Irish extraction) or smaller, sometimes cross-bred specimens of the heavy draught breeds. They could not be much over 1.60 m (15.3 hh) because of the height of the bridges along the towpaths.

THE STRENGTH OF THE BOATERS

Strength was of major importance to the barge horse, who regularly had to shift loads of 50–60 tonnes (45–54 tons). Indeed, in 1810 it was estimated that one horse and three men could move as big a load by barge as 60 horses and 10 men could transport over roads in a wagon. A boat horse pulled its load at the rate of 3.3 km/h (2 mph), but some single turnouts, when drawn by relays of trotting horses working in short stages, could cover 80–90 km (50–60 miles) a day.

In the mid-18th century, well before the railway revolution, barges carrying loads of up to 200 tonnes (196 tons) were hauled up the River Thames by teams of 14 horses. The slower and more laborious alternative was to employ gangs of 80 men on the tow ropes.

HIGH-SPEED FLY BOATS

A system of high-speed light freight and passenger transport, far more comfortable than any road transport, was developed by the end of the 19th century. These boats, called fly boats, only operated on certain canals in the UK, notably the Shropshire Union and the Grand Union, and carried passengers or urgent freight of up to 17–18 tonnes (15½–16¼ tons). They were light, shallow craft, drawing no more than 46 cm (18 ins) of water, and were pulled by two horses, one at the stern and one at the bow. On the Shropshire canal it was usual for the rear horse to be ridden by a postillion, who controlled the lead horse with his whip and voice. The boat was drawn at a steady canter, causing the bow to lift and the craft to assume a planing attitude. On the Grand Union the postillion rode the lead horse,

TANDEM
This sailing barge (c. 1784) is on a portion of the Duke of Bridgewater's Canal, later taken into the Manchester Ship Canal. It is being drawn by a tandem, with a postillion riding the lead horse.

which must have reduced his control of the situation. Even so, whatever the method, the boats, using teams of horses over 5–8 km stages (3–5 miles), could average speeds of 16–19 km/h (10–12 mph). Fly-boats had priority on the river, and to enforce this the bows were fitted with sharp scythe blades that would cut the rope of any barge that did not give way quickly enough. When the canals froze, broad-beamed ice-breakers were used. They were pulled, usually at a gallop, by up to 20 horses, while the boatmen rocked the barges from side to side so as to clear as wide a channel as possible.

Negotiating locks and changing horses were operations that demanded much skill and expertise on the part of the lockmen and horsemen, and the fly-boat men were no exception. They could work as fast as any stagecoach ostler, who reckoned to change a team of horses in 50 seconds.

PATHS, BRIDGES, AND TUNNELS

In order to survive, canal horses had to learn how to cope with towpaths, bridges, and tunnels. On smaller waterways, towpaths were often deep in mud. They might also have self-closing gates, or stiles marking boundary fences. These could be as high

as 0.9 m (3 ft) and had to be jumped. Barge horses were trained to negotiate these hazards, but they sustained many injuries. When the towpath changed sides the horse had to cross the canal, either over a simple hump-back bridge or on a "roving bridge", a spiral arrangement which let the horse cross over without being unharnessed. Otherwise the horse was ferried across the water or had to jump into a moving boat from a pier and jump out on the other side. Horses also had to assist in opening and closing of the locks, but where locks were impractical there were tunnels. Sometimes these had towpaths, but otherwise the horses were

led over the top or had to find their own way. The barge was poled through like a punt, or the men lay on boards placed across the bows, and pushed against the sides of the tunnel with their feet.

The canal horse was eventually ousted by the combustion engine. Early engines were often unreliable and took up freight space, and because of speed restrictions to prevent breaking down the canal banks, motor barges were no quicker and running costs not very different. But an engine could work all night, something that the horse could not do.

THE LEAPING HORSE
John Constable's The Leaping Horse, *painted in the Dedham Vale, Suffolk, illustrates how the "boaters" were trained to jump stiles on the towpath. These obstacles were often as much as 0.9 m (3 ft) high, and called for considerable agility, strength, and intelligence.*

A MODERN BOATER
This present-day "boater" is at work at Kintbury on the Kennet and Avon Canal in Berkshire, England, and is drawing a passenger barge. The height of the bridge limits the size of the horses to about 1.52 m (15 hh).

HORSE MINDER
The slow-moving "boaters" could take a little snack while they were on the move. It was quite usual for the docile canal horses to be managed by small children, as shown in this picture.

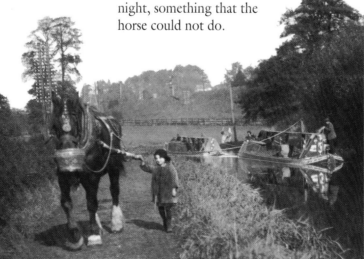

THE AGRICULTURAL HORSE

MEDIEVAL OX-PLOUGH

FOR OVER 4,000 years the horse was primarily used for war. There were, of course, numerous peaceful uses to which horses were put, but in Europe it was not really until the 18th century that horses finally supplanted oxen in the cultivation of the land. Teams of oxen were still being used in Europe after the First World War, while in the Middle East and Asia, where the employment of valuable horses for lowly tasks would have been unthinkable, the ox, the mule, and the donkey worked the land perfectly well, as they still do today. Tractors now do the work that used to be done by horses. Although they work more quickly, they pollute the atmosphere and, unlike a horse, do not have the ability to breed or produce natural waste-products that can be used to fertilize the soil.

RITUAL PLOUGHING

Although there are Bronze Age rock drawings in Northern Europe showing horses working at the plough, this was not a usual practice. It was, in fact, part of a religious ritual in which the horses were harnessed for the symbolic cutting of the first furrow, after which the job was taken over by oxen. Harness and horseshoes were not sufficiently developed for horses to undertake agricultural work until the 8th century AD, and even then the horses at that time were not big enough to perform more than a limited range of tasks. It was not until the 11th century that bigger, stronger war-horses had evolved, which provided the base for the eventual production of the modern heavy draught breeds such as the Belgian (see pp.274–75), Shire (see pp.288–89), and Percheron (see pp.94–95). The ox still remained the main draught animal well into the 18th century.

THE OLD MCCORMICK
The first American reaper was "The Old McCormick", which was worked by just two men and a pair of horses.

THE NEW SYSTEM

In the 18th century, the introduction of the three-crop rotational system (cereals and roots followed by the return to grass), and the subsequent invention of increasingly sophisticated farm machinery, were the primary factors in the development of the heavy agricultural horse. The quick, even action of the horse was better suited to the new equipment than the slow pace of the ox, an animal that has inherent disadvantages in a system designed to produce a variety of crops in quantity. It is much slower than the horse; is a ruminant, and so must be given time to chew the cud; and, because of its slow pace, it needs pasturage close to where it is working. Nonetheless, the use of oxen was championed by a number of leading agriculturalists well into the 18th century, on the grounds that they were cheaper to keep than horses, and could be fattened and sold profitably at the end of their working lives.

However, the Industrial Revolution in the 19th century, and the increase in population that accompanied it, created enormous demands for foodstuffs. A greater variety

ROMANTIC SCENE
This 19th-century pastoral scene, by the artist George Cole, is much romanticized but would have satisfied the city dweller. In reality the work was very hard and there was the ever-present fear of the crops being spoiled by rain.

of cereal and root crops was necessary, and huge quantities of grasses and clovers were needed to feed the animals that were integral to the expansion of both industry and agriculture. All these reasons, along with the continual innovations in implement design, contributed to the establishment of the agricultural horse.

HORSE-DRAWN MACHINES

A notable early invention in the field of agricultural implements was Jethro Tull's horse-drawn seed drill. It was developed in Britain, and was available in 1731. Significant improvements were also made in the design of the plough, culminating in the Arbuthnot swing plough, which was lighter than any other plough and turned the spit (the furrow slice) more cleanly and easily than anything else. It was the successor to the Rotherham plough and tests proved that when drawn by two horses, an Arbuthnot could till a greater area in one day than six oxen pulling the older type. By the middle of the 19th century the agricultural implement industry was in full swing, producing threshing machines, corn grinders, elevators, multi-furrowed ploughs, special sub-soiling ploughs, reapers, cutters, binders, and, in the US, the huge and heavy combine harvesters, which were pulled by teams of 40 horses. Indeed, American expertise in the operation of multi-horsed agricultural implements was unrivalled.

AMERICAN AGRICULTURE

The growth of American agriculture paralleled that of the country's rapidly expanding economy. By the end of the 19th century, American wheat acreage alone was half as large again as the whole of the cultivated area of Britain and was very productive. As a result, between the 1860s and 1914, the horse population of the US rose from around 7 million to 25 million.

Millions of acres of western prairie land were cultivated and harvested by thousands of huge machines. By 1890 the combine harvester had reached the zenith of its perfection. It was then 12 m (40 ft) wide, weighted 15 tonnes (13½ tons), and was drawn by teams of as many as 42 horses under the control of six men. So good was the machinery and the method of harnessing that one man could drive a 36-horse team to a set of harrows or drills. The massive four to five bottom ploughs, used on the prairie lands, were drawn by eight-horse teams and with every justification were called the "horse killers".

By 1940, 20 million horses in the US had been made redundant by the tractor and some 32,376,000 hectares (80 million acres), until then used to grow horse-feed, were released for other purposes. However, that benefit was counter-balanced to a degree by an increased used of fuel oil, causing an atmospheric pollution that did not arise in the horse era. In our enviromentally

AMISH PLOUGHMAN
The Amish people of Indiana, Pennsylvania, and Ohio rely solely on horses for farming and transport. This boy cultivates with a team hitched five abreast – no mean feat.

conscious times there is now recognition that tractors, though able to complete the work more quickly, have disadvantages. Apart from the pollution factor, they do not reproduce themselves like the horse, whose waste product enriches the land that feeds it without recourse to artificial fertilizers.

Although the heavy horse breeds no longer have a role to play in American agriculture, breed societies ensure that they do not disappear entirely. The tradition of the Clydesdale and Percheron still persists, while at the Kentucky Horse Park (see pp.240–41) Belgian Heavy Draught Horses are a popular working feature.

HORSE-POWER
The huge, very heavy combine harvesters of the Oregon wheat fields needed teams of 30 or more horses to work them.

THRESHERS
Shown here is a novel use of horse-power to thresh the corn in a specially constructed threshing ring, near San Rafael Mucachies, Venezuela.

MAREMMANA & MURGESE

DESPITE THE ITALIANS' PREOCCUPATION with the Thoroughbred (see pp.120–21), and their production of excellent trotting stock, riding horses of mixed blood are still bred in Sicily, Sardinia, the Po Valley, and the Tuscan province of Maremma. The horses of Maremma, also known as Maremmanas, are most closely associated with cattle raising. They are not bred with great selectivity, and their background has been obscured by much outcrossing. The Murgese is an older breed. It comes from the Murge district in the Puglia region of Italy, which was famous for centuries for a breed of high-quality horses.

CONVENT HORSE
The Murgese originated in the Puglia region, but this horse is at a breeding establishment in northern Italy that was once a convent.

THE MAREMMANA

Although the origins of the Maremmana are unclear, the breed is probably based on the Neapolitan blood, derived from Spanish, Arab, and Barb stock (see pp.108–9 and pp.64–67), for which Renaissance Italy was

NECK
Although weak and short in the neck, the Maremmana is a surprisingly versatile horse.

ORIGINS

THE MAREMMANA AND THE MURGESE originate on opposite sides of Italy. The Maremmana is raised in the northern province of Maremma in Tuscany, on the west coast, and the Murgese developed in the Murge district of the Puglia region in the south-east, where the dry, rocky hills produce horses with dense bone, hard feet, and strong constitutions. The Maremmana was originally bred at the stud at Grosseto as a light draught horse, but its use as the mount of the butteri, *the local cowboys, has given the breed a particular agility and an instinct to work cattle.*

renowned. Later, in the 19th century, the local animals would also have benefited from being crossed with English imports, notably the Norfolk Roadsters (see pp.122–23) and probably with half-bred stallions as well. There were several studs in the province of Maremma, and although some bred horses with semi-feral ancestry, they all made use of these English crosses as a means of upgrading the often coarse local stock.

It seems that the Maremmana developed as a distinctive type at the stud at Grosseto, where it was bred to be a heavy saddle or light draught horse. It has been described as "rustic", and is by no means handsome, but it is solid, enduring, very steady, and surprisingly versatile. It is a hardy animal, economical to feed, and well-suited to light agricultural work. In the past it was also a reliable troop horse, and was used in large numbers by both the cavalry and the police. The Maremmana's principal claim to fame,

HEIGHT OF MAREMMANA
1.60 m
(15.3 hh)

MAREMMANA

however, is that it is ridden by the *butteri*, who are the herdsmen or cowboys of the Roman countryside, and is much esteemed for its natural ability to work cattle.

The Maremmana is still somewhat common in appearance. However, the use of better-quality stallions, from the 1940s onwards, has resulted in offspring that have more correct limbs than the old type. Moreover, the horses that are used for herding cattle are notable for their strong hock joints – an essential attribute for work of that nature. The Maremmana is not capable of any great speed and does not have the best shoulders, but its strength and good-natured, willing temperament make it suitable for various purposes. The average height is around 1.60 m (15.3 hh), and all solid coat colours can be found in the breed.

THE MURGESE

The Murgese evolved in the dry limestone hills of the Murge district. Like the harsh Slovenian *karst*, the heartland of the old Lipizzaner (see pp.112–13), this area produces animals with good, dense bone, hard feet, and a sound constitution. In the 15th and early 16th centuries the horses bred in this region were in great demand as cavalry remounts. Then, about 200 years ago, interest in the Murgese died

out, and the breed virtually disappeared. It was revived in the 1920s, but the modern Murgese horse probably does not bear any direct relationship to the old breed. The new version is basically a light draught horse, of a sort similar, but inferior, to the Irish Draught (see pp.396–97).

The best specimens fulfil a useful role as light agricultural horses that can also be ridden. The mares provide a good basis for cross-breeding, for like the Irish Draught they are roomy and of substantial build. A good stamp of riding horse can be bred by putting Murgese mares to Thoroughbred or half-bred stallions, and the mares also produce the strong mules that are still needed in the area.

The Murgese has an obvious coldblood foundation with a possible trace of oriental influence, but its ancestry is undetermined. There is also a lack of uniformity in the type, a characteristic of Italian light horses, because their breeding is not subject to controls or breed society regulations. There are certain conformational faults, such as flat withers overloaded with muscle, and upright shoulders, and these inhibit free movement. Nonetheless, within the limitations of its structure, the Murgese is fairly active and energetic, and is very amenable, even-tempered, and economical to keep. It stands between 1.52 and 1.63 m (15–16 hh), and the usual coat colour is chestnut.

HEAD
The head is a little convex in profile but is not unattractive.

HIND LEGS
The hind legs give the appearance of being poorly muscled, but the hocks are strong enough to ensure a remarkable agility.

LEGS
The legs are clean and hard, although the shoulders are loaded and upright. The shanks are long.

FEET
The feet are hard-wearing and a good shape. The pasterns are short but not upright.

MURGESE

HEIGHT OF MURGESE
1.52–1.63 m (15–16 hh)

ITALIAN HEAVY DRAUGHT

THE ITALIAN HEAVY DRAUGHT, sometimes called the Italian Agricultural Horse, is the most popular heavy horse in Italy, and probably makes up one-third of the stallions at stud there. It is bred throughout northern and central Italy, principally in the area around Venice. However, its future is anything but assured. There is still a demand for a swift-actioned agricultural horse but, inevitably, there is increased competition from mechanization. In addition, some modern breeders, with an eye to the demands of a voracious meat market, concentrate on breeding for carcase weight and, in consequence, are not much concerned with improving conformational details applicable to work and the furtherance of the breed for that purpose.

BREED DEVELOPMENT

During the 19th and early 20th centuries, Italian breeders sought to improve their very moderate local stock by importing the massive Belgian Draught or Brabant (see pp.274–75). However, these horses, bred for working the heavy land of their own country, were ill-suited to the light, general farm work required by the Italians, and their offspring, though more powerful than the native stock, were too heavy and too slow for the work required.

To rectify this situation, the Italians imported the versatile Percheron (see pp.94–95) and the more active Boulonnais (see pp.266–67), which had a well-deserved reputation as an energetic trotting horse. Both breeds improved the stock, lightening the offspring and improving the action.

However, they still fell short of the type that was wanted. Finally, the answer was found in the quick-moving, lively Breton (see pp.268–69), a clean-legged horse that had inherited much of its swift trotting action from the heavy infusions of Norfolk Roadster blood (see pp.122–23) introduced in the 19th century.

Crossed with the common Italian mares, the Breton produced an ideal type for the needs of the small farms. It was smaller than the Belgian crosses but it was strong enough and had a kindly, docile temperament. It was hardy and economical to keep, but more importantly it had the speed that is as much appreciated by Italian farmers driving

NECK
The short, powerful neck and the attractive, alert head are reminders of the influence of the lively, well-built Breton.

MOUNTAIN PASTURE
A group of Italian Heavy Draught mares grazes on mountain pasture in Puglia in southern Italy, far from the traditional breeding area in Venetia to the north. The Heavy Draught is noted for its hardy constitution and is economical to keep.

HEIGHT
1.52–1.63 m
(15–16 hh)

country carts as by Italian motorists on the crowded city streets. That swift trotting action accounts for the breed's Italian title, *Tiro Pesante Rapido* – "Quick Heavy Draught". Another feature that appealed to Italian breeders was that it matured early, an advantage in an animal now produced as much for meat as for its working ability.

CHARACTERISTICS

Despite a tendency towards boxy feet and upright pasterns the Italian Heavy Draught is not unattractive. There is a noticeably close resemblance to the Avelignese (see pp.52–53), which, on geographical grounds, must have played a part in its evolution. The Avelignese has the same ancestors as the

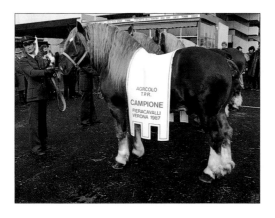

CHAMPION STALLION

The popular Tiro Pesante Rapido *is exhibited at the annual horse fair held at Verona in the principal Heavy Draught breeding area. This champion stallion with its striking coat colour is an excellent example of the breed.*

better-known Austrian Haflinger and the difference between the two is slight. The Draught Horse is, of course, bigger, standing at 1.52–1.63 m (15–16 hh), but it has a general outline similar to that of the Avelignese and usually retains something of the striking coat colour – the predominant coloration is an attractive liver chestnut with flaxen mane and tail, although there are also roans and chestnuts.

Unlike the Avelignese or the Breton, the Italian Heavy Draught retains coarse feather on the lower limbs. The limbs are often lacking in bone and the joints are small and rounded – a legacy from the generally poor quality of the base stock. Conversely, the breed has acquired some of the Breton's good conformational features, as well as some of that horse's compact outline. The chest is very deep with the forelegs spaced well apart, while the back is short and flat and the loins broad and muscular. The tail is carried high in the strong, rounded quarters and the head is surprisingly fine in relation to the overall bulk – long and tapering with a pleasingly alert expression. However, it is the ability to work at a good speed, together with the long walk and the energetic trot, that has made the Italian Heavy Draught so attractive a proposition.

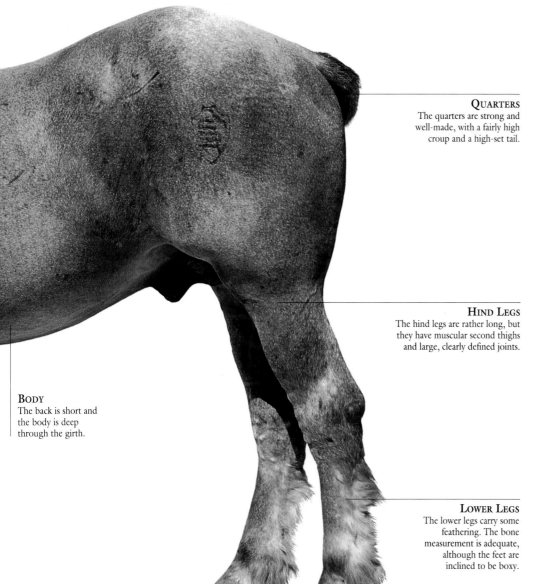

QUARTERS
The quarters are strong and well-made, with a fairly high croup and a high-set tail.

HIND LEGS
The hind legs are rather long, but they have muscular second thighs and large, clearly defined joints.

BODY
The back is short and the body is deep through the girth.

LOWER LEGS
The lower legs carry some feathering. The bone measurement is adequate, although the feet are inclined to be boxy.

ORIGINS

ITALY'S HEAVY DRAUGHT BREED comes from the northern part of the country, with some breeding also being carried on in central Italy. However, the principal area associated with the Italian Heavy Draught is in the region of Venetia, in the plain enclosed by the Dolomites and Julian Alps to the north and Slovenia to the east. There is an inevitable resemblance to the breed's close neighbour, the Avelignese mountain horse, which must have played a part in its evolution.

CAMARGUE

THE CAMARGUE HORSE LIVES IN THE RHÔNE DELTA in southern France, a harsh land that is fiercely hot in summer, and covered with cold, salt water at all other times. The *mistral*, the tearing, salt-laden wind, stunts the sparse scrub growth, the tough grasses, reeds, and saltwort on which the horses feed. The people who live there take pride in their stark swampland, calling it "the most noble conquered territory of man", while their horses have long been romanticized as "the horses of the sea". Together with the fierce, black fighting-bulls, the horses are the very essence of the Camargue.

LAND OF SALT WATER
For the most part, the land of the Camargue, which supports the white horses, is marshy and covered with light sheets of cold, salt water.

HISTORY

The Camargue is an ancient breed and was probably indigenous to the area in prehistoric times. However, like most ancient breeds its early origins are impossible to state definitively. Certainly, it bears a strong resemblance to cave drawings at Lascaux and Niaux dated c.15000 BC. In terms of proportion, it also relates to the remains of prehistoric horses found at Solutré during the 19th century, which are estimated to be as much as 50,000 years old.

In the pre-Christian era, Ostro-Goths and Vandals passed this way on Asian or Mongol horses in their invasion of Europe.

HEAD
The head is often coarse and heavy, and the neck is short, running back to flattish withers and a strong back.

Later, in the 7th and 8th centuries, a strong Barb influence (see pp.66–67) was introduced by the Moorish conquerors from the Iberian Peninsula. That association is evident in the saddlery and horse-lore of the *gardian*, the French cowboy, which is identical, down to the cage-type stirrup irons, to the one that developed in Spain and Portugal during the Moorish occupation. Since then the isolation of the Camargue has ensured that the horse herds, or *manades*, have remained free from outside influence.

The equipment used by the *gardians* to herd cattle comprises a rope and a trident. The rope, a horse-hair lariat some 11 m (36 ft) long, is used from the ground in the corrals, while the trident is used to handle cattle in the open. It can be employed to control unruly or aggressive bulls, or to help throw calves for branding.

Probably because of the independence of the *gardian*, the breed was not officially recognized until 1968, when an association

SHOULDERS
The shoulders incline to be upright, giving a short, stilted trot, but contributing to a distinctive high-stepping walk.

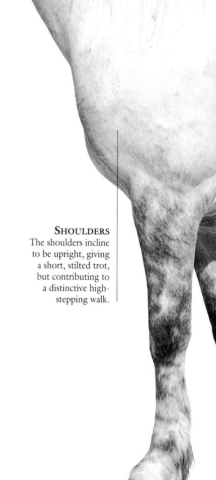

WORKING THE CATTLE
The Camargue is the traditional mount of the French cowboys, known as gardians, *who tend and work the black cattle of the Rhône Delta.*

of breeders was formed and annual stallion inspections were organized under the aegis of the Nîmes National Stud.

Today, much of the Camargue has been drained and given over to the cultivation of rice and vines, but horses are still used to work the cattle and to drive the bulls through the village streets during the traditional folk festivals. A huge area of the Camargue – the 6,880-hectare (17,000-acre) lagoon of Etang de Vacarès – is now designated as a nature reserve, and the tourist industry is creating a new use for the Camargue; there is no better way to see the wildlife than from the back of a horse.

CHARACTERISTICS

In fact, while the sight of a herd of pure white horses galloping in a curtain of sea spray has a certain romantic appeal, these horses are otherwise unprepossessing in

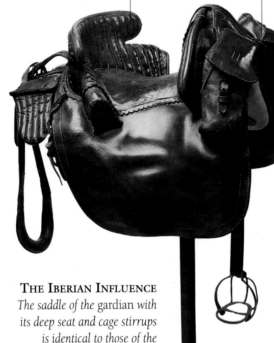

CANTLE
The high cantle is identical to that used on the Iberian Peninsula and gives great security to the rider's seat.

POMMEL
The pommel, in conjunction with the cantle, encircles the rider, giving strong support to the upper thigh.

THE IBERIAN INFLUENCE
The saddle of the gardian with its deep seat and cage stirrups is identical to those of the Iberian peninsula.

their appearance. The heads are often coarse and heavy, the necks short, and the shoulders are usually upright. The overall impression is of a "primitive" horse with overtones of the North African Barb.

To compensate for these deficiencies, the horses are deep through the girth, and have good backs. The croup slopes sharply, but is nonetheless short and strong. The limbs are also generally well-formed, and the feet, though wide to conform with the marsh environment, are hard and sound; so hard, in fact, that Camargue horses are rarely shod. They are incredibly hardy horses, possessed of great stamina and needing, or at any rate receiving, nothing more than what they can scavenge in the reeds.

The Camargue usually stands at about 1.42 m (14 hh), but may be smaller than that. It is slow to mature, not reaching adulthood until it is between five and seven years old, and is noted for its exceptional longevity, often living beyond the age of 25. Its coat, which is always white, is probably its greatest visual asset. It has a very distinctive action – the walk is long, high-stepping, and exceptionally active, but the trot is so short and stilted that the horse is rarely ridden at that pace. However, the canter and gallop are extraordinarily free. Agile, sure-footed, and possessed of high courage, the Camargue horse works the bulls in the area as instinctively as a sheepdog controls a flock of sheep.

BRAND MARK
The Camargue horses are branded with a "C" on the near quarter as a means of identification.

LEGS
The legs are short, strong, and well-formed with good, hard joints. The breed is particularly agile and active.

BODY
The body is deep-chested and the back strong and fairly short. The croup is short and slopes to a bushy tail.

FEET
The feet are very hard and sound, and in their own environment it is hardly necessary to shoe the horses.

ORIGINS

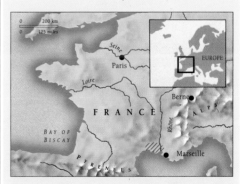

THE CAMARGUE *is an area of flat salt marshes in the Rhône Delta in southern France. It supports the manades of white Camargue horses, which live on sparse, hard grasses, reeds, and saltwort in extremes of climate; it is very hot in summer and very cold in winter. This environment produces a remarkable hardiness, and the famous fighting bulls of the Camargue, which can be fierce and unruly, contribute to the horses' courageous, cattle-wise character.*

HEIGHT
Average 1.42 m (14 hh)

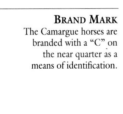

ARDENNAIS

THE ANCIENT ARDENNES BREED of heavy horse belongs to both France and Belgium. It is probably an almost direct descendant of the pre-historic horses whose remains were found at Solutré; certainly, primitive features such as the skeletal formation of the head, with its distinctive, squared-off nose, are still evident in the modern breed. The Ardennais was known to both Julius Caesar and the Greek historian Herodotus, who praised them for their hardiness and stamina. Originally small, broad-bodied draught horses, the Ardennais undoubtedly formed the basis for the great horses of the Middle Ages.

NECK
The neck is immensely strong and heavy, as befits so thick-set a horse, but it is in proportion to the huge shoulders.

THE OLD TYPE

During the 17th, 18th, and 19th centuries, the Ardennais horses were stocky, lively animals that were both ridden and used as excellent light draught horses. During the French Revolution (1789), and in the following years of the Empire, they became renowned as the best artillery horses in Europe. Large numbers pulled the French guns and transported food supplies during Napoleon's disastrous Russian campaign in 1812, and it was said that they were the only horses hardy enough to withstand the rigours of the winter retreat from Moscow and bring home a substantial part of the Emperor's wagon train. Some of those hardy, lighter Ardennes post-horses were still to be found in north-east France, in

HEAD
The massive, straight-profiled head is distinguished by a squared-off muzzle, prominent eye sockets, a low, flat forehead, and surprisingly small, pricked ears, spaced far apart.

Bassigny and on both sides of the upper Marne, around Chaumont, until the 1970s. Otherwise, there is little evidence of this old, lighter type remaining today.

THE MODERN ARDENNAIS

At the beginning of the 19th century the Ardennais was crossed with Arab blood to increase its energy and activity. Later, some Percheron, Boulonnais, and Thoroughbred crosses were introduced. However, the impact of these last three was transitory, except possibly in the related Auxois.

The trend towards a bigger, heavier animal was brought about in the 19th century by the changing demands of agriculture and the need for an increasingly powerful horse for very heavy draught work. Three distinct types of Ardennais evolved over the years: a smaller sort, nearest to the old type, which stands between 1.52 and 1.63 m (15–16 hh); the bigger and more massive Ardennais du Nord, also known as the *Trait du Nord*, which resulted from outcrosses to the Belgian Draught Horse (see pp.274–75), and the powerful Auxois.

ORIGINS

THE TRADITIONAL BREEDING AREA of the massive Ardennais breed is in the Ardennes region of France and Belgium. A hardy, quick-moving sort used to be bred on both sides of the upper Marne around Chaumont, but it is not much in evidence today. The harsh climate and severe winters in Lorraine, Champagne, and the Vosges foothills, home of the Ardennais, ensure the breed's strength of constitution. The Ardennais has influenced both the Comtois of Franche-Comté and the Auxois of Burgundy.

LEGS
The legs, "like small oak trees", carry a lighter-coloured feather, which is not as thick as that of many cart horse breeds.

The popular Ardennais du Nord (shown here) comes largely from Lorraine. Known as "the cart-horse of the north", it has a massive bone structure and correspondingly strong muscles. The powerful Auxois from Burgundy is similar to the Ardennais du Nord, but was more influenced by the 19th-century Percheron and Boulonnais crosses.

Thousands of Ardennais were used in the First World War, when the active, traditional horse again found favour for hauling stores, guns, and ammunition. Losses during both World Wars led to the importation of Dutch and Belgian stallions, but it is now no longer necessary to bring in foreign blood and such outcrosses are much less frequent. Today, the Ardennais is raised for the meat market as well as for use as a heavy draught horse.

CHARACTERISTICS

The modern Ardennais is more thick-set than any other draught horse and has been described as being built like a tractor. It has a wide frame and a rather short back with very muscular loins. The legs are quite lightly feathered, and the feet, in comparison with the massive body, are smaller than might be expected, although they are well-made, strong, and seldom flat or brittle. The Ardennais has small, pricked ears, which is unusual in heavy breeds. Because of the exceptionally good shoulders, the action of the smaller type of Ardennais is free, animated, and straight.

The climate in the French Ardennes in Lorraine, in Champagne, and in the foothills of the Vosges is harsh, and the winters are severe. In consequence the Ardennais is extraordinarily hardy, and has a very strong constitution. The breed has a reputation for extreme docility and exemplary gentleness, and can be handled easily, even by children.

The preferred colours, as stipulated in the breed standard, are roan, red-roan, iron grey, dark or liver chestnut, and bay. Bay-brown, light chestnut, and palomino are admissible, while black, dapple grey, and any other coat colours are not.

THE AUXOIS
The Auxois, the old horse of Burgundy, has co-existed with the Ardennais for centuries, and has benefited from Ardennais outcrosses.

BACK
The back of this wide-framed horse is broad and unusually short.

HEIGHT
1.60 m (15.3 hh) and above

QUARTERS
The quarters are wide and rounded, with the muscles being particularly short, thick, and powerful.

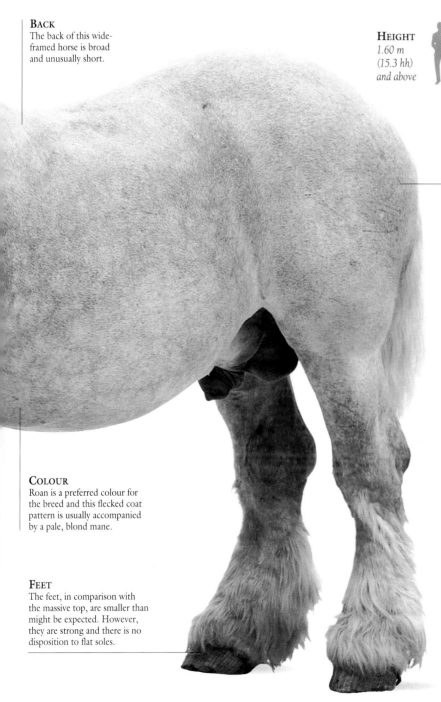

COLOUR
Roan is a preferred colour for the breed and this flecked coat pattern is usually accompanied by a pale, blond mane.

FEET
The feet, in comparison with the massive top, are smaller than might be expected. However, they are strong and there is no disposition to flat soles.

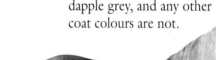

A RELATED BREED
The Comtois of eastern France is related to the Ardennais. It excels at light draught work, and is used in both the forests and the vineyards of the region. Like the lighter type of Ardennais, it is noted for its freedom of action.

BOULONNAIS

T HE HEAVY HORSE BREEDS may be described variously as being massive, majestic, powerful, or sometimes just ponderous. Of them all, however, none is more beautiful than the Boulonnais, native to north-west France, a breed that has been acclaimed as Europe's noblest draught horse. Its elegance and striking appearance are due to the repeated infusions of eastern blood that it has received. The first of these is said to have come from the Numidian cavalry that was encamped on the Boulogne coast prior to Julius Caesar's invasion of Britain (55–54 BC).

PRACTICAL PLAITING
It is traditional with the heavy horse breeds to plait up their tails. This is a practicality, ensuring that the tail does not get caught up with the reins when the horse is in harness.

HISTORY

There were ancient heavy horse breeds in this area of France in pre-Christian times. After the Roman occupation, more eastern blood was introduced during the Crusades, particularly through the work of two innovative breeders: Eustache, Comte de Boulogne, and Robert, Comte d'Artois.

In the 14th century the breed was employed as a war-horse. The increased use of heavy plate armour necessitated crosses with large, northern stallions and the then heavy German horses of Mecklenburg (now indistinguishable from the Hanoverian – see pp.144–45) to give greater weight and size. With the Spanish occupation of Flanders in the 16th century, there were generous infusions of superlative Spanish blood, itself much influenced by the Barb (see pp.66–67).

In the 17th century the breed became known as the Boulonnais, and two distinct types emerged. The smaller one, which stood between 1.55 m and 1.60 m (15.1–15.3 hh), was known as the *maréeur* or *mareyeur* (horse of the tide). It was used for the fast transportation of fish from Boulogne to Paris, a purpose for which it was ideally suited on account of its quick, energetic trotting gait.

The Boulonnais was almost destroyed by the effects of the First and Second World Wars, when the area around Boulogne was devastated twice in the space of 25 years and the mare band was scattered. Unhappily, the breed is now a victim of progress: fish is transported by road and rail, and it is doubtful if the swift *mareyeur* still exists, while the demand for the bigger type is restricted largely to the meat trade.

CHARACTERISTICS

The Boulonnais is distinguished by the expressive head, in which the Arab-like qualities are even more noticeably marked than in that of the Percheron (see pp.94–95), a similar horse that has also absorbed eastern blood. The graceful, flowing lines of the Boulonnais are unusual in draught breeds, while the fineness of the body tissues and the delicate veining are unique. The horse has been described as looking "like polished marble".

ORIGINS

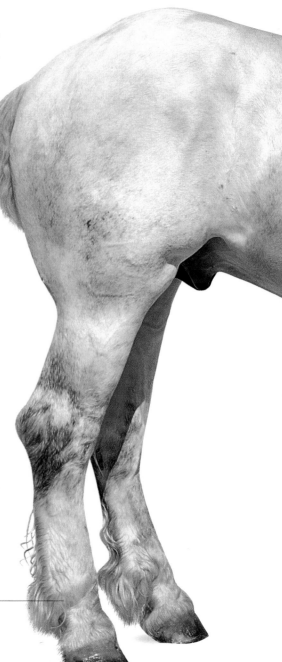

THE MAJESTIC BOULONNAIS belongs to north-west France, originating in the Boulogne-Calais hinterland, where breeds of heavy horses were raised in the pre-Christian era. One of the most renowned breeding centres was at the famous private stud of Eterpigny, just west of Arras, which for centuries was the property of the Barons of Herlincourt. Stallions reared there were sent all over the country, with the express permission of the government department controlling the national studs.

LEGS
There is little or no feather on the lower legs and the joints are large and solid. The thighs are noticeably strong and muscled.

NECK
The neck is short, thick, and gracefully arched. It blends perfectly into the muscular shoulders and the broad, powerful chest.

HEAD
The head is refined and even elegant, with large, bright eyes, erect ears, and rounded, well-spaced jowls.

BODY
The back is straight and broad. The fineness of the body tissues gives the appearance of "polished marble".

CHEST
The chest is broad and very deep, but this does not affect the straightness of the action.

HEIGHT
1.68 m
(16.2 hh)

SPIRIT
There is a look of the Arab in the striking head of the Boulonnais, and there is no doubting the spirit and courage of the breed.

FEET
The feet are usually beyond reproach and are proportionate to the size of the body.

The breed is clean-legged, without the Percheron's strength of build, but possessed of powerful, very muscular limbs with short cannons and good joints. The neck is almost always arched, even in mares, and is longer than in other draught breeds. The withers are also more clearly defined, and the shoulders are more sloped. As a result, the action is exceptional for a horse of this size (over 1.70 m, or 16.3 hh, for the large type), and is straight, quite long, and very swift and energetic. The breed is noted for its stamina, and can maintain a steady speed for long periods. As befits its eastern background, the Boulonnais' peculiarly bushy tail is set high in the quarters. At one time the predominant colour was grey, but in recent years breeders have returned to the old coat colours of chestnut and bay.

The unique quality of the Boulonnais, a breed that stands apart from the other heavy horses of Europe, with which it shares few roots, derives almost certainly from the unusual ancestry. It is worth examination because of the combination of the cold blood of European heavy horses with the hot blood of the prepotent eastern horses, whether Arab or Barb, and the Spanish blood that for 300 years was a dominant force in Europe. All three are evident in the modern Boulonnais and would have been even more apparent in the small, quick-trotting *mareyeur*. Had this last type been available today, it would have provided an almost perfect base for crossing with the Thoroughbred (see pp.120–21) or Anglo-Arab (see pp.78–79) to produce a competition warmblood.

BRETON

THE HORSE-BREEDERS of Brittany pursue the development of their breed with an enthusiasm that is more like a passionate obsession. Ever since the Middle Ages, Brittany has boasted its own variety of distinctive horse, or rather types of horse, which all derive from the same root – the primitive, hairy little horse from the Black Mountains in the west of Brittany, which was so strongly reminiscent of the Steppe Horse. This mountain horse was the ancestor of the medieval pacer, or *bidet*, as well as the later Sommier, a sturdy animal that, like the modern Breton, retained many of the mountain horse's characteristics.

EARLY BRETON HORSES

The Sommier was a typical Breton all-rounder, able to work in the plough, under pack, and at all sorts of light draught. From the Sommier the shrewdly skilful Breton breeders produced the Rossier, a lighter riding horse that became popular in southern and central Brittany because of its comfortable, inherited ambling gait.

The mountain influence was easily retained because the National Provincial Stud was sited at Lanagonnet, in the middle of the mountain country, until well after the Empire period. Eastern stallions were kept and used, followed later by Thoroughbreds (see pp.120–21). These important outcrosses produced the little-known, and now extremely rare, Cheval de Corlay, a general purpose ride-and-drive horse of about 1.52 m (15 hh) that nonetheless had the speed to take part in local races.

HEAVIER ANIMALS

In the north of Brittany other crosses were made, notably with the Boulonnais and the Percheron (see pp.266–67 and pp.94–95), while in the mountain areas the blood of the massive Ardennais (see pp.264–65) was used to create a heavier, stronger animal. But nothing could approach the improvement made by the introduction of powerful Norfolk Roadster blood during the mid-19th century (see pp.122–23). When crossed with the Breton these superlative trotting horses produced the Postier, the *beau idéal* of the light draught horse, which became the pride of the French Horse Artillery. The Postier was a compact, almost clean-legged, elegant sort, like a lighter

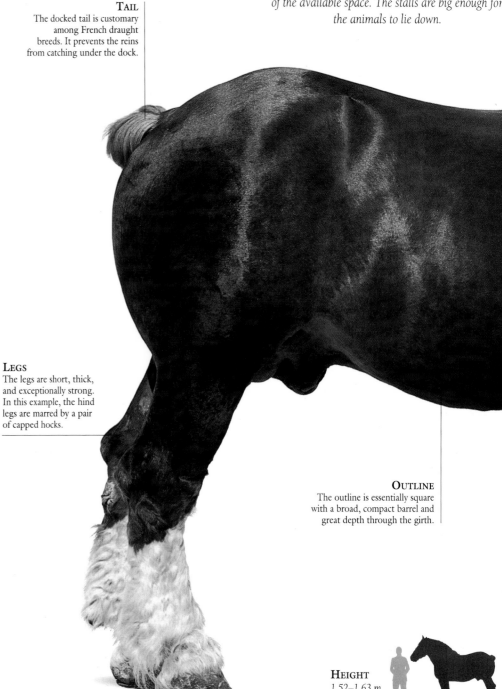

SPACE-SAVING ACCOMMODATION
It is customary in most established European studs to keep the horses in stalls so as to make maximum use of the available space. The stalls are big enough for the animals to lie down.

TAIL
The docked tail is customary among French draught breeds. It prevents the reins from catching under the dock.

LEGS
The legs are short, thick, and exceptionally strong. In this example, the hind legs are marred by a pair of capped hocks.

OUTLINE
The outline is essentially square with a broad, compact barrel and great depth through the girth.

HEIGHT
1.52–1.63 m
(15–16 hh)

version of the Suffolk Punch (see pp.290–91). Its action, in deference to its illustrious ancestor the Norfolk Roadster, was exceptionally energetic, and it was, and indeed still is, constitutionally as hard as nails.

MODERN BRETONS

Today, two types of Breton are recognized – the Postier and the Heavy Draught. The latter is an early-maturing horse that is ideal for meat production. It

is a heavier specimen, less compact and active than the Postier, but hardy and possessed of great stamina and strength.

Both types appear in the same stud book. Originally there were two books, both of which were opened in 1909, but these were combined in 1912 with a section for each type. Finally, a single book was introduced in 1926. To qualify for admission, Postiers must be of Postier parentage and have to pass performance tests in harness. These occasions become festival

FOREHEAD
The forehead is broad, with bright, widely spaced eyes.

HEAD
The square head has a straight profile with open nostrils. The ears, set low on the head, are small and mobile.

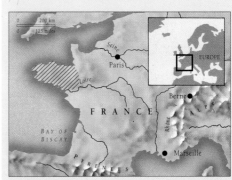

ORIGINS

THE BRETON HORSE originated in Brittany, in north-west France, and may be said to be indigenous to the region. Since the Middle Ages, the Breton horse-breeders have been considered to be among the most skilful in Europe. They based much of their stock on the little horse of the Black Mountains in western Brittany. Breton horses have been widely exported, and bred in small numbers, or used as crosses to improve the local stock, in places as diverse as Japan and the Balkans.

days and are an excuse for turning out in regional costume. No outside blood has been permitted since 1920, and the stud book has been closed since 1951.

The Breton is still a popular horse in France, and is exported as far as Japan and the Balkans. It is appreciated both as a work horse and as an ideal improver of less developed stock. In the UK it is used not only for its own sterling qualities but also as crosses to produce riding cobs.

The average height of this attractive, rather "squarish" horse is between 1.52 and 1.63 m (15–16 hh) and the colour is mainly red-roan. There are, however, some chestnuts, bays, and the occasional grey.

SUPERLATIVE TROTTERS
This pair of Bretons is drawing a break at the National Stud of Tarbes. The Postier type, formerly the pride of the French artillery, is still a superlative trotting horse in heavy draught.

FEET
The feet are medium-sized. The lower limbs are clean, carrying only a little feather.

NORMAN COB

THE NORMAN COB IS DESCENDED from the small horses, known as *bidets*, which lived in Brittany and Normandy from before the time of the Roman Empire. These hard, enduring little horses came out of Asia with the Celts and then passed through Russia, bringing with them the powerful genes of the Mongolian Horse and acquiring a little of the refining eastern influence along the way. The Romans, who were eminently practical, crossed the *bidet* with the heavy pack mares that serviced their legions, to produce a strong, round-buttocked utility horse, ancestor of the modern Norman Cob.

HISTORY

By the 10th century Normandy had become established as one of the world's best horse-breeding areas, its limestone sub-soil and abundant grass pastures providing the ideal nursery for rearing horses. In particular, the Norman breeders were famed for a war-horse that would now be considered as a draught type, although it was not as heavy as the massive heavy horses of Flanders.

By the 16th and 17th centuries this horse had become lighter as a result of outcrosses to Arab and Barb horses (see pp.64–67), and in the 19th century there were further crosses to the English Thoroughbred and the Norfolk Roadster (see pp.120–23) and to half-bred English "hunter" stallions, which were also influenced by the Roadster. This process led to the development of the Anglo-Norman, which then developed into the Selle Français (see pp.132–33).

FRENCH STUDS

The Norman Cob, in common with a number of French breeds, owes much of its development to the great French royal studs that were established in the 18th century to meet the seemingly unending demand for vast numbers of horses for military purposes. One of the first to be founded was the famous and magnificent stud at Le Pin. Louis XIV bought the estate in 1665 as a replacement for the royal stud at Montfort l'Amaury, but it was not completed and the

FRAME
The frame is powerful and stocky but without the massiveness of the true heavy breeds. The shoulders are strong and produce a noticeably free action.

SAINT LÔ
Norman Cobs form an important part of the complement housed at the National Stud of Saint Lô. These strong, lively horses are ideal for small business use, and can be employed as all-round farm horses on the small Normandy holdings.

HEIGHT
1.60–1.68 m
(15.3–16.2 hh)

first stallions installed until 1728. The stud at Saint Lô, in the La Manche region in Normandy, home of the Norman Cob, was founded by Imperial decree in 1806, and by 1912 it housed no fewer than 422 stallions. In 1944 the old stud farm was destroyed by enemy action but, in time, new buildings were put up on another adjacent site and by 1976 its stallion complement had risen to 186, of which 60 were Norman Cobs. Le Pin, too, was concerned with the Cob as well as with Trotters, Anglo-Normans, Thoroughbreds, and Percherons.

At the beginning of the 20th century a distinction was being made between the Norman horses of riding type suitable as cavalry remounts, and those of less quality and sturdier build that could be used in light draught. At Saint Lô and Le Pin it became the practice to dock the tails of the light draught horses. This was a practical rather than a fashionable measure, because it was thought that on a harness horse the reins might become dangerously trapped under a tail that was left in its natural state. Soon, the animals were being called cobs after the dual-purpose English cob which they so much resembled (see pp.410–11) and were recognized as a breed in their own right.

However, even though Norman Cob stallions are to be found at the national studs, especially at Saint Lô, no stud book is kept, although breeding is documented and in some parts performance testing of young stock is organized.

THE MODERN NORMAN COB

The Norman Cob is a powerful, stockily built animal, which was developed as an all-round agricultural horse for work on small farms. It is heavier than its Norman predecessors, which were bred for the military market, and which, in many instances, could have been classed as heavy-weight riding horses as well as being suitable for light draught. It is also heavier than its modern Welsh counterpart (see pp.184–85). Even so, it is not a true heavy breed, but a warmblood lacking the massive proportions of the heavy draught horse. The breed still retains the active, energetic paces of its forebears, particularly their great trotting ability and appealing "cob character". Cobs are still popular in their native Normandy in much the same way as the Welsh Cob is virtually integral to the rural life of the old Welsh county of Cardiganshire.

The Norman Cob stands at 1.60–1.68 m (15.3–16.2 hh), and is usually chestnut, although there are also bays and the occasional red-roan. Its survival is due to the existence of the government-administered network of French National Studs, which has maintained a consistent policy ever since the decree of the Council of Louis XIV, in 1665, involved the state in horse-breeding.

TAIL
The tail is set high in the quarters. The docking of tails is allowed in France but prohibited by law in the UK.

LEGS
The legs are short and thickly muscled in the second thighs.

HOCKS
The proportionate hocks are well-set on the hind legs. Both the cannons and the shanks are short. The joints are prominent and there is ample bone of good quality.

FEET
The feet are medium-sized and sound. There is some light feathering on the heels, which does not extend further up the legs.

ORIGINS

THE REGION OF LA MANCHE in Normandy is regarded as the centre of Norman Cob breeding, in the same way as the old county of Cardigan in mid-Wales is seen as the home of the Welsh Cob. The principal establishments keeping Norman Cobs are the National Studs of Le Pin and Saint Lô. Normandy's limestone sub-soil and high-quality, mineral-rich pasture are critical factors in any successful horse-rearing enterprise and they are reflected in the breed's size, bone, and substance.

POITEVIN & BAUDET DE POITOU

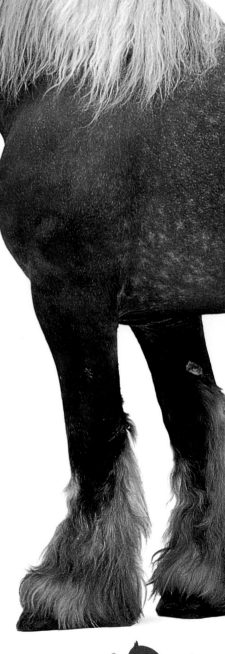

POITEVIN

THE POITOU REGION OF FRANCE, south of the Loire, is famous on three counts. There is the Poitevin horse or Mulassier, a heavy horse that has more conformational faults than most, is singularly unattractive in appearance, and has little potential as a working horse. Secondly, there is the gigantic Poitevin jackass, or Baudet de Poitou, which is used to sire the biggest mules in Europe. Finally, there is the mule industry based on these two animals, for which this part of France has been notable since the 19th century.

THE POITEVIN

The Poitevin is descended from the mainly Dutch, Danish, and Norwegian heavy horses that were brought to Poitou in the 17th century to help drain the marshes of La Vendée and Poitou. The mares were then bred to cross with Baudet de Poitou jackasses to produce valuable mule stock.

Poitevin mares have few redeeming conformational features. They are usually dun in colour, in accordance with a primitive background that must trace to the heavy Forest Horse of Northern Europe (see pp.14–15). The body is large and long, the head is heavy, and the ears thick and not very mobile. Shoulders are straight, the croup slopes away, and, as befits a marsh horse, they have very large feet. The mane and tail hair is thick, coarse, and shaggy, and the legs are heavily feathered, the rough hair growing in curly tufts around the knees and hocks. The breed is very strong but slow-moving and correspondingly slow and sober in terms of disposition – possibly more so than other European heavy breeds.

THE BAUDET DE POITOU

The Baudet de Poitou, on the other hand, is a remarkable animal by any standards. At 1.63 m (16 hh) it is almost the same height as the Poitevin. It is

ORIGINS

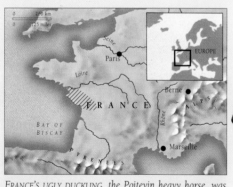

FRANCE'S UGLY DUCKLING, the Poitevin heavy horse, was brought to the Marais Poitevin in the 17th century, and is bred in this area and the Poitou region. It was used initially in the draining of the marshes of La Vendée and Poitou, and has the wide feet of the marshland inhabitant. The Baudet de Poitou is the huge ass of the Plaines du Poitou. It has been bred carefully over centuries, and its breeding is encouraged by the proximity of markets to which the Poitevin mule is traditional. Even today there is no shortage of buyers for the Poitevin mules.

POITEVIN HORSE FOAL
Essentially producers of mules, Poitevin mares are also put to Poitevin stallions to maintain the breed. Surplus animals can be sold through the meat market.

HEIGHT OF POITEVIN
1.63–1.68 m (16–16.2 hh)

unusually hardy for a donkey and bred carefully for its size and conformational strength. Its size, length of limb, and even the set of its shoulder contribute to a quick action and a longer stride than might be expected. There is a single stud book, opened in 1885, for both the Poitevin horse and the Baudet de Poitou.

POITEVIN MULES

Poitevin mules, famous for their versatility and exceptional strength, quickly became sought after in both Europe and the US

MULE FOAL
This is a typical dun-coloured Poitevin mare with her mule foal by a Poitou jackass. These very strong hybrids make excellent workers.

where mules formed an essential part of the agricultural economy. Ideal for work in difficult terrain where heavy horses are not a practical proposition, they were used in places such as Turkey, Greece, the south of France, Italy, Spain, and Portugal, and were even exported as far as Russia.

Between 1900 and 1914 there was a good trade for Poitou mules in the US, and until the First World War Germany was also a major purchaser. After the war numbers were seriously depleted, but during the 1920s the trade recovered. Further setbacks were experienced after the Second World War, but recently there has been a limited revival and there is no shortage of buyers for the stock produced.

Mules are very strong, have excellent constitutions, and are almost always sound in wind and limb. In addition they are willing workers, have a long working life of as much as 25 years, and are cheap to keep, managing very well on basic rations.

TAIL
The tail, especially in mares, is set low in sloping quarters. The tail hair is coarse.

HEAD
The head has a pleasing expression enhanced by the enormous ears.

LEGS
The legs are solid, and though the back and shoulder are naturally straight, the action is quick and sure.

LOWER LEGS
Coarse feather covers the lower legs. The feet are large and flat.

HEIGHT OF BAUDET DE POITOU
1.63 m (16 hh)

BAUDET DE POITOU

BRABANT

THE BRABANT, or Belgian Heavy Draught, is one of the most influential and, in its day, the most famous of the European heavy horse breeds. Known during the Middle Ages as the Flanders Horse, it played a considerable role in the development of heavy breeds such as the Clydesdale, the Shire, and the Suffolk Punch (see pp.290–91). In addition, it was probably used, centuries ago, to increase the size of the forerunners of the Irish Draught (see pp.396–97).

ORIGINS

The Brabant is an ancient European breed that has been a major factor in the history of horse development. Through the even older Ardennes (see pp.264–65) it may be a direct descendant of the primitive Forest Horse (*Equus sylvaticus*), one of the four early types of horse (see pp.14–15). The Ardennes (and by association the Brabant) was known to the Romans and given honourable mention in Julius Caesar's *Commentaries on the Gallic War* as a willing, untiring work horse. Despite its virtual eclipse in modern Belgium, the Brabant retains a strong following in the US.

SELECTION AND IN-BREEDING

Belgium, like other countries of mainland Europe, suffered from the tides of war that regularly ebbed and flowed over its territory, bringing and often leaving behind horses of alien blood. Belgian breeders, however, despite pressures to produce the lighter stamp of cavalry horse, were unswerving in their devotion to their own heavy horse, which made up 90 per cent of their country's horse population. It was one that suited their traditional skills, their climate and heavy, rich soil, as well as their economic reliance upon the land. They resisted the inclusion of foreign blood and practised a policy of stringent selection, in-breeding where necessary, to preserve or develop exceptional qualities. By doing so they established definitive lines that produced a unique heavy horse, more versatile than most heavy draught breeds and with quite exceptional power.

Increasingly, this all-Belgian creation took on the name of one of its breeding areas, Brabant, and was as often called *Race*

HORSE-POWER UNLIMITED
This impressive span of matching Brabants is making light work of a heavily loaded brewer's dray. The colourful harness accessories give emphasis to the stylish, free-moving horses.

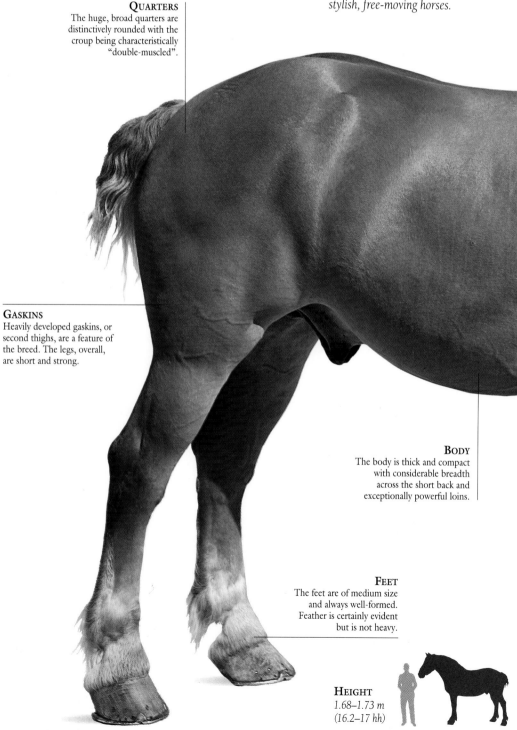

QUARTERS
The huge, broad quarters are distinctively rounded with the croup being characteristically "double-muscled".

GASKINS
Heavily developed gaskins, or second thighs, are a feature of the breed. The legs, overall, are short and strong.

BODY
The body is thick and compact with considerable breadth across the short back and exceptionally powerful loins.

FEET
The feet are of medium size and always well-formed. Feather is certainly evident but is not heavy.

HEIGHT
1.68–1.73 m (16.2–17 hh)

de Trait Belge. Both names are more befitting to its distinguished position among the heavy horse breeds than the modern, more pedestrian description of it as the Belgian Heavy Draught.

IMPORTANT BRABANT LINES

By about 1870 there were three main groups, although the distinction was more to do with bloodlines than with specific conformational differences. The first of the three groups was that of Orange I, forefather of the particularly massive, bay horses of the magnificently titled line Gros de la Dendre. The stallion Bayard founded the line Gris du Hainaut, which had grey, dun, and sorrel or red-roan colouring. Red-roan, in particular, reveals the ancient, "primitive" origin of the breed. The third Brabant line was founded by the bay horse Jean I, and was grandiloquently named Colosses de la Mehaïque. The horses from this bloodline were noted for the extreme strength and hardness of their legs.

FAMOUS BRABANTS

The demand for the *Cheval de Trait Belge* was much encouraged at the end of the 19th century by the success of Belgian horses in international competitions. The stallion Brillant, son of Orange I, won the International Championship at Paris in 1878 and repeated his victories in the succeeding years at London, Lille, and Hanover. In 1900 his grandson, Rêve d'Or, became world champion, and after him there was the "super-champion" Avenir d'Herse.

CHARACTERISTICS

The Brabant is a massive, powerful horse of about 1.68–1.73 m (16.2–17 hh). It is short-backed and compact, and its legs are very strong, short, and sturdily built, with ample feather. The head is small in proportion, square, and plain, but the expression is intelligent. The action cannot be described as showy or elegant, but it is well-suited to the work for which the breed is used and these horses have a particularly good stride at the walk. The Brabant is also notable for its kindly temperament.

CHEST
The chest is broad, and the neck short, thick, and strong enough for every sort of heavy draught purpose.

HEAD
The head is small and refined in comparison with many other heavy breeds, but remains proportionate and an attractive feature.

LEGS
The short legs are noted for their extreme strength and hardness. Soundness of limb is a prime requirement in all the Brabant lines.

DUTCH DRAUGHT
The Dutch Draught was developed from the Brabant after 1918 using Zeeland-type Dutch mares and an occasional outcross to the Belgian Ardennais. A massive horse, it is quiet in temperament, free-moving, and possessed of great stamina.

ORIGINS

THE BRABANT, ALSO CALLED the Belgian Heavy Draught, was known during medieval times as the Flanders Horse and as such had an important influence on numerous heavy horse breeds, including the Shire, Clydesdale, and Suffolk. The principal breeding area, from which it takes its name, is Brabant in Belgium, but the breed was once numerous throughout Flanders, covering the regions of Anvers, Hainaut, Limberg, Liège, Namur, and extending into Luxembourg. Today it is also bred in the US, where it has a particularly strong following.

JUTLAND & SCHLESWIG

THE HEAVY JUTLAND HORSE IS NATIVE TO DENMARK, and has been bred on the Jutland Peninsula for centuries. The first recorded mention of the breed is in the 12th century; at that time they were employed as war-horses, because they had the strength to carry a knight in full armour and the stamina to withstand the rigours of a military campaign. The Jutland is the foundation ancestor of the neighbouring Schleswig Draught Horse, which originated in the north German province of Schleswig-Holstein.

CITY DRAUGHT
A team of Jutlands drawing a smart brewer's dray is still a popular sight on the streets of Copenhagen, though the breed is not much used in agriculture.

THE JUTLAND

There is some evidence that the forerunners of the modern Jutland existed in the Viking period, which began in the early 9th century. Anglo-Saxon pictures show the Danish raiders rounding up prisoners while riding horses that appear very similar to present-day Jutlands. It has been suggested that the Vikings brought Danish horses to East Anglia in England, and therefore that such animals would have contributed to the base stock from which came the Suffolk Punch (see pp.290–91). In any case, England, along with Germany and France, imported horses from Jutland during the Middle Ages.

A principal influence in the evolution of the modern Jutland was the Suffolk Punch, and in particular the stallion Oppenheimer LXII, who was imported in the 1860s. The dark chestnut Oppenheimer is sometimes erroneously said to have been a Shire, but there is little doubt that he was a Suffolk horse. He was imported by the noted horse dealer Oppenheimer of Hamburg, who dealt consistently in Suffolk Punches, importing them to Germany for the Mecklenburg Stud. The horse was very successful at stud, and founded the most important bloodline through one of his many descendants, Oldrup Munkedal.

During the 18th century, the Danish Frederiksborg horse (see pp.114–15), which is of Spanish descent, was used on the Jutland in order to give the breed more active paces, and in the 19th century some not altogether successful crosses were made with Cleveland Bays (see pp.306–7) and their derivative the Yorkshire Coach Horse. In the 1950s there were 405 studs breeding Jutlands in Denmark, with a total of 14,416 mares and 2,563 stallions, but since then the numbers have dwindled. Few Jutland horses work on the land now, but the breed is still used for draught work in the cities and is a popular sight at horse shows.

Today, the similarity between the Suffolk, the Jutland, and the Schleswig is obvious. The modern Jutland bears a close resemblance to the Suffolk Punch in all respects except for the feathering on the

QUARTERS
The quarters in both breeds are round and muscular.

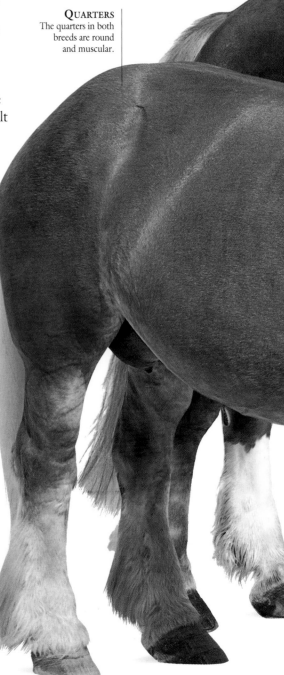

ORIGINS

THE DANISH HEAVY HORSE BREED takes its name from the Jutland Peninsula where it has been bred since the Middle Ages. At that time Jutlands were imported to England and may have had an early influence on the Suffolk Punch. Germany and France also made use of the Jutland horse. Later, as trade continued to develop between England and Denmark, Jutlands were improved by the import of British Clevelands and, very notably, by the Suffolk Punch. The Jutland is the foundation for the neighbouring Schleswig Draught Horse and outcrosses were being made up to 1938.

HEIGHT OF JUTLAND
1.57–1.63 m
(15.2–16 hh)

legs, and even so Jutland breeders still seek to reduce if not eliminate this feature. The horse is coarser than the Suffolk Punch, particularly about the head, but it has the compact, roly-poly body and the appealing roundness of the British breed. The Jutland is sturdy, active, and enduring, and is a willing work horse. It stands at between 1.57 and 1.63 m (15.2–16 hh), and the predominant colour is dark chestnut with an attractive flaxen mane and tail.

THE SCHLESWIG

The Jutland stallion Munkedal, through his in-bred descendants, the horses Prins of Jylland and Høvding, is virtually the foundation sire of the Schleswig breed. Initially, in the first part of the 19th century, the Yorkshire Coach Horse (see pp.306–7) and

JOWL
The modern Jutland and its offshoot the Schleswig are much less fleshy in the jowl than their predecessors and the head is less heavy.

LEGS
The legs are short and heavily feathered. The feet have improved.

SCHLESWIG

JUTLAND

HEIGHT OF SCHLESWIG
1.57–1.63 m (15.2–16 hh)

even the Thoroughbred (see pp.120–21) were also used to improve the soft and somewhat coarse native Schleswig. Selective breeding based on the Munkedal line was practised from 1860. In 1888 a breed standard was recognized, and three years later the Society of Schleswig Horse Breeding Clubs was formed. By the end of the 19th century the Schleswig Horse had evolved as a medium-sized, tractable animal of between 1.57 and 1.63 m (15.2–16 hh) that was much in demand for pulling buses and trams. The early Schleswig was predominantly chestnut, as a result of the Jutland influence, but grey and bay coats occurred in later years.

To maintain the breed, outcrosses to the Jutland were made regularly until 1938. After that, strict selection was practised within the breed in an effort to eradicate conformational deficiencies such as the flat ribs, over-long body, and the soft, flat feet. To accelerate this process, a Boulonnais and a Breton stallion (see pp.266–69) were used after the Second World War, with the Boulonnais having the greater influence. Like the Jutland, the Schleswig population has decreased greatly as its traditional functions have been taken over by machines.

VLADIMIR & RUSSIAN HEAVY DRAUGHT

HEAD
The head is large and fairly long, and has either a straight or convex profile. The muscular neck is of medium length.

HEIGHT OF VLADIMIR
1.65 m
(16.1 hh)

VLADIMIR

Bᴇꜰᴏʀᴇ ᴛʜᴇ Rᴇᴠᴏʟᴜᴛɪᴏɴ ᴏꜰ 1917, Russia had more horses per 100 persons than any European country except Iceland. The tradition of keeping horses resembled that of Central Asia, so heavy breeds were few compared with light farm, carriage, and saddle horses. After the Second World War the state studs concentrated on selective breeding, and both the Vladimir and the Russian Heavy Draught benefited from their carefully formulated policies.

THE VLADIMIR

The Vladimir Heavy Draught breed evolved at collective and state farms in the provinces of Ivanovo and Vladimir. It was developed on the basis of selective breed programmes that had been carried out at the Gavrilovo-Posadsk State Stables in the early years of the 20th century. There, the local mares were crossed with Clydesdales and Shires (see pp.286–89). The principal foundation stallions were the Clydesdales, Lord James and Border Brand, both foaled in 1910, and Glen Albin, who was foaled in 1923. The Shire crosses, though important, were less influential and they are found far back in the pedigrees, mostly on the dam's side. It seems that early experiments were also made with outcrosses to Percherons, Suffolk Punches, and Cleveland Bays (see pp.94–95, pp.290–91, and pp.306–7). By the mid-1920s inter-breed crossing was being phased out, as an increasing number of good cross-breds had by then been obtained. Selected cross-breds were then mated in order to fix the breed's type and character. This phase was completed in 1950, four years after the Vladimir horse had been officially recognized as a breed.

The Vladimir is well-built, and is usually bay in colour. The stallions stand at about 1.65 m (16.1 hh); they have exceptionally deep girths, and may measure as much as 2.07 m (6 ft 10 in) round the barrel. Most Vladimir horses have clean legs, but some carry substantial feather and, as a result, may suffer from cracked heels. If there is any deficiency in the breed it is in the back, which, though broad, can be rather weak in some animals. There is a pronounced slope to the quarters.

A good-natured horse, the Vladimir combines great pulling power with adequate speed. The action is free and energetic, and makes the breed well suited to pulling the famous Vladimir *troika* three-abreast. The horses mature quickly, an important quality

LATVIAN RIDING HORSE
This horse was developed in the late 1970s to meet the demand for competition horses in Latvia and neighbouring countries. The base was provided by the Latvian Harness Horse outcrossed to Thoroughbreds, Arabs, and Hanoverians.

for animals that are put to work at three years of age, and stallions have a very high fertility rate, of between 75 and 80 per cent.

THE RUSSIAN HEAVY DRAUGHT

This breed came into being at about the same time as the Vladimir, at the Khrenov and Derkul State Studs in the Ukraine. At first, Ardennes stallions (see pp.264–65) from Sweden were crossed with Ukraine mares and with a variety of others, including the Belgian Heavy Draught (see pp.274–75) and some Percherons. Orlov Trotters (see pp.342–43) were also used to give increased activity. Until the 1920s the breed was known as the Russian Ardennes, and it was not registered as the Russian Heavy Draught Horse until 1952. During the 1920s it was in decline, but then a breeding programme was initiated with the aim of producing an amenable horse with a good action, which was suitable for general agricultural work.

The Russian Heavy Draught is a smart horse, built like a heavy cob, with a strong frame and lively movement. It stands at 1.47–1.50 m (14.2–14.3 hh), and has short, clean legs that carry very little feather. As with the Vladimir, the back is not the best feature; sickle-hocks may also be a problem. The head is notable for its lightness and attractive expression, which may be a result of the Orlov cross. The usual colours are strawberry roan and chestnut.

The Russian Heavy matures very quickly; it is reckoned to have grown to 97 per cent of its full height, and to have reached 75 per cent of its full weight, by the time it is 18 months old. The horses also have a long life expectancy, and can still be used at stud at over 20 years of age, as well as carrying out agricultural work. The fertility rate for stallions is between 80 and 85 per cent, even higher than that of the Vladimir.

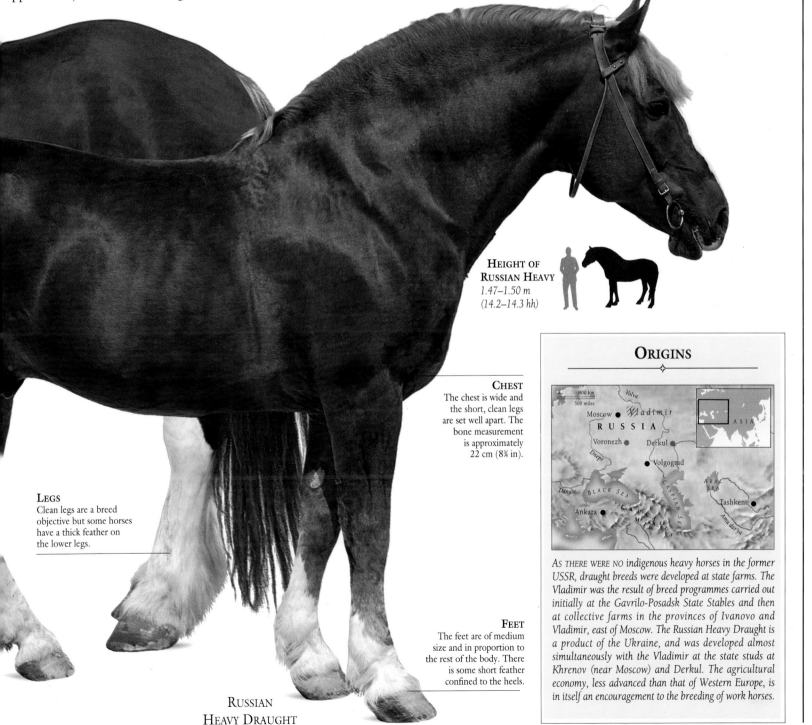

HEIGHT OF RUSSIAN HEAVY
1.47–1.50 m
(14.2–14.3 hh)

CHEST
The chest is wide and the short, clean legs are set well apart. The bone measurement is approximately 22 cm (8¾ in).

LEGS
Clean legs are a breed objective but some horses have a thick feather on the lower legs.

FEET
The feet are of medium size and in proportion to the rest of the body. There is some short feather confined to the heels.

RUSSIAN
HEAVY DRAUGHT

ORIGINS

As there were no indigenous heavy horses in the former USSR, draught breeds were developed at state farms. The Vladimir was the result of breed programmes carried out initially at the Gavrilo-Posadsk State Stables and then at collective farms in the provinces of Ivanovo and Vladimir, east of Moscow. The Russian Heavy Draught is a product of the Ukraine, and was developed almost simultaneously with the Vladimir at the state studs at Khrenov (near Moscow) and Derkul. The agricultural economy, less advanced than that of Western Europe, is in itself an encouragement to the breeding of work horses.

MURAKÖZI

THE GOLDEN AGE OF HORSE-BREEDING IN Hungary lasted from 1870 until the outbreak of the First World War in 1914. During that period many of the best Hungarian light horse breeds were developed, usually with the help of Arab blood (see pp.64–65). However, the cold-blooded agricultural horses, on which much of Hungary's rural economy depends even in the 21st century, were not neglected. The Noriker (see pp.50–51) filtered across Hungary's western border from Austria at the end of the 19th century, and the Noriker mares were put to Arab stallions. As a result, a new breed, the Muraközi, was created.

BREEDING

The breeding programme was centred on Muraköz, on the River Mura in southern Hungary, and the early foundation stock was sometimes referred to as Mur-Insulan (i.e. confined to the Mura region). The Arab blood that was used so extensively in Hungarian horse-breeding produced lighter offspring with a much greater freedom of action. Thereafter, good-quality Hungarian

LIGHT DRAUGHT
The quick-moving, active Muraközi is ideal for light draught work in a mixed agricultural environment, as well as for arable farming.

stallions were used, and both Percherons (see pp.94–95) and Ardennais from Belgium (see pp.264–65) were imported. In this way, a more or less fixed type of quick-moving, alert horse was created. Such horses were ideal for farm work, and were strong enough to be suitable for the tasks involved in intensive arable farming, even on heavy soils.

After the First World War, arable farming increased dramatically in Eastern and Central Europe. As a result, the Muraközi

HEAD
The face has an alert expression, and the head has some quality as a result of the infusions of Arab blood.

was in great demand and the breed flourished. By the mid-1920s, 20 per cent of the horse population in Hungary was made up of Muraközi horses. Even in the 1970s, 80–85 per cent of the horses in Hungary (of which there were about 231,000 in all) were still being employed for farming, and the hard core of heavy agricultural horses was composed of Muraközis.

The breed continued to go from strength to strength until the Second World War. By the end of the war the Muraközi breeding stock was much depleted, as was that of so many of the established breeds in Europe. A policy of introducing outside blood was swiftly implemented, and had the desired effect of revitalizing the breed and thus encouraging the regrowth of arable farming. Between 1947 and 1949, 17 stallions of the Ardennais breed (already a significant element in the Muraközi's genetic make-up) were imported from France, and some 59 from Belgium. These horses re-established the breed in a relatively short time.

CHARACTERISTICS

Among the heavy, cold-blooded breeds of Europe, the Muraközi is as distinctive as the Boulonnais (see pp.266–67) or the Breton (see pp.268–69), possibly as the result of the Arab influence in its ancestors. The breed

MANE
A flaxen mane and tail accompany the chestnut coat colour. Other body colours are bay, brown, black, and grey.

WITHERS
The withers, though not high, are more clearly defined than in most heavy horse breeds, and the shoulders are more sloped.

LIMBS
The limbs are light, with only a little feather at the heel, but the joints are hard and the forearms are muscular.

is still classed as a coldblood, and continues to be used for draught work and agriculture, but it has a particular refinement that perhaps accords with the Hungarian tradition of employing eastern outcrosses in order to improve the action and the general activity of the working paces.

There are two types of Muraközi: a heavy horse that stands at 1.63 m (16 hh) or more, and a lighter, more active, general-purpose sort. These horses are predominantly chestnut in colour, often with the flaxen mane and tail of their far-off Noriker ancestors, but bays, blacks, and greys also occur. The head is usually plain and honest in outlook, and is notable

ARABLE FARMING
This horse-hoe is being drawn by a typical Muraközi. The breed's quick action is ideally suited to this form of work. Interestingly, the horse wears Hungarian breast harness rather than a collar.

for the large, kind eyes. The Muraközi's physical structure is compact and very powerful, with plenty of depth through the girth. The legs carry only a little feather. They are short and strong, although the bone in some instances appears rather light in proportion to the body weight and for the work demanded of the horse. The tail is usually set low in a sloping croup, but the quarters are very well-muscled and attractively rounded. These horses mature early, and may be worked at only two years of age. Their temperament is calm and even, and their physical constitution is similarly dependable. A notable characteristic of the breed is its reputation as a most efficient converter of food into energy. This feature makes it economical to keep, an important consideration in an agricultural economy that is only minimally mechanized and so depends on the employment of horses. An additional benefit is the massive flesh structure, which makes the breed attractive to the meat market.

Muraközi horses are bred in Poland, and in the countries that formerly belonged to Yugoslavia, as well as in Hungary.

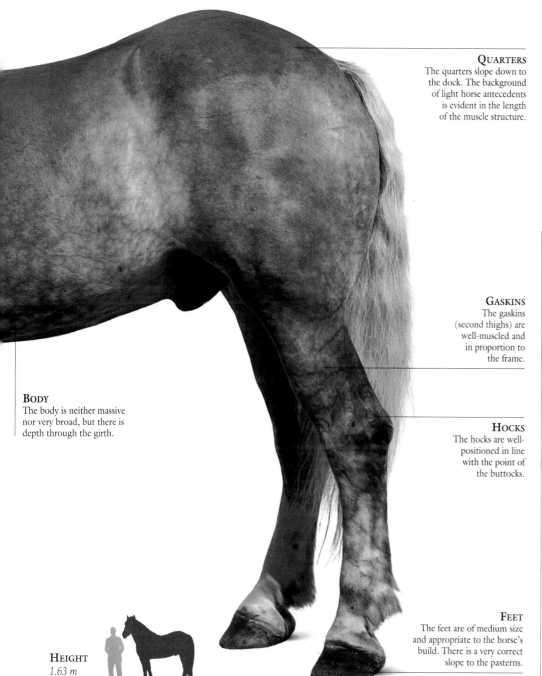

QUARTERS
The quarters slope down to the dock. The background of light horse antecedents is evident in the length of the muscle structure.

GASKINS
The gaskins (second thighs) are well-muscled and in proportion to the frame.

BODY
The body is neither massive nor very broad, but there is depth through the girth.

HOCKS
The hocks are well-positioned in line with the point of the buttocks.

FEET
The feet are of medium size and appropriate to the horse's build. There is a very correct slope to the pasterns.

HEIGHT
1.63 m
(16 hh)

ORIGINS

THE MURAKÖZI is an exception among Hungarian horses, which are usually of pronounced eastern type. It was developed as a general farm horse in western Hungary, principally at Muraköz on the banks of the River Mura. A popular farm horse in Eastern and Central Europe up to the Second World War, it was also bred in the former Yugoslavia and in Poland. The breed is economical to keep, active, and versatile, and is well-suited to work the medium type of arable soil in these areas, as well as being ideal for general farm work.

DØLE GUDBRANDSDAL & DØLE TROTTER

THE DØLE GUDBRANDSDAL, the "utility" horse of Norway, is an old breed from the great central valley of Gudbrandsdal. Although less well-known than the country's famous and widely bred Fjord Horse (see pp.192–93), it is, in fact, more numerous, and accounts for half the Norwegian horse population. The Døle Trotter, a Døle Gudbrandsdal cross, is a lighter, sporting horse that was developed in the 19th century.

GOOD GRAZING
The good quality grazing found in the valleys contributes to the growth of this Døle Gudbrandsdal mare and her strong foal.

THE DØLE GUDBRANDSDAL

The Døle Gudbrandsdal, bred on the rich grazing of Norway's mountain valleys, developed as a strong, hardy horse of around 1.52 m (15 hh), which could be used for all agricultural purposes as well as under pack. Like the British Dales and Fell Ponies (see pp.172–73), it has the most excellent, hard feet and is a great trotter, a characteristic that was exploited in the development of the lighter Døle Trotter. Nonetheless, the breed has the build, though not the massive proportions, of a draught horse, and in relation to its size can exert a remarkable tractive power, a characteristic quality in many breeds with a pack-horse background.

In appearance the Døle Gudbrandsdal much resembles the Fell and Dales Ponies. The strong similarity is hardly surprising, since all three of these breeds would have derived from the same prehistoric wild stock. Thereafter, Friesian merchants from the Netherlands introduced their own, not dissimilar, black horses to both Norway and the British Isles, and later, between AD 800 and 1066, there was much to-ing and fro-ing between western Norway and the north of England. Like the Dales Ponies, the Døle Gudbrandsdal horses were used as pack animals. Carrying goods, they serviced Norway's overland trade route, which ran through the Gudbrandsdal valley in central Norway, and connected the Oslo region with the North Sea coast.

ORIGINS

THE DØLE GUDBRANDSDAL originated in Norway's Gudbrandsdal valley, which is the principal overland trade route through the centre of the country and connects Oslo with the North Sea coast. These strong, quick-moving pack-horses were bred in the mountain valleys, where the grazing is plentiful and of good quality. The good trotting action was much encouraged by the development of harness racing in the 19th century. The lighter Døle Trotter, derived from the Døle Gudbrandsdal, was especially developed for harness racing, a popular sport in Scandinavia.

LEGS
The legs are short, thick, and strong, with an abundance of feather at the heels. The feet are good, hard, and well-shaped.

DØLE TROTTER

DØLE GUDBRANDSDAL

In the 19th century, when interest in the breed was at a peak and equestrian sports, particularly harness racing, were being encouraged, numerous outcrosses were made with the aim of increasing the speed at trot. The most notable, and the most long-reaching in their effect, were the crosses with the English Thoroughbred Odin, imported in 1834. This stallion produced a lighter type of horse, which had a longer, more economical stride at trot, but still retained the powerful thrust that resulted from the hind legs being engaged well under the body. Odin appears in all modern Døle pedigrees, and his grandson

Balder 4 (foaled in 1849) continued the influence. However, there was still a need to keep the heavier, more powerful type of horse for farming, particularly as the weight of agricultural implements increased. This was made possible through the skill of the Norwegian breeders and through one stallion in particular, Brimen 825.

Demand for the breed continued up to the Second World War, and much use was made of the horses during the German occupation. After the war, when forestry and agriculture became increasingly mechanized, interest waned until state breeding centres were established in 1962. Today, a lighter type of Døle Gudbrandsdal horse is more usually bred, as well as the Døle Trotter.

THE DØLE TROTTER

The basis for the Døle Trotter, a very tough, hard horse with a great trotting ability and capacious lungs, was the lighter type of Døle Gudbrandsdal. These horses were then crossed with imported trotting stallions, which were often Swedish. In Scandinavia, the former USSR, and Europe, the diagonal trotting gait predominates in harness racing and the Swedish horses are no exception. In consequence, the Døle Trotters are raced in that gait and show no inclination towards the lateral pacing movement. Much attention is given to the improvement of performance and to qualify for entry in the stud book Døle Trotter stallions are tested over 1,000 metres (0.6 miles). The time limit for the distance is three minutes.

The Døle Trotter looks similar to the Fell. Colours for both breeds are mostly black and brown, although bays can also be found in the Trotter.

HEAD
The refining Thoroughbred influence is apparent in the head of the Trotter, which is long and clean-cut, and tapers to a neat muzzle.

HEAD
The head has pony character. The profile is straight, the muzzle square, and the forehead wide.

HEIGHT OF DØLE GUDBRANDSDAL
1.52 m
(15 hh)

HEIGHT OF DØLE TROTTER
1.55 m
(15.1 hh)

FARM HORSE
The Døle Gudbrandsdal is a compact, well-made horse with very good, free action at walk and trot. It is especially suitable for the agricultural work in the region.

CANNON
The cannons are short and strong with a more than adequate bone measurement below the knee. The knees are flat and large.

NORTH SWEDISH & FINNISH

THE EMPHASIS IN HORSE-BREEDING in Northern Europe and Scandinavia is largely directed at the production of agricultural and forestry horses capable of working hard in difficult conditions. Both the North Swedish and the Finnish Horse are regarded as coldbloods, but neither are "heavy" horses in the European tradition. Both have been influenced by the growing interest in trotting, which has encouraged the breeding of lighter, livelier horses that are hardy and sound, and can trot competitively at speed.

THE NORTH SWEDISH

The North Swedish Horse has its origins in the ancient Scandinavian breeds and is closely related to the Døle Gudbrandsdal (see pp.282–83). Until the end of the 19th century the Swedish horse was a mixture of several imported breeds. After the formation of a breed society, efforts were made to achieve greater uniformity. Rigorous testing was introduced at the principal stud at Wangen to support a policy of strict selective breeding. Since the North Swedish is used extensively in forestry as well as in farming, tests directly related to forestry requirements were devised. One involves log-hauling over rough tracks and further tests of pulling power are measured against an ergometer. In maturity both stallions and mares are re-tested for draught capacity with a specially constructed vehicle. The legs and feet of all stock are checked radiologically.

The emphasis on performance testing and the care devoted to selectivity in breeding programmes has resulted in a compact, very active horse with a remarkable capacity to draw heavy loads. The breed is noted for its cheerful temperament, is exceptionally long-lived, and is claimed to be immune to the majority of common equine diseases. Crosses with the Døle produce a lighter horse that has the longer action that is required for harness racing, a sport that has a big following in Scandinavia.

The North Swedish stands at around 1.60 m (15.3 hh), and may be of any solid colour. It is a deep, little horse, set on good, short legs, which have ample bone. There is some feather on the lower limbs, and the mane and tail are abundant. The back inclines towards being long, but it is strong.

NECK
The neck is short, thick, and usually crested, to correspond with the somewhat heavy head that it supports.

HEAD
The head is squarish and fairly large in comparison with the overall frame.

SHOULDERS
The shoulders are fairly well-sloped and powerfully built. The body is carried on short limbs.

SHOW TEAM
This is a show team of North Swedish Horses. The breed traces back to the ancient Scandinavian horse, but the modern North Swedish evolved during the first decades of the 20th century, when a breed society was formed.

HEIGHT OF NORTH SWEDISH
1.60 m
(15.3 hh)

The lighter trotting horse, the world's only coldblood harness racer, is lighter-bodied, and has longer limbs and a more pronounced slope to the croup.

THE FINNISH HORSE

There used to be two types of Finnish Horse: the Draught, and a lighter type, the Universal. Neither of them were noted for their conformational beauty, but they did the jobs required of them. The Draught was a strongly built, common animal, with quick, active paces. There is still a need for horses of this type in both forestry and general agricultural work, where they are preferable to tractors because they are easier to manoeuvre and do not cut up the ground. In 1907 a stud book was opened

GENERAL-PURPOSE
The Finnish Horse is a general-purpose agricultural animal but the lighter specimens can be surprisingly fast when raced in harness.

COLOUR
Any colour is acceptable, except piebald and skewbald, although chestnut with a flaxen mane and tail is preferred.

BODY
The body is long, which is a usual feature of a harness racing horse.

ORIGINS

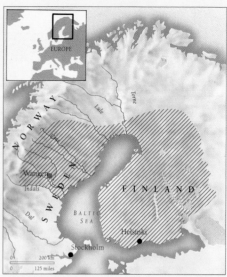

THE VERY ATTRACTIVE *North Swedish Horse is bred in the north of Sweden, and one of the principal studs is at Wangen. It has been developed, largely, as a forestry horse but has been as much influenced by climatic conditions which have ensured its exceptional hardiness. The Finnish Horse is also much used in forestry and is bred widely throughout Finland. Like its neighbour, the North Swedish Horse, it owes its constitutional strength to the environment, but the greatest encouragement to breeding is the popularity of harness racing, a very popular sport throughout Scandinavia.*

for both types and performance testing was also instituted. The modern emphasis is given to the lighter Universal type and today's Finnish Horse is mostly a general-purpose animal, well-fitted for light draught, but rideable at a pinch, and capable of harness racing at a respectable level. The modern stock has been developed from the native pony population crossed with both cold- and warmblood breeds, such as the Oldenburger (see pp.308–9).

Although relatively small-framed, standing at about 1.57 m (15.2 hh), the Finnish Horse has great pulling power, together with some speed and agility. The slope of the quarters and croup and the length of the body allow for energy and extension at trot, and are characteristic of harness-racing horses. The legs are well-made with little or no feather, and although the horses are ridden, the strong shoulders are predominantly of harness type. The breed is even-tempered, long-lived, and very enduring, and is noted for its excellent constitution.

HEIGHT OF FINNISH
1.57 m
(15.2 hh)

CLYDESDALE

THE CLYDESDALE ORIGINATED IN THE Clyde Valley, Scotland. It has only existed for about 150 years, but it is probably the most influential heavy horse apart from the Percheron (see pp.94–95). The breed was founded between 1715 and 1720, when the 6th Duke of Hamilton imported Flemish horses to improve and increase the size of the native draught stock. At the same time John Paterson of Lochlyoch also brought in Flemish horses, probably from England, and founded a strain that was to be a major influence at least until the mid-19th century. In addition, there were undoubtedly infusions of Shire Horse blood (see pp.288–89).

PERFECT MATCH
This magnificent pair of Clydesdales, both over 1.73 m (17 hh) and weighing one tonne, are working in sets of decorative harness traditional to the breed.

IMPROVING THE BREED

Two notable 19th-century breeders were Lawrence Drew, steward to the 11th Duke of Hamilton at Merryton, and his friend David Riddell. Both were dedicated to the improvement of the Clydesdale. They had little respect for the establishment and in 1883 set up the Select Clydesdale Horse Society, in opposition to the official *Clydesdale Horse Society Stud Book* which had been published five years previously. They were committed to the introduction of Shire mares, and firmly believed that Shires and Clydesdales were two wings of one breed. Riddell was also one of the first breeders to export Clydesdales, creating a tradition that was to become the hallmark of subsequent Clydesdale breeders.

FAMOUS SIRES

Both Drew and Riddell used the great 19th-century sires, Prince of Wales 673 and Darnley 222. The success of these stallions was consolidated by the lines created by one being put to the best daughters of the other. However, it is an earlier horse, Glancer 335, who is recognized as the breed's foundation sire. Glancer was the son of "Lampit's mare", who was foaled in 1806, and was believed to be descended from the Lochlyoch strain. His descendant, Broomfield Champion, appears in Darnley's pedigree, and sired Clyde (or Glancer 153), a horse who left a particular mark on the breed through his sons.

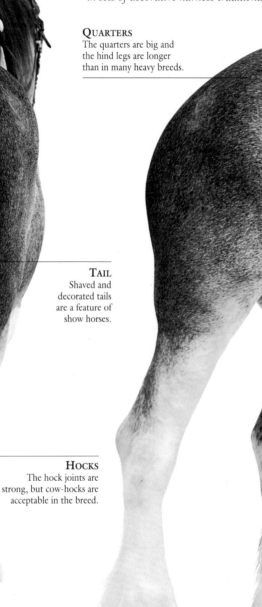

QUARTERS
The quarters are big and the hind legs are longer than in many heavy breeds.

TAIL
Shaved and decorated tails are a feature of show horses.

HOCKS
The hock joints are strong, but cow-hocks are acceptable in the breed.

CHARACTERISTICS

The Clydesdale is renowned for its action. According to the Clydesdale Horse Society, the breed has "a flamboyant style, a flashy, spirited bearing and a high-stepping action that makes him a singularly elegant animal among draught horses". More importantly, it is bred for the "wearing, enduring qualities of feet and legs". Judges will usually begin their examination of a horse by inspecting the feet. Being large, rather flat, but very

BODY
The body is deep, with clearly defined withers that are higher than the croup.

HEAD
The profile is usually straight rather than convex. The eyes are big and bright and there is great width across the forehead.

SHOULDERS
The shoulders are more sloped than those of the Shire, and the neck is proportionately longer.

HEIGHT
1.68 m
(16.2 hh)

FEET
The feet are somewhat flat, but sound and hard-wearing. There is a heavy, silky feather on the lower limbs.

open, with well-formed frogs, these feet suit the breed for work on ungiving city streets. However, they are less good for ploughing, as they can be too big to fit in the furrow.

The modern Clydesdale is lighter than those bred in the past, and is now distinctive in type and appearance. The average height is around 1.68 m (16.2 hh), although some are larger, and they weigh up to one tonne. The legs often appear long, and carry abundant silky feather. The joints should be big, the hocks broad and clean, and the knees flat. Cow-hocks are a breed characteristic, and are not viewed as a fault; sickle-hocks, however, are not acceptable. Breed enthusiasts want "close" movement, the forelegs being placed right under the shoulders and the hind legs close together.

Unlike the Shire, which has a Roman nose, the Clydesdale has a straight profile; it also has a longer neck. The colour is usually bay or brown, but greys, roans, and blacks are also found. White occurs on the face, the legs, and the underside of the body to a greater extent than in Shire horses.

WORLDWIDE POPULARITY

Clydesdales have been exported worldwide, although the preponderance of white markings and the heavy feather, which can cause an eczema-type condition on the legs, were a disadvantage in some markets. They worked the Canadian and American prairies, and they also earned the title "the breed that built Australia". They are still used in forests and in many cities, where "the glamour of the Clyde turns an ordinary beer delivery into a public event . . . ".

ORIGINS

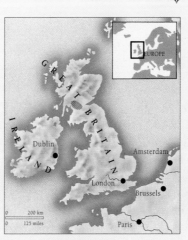

THE CLYDESDALE was founded in the early 18th century on Flemish horses imported into the Lanarkshire area of the Clyde Valley in Scotland. It was purpose-bred for the area, and also excels as a heavy urban draught horse. The environment has had no effect upon its subsequent evolution. The Clydesdale is among the most successful of the heavy breeds, and is found in Germany, the former USSR, Japan, South Africa, Canada, the US, New Zealand, and Australia, where it was called "the breed that built Australia". Surprisingly, the introduction of Clydesdale blood to Highland, Dales, and Irish stock was unsuccessful.

SHIRE

THE SHIRE HORSE is bred principally in the UK, in the Fen country and the counties of Leicestershire, Staffordshire, and Derbyshire. It descends from the English Great Horse of the Middle Ages, which in turn was derived from the heavy horses brought into England after the Norman Conquest. Those horses were descendants of the primitive, cold-blooded Forest Horse (see pp.14–15).

FROM GREAT HORSE TO SHIRE

From the evidence of 16th-century armour, it seems that the Great Horse was, in fact, a heavy cob type that measured about 1.57 m (15.2 hh) and bore little resemblance to the massive, modern Shire. The big, heavy draught horse did not appear in Britain until the end of the 16th century, when the Great Horse, no longer required to carry knights in full armour, was used to haul heavy

DRESSED TO PLOUGH
A pair of Shires, in an elaborately decorative harness, plough heavy land at a demonstration on a Devonshire farm.

wagons and coaches across the countryside, along roads that were no more than rough tracks, horrendously rutted in the dry summer months and deep in mud in winter.

Writing of the importation of heavy horses during this time, Thomas Blundeville (c.1561–1602) specifically mentions the Almaine or German Draught Horse, the Friesian (see pp.48–49), and the Flemish or Flanders Horse. The German horse does not seem to have had any lasting influence, but the Friesian and the Flanders Horse both played important parts. The Friesian

introduced a refining element and a better, freer movement, but it is the Flanders Horse, predominantly black like the Friesian, that had the greatest influence on the evolution of the British Shire. Again and again this large, slow-moving, heavy animal, bred on marshlands similar to the habitat of its far-off ancestor the Forest Horse, appears in the development of the Shire, and it is generally regarded as the breed's principal ancestor.

Large numbers of Flanders Horses were imported by Dutch contractors in the first half of the 17th century, when work began on draining the Fens in eastern England. When the work had finished, these horses remained and were bred in the area. At this time references to the Great Horse ceased, and the English draught horse became known as the English Black, a name given by Oliver Cromwell, himself a Cambridgeshire man and a noted agriculturalist. In fact, it is more likely that the future Lord Protector was referring to Friesian horses, but the name stuck and passed into general usage.

THE PACKINGTON BLIND HORSE

The foundation stallion of the Shire breed is generally recognized to be the Packington Blind Horse, who stood at Packington, near Ashby de la Zouche, between 1755 and 1770. He was black, and appears in the first

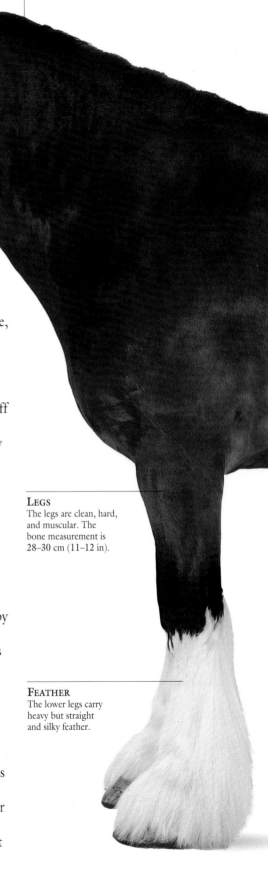

NECK
The neck is relatively long for a draught horse. It runs into deep, oblique shoulders, which are wide enough to carry a collar.

LEGS
The legs are clean, hard, and muscular. The bone measurement is 28–30 cm (11–12 in).

FEATHER
The lower legs carry heavy but straight and silky feather.

PASTORAL SCENE

This Shire mare and her foal are pictured in typical English countryside. Shires are bred extensively throughout England and Wales.

Shire stud book because of the large number of horses that were claimed to be descended from him.

THE SHIRE STUD BOOK

A society for the Shire, known as the English Cart Horse Society, was formed in 1876, and the first stud book was published two years later.

It changed its name to the Shire Horse Society in 1884. Five thousand animals were registered each year between 1901 and 1914, and breeders enjoyed a thriving export market to the US. However, after the Second World War, there was little need for the Shire either in industry or agriculture and the numbers dropped, although Shires were still used by the brewing companies. The subsequent revival of the Shire owes much to the breweries' support, and perhaps also something to the Drive of the Heavy Horses at London's Horse of the Year Show. Today the annual Shire Horse Show at Peterborough attracts over 300 entries and over 15,000 spectators.

COLOUR

Black is the most popular coat colour, but bay, brown, and grey are also found.

THE MODERN SHIRE

The modern Shire has greater quality than its forebears, and inclines more towards the type developed in the Midlands than to the coarser Fen strains. Its enormous strength can be gauged from weight-pulling records. For instance, at the Wembley Exhibition in 1924, a pair pulling against a dynamometer (a machine for measuring mechanical power) exceeded the maximum reading and were estimated to have exerted a pull equal to a starting load of 50 tonnes. The same pair, driven in tandem on slippery granite setts, shifted 18.5 tonnes, the shaft horse starting before his leader had even got into his collar. Black with white feathering is still the most popular coat colour, but there are numerous grey teams to be seen, and bay and brown are also acceptable.

BODY

The Shire is one of the biggest horses in the world and weighs more than 1 tonne (2,205 lb).

HOCKS

The hocks should be broad and flat and set at the correct angle for optimum leverage.

FEET

The feet should be open, and big round the top of the coronet, with plenty of length in the pasterns.

HEIGHT

Over 1.73 m (17 hh)

ORIGINS

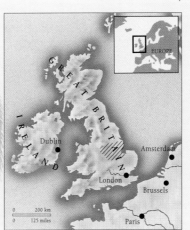

THE TRADITIONAL CENTRES of breeding for the great Shire Horse are the English counties of Leicestershire, Staffordshire, and Derbyshire and the Fen country of Lincolnshire. Work on the draining of the English Fens in the first half of the 17th century represented a significant factor in the breed's development. The Dutch contractors brought with them their own massive, wide-footed horses to provide the strength and weight necessary for the heavy work. It was these horses, staying on to work and breed, that provided the foundation for the Shire Horse. Before the First World War there was a thriving export market for Shires in the US.

SUFFOLK PUNCH

THE SUFFOLK PUNCH is an endearing and unmistakeable horse. The oldest of Britain's heavy breeds, it is defined in one dictionary as "a variety of English horse, short-legged and barrel-bodied, a short, fat fellow", which describes it admirably. Its early origins are obscure, but William Camden in his *Britannia* (published 1586) refers to the Suffolk breed as having existed for 80 years. Economical, adaptable, maturing early, and long-lived, the breed has influenced many European and Russian heavy horse breeds. It has also been exported to the US, and to Pakistan, where it has been used to produce army remounts and mules.

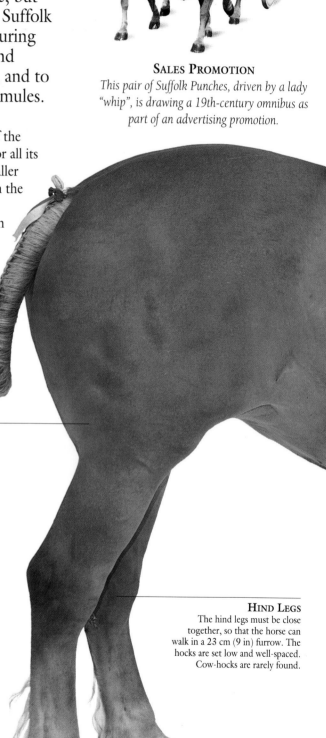

SALES PROMOTION
This pair of Suffolk Punches, driven by a lady "whip", is drawing a 19th-century omnibus as part of an advertising promotion.

THE HORSE OF UFFORD

Every Suffolk traces its descent to a single stallion, Thomas Crisp's Horse of Ufford, stud book number 404, which was foaled in 1768. ("Ufford" was probably a mistake, as the Crisps lived at Orford.) This stallion was used in the area around Woodbridge, Saxmundham, and Framlingham, which is still a centre for Suffolk Punch breeding. He was described as being a short-legged, large-bodied, bright "chesnut" standing at 1.57 m (15.2 hh), with a better head than most of his contemporaries. Crisp advertised him as "able to get good stock for coach or road" – a reminder of the background of trotting horse blood that was traditional to this part of the UK.

All Suffolks are "chesnut". The Suffolk Horse Society, formed in 1877, recognizes seven shades, ranging from a pale, almost mealy colour to a dark, almost brown shade. The most usual is a bright, reddish colour.

The stamina and pulling power of the Suffolk are unquestionable, but for all its strength and size it thrives on smaller rations than most other breeds. In the past, farm horses typically worked eight hours a day, between 6.30 am and 2.30 pm, and would have needed to be fed twice. The Suffolk only needed one feed.

TAIL
The long tail is plaited up and skilfully braided for work. This is both practical and traditional.

QUARTERS
The quarters are huge, rounded, and powerfully muscled.

HIND LEGS
The hind legs must be close together, so that the horse can walk in a 23 cm (9 in) furrow. The hocks are set low and well-spaced. Cow-hocks are rarely found.

ORIGINS
◇

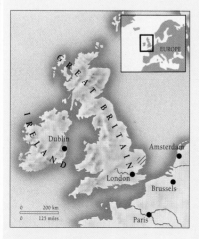

THE SUFFOLK PUNCH belongs firmly to the East Anglian county from which it takes its name, and in which it was developed to meet the local conditions. The clean legs of the breed and the activity of the paces make the Suffolk admirably suited to a system of arable farming involving heavy draught work. Suffolks were exported to Europe during the 19th century to up-grade the native breeds, and exports to Pakistan in recent years, where the Suffolks have been crossed to produce army remounts and mules, have been particularly successful. For such massive horses Suffolks have adapted to the climate of Pakistan remarkably well.

ESTABLISHING THE BREED

If the Suffolk Punch owes its existence to one prepotent horse, it owes much of its subsequent establishment to a single man, Herman Biddell, the Suffolk Horse Society's first secretary. He compiled the first stud book, *The Suffolk Horse History and Stud Book*, over a period of nearly 20 years. Published in 1880, it is a wonderfully comprehensive work, containing a history of breed and farming practice within the county, a register of 1,230 stallions and 1,120 mares, lists of prize-winners from 1840, and what is still considered to be an excellent "breed standard".

HEAD
The forehead is notably broad. The ears are alert, and relatively small for a heavy breed.

RIBBONS
For showing, the mane is plaited with straw and decorated with ribbons to accentuate the strongly crested neck.

PUNCH TESTS IN SUFFOLK

The Suffolk, developed specifically to meet local conditions, is exceptionally strong and clean-legged so it can easily work the heavy clay of its native East Anglia. Its strength also meant that in the past it was much in demand for heavy work in cities and towns.

At fairs in Suffolk, this strength was tested by hitching a horse to a fallen tree. Even if the horse did not move the tree, provided that it got down on to its knees it was considered to have passed the test. This pulling posture became typical of the breed. Another test was to ask the horse to rein back, which was an essential skill for work in city streets, although unnecessary for a plough horse. The exceptional tractive power of the Suffolk is greatly assisted by a low shoulder, a feature skilfully developed by early breeders and ideally suited for heavy draught work.

CHARACTERISTICS

The modern Suffolk is bigger than its forebears and stands around 1.63–1.70 m (16–16.3 hh). Its action is distinctive: its walk is sharp with a noticeable swing, while the trot, with only a modest degree of knee action, has a particular cadence not found in other heavy breeds. Because of the powerful chest, there is considerable width between the forelegs, which can sometimes result in a slightly round, dishing action.

FOREHAND
Muscular forearms, good bone, and minimal feather characterize the breed. Tractive power is helped by the low-set shoulder.

HEIGHT
1.63–1.70 m
(16–16.3 hh)

GIRTH
The girth can measure up to 2.03 m (80 in), which is more than either the Shire or the Clydesdale.

LEGS
The big body is set on short, stout legs of very great strength.

AT WORK
A team of matching Suffolk horses, harnessed abreast, ploughs the stubble on a Suffolk farm. The lack of feather is an advantage for ploughing on land with heavy soil.

AUSTRALIAN STOCK HORSE & BRUMBY

THE FIRST HORSES brought to Australia were from the South African Cape, and arrived in 1788. Thereafter, more and more were imported, particularly Thoroughbreds (see pp.120–21) and Arabs (see pp.64–65). These two breeds gave rise to the Waler, which evolved mainly in New South Wales. The descendants of those first horses are the Australian Stock Horse, which derives from the Waler, and the Brumby, the wild horse of the outback.

THE WALER

The original Waler was bred as a working horse on the vast sheep stations, and was used in harness as well as under saddle. It was also regarded as an excellent cavalry remount; R.S. Summerhays said in his *Observer's Book of Horses and Ponies*, 1968, that between the Battle of Waterloo (1815) and the Crimean War (1854), Australia had probably the world's best saddle horse.

Until the 1930s the Indian cavalry took many Walers, and during the First World War Australia provided some 120,000 for the allied forces. Like those used by General Allenby's Desert Mounted Corps, "they did not come home". The Sydney memorial on which those words appear virtually marked the end of the Waler, although the name and some horses persisted until after the Second World War. By then the Waler, originally bred from Arabs, Thoroughbreds, and Anglo-Arabs, was "close to being a pure-bred Anglo-Arab, in many cases with a preponderance of Thoroughbred blood" (W.J.B. Murphy, in Richard Glyn's *The World's Finest Horses and Ponies*, 1971).

The Waler was a type rather than a breed. Although it was not exceptionally fast, it was agile and had remarkable stamina. It stood between 1.52–1.63 m (15–16 hh), had plenty of bone, and could carry 102 kg (16 stone). It was hardy, resistant to heat, and had a sound constitution. This amenable horse could also jump – in 1940 a Waler was recorded as jumping 2.54 m (8 ft 4 in).

THE AUSTRALIAN STOCK HORSE

The Waler's successor, the Australian Stock Horse, has not yet achieved a fixity of type. It usually resembles a good-class hunter, but the height may vary. Essentially, it is still an Anglo-Arab, tending very much towards the Thoroughbred in its outlook, but infusions of outside blood have led to wide variations in appearance. There is a small pony influence, some Percheron (see pp.94–95),

OUTLINE
The outline is that of a good, all-round saddle horse of Thoroughbred type.

HEAD
The head is sharp and intelligent, and the better specimens often show some quality.

CONFORMATION
In general, the body shape is poor and degenerate. However, the best Brumbies have some conformational merit.

WORKING HORSE
This Australian stockman at work is riding a compact, well-made horse that shows an Arab influence in the neat, intelligent head.

HEIGHT OF STOCK HORSE
1.52–1.68 m
(15–16.2 hh)

AUSTRALIAN STOCK HORSE

IN THE WILD
Brumbies have spread all over the Australian outback, and still survive in large numbers. This group is in the Finke Gorge National Park, in Australia's Northern Territory.

and, perhaps more importantly, some input from the very popular Quarter Horse (see pp.230–31). This breed was introduced to Australia in 1954, and now has its own Quarter Horse Association. The Stock Horse is promoted and represented by the Australian Stock Horse Society, which aims to standardize the "breed". It has had considerable success in this task.

The Stock Horse is still used on the big stations as an all-rounder. Like the Waler, it is an enduring, even-tempered horse, and is notable for very good legs and feet, ample bone, and natural balance. It is still the largest single group of horses in Australia, and reflects the Australian preference for a versatile horse of Thoroughbred character.

THE BRUMBY

After the great Australian Gold Rush of 1851, many horses escaped from the mining settlements and ran wild in the

ORIGINS

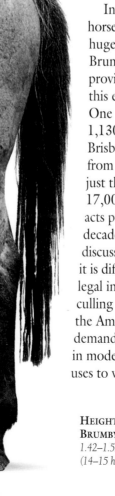

THE WALER, forerunner of the modern Australian Stock Horse, evolved in New South Wales, and acquired its special character as a result of its natural environment and the work expected of it. The Waler learned to work long hours carrying a man and his gear over rough ground, sometimes at speed, and it adapted to withstand the effects of a hot, dry climate in which water was limited. Similarly, the Brumby stock developed their tenacious and enduring character as a result of running loose in the wild outback country.

scrublands. These horses came to be known as Brumbies. Although some have been caught and tamed, they are usually far too wild to be of any practical use. The Brumbies degenerated in quality, but developed a survival instinct that enabled them to withstand the harsh climate and avoid the stockmen who hunted them.

In the 1960s the number of horses was such a problem that a huge culling operation took place. Brumbies were already hunted to provide meat for pet food, but this exercise was sheer slaughter. One herd of about 8,000 horses, 1,130 km (700 miles) west of Brisbane, was pursued and shot from light aircraft and Jeeps. On just three properties, an estimated 17,000 horses were killed. Such acts provoked global outrage, and, decades later, the issue is still under discussion. The problem remains and it is difficult to see a solution, beyond legal insistence on defined, humane culling methods. Unlike some of the American Mustangs, there is no demand for Brumbies as riding horses in modern Australia and no practical uses to which they could be put.

LEGS
The legs are slender but strong, and the horse is agile and quick-moving. In poorer specimens, cow-hocks and a general weakness in the quarters are evident.

FEET
The feet are hard, and can withstand wear on rough ground.

BRUMBY

HEIGHT OF BRUMBY
1.42–1.52 m
(14–15 hh)

LINES OF COMMUNICATION

ROMAN ROAD

THE WORLD'S SYSTEMS of communication allowed empires and civilizations to be built, extended, and sometimes destroyed, and they were, for the greater part of our recorded history, dependent upon the use of horses. Similarly, the delivery of a simple letter relating the family affairs of ordinary people was made possible by the same means. Some form of communication was a necessary part of even the primitive societies and the creation of effective communication systems became even more essential as early societies expanded into major powers and civilizations. Even after the introduction of the railway in the 19th century, horses, collecting and delivering mail at the railheads, remained integral to the complex postal systems of Europe and the US.

EARLY COMMUNICATION SYSTEMS

As long ago as the 3rd century BC the Persians had developed a highly efficient mail system that stretched from Egypt to Asia Minor and from India to the Greek Islands. The civilizations of Greece and Rome had similar systems, with Rome building a road network giving access to the furthest corners of its empire. Genghis Khan (see pp.72–73) followed in the 12th century with the *Yam*, a reliable courier system that enabled him to govern his huge empire. Using the *Yam* it was said that "a virgin with a pot of gold" carrying the seal of the Khan, could cross the Mongol Empire without danger.

THE AMERICAN PONY EXPRESS

That would certainly not have been the case 600 years later when America's legendary Pony Express courier system carried the mail between Missouri and San Francisco. Epitomizing the frontier spirit,

MAIL WAGGON

The French mail waggons of the early 19th century were drawn by a pair of horses driven by postillion. The post-boy wore the heavy seven-league boots, which were so-called because they only touched ground at the mail stops, which were placed seven leagues apart.

"The Greatest Enterprise of Modern Times" was set up by William H. Russell, the "Napoleon of the Plains".

The service was inaugurated in April 1860 before the coming of the telegraph. A series of riders took the mail in relays

SEVEN-LEAGUE BOOTS

through what was more often than not hostile Indian territory, each man riding 96 km (60 miles) as fast as his ponies could carry him. The route was from St Joseph, Missouri, through Kansas, Nebraska, Colorado, Wyoming, Utah, and Nevada to Sacramento, California. The distance of 3,164 km (1,966 miles) was covered in 10 days, using 400 ponies. At one time there were 100 riders, "young, skinny, wiry fellows, not over 18", each equipped with a rifle, a pair of revolvers, and a Bible. They were supported by 400 horses, 190 relay stations, and a 400-strong station staff.

The fastest run was made in March, 1861, by "Pony Bob" Haslam. He carried the mail 193 km (120 miles) from Smith's Creek to Fort Churchill, Nevada, in eight hours and 10 minutes. This was an extraordinary performance because Haslam,

PONY EXPRESS

America's famous, if short-lived, Pony Express was inaugurated in 1860 to carry the mail the 3,164 km (1,966 miles) between Missouri and San Francisco.

WELLS FARGO STAGE COACH

The Wells Fargo Overland Stage was the successor to the Pony Express. Heavily armed, the coach travelled through largely hostile Indian territory.

whose relief had been killed, actually rode 612 km (380 miles) with a bullet wound in his arm and his jaw broken by an arrow.

The Pony Express closed down after only two years because of the losses incurred, but it had, nonetheless, pioneered the most practical route across the continent, one which was subsequently followed by the famous Wells Fargo Overland Stagecoach.

POSTAL SERVICES

Long before the short-lived Pony Express, a postal service operated between the principal eastern cities of the US. For example, as early as 1717 a regular Post Rider service operated between Boston and New York. The 250-mile journey took about two weeks, the rider averaging only about 27 km (17 miles) a day, largely because of the rough country that had to be crossed.

Nonetheless, 50 years later, the service, by then extending from Montreal, Canada, to St Augustine, Florida, had improved, and was more reliable. The first regular coach service carrying mail was between Boston and New York and began on 25 June 1777.

In Europe similar and more extensive services were in operation more than a century earlier but until the establishment of the Royal Mail service in Britain by John Palmer in 1784, mail was carried in carts and by mounted post-boys. The British mail system led the way in Europe largely because of the excellence of the roads and the availability of surplus Thoroughbred horses that could cover the stages at a regular

16 km/h (10 mph). The countries of mainland Europe soon established similar systems, although for some years reliance was still placed on post-boys and mail carts.

The post-boys, who later rode postillion to the Post Chaise, which carried travellers more quickly and expensively between post houses (inns), were rarely well-mounted. To mitigate the discomfort of long hours in the saddle on a common, rough-actioned horse, they "posted" to the trot. That is, they rose from the saddle at every other stride. This was just as popular elsewhere in Europe and was often called "the English trot".

By the end of the 19th century the postal services were sophisticated and highly organized.

The railways had taken over from the mail coaches, but distribution from the railway stations to local offices remained dependent upon horse-drawn vans.

The British Post Office, whose system was duplicated throughout Europe, used contractors to "horse the mails". In the 1890s the London contractor was Messrs McNamara. They kept 600 horses at their headquarters in Finsbury and more at suburban out-stations for the parcel coaches to the south. Mail-cart horses worked a seven-day week and as well as the regular inland mails, collected the foreign mail at all sorts of unexpected times, because of the unpredictability of sailing schedules over long distances.

JAVA POST

The Java-style postman c. 1905 delivered mail on a horse of obvious Arabian ancestry. He is riding in a saddle that is almost certainly of Mongolian origin.

NED. INDIE

20 CENT.

LA POSTE AUX INDES NÉERLANDAISES (Java)

REPLICA OF ELIZABETH I'S COACH

THE GOLDEN AGE OF COACHING

THE 100 YEARS between 1750 and 1850 was possibly the most significant century in the history of communication and passenger transport. This was the period when Britain's coaching network was at its height, before it gave way to the railway system. It culminated gloriously in the final quarter of a century which came to be known in coaching history as "the Golden Age". The American equivalent of the British coaching era began almost simultaneously, and was based on the famous Concord coaches made by Abbot-Downing Co. at Concord, New Hampshire. These coaches covered the American long-distance routes, often at speeds of 23 km/h (15 mph). They were introduced into Australia in 1853, where they provided a service covering 9,655 km (6,000 miles) in New South Wales and Queensland.

THE HUNGARIAN KOCSI

The coach was first produced in the late 15th century in the Hungarian village of Kocs, in the Komorne area, a place famed for the skill of its wainwrights. The word "coach", or *kocsi*, comes from the name of the village. The distinguishing features of the Hungarian design were the smaller front wheels that allowed the fore-carriage to turn on a very full lock, the lowered centre of gravity, and the lightness of construction. These all contributed to greater manoeuvrability and increased safety, while allowing the vehicle to be driven much faster than had previously been possible with the enormously heavy, cumbersome road coaches. The *kocsi* was introduced to England in the reign of Queen Elizabeth I (1558–1603). It was initially condemned as a "senseless luxury", and even viewed as a fashion that would "make men effeminate". However, the use of the coach quickly gained favour, particularly after the introduction of two further Hungarian inventions: the body supported on leather slings, like a hammock, and then, finally, the system of multi-leaved springs.

THE GOLDEN AGE

During the reign of George II (1683–1760) English coachbuilding supplanted the German industry, which to that point had been the dominant influence in Europe. The new system of springing, as well as giving greater comfort to the passengers, improved the vehicle's performance appreciably. A sprung vehicle can be driven faster and is safer since it is far less likely to overturn. Moreover, the "floating" weight load is far less tiring for the horses. The light,

HEAVY GOODS TRANSPORT
This stage wagon of 1820 was designed to carry large quantities of goods. The wide wheels helped to prevent the vehicle from sinking in soft ground.

well-sprung coach, soon improved further by efficient axle-boxes obviating the broken axles and lost wheels which had in earlier times bedevilled coach transport, was an important factor in the development of a speedy system of transport more reliable and regular than any other in the world of that time. It was "the wonder of the age and the envy of Europe".

In addition, patterns of harness were devised and superbly crafted from English leather that were lighter, stronger and superior in all respects to those made on the Continental mainland.

The most significant factor in the development of an efficient transport system was the increased availability of horses. By 1770 the English Thoroughbred had been bred selectively, enthusiastically, and to a consistent pattern for 100 years for the purposes of racing. If anything, the situation

THE OUTSIDERS
Only four passengers could be accommodated inside a coach, while eight sat on the outside, on top of the vehicle. For the "outsiders", coach travel was often a matter of extreme discomfort.

ROYAL MAIL

This picture shows the Royal Mail coach taking on the mail at the Post Office, Lombard Street, London. Mail coaches frequently travelled through the night to the principal cities.

mail box, armed with a blunderbuss and carrying the "yard of tin", the coaching horn with which he warned inn-keepers and toll-gates of the coach's approach.

PUBLIC COACHES

The success of the mail coaches encouraged private operators to run passenger coaches to the same exacting standards. These carried 12 passengers, four inside and eight outside. As early as 1825 the Wonder coach between London and Shrewsbury covered the 254 km (158 miles) at a rate of 16 km/h (10 mph), using 150 horses for each journey. The largest operator among the coachmasters was William Chaplin, who ran coaches from five London inns, employing 2,000 men and 1,300 horses for his fleet of 60 coaches. At Hounslow alone, which was the first change for coaches going west out of London, there were over 2,000 stabled horses. Only "blood" horses could attain the speeds required, and on a fast 16 km/h (10 mph) coach their life expectancy would not exceed three years. "Working to death" was commonplace, and was regarded objectively in an industry that held its commercial interests very close to its heart.

was one of over-production, and there was a surplus of animals that could be used to supply harness teams. Another important element was a system of good roadways. By 1780 the *via strata* of Roman Britain, which had extended 8,000 km (5,000 miles), had been re-made by the road commissioners and the turnpike trusts. Fifty years later, largely due to the work of Thomas Telford, the bridge and road builder, and that of John McAdam, who perfected "tarmacadam" or "macadam" road surfaces, there were 32,000 km (20,000 miles) of good roadways, and the coaching era was under way.

MAIL COACHES

The incentive for the development of a passenger service was the mail coach, which superseded the often unreliable, mounted post-boy and also, to a large degree, the mail carts. The mail coach carried four passengers inside the coach in relative comfort, and four "outsiders" on top. The guard, employed by the Post Office, sat over the

THE US CONCORD COACH

In the US, the strongly built "Concord" stage coaches were used. Here, a six-horse team draws a Concord stage coach through rough country in Montana during the 1880s.

HOLIDAY COACH

Passenger coaches, such as this one in England taking Whitsun holiday-makers from Charing Cross to Greenwich, were often over-loaded and under-horsed.

PRIVATE DRIVING

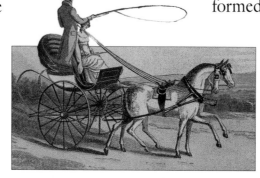

WAGONETTE BREAK

THE COACHING ERA, from 1750 to 1850, marked the apex of a great driving tradition, and also inspired the "private driving" exemplified by the Regency bucks of 18th-century England. The popularity of commercial road coaches encouraged a proliferation of amateur driving clubs, whose members raced against each other, often laying large sums on the outcome. The Prince Regent, later George IV (1820–30), often took part in such races, and at least once drove the notoriously difficult "random" (three horses harnessed in front of each other in tandem fashion) from London to Brighton. Famous clubs include the Four-in-Hand, which was established in 1856, and the Coaching Club, formed in 1871, both of which still survive.

HORSE-DRAWN VEHICLES

The interest in private driving gave increased impetus to the building and design of carriages and carts for the owner-driver. As a result, there is a huge variety of vehicles, most of them originating in the 18th and 19th centuries, that are suitable for private driving. Most of them, however, can be categorized in one of four principal groups. These are phaetons, gigs, dog carts (of which one variation was the Governess Cart), and the larger carriage, which included the various types of break and wagonette. Otherwise there are the usually rare vehicles of individual design, such as the Curricle and the Cabriolet. Broughams,

THE CURRICLE

This shows the Prince Regent (later George IV) on his way to Brighton in his Curricle. The Curricle was the only two-wheeled vehicle that took a pair of horses.

DRIVING IN HYDE PARK

This picture by J. Pollard, painted in 1844, shows fashionable turnouts at Hyde Park, London. The postillion team on the left is drawing a Barouche.

Landaus, and Victorias were driven by a coachman, and do not come within the parameters of private driving.

PHAETONS AND GIGS

Phaetons are light, four-wheeled vehicles, which originated in a variety of forms in the late 18th century, and were designed to be driven by the owner. The name "phaeton", first used in 1788, is taken from Phaëton, the son of the Greek sun god Helios. According to legend, Phaëton drove his father's sun chariot. The horses bolted, and almost set fire to the earth before they were stopped. There are about 40 types of phaeton ranging from the high Crane-neck,

through the Mail and Demi-Mail (the largest and heaviest of the phaetons), to such exotics as the American two-seat, Canopy-type Surrey ("the Surrey with the fringe on top") and the Siamese Phaeton, which was first built by Mulliners, the coachbuilders who later made some of the most elegant Rolls Royce car bodies.

There are almost as many types of gig as there are varieties of phaeton. The gig probably derives from the old unsprung Sedan Cart, and first appeared in its improved form in the late 18th century. It has two wheels and a forward-facing seat for two people, and is drawn by one horse. Before the railways, gigs were the most common vehicles on the roads. They were popular with commercial travellers and were much used by suburban commuters. Many gigs, such as the Stanhope, were named after their designers, or, like the Tilbury, after their coachbuilder. Some, such as the Round-Back and the Stick-Back, derive their names from the body shape.

OWNER-DRIVEN
Here, a single-horse phaeton is being driven to a meet. This particular turnout won first prize for action and pace at the Islington Horse Show, London, in 1872.

AMERICAN ELEGANCE
The Spider Phaeton, usually drawn by a pair, is one of the most elegant phaeton carriages. It originated in the US, and was popular for park and town use.

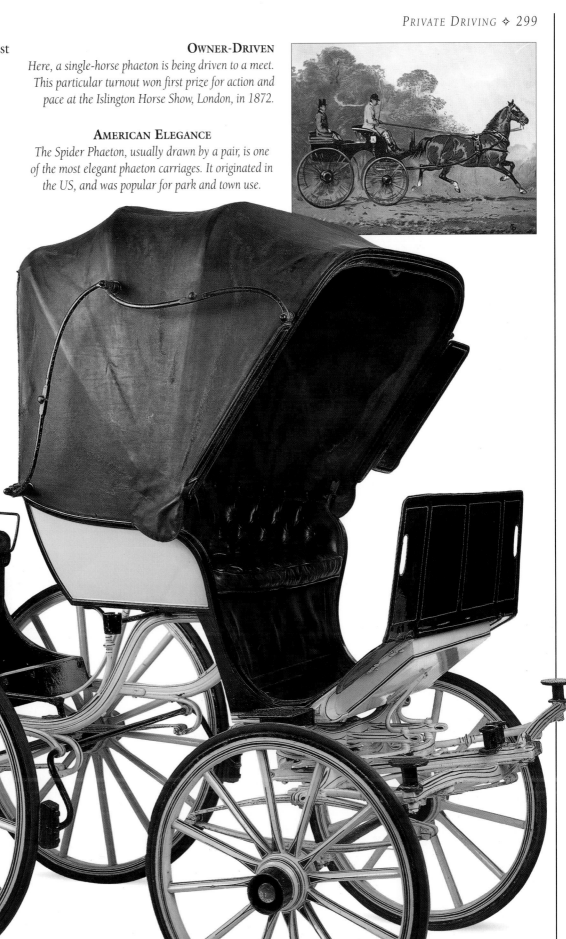

DRIVING FURIOUSLY
This painting, by A.D. Wray, is a spirited depiction of
Mrs Celestine Nichols and her grandchildren, driving
a phaeton in Richmond Park, just outside London.

DOG CARTS AND BREAKS

The family of dog carts is, if anything, even
larger then those of the phaetons and gigs.
Throughout the l9th century, dog carts were
built in large numbers. They were either
two-wheeled or four-wheeled, and were
usually sporting vehicles with enough room
for the driver's shooting dogs under the
back seats. All sorts of carts evolved from the
basic pattern; Cocking Carts, used for
transporting fighting cocks, Governess
Carts, Ralli Cars, and even the back-to-back
Indian *tonga*, which carries four people.

Governess Carts were popular and
numerous at the turn of the 20th century.
They were originally designed so a governess
could take children for drives in reasonable
safety. The tub-like body was fitted with a
door at the back, which could be tightly
secured once the children had got in. The
seats ran along the length of both sides of
the cart, and the driver sat sideways at the
rear of the seat on the right-hand side.

The Ralli Car, named after the England-
based Greek shipping family named Ralli,
appeared towards the end of the
19th century. It had side panels curving out
over the wheels to form splash boards, seated
four people, and had room for luggage.

Breaks were open, four-wheeled country
vehicles that could accommodate sportsmen
together with their guns and dogs. Most of
them carried a minimum of six people. A
wagonette was a similar vehicle with plenty
of room for passengers to sit on inward-
facing seats, and ample space for luggage.
An even larger version was called a wagonette
break, and was much used for attending race
meetings or other sporting events, or for
conveying servants and luggage.

MODERN PRIVATE DRIVING

These days "Private Driving" predominantly
takes place in the show ring, although
privately owned coaches were operated over

ROOM FOR FOUR
The four-wheeled Ralli Car was an offshoot of the
sporting dog cart. It seated four people and had
luggage space under the seat.

MULE TEAM

A splendid turnout of matched mules pulls an open sporting break. They are dressed for the feria *at Jerez de la Frontera, Spain.*

some of the old coaching routes right up to the First World War by enthusiasts such as the 8th Duke of Beaufort and the American Alfred Vanderbilt. Some coaches even continued to run until the outbreak of the Second World War in 1939.

In the show ring, the Private Driving classes on the English pattern exclude the show buggy vehicle. Instead, the traditional carts and carriages, designed for the owner-driver not engaged in trade, are used. They are drawn by a great variety of horses and ponies driven in single, pair, and tandem combinations, although a distinction is made between animals of Hackney (see pp.402–3) and non-Hackney type. Private Driving does not include the Hackney classes, in which Hackneys draw light, show wagons fitted with wire-spoke wheels and pneumatic tyres, or the Light Trade classes for commercial vehicles. At some shows the exhibitors are sent out for a drive in convoy, starting and finishing at the show ground. A popular class in countries with a driving tradition is the *Concours d'Elegance*,

in which the infinite attention to detail in all respects contributes to the aesthetic perfection of the turnouts.

In Europe, the Netherlands probably produces a greater variety and a greater number of turnouts than any other country, with the possible exception of the UK. In fact, there are just as many Hackneys in the Netherlands as there are in the UK. There

are also the high-moving, enormously impressive Gelderlanders (see pp.126–27), driven to every sort of gig, as well as the black Friesians (see pp.48–49), driven to the traditional Friesian Chaise with white rope traces and reins. Elsewhere in Europe, driving, although practised widely and with great expertise, more often takes the form of spectacular displays at stud open days or at major equestrian events. Spain and Portugal, nonetheless, are famous for their fiestas, in which splendid carriage processions, horsed by noble Andalucians and Lusitanos (see pp.108–9), play so prominent a part.

The US, Canada, South Africa, Australia, and New Zealand all have a range of driving activities with a national flavour. Australia and South Africa specialize in multiple-horse hitches, or spans, as main-ring attractions; at South Africa's Rand Show mules feature in the spans as well as horses. The US and Canada have their own Heavy Harness Horse Classes. There are at least as many coach horses in North America as in England, and they are shown in traditional English style.

Improbably, perhaps, coaches are also to be seen at the national shows of India and Pakistan. The classes, always well-filled, are made up of regimental coaches, or drags, in a tradition inherited from the British.

PERFECT MATCH

This Welsh Section C Pony is driven in a Liverpool bit, which allows for a variety of rein positions according to the contact required.

THE ROYAL MEWS

The royal stables in the UK's capital city

FALCON MEWS

Up to the time of Henry VIII the English royal household maintained mews in London for its hunting falcons.

IN THE MIDDLE AGES a "mews" was a place where falcons were kept during the "mewing" period, when the birds change their plumage. Until the reign of Henry VIII (1509–47), the English kings kept a mews in London at Charing Cross especially for this purpose. It was only in 1537, after a fire destroyed the royal stables (in modern-day Bloomsbury), that the falcons were moved to make way for Henry's stud of horses. George III (1760–1820), who bought Buckingham House (later Buckingham Palace) in 1762, made use of its stables, and employed John Nash to design and build the present Riding House in 1764. In 1820 Nash was commissioned by George IV (1820–30) to redesign the stables and coach house. In 1825 these became the Royal Mews. Today, the Mews, which is a working establishment, houses the state coaches, carriages, carriage horses, and a collection of the Queen's cars, as well as accommodating staff. The four great state Coaches, known as "glass" coaches, are the Gold State Coach, the Irish State Coach, the Glass Coach, and Queen Alexandra's Coach. There is also a unique exhibition of saddlery and harness, including items given to the Royal Family by foreign monarchs and governments. At present there are about 30 horses at the Mews: the Bays, most of which are Cleveland Bays (see pp.306–7), although there are also some Dutch bay horses; and the Windsor Greys, which only draw the Queen's carriages. In the past dun, cream, and black horses were also kept; chestnuts have never been used. The Windsor Greys, so-called because they were always kept at Windsor until they were moved to London by George V (1910–36), are not a special breed. For many years, the best-known royal horses were the Creams, introduced by George I in 1714. George I also imported Hanoverian stock, and such horses were used well into the 20th century. More recently, the Royal Family has also bought Holsteiners and Oldenburgers (see pp.142–43 and pp.308–9).

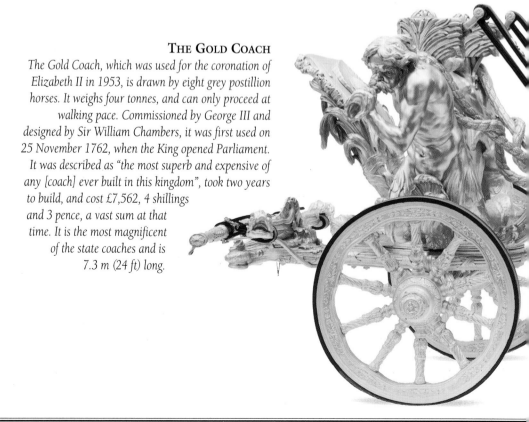

THE GOLD COACH

The Gold Coach, which was used for the coronation of Elizabeth II in 1953, is drawn by eight grey postillion horses. It weighs four tonnes, and can only proceed at walking pace. Commissioned by George III and designed by Sir William Chambers, it was first used on 25 November 1762, when the King opened Parliament. It was described as "the most superb and expensive of any [coach] ever built in this kingdom", took two years to build, and cost £7,562, 4 shillings and 3 pence, a vast sum at that time. It is the most magnificent of the state coaches and is 7.3 m (24 ft) long.

NASH'S GATEWAY

This is the gateway to the Royal Mews in London's Buckingham Palace Road. George IV commissioned the Mews in 1820 and it was built to the design of John Nash.

A STATE OCCASION
A state occasion at the Royal Mews is an event involving the whole of the Mews staff. The horses are a team of Windsor Greys in full state harness.

GILDED COACH
The figures at the rear carry the Imperial fasces (bundles of rods symbolizing official authority) topped with tridents. The three cherubs on the roof represent England, Scotland, and Ireland. They support the crown and hold in their hands the Sceptre, Sword of State, and Ensign of Knighthood, respectively.

ROYAL CARRIAGE HORSE

T HE ENGLISH MONARCHY, like the other royal families of
Europe, maintained large numbers of carriage horses
from the 16th century onwards. Over the centuries it has
relied heavily on importing carriage breeds from other
European countries, particularly Germany, the original
home of the Hanoverian monarchs. Today, the UK is
almost the only country in Europe to use horse-drawn
carriages for all state occasions, and in so doing
heightens the splendid pageantry of such events.

HORSES FROM EUROPE

In England, the royal family had been using
carriages and other horse-drawn vehicles
since the time of the Tudors in the 16th
century. Lupold von Wedel, a Pomeranian
nobleman who visited the country in 1584,
describes Queen Elizabeth I riding in a gilt
carriage drawn by "four brown horses,
royally attired". Later in the same month,
he mentions a richly-upholstered sedan chair
carried by "two cream-coloured horses with
yellow manes and tails". This reference to
cream-coloured horses is surprising, since
it is generally accepted that George I
(1660–1727) first introduced cream horses

CLEVELAND BAY CROSS

*Cleveland Bays replaced the black Hanoverian horses
in the royal stables in the 1920s, and much use
is now made of the lighter Cleveland cross.*

BROWBAND
The browband and rosette are part
of the bridle for the horses that
draw the monarch's carriage.

BEARING REIN
The bearing rein is
attached to the bit,
and assists the
carriage of the head.

NOSEBAND
The noseband and face-
piece bear the crown
and royal cipher.

BIT
The Buxton-cheek
driving bit carries
the royal cipher.

DRIVING BRIDLE
The driving bridle forms
a part of the semi-state
livery harness.

COLLAR
The harness collar
has richly decorated
brass hames.

BLINKER
The blinkers are
decorated with brass,
and are sometimes
known as "winkers".

FALSE MARTINGALE
The false martingale
is attached to the base
of the collar.

QUEEN VICTORIA'S CHARABANC
*A royal party enjoys a drive at Windsor in Queen Victoria's
charabanc. The vehicle is drawn by Windsor Greys, which are ridden
by postillions wearing semi-state livery.*

to the royal stables (see pp.302–3). However, Elizabeth's creams may possibly have been part of a small consignment of grey Hungarian horses, which had been imported from Holland in 1581 and had their manes and tails dyed orange.

Charles I encouraged the importation of coach horses from Europe, and stipulated that they should be "not under 14 hh high". Oliver Cromwell, under whose rule Charles I was executed, is recorded as being involved in an accident in Hyde Park while driving, rather inexpertly, a team of grey Oldenburgers (see pp. 308–9) that were presented to him by Count Anton Gunther von Oldenburg. In more recent times, both Oldenburgers and Holsteiners (see pp. 142–43) have been purchased for use in the royal stables.

HANOVERIAN HORSES

George I introduced horses from his huge stud in Hanover; in particular, he imported the renowned Hanoverian creams exclusively for the German royal family. The creams were used to pull the British sovereign's carriage until the reign of George V, and drew the Gold Coach at his coronation in 1910. They were bred at the royal stud at

WINDSOR GREYS
This royal postillion wearing full state livery is tending to two Windsor Greys at the Royal Mews in London. The horse on the left wears the postillion's saddle.

Hampton Court, but by 1920 in-breeding had become a problem, due to difficulty in obtaining new stock, so they were replaced with greys from Windsor. "Windsor Greys" had been kept at Windsor since before Queen Victoria's reign (1837–1901). They were named after both their home and the royal family, whose name had been changed from Saxe-Coburg and Gotha by George V. They are still used only for the monarch's coaches. Although almost identical, they are of no particular breed.

Up to the early 1920s many of the royal carriage horses were black Hanoverian stallions, described as being less graceful than the creams, but "more serviceable-looking". They were replaced in the 1920s by bay horses, which are mainly Cleveland Bays (see pp.306–7), with some Dutch, Irish, and Oldenburg horses. Cleveland Bay/Thoroughbred crosses are also used.

HARNESS AND DECORATION

There are eight sets of state harness, the most opulent being the red morocco harness worn by the Windsor Greys to draw the state coach. The sets, each weighing 50 kg (110 lb) and richly ornamented with gilt ormolu, were made in 1834, to replace sets first made in 1762. By tradition, the manes of the "state horses" have always been plaited: the greys are plaited with royal purple ribbons, and the bays wear scarlet.

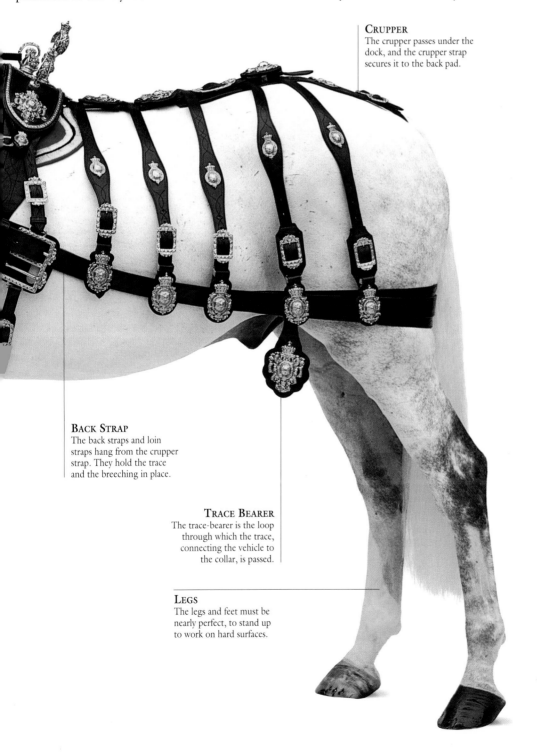

CRUPPER
The crupper passes under the dock, and the crupper strap secures it to the back pad.

BACK STRAP
The back straps and loin straps hang from the crupper strap. They hold the trace and the breeching in place.

TRACE BEARER
The trace-bearer is the loop through which the trace, connecting the vehicle to the collar, is passed.

LEGS
The legs and feet must be nearly perfect, to stand up to work on hard surfaces.

HEIGHT
About 1.70 m (16.3 hh)

CLEVELAND BAY

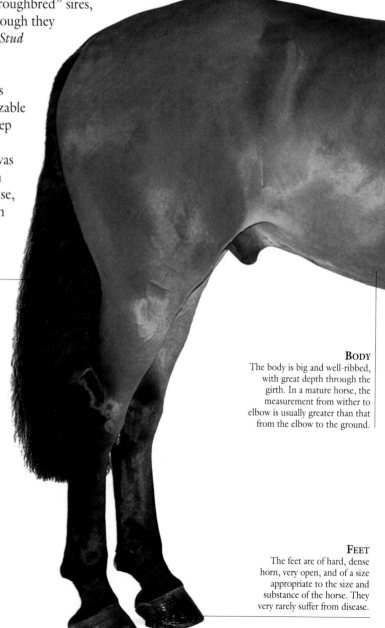

Oᴛʜᴇʀ ᴛʜᴀɴ ᴛʜᴇ ɴᴀᴛɪᴠᴇ ᴘᴏɴɪᴇѕ, the Cleveland Bay is the oldest indigenous horse breed in the UK. Its ancestor, the Chapman (known as the Vardy if it was bred north of the River Tees), was a bay pack horse with black points. It was recorded in the Middle Ages as being bred in the Wapentake of Langbaurgh, an area corresponding to north-east Yorkshire and Cleveland. Since the reign of George II (1727–60) the breed has enjoyed royal patronage, and the *Cleveland Bay Stud Book* was published in 1884. The breed is still a feature of the royal stables (see pp.304–5).

THE CHAPMAN HORSE

The Chapman was the horse used by travelling salesmen of the day (chapmen) to carry their merchandise. It was also vital to the area's mining industry and transported ironstone, and later potash and alum, from the hill mines to the sea or the nearest navigable river. The breed was clean-legged, an essential feature in a country of deep clay. Although it was much smaller than the modern Cleveland, perhaps no more than 1.42 m (14 hh), it was clearly powerful, for we know that it could carry a 100-kg (2-cwt) load over rough, deep, difficult ground.

OTHER INFLUENCES

There is no doubt that the Chapman was the root stock from which the Cleveland Bay derived, but it is less certain what outcrosses were used and when. The proud boast of the Cleveland breeder is "No taint of Black nor Blood", meaning that the horse is untouched by either cart-horse or Thoroughbred introductions. There is no suggestion that cart-horse blood was involved in the breed's evolution, and two early, influential "Thoroughbred" sires, Jalep and Manica, although they appear in the *General Stud Book* (see pp.120–21), were used well before the Thoroughbred was recognized or recognizable in its present form. Jalep was a grandson of the Godolphin Arab and was probably more Barb in character than otherwise, while Manica was a son of the Darley Arabian.

COACH HORSE SUPREME
HRH The Duke of Edinburgh used to drive a team of Cleveland Bay/Thoroughbred crosses from the Royal stables, and regularly competed in international driving events as a member of the British team.

TAIL
The tail hair, like the mane, is thick and luxuriant. The Cleveland's mane and tail are always black.

BODY
The body is big and well-ribbed, with great depth through the girth. In a mature horse, the measurement from wither to elbow is usually greater than that from the elbow to the ground.

FEET
The feet are of hard, dense horn, very open, and of a size appropriate to the size and substance of the horse. They very rarely suffer from disease.

ORIGINS

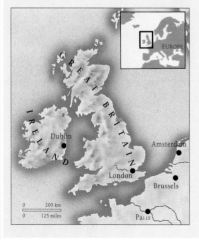

THE CLEVELAND BAY *is bred in a part of north-east England that includes Cleveland and the north-east corner of Yorkshire's North Riding. This area is noted for its heavy clay soil. The ancestors of this enormously strong horse were bred here in medieval times, often at the great monasteries in this part of Yorkshire. Spanish blood was introduced during the English Civil War (1642–49), and the constant traffic between the north-eastern sea-ports and the Barbary Coast of North Africa, in the 17th century, allowed for the influence of the Barb, which played an important part in the evolution of England's oldest horse breed.*

0   200 km
0   125 miles

However, it is reasonable to assume that the Barb (see pp.66–67) played an important part in the formative years of the Cleveland Bay. The marriage of Catherine of Braganza to Charles II in 1661 brought the North African port of Tangier to the British crown, and when the Tangier harbour works were being built by contractors from north-eastern English sea-ports there was constant traffic between the two. Given the popularity of racing in England and the prominence of Yorkshire breeders in the sport, it is probable that horses from the Barbary coast were imported.

In the last half of the 17th century, after the English Civil War, there were many Spanish horses in north-east England. They were, or had been, the property of redundant general officers and would have been available to breeders. There is still visual evidence of the Spanish forebears in the profile of the modern Cleveland Bay.

After the 18th century there is no evidence of further infusions of alien blood. By then, the Cleveland was fixed in its type and its resultant prepotence led to it being exported to improve many of the European breeds. Up to the reign of George II it was acknowledged as the best and most powerful coach horse in Europe, but after the introduction of macadamized roads it was deemed too slow to maintain the speeds demanded. As a result the Yorkshire Coach Horse, a Cleveland/Thoroughbred cross, came into being and its stud book remained open until 1936. The Cleveland was also employed in farming in north-east England, where it was the only horse that could work the clay land. It could haul very heavy loads in deep going and it established itself as a heavyweight hunter able to jump out of clay almost from a standstill.

MODERN REVIVAL

The Cleveland Bay went into decline after the Second World War and by 1962 there were only four pure-bred stallions in the UK. It was saved by HM Queen Elizabeth II, who bought the stallion Mulgrave Supreme, who was to have been sold to the US. He was used on pure-bred and part-bred mares with great success, and within 15 years there were 36 pure-bred stallions in the UK. The royal stables employ numerous Clevelands and Cleveland crosses and great encouragement was given to the breed by HRH The Duke of Edinburgh who, until recently, drove Clevelands in international driving events. The breed crosses well with the Thoroughbred to produce showjumpers and quality hunters.

HEAD
The head has a "ram-like" or "hawk-like" profile, very like the heads of the Spanish breeds from which the Cleveland Bay is descended.

COLOUR
All Clevelands are bay with black points.

HEIGHT
1.63–1.68 m
(16–16.2 hh)

NATIVE HEATH
These top-class Cleveland mares are in their natural habitat on the Cleveland Hills. In winter this area suffers the harshest weather, and this factor, allied to hundreds of years of careful breeding, has ensured the Cleveland's remarkable strength of constitution.

LEGS
The clean, powerful legs have short cannons, a 23 cm (9 in) bone measurement, and big, solid joints.

OLDENBURGER

THE OLDENBURGER was developed in the 17th century as a coach horse that could also work in agriculture. Over the centuries, breeders adapted the horse to the needs of the market, outcrossing to chosen breeds while operating selection policies to ensure uniformity of type. The 17th-century Oldenburger had a typical harness horse action, with high knee flexion, and shoulders that were upright enough to take a collar comfortably, but within the next 100 years it developed into a more elegant riding and carriage horse.

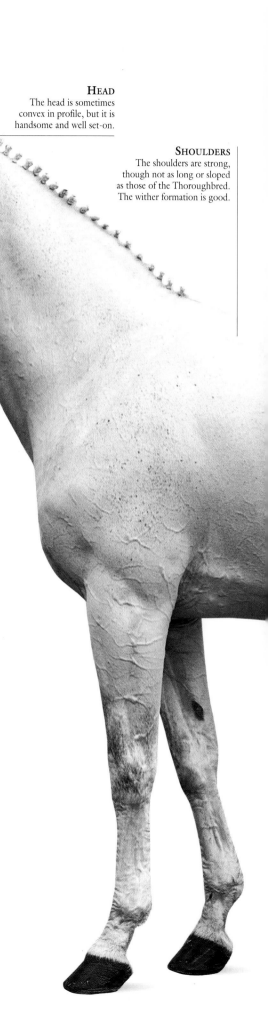

HEAD
The head is sometimes convex in profile, but it is handsome and well set-on.

SHOULDERS
The shoulders are strong, though not as long or sloped as those of the Thoroughbred. The wither formation is good.

EARLY INFLUENCES

The Oldenburger originated in the provinces of Oldenburg and East Friesland, and was based on the old Friesian horses found in the region between the River Weser and the Netherlands (see pp.48–49). Its development as a coach horse, however, was due largely to the sustained enthusiasm of the Count of Oldenburg, Anton Günter von Oldenburg (1603–67). The Count imported Spanish and Neapolitan horses, which both had a background of Barb blood (see pp.66–67)

SHOWJUMPING
This picture shows the Oldenburger Henderson Gammon being ridden by the British international rider John Whitaker. Oldenburg horses are used increasingly for showjumping.

and were then acknowledged as the most significant and valuable to be found in Europe. He made great use of the grey stallion Kranich, a descendant of notable Spanish lines and probably similar to the Czechoslovakian Kladruber (see p.158), which was established at Kladrub in 1572.

COACH TO CARRIAGE HORSE

Over the next century, the Roman-nosed Oldenburger coach horse gave way to a more refined carriage horse, which at a pinch could go quite well under saddle. Although it was a better quality horse than its predecessors, it retained the size, depth, and early-maturing character of the breed (a very unusual feature in such a massively framed animal).

THOROUGHBRED BLOOD

In the last part of the 18th century, together with the Spanish, Neapolitan, and Barb blood, half-bred English stallions were also introduced. These half-breds, which were influenced by the the early Thoroughbred blood strains and the influential trotting Norfolk Roadsters (see pp.122–23), were introduced to create an important refining element. After this, there followed a sensible period of consolidation, and there was no further major influx of outside blood until the late 19th century.

Around 1897 English Thoroughbreds (see pp.120–21) were used, at least one line tracing back to the unbeaten racehorse Eclipse, descendant of the Darley Arabian and founder of one of the four acknowledged Thoroughbred tail-male lines.

CLEVELAND BAY CROSSES

As well as Thoroughbreds, considerable use was also made of the prepotent Cleveland Bay (see pp.306–7). Once influenced by Spanish blood and unsurpassed as a coach horse of stamina and strength, the Cleveland Bay is a natural cross to the Thoroughbred and is also a powerful jumper under saddle. Some Hanoverian crosses were also used, but the most important influence was that of the Norman Horse (the basis for the Selle Français – see pp.132–33), through Normann 700, a stallion descended from the pervasive Norfolk Roadsters, which were also of the Darley Arabian blood.

After the First World War, the emphasis shifted back to the production of a strong, agricultural, utility horse. The need for this type of horse declined after the Second World War, and breeders followed the market demand for a useful, all-round riding horse, which was up to weight but had good paces and a greater freedom of action. This was the prototype for the modern Oldenburger, still a big, impressive horse, but more refined than its forebears.

BRAND MARK
The Oldenburg brand mark, an "O" with a ducal coronet, is put on the near-side quarter.

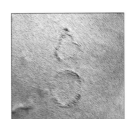

THE MODERN OLDENBURGER

In the 1950s, when the emphasis was firmly on producing riding horses, a Norman stallion called Condor, who carried 70 per cent Thoroughbred blood, was used. At about the same time, the Thoroughbred Lupus was imported. Since then outcrosses have been predominantly Thoroughbred with some Hanoverian (see pp.144–45). Used judiciously, this has helped to maintain the equable temperament for which the breed is noted. They have also combined to improve the shoulders and the riding action.

The modern Oldenburger stands between 1.68 m and 1.78 m (16.2–17.2 hh), and is usually brown, black, or bay. The powerful build is not conducive to speed, but careful selection, incorporating obligatory performance testing, has resulted in very correct paces. The action is straight, elastic, and rhythmical, although still a little high. However, this is no disadvantage in a dressage or jumping horse. The feet are uniformly good, whereas they are sometimes a failing in other European warmbloods.

HEIGHT
*1.68–1.78 m
(16.2–17.2 hh)*

QUARTERS
The very strong, wide quarters contribute to the Oldenburger's powerful action.

BODY
The body and the chest are deep, and still retain the length and outline of the coach horse. The back is rather long for a jumping horse.

LEGS
Strong, stocky legs are needed to carry such a large-bodied horse. The joints are big, the cannons fairly short, and the bone measurement around 23 cm (9 in).

FEET
Particular attention is paid to the feet. They must be in proportion to the large frame, open at the heels, and sound.

ORIGINS

THE OLDENBURGER DERIVES *from the old Friesian horses living between the River Weser and the Netherlands. The breed originated in the provinces of Oldenburg and East Friesland, when the former was owned by Anton Günter, Count von Oldenburg (1603–67). The climate is temperate, but otherwise has little to do with the horse's development, which has depended on the judicious introduction of outside blood. The Society of Breeders of the Oldenburg Horse is centred in Oldenburg.*

MOUNTED POLICE

POLICE ON HORSEBACK were first used in the 18th century when they replaced army units controlling civil disorder in Europe. The oldest recorded force is the London Bow Street Horse Patrol, established in 1758. Following a spate of riots in the late 1830s, a mounted police force was mobilized in inner London to keep public order and to regulate processions, ceremonies, and large gatherings, as well as to carry out street patrol duties. That remains the principal function of the mounted branch today. The employment of similar mounted units in Britain's larger cities followed, and mounted forces were soon in use all over Europe. Similar forces were then established in the US, Australia, and India.

KEEPING THE PEACE

By the mid-19th century, most European countries had mounted units recruited from what had formerly been municipal guards. The mounted division of the Barcelona Municipal Police, for example, was founded in 1856 and, unusually for a mounted police force, rides stallions. The horses, of the Andalucian breed, are trained to perform a unique heels-first advance, a most effective deterrent to an unruly crowd.

France, Sweden, Germany, Belgium, Italy, and the Netherlands are all countries maintaining a force of highly trained mounted police. One Dutch unit has a particular distinction: during the summer the force patrols beaches at the Hague, and its horses are trained in life-saving duties. They stand quite still while their rider throws a line to a swimmer in difficulties and will, in emergencies, plunge into the sea to make a rescue.

American cities – particularly New York, which has the largest branch in the world – rely heavily on the mounted police to control both crowds and heavy traffic. They are also invaluable in patrolling the extensive parks and public gardens.

Japanese mounted police in Tokyo help to control the world's most congested traffic; and there are mounted police in the Middle Eastern states, often riding Arab horses, and in Jamaica, Fiji, and Africa.

Many cities in India support mounted police units, most of those in the North being mounted on Kathiawari horses. They are especially useful during religious festivals and the great pilgrimages to the bathing ghats along the banks of the sacred Ganges, when there are crowds numbering tens of thousands. India also maintains a unique, virtually paramilitary formation in its Border Security Force (BSF), which has its own Academy at Tekanpur, Gwalior. The BSF is responsible for patrolling the long and volatile border with Pakistan, which would be an impossible task without a trained mounted force of considerable strength. Indeed, it is likely that India, allowing for its specialist BSF, employs more mounted

MOUNTED PATROL
Mounted policemen are used on a regular basis to patrol the huge areas of the national parks throughout America.

THE RULE OF LAW
American mounted police wearing riot gear quietly and effectively control a potentially violent anti-war demonstration outside the United Nations building.

police and makes greater use of them than any other country.

The maintenance of a mounted police force was just as essential to 19th-century Australia. The first mounted force was a 13-strong patrol raised by Governor Brisbane in 1826 to take on duties performed previously by the New South Wales Militia. As the force expanded, the rule of law was taken to the "outback", where the Trooper Police protected the early settlers as well as enforcing the law in remote areas and even taking responsibility for the issue of birth, marriage, and death certificates. To this day, a reduced number of mounted police are still retained in most Australian states.

THE CANADIAN "MOUNTIES"

The most famous and romantic of all the mounted police units is the Royal Canadian Mounted Police, the "Mounties", which became a role-model for the policing of vast, inhospitable, and often hostile areas not dissimilar to the North West frontier of the old Indian Empire. These

COUNTRY CONSTABLE
Mounted constables, often using Kathiawari horses, play a large part in policing the country areas of India, as well as carrying out duties in the cities and towns.

huge tracts of country in the north-western interior of Canada were known as the North-West Territories. Stretching over 300,000 square miles (an area as large as Europe), its government, under the law, was entrusted to what was initially a small, but well-equipped, paramilitary force raised in 1873 as the North West Mounted Police (NWMP).

Its duty was to maintain the peace between the indigenous Indian population and the increasing flow of traders and settlers encroaching on the Indian lands and threatening the native way of life, which was largely dependent on the buffalo herds. In contrast to the American experience, the Canadians made just and acceptable settlements with the Indian tribes, protecting their livelihoods and earning their respect.

It was the responsibility for the security of the border with America, which was increasingly being crossed by American whisky traders, that provoked the great "March West" by the fledgling force in 1874. A company of 300 set off on a 1,200-km (745-mile) overland trek to the foothills of the Rockies that was to become an epic of endurance and the founding myth for the new organization.

Loosely modelled on the Royal Irish Constabulary and the methods of policing employed in British India, NWMP officers, as well as being police officers, were also administrators with legal and penal powers. The Klondike Gold Rush of 1896–97, when thousands of miners poured into a country without communication links or government and subject to the harshest of climates, provided the "Mounties" with their greatest challenge. They met it in the best traditions of law enforcement: maintaining order, apprehending criminals, and providing the services of government in registering claims, acting as an arbitration service, collecting customs, and even carrying the mail. The title changed to the Royal Canadian Mounted Police in 1920 and between the World Wars the force still used horses on general duties.

MAINTIENS LE DROIT
The Mounties lived up to their motto, "Maintain the law", in the Klondike Gold Rush.

THE ROYAL FORCE
Canadian Mounted Police, male and female, in dress uniform prepare for the musical ride with their traditional black horses.

POLICE HORSE

WITH NOTABLE EXCEPTIONS, such as the Andalucian horse in Spain (see pp.108–9), the police horse is not a breed, but the majority of mounted police forces select horses of a particular type. London's Metropolitan Police, for instance, use hunter-type horses as shown here, which are usually half- or three-quarter-bred, i.e. 50 or 75 per cent Thoroughbred, and this policy is usually followed by mounted units elsewhere in the UK. What is common to all police horses is a calm temperament combined with courage, which enables them to work in the heaviest traffic conditions and, on occasion, to control hostile crowds that may respond with extreme violence.

ON PATROL
Mounted police, wearing riot gear, patrol a street in London. The horses are trained to work in heavy traffic conditions.

LONDON'S POLICE HORSES

Part-Thoroughbred, hunter-type horses (see pp.394–95) are regarded as the ideal choice for police work in London, provided that they have a suitably steady temperament. The Thoroughbred blood gives them agility and courage, while any draught or carriage horse elements provide strength, size, and substance, and perhaps a quieter nature as well. The majority of London's police horses come from Yorkshire, and some, therefore, may have a relationship with the Cleveland Bay (see pp.306–7). The horses have to be sound, with very strong limbs and feet, so that they can withstand the long hours of roadwork, and they must be at least 1.63 m (16 hh) in height.

British police horses are bought at three or four years of age, and are usually unbroken. The horses that work in London then undergo a training period of about 40 weeks at the Metropolitan Police Centre in south-west London. This training is intensive and comprehensive, and the progress of each horse is

VISOR
A plastic visor protects the face and eyes from injuries that could be caused in riot situations.

CHAIN
The chain is fastened to the headcollar. It is fitted with snap hooks, and can be used to tether the horse.

KNEECAPS
Kneecaps and boots protect the legs in the event of the horse falling or being brought down on a tarmac surface.

RIOT GEAR
Modern mounted police and their horses may have to face violence when they are used in situations such as demonstrations and football matches. In those circumstances, riot gear gives humans and animals at least partial protection.

carefully monitored. Steadiness in traffic is an essential quality in a police horse, and great emphasis is placed on this particular aspect in the training programme. Some horses, especially the more highly strung ones, will not tolerate heavy traffic, and those that are likely to be traffic-shy are rejected during the basic training period. Great attention is also given to matching horse and rider; the two have to be entirely compatible for the partnership to be a successful one. In the situations that police horses and their riders

THE BLUE LINE
A line of London's mounted police leads a good-natured crowd down the Mall from the Victoria Memorial. The Mounted Branch plays a vital role in crowd control, especially on state occasions.

BRIDLE
The bridle follows the military pattern and is fitted with an "angle-cheek" Pelham bit. The noseband doubles as a headcollar.

BREASTPLATE
The breastplate is a traditional piece of military equipment. It helps to keep the saddle in place, and prevents it from sliding backwards.

HEIGHT
1.63 m
(16 hh)

sometimes have to face in support of public order, they must be able to depend on each other almost completely.

Special training in demonstration and crowd control is given to all Metropolitan Police horses at a purpose-built centre in west London. There, trainee policemen, acting the part of rioters, jostle the horses realistically, pelt them with harmless, soft objects, shout and yell slogans, wave banners, let off smoke bombs, and create minor explosions. Meanwhile, the horses are encouraged to push the crowd back and to disperse any large groups, if necessary by charging in formation.

The horses and the riders are provided with protective riot gear when engaged in crowd control, but even so both may sustain injuries, and there are all too many instances of horses being stabbed, burnt with lighted cigarettes, or badly hurt by missiles such as bricks or stones.

OFF-DUTY HORSES

Each year, every horse is sent back to the centre in west London to take a refresher course. Horses that show any signs of unsteadiness are sold out of the force. The average working life of a police horse is about 14 years. Off duty, police horses can be seen at a number of the major horse shows during the summer season. They may stage musical or activity rides on the military pattern, but some shows also put on a programme of classes confined to police horses. Tent-pegging and skill-at-arms events and "nuisance" tests are always popular. Increasingly, there are dressage competitions, which follow the standard civilian tests.

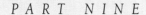

PART NINE

THE HORSE AT WAR

THE EARLY CIVILIZATIONS of the Hittites, Assyrians, Sumerians, Persians, Greeks, and Romans were created and destroyed with the help of large numbers of horses, while the ever-present threat of marauding steppe horsemen acted as a catalyst in the formation of powerful cavalry in later, western societies. Although the widespread introduction of firearms and artillery in the 16th century may have changed the role of cavalry, for the next 400 years the presence of huge numbers of horses still dominated the shifting fortunes of a western world that was almost constantly engaged in armed hostilities. In fact, cavalry and horse transport on a massive scale survived well into the 20th century, and was an important factor in both World Wars.

The charge of the Scots Greys at Waterloo, 1815. A detail
from *Scotland Forever* by Lady Butler (1810–80)

THE HORSE IN BATTLE

MAMELUKE WARRIOR

THE HORSE HAS BEEN used in warfare since the early days of domestication. The turning point came in the 16th century with the invention of firearms and artillery, but it took almost 400 years before the preponderance of effective fire-power compelled the acceptance of cavalry as a supportive, reconnoitring arm. Indeed, it is possible that the cavalry hierarchy never fully accepted it. Right up until the First World War many of them continued to be mesmerized by "the speed of the horse, the magnetism of the charge and the terror of cold steel", even though it was a largely outdated form of warfare. Indeed, there were still horsed regiments at the outbreak of the Second World War. At least one Indian regiment sharpened its swords on the day war was declared.

EARLY TACTICS

The European cavalry derived largely from the model exemplified in the first instance by Charles Martel and his Frankish knights (see pp.68–69), who relied on the weight and momentum of the charge by heavily armoured horsemen locked in tightly closed ranks. This was unlike the tactics of earlier armies such as those of the Greeks, who had neither stirrup or saddle, and used their cavalry to harry the enemy formations, discharging a hail of javelins at close-packed bodies of the enemy without ever getting too close. Most importantly, the cavalry was used to scout ahead of the main body.

Similarly, the 12th-century Mongols, who had the advantage of both saddle and stirrup and were primarily horse-archers, were masters of the hit-and-run tactic. They never sought to emulate the European steel wall and, furthermore, never launched an attack until the ground ahead and the dispositions of the enemy had been carefully reconnoitred. It was a lesson that European cavalry took a long time to learn.

THE HUNGARIAN HUSSARS

The natural successors to the Mongols were the Hussars, the dashing light horsemen of the Hungarian plains. The name is derived from *hazar*, meaning "20th", and refers to the corps raised by Matthias Corvinus, King of Hungary, in the 15th century, when one man in 20 from each village was required to do military service.

Like the Mongols, the Hussars were exceptionally mobile and not reliant upon slow-moving supply trains. They disdained the set-piece battle and were, perhaps, the first exponents of the *Blitzkrieg* attack (the "lightning strike", perfected in the Second World War by the German armies, when fast-moving armoured divisions penetrated the enemy line and swept onwards to turn the flank). Using the element of surprise, they hit swiftly with devastating effect and were adept at pursuing a broken enemy. The loose, open formations they adopted made any sort of counter-attack a matter of some difficulty. Their tactic became known as the *coup d'huzzard*. Like their forebears, the Hungarian Hussars rode with bent knee, short stirrups, and with the trunk inclined forward, for all the world in the position which Caprilli (see pp.346–47) was to advocate at the end of the 19th century.

LIGHT HORSEMAN
The Hussars were raised by the King of Hungary, Matthias Corvinus, in the 15th century. They rode with a short stirrup, in contrast to the long stirrup and forward-thrust leg of their contemporaries in Europe.

GUNS IN THE ENGLISH CIVIL WAR
The surrender of Leicester to the Royalist Prince Rupert (the nearest mounted figure) in 1645 was achieved largely by artillery supremacy. The pieces were brought to the field and positioned by gun horses.

It was the antithesis of the long-leg, braced seat that the heavy cavalry had continued to use since the battle of Poitiers in AD 732.

WESTERN EUROPEAN CAVALRY

Western Europe did not follow Hungary's example exactly. Its horses were not always suitable or its commanders flexible enough. There was also a need to retain the traditional cavalry role – breaking the enemy line, routing infantry formations and exploiting any advantages made by the light horsemen. (Modern warfare follows the same precept – the heavy tanks with their greater fire-power follow up to consolidate the breakthrough made by the faster light tank squadrons.) But in the end the light cavalry role, exemplified by the Hussars, was accepted throughout Europe, and the Hussars were

often viewed as the cavalry élite. Inevitably, there had to be a merging of the two concepts and a recognition that elements of both had their place in warfare.

BRILLIANT COMMANDERS

The 17th and 18th centuries witnessed commanders whose handling of the cavalry was exemplary. Gustavus Adolphus of Sweden, for example, perfected the shock tactic in the Thirty Years' War (1618–48). Keeping his troops under tight control, he had them trot to the enemy, fire their pistols, and then "fall on" with the sword. In the English Civil War (1642–49), Prince Rupert's troops charged in line, epitomizing the highest aspirations of the cavalryman. But Rupert's cavalry, while never lacking courage, was not sufficiently disciplined to exploit any advantage gained, which would not have been so with the horsemen of Gustavus Adolphus. Oliver Cromwell also held his troops well in hand. Unlike Rupert's cavaliers, the Roundheads charged, not at the gallop, but at "a good round trot". Rupert was a dashing cavalryman but Cromwell was the better commander.

Under commanders of this calibre and men like Charles XII of France, the Duke of Marlborough, and Frederick II of Prussia,

THE BATTLE OF MARSTON MOOR, 1648
Cromwell's Roundheads break the Royalist line. Part of the King's cavalry was commanded by the Duke of Newcastle, a great horseman but a poor soldier.

LA PIE
The favourite charger of the Viscount de Turenne, Marshal General of the Armies of France, was – unusually for the time – a mare. She was a Limousin named La Pie. In 1678, during a battle against the Austrian army, her master was killed, and the riderless La Pie led the assault on the Austrian guns.

the cavalry reached heights which were rarely surpassed later. Theirs was the real "cavalry spirit" so often misunderstood by the officers of the 19th century.

Frederick II of Prussia added a new dimension to the battlefield by introducing galloping horse artillery to support the cavalry. The light guns, drawn by six horses, kept up with the cavalry and could be used to disperse any threatened action against them.

THE MAMELUKES

The Mamelukes, originally steppe Turks from Central Asia, were an élite group of slave soldiers used by Islamic states. They perfected the furusiyya, a system of mounted skill-at-arms. Mameluke armies fought Napoleon in Egypt in 1798.

CAVALRY MANAGEMENT

The 19th century witnessed the employment of cavalry on a huge scale, despite the increasing effectiveness of small-arms fire and the more sophisticated use of artillery. In almost every mounted engagement the "cavalry spirit" was strongly evident, but it was not always matched by the professionalism of the officers, although their courage was never in question. As a result there were some disastrous actions. Furthermore, the standard of horse management in the cavalry of Europe was often, in the words of Major-General Brabazon, who conducted an enquiry following the Boer War (1899–1902), a "shameful abuse of horse flesh".

Napoleon, who was by training an artilleryman – and one of genius – employed massed cavalry brilliantly, if in prodigal fashion, but the French troopers were rarely good horsemen or good horsemasters. Murat, a very good cavalry commander, manoeuvred his troops at trot to hide their equestrian deficiencies, but he lost 18,000 horses in two months in the Russian

campaign in 1812 and another 30,000 in the retreat from Moscow. As General Nansouty, Commandant of the Cavalry of the Guard, wryly observed, "The horses of the Cuirassiers not, unfortunately, being able to sustain themselves on patriotism, fell down by the roadside and died".

THE BATTLE OF WATERLOO

In effect it was the Battle of Waterloo in 1815 that represented the last major European engagement of large bodies of cavalry handled in the conventional copy-book manner. Napoleon had 16,000 horses at his disposal, while Wellington, not including the horses of the Prussian allies, had 13,000. Despite an inevitable impetuosity, which prevented a controlled pursuit of the enemy after the victory, the British cavalry behaved magnificently. The heavy brigades, launched at the optimum moment, routed an infantry corps and a whole cavalry brigade, and overran many of the field batteries whose guns had constantly raked the square formations of British infantry with tormenting fire. (The practice of forming the infantry into a square that afforded all-round protection persisted to the end of the century. The square was three ranks deep on each side. When the front rank had fired its muskets from a kneeling position, it moved to the rear to re-load, and its place was taken by the second rank and so on. Controlled volleys fired by steady, disciplined troops could be devastating in their effect.) The French were equally

heroic. Under Marshal Ney, "the bravest of the brave", they launched repeated attacks on the British squares and were as repeatedly repulsed, leaving walls of dead and dying horses and men piled in front of Wellington's stubbornly resolute infantry. Ney himself had five horses shot from under him, and both sides suffered terrible casualties. Much credit for the victory belonged to the Horse Gunners (Horse Artillery), whose support of the infantry was crucial. Mercer's Troop, for instance, was able to direct a devastating fire on the advancing French cavalry until the last moment, when it galloped back to the shelter of the squares before once again returning to the guns to harass the enemy as they were forced to withdraw. Nonetheless, despite the carnage at Waterloo, cavalry was to remain integral to warfare long after Napoleon's defeat by the combined forces of Europe.

BAGGAGE TRAIN

Well into the 19th century, European armies were supplied by baggage wagons carrying food, equipment and any regimental wives permitted to accompany their men. The women supported their men and often cared for the wounded and the dying.

DRILL BY NUMBERS

Sword drill and skill-at-arms exercises were practised and perfected on the ground, before cavalry troopers were expected to cope with controlling a horse while wielding a sword or lance in earnest. The sword could be used with either a slashing or a thrusting action.

THE MYTH OF WAR

The Charge of the Light Brigade took place at Balaclava on 25 October 1854. It was actually a costly military blunder, but it was later to be immortalized by poets and painters as a glorious episode in the history of British warfare.

INTO THE VALLEY OF DEATH

In the reign of Queen Victoria (1837–1901) and the heady days of Imperialism the British conducted over 80 campaigns, in all of which cavalry featured prominently and sometimes tragically. The best-known cavalry engagement of the period is probably "The Charge of the Light Brigade", which took place at Balaclava during the Crimean War (1854–56) and was immortalized by the Poet Laureate, Alfred Lord Tennyson.

Controversy still abounds as to the reason for the catastrophe. "Someone had blundered", most certainly, but to be fair it was not all the fault of the incompetent commanders concerned – the indecisive Lord Lucan, commander of the cavalry division, and Lord Cardigan, the arrogant commander of the Light Brigade.

The order to advance up the South Valley to attack the Russians guns on the heights was as ambiguous as any military order ever given. But Lucan, having received it, passed it to Cardigan who in turn, ordered his

Brigade, made up of the 17th Lancers, the 11th Hussars, 4th Dragoons, 13th Light Dragoons, and 8th Hussars, to advance.

"Brigade will advance. Walk march! Trot!" and, in perfect order, it did just that, to be shot to pieces from the heights in front and on both sides of the valley. Of the 673 horses, 470 were killed, 42 were wounded and 43 had to be destroyed. Thereafter many horses died of starvation and within two months the cavalry had lost 1,800 of its 2,000 horses.

The only redeeming feature of the campaign was the charge of the Heavy Brigade, which secured Balaclava against a Russian force outnumbering them by 10-1. It was one of the most astonishing feats of arms ever achieved by British cavalry.

A SALUTARY LESSON

The British cavalry learnt its most salutary lesson during the Boer War (1899–1901), when it was finally compelled, by the irregular Boer commandos who had no military experience at all, to adopt the tactics of the more flexible colonial mounted infantry. The colonial mounted infantry followed the practice of the cavalry of the American Civil War (1861–65), many of whom rode to battle and dismounted to

fight as infantry. Indeed, it was the lack of a strong mounted army that largely contributed to the Confederate defeat.

Most of the British horses losses in the Boer War were caused by poor management, resulting in a total loss of 326,000 horses out of 494,000. Nonetheless, the British learnt their lesson well, and by 1914 were superior to any other mounted formation in Europe.

PRACTICAL TACTICS

This cavalry captain in the American Civil War (1861–65) would probably have fought as a mounted infantryman. By 1865 the North had perfected the use of cavalry as mounted infantry, relying on fire-power rather than the shock-tactic of the charge.

NAPOLEON & MARENGO

The horse who carried an emperor

NAPOLEON BONAPARTE

ALTHOUGH the Emperor Napoleon I had 130 horses for his personal use, he is most closely associated with the little white Arab stallion, Marengo, who was named after the battle in 1800, in which he carried his master so courageously. Marengo was imported from Egypt as a six-year-old in 1799, after the battle of Aboukir, and was probably bred at the famous El Naseri Stud. He stood at only 1.45 m (14.1 hh), but was the perfect partner for Napoleon, who was short-legged and portly, and according to the Master of the Horse, General de Caulaincourt, was hard on his horses and not the most elegant of horsemen. He had been known to ride 80 km (50 miles) from Vienna to Semering before breakfast, and more than once galloped the 129 km (80 miles) from Valladolid to Burgos in five hours. Marengo seems to have had an extraordinary constitution. He was swift, handy, absolutely steady under fire, and courageous – a quality not lacking in his Imperial master, whose appearance at moments of crisis invariably rallied and inspired his troops.

Marengo, who was wounded eight times in his career, carried Napoleon at the battles of Austerlitz (1805), Jena (1806), Wagram (1809), and finally at Waterloo (1815). He was among the 52 horses that made up Napoleon's personal stud on the ill-fated Russian campaign in 1812, and survived the dreadful retreat from Moscow. At one point, he shied at a hare on an icy road, unseating the Emperor. The news of the fall lowered morale, and was generally seen as a foreboding of disasters ahead. Marengo was captured after Waterloo and taken to England by Lord Petre, where he was purchased by General J.J. Angerstein of the Grenadier Guards. He stood at stud at New Barnes, near Ely, when he was 27, but this was not a successful experiment. He died aged 38. His skeleton, minus one hoof, was put in the National Army Museum at Sandhurst. The hoof was made into a snuff box and presented by General Angerstein to the officers of the Brigade of Guards.

STYLIZED FLATTERY

Claude-Joseph Vernet's wooden portrayal of Napoleon and Marengo at the battle of Austerlitz in 1805 flatters the Emperor, but does not do much for his horse. In battle the little horse was as courageous as the Emperor and was the perfect foil for his charismatic master.

THE BATTLE OF MARENGO
Louis Lejeune's picture shows the battle of Marengo in 1800, after which Napoleon named his favourite Arab charger. The composition of the picture is as confused as the action itself but a closer study reveals much interesting detail.

WELLINGTON & COPENHAGEN

They shared "the glory of that glorious day"

COMMEMORATIVE PORTRAIT
Etching of the statue of Wellington and Copenhagen, which stands opposite London's Royal Exchange.

COPENHAGEN, the chestnut charger of Arthur Wellesley, Duke of Wellington, received the sort of adulation in his lifetime that would be reserved today for horses such as Arkle, Red Rum, and Desert Orchid. He stood a shade over 1.52 m (15 hh) and was typical of the early 19th-century Thoroughbred, retaining strong Arab characteristics. His pedigree carried lines to both the Darley and Godolphin Arabians (see pp.120–21). He was sired by Meteor, a son of Eclipse, who ran second in the Epsom Derby. His dam was Lady Catherine, the charger ridden by General Grosvenor at the Siege of Copenhagen. Wellington bought him in Spain in 1812 from Sir Charles Stewart and rode him throughout the Peninsular Campaign, as well as hunting him with a pack of hounds brought out from England. Copenhagen endeared himself to the troops by greeting detachments with excited neighs, but his other peculiarity, that of kicking out

if approached too closely, assured him of much the same respect as that accorded to his austere master. Copenhagen's "glorious day", shared with his master, was 18 June 1815, the date of the battle of Waterloo, which saw the final defeat of Wellington's old adversary, Napoleon Bonaparte. On the day before the battle the Duke rode Copenhagen from 10 am to 8 pm with scarcely a pause. On 18 June he rode the horse for 15 hours during which he took complete control of the battle, galloping from one vantage point to the other to steady and encourage his troops. When at the end of the day Wellington dismounted, Copenhagen had sufficient energy to lash out behind, missing his noble master by inches. Copenhagen died in 1836 at the age of 28 and was buried with full military honours at Stratfield Saye, the Duke's country seat in Hampshire. His headstone bore a couplet from the commemorative poem "Epitaph" written for him by R.E. Egerton Warburton. The Duke wrote of him: "There may be faster horses, no doubt many handsomer, but for bottom and endurance I never saw his fellow".

BOEHM'S STATUE
Edward Boehm's statue of Wellington and Copenhagen, which stands at Hyde Park Corner in London, emphasizes the strong Arab character of the horse, and does not attempt to disguise the Duke's less than elegant seat.

HERE LIES
COPENHAGEN
THE CHARGER RIDDEN BY
THE DUKE OF WELLINGTON
THE ENTIRE DAY, AT THE
BATTLE OF WATERLOO.
BORN 1808. DIED 1836

R.I.P.
Copenhagen died in 1836 at the age of 28. He was buried with full military honours at Stratfield Saye, the estate presented to the Duke by a grateful nation. His epitaph reads "God's humbler instrument, though meaner clay, should share the glory of that glorious day".

THE BRITISH SQUARE
The Duke of Wellington often took personal control of the infantry squares at the battle of Waterloo (left). R.A. Hillingford, the painter of this scene, was not born until 10 years after the battle, and his depiction of Copenhagen, who was chestnut, is certainly inaccurate.

THE TWO WORLD WARS

GERMAN LANCER,
FIRST WORLD WAR

IRONICALLY, THE END of the cavalry era witnessed some of the greatest achievements in the history of mounted warfare. The definitive, classic example of a cavalry engagement on a large scale remains the victorious Palestine Campaign in the First World War led by General Sir Edmund Allenby against the Turks in Palestine in 1917–18, in which he employed a Desert Mounted Corps made up of Australian, New Zealand, Indian, and British Yeomanry regiments, supported by machine-gun squadrons and a brigade of Royal Horse Artillery. Although dismounted action with rifles and the brilliant handling of machine-gun and artillery units were a major feature, the success of the year-long campaign was equally dependent upon sabre and lance, the speed and dash of the charge, and the indomitable cavalry spirit.

THE FIRST WORLD WAR

The First World War saw the employment of millions of horses. They were used extensively in both conventional cavalry formations and also in transportation – hauling supplies through the deep, clinging mud, bringing up the guns, and drawing ambulances. The horse casualties on the Western Front, many of which were caused by disease and mismanagement, were appalling. Britain alone lost half a million horses between 1914 and 1918, mostly due to the unavoidable effects of exposure.

The cavalry did not make any significant breakthroughs on the European battlefield, owing to the static nature of trench warfare and the ever-present inhibiting mud. Once the barbed-wire entanglements festooned the desolate battlefields of France and Belgium, the cavalry was compelled to dismount and fight in the trenches with rifle and bayonet.

Nonetheless, in the early part of the war, the conduct and achievements of British cavalry were exemplary. They sustained high levels of horse management, as they did throughout the hostilities, and were brilliantly handled in the early rear-guard actions. Their professionalism ensured that they remained operational, if in a limited cavalry role, up to 1918. It was a different story with the French and Germans, whose poor standards of management caused huge losses of horseflesh and often rendered mounted formations unfit for service.

Better use could be made of the cavalry away from the mud of Europe. It reached its apotheosis in the Palestine Campaign of 1917–18, led by General Sir Edmund Allenby (later Fieldmarshal Lord Allenby). Allenby was arguably the most gifted

CLASSIC CAMPAIGN
This painting shows General Sir Edmund Allenby's 6th Mounted Brigade routing the Turks at El-Mughar in the 1917 Palestine campaign. Allenby's masterful handling of the desert campaign remains the classic example of large-scale cavalry deployment.

commander of the First World War on either side. He was made Inspector-General of Cavalry in 1910, and was largely responsible for the high levels of professionalism in the cavalry in 1914.

Allenby launched his cavalry offensive to break the Gaza–Beersheba Line in October 1917. The 4th Australian Light Horse Brigade took Beersheba at the gallop, and captured some 1,000 Turks and nine guns for the loss of only 32 killed.

In September 1918 Allenby fought the decisive battle of Megiddo, breaking the Turkish line along the coast of Arsouf and loosing his cavalry down the Plain of Sharon. The campaign ended in October

CAMOUFLAGING HORSES
The Royal Scots Greys, 5th Cavalry Brigade, halted on the Belgian frontier in August 1914, 13 days after war had been declared on Germany. Later in the campaign, their grey horses were stained chestnut to make them less noticeable and to prevent the unit from being identified. Here, the horses are lined up to be stained.

1918 with the fall of Aleppo, a city founded by one of the first horse people, the Hittites. Aleppo is only 96 km (60 miles) from Alexandria, where Alexander the Great (see pp.40–41), an earlier commander of genius, won his first victory over the Persian King Darius in 333 BC.

What followed was shameful betrayal of the horses that the British Premier, Lloyd George, had described as being "as unbeatable as the riders". Twenty thousand were sold in Egypt to lives of brutal neglect and cruelty. To right some little part of that disgraceful wrong, Dorothy Brooke, wife of Sir Geoffrey Brooke, who commanded the Cavalry Brigade in Egypt in 1930, founded the Brooke Hospital for Animals in Cairo. It exists today as a memorial to a lady who "hated to remember, but could not forget".

THE SECOND WORLD WAR

Cavalry and horse transport survived into the Second World War. Poland, almost the last nation to rely heavily on horses, entered the war with about 86,000 horses. Too

SPAHI FIGHTER
This North African Spahi of the French army was in action on the Western Front during the First World War. His Barb horse wears the traditional Moroccan saddle, with the sword fitted horizontally to lie under the rider's leg.

many of them fell before the German armour. In 1939 the Pomeranian Cavalry Brigade lost 2,000 horses, out of 3,000, within half an hour when attacked by dive-bombers.

The Germans also employed thousands of horses, particularly on the Eastern Front, although not nearly as many as the Russians. The Russians had no fewer than 30 cavalry

divisions supported by horse artillery, as well as 800,000 draught horses, a total of about 1.2 million. In November 1941, the 44th Mongolian Cavalry Division attacked the German 106th Infantry Division and its supporting artillery near the village of Musino. They charged, knee-to-knee, with sabres drawn. Astonished, the German infantry opened fire. Within minutes 2,000 horses and riders lay dead or dying on the field. There were no German casualties.

Almost every cavalry action was magnificent. Too many had little to do with either war or common humanity.

ARTILLERY HORSES
During the invasion of France in 1940 much of the German heavy artillery was still being pulled by horses. This picture shows a 105 mm howitzer being moved over a pontoon bridge by a six-horse team.

BELGIUM, 1940
The German army used mounted troops and horse transport during the Second World War. In 1940, while the German panzer (tank) divisions were preparing to sweep through France to reach the Channel ports, the cavalry units spearheaded the offensive against Belgium.

THE MODERN WAR-HORSE

BOSNIAN WAR, 1993

A T THE START OF THE third millennium it is astonishing to find that there is still a place for the horse in the bloody business of warfare. Amidst and alongside the highly sophisticated, computerized armoury of the nuclear age, which can identify and strike targets with pin-point accuracy, the anachronism of cavalry and horse transport continues to fulfil a basic requirement in the more remote areas of the world. It is only in peacetime that mankind continues to cling to the pageantry and imagined glory of battle in colourfully caparisoned mounted squadrons, whose brilliant uniforms and extravagant accoutrements are the living reminders of the myth and legend of the cavalry tradition, even if they have little to do with its grim reality.

RECENT CONFLICTS

In 1979 the powerful, professional army of the USSR invaded Afghanistan and earned the condemnation of the world for what was seen to be an indefensible act of aggression against a country poorly equipped to defend itself against the force of modern arms. In the event, the Russian troops were harried, often out-manoeuvred, and finally humiliated by the Mujahideen guerrillas whose greatest ally was their own wild, barren, mountainous country. Armoured supremacy on the ground, supported by air cover, ensured that the Russians controlled the rudimentary road system, but the hills belonged to the guerrillas as they had from time immemorial. From these rocky strongholds the tribesmen constantly harassed the Russian troops and their lines of communication. They subjected the hapless Russians to continual small arms fire and attack by mortars and rockets.

HORSE TRANSPORT
In the conflict between Armenia and Azerbaijan over the area of Nagorno-Karabakh (which started in 1991), the absence of roads and motorized transport compelled the antagonists to use horses to move supplies and ammunition in rough country.

They were able to do so largely because of their ponies and horses, which conferred a mobility in desperately difficult terrain that was denied entirely to their enemies, and were also the means of transporting guns, launchers, and ammunition. The wiry, sure-footed Kabuli and Turkmene-type horses carried huge loads up and down the steep, rock-strewn mountainsides, picking their way through the boulders and virgin scree where no paths existed. Small strike groups used them to make lightning raids on Russian positions, afterwards withdrawing just as speedily to the safety of their impenetrable hills. These horses, as tough and resilient as the hillmen, would only rarely, if ever, have been shod, and, like the men, existed on no more than basic rations.

More recently, in the mountainous regions of Armenia and Bosnia, horses have once more played a role in modern warfare. They pull carts laden with possessions as streams of refugees flee before the advance

MOUNTED STRIKE
In the Afghan War (1979–89) the Mujahideen depended on their horses to maintain mobility in a difficult terrain, and to increase their capacity to harass their enemy effectively. The wiry little eastern horses, bred for life in the hills, are quick, very agile, and sure-footed.

of opposing factions. Both sides ride them or use them as pack horses, carrying machine guns, mortars, ammunition, and medical supplies along the steep hill tracks. For guerrilla purposes, a few ponies used over that ground can be as effective and as potentially destructive as an air strike; moreover, they are more easily deployed, and far more economical.

CEREMONIAL CAVALRY

Putting aside the reality of armed conflict, countries in all parts of the world preserve the heroic image of war in mounted squadrons that contribute to the pomp and pageantry of the state occasion. French ceremonial is splendidly enhanced by the panache and brilliance of its legendary *Garde Républicaine*. The Republican Guard of Paris is part of the *Gendarmerie Nationale* and is the only surviving cavalry regiment in the French Army. It stems from the Royal Watch and the Company of Constabulary, raised in 1666. It is commanded by a colonel, and is made up of two groups of squadrons, a motorcycle squadron, a mounted band, and a training school. With other police units, it is responsible for the maintenance of law and order, but it performs additional ceremonial duties such as providing state escorts and forming honour guards. On these occasions the Guard wears the dress uniform as laid down in 1873: crested, plumed helmets, blue tunics with scarlet facings, and blue breeches. White breeches are worn only if the President of the Republic is present.

The ruler of Morocco has his colourful bodyguard magnificently mounted on Barb and Arab horses (see pp.64–67), while India

retains her 200-year-old President's Body Guard, whose men and horses occupy the same quarters in New Delhi's Rashtrapati Bhavan as when it formed the personal bodyguard of His Excellency the British Viceroy. The President's Body Guard was first raised on 30 September 1773 at Benares, by Governor Warren Hastings, and was known initially as "The Governor's Troop of Moguls". The Body Guard is made up of Jat Sikhs and Punjabi Mussalmans, all of whom must be 1.85 m (6 ft) tall. It is

CEREMONIAL SPLENDOUR
In India, the President's Body Guard, which is 200 years old, complements the splendid rose-pink architecture of Lutyens' New Delhi. The Body Guard plays an integral part in state ceremonial, but its troopers are all trained parachutists as well.

commanded by a colonel and mounted on Indian-bred horses (see pp.166–67) that are bay with no white points. All personnel are trained as paratroopers and taught how to handle armoured cars.

FULL DRESS
France's Garde Républicaine is shown here in the dress uniform of 1873. It is the only surviving cavalry regiment in the French Army.

OPEN ORDER
This colourfully apparelled band are part of the bodyguard for King Hassan of Morocco. They favour a rather loose order, and ride Arab and Barb horses.

TROOP HORSES

THE HOUSEHOLD CAVALRY and the King's Troop are the only mounted units now remaining in the British Army. The Household Cavalry comprises the two senior regiments of the British army: the Life Guards, and the Blues and Royals (formerly the Royal Horse Guards). These two regiments are specially responsible for guarding the sovereign – the mounted squadrons, which are stationed in London, escort him or her on state occasions as well as fulfilling routine ceremonial duties. The King's Troop, Royal Horse Artillery, so named by HM King George VI in 1947, is also stationed in London, at St John's Wood. It carries out ceremonial duties in the capital throughout the year, as well as giving displays of the famous "drive" at shows throughout the country.

CHARGER IN FULL DRESS
This charger belonging to an officer of the Blues and Royals is in full ceremonial saddlery. The sheepskin is black, unlike those of the Life Guards, which are white.

THE HOUSEHOLD CAVALRY

The Life Guards are distinguished from the Blues and Royals by the fact that they wear scarlet tunics and white helmet plumes, while the latter wear blue tunics with red plumes. Both regiments ride the Household Cavalry Black horses, a tradition that goes back some 300 years. Like British police horses, the blacks are of no particular breed, although the regiments are adept at obtaining horses of a very distinctive type. The horses are bought at three or four years of age, in Yorkshire or in Ireland, and are of the half-bred hunter type. They must be able to carry a trooper in full ceremonial uniform, and they should stand at 1.63 m (16 hh) or a little more. After the Second World War the regiments had black horses that had been captured in Germany, many of which had been left to run loose in the countryside as the German troops retreated. Warmbloods and warmblood crosses have also been used where they fulfilled the necessary criteria of size, ability to carry weight, and colour.

All the Household Cavalry chargers go

HIND LEGS
Good hind legs with strong, muscular second thighs and clearly defined joints are a prime requirement in the troop horse.

HOCKS
The hocks, like those of a good-class, half-bred hunter, have to be well-formed and free from any irregularity or disease that might prevent their effective function.

SADDLE
As well as a girth, the army saddle is further secured by a leather surcingle passing over the seat, and the breastplate, round the chest.

TROOPING THE COLOUR
The officer commanding salutes HM the Queen at the march past of the Life Guards at the Trooping of the Colour at Horseguards Parade, London.

through army remount training. They must also become used to crowds, bands, and the attentions of the tourists who stop to admire them and to pat their noses when they are on guard duty. The horses never have plaited or hogged manes; instead, the mane is pulled to a uniform length, and lies loose on the near side of the neck.

While the squadrons ride black chargers, the Household Cavalry trumpeters are always mounted on greys. The splendidly caparisoned drum horses, which are larger and heavier than the blacks, are traditionally either skewbald or piebald.

THE KING'S TROOP

The first use of horse artillery as a quick-moving, mobile unit that was fast enough to give support to cavalry formations and to keep up with them in action was made by Frederick the Great of Prussia (1712–86). The example was quickly followed by other European armies, including that of the UK, which formed a Riding House Dept. in 1803, later the Riding Establishment, R.H.A.

KING'S TROOP, ROYAL HORSE ARTILLERY
The troopers or gun-horses belonging to the King's Troop, Royal Horse Artillery are mostly of Irish Draught breeding, like the typical example shown here. The gun-horses always have hogged manes, unlike the cavalry chargers.

The horses of the King's Troop are different from the Household Cavalry Blacks. Almost all of them come from Ireland, and many are of Irish Draught descent (see pp.396–97). The gun horses are bought at the age of four or five, then schooled for one year before they are deemed strong enough to work at the gallop in draught.

The guns and limbers of the King's Troop are pulled by six horses. The heavy gun limbers have no form of brake, so they are slowed and stopped by the "wheel" horses – the pair at the back, nearest to the limber. The wheel horses must be very steady and reliable, as must the lead horse on the near side. This horse's "driver" dictates the speed and the direction of the team. He must control the pair horse on his off side, while riding his own horse with his left hand.

The horses of the King's Troop stand at about 1.60 m (15.3 hh). Unlike the cavalry chargers, the Troop horses have hogged manes.

MANE
Chargers of the Household Cavalry always wear full manes, pulled to a hand's width (10 cm [4 in]).

TETHER CHAIN
A tethering rack-chain is attached to the head collar, which also does duty as a noseband.

LEGS
Cavalry horses must have sound legs, joints, and feet if they are to carry the weight of a trooper in full dress.

JACKBOOTS
Black jackboots are of polished, not patent, leather. Troopers in the Blues and Royals wear blue tunics and red helmet plumes.

CAVALRY HORSE HEIGHT
Over 1.63 m (16 hh)

MULE

THE MULE IS ONE OF THE WORLD'S most useful working animals and has been employed for many purposes throughout history. When properly treated, it can be highly intelligent. It is also tough, adaptable, and resilient. Mules are stronger than horses, and are capable of sustained hard work to a far greater degree. By nature, they are brave but usually calm, and have an independent disposition that is sometimes interpreted as being stubborn, although it may, in fact, be a reflection of the mule's highly developed sense of self-preservation.

MULES IN INDIA
Mule transport is a deeply rooted tradition with the Indian Army, which makes extensive use of mule companies in mountainous areas.

HISTORY

In ancient times the mule was revered above the horse. For instance, the Hittites, who were among the most powerful of the early horse peoples, valued mules at 60 shekels, while they fixed the price of chariot horses at only 20 shekels. The kings of Israel rode mules, and among the Amhara people of Ethiopia, who were possibly influenced by their ancient Semitic ties, the mule enjoyed the highest status. Prelates of the medieval church, following the Jewish preference, expressed their Christian humility and their appreciation of the comfortable ambling pace by riding richly caparisoned mules rather than the proud chargers used by the armoured knights.

MULES AT WORK

In fact, the greater value of the mule lay in its versatility. In many parts of the world a mule is more practical than a horse because of its smooth pace under saddle as well as its sure-footedness on mountain trails that would be too steep and rough for horses. Mules are still essential in Mediterranean Europe, where they plough, carry heavy loads under pack, and can be driven in harness. At one time they were also worked in huge numbers in the southern states of the US, where they were used for every sort of transport as well as in agriculture. Mules are much faster than oxen, almost as strong, and they are far more economical to keep than horses. Moreover, they adapt to heat more easily and are better able to work in hot climates than most horses. A further advantage is that appropriate types of mule can be created for specific purposes, by

HEAD
The big head has a slightly convex profile with characteristic long ears.

NECK
The neck is fairly short, but very strong and powerful.

LEGS
The legs are strong and short, with rounded joints like those of a donkey.

FEET
The feet are narrow, upright, and straight-sided, never rounded. They are exceptionally hard, and can withstand much wear.

HINNY
A hinny is the result of a cross between a male horse and a donkey mare. It is regarded as being much inferior to a mule in terms of strength and capacity for work. Like all of its kind, the hinny shown here has a body distinctly shaped like that of a donkey. Hinnies can be any colour, but are usually grey.

selecting suitable mares and putting them to a comparatively small range of jackass types. For instance, the Poitevin jackass, crossed with the Poitevin mare, produces heavy draught mules (see pp.272–73), while the smaller Maltese and Indian jackasses will get more or less lighter types according to the mares with which they are mated.

Mule transport featured prominently in both World Wars, being used widely in Burma and Italy for example, during the Second World War. Many of the mule transport companies in those war zones were drawn from the Indian Army, which has always been notable for its use of mules. The modern Indian Army still employs large numbers of mules, and in the post-war border disputes, particularly in the mountainous terrain of Kashmir and its neighbouring areas, the mule transport companies played a vital role. India also maintains its legendary Mountain Artillery, which operates with unrivalled efficiency in difficult country where it would be impossible to use conventional wheeled or tracked vehicles. Mules carry dismantled screw guns – carriage, wheels and axle, pivot, trail legs, and barrel – as well as heavy ammunition boxes, over precipitous and rocky mountain tracks.

MULES AND HINNIES

A mule is a cross between a jackass and a horse, while a hinny is the result of a mating between a horse and a donkey mare. There are differences between the two, and the mule has always been regarded as the superior animal. A mule resembles its jackass parent at its extremities – the ears, legs, feet,

SURE-FOOTED ON THE MOUNTAIN TRAILS
No other equine is more sure-footed than the mule. It is the natural and popular choice for tourists riding along the trails in the Grand Canyon.

QUARTERS
The quarters are very strong, the croup is sometimes sloped, and the tail is set low.

TAIL
The tails of both mules and hinnies are usually a little more like that of a donkey than of a horse.

BODY
The chest is wide and fairly deep. The withers and back are usually flat, and the back is rather long.

HIND LEGS
The mule's hind legs, particularly the hocks, are disproportionately strong for its size, although they do not appear so.

HEIGHT
1.42–1.63 m (14–16 hh)

and tail. It has been described as having a horse's body on donkey legs, and as looking like a donkey in front and a horse behind. Conversely, the hinny resembles the male (horse) parent in its extremities, and usually has a donkey-type body. A male hinny, like a donkey, has rudimentary teats on the sheath.

Both are marked by the long ears and head. Their tails, which are usually low-set, resemble that of a donkey rather than the full tail of a horse. Their feet are hard but narrow and straight-sided. The withers and back are flat. Mules are usually uniformly coloured, although occasional piebalds and skewbalds can occur. Hinnies may be any colour, but are usually grey. The size is variable, and depends on the choice of parents. The big Poitevin and the American mammoth mules may stand at over 1.63 m (16 hh), while those employed in pack companies will be around 1.42 m (14 hh). Hinnies lack the mule's hybrid vigour, and so are less valuable as workers.

Neither mule nor hinny has the ability to reproduce its kind. The hinny is difficult to breed as perhaps only one in seven donkeys will conceive if served by a horse or pony. Regarding the mule's sterility, the British politician John O'Connor Power is quoted in H.H. Asquith's *Memories and Reflections* as likening his political opponents to "the mules of politics: without pride of ancestry, or hope of posterity".

PART TEN

THE SPORTING HORSE

HORSES MAY WELL HAVE BEEN USED for sport and competition from the earliest days of domestication. Horse racing, either ridden or in harness, was well established in the classical civilizations of Greece and Rome, and in present-day Mongolia it is carried on in much the same fashion as it was 3,000 years ago. Many of the modern equestrian disciplines, such as eventing, showjumping, dressage, and long-distance riding, together with the more obvious skill-at-arms competitions, such as tent-pegging, have their origins in military practice.

Call to Hounds by George Wright (1860–1942)

FULL STRETCH

FLAT RACING

RACING IS OFTEN termed "the sport of kings" due to its close association with the British monarchy from the Stuart kings onwards. It was the evolution of the Thoroughbred racehorse (see pp.120–21) in 17th-and 18th-century England that was the origin of today's organized modern racing, in which the British pattern is the one that is followed worldwide. From the outset, betting was a central element in the sport and still underpins today's huge multinational industry, in which horses can change hands for unimaginably high sums. Lammtara, winner of the 1995 Derby, for instance, was sold to stand at stud in Japan by the most successful racing operation of the late-20th century, the Godolphin enterprise belonging to the Maktoum family, the rulers of Dubai, for $30m, without his stock having proved themselves on the racecourse.

NEWMARKET AND THE EARLY DAYS

Newmarket is the headquarters of British racing, largely due to the patronage of James I (1603–25), Charles I (1625–49), and Charles II (1660–85). Charles II's amorous adventures earned him the nickname "Old Rowley", after his favourite black stallion, and this name is immortalized in racing's best known 1.6-km (1-mile) course, the Rowley Mile at Newmarket. Charles II also instituted the famous Newmarket Town Plate race in 1665, which he won on two occasions. This race, run over 6.4 km (4 miles), is open to amateurs, and is still held annually on Newmarket's Round Course, with riders having to carry a weight of 76 kg (12 st). Today, Newmarket, like its counterpart in the US, Lexington, Kentucky, still revolves round the horse. Some 50 trainers have their yards in the town, and until the recession of

NEVER ECLIPSED
This painting of Eclipse is by the 18th-century artist George Stubbs. Eclipse, England's most famous racehorse, was never beaten. He founded the principal male line in English Thoroughbred breeding and sired 335 winners.

NEWMARKET HEATH
This oil painting by John Wootton (1686–1765) portrays racing on Newmarket Heath, and illustrates both the artist's ability to cope with a massive composition and the great popularity of the sport.

the 1990s over 2,500 horses were trained there. The Jockey Club, the governing body of flat racing in Britain, is also based at Newmarket. It owns the 16,000 hectares (4,000 acres) that make up Newmarket Heath, and also owns the 1,000-hectare (2,500-acre) site that makes up the two racecourses. The Jockey Club was founded in about 1752 by a group of interested gentry and aristocrats, and was granted a Royal Charter in 1970. Similar organizations exist in all racing countries.

THE UK AND THE CLASSICS

In relation to its size, the UK has more racecourses and more races than any other country. In all, there are 59 courses. Of these 25 are devoted to National Hunt racing over fences; 18 stage meetings on the flat and over fences; and 16 are devoted to the crowded flat-race calendar between

PRIDE OF KENTUCKY
The course at Churchill Downs, Louisville, Kentucky, where the Kentucky Derby is run, is a "dirt track", as is usual in the US. In Europe, racing takes place on prepared grass courses.

March and October. Courses vary between the fashionable magnificence of Royal Ascot, laid out in 1711 on the initiative of Queen Anne, and homely, small jumping courses such as those at Bangor-on-Dee and Cartmel.

In the first half of the 18th century the emphasis was put on distance races of up to 6.4 km (4 miles). These were often run in heats, a practice that put a premium on stamina. In the last part of the 18th century, however, shorter, speed races became usual.

This trend is reflected in the British Classic races for three-year-olds, which are made up of five events and act as a pattern for similar arrangements throughout the world. The St Leger is run in September at Doncaster, over a 2.8-km (1¾-mile) course. Racing has taken place there since 1695, and the course also has the distinction of opening and closing the racing season with the Lincoln Handicap in March, and the November Handicap. The St Leger, named after Colonel St Leger of Park Hill, was first run in 1776. The 2,000 Guineas

and the 1,000 Guineas (a race for fillies), which were first held in 1809 and 1814 respectively, are run at Newmarket in April, over a 1.6-km (1-mile) course. The remaining Classics, the Derby and the Oaks, are run over 2.4 km (1½ miles) at Epsom in early June. Racing has taken place on Epsom Downs, no more than 24 km (15 miles) from the centre of London, since the 15th century. The first Derby, run in 1780 and named after the 12th Earl of Derby, was won by Diomed, owned by Sir Charles Bunbury, who tossed a coin with the Earl for the privilege of naming the race. The Oaks, a race for fillies, was first run in 1779, and was named after the Earl's Epsom residence. The first race, appropriately enough, was won by Lord Derby's horse Bridget. The Triple

RACING IN FLORIDA
As the winter weather immobilizes the cities of the north and shuts down race tracks throughout the US, the racing fraternity makes for the warmth of Florida, and the first-class racing that it offers.

Crown, racing's greatest accolade, is the composite term given to the 2,000 Guineas, the Derby, and the St Leger.

THE GREAT AMERICAN RACES

The American equivalent of the British classics, a group of races which act as a pattern for similar arrangements throughout the world, are the Kentucky Derby, the Preakness Stakes, the Belmont Stakes, and the Coaching Club American Oaks. The first three constitute the prestigious Triple Crown. The Kentucky Derby – 0.4 km (¼ mile) shorter than the Epsom prototype – is held at Churchill Downs, Louisville,

Kentucky. The Belmont Stakes and the American Oaks are held at Belmont Park, close to where the first American racecourse was laid out in 1664 by the first Governor of New York, Richard Nicolls. The Preakness is held at Pimlico at Baltimore, Maryland. In the US, horses are trained on the tracks and raced on "dirt", unlike in the UK where they are trained off-course and run on grass.

IMPACT OF DUBAI

The Maktoums' Godolphin enterprise, supported by enormous wealth, added a new dimension to racing at the end of the 20th century. Based at Newmarket and Dubai, the Maktoum family have become patrons of the sport in the manner of its early founders. In the years immediately preceding the Millennium Godolphin produced world-beating horses of the calibre of Daylami; Kayf Tara, winner of the Ascot gold Cup in 1998 and 2000; and the phenomenal but short-lived Dubai Millennium. In the succeeding years its expansion continued to the point at which the "Dubai Impact" is seen as an underpinning element in the structure of world racing.

THE ENGLISH DERBY
The most famous race in the world is the English Derby, held at Epsom. The 2.4-km (1½-mile) horseshoe-shaped course is marked by the steep descent to Tattenham Corner, where more than one race has been lost or won. The Derby was first run in 1780.

STEEPLECHASING

STEEPLECHASING

THE SPIRITUAL HOME of steeplechasing is in the UK and Ireland, where it attracts large audiences. There is no equivalent scenario elsewhere. The US stages its Maryland Hunt Cup over open country and post-and-rail fences but lacks the grandstands and betting rings of the British sport. In Europe, racing takes place on a small scale over natural country in France, and in the Czech Republic the Gran Pardubice is run cross-country over numerous and formidable natural obstacles. In the UK, the modern sport is run by the National Hunt Committee, appointed by the Jockey Club in 1863. The first "match" took place in Ireland over a century earlier when, for a bet, Messrs. O'Callaghan and Blake raced the 7.25 km (4½ miles) between the steeples of Buttevant and St Leger churches, giving rise to the word "steeplechase".

BACKGROUND

Steeplechasing has its roots in both the hunting field and flat racing, where at early meetings races were often held for hunters over the flat-race course. These were often abused by flat-racers, so in 1811 the Clerk at the Bedford Course built four fences 1.37 m (4 ft 6 in) high to discourage them. The sport was first put on a regular footing by a former racehorse trainer in St Albans, Tom Colman, who initiated the St Albans Steeplechase in 1830. This race was run every year until 1839, when the Grand National at Aintree, Liverpool, was first run in its established form.

A WATER JUMP IN THE GRAN PARDUBICE
The Gran Pardubice, the most testing race in mainland Europe, is run over 6.4 km (4 miles). Many of the obstacles are natural hazards of formidable proportions.

OVER THE TIMBER
America's Maryland Hunt Cup is the only steeplechase to be run over fixed post-and-rail fences, and it demands specially schooled horses.

THE ENGLISH GRAND NATIONAL

The Grand National of 1839 is accepted as the first official Grand National, although earlier "Nationals" had been run in 1837 and 1838. The 1839 race was won by Jem Mason, thought to be the finest horseman in England, on a bay horse called Lottery.

The Grand National is the most famous and most demanding steeplechase in the world. It is run over 7.22 km (4 miles 856 yds) and includes 30 large fences, some of which have very big drops on the landing side. One of the most famous is Becher's Brook, which has to be jumped twice. It is named after Captain Martin Becher, an early

GRAND NATIONAL
The greatest jumping race in the world, the English Grand National Steeplechase, is run annually at Aintree in Liverpool. It covers a distance of 7.22 km (just under 4½ miles) and includes 30 of the stiffest fences in the sport.

competitor who fell into it. It continues to take its toll, although it has been modified since Becher's time. Major alterations were made to the fences in 1961, when they were changed from having an upright apron to having the more usual sloping one.

The National has been run annually since 1839, except between 1941 and 1945. The race was cancelled in 1993 because of faulty starting procedures, although almost half the field continued, unaware of the recall flag. Scotland, Ireland, and Wales stage their own Grand National races.

The greatest performer at Aintree was Red Rum, who won in 1973, 1974, and 1977. Before him, only six horses had won twice: Peter Simple (1849, 1853); Abd El Kadr (1850, 1851); The Lamb (1868, 1871); The Colonel (1869, 1870); Manifesto (1897, 1899); and Reynoldstown (1935, 1936).

CHELTENHAM AND THE GOLD CUP

Cheltenham, and particularly the Cheltenham National Hunt Festival, is the focal point for steeplechasing in the UK. The most prestigious race of the Cheltenham Festival is the Gold Cup, run over 5.2 km (3¼ miles)

with a testing uphill finish. It was first run in 1924, when it was won by Red Splash. Since then, winners have included the very best of the world's 'chasers. Arkle, the Duchess of Westminster's horse, made the race his own in 1964 and 1965, when he beat the great Mill House, and then again in 1966, when he romped home after making a near-fatal mistake at the fence in front of the stands. However, the Gold Cup record belongs to the extraordinary Golden Miller, who had five consecutive wins between 1932 and 1936, and who in 1934 created another record when he also won the Grand

National. Another Gold Cup record was made in 1983, when the trainer Michael Dickinson saddled the first five home: Bregawn, Captain John, Wayward Lad, Silver Buck, and Ashley House.

The Cheltenham Festival also includes the Champion Chase, and the better-known Champion Hurdle. Hurdle races are run over flights of hurdles, which are lower than 'chasing fences and give way if hit hard. The Champion Hurdle is run over 3.2 km (2 miles) and is one of the special events in the racing year. Since 1927 it has produced some spectacular performances.

POINT-TO-POINT RACING

The UK and Ireland also have the amateur sport of point-to-point racing. Races, which are open to both men and women, are run during the season from February to late April, or even May, by almost every recognized hunt. The races are restricted to horses that have been hunted with a recognized pack and are now run over oval, built-up courses not unlike the professional steeplechases. The minimum distance for a point-to-point race is 4.8 km (3 miles), and there are at least 18 fences. A dozen or more point-to-point meetings take place every weekend during the season.

POINT-TO-POINT
Point-to-point racing is the amateur sport organized by recognized hunts in Ireland and the UK. Races are open to both men and women, and hundreds of meetings are held during the season, attended by large crowds.

HARNESS RACING

HARNESS RACERS

Horses have raced in harness from the earliest times. The first evidence of a sophisticated use of horses in harness is given by the training manual of Kikkulis, Master of the Horse to the Hittite King Sepululiamas. Dated around 1360 BC, it details a comprehensive training programme for chariot horses. The war chariot, and then the lightweight, skeletal vehicle developed in the Roman circus, can be considered as the forerunners of the modern racing sulky. Modern harness racing has a huge following in the US, Europe, and Australasia, and both national and international races carry prize money equivalent to that offered on the flat. In the US, which is regarded as the world's leading harness-racing nation, the sport attracts audiences of over 30 million and in popularity is second only to Thoroughbred racing.

TROTTING AND PACING

In the US the pacing horse (which moves its legs in lateral pairs) predominates almost to the exclusion of the conventional trotter (which moves its legs in diagonal pairs). They are preferred because their action, which is assisted by hobbles (a harness connecting the fore- and hind legs above the knee and hock respectively), is less prone to "break" than that of the trotter. This is a prime consideration in a country in which heavy betting is a feature of the sport. Any horse that breaks into a gallop loses ground because it is obliged to move to the outside. When this happens in a field that is travelling at almost 65 km/h (40 mph), there is little chance that the offender will win the race.

Trotters are generally preferred in Europe, Scandinavia, and Russia, and in France there are races for trotters under saddle as well as in harness. Most countries have races for trotters and pacers, although in none do the two race against each other.

THE MOSCOW HIPPODROME
Harness racing is a popular sport in Russia, and regular meetings are held at the Moscow Hippodrome. Most races are for conventional diagonal trotters rather than for pacers.

RACING IN THE US

At the beginning of the 1990s, the US had more than 70 major raceways of a standard, basic design. All are left-handed, oval in shape, and equipped with all-weather surfaces and flood-lighting. Evening racing, first introduced at the Roosevelt Raceway, Long Island, New York, in 1940, is the norm. The leading raceway in the US is Meadowlands at East Rutherford, New Jersey. Opened in 1976, it stages some of the world's most valuable harness races, with prize-money reckoned in millions of dollars.

Like flat racing, harness racing also has Triple Crown races, one each for trotters and pacers. The trotting Triple Crown comprises the Hambletonian at Meadowlands, the Yonkers Trot at Yonkers Raceway in New York State, and the Kentucky Futurity at Lexington's Red Mile Raceway. The pacing equivalents are the Cane Futurity (Yonkers), the Little Brown Jug (Delaware, Ohio), and the Messenger Stakes (Roosevelt).

TECHNICAL INNOVATIONS

The bike-wheel racing sulky and the mobile starting gate are the two most important inventions in harness racing. The first was invented in 1892 and substantially reduced

HIGH-WHEEL SULKY

This print of the trotter mare Sunol was made in 1891, well before the introduction of the light bicycle-wheel modern sulky. The mare is wearing a very light harness, and is without protective boots.

racing times over the mile. It was improved in the mid-1970s by an engineer called Joe King, who made it out of steel instead of wood, and straightened and shortened the shafts. It resulted in a rise in the number of recorded two-minute miles – from 685 in 1974 to 1,849 in 1976.

The mobile starting gate first appeared in 1946 at the Roosevelt Raceway. The gate ensures a fair start and is made up of a pair of retractable wings set on a truck. The truck, with the wings extended the full width of the track, drives in front of the horses up to the starting line. Then it accelerates, closes the wings and pulls away, leaving the track open to the horses.

EUROPE

In Europe, harness racing is more popular than flat-racing. In Italy more trotting horses are bred than Thoroughbreds, and in France the sport is very highly organized. The *Hippodrome de Vincennes,*

PACERS

Standardbred pacers racing at the Red Mile Raceway, Lexington, Kentucky, wear hobbles to prevent them from breaking their gait. Most horses wear sheepskin nosebands, known as "shadow rolls", to limit vision and to keep them from shying at shadows.

SLEIGH SULKY

At St Moritz in Switzerland the racing sulky is a lightweight sleigh. The majority of races are for conventional trotters. Although diagonal-gaited horses are numerous in mainland Europe, elsewhere the pacer is preferred.

France's most important track, stages the *Prix de Cornulier*, the premier ridden trotting race in France, and the *Prix d'Amerique*, the driven equivalent of flat-racing's *Prix de l'Arc de Triomphe*. Vincennes stages 1,000 races a year, and is unique in having a downhill start and a long, demanding uphill finish.

AUSTRALASIA

In Australia and New Zealand trotting is virtually a national pastime. New Zealand produced the famous Standardbred gelding, Cardigan Bay, who was foaled in 1956 at the Matura Stud, Southland. He raced successfully in both the US and Australasia. At home, in New Zealand, he paced the mile (1.6 km) in 1 minute 16.3 seconds. He won 80 races in Australia, New Zealand, and the US, held two world records, and was the first Standardbred to win $1m, and be commemorated on a stamp.

AMERICAN STANDARDBRED

THE AMERICAN STANDARDBRED is the world's foremost harness racer, and in its own country it is as valuable as a top-class Thoroughbred. In the US, harness racing or trotting is second only to Thoroughbred flat racing in popularity, while in many European countries, and certainly in Russia, harness racing is even more popular than Thoroughbred racing. (In Italy it is likely that more trotters are bred than Thoroughbreds.) The term Standardbred was first used in 1879 and derives from the early practice of establishing a speed standard as a requirement for entry into the Register. The standard, which was originally 3 minutes, was later set at 2 minutes 30 seconds for conventional trotters over the mile (1.6 km) and 2 minutes 25 seconds for pacers. Today, speeds of less than 2 minutes over the mile are commonplace.

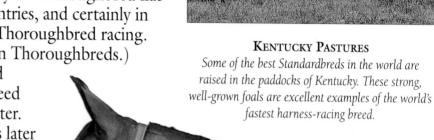

KENTUCKY PASTURES
Some of the best Standardbreds in the world are raised in the paddocks of Kentucky. These strong, well-grown foals are excellent examples of the world's fastest harness-racing breed.

HISTORY

The Standardbred was founded in the late 18th century on an English Thoroughbred called Messenger, and since then has contributed materially to most of the European trotting breeds. Messenger, the son of Mambrino out of an unnamed mare by Turf, was imported into the US in 1788, having raced successfully on the flat in England. Like all early Thoroughbreds, he also had trotting connections with the old Norfolk Roadster (see pp.122–23). Messenger's pedigree, which appears in

HEAD
The head is plain but not unattractive. It is, however, heavier and less refined than that of the Thoroughbred.

Vol. 1 of the *General Stud Book* (the UK Thoroughbred stud book) includes crosses to all three of the Arab foundation sires of the Thoroughbred, particularly the Godolphin (see pp.120–21). Messenger spent 20 years at stud in Pennsylvania, New York, and New Jersey. He died in 1808 (the year in which Vol. 1 of the *GSB* was published) at the age of 28 and was buried on Long Island.

Messenger never actually raced in harness but his sire Mambrino, the grandson of Sampson by Blaze (the patriarchal sire of trotters), did trot, and his owner, Lord Grosvenor, once made a wager of 1,000 sovereigns that the horse could "trot 14 miles [24.4 km] to the hour".

Messenger was bred to all sorts of mares, including Morgans (see pp.232–33) and Canadian and Narragansett Pacers (see p.234). These last two breeds, which now no longer exist, contained much blood from "ambling" horses. This came from English sources as well as from the strain

ORIGINS

THE AMERICAN STANDARDBRED was first established in the eastern states of the US. The breed's founder, Messenger, by Mambrino, was an early Thoroughbred imported in 1788. He spent 20 years at stud in Pennsylvania, New York, and New Jersey, dying on Long Island in 1808. Standardbreds are now raised in various parts of the US. They are also bred and used for crossing in other harness-racing countries, including Australia and New Zealand, and have up-graded European breeds.

LIMBS
The limbs have strong forearms and are in all respects iron-hard to withstand the effects of racing at speed.

FEET
Good, absolutely sound feet and a perfectly straight action are essential requirements.

of Spanish Jennets that survived from the 16th-century Spanish imports introduced by the conquistadores (see pp.216–17). It was these Spanish Jennets that introduced the lateral pacing gait (moving the legs in lateral pairs rather than diagonal ones) that is now favoured in American harness racing (see pp.338–39) where pacers outnumber trotters by four to one. In Europe diagonal trotters still outnumber pacers in a number of countries.

Two other important bloodlines that feature in the Standardbred are the Morgan horse, through its founder Figure, later called Justin Morgan, and the lesser known Clays, another early trotting strain, descended from a Barb stallion imported from Tripoli in 1820.

Nonetheless, it was the Thoroughbred Messenger, whose progeny were lower in action than the Morgan, moving from the shoulder with less knee lift, and possessed of greater courage than the Clays, who stamped his influence overwhelmingly on the breed through his closely in-bred descendant Hambletonian 10 (Rysdyk's Hambletonian).

HAMBLETONIAN

Foaled in 1849, Hambletonian sired no fewer than 1,335 offspring between 1851 and 1875 and is rightly regarded as the foundation sire of the modern Standardbred. Hambletonian never raced, although he was

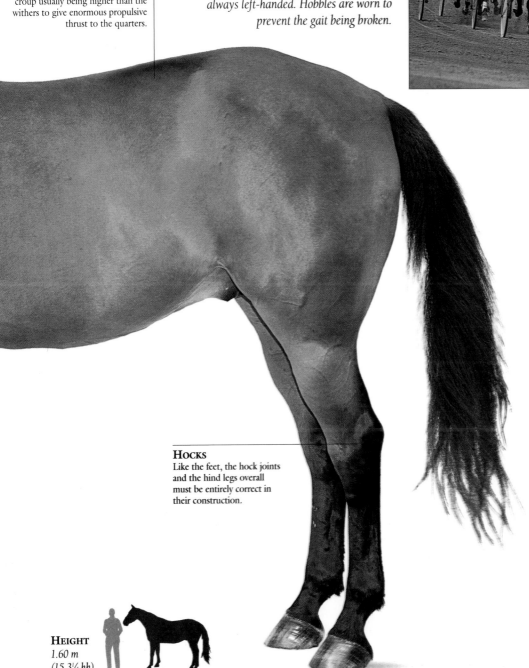

BODY
The body is long and low but is still powerful and deep through the girth. The overall build is powerful, the croup usually being higher than the withers to give enormous propulsive thrust to the quarters.

IN ACTION
Standardbred harness racers compete at the famous Red Mile Raceway in Lexington, Kentucky. The Standardbred races at the lateral pacing gait rather than the conventional diagonal trot and tracks are always left-handed. Hobbles are worn to prevent the gait being broken.

said to have trotted a trial mile (1.6 km) in 2 minutes 48.5 seconds. Although like most modern Standardbreds he was not very refined when compared with the Thoroughbred, he was powerfully built. When mature, he measured 1.55 m (15.1¼ hh) at the wither and 1.60 m (15.3¼ hh) at the croup; his build thus allowed for enormous thrust from the quarters. Hambletonian's dam, the Charles Kent mare (it then being a usual practice to name a horse after its owner), was as closely in-bred to Messenger as Hambletonian. She inherited trotting ability from her sire, Bellfounder, a direct descendant of the renowned Norfolk Trotter, Old Shales. Hambletonian was a prolific sire of trotters and, just as importantly, of trotting sires.

One outstanding son of his was Dexter who, in the 1860s, trotted the mile (1.6 km) in a record 2 minutes 17.25 seconds. He might have improved on this had he not been bought for $25,000 by Robert Bonner, a great enthusiast, who for moral reasons did not race or bet, driving his horses solely for pleasure. The first sub-two-minute miler was a pacer called Star Pointer, who clocked 1:59.25 at Readville, Massachusetts in 1897.

Nearly all Standardbreds descend from Hambletonian through his sons George Wilkes (foaled 1856), Dictator (foaled 1863), Happy Medium (foaled 1863), and Electioneer (foaled 1868).

HOCKS
Like the feet, the hock joints and the hind legs overall must be entirely correct in their construction.

HEIGHT
1.60 m
(15.3¼ hh)

ORLOV TROTTER

EVEN TODAY, THE FORMER USSR breeds huge numbers of horses for agriculture and transport, and in the remote eastern provinces horses are as much part of the economy as they were in the early days of the Mongol tribes. There are, however, many breeds that were developed at studs for specific purposes and to suit the requirements of the wealthy elite. The Orlov Trotter, one of the oldest and most popular, was developed in the 18th century both as a smart carriage horse and for racing.

FOUNDING THE BREED

The Orlov Trotter was developed by Count Alexis Grigorievitch Orlov (1737–1808). He began his work some time after 1780, when he crossed the white Arab stallion Smetanka, which he obtained from the Sultan of Turkey, with the best Danish, Dutch, Mecklenburg, and Arab mares at his Orlov Stud outside Moscow. In 1788 he transferred his operations to his newly formed Khrenov Stud in the province of Voronezh, where the evolution of the breed was continued with the expert assistance of his manager, V.I. Shishkin. It soon became clear that the best results were obtained by using the Arab on Danish and Dutch mares. It was this combination that produced the Orlov Trotter's foundation sire, the grey Bars I, born in 1784. He was the grandson of Smetanka and son of Polkan I (whose dam was Danish), who was one of the five offspring that Smetanka produced in his

ELEGANT TROTTER
At its best, the Orlov Trotter is an elegant, free-moving horse. It still holds its own in the raceway but is used increasingly to up-grade other breeds.

short stud career. When Polkan was mated with Hartsdraver, a big Dutch mare with substantial bone and substance who moved with the necessary freedom and energy at the trot, Bars I was the result.

Bars I served mares of the breeds from which he himself derived: Arabs, Dutch, and Danish, as well as some Arab/Mecklenburg crosses. To fix the desired type, in-breeding to Bars I and his sons was then practised extensively. All pure-bred Orlovs to the present time show a strong Bars connection.

SPORT AND CROSS-BREEDING

Systematic training and graded trotting race programmes, held in Moscow from 1834, encouraged improvements and increased the speeds attained, although in this respect the Orlov could never approach the American Standardbred (see pp.340–41). It was for this reason that the faster Russian Trotter (see pp.344–45) evolved as a result of crossing Standardbreds with Orlovs. Indeed, between 1890 and 1917, 156 Standardbred stallions and 220 mares were imported. The supply stopped during the First World War and the cross-breds were increasingly interbred with back-crosses to the Orlov. In the 1930s more use was made of the

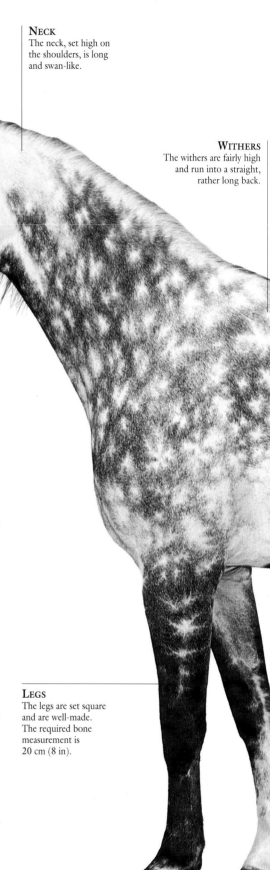

NECK
The neck, set high on the shoulders, is long and swan-like.

WITHERS
The withers are fairly high and run into a straight, rather long back.

LEGS
The legs are set square and are well-made. The required bone measurement is 20 cm (8 in).

Standardbred/Orlov cross, and in 1949 the Russian Trotter was recognized as a breed, although it by no means ousted the traditional and well-established Orlov.

THE MODERN ORLOV

The Orlov is hardly a perfect conformational specimen. Indeed, it can be a bit hairy about the heels (i.e. common in appearance) but it is reasonably large, standing 1.63 m (16 hh), and is proportionate in its outline. The head, though small, tends to be plain and somewhat coarse, and the less well-made types can be rather long in the leg with insufficient depth of girth. They are sometimes prone to

ORLOV TROIKA
These heavier Orlovs are harnessed in troika fashion with three horses abreast. The centre horse trots, while the outspanners must canter to keep pace.

tendon weaknesses, a legacy of the later over-use of Dutch mares. The type varies according to the stud at which the animals are bred, but the best and most characteristic are those bred at Khrenov. Others, such as those bred at Perm in the Urals, are more common in appearance, while both the Tula and Dubrov types are nearer to the heavier harness conformation than to that of a harness racer. They are, nonetheless, useful crosses which can be used to improve a wide variety of stock, a purpose that has always been part of the Orlov breeding policy.

The present-day Orlov is still being improved as a racing trotter. Emphasis is placed on preserving height, elegant conformation within a powerful but light frame, and strong tendons, as well as on improving the performance. However, in past years the objective has been increasingly to use the Orlov to up-grade other breeds. In this role the Orlov has exerted a powerful influence on Russian breeding, and has contributed to the evolution of the Don, the Tersk, and the Russian Trotter (see pp.80–81, pp.88–89, and pp.344–45), and some heavy breeds.

In pre-revolutionary Russia the Orlov was bred at perhaps as many as 3,000 stud farms, and it is probable that today there are still some 30,000 pure-breds in the countries that make up the former USSR.

TAIL
The tail is set well-up in somewhat short-crouped but muscular quarters. In movement it is carried high.

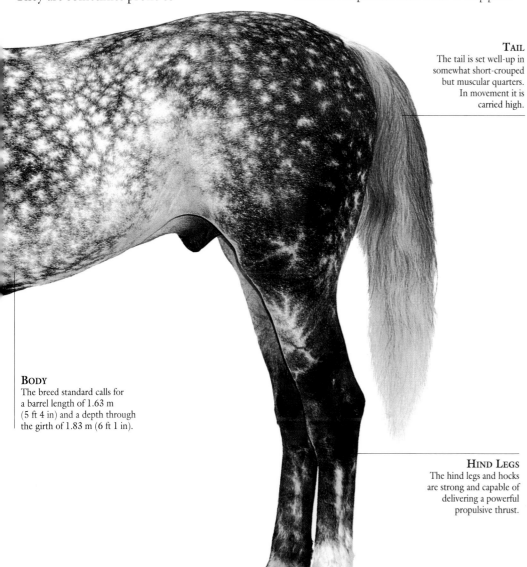

BODY
The breed standard calls for a barrel length of 1.63 m (5 ft 4 in) and a depth through the girth of 1.83 m (6 ft 1 in).

HIND LEGS
The hind legs and hocks are strong and capable of delivering a powerful propulsive thrust.

ORIGINS

THE EVOLUTION of the new Orlov breed began in earnest in 1788 when Count Alexis Orlov concentrated his breeding operation at his new Khrenov Stud in the province of Voronezh. The best of the modern Orlovs are still bred at Khrenov. A more common animal is bred at Perm in the Urals and heavier types are bred at Tula and Dubrov. Today, there are probably as many as 30,000 Orlovs in Russia and its former republics and Orlov Trotters are still raced.

HEIGHT
1.63 m (16 hh)

RUSSIAN TROTTER

HARNESS-RACING HORSES have been bred with enthusiasm in Russia ever since the Orlov Stud began to develop the Orlov Trotter (see pp.342–43) in the 18th century. Since then, trotting has become one of the most popular equestrian sports of the former USSR. The Russian Trotter is far more recent, and was not recognized as a breed until 1949. More common in appearance than the Orlov, it is, nonetheless, a good performer and fast enough to compete at international level. It was created by crossing the Orlov and the American Standardbred (see pp.340–41).

THE AMERICAN INFLUENCE

By the second half of the 19th century the American Standardbred had established its superiority over all the other trotting breeds. To compete internationally with any hope of success it was necessary for Russian breeders to improve the performance of the out-classed Orlov dramatically, while still retaining some of its best characteristics.

The obvious solution was to use the best of the Orlov stock as a base and to cross it with imported American Standardbreds. In consequence, some 156 stallions and 220 Standardbred mares were imported to Russia between 1890 and the beginning of the First World War. Among these were some high-quality horses, including General Forrest who trotted the mile (1.6 km) in 2 minutes 8 seconds, Bob Douglas who trotted it in 2 minutes 4 seconds, and the world record holder of the time, Cresceus, who had trotted it in 2 minutes 2 seconds. Crossings between selected Orlov stock and some of these horses, even though only half-a-dozen or so produced offspring of any prominence, resulted in animals that were faster, but smaller and less elegant than the Orlov. Furthermore, these horses were not of a type suitable for up-grading agricultural horses, a role in which the Orlov was particularly successful. A programme was therefore introduced with the object not only of continuing to increase the trotting speed but also of improving the size and conformation.

FIXING THE TYPE

The First World War prevented further American imports, but while the existing imported stock continued to be used, a programme of interbreeding the cross-breds was initiated, which sometimes employed the sound genetic practice of crossing back to the old Orlov. In 1928 an average Russian

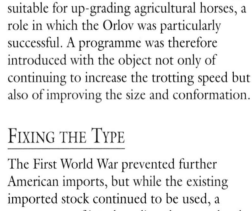

HEAD
The head is plain, straight in the profile, and broad across the forehead with the eyes set well to the outside. There is some thickness through the jowl.

SHOULDERS
These typical trotting shoulders show some wither development and corresponding depth of girth in a light frame.

LEGS
The legs are muscular but by no means exemplary. The breed standard calls for 19.9 cm (7¾ in) of bone below the knee, but the cannons are noticeably long and the pasterns are upright.

PERFORMANCE
The Russian Trotter races at the conventional diagonal trotting gait. It is considered a useful but not outstanding performer in relation to other breeds. However, it does mature quickly, even though the optimum trotting speeds are not attained until the horse has reached five or even six years old.

Trotter mare still stood not much more than 1.55 m (15.1 hh), with a girth measurement of 1.75 m (5 ft 9 in), and had a bone measurement below the knee of 19 cm (7½ in). By the early 1930s the carefully conceived programme had increased the height and improved the frame, body measurements, and overall conformation. It had also, in part, regained something of the old Orlov hardiness of constitution.

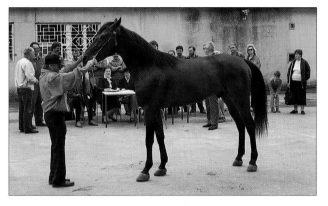

THE MODERN BREED

As with all the officially recognized breeds of the former USSR, stringent breed standards were imposed, with much emphasis given to body measurements. The modern standard calls for a height of 1.63 m (16 hh) for stallions and 1.60 m (15.3 hh) for mares. The barrel length is fixed at 1.63 m (5 ft 4 in), and the depth of girth is set at 1.84 m (6 ft 1 in) for a stallion and a little less for mares. A bone measurement of 19.9 cm (7¾ in) is required below the knee.

Initially, and for some years after the breeding programme had been established, efforts were concentrated on the production of three distinct types, "thick", "medium", and "sporting", a practice that may have detracted from the main purpose, which was to perfect a racing trotter. The "thick" type had the proportions of a heavy horse. It was big-bodied, somewhat long in the back, and stood on short, generally strong legs, which had good bone. However, the outcrosses to heavier farm horses that must have been made to produce such a horse seem to have given the animal a sounder constitution than the trotting or "sporting" type, which for some years was less robust than the old Orlov breed. This heavy Trotter would have been the equivalent of the 19th-century European coach or heavy gun horses. The "medium" type was lighter, and was an active, light agricultural horse of some substance.

The build of the "sporting" type, the modern Russian Trotter, is light but has pronounced muscular development and fairly hard, clean limbs. The feet are sound and strong, and the cannons are short with better ligaments and tendons than before.

Failings in conformation are concerned with occasional instances of sickle- or cow-hocks, over-sloped croups, and sometimes a shortening of the body length, which acts against the trotting action.

FEET
The feet are usually very sound and able to sustain concussion.

HEIGHT
1.60–1.63 m
(15.3–16 hh)

GRADING
Russian Trotters are graded to strict standards relating to type and conformation, and must meet the measurements stipulated in the breed standard in regard to bone and proportion. The Trotters are also performance tested on the raceway.

The predominant colour is bay, although black, chestnut, and grey also occur. The breed is quick to mature, reaching its full height at four years old. However, maximum trotting speeds are rarely attained by horses under the age of five or six. The action is low and surprisingly long, but because of the strong Standardbred influence there is a tendency in some strains to pace rather than to use the diagonal gait. Sub-two-minute miles (1600 m) are not unknown, and the Trotter is now significantly faster than the average Orlov.

The breed is kept pure, although occasional exceptions have been made to introduce the blood of other trotting strains. In the late 1970s and early 1980s the popularity of the Russian Trotter, and its consequent export potential, made it necessary to import more American Standardbreds to further improve the speed of the Russian horses. Among trotting breeds, the Russian has to be rated as a useful performer of moderate but not outstanding ability, but one well-suited to the harness-racing sport in its own country.

ORIGINS

THE RUSSIAN TROTTER is bred principally in the Moscow area, also the home of Moscow's most important raceway, the Moscow Hippodrome. The two constituent elements in the creation of the breed were the Orlov, Russia's traditional harness racer, and the imported American Standardbred, both of which were easily available in and around the harness-racing centre and its facilities for performance testing. Considerations of climate have little bearing on the breed.

Caprilli & the Forward Seat

A watershed in the development of riding

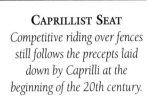

CAPRILLIST SEAT
Competitive riding over fences still follows the precepts laid down by Caprilli at the beginning of the 20th century.

THE TEACHINGS of Captain Federico Caprilli (1868–1907) represent a landmark in equestrian history, dividing one era of horsemanship from the next. Quite rightly, he is regarded as the greatest influence in the development of modern active, outdoor riding. When he was teaching at the Italian cavalry schools of Tor di Quinto and Pinerolo, where he became a chief instructor, riding in Europe was dominated by military practice based on classical precepts, which were increasingly irrelevant on a battlefield that was dominated by the huge developments in fire-power. Caprilli appreciated that in such a situation the knee-to-knee, set-piece charge of squadrons in line was no longer an option and that the role of cavalry was confined largely to aggressive reconnaissance, carried out by formations that could ride across country swiftly, negotiating whatever natural obstacles lay in their path. To this end he trained horses and riders over the sort of country in which they might be called upon to operate. Instead of the dominated, collected school horse, he asked for unfettered extension, teaching his riders to conform to the horse's natural outline and to ride with a shortened stirrup, perching with their bodies forward so that the weight was carried as far over the horse's advancing centre of balance as possible, where it would be the least encumbrance to free movement. The riders sat forward over every type of fence, even when riding up and down fearsome inclines. In essence they were using the same seat as that adopted by generations of steppe nomads and eastern horsemen. As a result of Caprilli's teaching, the Italians became pre-eminent in international jumping competitions and the basis of his system was adopted by cavalry schools worldwide. Since his death, horsemen have blended the classical precepts with those of "*il sistema*", but the world continues to sit forward over its fences in the Caprilli manner.

AHEAD OF HIS TIME
This 17th-century painting by the Dutch painter Rembrandt shows a Polish light cavalryman employing the forward seat, which was advocated by Caprilli two centuries later.

Seat Analysis

Eadweard Muybridge's photographic sequence shows the jumping seat adopted at the end of the 19th century, before the acceptance of the Caprilli system. Although the bareback rider does not interfere with the horse's mouth, his weight is carried out of balance.

"Il Sistema"

This is a modern horseman demonstrating Caprilli's sistema almost to perfection. The weight is positioned over the advancing centre of gravity, the hand follows the mouth, and the leg position ensures security. In essence, the rider conforms to the natural outline and movement of the horse.

THE EQUESTRIAN OLYMPICS

BARON DE COUBERTIN

HELD AT OLYMPIA on the Peleponnesus in the year 776 BC, the first-ever Olympic Games formed part of a religious festival honouring, among other deities, the fertility goddess Rhea, mother of Zeus. Ironically, all married women were barred from attending, an example of the kind of discrimination that was to persist to within half a century of the Millennium. Horse sports, in the form of chariot racing, were introduced at the 25th Olympiad which took place in 680 BC. The Games were held at intervals of four years until AD 393 when they were banned by the Christian Emperor of Rome, Theodosius I. The modern Olympics were revived by Baron Pierre de Coubertin in 1896 and were held, appropriately, in Greece. The first mounted events were held at the 1912 Stockholm Games.

ANCIENT HEROES

Among the most notable competitors of the ancient Games was Alcibiades of Athens, a man of enormous wealth who entered no less than seven four-in-hand teams for the Games of 416 BC. Hieron, King of Syracuse, was the winner in 476, 472, and 468 BC, while the Emperor Nero drove a 10-horse chariot to take the victor's wreath in AD 67. In fact, he contrived to overturn his team but, as the ruler of the known world, and, one presumes, because of his reputation, he was still proclaimed the winner!

Ridden races, which did not enjoy the same social acceptance as chariot racing, were held in 647 BC, but from 256 BC, when stallions were first raced, the events began to gain in prestige and popularity. The "medallists" of the Ancient Games were honoured with the traditional olive wreath, although, in fact, these were awarded to the owners, the drivers receiving a more humble headband of sheep's wool.

The equine hero, or rather heroine (for it was a mare), of the ancient Olympics was without doubt the horse belonging to Pheidolas of Corinth. Losing her rider, she ran on to pass the post first and then of her own accord took up the winner's position in front of the judges. She was awarded the race and honoured by having her statue placed alongside those of her peers in the Sacred Grove.

The mare may be considered to have struck the first much-needed blow for female emancipation in the Olympics, which for centuries were dominated by male participation. For instance, it was not until 1928 that track and field events for women were included in the modern Olympics, and, following the collapse of several runners, the 800 m event was discontinued until 1964. Indeed, up until 1952, no women competed in the equestrian events, but today they compete on equal terms with the men and in almost equal numbers.

THE MODERN GAMES

The modern Games of 1896 were held in Athens. These Games marked the appearance of the Olympic logo, which has been used ever since. 1896 was also the date when the Olympic motto, *Citius, Altius, Fortius* was first coined. It refers respectively to the throwing, jumping, and running events – "Further, Higher, Stronger".

The inclusion of the horse events in the Games at Stockholm in 1912 was due almost entirely to the efforts of Count Clarence von Rosen, Master of Horse to the King of Sweden. Stockholm was the first occasion the modern events of dressage, showjumping, and the three-day event

THE SIGNIFICANCE OF THE RINGS
The Olympic rings represent the five continents – every national flag contains at least one Olympic colour. The logo was first used in 1896.

OLYMPIC CHARIOTS
The first Olympic horse sports were for chariot teams usually of four horses harnessed abreast. However, Nero won the event in AD 67 with a ten-horse team.

(horse trials) were staged in recognizable form, although there were obvious differences, notably in content and in the scoring methods.

The three-day event, then known as "The Military", comprised a 53-km (33-mile) long distance ride, a 3.2-km (2-mile) steeplechase, showjumping, and finally a dressage test – the latter a reversal of the modern order, in which the dressage phase opens the competition. Seven teams of serving officers on military horses competed, with the host nation taking the team and individual gold medals, the latter being won by Lieutenant Norlander riding a British Thoroughbred. Indeed, 15 of the 31 horses competing were British bred. Sweden also won the team showjumping. There was no team dressage but, once more, it was Sweden who won the individual gold. In fact, in the first Games after the First World War, at Antwerp in 1920, Sweden won all three individual dressage medals as well as taking the team golds again in showjumping and the three-day event.

The three-day event in its present form was first held in 1928, when team dressage was also introduced. America won its first three-day-event team gold at Los Angeles in 1932, when no team completed the showjumping course but the individual gold went to the Japanese entry, Lieutenant Baron Takeichi. Clarence von Rosen, son of the horse Games' instigator, won bronze.

A far cry from the Olympic ideal was Hitler's 1936 Games in Berlin. They were the biggest, the most nationalistic, and the most ominous ever staged. They were also a watershed in the Olympic equestrian events. Germany swept the board in all three disciplines with what are still acknowledged as the finest teams in he history of equestrian competition.

Britain, despite the pond fence into deep water that accounted for 28 of the entry of 46, gained a team bronze in the three-day event and became established as a force in international competition.

In 1948, the first of the post-war Olympics, Britain, led by Lieutenant Colonel Harry Llewellyn, squeezed another bronze in the showjumping, while the Americans won the three-day event.

MEDALS FOR WOMEN

In 1952, civilians at last took over from the military and under Llewellyn, riding the legendary Foxhunter, Britain won the showjumping gold. The team made history again in 1956 when Pat Smythe became the first woman to share a team medal (a bronze) at Stockholm. A young Belgian woman, Brigitte Schockaert, also competed in these Games. The first woman to win an individual jumping medal was Marion Coakes of Britain who rode the pony-size Stroller to win the silver at Mexico in 1968, the same year that the British again made history by including another woman, Jane Bullen, with a similarly diminutive mount, Our Nobby, in the gold-medal event team.

THE FIRST LADY
Pat Smythe pioneered female participation in Olympic jumping when she became the first woman in a medal-winning team at Stockholm in 1956.

The first women to win team golds for showjumping were Leslie Burr and Melanie Smith of the 1984 US team at Los Angeles.

THE FUTURE

While both showjumping and dressage are firmly established disciplines that can be incorporated at the centre of an Olympic complex without difficulty, that is not the case with the three-day-event competitions. The very nature of the sport and the disproportionately large area that is needed to stage the event and provide stabling facilities, etc., create organizational problems that are not present in other disciplines. The very complexity of the competition and the number of persons involved in running it safely and successfully are also important considerations, particularly for those countries that do not have a tradition of cross-country riding.

The introduction of a new, shortened format for the three-day event (see p.360) is a serious attempt to respond to those logistical problems.

PURE GOLD
David O'Connnor won the individual gold medal for the US at the Sydney Olympics in 2000 with a masterly performance on the highly talented Thoroughbred Custom Made.

SHOWJUMPING: THE HISTORY

INDIAN ARMY
SHOWJUMPER

ALL OF THE EQUESTRIAN sporting disciplines have their origin in the practices of war. They began as essential training exercises for cavalry, with the initial emphasis on cross-country riding. Jumping training was mentioned in the French Cavalry manual as early as 1788 but the first definitive account of competitive arena jumping records the "leaping" competitions staged by the Royal Dublin Society at Leinster Lawn, Dublin, in 1864. There was a High Jump, which remained a feature of the Dublin Horse Show until the late 1950s, and a Wide Leap. Both were intended as practical tests for hunters, the production of which was very much a thriving Irish industry. Another notable inclusion were the famous Irish Bank obstacles, which, though now of less importance, are still retained in the main ring at Dublin.

THE FORWARD SYSTEM

The most significant development not only in showjumping but also in general equestrian theory and practice was the forward system of riding introduced by Captain Federico Caprilli (see pp.346–47) as Chief Instructor at the Italian Cavalry School of Pinerolo. The theory has not survived in its entirety, but the world still sits over its fences in pretty much the same manner as that prescribed by Caprilli. The system was not intended specifically for showring jumping but such was the outstanding success of the early Italian teams that, by the time of Caprilli's death in 1907, it had been officially adopted by the Italian cavalry and was being introduced into the military schools of Europe and the Americas by officers who had attended the courses at Pinerolo.

THE HIGH JUMP

From the 1880s showjumping was becoming established as a sport, albeit with some very haphazard rules.

The US held its first recorded jumping competition in 1883 at the first National Horse Show in Madison Square Garden, and it included a high jump. It is likely, however, that competitions were held in the US previous to that date, since American hunter classes were at that time being required to jump in the ring, as they are today. Subsequently, it was customary to enter hunters in both jumping and hunter classes.

The National's high jump was won in 1883 with a leap of 1.9 m (6 ft) and in the following year a hunter, Leo, jumped 2 m (6 ft 6 in). Four years later a 1.50 m (14.2½ hh) pony mare, owned by George Pepper cleared 2.1 m (6 ft 10 in) and in 1901 S. S. Howland's Ontario set a record at 2.2 m (7 ft 1 in). A further, though unratified, record was set in 1902 in Richmond, Virginia, when the Thoroughbred mare Heatherbloom, owned by Howard Willett and

GERMAN ACE
Hans Günter Winkler of Germany won five Olympic Gold medals in his 30-year career. Here, he is riding his famous Hanoverian mare, Halla.

PAU BANK
This French magazine cover of 1905 shows a horse and rider negotiating a bank obstacle typical of the Pau country in France.

ridden by Dick Donnelly, jumped 2.5 m (8 ft 2 in). To date, that record has never been exceeded.

Additional impetus to international competition was given by the inauguration of the International (later the Royal International) Horse Show held at Olympia, London, in 1907 under the presidency of the legendary Earl of Lonsdale, the "Yellow Earl", whose personality was to dominate the Show for 20 years. It was a brilliant affair, recognized subsequently as a feature of the London "season", and it set a pattern for all future international events.

In 1909, the first Nations Cup, for the King Edward VII Gold Cup, was staged at Olympia and was open to teams of three military riders. Indeed, jumping generally was dominated by the military up to the Second World War.

The first Cup was won by the French team, who won it again in 1911, but the Russian team achieved a remarkable hat-trick of wins between 1912 and 1914, winning the Cup outright. After the Revolution, the original Cup disappeared and was never seen again. It was replaced in 1920 by the Prince of Wales Cup, which is still competed for as Britain's Nations Cup.

Courses, however, even up to the Second World War, were rudimentary in comparison with the brilliantly designed and meticulous tracks built today. There were also enormous variations in the rules between competing nations.

For many years, riding style was a major consideration in the judging of a competition. In the 1911 Nations Cup, Holland and Canada tied for first place, but the coveted first prize was awarded to the Dutch who were deemed by the judges to have ridden in better style throughout the race.

Until after the Second World War and the formation of standardized international rules by the FEI, the International Equestrian Federation that was founded in 1921, national associations in both the US and UK persisted in using their own rules. These included the use of slats (called slip fillets in the US) laid on the top of fences,

RUSSIAN TEAM
The Russian team won the King Edward VII Gold Cup at Olympia outright after achieving a remarkable hat-trick of wins between 1912 and 1914.

FOXHUNTER
Col. Sir Harry Llewellyn and Foxhunter led the British team to a bronze medal at the 1948 London Olympics and gold at Helsinki in 1952.

with marks being deducted for their dislodgement. The arcane rules and the absence of timing (competitors could take as long as they liked and could even circle in front of a fence to find the right approach) were largely responsible for the sport's decline in Great Britain and, prior to the Second World War, many county shows did not even include jumping competitions.

NEW RULES

Today's rules are easy to follow by competitor and spectator alike. Four faults are given for a knockdown; three for the first refusal; six for the second, and elimination for the third. Eight faults are incurred for a fall of horse and/or rider. In timed jump-offs or speed competitions, faults are expressed in seconds.

LONDON'S INTERNATIONAL
A French officer jumping at the International Horse Show at Olympia, which was first held in 1907 under the presidency of the charismatic Lord Lonsdale. It was to become a spectacular feature of the London "season".

MODERN SHOWJUMPING

The calendar of jumping fixtures, both national and international, extends over the whole year, unlike horse trials, for instance, which are necessarily held outdoors in the spring and summer months. The national federations of countries participating in the sport are affiliated to the world governing body, the International Equestrian Federation (FEI), and operate under its rules. The variety of classes is very large but, in all competitions, time is a deciding factor either in a jump-off or in speed events "against the clock". While all classes impose a time limit for the completion of the course, this is hardly a factor in the Puissance test, in which horses jump a limited number of big fences, usually ending, after jump-offs, in a high wall obstacle and one wide spread

POSING PROBLEMS

Problems are created in a course by the use of a number of combination and related fences. Combinations may be "doubles", incorporating two elements, or "trebles", which have three. The distances between the fences are based on the length of an average canter stride of 3.7 m (12 ft) but will vary according to the structure of the fences, i.e. whether upright or spread. Related fences are those placed between 12 m (40 ft) and 24 m (80 ft) apart and cause their own problems in respect of the rider's ability to adjust the length of the stride.

TYPES OF FENCES

An "upright" fence is one in which all the elements are in the same vertical plane, as they are in fences constructed of planks or poles. Walls and gates are all termed "upright". (A "ground-line" provided by a pole placed a little in advance of the fence makes it easier for the horse to judge his take-off point; conversely, the absence of a ground-line increases the difficulty.)

Two or more uprights can be combined to form a "spread" fence. The easiest of the spread fences is the "staircase" – a triple bar of ascending heights.

THE PUISSANCE WALL
The wall may be as high as 2.1 m (7 ft) and calls for a brave horse and a bold rider. This is the modern version of the old High Jump.

A "true parallel" is a spread fence made up of two parts of equal height, and is more difficult than a parallel fence in which the first element is set lower than the second. When a "brush" fence is placed between the two elements of a parallel it becomes an "oxer" and is more challenging because of the false ground-line it creates. The most usual form is a "reversed oxer", in which a brush fence is set in front and behind a central set

TRUE PARALLEL
A brilliant shot of horse and rider clearing a big parallel in style – the horse jumping both high and wide with great athleticism.

of higher poles. Less common is the "pyramid" fence, in which the first and last elements are of the same height but lower than the central pole. It can, however, be jumped from both directions.

PRINCIPAL COMPETITIONS

The international competitions are the Olympic Games, held every four years and comprised of an individual competition and the Nations Cup, a team event; the World Games, held in the even year between one Olympics and the next; and the European Championships, Pan-American Games, etc., held every two years in the year between the Olympics and the World Championships.

THE DERBIES

The Derbies originated with the Hamburg event held in 1920 and are now held at arenas in Spain, Ireland, the US, and Portugal, as well as being a principal feature at the UK's All-England Arena at Hickstead. These are unusual competitions taking place over a long course, 1,300 m (1,420 yd), i.e. 500 m (547 yd) longer than the Olympic course. They include cross-country type obstacles such as banks (very big ones) and ditches, and they put a premium on stamina as well as speed and jumping ability

DISTANCES

The following table is a guide to the "easy" distance between elements of a combination fence. In international competitions additional difficulty is imposed by increasing the distances between elements so as to produce half-strides that cause the horse to either shorten or lengthen.

Upright to Upright
7.3 m (24 ft) = One non-jumping stride
10–10.7 m (33–35 ft) = Two non-jumping strides

Upright to Spread
7 m (23 ft) = One non-jumping stride
9.8–10.4 m (32–34 ft) = Two non-jumping strides

Spread to Upright
7.6 m (25 ft) = One non-jumping stride
10.7–11.2 m (35–37 ft) = Two non-jumping strides

Spread to Spread
7.3 m (24 ft = One non-jumping stride
10-10.7m (33-35ft) = Two non-jumping strides

THE BANK
A British rider negotiates the famous Hickstead Bank in perfect form. Straightness in the descent is crucial to a successful conclusion.

PERFECT STYLE
Mark Todd, arguably the finest event rider of the 1990s, is also an accomplished showjumper. His horse in this picture, Kleenex Double Take, is jumping with great scope and confidence and in perfect style, with forelegs and hind legs tucked up.

SARDINIAN & SALERNO

WITH THE EXCEPTION OF ITS superlative Thoroughbreds, Italy is not noted for its riding horse breeds. However, in recent years much use has been made of the Thoroughbred cross to improve the Salerno, which has become a very good horse with ample potential for competition. The less well-known Sardinian has suffered from a lack of systematic breeding, but is interesting for being the product of traditional crosses between Barb, Arab, and Spanish stock.

NECK
The light, elegant neck arches gracefully, joining smoothly with an attractive, intelligent head.

HEIGHT OF SARDINIAN
1.57 m
(15.2 hh)

THE SARDINIAN

For many centuries Sardinia imported a lot of horses, basing its island breed on crosses between Arabs and Barbs (see pp.64–67). A distinctive type began to appear in the 15th century, after Ferdinand of Spain (1452–1516) founded a stud of Spanish horses (now called Andalucian – see pp.108–9) near Abbasanta. The stud made stallions available to local breeders and other studs were subsequently established at Monte Minerva, Padromannu, and Mores. The horses produced became famous as tough, enduring saddle horses with great stamina. When Sardinia passed from Spain to the House of Savoy in 1720, horse breeding declined and it was not until 1908 that Arab horses were imported to improve the stock.

The best of the modern Sardinian horses are of pronounced eastern appearance, and have acceptable riding horse conformation.

It is claimed that a good Sardinian is bold, intelligent, and has great jumping talent. The main colours are bay and brown, and the horses stand at about 1.57 m (15.2 hh).

THE SALERNO

The Salerno originated in the 18th century in the Campania region of Italy, and is one of the most attractive of the Italian warmbloods, although it is now reduced in numbers. It evolved at the Persano Stud, which was founded by the Bourbon Charles III, King of Naples and then of Spain, in the first half of the 18th century. The horses bred at Persano, which were known as Persano Horses, were based on the Neapolitan, a horse bred near Sorrento and

POLICE HORSES
Thoroughbred outcrosses to the Salerno breed produced good-quality cavalry remounts, which are now used in mounted police formations. The horses are sensible, well-made, and noted as having above-average jumping ability.

SARDINIAN

Naples and full of Spanish and Barb blood. Although coarse in comparison with the Iberian horses it was regarded in Italy as one of the best school horses of its day and was much admired for its high, fiery action and exceptional strength of limb. These horses were crossed with the local horses of the Salerno and Ofanto valleys, and then Arab and Spanish imports were used to produce a distinctive, quality riding horse. The stud was closed after the Italian Republic was established in 1860. When breeding was revived in 1900 the old name lapsed and the breed was known increasingly as the Salerno. The introduction of Thoroughbred blood (see pp.120–21) improved the stock, and produced a good cavalry-type horse. It was bigger than before, attractive, had good action and conformation, and jumped well.

Some notable horses were produced at the Morese Stud, close to the original Persano Stud. These include two of the greatest Italian showjumpers, Merano and Posillipo, both ridden by the Italian ace Raimondo d'Inzeo. Merano and d'Inzeo won the World Championship in 1956, having been reserve to the German rider, Hans Winkler, in 1955. D'Inzeo was also riding Posillipo when he won the individual gold medal at the 1960 Olympics in Rome.

The Salerno now carries yet more Thoroughbred blood, and is even more refined. It has a good riding shoulder and the conformation of a quality horse with scope. In consequence the action is correspondingly free and athletic. No one colour predominates, and at over 1.63 m (16 hh) it is bigger than its predecessors.

HEIGHT OF SALERNO
Over 1.63 m (16 hh)

HEAD
The head is fine and shows a Spanish influence.

LEGS
The legs are well-shaped with fine joints.

SALERNO

ORIGINS

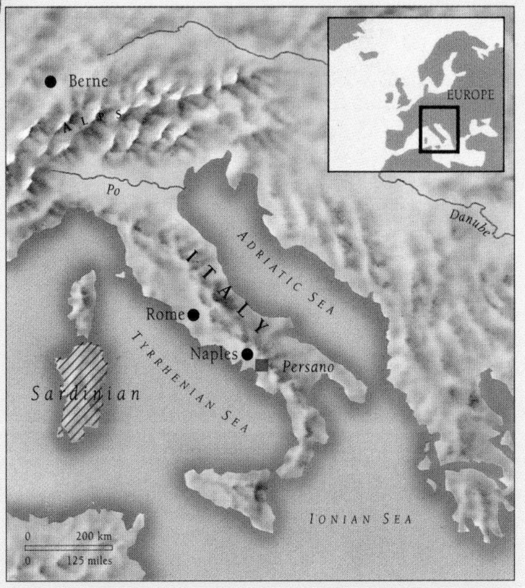

SARDINIA HAS A LONG *horse-breeding tradition. Being within easy reach of North Africa, the Sardinians were able to import Barbs and Arabs, and these, with the Thoroughbred, resulted in the modern Sardinian horse, which is now very much Anglo-Arab in type. The Salerno is still bred in the Campania region of Italy, where it originated in the 18th century. The Morese Stud was a principal centre, and produced some notable competition horses including some of the greatest international showjumpers. It is situated close to where the Bourbon stud of Persano was founded in the early 18th century.*

DRESSAGE

COMPETITIVE DRESSAGE is the fastest growing sport among the nations involved in the Olympic equestrian disciplines and offers, through carefully constructed tests, opportunities for riders at every level. While there is the obvious satisfaction to be gained from improving one's own riding and the performance level of the horse, dressage also has the advantage of being a lower risk sport, an important consideration for those with family and business responsibilities. The word "dressage" comes from the French verb *dresser*, used in the context of training the riding and harness horse. It is now practised at all levels in the Pony Club and within the riding clubs' movement.

ORIGINS

While the origins of the sport are with the classicism of the Renaissance schools and their successors (see p.91), the forerunners of competitive dressage were the cavalry "best-trained-charger" tests, which assumed Olympic standing at the 1912 Olympics in Stockholm, Sweden.

As with all the Olympic disciplines the sport is conducted under the aegis of the International Equestrian Federation (FEI), which defines the paces and movements involved and the overall objectives implicit in the tests.

It defines the object of dressage, for instance, as follows:

"... the harmonious development of the physique and ability of the horse. As a result it makes the horse calm, supple, loose and flexible, but also confident, attentive and keen, thus achieving perfect understanding with his rider".

DRESSAGE COMPETITIONS

The FEI is responsible for tests used in international competitions, and these in turn provide the basis for the national tests that are written by individual countries in

GERMANY VICTORIOUS
The Sydney Olympics gold medal team comprised (left to right) Nadine Capellmann (Farbenfroh), Isabell Werth (Gigolo), Alexandra Simons de Ridder (Chacomo), and Ulla Salzgeber (Rusty).

THE INDIVIDUAL CHAMPION
Anky van Grunsven of Holland is a World Champion and won the individual gold at the Sydney Olympics in the Millennium year.

TEAM BRONZE MEDALLIST
Susan Blinks with Flim Flam was a member of the American Olympic bronze-medal team in Sydney and is a successful international rider.

elementary and medium tests, in which a degree of collection is introduced; and continue on to advanced classes.

Competitions take place within a prescribed flat area, usually enclosed with boards. Lower level tests are held in an arena measuring 20 m x 40 m (65.5 ft x 130 ft) and the higher and advanced tests in the larger 20 m x 60 m arena (65.5 ft x 197 ft). Markers, indicating the points at which the movements must be performed, are provided by letters placed at fixed points. The letters are positioned in a set sequence but their significance, if there is one, is unknown.

While there is no specific type of dressage horse, the Warmbloods are probably the most popular – the German breeds, in particular, being

virtually purpose-bred for the sport. Good conformation is an essential factor in a top-class dressage horse along with a high degree of athleticism and, most importantly, a calm, willing temperament.

BAROQUE HORSE

In recent years, the attractive Iberian breeds – Andalucian, Lusitano, and Alter – have been increasingly evident and have become a major influence in competitive dressage. They are, indeed, closer than any other breed to the classical, baroque horse. While there is great elevation in the paces they do not all have the ability to extend, but they bring a new, exciting dimension to the sport that is, perhaps, nearer to the classical art-form.

accordance with their own specific needs and perceived objectives. A dressage test is comprised of a series of movements, each being marked out of a possible ten. The scale of marks is as follows: 10. Excellent, 9. Very Good, 8. Good, 7. Fairly Good, 6. Satisfactory, 5. Sufficient, 4. Insufficient, 3. Fairly Bad, 2. Bad, 1. Very Bad, 0. Not Performed.

The two FEI Grand Prix tests at Olympic level, for individual and teams respectively, include the most difficult movements in competitive dressage and ask for *piaffe*, *passage*, the canter *pirouettes*, and the flying changes of leg at every stride. The lowest level FEI test is the Prix St George, which is succeeded by *Intermediaire* 1 and 2, the latter including the *piaffe*.

There is also the very popular *Kur*, or Freestyle, test usually ridden to music of the rider's choice.

DRESSAGE ARENAS

Most national classes begin with simple preliminary and novice tests performed at walk, trot, and canter; pass through

SPANISH HORSE
Ignacio Rambla Algarin, a member of the Spanish Team, rides the free-moving and spectacular Andalusian stallion, Granadero, in the team dressage competition in the World Equestrian Games, Jerez, Spain, in 2002.

CAPT. HANS SCHWARZENBACH

EVENTING: THE HISTORY

O F ALL THE EQUESTRIAN disciplines none is more comprehensively demanding than eventing, which is also known as horse trials. The French call it *concours complet*, the complete test, and its origins, in common with those of other horse sports, are in the cavalry competitions and training exercises that were designed to test the horse's endurance, speed, and stamina, as well as the character and ability of the rider. During the past 50 years or so eventing, which is now in the civilian domain and attracting a large female entry, has grown significantly and at the advanced levels the sport is increasingly dependent on sponsorship. In essence, the object and philosophies of long ago remain but with an altered emphasis that puts a premium on riding skills.

TEST OF STAMINA

During the 19th century, the armies of France, Germany, Sweden, and the US included "endurance rides" in their cavalry training programmes, the rides varying in length between a modest 30 km (18½ miles) and a staggering 725 km (450 miles). No jumping was required, but speed and stamina were important considerations. A more comprehensive test, *Championnat du Cheval d'Armes*, was devised by the French cavalry authorities in 1902.

The *Championnat* was comprised of four distinct phases: a "dressage" test along the lines of a "best-charger" competition; a steeplechase; a 50-km (30-mile) ride over roads and tacks; and, for the first time, a final jumping competition.

This format formed the basis of the three-day event, which was initially titled "the Military" and later in its development "Combined Training".

DOUBLE VICTORY
A star of the 1960s, Anneli Drummond-Hay won the the Badminton and Burghley events in 1962 with the legendary Merely-a-Monarch.

FLOWERS ALL THE WAY
A competitor at the 1988 Olympic Games, Seoul, South Korea, on the roads-and-tracks section leading up to the steeplechase phase. There is a further roads-and-tracks section before the cross-country.

BADMINTON

The military connection was maintained up to the end of the Second World War, when participation became wholly civilian.

The greatest impetus given to the "new" sport occurred in 1949 when the first Badminton Horse Trials was staged in Britain on the Duke of Beaufort's Gloucestershire estate.

It is still held there at the beginning of the event season and is acknowledged as the sport's premier competition attracting top-class international fields.

With its strong tradition of hunting and cross-country riding it is not surprising that the sport of eventing has centred largely on the UK where there are more opportunities to compete at all levels than elsewhere in the world.

Nonetheless, while British riders do maintain an enviable record in world competition, they are far from dominating the international scene. Australia and New Zealand, many of whose event riders base themselves in Britain to take advantage of the opportunities offered there, are just as successful, and the powerful German teams are equally prominent with teams from France and Holland close behind.

LUCINDA GREEN
Lucinda Green was the world's leading event rider in the 1970s and 1980s, winning the Badminton Horse Trials on a record six occasions and becoming the European Champion in 1973. She won the individual gold medal at the 1982 World Championships.

COURAGE OF A THOROUGHBRED
A big effort by horse and rider takes this bold and determined pair cleanly over an uphill obstacle at the 1989 Badminton Horse Trials. Fences of this sort call for agility, athleticism, and the courage of the Thoroughbred horse.

MODERN EVENTING

Today, eventing is conducted under the rules of the International Equestrian Federation (FEI) and event horses are graded according to performance records, following in Europe a carefully devised progression from novice and pre-novice events to the four-star international championships. The predominant equine influence in eventing remains that of the English and Irish horses and the Thoroughbred blood lines. Despite the physical and mental demands of the sport, or perhaps because of them, top-class eventers are often 14 or 15 years of age.

THREE PHASES

The sport in its modern form involves three separate phases: dressage, cross-country, and arena jumping. In one- and two-day events the dressage test is ridden first, followed by the arena jumping phase, and then the cross-country.

Dressage is also the opening phase in the three-day event. On the following day the cross-country course is ridden and on the third day, after a veterinary inspection, the arena jumping concludes the event.

The relative influence of each phase is traditionally calculated as being in the ratio of dressage 3; cross-country 12; arena jumping 1. Nonetheless, there have been times when both dressage and arena jumping have exerted undue influence to the detriment of the guiding philosophy. The purpose of dressage is to display a horse at peak fitness that is still obedient and submissive; the cross-country, central to the event, tests the ability, speed and courage of the combination under pressure; while the jumping test confirms that the horse remains "fit for service".

THE SHORT FORMAT

Until the adoption of the "short format" (see p.349) the cross-country course was preceded by 6 km (3½ miles) of roads and tracks followed by a 3-km (2-mile) steeplechase course. After that competitors completed another 9 km (6 miles) on roads and tracks before taking a 10-minute break and setting off over the cross-country course of some 32 fences; although, allowing for combination fences involving two or three obstacles, the horse had to make many more than that number of jumping efforts.

The maximum dimensions of obstacles have not changed for many years. The maximum height is 1.2 m (3ft 11in), the spread should be no more than 2 m (6½ ft), and the maximum drop is also 2 m (6½ ft).

The short-format event abolishes the roads and tracks and the steeplechase retaining only the cross-country element. The endurance element is therefore much

TOUJOURS L'AUDACE
A formidable obstacle on the cross-country course at Saumur, France. It demands a bold horse and an athletic one, too.

THE BIG DROP
A German combination tackle a big drop fence at the Sydney Olympics. The rider is in perfect balance with his horse.

BURGHLEY HORSE TRIALS

British rider Rodney Powell comes off the bank obstacle in front of Burghley House. The rider's position is beyond criticism.

PRIZE MONEY

Prize money has improved somewhat over the years but remains almost derisory when compared with far less demanding sports. For example, the first prize at Badminton is £50,000, which is less than a third of that offered at a major snooker championship and may be less than a week's wages for a "top-class" football player. The biggest prize on offer in the early years of the century was the Rolex Grand Slam, amounting to some $250,000 for the rider who could win the Kentucky, Badminton, and Burghley events in the same year. To date this prestigious prize has been won by only one rider, the hugely talented Pippa Funnell of Great Britain, who completed the hat-trick in September 2003 on Primmore's Pride.

reduced, the course is more technically demanding, and the character of the event is changed in consequence. The Badminton catalogue acknowledges the change of emphasis and concludes that "the ability of the rider is now probably more important than the qualities of the horse".

In the old format the roads and tracks and the steeplechase gave the rider time to settle the horse before embarking on the cross-country, while also providing a test of stamina. In the short-format event it is necessary to provide an adequate warm-up area in which to prepare the horse before the cross-country phase. It does not, however, constitute a test of stamina.

Otherwise, management of a big event is made easier, the area required is smaller and it is probable that the competition is better suited to less experienced nations and the type of horse available to them. It does, however, increase the premium placed on the design and construction of the cross-country course if the essential ratio between the three phases is to be maintained and safety considerations observed.

GRAND SLAM

Pippa Funnell (GB), winner of the Rolex Grand Slam, riding Primmore's Pride at Kentucky in 2003. In the same year she also won at Badminton and Burghley.

PARK DRIVING

COMPETITIVE DRIVING

COMPETITIVE driving was well-established in mainland Europe by the late 19th century, particularly in Germany, Switzerland, Austria, Hungary, and other countries in Eastern Europe. The first competition to award a gold medal for driving was held at Baden-Baden in 1882. It was won by Benno von Achenbach, who later perfected the Achenbach or "English" method of driving (so called because he learnt his skills from the English professional Edwin Howlett). The first Hamburg Driving Derby was held in 1920, and classes for four-in-hand teams have been a feature at the Aachen Show for over 50 years. At the instigation of HRH Prince Philip, then the President of the International Equestrian Federation (FEI), driving was internationally recognized as a competitive sport in 1969 and has since grown in popularity.

DRIVING TRIALS

The first international driving trial, for teams of four horses, was held in Switzerland in 1970. Since then there has been a European or World Championship every year, as well as international trials involving some 20 nations. In addition to the four-in-hand teams, these trials cater for pairs, tandems, and some single horse and pony turnouts.

The driving trial, or competition, is based on the ridden three-day event. It is made up of three competitions, A, B, and C, and a mini-competition, originally termed Presentation, involving an appraisal of the turnout of each competitor. However, this weighted the competition in favour of UK conventions, for example the top hat, and was replaced in 1988 by a general impression mark given during Competition A, dressage.

Competition A takes place in an arena of 100 x 40 m (110 x 44 yds) or, for pairs and singles, in one of 80 x 40 m (88 x 44 yds). The movements judged are straightforward, since the length of a four-horse team and carriage is about 10 m (33 ft). Marks are also given for obedience, impulsion, the quality of the paces, style of driving, and so on.

THE MARATHON

Competition B is the marathon. It is the equivalent of the three-day event's speed and endurance phase, and is expected to have three times more influence on the final result than the dressage test. Covering a distance of

MARATHON
This team of Gelderlanders is participating in an International Coaching Marathon at the Royal Windsor Horse Show, Berkshire, UK. Dutch Gelderlanders are becoming increasingly successful in international competition.

CROSS-COUNTRY COURSE
Shown here is a British competitor, Alwyn Holder, making up time on the World Championship cross-country course at Apeldoorn, Netherlands, in 1982. The UK won the team gold medal at this event.

24–27 km (15–17 miles), it consists of five sections with two obligatory 10-minute halts, and must be completed in two hours.

Section A is a 10-km (6¼-mile) route over roads and tracks, at a speed of 15 km/h (9½ mph). It is usually taken at a trot, but any pace may be used. Section B is over 1.2 km (¾ mile). It must to be driven at a walk, at a speed of 7 km/h (4½ mph). It is followed by the first halt. With Section C the marathon enters a more demanding phase, over a hilly, twisting course and timed for a speed of 18–19 km/h (11–12 mph). No cantering or galloping is allowed, so the pace has to be a good, sharp trot. Section D is the second of the walk stages, and during the 10-minute halt a veterinary check is made. The final section, Section E, is over 10 km (6¼ miles). It is timed at 15 km/h (9½ mph), and includes eight obstacles (called "hazards") situated fairly close together at the end of the course. Initially, the hazards were meant to be natural ones, such as water-crossings, but they are now almost all artificially constructed, though planned carefully in relation to factors such as the ground condition or distances.

Competition C is the obstacle competition, known generally as "cone driving". The course consists of up to 20 obstacles created by traffic cones. Penalties are incurred for striking a cone and displacing the ball on top, and for exceeding the usually very tight time limit. The competition tests the driver's skill and judgement, and is designed to ascertain the ability of the horses to perform after the previous day's marathon.

VEHICLES AND HORSES

Marathon competition vehicles, or "battle wagons", are built specially for this sport, and are designed for practicality rather than elegance; in fact, many are fitted with a type of disc-brake, like in cars.

Most of the horses used in driving trials are warmbloods derived from the European coaching breeds – Holsteiners, Oldenburgers, and so on. But Cleveland Bays and Cleveland crosses, Welsh Cobs, and Fell Ponies are all used, along with the imposing Dutch Gelderlanders and the Lipizzaners of the dashing Hungarian teams.

The Hungarians employ their traditional, unique driving method, using breast harness and including coupling buckles adjustable

TIGHT TURNS
A well-judged turn takes this team safely through a demanding obstacle on the course at Aachen, Germany. The team is wearing the breast harness preferred by many competitors.

HAFLINGERS
A team of flaxen-maned Haflinger ponies take their "battle wagon" boldly through the water hazard at Windsor, Berkshire, UK.

close to the driver's hand. The standard method in most other places in the West is the less flexible Achenbach style, which is described in *The Art of Driving* (published in 1966) by Colonel Max Pape.

SCURRY DRIVING

This sport involves mini obstacle races against the clock. These are contested by pony pairs in two height divisions, 1.22 m (12 hh) and under and 1.22–1.47 m (12–14.2 hh), put to light, pneumatic-tyred, four-wheeled vehicles. A groom rides with the driver and leans out to maintain stability. Fast, agile ponies, often of Welsh extraction, are the best for this hell-for-leather sport which has been called "the equestrian version of stock-car racing".

INDIAN TEAMS
Turnouts for the driving class wait in the collecting ring at the Delhi Horse Show, India. There is great rivalry between the private coaches entered by army units.

ENDURANCE RIDING

DISTANCE RIDING

IN COMMON with most equestrian disciplines endurance riding has its origins in military practice. European cavalry, particularly that of Germany and the old Austro-Hungarian Empire, were conducting distance rides up to and beyond the first years of the 20th century. The objective was to improve the quality of cavalry remounts, but, unhappily, the rides often deteriorated into races of such severity that horses were ridden to death. In contrast, the supervised rides held by the American Cavalry put the emphasis on high standards of management as well as being tests of endurance and speed. Today, the US is still a major influence in the sport, staging upwards of 500 rides each year of varying length and severity. Nonetheless, the sport is increasingly popular in Europe, where numerous major rides are held over exacting courses.

FOUNDATIONS

European and World Championships are staged under the aegis of the International Equestrian Federation (FEI), as are the other major equestrian sports.

In 1919 the US Cavalry rides were being conducted with the object of assessing the qualities of Arab and Thoroughbred horses as remounts. The tests were over 480 km (300 miles) and were run over five days in stages of 96 km (60 miles), with the horses carrying 91–111 kg (200–245 lb). These rides encouraged similar civilian events, one of the earlier ones being the Vermont 100-Mile, and led to the formation of numerous Trail Ride Associations.

The most famous, and certainly the toughest, of the American events is the 100-mile Western States Trail Ride, known as the Tevis Cup Ride. It first took place in 1955 when Wendell T Robie, a prominent Arab enthusiast, rode with four companions from Tahoe City, Nevada, to Auburn, California. The journey took 23 hours and involved crossing the steep and hazardous Sierra Nevada. The route taken involves a descent of 4,648 m (15,250 ft) and a daunting climb over rough terrain through the Squaw Pass to the El Dorado Canyon. The track climbs to an altitude of 2,896 m (9,500 ft) and temperatures may reach as much as 38° C (100° F).

Today's Tevis Cup Ride takes place against the background of stringent veterinary checks made at intervals over the course and entries are limited by qualifying rides, practices that are now universally adopted. Modern-day riders complete the course in between 11 and 12 hours, and all those finishing within 24 hours win the coveted silver-and-gold buckle.

WORLD CHAMPION 2006
Individual World Endurance Champion Miguel Vila Ubach of Spain riding the Arab Hungares. The team medal was won by France.

ARAB INFLUENCE

Wendell Robie won the Tevis in 1956, 1957, and 1958 over the course he had pioneered. His horses were all Arabs, his first and most famous being the grey stallion Bandos, by Nasr. Subsequently, it is the Arab and Arab crosses that have become the supreme long-distance horses.

In Australia, another country pioneering the sport, the equivalent of the Tevis Cup is the Tom Quilty Ride, which is run over the same distance and on terrain that is just as demanding for horse and rider.

Distance riding in Europe, encouraged by the continuing military requirement for cavalry horses, also recognized the importance of Arab blood. In the UK, the British Arab Horse Society were staging rides, called "endurance races", in the early 1920s with the object of "demonstrating to the War Office the phenomenal stamina and recuperation powers of the breed, with a view to an infusion of Arab blood into the cavalry horse". The Arabs, standing no more than 1.52 m (15 hh), carried 82.5 kg (13 st) and, as with the US Cavalry tests, covered the 480-km (300-mile) course in five consecutive days.

The first competitive rides in the UK of a 160-km (100-mile) course were those organized by the iconic *Country Life* magazine in 1937 and 1938. They were well run but hardly as demanding as the modern equivalent, the 1937 ride being described as "a summer holiday on horseback".

After the Second World War fresh impetus was given to the UK sport by the Golden Horseshoe Ride, which was held over the testing going of the Exmoor National Park.

Endurance riding was quick to gain support throughout Europe, while in the Middle East the Maktoum family, rulers of Dubai, have been active patrons of endurance riding and are responsible for the prestigious Dubai Championships.

At the 2006 World Equestrian Games, held in Aachen, Germany, the Endurance Championship attracted 159 entries from 42 nations, the team gold was won by France and the individual championship by Miguel Vila Urbach of Spain, who completed the course in 9 hr 12 mins 27 secs riding the Arab, Hungares.

CHECK POINTS

Veterinary check points are mandatory throughout the sport, from the introductory pleasure-ride level, through competitive trail rides (more complicated in their rule structure and calling for the distances to be covered at stipulated speeds) to the endurance ride, which is actually a race in which the first past the post, having passed the veterinary judging, is the winner. In the trail rides checks are carried out during the compulsory halt period (usually 30 mins) and are conducted just before the horse is due to leave the check point. Endurance rides, however, employ the system of "vet-gates", which essentially put the onus on the rider to ensure that the horse's recovery rate (pulse, respiration, dehydration, etc), as well as the animal's overall condition and ease

THE BACK-UP TEAM

At the constant veterinary checks, the well-drilled and expert back-up team goes into action to examine their horse and make it comfortable. In this instance, the farrier has to attend to an ill-fitting shoe.

of movement, is satisfactory before presenting the horse to the veterinarian for a health inspection.

Clearly, the veterinary check is central to the sport and in endurance rides the time spent at the vet gate is critical to the final placing. The responsibility on the rider's part to get the horse to each gate with the horse's pulse and respiration rates as near to normal as possible is a matter requiring fine judgement and considerable skill. Thereafter, the horse is taken over by the "crew", a well-drilled group of experienced handlers that attends effectively to the horse's needs and comfort. The "crew" has, indeed, become an essential element in the modern-day sport.

Ultimately, the veterinary team has three options: to pass or fail the horse, or to allow for a re-inspection within a specified time, which is usually 10 minutes. A 10-minute delay, however, may well cost the rider a placing in the final result. If the horse fails the re-inspection it is eliminated.

THE DESERT RIDE

The Maktoum family, rulers of Dubai and powerful supporters of Thoroughbred racing, also take part in endurance riding. Here, Sheikh Mohammed bin Rashid Al Maktoum and the two princes compete in Dubai's World Endurance Championships.

ROCKY MOUNTAIN HORSE

THE ROCKY MOUNTAIN HORSE is a relative newcomer to the vast and infinitely varied repository of breeds and types to be found in the American continent. It is, indubitably, in the gaited tradition of the southern states of the eastern seaboard, although not nearly so established as its more famous and more fully documented cousins: the Saddlebred (see p.234), the Missouri Fox Trotter (see p.236), and the Tennessee Walker (see p.238). For all that, it is a typical product of the vigorous American horse culture and its natural ambling gait makes it a very comfortable mount over long distances.

AMBLING GAIT
The lateral ambling gait of the Rocky Mountain Horse is inherited from America's early Spanish stock. The gait is natural to the pony and is very comfortable over long distances.

ORIGINS

In common with much of the American horse population, the Rocky Mountain Horse has its origins in the early Spanish horses brought to the New World in the 16th century by the conquistadores (see p.216), many of which were from the comfortably gaited strains that were so prized in 16–17th century Europe.

Otherwise, the history of the breed is relatively obscure and to some degree based on hearsay and conjecture. The breed society is the Rocky Mountain Horse Association of Mt. Olivet, Kentucky, and the Register was opened in 1986.

The Rocky Mountain Horse is always referred to as a "breed", a term used more generally throughout America. It would not, however, meet the criteria for breed status as

it is applied in Europe. In the past the Rocky Mountain was often classified as a pony, probably because of the conventional division between horses and ponies being set, arbitrarily, at 1.42 m (15 hh). That convention is, in fact, misleading because the difference between horses and ponies is actually as much concerned with proportion as with size.

CHARACTERISTICS

The European definition of a breed is dependent on the existence of a Stud Book recording the pedigrees of each entry. Animals so recorded must be the progeny of animals already in the Book and, in turn, their progeny are entitled to entry. This is the definition of a "closed" Stud Book, i.e. one that is confined to pure-bred stock and does not admit the use of outcrosses from other breeds, although it may operate a controlled "register" for approved part-bred animals.

An "open" Stud Book, like that maintained by many warmblood societies, allows for approved outcrosses to animals entered in other stud books.

In simplistic terms it can be said that the word "breed" may be applied to a group of horses that have been selectively bred over a sufficient period of time to ensure the consistent production of stock that has in common clearly defined characteristics of height, colour, conformation and action.

The existence of a Register for the Rocky Mountain Horse and the practice of examination for specified characteristics is a powerful tool in

HIND LEGS
The hind legs have to be strong and sufficiently sound to stand up to plenty of work.

ORIGINS

IT IS CLAIMED THAT THE ROCKY MOUNTAIN HORSE originated in the Appalachian foothills of eastern Kentucky in about 1890 but there is very little evidence in existence from the period to support the assertion. Nonetheless, the existence of a strain of comfortably gaited horses, sure-footed over the rough ground of the area and well able to tolerate the Appalachian winters, is incontrovertible and a register was opened by the Rocky Mountain Horse Association in 1986.

achieving, in time, a recognizable uniformity in type. The outstanding characteristic that is inherent in the Mountain Horse stock is the gait, which is already firmly established as being central to the character of the breed.

AMBLING GAIT

The Rocky Mountain Horse has a natural ambling gait, involving four distinct beats rather than the faster, two-beat, lateral pacing gait. The amble is more comfortable than the pacing action and this reassuringly sure-footed horse is able to maintain a steady 11 km/h (7 mph) over rough ground. On better going it is claimed that it can reach speeds of 25 km/h (16 mph).

Any solid colour is acceptable but the unusual chocolate shade, accompanied by a flaxen mane and tail, is a distinctive and much prized attribute. It stands at 1.42–1.63 m (14–16 hh) and has good proportions for the jobs required of it, as well as excellent feet. It is noted for its extreme hardiness and is well able to tolerate the severe Appalachian winters of eastern Kentucky.

The Rocky Mountain Horse Association states in its "rendition of the history of the breed" that a gaited colt was brought from the Rocky Mountain area to the foothills of the Appalachians around 1890. He was, it is claimed, chocolate coloured with flaxen mane and tail and was noted for his ambling action. The colt is credited as the foundation sire of the breed. There is little on record to prove this story, but it probably carries an element of truth.

OLD TOBE

What has also to be considered is that the horses of the Appalachian foothills would have felt the influence of forebears of the Saddlebred (originally called the Kentucky Saddler), Missouri Foxtrotter, and the Tennessee Walker, all of them descended in some measure from the Narragansett Pacer (see p.324), a horse that had a profound influence on the American gaited breeds.

Again there is no definitive evidence. What is incontrovertible, however, is the existence of Sam Tuttle of Sport Springs, Kentucky, and his stallion Old Tobe. In the 1960s Sam had the riding concession at the Natural Bridge State Park in Powell County and used Old Tobe as a trail horse there as well as for breeding.

Old Tobe was noted for his calm disposition, his sure-footedness, and his outstandingly comfortable ambling gait. He was still active at 37 years of age and proved to be a highly prepotent and prolific sire, transmitting his own excellent qualities, particularly the gait, to his long-lived offspring and occasionally throwing some chocolate-coloured stock.

Because of his influence and an acceptable degree of documentation, Old Tobe might, perhaps, be seen as a foundation stallion of the Rocky Mountain Horse.

HEAD
This fine, intelligent head is free from fleshiness through the jowl and has an alert expression.

HEIGHT
1.42–1.63 m
(14–16 hh)

HORSE PACKING
Trail riding and horse packing are popular leisure pursuits for visitors to the state parks of the US and the wild countryside of states such as Montana and Wyoming. Knowledgeable trail leaders and reliable horses are a necessity.

LEGS
The legs are slender but there is sufficient bone measurement and pasterns are well shaped.

POLO & BUZKASHI

Polo is one of the world's oldest and most popular galloping games. It originated in the East and was certainly played as much as 2,500 years ago, by both men and women, in Persia and neighbouring areas, as well as in Ancient China. From there it spread into India. In the Persian tongue the game was called *changar*, meaning mallet, but the word "polo" derives from the Tibetan *pulu*, the word for a ball.

There are also other games, which are tenuously related to the polo depicted in 16th century Mogul art. They are played in the wild parts of Asia, in Afghanistan, and in the Uzbek and Tajik regions spanning the former Russian border. These are elemental, ferociously brutal equestrian contests involving as many as 100 players. Afghanistan's game of *buzkashi* is one of the fiercest of these.

BUZKASHI

Buzkashi is Afghanistan's foremost galloping game. In the place of a ball, the Afghan horsemen use the carcase of a decapitated goat or, on special occasions a calf, which may weigh up to 40 kg (90 lb). The object is for a team of *chapandazan* (riders) to pick up the *buz* (the carcase), carry it the length of the field, and then return it to a circle at the opposite end. The game is played as a battle between two teams of over 40 powerful men, each of whom must be over 30 years of age; the rules are rudimentary and unwritten, and no quarter is given or asked, the horses being encouraged to bite and kick as their riders, flailing their heavy whips, attempt to force a way into the circle. The ground is 0.8 hectares (2 acres) in extent, and a specified time-limit is set for the completion of the game. Possibly *buzkashi* has its origins in the war games of Genghis Khan's Mongol warriors, who surged into the tribal lands of the Hindu Kush from their Central Asian steppes over 700 years ago. Certainly it bears all the hallmarks of those ruthless horsemen.

POLO

British soldiers and civilians serving in India in the 19th century were the first Westerners to come into contact with polo. Working in Manipur, the small state between Assam and Burma, where polo was the national game and villages and groups of villages had their own teams, a handful of British officials learnt it from the local people. The Manipuris copied and probably adapted the game from Tibet, using the Tibetan word *pulu* as well as their own name, *kán-jāi-bazèè*.

In 1854 the British were establishing tea plantations in Manipur's Cacher Valley and five years later, in 1859, the first European polo club was formed there by Captain Robert Stewart, Superintendent of Cacher, and Lt. Joseph Sherer of the Bengal Army. Sherer later gained the rank of Major-General and became known as "the Father of Modern Polo". By 1870 the game was being played throughout British India, often on very small ponies (see pp.202–3). The Manipuri ponies were no more than 1.27 m (12.2 hh), and even today rarely exceed this height.

Polo was first played in the UK in 1869, by officers of the 10th Hussars at Aldershot, and was known as "Hockey on Horseback". A year later, the Hussars played against their great rivals, the 9th Lancers, at Hounslow, fielding eight players a side. The game

POLO FOR POSTERITY
This glazed pottery figure of a polo player is from a Chinese tomb of the Tang Dynasty.

FEROCIOUS BUZKASHI
Afghanistan's ferocious equestrian contest, buzkashi, is a battle fought over a goat's carcase by as many as 100 players. Similar games are played in most of the Asian republics of the former USSR.

NATIONAL SPORT
The cradle of modern polo is in the Cachar Valley of Manipur, Assam, where it is played as a national sport. Riders use the quick-moving little Manipuri ponies, most of which are no more than 1.27 m (12.2 hh) high.

quickly became part of the fashionable "London Season", and was centred at Hurlingham, near London. Hurlingham became the headquarters of the sport, and the Hurlingham Club formulated the rules.

The Americans, encouraged by the newspaper tycoon, James Gordon Bennett Jr., took up the sport in 1878, and the Meadow Brook Club, fulfilling the same role as Hurlingham, was formed in 1882. International matches began in 1886, with the British and the Americans competing for the Westchester Cup. The Americans, superbly drilled and well mounted, had achieved international supremacy by 1909, when, riding Argentinian ponies, they won the Cup in the UK.

Polo had been introduced into Argentina in 1877 by the British, and since the 1930s the Argentinians

HOCKEY ON HORSEBACK
Polo was introduced to the UK from India in the 19th century. It was originally called "hockey on horseback", and was played enthusiastically by army officers stationed around London. This particular game took place in 1872 on Woolwich Common.

have been the world's leading polo players. They have a plentiful supply of horses, and produce world famous polo ponies, which are trained by professional horsemen to whom the game is a way of life.

THE RULES OF THE GAME

Polo is played at the gallop, and is one of the fastest games in the world. The object is to score more goals than one's opponents by hitting an 8 cm (3 in) diameter willow ball with a bamboo mallet through goalposts, which are 3 m (10 ft) high and 7.3 m (24 ft) apart. The ground measures 275 x 180 m (300 x 200 yd), and is usually enclosed by low boards. The average height of a modern polo pony (they are always called "ponies") is now 1.52–1.60 m (15–15.3 hh). The British originally introduced a height limit of 1.47 m (14.2 hh) but, largely at the instigation of the Americans, this was abolished in 1916. In 1886 the number of players was fixed at four per side: numbers 1 and 2 were the

forwards, 3 played the centre field, and 4 was the back. Players are handicapped according to the American system, which was universally adopted in 1909, and is graded from –2 to +10 goals. A player on a –2 handicap is on the lowest grading. In "high-goal" polo the team aggregate handicap is 19 and over, and in "medium-goal" polo it is between 15 and 18 goals.

A match lasts a little under an hour, and is divided into *chukkas*, which last for seven and a half minutes each. A high-goal match is divided into five or six *chukkas*, and a lower-rated event into four. Ponies are changed after each *chukka*, and no pony plays more than two *chukkas* in a match. There is no off-side rule in polo, as there is in soccer, but free hits are given against a player crossing another's right of way, for bumping another horse deliberately, for zigzagging, or for using the stick improperly. However, it is permissible to hook an opponent's stick, or to "ride him off" the ball.

DRAW-REIN
A draw-rein contributes to the rider's control by "drawing" the head inwards.

TAIL
The polo pony's tail is always plaited up short so as to prevent it being caught up with the mallet (stick).

GAG-BIT
The gag-bit raises the head and with the martingale increases control.

MARTINGALE
A polo standing martingale governs the degree to which the head can be raised.

LEGS
All four legs are bandaged, both for support and as protection against blows.

POLO KIT
This Indian polo player rides a good sort of high-goal pony. The bitting arrangement of gag and draw-rein, and the near-obligatory martingale, ensure maximum control.

THE KING OF GAMES

"Let other people play at other things – the King of games is still the game of Kings". This is the verse engraved on a stone by the polo ground at Gilgit, high above Srinager in Pakistan's North-West Frontier Province, where, at the annual *jhalsa* in the early 19th century, matches between the kingdoms of Hunza and Nagar, and Punial and Yasin, used to be played out with a ferocious passion, if with scant respect for the rules of the game. In modern polo, one of the fastest and the most

PRACTISE MAKES PERFECT
A rider at the Escondida Polo School, Argentina, plays the first of the four basic polo shots – the offside forehand.

complex games in the world, the rules are always strictly enforced by the umpire, and penalties are awarded for any infringement.

SPEED AND ACCURACY

Above all, polo is a team game that, despite the speed involved, is often likened to a game of chess. It calls for almost telepathic communication between players at speeds of up to 64 km/h (40 mph), each member appreciating the significance of his position in the team.

Numbers 1 and 2 are forwards, number 2 being the midfield attacker and usually the stronger player of the two. Number 1 marks the opposing number 4, and number 2 the opposing number 3. Three is the pivotal position and the one from which the run of play can best be controlled. It is the most important place on the field and is usually taken by the captain. Number 3's job is to get the ball up to his forwards and to be ready to intercept attacks as they are mounted on his own goal. He has also to mark the opposing number 2. Number 4 is the back whose responsibility is for the defence of his goal. He has to be a steady player and a strong, safe, accurate hitter with a particular ability to hit backhand

strokes. Above all, number 4 is responsible for marking the opposing number 1 very closely throughout the game.

While maintaining these positions and the marking of opponents form the basis of the game's tactics, positions are essentially interchangeable according to the needs of the moment. The back, if he finds himself unmarked, for instance, and in a favourable position, may gallop forward in attack. Number 3 will then assume the back's position while number 2 fills in for number 3. Good marking involves good riding off, a skill which is integral to the game. A good team player chases the man first and then the ball. Riding off is consequently an essential accomplishment. To ride off an opponent it is necessary to place the knee in front of his knee so that one's pony's weight is a little in front of that of one's opponent. The pony by neck rein, bodyweight, and leg is pushed over against the other pony, the rider leaning hard against his opponent's shoulder to guide them off the line. It is not a question of bumping the opponent, which can cause injury, but more of exerting irresistible persuasion to move over.

Although shouting at and between players during play is generally discouraged, there are accepted vocal instructions essential to the play, which are usually made by the captain at number 3. "Leave it!" shouted by a player from behind the man in possession means that he may see a better opportunity if he takes the ball himself. "Take the man!" is a command to ride off the nearest opponent and let the man following up take the ball. "Ball!" means simply, "Keep with the ball, or hit it; I'm backing you up".

CALLING THE SHOTS

There are four basic polo shots, two on each side of the pony: offside forehand and offside backhander; nearside forehand and nearside backhander. They are supplemented by shots made under the pony's neck in both directions, and similar shots made under, or behind, the pony's tail. Then, to complete the repertoire, there are the cut shots in both directions that are designed to

ATTACK, ATTACK, ATTACK!
A formidable Argentine player mounts a ferocious, high-speed attack in an international semi-final and outrides his opponents.

POLO IN THE SNOW
Well-rugged polo ponies exercise at St Moritz, Switzerland, where the game is played with great enthusiasm.

hit the ball at an angle of 45 degrees to the pony's body, using either the forehand or backhand stroke.

Penalties given for rule infringements are referred to by numbers. Number 1 is the most serious penalty, when a goal is awarded for a foul in front of the goal area. It is the only time a goal is not followed by the teams changing ends. Instead, the ball is thrown by the umpire into a line-out 9 m (30 ft) in front of the goal. Penalty number 2 is for fouls made within the 30-yard line, and a free hit from that line is awarded. Similarly, penalties 3 and 4 involve free hits from the 40- and 60-yard line, respectively. There are then penalties 5A and 5B, which earn a free hit, in the first instance, from the point where the foul occurred and, in the second, from the centre line.

The rules are those devised by Britain's Hurlingham Polo Association, the world's guiding body for the sport.

CLOTHING AND EQUIPMENT

Since its inception in England in 1869 equipment for ponies and riders has, inevitably, changed.

Initially, the stick used by the 10th Hussars at Aldershot in the first polo matches very much resembled a hockey stick, giving rise to the title "hockey on horseback". Modern sticks have a cigar-

"TAKE THE MAN!"
In a fiercely contested high-goal game at St Moritz, the players are in robust physical contact and going hard for possession of the ball.

shaped head fitted to a cane shaft of one kind or another and with a shaped rubber grip, or occasionally one covered in towelling, and a wrist loop. Variations on the cigar head occur in the RNPA (Royal Naval Polo Association) pattern and in the Skene, a head perfected by the Australian-born 10-goal player Robert Skene.

Cane shafts range from stiff to whippy, the latter adding to the power of the stroke but being more difficult to use. The average weight of stick is 450–500 g (16–18 oz) for a man and 375–450 g (13–16 oz) for a woman. The length is of great importance. On a 1.52–1.57 m (15–15.2 hh) pony 130–132 cm (51–52 in) is the most satisfactory. (Sticks made of a composite synthetic are now available although far from being universally adopted. They improve the hitting power and are generally lighter in weight.)

The best polo balls are the plastic ones, which were developed in the US. Originally, they were made from bamboo root or local woods, while the English polo ball was traditionally made from willow.

Between the Wars, international teams were turned out in immaculately tailored white breeches, highly polished brown boots of similar quality, and one or other variation of the pith helmet.

Today, the turnout is practical but less stylish. The breeches are often loose fitting and the elegant boot of yesteryear has been replaced by a boot fastening with a zip up

the front. The pith helmet is now rarely seen, players wearing the well-designed peaked polo helmets with a chinstrap and often fitted with a face-guard. Knee-pads are in almost universal use.

Similarly, the pony's equipment has altered, sometimes in accordance with a change in the style of riding. Boots and leg-bandages remain much the same and are as essential as ever to prevent accidental striking of the pony's legs.

THE GAG BRIDLE

It is in the bitting arrangements, however, that the greatest differences are noticeable. In between the World Wars, the emphasis was firmly placed on the double bridle or Pelham, usually used in conjunction with the standing martingale. The accent in equitation since the Second World War has shifted from the double bridle to the snaffle and the drop-noseband, and in polo to the gag bridle supported by a variety of auxiliaries. As well as the standing martingale, the action may be supported by a drop-noseband. Often there is a running rein, and sometimes side-reins are used too. While occasionally earning the disapproval of the more purist element, this arrangement has the advantage of allowing the rider to exert maximum control.

POLO PONY

THE POLO PONY evolved with the game of polo (see pp.368–71) and spread to the western world. The Manipuri ponies (see pp.202–3) on which the British first played in the 19th century were no bigger than 1.27 m (12.2 hh). By 1870, however, the average height of the ponies used had increased to 1.37 m (13.2 hh). In 1899 the British brought in the height limit of 1.47 m (14.2 hh). That ruling was abolished in 1916, largely at the instigation of the Americans, and from that date the height increased to 1.52–1.60 m (15–15.3 hh). The modern mount is actually a small horse, although it is always called a "pony".

DELHI POLO PONIES
Polo ponies are led to their lines at the ground of the President's Body Guard, Delhi, during the spring tournament season.

TYPES OF POLO PONY

The polo pony is not in strict terms a breed, although its character is more fixed in detail than that of many European breeds. The western game was born in the state of Manipur, between Assam and Burma. It is still played there, on small, Mongolian-type ponies. On village "grounds" throughout the Hindu Kush and beyond, a variety of nimble ponies of a distinct Turkmene stamp play the game, under rules that in no way resemble those of the Hurlingham Club, London. In Africa, Basuto Ponies (see pp.208–9) can be pressed into service, and in the Gulf States the game may be played on Arabs. In the western world, however, and in India and Pakistan, it is the Thoroughbred or near-Thoroughbred pony that predominates.

who pioneered the evolution of the polo pony. They had the advantage of their own excellent native pony breeds, particularly the Dartmoor, the New Forest, and the Connemara (see pp.174–77 and pp.180–81), as well as plenty of small Thoroughbred stallions of the best quality. In fact, the National Pony Society, when it was founded in 1893, was originally called the Polo and Riding Pony Society, and had as a prime objective the encouragement of " . . . the breeding and registration of Polo and Riding Ponies".

POLO IN THE UK AND THE US

Western polo was developed in the UK from tentative beginnings at Aldershot in 1869, and, not surprisingly, it was the British

SHOULDERS
Excellent shoulders, muscular forearms, hard joints, and the best of feet are necessities in the polo pony.

THE GALLOPING GAME
This polo match is being played at the Delhi ground. Polo is largely supported by officers in the Indian Army, but there is also considerable civilian participation in the game at the principal centres.

FEET
Sound feet, some slope to the pasterns, and clean joints absorb some of the concussion caused by galloping on hard ground.

The game was introduced to the US in 1878, and the first match for the Anglo-American Westchester Trophy, the top prize in polo, was played eight years later. The Americans rapidly developed a distinctive pony from stock obtained largely from South America, in particular Argentina. Possibly to safeguard their own interests, the British, who had virtually cornered the market, brought in a 1.47 m (14.2 hh) height limit in 1899. The Americans had the rule abolished in 1916, and from that point the emphasis shifted increasingly to the fast

Argentinian pony, which could be produced in considerable numbers and comparatively cheaply by very skilled horsemen. Very good Thoroughbred ponies continued to be bred in the UK, as they are today, but in terms of economics they could not compare with the Argentinian product, which had the lucrative American market on its doorstep.

ARGENTINA

Polo was brought to Argentina in 1877 by the British community, and rapidly became so popular that in the space of 50 years Argentina had become the leading nation in polo. The reason for the Argentinian supremacy lay primarily with the country's traditional horse culture. The *gauchos* of the pampas are among the world's greatest natural horsemen, and Argentina is also the

POLO PRACTICE
The best way for a polo player to perfect his strokes is by practising regularly on the polo horse, a simple but effective teaching aid.

home of excellent ball-game players. The game quickly became a part of a way of life that could be supported by a virtually unlimited supply of horse flesh.

Argentina first imported Thoroughbreds, to cross with its native Criollo stock (see pp.220–21), which is one of the toughest and soundest breeds in the world. The Thoroughbred was then put back to the subsequent progeny until a distinctive, lean, wiry pony, which was very Thoroughbred in character with exceptional hocks and quarters, had evolved.

The modern Argentinian pony stands at about 1.55 m (15.1 hh). It is to all intents and purposes Thoroughbred, but has the strong limbs, ample bone, and good feet of its Criollo forebears. It is customary for polo ponies to have their manes hogged to avoid interference with the stick, and to have their tails plaited and tied up in a short polo "bang", also to prevent them from being caught up with the stick.

The Argentinian pony is very skilful, and is able to turn and twist at full speed. It also has stamina, courage, and what amounts to an innate "ball-sense", following the ball in the same way as a cow-pony works cattle. Although any pony can become ball-shy and attempt to avoid the more robust aspects of the game, it is rare for an Argentinian animal to display such reluctance.

QUARTERS
Good galloping quarters run into broad loins and a strong back. The muscles at the croup are well-developed.

HIND LEGS
The excellent hind legs are long from the hip-joint to the hock, with the second thighs strongly muscled. The conformation is conducive to speed.

OUTLINE
This mare is beautifully balanced in her conformation, deep through the girth, and wonderfully intelligent in her outlook. The whole outline is indicative of speed and agile athleticism.

HOCKS
The hock joints are big in relation to the proportions of the leg.

HEIGHT
*1.52–1.60 m
(15–15.3 hh)*

Pig-Sticking & Tent-Pegging

A Hog Jinks

Even before the ancient civilizations of Greece, Rome, and Persia, 3,000 years ago, men hunted wild boar from horseback armed with a spear. Today, pig-sticking, or hog-hunting, is still practised in the Indian sub-continent, where British officers and civilians in India took up the sport in the 18th century, and hard-riding officers of the modern Indian army still carry on the tradition today, though on a much reduced scale. As well as being probably one of the oldest equestrian sports, pig-sticking is also the most dangerous. It combines the perils of riding at full speed, over rough, blind country, with the dangers involved in facing and fighting one of the most ferocious animals in the world, and sets a premium on horsemanship and on the courage of both horse and rider.

Pig-Sticking in India

A full-grown boar can measure up to 1 m (39 in) at the withers, and can weigh 150 kg (330 lb). It has razor-sharp tushes, and over the first 0.8 km (½ mile) can run as fast as a Thoroughbred horse. When hard-pressed, it will leap sideways (jink), swerve, and double back, or may squat in thick cover. Finally, a hunted boar, choosing its time with great cunning, will charge at its pursuers with a characteristic "whoof-whoof" of rage. Given the chance, it will launch itself at horse and man, slashing upwards with its tushes. There have been many instances of horses being knocked over by a boar's charge, and furious boars are known to have attacked elephants.

The best hunting areas in India were, and still are, the Kadir or riverine jungle country bordering the Ganges and the Jumna at Meerut and Muttra. The ground is hard and broken, often intersected with *nullahs* (dry stream beds), and pocked with holes and other hazards, all of which are hidden from view by tall, waving yellow grass and tough bushes of *jhow* (tamarisk). Riders in this area employ a 2.1-m (7-ft) underhand bamboo spear, whereas in Bengal in upper India shorter, jabbing spears used to be employed because of the thickness of the jungle. To ride across this country the horseman has to trust his mount. He must ride flat out on a loose rein, relying on his horse to keep its feet while he fixes his eye on the boar.

Horses for pig-sticking need to be well-made, fast, reliable, sure-footed, and very brave. Australian Walers (see pp.290–91) were probably the best, but many good ones were Indian-bred at army remount centres such as the one at Saharanpur. In the mid-19th century some of the most successful hog-hunters favoured Arab horses, but these were not much in evidence in later years. The optimum height for a pig-sticking horse was around 1.57 m (15.2 hh).

Hunting the Boar

This painting by an Indian artist, dated 1835, portrays the Maharana Jawan Singh and his retainers hunting wild boar. The use of a slashing sword rather than a thrusting spear was unusual, even at this time.

FULL GALLOP

A competitor strikes the peg at full gallop during a competition at the Delhi Horse Show. The rider must carry the peg for a distance of 15 m (49 ft) to obtain full points.

Hog-hunting was organized around tent clubs. These had fixed boundaries, were responsible for upholding hunting rules, and kept a staff of *shikaries* (game-keepers) who located and harboured pigs. Tent clubs were so called because the members attending a meet camped in the jungle. The "blue riband of pig-sticking" was the contest for the Kadir Cup, which took place at Sherpur, near Meerut. First held in 1874, it was run annually until 1939, apart from a break during the First World War. The competition was run in heats of three or four riders, supported by beaters and up to 50 elephants to carry spectators. The victor, or "first spear", was the first rider to draw blood. One of the best hog-hunters was Brigadier J. Scott-Cockburn (4th Hussars), who won the Cup in 1924, 1925, and 1927.

TENT-PEGGING TURNOUT

This is typical tent-pegging turnout for both horse and rider. The horse's bright red puggaree (turban) martingale is commonly used in India. For the sake of balance, the spear is weighted at the base.

TENT-PEGGING

Tent-pegging is related to pig-sticking, but is far less dangerous. It is still very popular in the Indian Army and in northern India, Rajasthan, and Pakistan, where competitions are held at festival times. An individual, or a team of four riders, gallops down a prepared track (*pathi*), at the end of which are balsa wood tent pegs set at 60° to the ground. Each peg is 6 cm (2½ in) wide, and projects 12.5 cm (5 in) out of the ground. The rider must strike a peg and carry it on the lance for 15 m (49 ft) in order to gain full points. Fewer marks are awarded for a "strike", or a peg lifted but not carried. Style and pace are also taken into account. In the final run, the peg may be turned sideways to present a face of about 2.5 cm (1 in). Riders often shout "war-cries" (actually prayers for a good strike) as they gallop for the peg, and may indulge in fancy play with the lance, twirling it extravagantly in celebration of a good "carry". The sport had a military origin: cavalry attacking an enemy camp could cause chaos by galloping through the lines and collapsing the tents by lifting the pegs.

THE PONY CLUB

PONY CLUB JUMPING

ONE OF THE WORLD'S most remarkable and enduring institutions is the Pony Club, an international youth movement based on the ideals of good horsemanship and the proper care of horses and ponies. It was founded in England in 1929 as a junior branch of the Institute of the Horse, the organization which in 1947 amalgamated with the National Horse Association to become the British Horse Society. The Club was the brainchild of two military men – Brigadier Tom Marchant, the Institute's secretary, and Major Harry Faudel-Phillips, who became the first Chairman of the Central Committee of the newly named Institute of the Horse and the Pony Club.

MILITARY STYLE

Retired soldiers, the early ones products of the cavalry schools at Weedon and Netheravon, played a leading part in the Pony Club throughout its history. One was Colonel V.D.S. Williams, named the "Father of British Dressage" by Alois Podhajsky, a long-time Director of Vienna's Spanish Riding School. Another, perhaps the most notable, was Colonel the Honourable Guy Cubitt, who was the Club's Chairman for 25 years and its first Life President.

Through these retired officers there evolved a sound organizational structure which, in its essentials, survives to this day. They were also responsible for the publication of valuable instructional manuals and booklets culminating in the *Manual of Horsemanship*, which is still the "bible" of the organization. The declared "aims" and "objects" of the Pony Club, as they appear in the Golden Jubilee celebration booklet, are:

"To encourage young people to ride and to learn to enjoy all kinds of sport connected with horses and riding.

"To provide instruction in riding and horsemanship and to instil in members the proper care of their animals.

"To promote the highest ideals of sportsmanship, citizenship and loyalty, thereby cultivating strength of character and self-discipline."

Faudel-Phillips' motto was, "Do to all animals as in similar cases you would wish them to do to you and in training your pony make haste slowly." Guy Cubitt defined the Pony Club ideal as, "a child riding

PONY RACING
Racing is a new and exciting dimension to the complement of Pony Club competitions and has proved to be very popular.

with happiness, safety and comfort on a pony equally happy and comfortable and free from pain, fear or bewilderment."

HUNTING CONNECTION

At the outset, and in tune with the context of the time and the background of its founders and their ever-growing band of dedicated volunteers, hunting, as well as an understanding of the countryside in which it was often a central element, was integral to the concept of the Pony Club. This may have contributed to an elitist image, which, though unjustified, was refuted only in the closing years of the 20th century.

After the Second World War, and the expansion of recreational riding into towns

IT'S ALL ABOUT FUN
Typical of the Pony Club events is the popular and often hilarious sack race, which nonetheless calls for skills of a high order.

and cities, there was a shift in emphasis towards the competitive sports.

Initially, it was the hunt structure that provided the most convenient base for the Pony Club branch organization, and it was hunting people who initiated and controlled the branch activities, as in many instances in Britain they do to this day. The first branches (14 initially) were named after the local hunt, to which they became and remain closely connected, for example, the Quorn Branch of the Pony Club or the Banwen Miners' Hunt Branch. Where there was no hunt, the branch took the name of the town or locality.

DIVERSITY

Each branch is the responsibility of a District Commissioner and is self-contained, self-governing, and self-supporting while under the overall control of the Pony Club Headquarters. Branches, as a result, develop a character of their own. Some may be markedly competitive; others may offer minority sports like polo or polo-crosse; and there will be those that emphasize countryside studies or, if the membership is young, will concentrate on basic instruction. There is, in theory, no minimum age for a Pony Club member. At the age of 18, members are known as Associates, and their membership ceases three years later.

Branches in the UK, some 366 with a total membership averaging about 30,000, are divided into 19 geographical areas, a system that allows for inter-branch and inter-area competition, the latter culminating in the annual National Championships.

The Pony Club is involved at a commendably high level in competitions covering the major disciplines: horse trials, showjumping, and dressage. It organizes a tetrathlon competition and, on a smaller scale, there are championships for polo and polo-crosse.

A feature of the Pony Club is the Mounted Games, popularly known as the Prince Philip Cup Games since their inauguration by the Duke of Edinburgh in 1957, the finals of which are held annually at London's Horse of the Year Show.

While competition is an important aspect of the Club's activities, it is the working rallies and, for most branches, the annual Pony Club Camp that is at the very core of the organization. It is at these that members can be prepared for the tests devised to gauge progress and to give incentive for improvement. There are four tests from D, the simplest, to the A test, which is acknowledged as calling for a very high standard of all-round riding ability and horse management.

But while the Pony Club has the greatest influence on the national scene in Britain, it has from its early

RELAXATION
Pony Club members away at camp treat their ponies to a refreshing dip in the river at the end of the working day.

beginnings been truly international in its appeal. Although numbers will naturally fluctuate, overseas branches, most of them affiliated to the parent body, number around 1,800 at any one time, giving world-wide membership exceeding 100,000 and providing the opportunity for organized visits and competitions between countries.

The two countries with the greatest number of branches are Australia, with over 900, and the US with in excess of 500. Both organizations have developed a strong national character of their own.

The first Pony Club branch in Australia was the Mountain District Branch in Victoria, formed in 1944. Overall administration is vested in the Australian Pony Club Council, which includes representatives of the six State Pony Club Associations. In general, the Australian Pony Club branches follow the British pattern as closely as circumstances allow.

The American Pony Club – and each branch is termed a Club – was started in 1935 by Mrs Barbara Taylor, following a visit to England. However, the war years intervened, and it was not until 1950 that Mrs Dean Bedford started a branch in Harford County, Maryland. Four years later, the United States Pony Clubs Inc. was granted a charter. It is not officially associated with the parent body in Britain, but it has in most respects adopted its programme, standards, and training methods, holding its own national events. It maintains links with the British Pony Club and the American hunt clubs.

POLO-CROSSE

Polo-crosse is a derivative of polo and can be played on almost any pony. The game is fast and not without physical contact.

GALLOPING GAMES

COSSACK HORSEMAN

IN THE PAST, games that were played on horseback, and skill-at-arms competitions involving the use of sword, pistol, and lance, were regarded as useful training exercises for cavalrymen, and were practised in most of the world's mounted formations. Among the peoples of Asia, traditional mounted games, which were probably rooted in the ancient equestrian culture of the Scythians, are still played with enthusiasm by adults. Official All-Union competitions based on these games were organized under established rules of play during the years before the collapse of the former USSR. In contrast, in Western Europe today mounted games are played almost exclusively by young people. The British Pony Club organization, in particular, has developed a complex competition structure.

TRADITIONAL GAMES

The brutal sport of *buzkashi* (see pp.368–69) is perhaps an extreme example of the old mounted contests. There are also many less ferocious games, most of them demanding exceptional riding skills, which are played with enthusiasm throughout Central Asia, Iran, and Afghanistan.

A colourful game, popular in varying forms throughout the Asian republics, is *khis-koubou* or *kyzkuu*, which is based on the bridal chase of the nomadic horse peoples. In the original form, several men might pursue a young woman, intent on claiming a kiss from her. She, however, would be armed with a stout whip, and would repel their advances while riding towards the goal, usually a pole stuck in the ground (which, it is suggested, was a form of fertility symbol). On the other hand, of course, she might submit to a particularly favoured swain.

The modern game is run over a distance of 300–400 m (328–438 yds). If, at the end of the course, the man has not been able to claim his prize, the woman turns and pursues him back to the start, all the time beating her erstwhile suitor with her whip.

Dzhigit riding involves many acrobatic exercises, such as *Tenge-Lyu* (picking a handkerchief from the ground at full gallop). Another game is the light-hearted *Papakh-oyuno* (pulling off the hat), a popular pastime in Azerbaijan, in which the players try to take the hats of their opponents. Further east, in Kazakhstan and Kirghizia, the people play *Oodarysh* or *Sais*, which involves wrestling on horseback within a rectangular pitch.

In Europe, the *Czikos* horsemen of Hungary have games similar to those played by the Asian peoples. They also excel at activities such as standing on the saddle of a galloping horse while driving two others, and other extraordinary feats.

EUROPEAN GYMKHANAS

The word *gymkhana* is of Indian origin. Gymkhana games were brought to Europe, and particularly to the UK, by army officers returning home during the 19th century, and they are the source of the Pony Club mounted games. There are countless games that can be played from the back of a pony. The best known events are the bending race, where the rider zig-zags at speed

TRAINING GAME
Picking up the handkerchief is a game played the world over, and often forms part of the training of cavalry troopers such as this Indian horseman.

WRESTLING ON HORSEBACK
Horse sports in Kazakhstan and Kirghizia include this form of wrestling on horseback, called Oodarysh *or* Sais. *The horses seem to enter into the spirit of the game and attempt to co-operate with their riders.*

TRICK HORSEMANSHIP

The Czikos horsemen of the Hungarian puszta specialize in trick horsemanship based on driving horses while standing on the backs of others – it is as difficult as it looks.

MOUNTED GAMES

A competitor at the Windsor Horse Show, in the UK, takes part in a qualifying heat for the Pony Club Mounted Games Championship. This event was instigated in 1957 by HRH the Duke of Edinburgh.

through a line of poles; the sack race, in which the rider leads the pony while hopping beside it in a sack; stepping stones, which involves leading the pony while running down a line of upturned pots; and all sorts of relay-type team races. There is a sharpshooters' race, when two riders have to ride one pony, one of them having to leap off to throw a ball at comic figures or something similar. The flag race calls for a flag to be lifted in and out of a bucket; the sword race involves removing rings from a post on the point of a wooden sword; and then there are races in which children have to wriggle through tyres. They are all fun events, but they demand balance, agility, suppleness, and highly developed riding skills. The ponies used need to be well-schooled, for they are ridden mostly on

one hand. They have to be quick and responsive, and yet be temperamentally suited to games that are potentially very exciting for both ponies and riders.

In the UK a Pony Club Mounted Games Championship was instigated in 1957 by HRH Prince Philip, and this is still called the "Prince Philip Games". Teams from all over the country compete at area and zone finals during the summer, and the event takes place at London's Horse of the Year

Show in October. The games are limited to riders aged 15 years and under, and to ponies under 1.47 m (14.2 hh).

Finally, there is the Mock Hunt, which can be organized to suit the competence of the young riders taking part. A route is planned, incorporating a number of fences, which can be built with a way round to save over-facing the more novice riders and ponies. The "Fox", a competent, usually adult rider, lays a trail of sawdust or wood-shavings, which is hunted by "Hounds" under the direction of a "Huntsman". They are followed by the "Field" until the "Fox" is caught at some predetermined spot. The Mock Hunt is a very suitable fun event for both pony clubs and adult riding clubs and is very popular with both.

HORSE RACING IN MONGOLIA

Horse racing is endemic to the Mongol way of life, and is often central to religious festivals. In Mongol races the ponies are ridden by young boys and girls, rather than by heavier adults, over a distance of 32–64 km (20–40 miles).

RODEO

BULL RIDING

RODEOS DEMONSTRATE the skills developed by the cowboy in the early days of cattle-ranching, and have their origins in informal contests that were held at round-ups and which subsequently became a principal feature at Western fairs. The first commercial rodeo (which means "round-up") was held in Arizona, in 1888. A hundred years later over 700 rodeos were being held in the US and Canada under the rules of the Professional Rodeo Cowboys' Association, formed in 1936. It now has a membership of thousands, together with "apprentice" permit holders who must qualify, in terms of prize-money, before being admitted as full members. The top events are the Calgary Stampede and the annual National Finals Rodeo in Las Vegas, where prize money is over $2 million. The title of World-Champion All-round Cowboy goes to the rider who wins a final event involving the top 15 money-winners of the year.

CLASSIC RODEO EVENTS

There are six basic competitive rodeo events: saddle-bronc riding, bareback riding, bull riding, steer wrestling, calf roping, and team roping. Other events include chuck-waggon racing, barrel racing, and pole bending.

Saddle-bronc riding, the classic rodeo event, is the most difficult, but surprisingly, it is not the most dangerous event and casualties are rare. The horse is saddled with a bucking strap fastened tight round its loins and wears a stout headcollar with a single plaited rope for the rider to grasp. It is mounted in a closed chute and when the gate is opened comes out bucking hard. The rider has to stay in place, riding with only one hand, for eight seconds, and is marked on the style of the ride as he rakes the horse from shoulder to flank with his blunt rowelled spurs. The rider's movements have to be synchronized with those of the horse. The cowboys hope to draw a horse that bucks rhythmically and so gives a better chance of scoring good marks, rather than one that bucks and twists wildly in no pattern. Horses are often bred specifically for the rodeo and some are as famous as their riders.

Bareback riding is as difficult as the saddle-bronc event but more dangerous. The horse wears neither a headcollar nor a bridle and the rider has only a hand-loop fastened to a surcingle to help him stay on. "Style" is the deciding factor and the rider must sit the bucking horse, spurring with the legs from front to rear, for eight seconds.

Even more in line with the elemental, gladiatorial nature of the rodeo is the riding of the quick-moving, horned Brahma bulls. It is judged in the same way as the ridden contests, but with the bull it is necessary to have men on foot to distract the enraged animal when the rider parts company.

Steer wrestling is an individual competition but the cowboy needs the help of a "hazer" to position the steer so that he can leap onto it and bring it down. The event is judged on time and usually the steer is put down within three or four seconds.

BUCKING BRONCO
Saddle-bronc riding is the classic rodeo event. The horse wears a tight "bucking strap" round the loins, and the cowboy is only allowed to use one hand.

SPEED AND AGILITY

Barrel racing is open to women as well as men and the women are often the most successful. The Quarter Horse is considered the best barrel racer of all.

Time is also of the essence in the calf roping event, in which the rider ropes the calf and then dismounts quickly to hog-tie the animal while the horse holds the rope taut. In this partnership of man and horse it is the Quarter Horse (see pp.230–31) that is unrivalled for speed, agility, and intelligence. Quarter Horses are also the best performers in the team roping. A team of two riders and their horses work in unison to immobilize the steer. The practical application of team roping is to catch animals for treatment or branding and it is still practised on the cattle ranches.

AGAINST THE CLOCK
Calf roping is a timed event and the cowboy, having roped the calf, has to dismount and hog-tie the animal, while his horse holds the rope taut.

One rider and his horse act as the "header", the other as the "heeler". The header has to stop the steer by roping either the head and one horn or by roping both horns. He then turns the steer so his partner can lasso the steer's heels. Both horses then pull the rope taut and the clock stops once they stand facing each other on either side of the steer.

CHUCK-WAGGONS AND BARRELS

Chuck-waggon racing and barrel racing are the two racing rodeo events. Chuck-waggon racing, regarded as a "fun event", is a modern version of the Roman chariot races and is just as dangerous. To drive a team of four at full gallop on an oval track calls for great skill. Barrel racing, unlike the other rodeo events, is open to women as well as men and the cowgirls are often the most successful. The Quarter Horse is the best mount because of its exceptional agility and acceleration. Riders race in turn around three barrels set on a triangle, and are timed electronically from the start to when the horse's nose crosses the finishing line.

SHOW CLASSES

There are some half-dozen competitive Western show classes, all of them demanding high standards of horsemanship. The most popular of these classes, and the one within reach of most riders, is the Western Pleasure Class, which

NO SADDLE
The cowboy has only a hand-strap to help him stay on when he is taking part in the bareback riding competition, the most dangerous rodeo event.

demonstrates the paces and obedience of the horse. Trail classes are more advanced and include mandatory obstacles, as do the Western Riding classes. Perhaps the peak of the Western equestrian art is represented by the reining classes, the equivalent of the dressage test, but with the movements being carried out at full speed.

WESTERN RIDING

WESTERN SADDLE

THE ORIGIN OF WESTERN-STYLE riding can be traced to the Spanish Conquests of the 16th and 17th centuries, and more particularly to the Spanish settlers who brought cattle ranching to the Americas and created a huge industry, first in leather and later in meat. With them came an age-old horse culture, as well as a distinctive system of saddlery and bridling. However, the subsequent development of the Western style has produced a form of horsemanship that is wholly original and in stark contrast to the European practice, or even to that of its Iberian progenitors. At its highest level, it exemplifies the near-perfect harmony that can occasionally exist between horse and rider.

WESTERN VERSUS EUROPEAN

For many, the attraction of "riding Western" lies in its seemingly relaxed informality, and this is especially true of holiday riding, which forms a notable part of the US tourist industry. In this context, riding Western is, indeed, relaxed and informal, the greatest pleasure to be had from riding a calm, responsive horse with smooth, comfortable paces. The whole adds up to a comforting feeling of reassurance for the less experienced rider, a feeling strengthened by the security of the Western stock saddle.

Trail riding is deservedly popular, and American show programmes include trail-riding classes designed to test and encourage the all-round ability of the trail horse. However, Western riding at more advanced levels, particularly in the show classes, has its own strictly observed conventions, and it can achieve a formality and attention to detail far in excess of its European equivalent. What is not always appreciated in the European horse world – dominated, largely, by the three major disciplines of dressage, showjumping, and horse trials – is that Western horsemanship at its highest level is on a par with that of the "classical" schools of Europe. It may have no relevance to the European disciplines, but it requires, nonetheless, just as much skill, dedication, and devotion to basic training principles. It may, indeed, come closer to the classical ideal in its insistence on the purity of the paces and in obtaining in the highly schooled Western horse a perfectly balanced self-carriage with minimal rein support, often amounting to no more than the weight of a looping rein.

Both schools have common objectives: lightness, obedience, relaxation in movement, and the maintenance of a supple, fluid balance – in short, a horse that is a pleasure to ride. However, they differ in purpose, method, and emphasis. The European system – with the exception of the hunter, either Irish or English, and to an extent the long-distance horse – is primarily concerned with competition in the major disciplines, with lip-service being given to the overlay of "classical" horsemanship. The Western system has the practical objective of producing an all-round working horse against the background of handling cattle.

In Europe, the emphasis is on collection, with the horse being dependent on the will of the rider expressed through the application of the "aids" (in the US known as "cues" – a more descriptive word, perhaps, for the signals given by the rider's hands, legs, and body weight).

The dressage rider uses a more or less continual mix of driving aids, applied through the legs and seat; and halting aids, made through the seat again, combined with a slight backward inclination of the trunk, and both hands, connected in advanced competition to the obligatory double bridle. In this manner, the rider seeks to encourage the propulsive engagement of the hocks beneath the body, to maintain the rhythm and fix the outline within the frame imposed by leg and hand.

BACK-UP
The Western horse performs the back-up (rein-back) with head tucked in and on a looping rein. The rider's "cues" are minimal.

cotton thread to the most powerful of curb bits, while modern displays are often ridden without a bridle, to show that the horse is not reliant on the bit.)

The regularity and quality of the paces is central to the training of the Western horse, as with its European counterpart. The definitive Western paces are the jog and lope, taught from the basis of an established working trot and canter, of which they are essentially scaled-down versions with a somewhat shorter stride. Both demand great suppleness and strength and the necessary powerful engagement of the quarters. The paces should be flat and smooth to give a comfortable ride and preclude any lift in the knee and hock action. Basic requirements are the ability to rein-back, move sideways, and execute turns on the quarters as well as on the forehand.

ADVANCED WORK

Advanced work calls for lead changes, i.e. the flying change of leg at canter and the roll-back, when the horse turns on the pivot of the haunches through 180° and does so at speed, with the turn made following a halt from the lope. This is followed immediately by a swift roll-back from which the horse goes away in lope in the opposite direction. The Western spin is a pirouette carried out at speed on the pivot of the inside hind leg, with the horse maintaining a rounded back and crossing the fore legs with smooth fluency. It must be executed in balance, with the inside shoulder kept high.

The spectacular sliding stop is purely a show movement. It is, also, a punishing manoeuvre, putting tendons and joints at risk. Its artificiality is emphasized by the use of special, sliding shoes, a prepared surface, and the fitting of protective boots. It is taught from the halt preceding the roll-back and necessitates full engagement of the hocks under the body. Rein contact is minimal, and very advanced horses can perform the stop without a bridle at all. At its very best (or worst), a sliding stop is made from an accelerating gallop and can involve the horse sliding along the ground for up to 9 m (30 ft) on the hind legs.

Western riding associations exist in Europe and enjoy considerable popularity.

ROLL-BACK
In a roll-back, the horse turns on the pivot of the haunches with its head lowered. The rider carries the reins in one hand.

The Western horse is no less balanced. The hocks are just as much engaged and the topline as softly rounded, but the outline differs since head and neck are held lower and more extended, although the horse "tucksin" easily when asked to rein-back, for instance. The finished Western horse is ridden with one hand, although in the training progression both hands are used to emphasize the changes of direction that are required. For the Western horseman the principal "cues" are made through the disposition of the seat and body weight, little reliance being placed on the legs, as in the European fashion. There is an influence through the reins, but so subtle that in the trained horse it is virtually imperceptible. This is achieved through the hackamore system (see pp.446–47) involving a progression of *bosal* (noseband) of varying weights, and culminating in a potentially severe curb bit brought minimally into play by no more than a slight upward movement of the hand. The horse is thus effectively "mouthed" through the nose and can be ridden on no more than a floating-rein contact, the opposite of the European practice but consistent with the "classical" ideal. (The great Western horsemen used to demonstrate rein contact by attaching a

SLIDING STOP
The movement is carried out with light rein contact and with hind legs fully engaged under the body.

SLIDING STOP

WESTERN SHOW CLASSES

APART FROM THE USUAL rodeo events, the Western-trained horse can compete in a variety of show classes. Most come under the overall aegis of the American Quarter Horse Association, a situation that reflects the still-booming "Quarter Horse industry" in the US. Show-class events are not confined solely to the Quarter Horse breed, however, and there are specialist associations, like the National Reining Association, controlling their respective sports. All the Western-ridden show classes are based on the practical use of the working horse. Accordingly, exhibitors turn out in correct Western clothes that evolved as the cowboy's working dress. However, a certain individuality in the choice of dress is apparent and is not discouraged in this increasingly popular sport.

A PLEASURE TO RIDE

The most popular class, and probably the one best suited to the beginner, is the Western Pleasure, in which the horse shows that he is, indeed, a pleasure to ride at all paces. Horses are ridden in both directions at walk, jog, and lope and are required to rein-back (back-up). With exceptions for young horses, the reins are held in one hand and are reasonably loose.

Although trail-riding classes may reflect the popularity of this leisure activity, they are highly competitive and represent a comprehensive test of the horse's training and calm acceptance of unusual situations. Once more, the tests are ridden with one hand. Competitors are required to complete a course that includes three mandatory obstacles. These are a gate to be opened, passed through, and closed; a grid of at least four logs, which may be set in a straight line or on a curve or zigzag, and which may be raised off the ground by as much as 30 cm (12 in); and an obstacle constructed for the horse to back through or around. Variations in this obstacle may include L-, V-, or U-shaped patterns; three markers set in line or on a triangle to be backed through and around; and the very difficult wine-glass shape with an overall length of 4.88 m (16 ft). Other tests may involve a water hazard or a wooden bridge, which has to be calmly negotiated. Competitors may also be asked to carry an article over a stipulated length of the arena. A very practical test involves putting on and taking off a waterproof (a slicker) from the saddle. Horses are expected to move sideways, sometimes over a 30-cm (12-in) high obstacle, to rein-back through a series of poles, and, in a particular test of handiness, to step into a square of poles laid on the

TRAIL-RIDING OBSTACLE
The gate that has to be opened, passed through, and closed again afterwards is one of three mandatory obstacles in the demanding trail-riding classes of the Western discipline.

ground, perform a 360° turn within the square, and then step quietly out again. Ground-tying or hobbling the horse is sometimes required and, at the other end of the scale, there is usually mail to be posted in a box, in the manner of an English gymkhana event.

Horses are judged not only on their performance at the obstacles but also on a number of other criteria: their overall way of going, the correctness of the paces, and the style in which the test is accomplished.

By any standard, the trail class is a demanding test of horse and rider and judging is exacting, allowing for little or no deviation from the stated requirement.

The horsemanship (equitation) class is judged on the ability of the rider to perform

PURPOSEFUL RELAXATION
The Western Pleasure class is one of the most popular in the show programme. Its laid-back style provides the best sort of introduction for beginners into the Western show classes.

a prescribed set of manoeuvres with a high degree of precision, while demonstrating correctness of seat and the subtle application of the cues. A "pattern" (course) may include work at walk, jog, and lope on curves, serpentines, or circles; a stop; back-ups (rein-back); leg-yielding; and even flying change of leg, which is again an accepted advanced movement. Instructions on what constitutes a correct seat are detailed in the extreme and are applied even when entrants are asked to ride without stirrups, a matter which is at the discretion of the judge.

THE REINING CLASS

The Western horseman's equivalent of the dressage test is the reining class, employing set "patterns" of varying degrees of difficulty ridden at speed and subject to judging criteria of particular severity. The reining classes, like the advanced dressage tests, demonstrate a very high level of schooling calling for fluency and great accuracy and, as in the dressage test, resistance of any sort, tension, and lack of accuracy are penalized.

The patterns are ridden in an arena set with three markers at either side. These are placed on the centre line and at least 15 m (50 ft) from each end of the arena.

Each pattern is required to be ridden one-handed and with virtually imperceptible cues on the part of the rider. The patterns, performed at the lope with variations of

PROPER TURNOUT
This competitor and her horse are correctly turned out for Western competition classes, in which turnout is an important consideration.

speed, include all the movements of the Western school: spins, roll-back, lead changes, fast and slow circles, and the sliding stop. The stop is defined by the National Reining Horse Association, the sport's governing body, as "the act of slowing the horse from a lope to a stop position by bringing the hind legs under the

horse in a locked position sliding on the hind feet. The horse should enter the stop position by bending the back, bringing the hind legs further under the body while maintaining forward motion, ground contact, and cadence with the front legs. Throughout the stop, the horse should continue in a straight line while maintaining ground contact with the hind feet."

On completing the pattern, riders are required to dismount and "drop the bridle to the designated judge".

EUROPEAN FOLLOWING

There are a number of Western horse associations in Europe, and the Western style has a small but active following in Britain. The UK's Western Equestrian Society, for instance, was founded in 1985 and publishes a rule book with detailed information on Western classes and regulations. This Society stages its own shows and holds a Championship weekend, where classes are usually judged by a prominent expert from the US. The reining classes are affiliated to the British Reining Horse Association and are held under its rules. There is also a freestyle reining to music class, in which specified movements – stops, spins, lead changes, back-ups, and circles varying in size – are obligatory. This is the Western equivalent of the dressage *Kur* (freestyle test) and has great spectator appeal. Interestingly, and with commendable pragmatism, its published Constitution recognizes the prejudice of the European horseman towards Western riding and the misunderstandings that arise as a result.

The Society's first object is concerned with the promotion of "... true high standards of Western equitation as practised in the United States of America". It goes on to state as further objectives: "To stimulate growth of this riding discipline to the detriment of the movie image and to maintain its acceptance within the British Isles"; and then: "To actively discourage ridden games or rodeo events that act to the detriment of the image of Western equitation in the British Isles."

HALTER CLASS CHAMPION
A splendid pair exhibit in a Western part-bred halter class, with both horse and rider immaculately turned out. This is a very good example of an all-round Western horse.

CUTTING HORSES

CUTTING HORSE IN ACTION

THE PRIMARY USE of the horse in the American West and the Canadian prairies – "the empire of woods and wheat" that nonetheless raises a million head of cattle a year – was as an indispensable aid in herding livestock. Canada, up until the 1980s, employed half-a-million horses on the cattle ranches of the West, and the US had many more. Both countries recognized the Cutting Horse as the king of cow-ponies, but it was Canada that actually bred a horse specifically to fill that role and gave it the title of "Cutting Horse". Although the animals are trained for the work, no amount of training can compensate for the innate intelligence and instinctive behaviour, known as "cow sense", found in some Quarter Horse lines, which makes them particularly suited to this type of occupation.

BRED FOR SUCCESS

The first horses to be introduced into Canada were those taken there by the French settlers of the mid-17th century. Later, the British imported quality English and Irish horses into the country, which produced, in time, a recognizable Canadian hunter with great jumping ability.

It was to be the basis, with a judicious infusion of Cutting Horse blood, for the remarkably successful horses that made up the Canadian Olympic teams. Canada won the three-day-event bronze medal in 1956 and the team showjumping gold at the Mexico Olympics of 1968, and has an enviable record in World Cup events, as well as a formidable list of individual medal winners. The 1976 Olympics were staged by Canada at Bromont, Montreal. Additionally, Canada became deservedly famous for its Percheron heavy draught horses (see pp.94–95), thousands of which were sent to France after 1915 to replace the enormous number of horses lost in the First World War.

In 1926, the Canadian Hunter and Light Horse Society was founded, and in 1933 a stud book for the Canadian Hunter was opened in Ottawa.

Over the years, provincial breeders had created in the Canadian Cutting Horse yet another very recognizable working horse for use in the extensive ranching industry. It was, in fact, a relation – a cousin, perhaps – of the famous all-American product, the American Quarter Horse, the oldest and most popular of the American breeds (see pp.230–31), which was being bred early in the 17th century in Virginia and the settlements along the eastern coast.

The Royal Canadian Mounted Police (see pp.310–11) were mounted on Canadian Cutting Horses up to 1940, when Commissioner Wood created the RCMP stud around the old Fort Walsh, built in 1874, to produce the force's distinctive black and dark bay horses through the crossing of Thoroughbred sires with half-bred and Cutting Horse mares.

Today, the emphasis in Canada has shifted towards the production of the sports or competition horse, as is the case in Europe and elsewhere. The Canadian Cutting Horse, as such, is perhaps not so much in evidence now, and there is a far greater Quarter Horse presence nowadays than there was in the past.

Nonetheless, it was teams of Canadian Cutting Horses that introduced the sport of cutting to British audiences in the 1960s and 70s, and they were also a considerable influence throughout Australia, a country that raises large numbers of cattle on the vast stations of the outback, along with its ubiquitous sheep.

FROM RANGE TO ARENA

On the working ranches of the western United States and in Canada the most valuable horse in the *remuda* was the Cutting Horse. Canada had its own horse, and in the US it was the remarkable Quarter Horse that, increasingly, filled this role.

In the early days of ranching, the prairies were virtually unfenced and so the cattle were herded, gathered, and separated on the open range. Once a cow had been selected it was the job of the Cutting Horse to ease into the herd, causing the very minimum of disturbance, and to drive the cow out and hold her out. When the "cut" (a group of cows that had to be separated from the main herd) was started, the Cutting Horse drove the selected cow to the "cut" and prevented her from returning to the herd. In the meantime, one group of riders held the herd, while other riders positioned themselves to hold the "cut".

In its essentials the sport of cutting, controlled by the National Cutting Horse Association, holds closely to the practice of the open range. The difference is that prize purses, often in excess of $2 million, have

CANADIAN CUTTING HORSE

A highly schooled Canadian Quarter Horse, bred "to cut", works almost independently of the rider and has exceptional intelligence.

LOOK, NO HANDS!

A Cutting Horse demonstrates its innate skills and its obedience in a display ridden without a bridle. This is the acme of the Western schooling system.

made cutting the world's richest equestrian arena sport and the Cutting Horse almost as valuable as a Thoroughbred racehorse.

In the arena, horse and rider approach the herd quietly, while the rider selects the calf to be cut out. Once the choice is made, he is not permitted to change to another. As on the range, he cuts out the calf without upsetting the herd, and it is driven to the middle of the arena. The "turnback" men, in order to increase the excitement for the spectators, push the calf back towards the Cutting Horse. Without touching the rein or otherwise "cueing" his horse, the rider must then allow the horse to control the calf on his own initiative and prevent it returning to the herd. If the calf escapes or the horse misjudges and turns away from it, penalties are incurred. More than one calf may be cut, but the rider has just two-and-a-half minutes to demonstrate the skill and lightning-quick reactions of his horse.

Because of the horse's speed in turning to head off the calf, most riders prefer to use a saddle with a higher fork and cantle and a deeper seat that gives more security. It goes without saying that the rider of the Cutting Horse must be as fit and supple as his horse if he is to avoid injuries caused by the speed and violence of the movement.

COW-SENSE

The conformation and, just as important, the innate intelligence and cow-sense of the Quarter Horse, make the breed an ideal choice for this sport. The Quarter Horse is naturally balanced, with the ability to bring the hindlegs well under the body so as to provide the maximum propulsive thrust. He is explosively fast (the fastest horse in the world over short distances) and very athletic and supple, as well as being immensely agile.

Of course, the Cutting Horse has to be trained for the work, but no amount of training will make up for the inherent and possibly inherited cow-sense found in some Quarter Horse lines.

In fact, if the horse does not "show cow" at an early stage, it would not be worth persevering with the training. "Showing cow" means that the horse can be seen instinctively watching the selected calf throughout, before acting of its own volition to maintain the head-to-head position so that it blocks the calf's efforts to return to the herd. A natural Cutting Horse, just like a sheepdog, works instinctively and has the capability to out-think and out-manoeuvre a calf far quicker and far more effectively than its rider.

No branch of equestrian sport combines the infinitely subtle control exercised by the rider with the complete freedom to work on its own account that is the unique quality of the Cutting Horse.

In no other sphere of horsemanship is the partnership between man and horse quite so evident as in this.

THE WORKING HORSE

Quarter Horses take part in a "team penning" competition where a group of animals is cut out from the herd.

CALGARY STAMPEDE

"The Greatest Show on Earth"

RIDING THE BULL
Bull riding provides an interesting, and a dangerous, variant to the saddle-bronc events.

CANADA HAS A RICH, if somewhat understated, horse culture that combines the influence of both the French and British settlers (see pp.386–87). Much of the interest in horse sports and associated equestrian recreational activities has been due to a handful of influential enthusiasts. One of these was E.P. Taylor, whose interest in Thoroughbred racing encouraged some of the best facilities in the world. Mr Taylor and Windfields Farm were also responsible for Northern Dancer, leading sire of North America in 1971 and sire of the super-horse Nijinsky. Another great contribution to the Canadian scene was made by an American cowboy, Guy Weadick, who in 1912 started the Calgary Stampede, "the biggest show the world has ever seen". Toronto is considered to be the capital of Canada's equestrian sport, but it is Alberta's Calgary Stampede that captures the imagination of the public. The Calgary Stampede is the largest of the three top rodeos – the trio being completed by the Pendleton Round Up (Oregon) and the Cheyenne Frontier Days (Wyoming). Weadick's first one-day show in 1912 was a flop. The people liked it, but it lost money. He returned in 1919, and this time it was a success. With the amalgamation of the Calgary Industrial Exhibition and the Stampede committee in 1923, the show was firmly established. Since then, for ten days in July, Calgary and the whole of Alberta goes Western. The Stampede opens with the Grand Parade, which may be up to 8 km (5 miles) long, through the streets of Calgary. Brightly dressed horsemen and women on every sort of horse, from the recognizable Canadian Hunter to the extravagantly caparisoned Parade horses, striking Palominos, colourful Appaloosas, or the flashiest of Arabians, pass through applauding crowds, most of them dressed for the occasion in Western style. The Mounties ride past, there are decorated and crowded chuckwagons and floats, and possibly as many as 30 marching bands, all contributing to the carnival atmosphere. More significantly, and of greater social importance, is the strong Indian presence drawn from the five Plains tribes. They are as integral to the Calgary Stampede as they are to Canadian life, and the Stampede acts as an unmistakable celebration of Canada's harmonious mix of cultures and races. Combined with the Stampede is a fairground as big as any in the world, with a mammoth roller-coaster. There are exhibitions of every kind, displays, concerts, and a large and important agricultural section in which over 1,000 cattle compete for six-figure prizes. The whole extravaganza closes with a giant fireworks finale. But, of course, the heart of the Stampede is the rodeo held in Stampede Park. As with all rodeos, saddle-bronc riding, on animals often raised specifically for the purpose, is the classic event and carries the biggest prize-money. A particular feature at Calgary are the spectacular chuckwagon races for teams of four attended by outriders, and they always attract a large entry.

FAST AND FURIOUS
Chuckwagon racing is a highlight of the Calgary Stampede. Accompanied by whooping outriders, the four-horse teams race at breakneck speed, urged on by the enthusiastic crowd.

SADDLE-BRONC RIDING
The focus of the Calgary Stampede, the world's largest rodeo, are the eagerly awaited saddle-bronc events. The rider has to stay in place for eight seconds on specially chosen horses that are "mean" enough to have learned every trick of the game. He sits out the bucks and twists riding with one hand, while synchronizing his body with the unpredictable movements of the horse.

HUNTING: THE HISTORY

Sᴵɴᴄᴇ ᴘʀᴇʜɪꜱᴛᴏʀɪᴄ ᴛɪᴍᴇꜱ, hunting has been practised both for food and for sport. Hunting quarry by its scent with a pack of hounds came later but was well known in Ancient Greece; the Greek general, historian, and agriculturalist Xenophon (c.430–355 ʙᴄ) wrote at length on the breeding and management of hounds. In Europe, France has the oldest tradition of organized hunting. It was introduced into Britain in the 11th century, when the recognized "beasts of the chase" were the stag, the boar, and, at one time, the wolf. Hunting with hounds on horseback is now found mainly in the UK and Ireland, parts of mainland Europe and the British Commonwealth, and the US.

HUNTING IN FRANCE

Hunting in France is still carried on in its traditional form with great style and splendour. There are 75 packs of hounds, which are termed *équipage* when the stag is the quarry and *vautrait* when the wild boar is hunted. French hunting is a very stylized, musical affair, the phases of the chase being attended by varying calls on the curled French horns. These calls are known as *fanfares de circonstance*. The hounds, which are usually heavier in build than the faster English foxhounds, are from old French strains and bred for their "nose" (scenting ability) and their "tongue" (voice). Among the principal strains of French hound are those of the *Grand Bleu de Gascoyne*, the *Gascon Saintongeais*, and the *Française Tricolore*. For the most part, these have been crossed with English foxhounds to improve their speed and stamina.

French hunting is often regarded as something of an art form and is far removed from the dash and hurly-burly of the English hunting field. Nonetheless, although no jumping is involved, the days are long, and the sport calls for stamina on the part of both horse and rider, and from the latter a deep knowledge of the intricate etiquette of the chase.

THE UK AND IRELAND

Much of the language of the chase is based on early French terms. The well-known "Tally-ho", for instance, which indicates that the fox is away, has its origins in *Ty a haillaut* or *Il est hault* (he is off).

Towards the end of the 17th century the English began to hunt foxes, having previously been more concerned with hare- and stag-hunting. The fox, then classed as vermin, ran straighter and more strongly than the circling hare, and, because its scent was not as powerful as that of the stag, it was considered to present a greater challenge to the skills of the huntsman. Despite the legislation of 2004 banning "hunting with dogs" (see p.392), fox-hunting remains the most generally practised form of hunting in the UK and Ireland. In both countries there are a number of harrier packs (hunting hare), while three packs in the south-west of England continue to hunt stag within the dictates of the law. Supporters claim that

THE IRISH SPIRIT
Irish hunting countries are big and demand the best sort of horse. Here, a follower of the Limerick hounds tackles a wide, water-filled ditch in some style. The Irish countryside is also famous for its formidable bank obstacles.

hunting is the most efficient and humane way of culling the red deer selectively. The fox-hunting season proper extends in the UK and Ireland from November until April.

The enigmatic properties of scent have occupied the attention of hunters for centuries. Scent is exuded from the pads of a fox and from beneath the brush (hunting parlance for the tail), and it varies in its intensity according to the vagaries of the weather, being stronger in cold, damp conditions than it is on dry, sunny days.

Hunting in the UK, where there are over 200 packs of hounds, attracts large "fields" (the term for the riders who follow hounds). It also supports a sizeable industry, giving employment to breeders, farriers, makers of equipment, and so on. The cream of the hunting countries (the areas covered by

DEER HUNTING IN THE FOREST OF COMPIEGNE
This print of 1860 shows French hunting in its traditional form. Far more formal than its British counterpart, the hunt livery is elaborate and the chase is accompanied by grand fanfares on the curled French horns.

OVER THE RIVER
A 19th-century example of the school of British sporting art that is typical of the genre. It personifies the hard-riding tradition of 19th-century hunting.

hunts) is in the Midlands – in Leicestershire, Warwickshire, Northamptonshire, parts of Lincolnshire, and Rutland (the smallest of the English counties). The Shire packs are the Pytchley, Quorn, Fernie, Belvoir, and Cottesmore, which hunt over strongly fenced, grassed countries. They attract fields so large that numbers have to be limited, and the subscription allowing a rider to hunt with one of these packs is necessarily high. For these hunts nothing but the best horses will do. Most of them are nearly Thoroughbred, and they must be fearless and able to jump and gallop. It is the custom in the Shires to change to a second horse halfway through the day, as a single horse is not capable of lasting through the afternoon. There are, nonetheless, many hunts in which a full day can be enjoyed on a single horse. Such hunts, outside the Shires, are termed "provincial" but still provide great sport.

THE BEAUFORT HUNT
A young member of the Beaufort field shows the way over a post-and-rail fence. The Beaufort Hunt is centred on the Duke of Beaufort's Badminton estate, in Gloucestershire.

In the UK and Ireland, fox-hunting is carried on under the authority of the Masters of Foxhounds Association. The ownership of a pack of hounds is usually vested in a committee, which appoints a Master or Joint-Masters to hunt the country and be responsible for the daily running of the establishment. The committee guarantees the Masters an annual sum (largely provided from the subscriptions paid by members of the field) to provide sport on a given number of days per week.

The Masters are responsible for paying the wages of the professional hunt servants that they employ: a huntsman, or a kennel-huntsman if the Master "carries the horn"

HOUNDS OF ARIZONA
The High Country Hounds of Flagstaff, Arizona, hunt the coyote in the absence of fox and often do so with a coating of snow on the ground.

(i.e. hunts the pack); whippers-in, who assist the huntsman in the field; and various kennel and stable staff. A Field-Master is appointed, often the Master or one of the Joint-Masters, and he has authority over the field in every respect. The huntsman alone hunts hounds, and his means of communicating with them, his assistants, and the field is through calls blown on his hunting horn. He alone carries a horn.

FOX-HUNTING IN THE US

American hunting originated in the richly historic states of Virginia, Maryland, and Pennsylvania on the east coast, where the early 17th-century colonists were quick to establish the sport along English lines. For the most part, American packs hunt the grey fox, in the absence of the English red fox. It is generally thought not to run as straight, but nonetheless it provides exciting sport.

MODERN HUNTING

DRAG HUNTING IN GERMANY

IN GREAT BRITAIN, to all intents a country central to the sport of foxhunting, "hunting with dogs" was banned by Act of Parliament following the landslide victory of the Labour government in 1997. In fact, while the Labour Party had been to all intents committed to the abolition of hunting long, the issue has always been recognized as a highly controversial one, and in many respects one that is often considered to be dependent on the conscience of the individual. Indeed, the Bill did not become law until 2004 and, even then, it was only after more than 700 hours of Parliamentary debate and after widespread consultation to arrive at a workable solution.

RENEWED POPULARITY

Despite the efforts of Parliament, protests by opponents of the Bill, made manifest in marches through the capital, lobby groups, and even an appeal to the European courts, reached unprecedented levels. Nonetheless, despite the worst fears of the Bill's opponents, many of whom had argued that huge job losses would be sustained by the industry, hunting, "within the law", not only continued but was actually expanded, with many hunts increasing their membership figures quite dramatically. Jobs in the industry were not lost and hunts maintained a full staff complement.

THE LAW

Hunting has survived and prospered in Great Britain, admittedly in a somewhat altered form, because the Act provides for the continuance of the sport within certain permitted parameters. It is "within the law" for hounds to follow a scent (so long as only two hounds are used) and flush out the fox to be shot. In some instances, hunts use a bird of prey to despatch the fox, thus

BEAUFORT HUNT
Fields attending meets of the Beaufort Hunt are larger than ever since the hunting act was passed in 2004. Many other hunts have increased membership.

combining two of the principles of venery. Hounds may also hunt a previously laid trail when it is recognized that they may sometimes kill foxes "accidentally" if they pick up their scent, which is both natural to them and inevitable.

In common with much legislation the Act is far from perfect and without doubt is in need of some amendment. Contrary to its intention for instance, more foxes and hares are being killed than before the law was introduced, very often as a result of shooting, which may wound rather than kill the animal outright resulting in prolonged suffering. There has also been a marked increase in trapping and poisoning.

DRAG-HUNTING

Hunting a drag, a laid trail over a fixed line of country, may not have the uncertainty and excitement of fox-hunting, but it is very popular and has an important place in the traditional concept of hunting with hounds. Moreover, it provides an exciting cross-country sport when natural facilities are limited by roadways, conurbations, and so on. It is, too, a sport for those with limited time at their disposal. The drag-hunter can go out at 11 a.m. in the certain knowledge that he or she can be home soon after lunchtime. It is the ideal sport for young thrusters (undergraduates or soldiers), or for anyone who hunts to ride, rather than those who ride for the more esoteric appreciation of true venery.

Drag-hunts are not reliant upon the keeping of a large pack. Ten or eleven couple is a popular number, but it is quite possible to hunt with as few as five couple

("couple" is hunting terminology for two hounds, and a pack is always referred to as being composed of so many couple of hounds). The hounds used are principally drafts from established packs of foxhounds. It is important to have a level pack in terms of size and conformation so that they all run at a similar speed.

Hounds hunt a "drag", a strong-smelling lure made up principally of animal excreta – that of fox is the most usual, spiced with aniseed. The drag-man, either on foot or mounted, pulls the lure behind him over a pre-determined line, which can be planned to simulate natural hunting.

The length of the line is dependent on a number of factors but is usually about 8 km (5 miles), although the established hard-

HUNTING THE MAN
Instead of a drag-line, bloodhounds hunt the "clean boot" (left) – following the scent of a man. The bloodhound is the oldest of hunting dogs and has great scenting ability.

RIDING THE LINE
Efforts are made to include as many natural obstacles as possible in the line. They add a welcome variety to specially built hunt fences.

riding hunts may sometimes follow a line as long as 24 km (15 miles). Usually, the line is divided into three or four legs, the field (followers) following on from one another. In the absence of a live quarry, hounds are always rewarded for their persistence at the end of the day.

Because of the strength of the scent, hounds can hunt at speed, and it is the fences that are central to the concept of modern drag-hunting. Fences vary in number according the the country and the competence of the field. The famous Hickstead line in the UK has over 80 fences.

Drag-hunting takes place all over Europe, of necessity in those countries where rabies is endemic and the hunting of live animals is therefore prohibited. Both the US and Canada also support numerous drag-hunting packs.

THE "CLEAN BOOT"

Hunting with bloodhounds is organized in much the same way as drag-hunting, but, instead of a drag, the hounds hunt the "clean boot" – the scent left by a man. The sport is controlled by the Masters of Bloodhounds Association (MBHA). The bloodhound's scenting ability is highly developed, it will persevere on a given line, and, although slower than a foxhound, there is the added bonus of hearing the bloodhound's resonant tongue (baying) when on the scent of its quarry.

THE "CLEAN BOOT"

THE BLOOD HOUNDS

HUNTER

HUNTERS ARE FOUND IN EVERY COUNTRY IN which hunting with a pack of hounds takes place. The type of horse favoured varies according to the country itself and the terrain that has to be crossed. The best examples are those bred in countries with a long hunting tradition, in particular Ireland, the UK, and, to a degree, the US, where the Thoroughbred horse (see pp.120–21) is much in evidence in the principal hunts. Exceptionally good English and Irish hunters, allowing for the need for a special talent, may often be potential event horses (see pp.358–59).

NECESSARY QUALITIES

The criterion by which a good hunter might be judged is that it should be able to carry a rider quickly and safely over the rider's chosen hunt country and to do so on,

perhaps, two days a week during the hunting season, which extends from November to April. The horse should be able to sustain this effort without suffering strain leading to unsoundness, without signs of distress, and without losing condition – matters that would prevent the animal's regular and effective participation in the sport.

In Europe hounds usually meet at 11 a.m., with horses possibly setting off earlier. The day ends in the failing light at about 3.30–4.00 p.m., and by then the horses will have been working constantly for some four or five hours, much of the time being spent galloping and jumping. Additionally, since hunting is a winter sport, the ground may be wet and heavy and thus add to the exertion. A horse that can cope

with these exacting conditions has to be strong, both physically and constitutionally; have stamina and reasonable speed; be a bold and capable jumper; be inherently sound; and possess a suitable temperament.

TYPES OF HUNTER

Preferred types vary according to the requirements of the different hunting countries. In the old pasture of the English Shires, the cream of the world's hunting countries, which embraces part of the English Midlands (Leicestershire, Rutland, Warwickshire, Northamptonshire, and parts of Lincolnshire), a big, galloping, near-Thoroughbred horse with sufficient scope to jump a strongly fenced country is needed.

HEAD
There is no set pattern for the hunter head, but it should have quality and give an impression of lively intelligence.

SHOULDERS
The shoulders should be strong, sloped, and with defined withers if the horse is to gallop and jump.

SUNNY FLORIDA
Hunting is firmly established in many countries, including the US. The Palm Beach Hunt pursue the sport in sunny Florida.

FOREHAND
The chest is broad and deep but not too wide. The forearms are strong, the joints big, and the tendons clean and hard.

(In fact, in the Shires it is customary, or at any rate advisable, to have a second horse for the afternoon's sport.)

In more enclosed countries, in ploughlands, or on the hills, a powerful, short-legged type, possibly half- or three-quarter-bred, that will jump tricky places, may be more suitable. Generally, the greater the amount of Thoroughbred blood, the greater will be the speed and scope. Whatever the country, a horse with good conformation and, therefore, natural balance is a necessity.

BRITISH AND IRISH HORSES

The essential quality required in a hunter is courage. In Irish and British horses this attribute is provided by the Thoroughbred,

but it is also present in full measure in the other elements with which Thoroughbreds are crossed. It is the bold temperament, along with an almost atavistic instinct for going across country, that puts the Irish and British animals a distance ahead, in their field, of most of the coach-horse based breeds of Europe.

The Irish hunters, still regarded as some of the best cross-country horses in the world, are based on the Thoroughbred/Irish Draught cross (see pp.396–97). Like the Quarter Horse (see pp.230–31) and the polo pony (see pp.372–73), they seem to have an innate instinct for their job. Irish horses are often hunted as three- and four-year-olds and almost always in a plain snaffle bridle. They learn quickly how to cope with obstacles and to look after themselves in all sorts of situations. The damp climate provides ideal growth conditions for high-nutrient grass and

FRENCH HUNTING
Hunting in France is carried on its traditional form with some style and splendour. The quarry is either stag or boar and the French hunting ritual is slower and far more formal than in the UK.

the mineral-rich limestone subsoil ensures that young stock have strong bone structure and develop naturally into big, upstanding yearlings and two-year-olds.

There are other possible crosses with the Thoroughbred that will produce a high-class hunter. The Cleveland Bay (see pp.306–7), for instance, is a hunter in its own right and possibly the most powerful in the world. It can carry a man of 114 kg (18 st) for a day's hunting and in its native country will jump big obstacles out of and into deep, heavy clay. Crossed with a Thoroughbred, the progeny will be faster and lighter but will still retain much of the Cleveland's strength and massive bone. Many good heavyweight hunters have also been bred against the background of the English heavy horse breeds, the Shire and Clydesdale in particular, and also from the English-bred Percheron (see pp.286–89 and pp.94–95).

As good as any, and better than most, are the crosses and second crosses to the British native pony breeds (see pp.172–85). They have a distinctive, lively character, as well as stamina, initiative, intelligence, and soundness. Together with the Irish Draught cross, they are unmatched in terms of sheer ability. Any of the larger British pony breeds will also carry a lightweight adult very well in most hunting countries.

In the UK many hunters are bred by the Thoroughbred sires that are made available under the Premium Stallion Scheme. This scheme is administered by the National Light Horse Breeding Society (Hunters' Improvement Society), which in turn receives grants from the Racecourse Betting Levy Board.

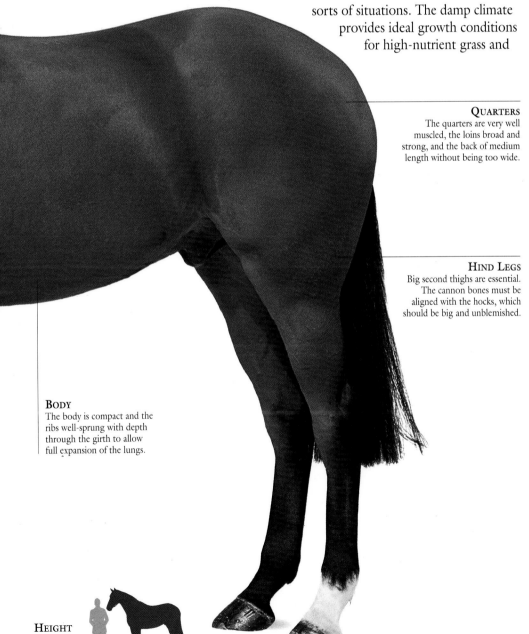

QUARTERS
The quarters are very well muscled, the loins broad and strong, and the back of medium length without being too wide.

HIND LEGS
Big second thighs are essential. The cannon bones must be aligned with the hocks, which should be big and unblemished.

BODY
The body is compact and the ribs well-sprung with depth through the girth to allow full expansion of the lungs.

HEIGHT
*1.52–1.83 m
(15–18 hh)*

IRISH DRAUGHT

THE IRISH DRAUGHT, the foundation of the celebrated Irish hunter, is derived from the Great Horses of France and Flanders, which were imported after the Anglo-Norman invasion of AD 1172. These strong mares were then crossed and improved with imported eastern and Andalucian horses (see pp.108–9). This eventually resulted in the draught horses that were used on small Irish farms, both in harness and under saddle.

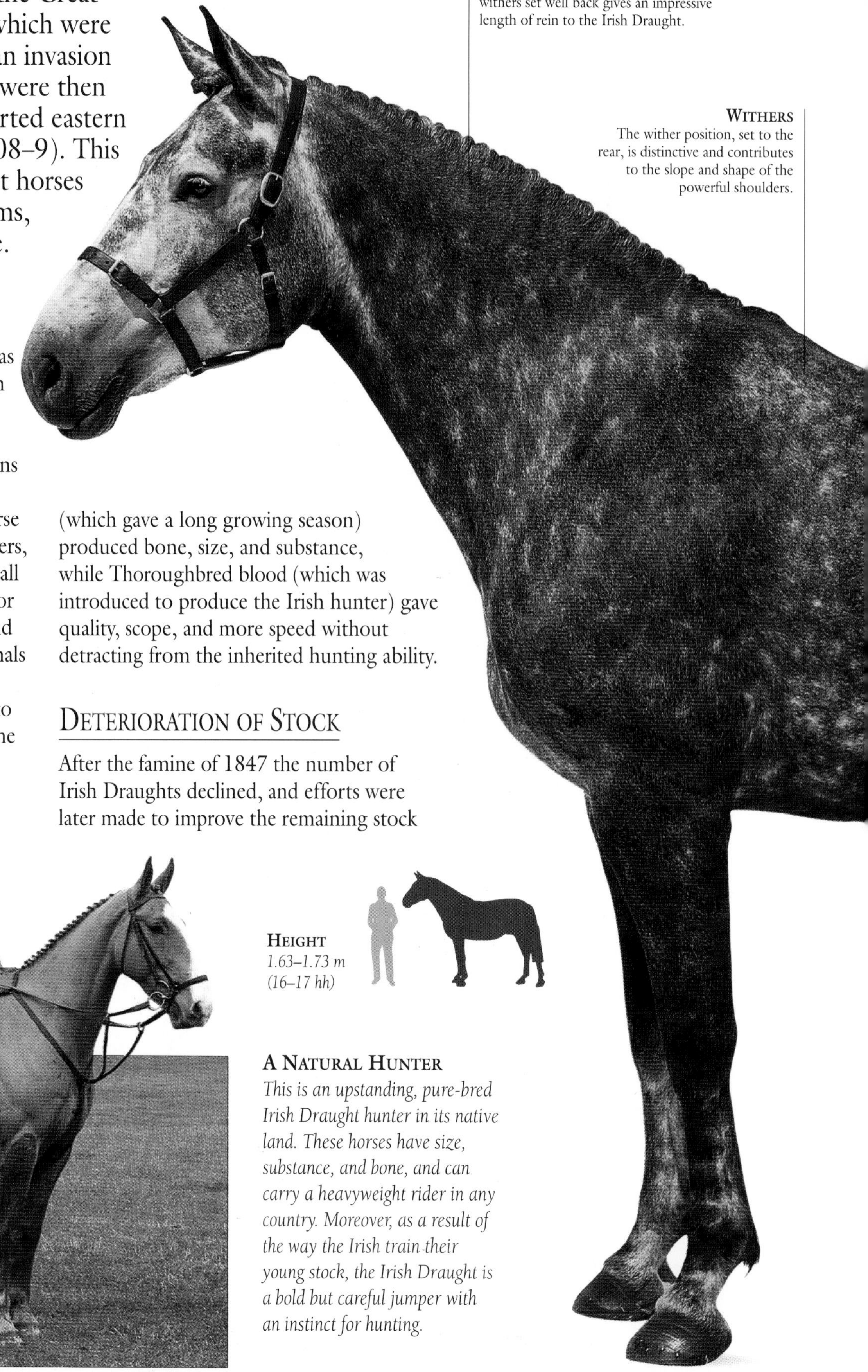

THE OLD TYPE

In 1850 the Irish Draught was described as a low-built animal, standing no more than 1.57–1.60 m (15.2–15.3 hh) with much bone and substance and short, strong, clean legs. The back was short and the loins strong, but the quarters tended to droop and goose-rumps were prevalent. The horse was generally rather upright in the shoulders, but the neck was strong, and the head small rather than coarse. The action, allowing for the slope of the shoulders, was straight and level, though not extravagant. These animals could both trot in harness and canter and gallop under saddle. They were also said to jump very well; this quality arose out of the Irish love of hunting, which encouraged the Irish horses to develop their innate talent for going over the most fearsome of obstacles. The rich limestone pastures and the wet, mild climate (which gave a long growing season) produced bone, size, and substance, while Thoroughbred blood (which was introduced to produce the Irish hunter) gave quality, scope, and more speed without detracting from the inherited hunting ability.

DETERIORATION OF STOCK

After the famine of 1847 the number of Irish Draughts declined, and efforts were later made to improve the remaining stock

NECK
The long, arched neck combined with withers set well back gives an impressive length of rein to the Irish Draught.

WITHERS
The wither position, set to the rear, is distinctive and contributes to the slope and shape of the powerful shoulders.

HEIGHT
1.63–1.73 m
(16–17 hh)

A NATURAL HUNTER
This is an upstanding, pure-bred Irish Draught hunter in its native land. These horses have size, substance, and bone, and can carry a heavyweight rider in any country. Moreover, as a result of the way the Irish train their young stock, the Irish Draught is a bold but careful jumper with an instinct for hunting.

with Clydesdale and Shire crosses (see pp.286–89). These were not successful and had a coarsening influence. The Clydesdale is also held responsible for the breed becoming rather tied-in below the knee, a fault that has taken a long time to eradicate. In 1897 Thomas Meleady spoke bitterly of the effect of "the Scotch horses" on the Irish stock. He called them "heavy-legged horses, easily tired", and claimed that the Clydesdale had also destroyed the pony stock of Co. Mayo, Wicklow, and Wexford.

IMPROVEMENT

The breed was much improved by the stallion subsidies made available in 1904. Ireland, unlike England, always recognized

HORSE TRIALS

The Irish Draught is an excellent performer at horse trials at international level and has a natural talent for cross-country jumping.

its horses as a national asset, and encouraged their breeding and sale accordingly. In 1917 a *Book for Horses of the Irish Draught Type* was introduced, in which 375 mares and 44 stallions were entered. Until the Second World War there was a good trade in vanners, army remounts, draught horses, and the half-bred hunter. Inevitably the war brought about a decline in standards, but since then there has been a revival.

THE IRISH DRAUGHT SOCIETY

The Irish Draught Society was formed in 1976, followed in 1979 by the Irish Draught Horse Society (GB), which soon became one of the most progressive British horse societies. It operates a grading system to produce animals suitable for registration, and its influence on hunter breeding has been remarkable. If the national mare band is not yet sufficiently large for comfort, the choice of top-class stallions is wide. Used on Thoroughbred mares, the Draught stallions pass on bone, substance, size, and usually their jumping ability as well. Irish Draughts and their progeny are easily managed, have an equable temperament, are rarely sick, and thrive on smaller, plainer rations than other breeds of comparable size.

Irish Draughts are bigger than they were a century ago, most of them standing 1.63 m (16 hh), while stallions often reach 1.73 m (17 hh). The quarters and the set of the tail are much improved, and although they retain the massive limb and bone, most of them are extraordinarily athletic – many of the stallions standing in the UK are regularly ridden, hunted, and jumped.

QUARTERS
The quarters slope downwards from the croup to the junction with the tail, but the latter is carried high in movement.

HIND LEGS
The hind legs are very powerful with strongly muscled thighs and big hock joints. This ensures exceptional jumping ability.

BODY
The body is deep with an oval rib cage and deep chest, although the back may be a little long.

LEGS
The legs are massive and carry minimal feather. The bone is flat and hard and the joints big and well-shaped.

ORIGINS

THE IRISH DRAUGHT *originated in Ireland, although today it is also bred in the UK under the auspices of the Irish Draught Horse Society. Initially developed as an all-round farm horse, it derived bone, substance, and size from the limestone pastures and rich grass, which result from the mild, damp climate. The Irish Draught was also affected by the Irish love of hunting, which encouraged its innate talent across-country. Crosses to the Thoroughbred produced the Irish Hunter – probably the world's best cross-country horse. Today, greater quality in the Draught mares results in faster event-type horses, with greater scope over fences.*

EUROPE

GREAT BRITAIN

IRELAND

Dublin

Amsterdam

London

Brussels

Paris

0   200 km
0   125 miles

HORSE SHOWS

CONFORMATION CLASS, FLORIDA

IN EUROPE, horse shows have their origins in the medieval fairs at which animals of all kinds were exhibited and put up for sale. Such fairs are still held all over the world. Some have developed into sophisticated horse sales, like many in mainland Europe, while others retain their traditional ambience. Essentially, the purpose of the modern horse show, where animals are brought together in competition against each other, is to encourage improvement in the breeds or types exhibited. In a commercial sense, the horse show provides a "shop window" for breeders and owners who wish to buy or sell horses, as well as setting and maintaining the standards expected of the various breeds and types. In European countries, much emphasis is placed on performance testing as well as on the assessment of conformation and movement.

SHOW-RING CLASSES

Traditional British show-ring classes take place at horse shows held in Britain and Ireland, as well as those held in Commonwealth countries such as Australia, South Africa, and Canada, and even at some of the national shows in India and Pakistan.

The huge American show circuit differs from the traditional shows. It offers the widest diversity of classes to cover the three riding styles – hunt seat, saddle seat, and stock seat. The criteria and the method of judgement for ridden classes vary considerably, but the judgement of led classes varies only in detail.

THE TRADITIONAL SYSTEM

The UK-pattern show classes are almost as wide-ranging as those held throughout the US, and there are often more horse shows held per annum in the UK than occur in much larger countries.

Under the British system, which may be said to rely on the expert opinion and experience of the judges rather than on specific requirements, the basis of judgement in both ridden classes and "in-hand" (led) classes rests upon four pillars: presence, conformation, ride, and manners. In breed classes there will be the additional consideration of breed type. The term

"presence" may be directly interpreted as "personality". It is the star quality that attracts and demands immediate attention. This quality is usually found only in animals of good conformation, and therefore it can be seen as a corollary of physical excellence. "Conformation" refers to the correctness of

JUDGING HUNTERS

In the UK, the judges must ride the entries before having the saddles removed to assess the individual conformation. Show hunters in the UK do not jump in the ring, although working hunters are required to do so over a course of rustic-type fences.

a horse's physical structure in relation to the purpose for which it is intended. This factor will govern the quality of the horse's action.

In the ridden classes for show hunters, working hunters, riding horses, hacks, and cobs, the judge or judges (there are never more than two) ride each horse. Great emphasis is given to "the ride", since it is held that however beautiful a horse may be, he is of no use unless the ride he gives is also of a high standard. In led classes for

AN IBERIAN IDYLL

National dress is worn by this owner at the prestigious Lisbon Horse Show, Portugal. The lovely mare and her well-grown foal are of Portugal's indigenous breed, the Lusitanian, around which the entire show revolves.

potential riding horses, the judge must assess the possible ride from the action and conformation. The horse's manners are a further consideration in all show classes. Classes are held for children's ponies (in three height divisions); for working hunter ponies, again divided by height; and for show hunter ponies, the more substantial version of the show pony. Shows also stage classes for specific breeds, which encompass breeding and young stock, and other classes, such as those for driving turnouts.

AMERICAN SHOWS

The American circuit caters for a wealth of different breeds, together with the riding classes and a great variety of "halter" classes for horses shown "in-hand". Hunt seat (or English seat) classes correspond most closely to the UK-pattern hunter classes. The main differences are that hunters in the US are

NEW ZEALAND CHAMPIONS
New Zealand horse shows stage pony classes on the British pattern and the quality of entry is high. These two champions and their immaculately turned out riders are excellent examples.

not ridden by the judge, unlike their British counterparts, and all American hunters, whether working, handy, or junior, have to jump and are judged on their ability to do so in an acceptable style. Although British working hunters are asked to jump a course of obstacles, 60 per cent of the marks available being given for performance and the remainder for ride and conformation, the show hunters are not required to prove their jumping ability. Instead, they are assessed on what the judge considers to be the qualities most desirable in a potential hunter. The American system provides suitable experience for the budding showjumper or even event horse, and that could also be the case with the British working hunters.

American stock seat classes are those ridden in Western style. They include the popular Western pleasure classes; the trail class, which has what is almost an obstacle course; the Western riding classes, which display the three paces of walk, jog, and lope; and the reining classes, which call for advanced movements carried out at speed.

Saddle-seat classes are only for the gaited horses: Saddlebreds, Missouri Foxtrotters, and Tennessee Walkers (see pp.234–39).

A BREED CLASS
The show ring provides a "shop window" for breeders, and helps to establish standards for the breeds. The horses, like this in-foal Suffolk Punch, are trotted out so that the quality of the action can be assessed.

THE AMERICAN SHOW SCENE

COSTUME CLASS

WHILE THE BRITISH and Irish show circuit is rich in its diversity and the number of shows held, it cannot compare to the sheer scale of the US show scene. Nothing short of an American industry, the bigger shows, State Fairs, and breed societies are run like businesses, and often employ permanent secretariats equivalent in size to those of any large-scale commercial enterprise. In contrast, the showing of horses in mainland Europe, where the criteria of judgement is influenced by performance testing and the imposition of set standards, is altogether more pragmatic. Horsemen from mainland Europe are known to regard the British system with bewildered amusement, and would probably view the American scene with total incomprehension.

A HORSE-CRAZY COUNTRY

The first recorded horse show in the US took place in 1883 when the horse population was reckoned to exceed 25 million. It had fallen to about seven to eight million by 1972, according to an estimate made by the American Horse Council; since then, in the words of a distinguished commentator, "America has gone horse crazy" and numbers continue to rise.

The American Quarter Horse Association, in Amarillo, Texas, has registrations world-wide numbered in millions, and that takes no account of animals as yet unregistered. The Association gives its approval to well over a thousand shows a year. The Arabian presence in the US does not approach the Quarter Horse figures, but it is the largest Arab horse population in the world. The Arabian Horse Registry of America published its first stud book in 1909, registering 62,000 horses in 1970 alone. Registrations are now approaching the million-mark.

California is the principal centre for the Arabian horse, and National Arabian Championship classes were established in 1957, while the first Arabian International Cutting Horse Jubilee was staged at Filer, Idaho, in 1970. Arabians compete, on equal terms with other breeds, in pleasure classes, trail riding, ranch work, parade classes, and in harness.

Recently, the American influence has stamped itself indelibly upon the British and European show rings. The staid, bowler-hatted, garden-party ambience of the British Arab Horse Show has given way to the show-biz atmosphere of the American show circuit. The sombre-suited and Ascot-hatted attendants have been replaced by white-trousered, plimsoll-shod, and fancy-

THE GAITED TRADITION

The American Saddlebred is integral to the American Show, and while the action is artificial, it is nonetheless undeniably brilliant.

HALTER CLASS

An American Saddlebred is shown in a halter class. This is a very good example of the breed with an exceptionally noteworthy shoulder.

waistcoated handlers performing what a correspondent of the leading British journal *Horse and Hound* described as "a simulated love affair with a long whip, decorated with a tassle of lavatory paper." In these circumstances the presentation of horses in-hand, or in "halter" classes, is unashamedly theatrical. Horses are not exactly shown at the full "stretch" or "camp", so beloved of the American rings, but the head and neck are nonetheless stretched upwards and outwards, while much emphasis is given to running out young stock at speed after the manner of the Welsh Cobs, who are far better equipped physically for the practice.

UNNATURAL POSTURE

The full stretch – with hind legs pushed out behind (in the position adopted by the horse when urinating) and fore legs extended well beyond a line with the wither – was taught originally to keep the horse still.

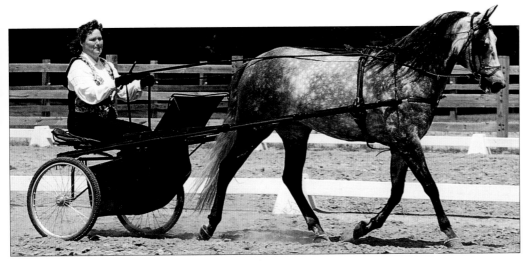

POPULAR CLASSES

This pleasing entry in a Pleasure Driving class is an Andalucian (Spanish) mare shown moving naturally in appropriately simple harness.

Carriage horses assumed this posture so that ladies, in voluminous skirts, might enter and leave the carriage safely. It was also taught to the military drum-horse to ensure it maintained a fixed position on parade. It persists, often for no good reason, in many of the American halter classes.

Similarly, the practice of running out young horses at speed in order to display the movement is, in most instances, detrimental to the animal. When a young horse is encouraged to trot out at a fast pace it is likely to compensate for the lack of physical maturity and co-ordination by carrying the hindlegs outside of the track made by its forelegs. The animal is then deemed to be "going wide behind" or, more graphically, to be demonstrating the "wet-knicker trot". The practice can cause damage to the joints and strain on undeveloped tendons and muscles.

OFFICIAL RECOGNITION

The principal American shows are all officially recognized by the American Horse Shows Association (AHSA). It publishes a rule book, setting the standards for show rules in the US, and classifies shows according to the amount of prize-money on offer and the number and variety of classes – all of which are very large in comparison with the European equivalent.

While in so vast a country shows will specialize in one or more of the 20-odd AHSA divisions for hunter and jumper or saddle-horse classes, the majority include a bewildering array of halter classes for animals as varied as Shetlands and miniature horses to Thoroughbreds and the gaited horses within the Saddle Horse, Walking Horse, and Quarter Horse divisions. Almost all, however, stage an equitation division with a points system for champion hunters and jumpers. Qualified riders are entitled to compete in the national horsemanship awards at the National Horse Show in New York in the fall of the year. Championships cover hunter seat and saddle seat, and also the stock saddle seat for Western riding.

All American hunters jump in the arena, the marking being heavily weighted on performance, usually a highly polished one. Many talented junior riders have been discovered in the equitation division, some of them being selected for further training at the United States Equestrian Team headquarters at Gladstone, New Jersey.

Some 50–60 affiliated associations hold their own specialist shows, and there are countless smaller local shows.

A highlight of the big shows are the extravagant Parade Classes. Possibly "over the top", they are nonetheless a unique spectacle. The trappings of the horse and the costume of the rider are intricately and expensively embroidered in silver trim, and the paces employed – the animated walk and the high-prancing, 8 km/h (5 mph) parade gait – have particular brilliance.

COMMERCIAL ELEMENT

A feature of the US circuit is the system of judging, which employs professional judges paid for their services. Judging for these experts, approved by the appropriate Associations, is, therefore, a business – in contrast to the firmly amateur status of European judges. The practice can be seen, however, as being entirely compatible with the highly competitive and inevitably commercial US scene, in which turnout and presentation assume major importance.

One US author in an instructional book on show-ring competition and technique advised his readers to "notice carefully the proper length and thickness of tails and the way the foretop and mane are prepared for the ring. Note whether it is currently fashionable to leave some hair on the withers ..." Similarly, braiding (plaiting) of the mane is a matter for serious consideration, if not always taking into account the basic purpose, which is to accentuate the neck's good features and disguise any failures in its conformation.

While the magnitude of the US show scene is remarkable and admirable in so many ways, it has, nonetheless, a less attractive and sometimes unacceptable face by European standards. Allowing for a more robust tradition, there is still a lingering disquiet about training methods and the equipment used in the production of Western horses (the latter openly offered for sale in catalogues). In the case of the brilliant, gaited saddle horses, the shoeing of the feet can be a cause for concern. Both practices detract from what are otherwise immensely skilful feats of horsemanship.

ALL CORRECT

An elegantly turned-out pair competes in a show-ring class. It would be difficult to fault the appearance of either horse or rider in a class in which correctness is a paramount consideration.

HACKNEY & HACKNEY PONY

T HE HACKNEY, AND THE RELATED HACKNEY PONY, are undoubtedly the world's most impressive harness horses. The Hackney has a distinctive conformation, and its brilliant, unique action has been described in the breed description as "effortless in the extreme", "electrical and snappy at its zenith", and giving "the impression of a mystic, indescribably deliberate, instantaneous poise". In part this extravagant movement can be taught and refined by skilful training, but much of it is inherited and derives from years of careful selective breeding and the foundation of trotting blood, from which it originated in the 18th century.

SHOWING IN-HAND
This Hackney stallion, wearing the appropriate "harness", is being shown in-hand at Britain's annual Hackney Horse Society Show in 1990.

ORIGINS

The Hackney Horse developed from the great trotting horses of the 18th and 19th centuries, which were traditional to England and left their mark upon many breeds in Europe and some notable ones in the US. However, the word Hackney probably comes from the French word *haquenée* (see pp.404–5) and "hackney" (without the capital letter) was used to mean a riding horse from the Middle Ages onwards.

There were two regional types of trotting horses in the UK, known as Trotters or Roadsters: the Norfolk and the Yorkshire. These shared a common ancestor, Original Shales, who was born in 1755 out of a "hackney", or riding, mare by Blaze. Blaze, who is considered as "the principal figure in the first chapter in the Genesis of Great Trotters", was the son of Flying Childers, the first great racehorse. He, in turn, was a great grandson of the Darley Arabian, one of

the three founding sires of the Thoroughbred (see pp.120–21). Blaze is also connected with the American Standardbred (see pp.340–41) through his great-great-grandson Messenger. However, it was Blaze's son Shales, and Shales' two sons, Driver and Scot Shales, together with another horse, Marshland, who had Scot Shales on both sides of his pedigree, that were the prime influences on the

HEIGHT OF HACKNEY HORSE
1.42–1.60 m
(14–15.3 hh)

HOCKS
The hock joints must be set low to the ground if they are to contribute to the "brilliance" of the action.

HACKNEY HORSE

HACKNEY PONY

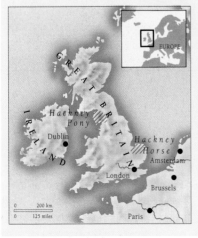

ORIGINS

THE MODERN HACKNEY HORSE derives from the famous trotting "Roadsters" of Norfolk and, to a lesser extent, the Yorkshire Roadsters, which shared a common ancestry with the Norfolk breed. The Hackney Pony, created in Cumbria in the 19th century, has an obvious connection with the Hackney Horse bloodlines of the day, but was principally based on a foundation of Fell Pony stock. Hackneys, both horses and ponies, are now bred worldwide. The Netherlands probably produce more Hackney stock than any other country in the world. The breed also enjoys great popularity in both the US and Canada.

Norfolk Trotter. It was their progeny, when crossed with Yorkshire mares, that produced the northern trotting strain.

Today, the regional variations are long gone, and the best characteristics are brought together in the elegance of the modern Hackney. The Hackney Horse Society was founded in Norwich, England, in 1883. The records of these early trotting horses, who were trotted and raced under saddle long before they were used between the shafts, are very impressive, and explain something of the high courage and stamina of their modern descendants.

HEAD
The head is slightly convex in profile, with small, neat ears and a fine, quality muzzle. The eyes are large and bold.

Bellfounder, with a direct line to the racehorse, Eclipse, trotted 3 km (2 miles) in six minutes, and 14 km (9 miles) in 30 minutes. His dam Velocity had trotted 25 km (16 miles) in an hour. The mare Phenomena, who was by the Norfolk Phenomenon, was barely 1.42 m (14 hh), but she trotted 27 km (17 miles) in 53 minutes, and in 1832 Nonpareil was driven 160 km (100 miles) in 9 hours 56 minutes and 57 seconds.

THE HACKNEY PONY

The Hackney Pony, which does not exceed 1.42 m (14 hh), shares the same stud book as the Hackney Horse, and to a great extent has a common ancestry in the great lines of Norfolk and Yorkshire Trotters. Nonetheless it is a real pony, not just a little horse. The modern Hackney Pony is confined to the show ring, where its action is the equal of that of its larger counterpart. The breed was essentially created by one man, Christopher Wilson of Cumbria. By the 1880s he had created a distinctive type

IN ACTION
A Hackney Pony draws the conventional pneumatic-tyred show buggy and displays all the brilliance and stylish movement expected of the breed.

SHOULDERS
The shoulders, of pure harness type, are exceptionally strong, and the withers are low, quite unlike those of a modern riding horse.

HARNESS
Both horse and pony are wearing stallion in-hand showing harness, comprising body-roller (to which side-reins can be attached), crupper, and dock-piece. The crupper compels a high tail-carriage.

FEET
The feet are allowed to grow longer than usual so as to give emphasis to the "snap" of the action.

based on trotting blood crossed with local Fell Ponies (see pp. 172–73), or occasionally with Welsh ones. The most important Hackney Pony sire was Wilson's champion pony stallion, Sir George, who was by a Yorkshire Trotter and could trace his descent back to the racehorse Flying Childers. Wilson mated Sir George's female progeny from selected mares back to their sire to produce outstandingly elegant ponies with brilliant harness action. The "Wilson Ponies", as they were known, were kept to their required limit by being wintered out on the fells where they were left to fend for themselves, a practice which ensured a remarkable hardness of constitution.

HEIGHT OF HACKNEY PONY
Up to 1.42 m (14 hh)

HACK

THE HACK IS VIRTUALLY A BRITISH PHENOMENON, although it has been adopted by show-ring exhibitors in South Africa and Australia. The word "hack", like Hackney, derives from the Norman French word *haquenée*, which referred to a light riding horse. In the 19th century, two types of hack were recognized in the UK: the "covert hack" and the "park hack". Today, motorized transport has superseded the "covert hack" that carried its rider to the meet, and London's socialites no longer ride the elegant "park hacks", so the modern hack is confined to the show ring, where it evokes a more gracious age.

NECK
The neck is light, long, and elegant, running smoothly into prominent withers and long, perfectly sloped shoulders.

HEIGHT
1.47–1.60 m
(14.2–15.3 hh)

19TH-CENTURY TYPES

The use of both covert and park hacks became increasingly popular during the 19th century, due to the availability of Thoroughbreds (see pp.120–21) in the UK as well as the preferences of the English gentry at that time.

The covert hack was a good-looking, or even handsome, Thoroughbred riding horse, which carried its rider at a smooth "hack canter" to the meet on hunting days. It was most frequently ridden by the splendidly tailored swells who could cut a dash riding to the meet, while most other participants sent their hunters on with a groom and followed in a carriage or, perhaps, in a smart, workmanlike dog cart. This hack was required to be well-mannered

HEAD
A neat, quality head tapering to the muzzle, but without concavity in the profile, is the hall-mark of the hack.

and comfortable to ride. It was a showy horse of attractive appearance, but lighter in build than the hunter and without the latter's substance and bone. The overriding criteria were elegance, presence, and smoothness of action. Bone, strength, stamina, or even galloping ability were not considerations for the covert hack, which was not expected to carry weight across country for a full day's hunting.

Covert hacks no longer exist either in the hunting field or in the show ring. Their nearest equivalent may be seen in show classes for riding horses. These are quality horses, but like the covert hack they do not have the hunter's substance, nor the extreme quality and brilliance of the animals exhibited in the pure hack classes. The park hack, on the other hand, corresponds exactly to the modern exhibit in hack classes. Far

LEGS
The legs are long and graceful with 20 cm (8 in) of bone expected below the knee.

SIDE-SADDLE

Classes for ladies' hacks, and for ladies' hunters, are ridden side-saddle and are one of the attractive sights to be seen in British show rings. The rider has only a single leg with which to give the aids and on her off-side has to rely on her cane, so the side-saddle horse must be exceptionally well-schooled and responsive.

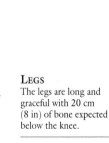

THE MODERN HACK

The present-day hack is expected to have the same attributes as the 19th-century types. It must be light and graceful, and should be an example of proportionate conformation, with not less than 20 cm (8 in) of bone below the knee. The "blood weed", a weak, insubstantial type of Thoroughbred, is not tolerated. Overgrown riding ponies and animals of pronounced Arab character are also viewed unfavourably. Most hacks are Thoroughbred, but there have always been a few Anglo-Arabs (see pp.78–79).

The action of the hack has to be as near perfect as possible. It must be straight and true, with the hind feet consistently "tracking up", or falling into the imprints left by the forefeet. The walk is free, with the horse covering a lot of ground at each stride. At the trot the movement is low and floating, with the toes extended. There must be no tendency towards dishing, nor any lifting of the knees. The canter is oily smooth, slow, light, and in perfect balance.

GOOD MANNERS
The hack is supremely elegant with beautifully light paces and manners to match. There is no difficulty in riding it with one hand.

In all the gaits, the horse's movement is distinguished by a brilliance rarely seen outside these classes.

There are three classes for single hacks, and classes for pairs. The single hack classes are for small hacks standing at 1.47–1.52 m (14.2–15 hh), large hacks of 1.52–1.60 m (15–15.3 hh), and ladies' hacks between 1.47 m and 1.60 m (14.2–15.3 hh), these last being shown under side-saddle. Hacks are shown at walk, trot, and canter. They are not required to gallop, but each exhibit must give an individual display, which calls for riding skill and showmanship of a very high order. In addition to the individual show, the horses are ridden by the judge, in accordance with the British convention, and are expected to give him or her a smooth, trouble-free ride.

---

more refined than the covert hack, the park hack was a beautiful, near-perfectly proportioned animal that was schooled to perfection. In the fashionable days of riding in Rotten Row, in London's Hyde Park, hacks paraded their well-tailored owners (female as well as male) before the appraising eye of an often critical public. In order to show off its rider to best advantage, the horse needed to be full of presence. It had to have good manners, so that the rider could strike exactly the right note of casual insouciance by controlling it with one hand in a light, single curb bit. The hack moved as lightly as a feather, but with a gaiety and freedom that had nothing in common with the disciplined accuracy characteristic of the dressage arena and its powerfully moving warmblood horses.

BODY
The body and the line of the back are as near perfect as possible. The horse is deep through the girth and the ribs are well-sprung.

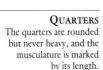

QUARTERS
The quarters are rounded but never heavy, and the musculature is marked by its length.

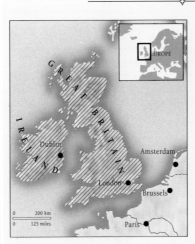

ORIGINS

ESSENTIALLY, THOROUGHBREDS are bred to race, but some that are found unsuitable for that purpose may find their way to the show ring as hacks. The hack is not bred deliberately, but is found all over the UK and Ireland where there are Thoroughbred or Anglo-Arab horses available. Hacks are also produced, almost always from Thoroughbreds, in South Africa and Australia, where show classes incline towards the British pattern. Similar animals may be bred elsewhere in the world where there is a Thoroughbred availability, but in the absence of show-ring classes must, of necessity, fulfil some other role.

200 km
125 miles

RIDING PONY & PONEY FRANÇAIS DE SELLE

A FTER THE THOROUGHBRED, the English Riding Pony is the most notable achievement of selective breeding in equestrian history. In terms of proportion and quality it is arguably the most nearly perfect equine specimen in the world, particularly when it is in the 1.37 m (13.2 hh) bracket. The formation in the 1970s of French Pony Clubs, along the lines of the British movement, has encouraged French breeders to produce a similar pony based largely on the Landais stock (see pp.188–89). The *Poney Français de Selle*, as it is called, is becoming established as a distinguishable type.

SHOW CLASS
Show classes for Riding Ponies in the three height divisions are a prominent feature at all of the principal British horse shows.

THE RIDING PONY

The Riding Pony, the juvenile rider's equivalent of the Thoroughbred show hack, was developed by a handful of dedicated, forward-thinking British breeders from a blend of Arab, Thoroughbred, and British pony blood (see pp.64–65, pp.120–21, and pp.170–71). It began to attract attention in the 1940s when a further use was sought for the smaller Thoroughbred polo pony sires. From the outset the base stock was chiefly Welsh and to a lesser degree Dartmoor (see pp.174–75), a pony with some Welsh blood. There was, of course, a tradition of riding ponies in the *Welsh Pony and Cob Society Stud Book*, the Section B being described specifically as being "of riding type".

HEAD
The head is the ultimate in refinement, but it is that of a pony, not of a horse.

The Arab, however, has also played a most significant part and is responsible for one of the two premier dynasties through the grey stallion, Naseel. This horse, who was by Raftan out of Naxina, was bought from Lady Yule's Hanstead stud by Mrs Christopher Nicholson of Kells, Co. Meath, Ireland. She put him to Gipsy Gold, who became the foundation mare for an illustrious line. Gipsy Gold was by a Thoroughbred polo pony sire, Good Luck, and out of Tiger Lily, a

RIDING PONY

IT IS NOT POSSIBLE to be definitive about the British Riding Pony's place of origin, although mid-Wales was an area whose native stock was highly influential in the pony's formative years. Similarly, there is the powerful pony dynasty descended from the Arab stallion Naseel, which originated in Co. Meath, north-west of Dublin in Ireland. Today, studs producing Riding Ponies are to be found throughout the UK and Ireland. There are large entries in show-ring breeding classes at major shows and smaller events for young stock, brood-mares, and stallions. They are a reflection of what has become a small industry with an increasingly popular product.

HEIGHT OF RIDING PONY
1.27–1.47 m (12.2–14.2 hh)

FEET
The feet are open, well-formed, hard, and of equal size. There is an adequate slope to the pasterns and no feather at the heels.

RIDING PONY

Welsh Mountain mare. The best-known of their progeny was the mare Pretty Polly, who was a champion throughout the 1950s at the Horse of the Year Show, London, and at the Royal International Horse Shows. She bred 11 foals, of which nine were champions. These included the outstanding Pollyanna and Polly's Gem, who were both dams of champions. Polly's Gem bred Gem's Signet, sired by Bwlch Hill Wind, one of the most remarkable ponies since the 1960s, while Pollyanna went to the US to prove the practical use of the Riding Pony by sweeping the board in American performance classes.

NECK
The neck, like the shoulders, is rather short.

QUARTERS
The quarters are perfectly proportioned. They are well-muscled, but not heavy or too rounded. The tail is set high.

BODY
The body is deep, and the outline more thick-set than that of the British Riding Pony.

LEGS
The legs are acceptable but the joints incline to roundness. There is some plebeian feathering at the heels.

PONEY FRANÇAIS DE SELLE

The mating of Polly's Gem with Bwlch Hill Wind united the two great Riding Pony lines, for Bwlch Hill Wind, by Bwlch Zephyr, was the grandson of the legendary Bwlch Valentino. Valentino, on his own account, and then through his son, Bwlch Zephyr, and grandson, Bwlch Hill Wind, played a leading role in establishing a virtually fixed pony type, of Thoroughbred proportion, movement, and form, but still retaining all the pony characteristics.

Valentino inherited his brilliant action and quality from his sire Valentine, who was a polo pony. Valentine was registered in the Argentine Stud Book, and was one of the band of small Thoroughbreds who exerted a great influence on most of the pony breeds. His paternal grandmother was Arab. His

HEIGHT OF PONEY FRANÇAIS DE SELLE
1.27–1.47 m
(12.2–14.2 hh)

PONEY FRANÇAIS DE SELLE

THE FRENCH EQUIVALENT of the British Riding Pony, the Poney Français de Selle, was developed fairly recently. It is certainly based originally on the Landais stock. The Landais, a native French pony breed, is indigenous to the Landes region in south-west France, a narrow coastal area extending south of Bordeaux and running down to Biarritz near the Spanish border. It is an ancient breed which was once termed semi-wild, and has been strongly influenced by Arab blood.

dam, Bwlch Goldflake, was by Meteoric, a small Thoroughbred, out of the part-Arab Cigarette, whose dam was a Thoroughbred/Welsh cross. Goldflake thus represents the essential trinity of bloods.

The Riding Pony competes in the show ring in three height divisions – 1.27 m (12.2 hh), 1.37 m (13.2 hh), and up to 1.47 m (14.2 hh). It provided a base for both the Working Hunter Pony, which performs in the ring over a jumping course, and the more substantial Hunter Show Pony which, at its best, is a miniature middleweight hunter.

PONEY FRANÇAIS DE SELLE

This pony, still in its early years, is not yet in the same class as its English counterpart, but relies on a similar mix. The object is to produce a pony version of the Selle Français (see pp.132–33), using the Landais as a base. The Landais itself has been heavily outcrossed to Welsh Section B, supported by Arab blood. Some Connemara and New Forest Ponies were also used on the embryo Poney Français de Selle. Less use has been made of the Thoroughbred, for the French, lacking a comparable show-ring circuit, do not need the quality of the English pony, and are more interested in an all-rounder suitable for Pony Club activities.

THE HORSE FAIR

THE *FERIA*, SEVILLE

Long before the organized agricultural shows or the horse sales conducted by auctioneers, the old horse fairs were an essential part of rural Britain. In mainland Europe, in the countries of Spain and Portugal, the *feria* is as traditional as the breeding of Iberian horses and continues to bring a special vitality to the national life. Just as colourful and deep-rooted are the fairs of India, and particularly Rajasthan, where horses and horsemen are integral to the warrior history of the Rajput states. If there is a common link between these fairs, it is provided by the pervasive presence of the Romanies, the travelling people, to whom dealing in horses is a way of life.

ROMANY CULTURE

The fairs are a part of the Romany culture, and the travellers are to be found at Britain's ancient Appleby Fair in Cumbria; about the fringes of the *ferias* at Jerez, in Andalucia, at Golega, and at Santarem in Portugal; and around the camp-fires at Pushkar, Nagaur, Jaisalmer, and a dozen more desert towns in Rajasthan, India. Trading horses at the annual fairs is an essential part of the calendar, giving a point of stability to a near-nomadic existence.

Nowhere is the colourful presence of the travellers so evident as at Appleby-in-Westmorland New Fair in Cumbria, possibly one of the largest traditional horse-trading gatherings in the western world.

THE ANCIENT FAIR AT APPLEBY

The travellers converge on Appleby in early June each year from all over Britain and Eire, and even from the US and Australia. Horse-traders, tinkers, potters, they come in hundreds of trailers and opulent mobile homes – the modern equivalent of the decorated gypsy vardo, which had its origin on the Asian steppes 3,000 years ago.

They are there to renew old acquaintances; to present, admire, and talk horse; and to buy, sell, or exchange hundreds upon hundreds of horses. Many will be coloured horses – piebald, skewbald, or spotted in the fashion of the Appaloosa – for colour and decoration is dear to the heart of the Romany. But there will be cobs and trotting horses, often raced through the streets as well as shown off at an organized evening meeting, and heavy horses and pony crosses, and, while they will carry no proof of pedigree, their breeding and background, passed on by word of mouth, is never unknown or in doubt.

Possibly the last of the old horse fairs left in Britain, Appleby Fair enjoys a special distinction since it is held under a Royal

HORSE FOR SALE
Young men ride through the streets of Appleby showing off their horses to potential buyers in the age-old tradition of the horse fair – and most of them will be sold.

Charter of 1685, granted by James II for the sale of "goods, cattle and horses".

The fair begins with a market on New Fair Sunday. Tuesday is devoted to trotting races, and Wednesday provides the climax to the week. Early in the morning, in a ritual going back some 200 years, the horses are taken to the River Eden to be washed, just in case the coat patterns might have been improved by a judicious dab of colouring. Thereafter, the trading begins, with horses being everywhere run up and down. Prices are not low, and many animals will change hands for huge sums, the money being paid

COME TO THE FAIR
Appleby-in-Westmorland New Fair, granted a Royal Charter in 1685, attracts "travellers" and their horses from all over Britain and Eire. Coloured horses are the most numerous and popular.

from an elastic-banded roll of notes. On Thursday, the great exodus begins, many of the participants nursing sore heads, and the little town resumes again its normal life – until the same time next year.

THE *FERIAS*

While the *ferias* of Golega, Santarem, and Jerez have their gypsy following and are an undoubted attraction for tourists, they are altogether more refined, and it would be impossible to imagine the appearance of a piebald horse. They have, too, a competitive element in the numerous show classes that are held amid the festivities.

But, like Appleby, they are still family affairs, if at the level of landed gentry, where horses are brought together for assessment and to display the skills of their breeders and riders. What is remarkable and entirely unique is the opportunity to see the spectacle of pure-bred horses of great quality, hundreds of them, schooled, ridden, and displayed in the true classical manner by riders turned out impeccably in riding clothes that must be correct in every detail.

Most of the splendidly caparisoned horses will be capable of the advanced movements of the High School: Spanish Walk, *passage*, and *piaffe*. At Jerez (see pp. 104–5), there is the additional bonus of the Andalucian School of Equestrian Art, the pinnacle of true classicism and unforgettably vibrant and colourful.

THE FAIRS OF INDIA

In Rajasthan the fairs are all linked with a special religious occasion, the change of season, or the celebration of the harvest. Cattle and camels are for sale as well as horses. The festival atmosphere is heightened by displays of dancing and folk music and, doubtless for the benefit of the tourists for whom the fairs are a focal point, there are whole townships of stands selling craft goods in bewildering variety. In addition, there are numerous desert camps offering accommodation and facilities.

Pushkar Fair, near the historic city of Ajmer, takes place in November and is one

CELEBRATION OF THE HORSE
The Spring Fair at Seville sees the streets filled with elegant caballeros *on beautiful horses with their brightly-dressed* señoritas *riding pillion.*

of the most important events in Rajasthan. However, despite the very secular nature of the Fair (it even incorporates a funfair with a giant wheel and roundabout), the vigorous exploitation of the tourist potential does not intrude upon what is essentially a religious festival; rather, indeed, it acts in a strangely complementary role.

Pushkar, built round the holy waters of Pushkar Lake, which formed miraculously on the spot where petals of the lotus blossom fell from the hand of the Lord Brahma, the Creator, is an ancient religious settlement. It becomes a bustling little town during the time of the Fair but is otherwise a place of peace and tranquillity.

During the 12 days in the month of Kartik, thousands of pilgrims come to bathe from the holy ghats giving on to Pushkar's lake, while above the town hundreds of cattle, camels, and horses are tethered.

The horses are of the Marwari breed with a percentage of Kathiawari (see pp. 162–65), and owners and breeders set up their camps in the sands where they can entertain, when necessary, potential buyers.

Horses are continually paraded, at speed and often dangerously, up and down the avenues at the desert pacing gait of the *revaal*, while on the maidan, the central area of the Fair, colourfully caparisoned horses give impromptu displays of the Indian version of the *Haute École*, performing recognizable levades, caprioles, and a form of *piaffe* and *passage*. There are also the "dancing" displays, given in long reins under spotlights with the horses traditionally decorated. Deals are struck, behind cupped hands, and money paid over in much the same way as at Appleby, 8,000 km (5,000 miles) away.

The gypsies are here, too, quite possibly in the land from which the Romany originated. They come in carts drawn by horses or camels, and they do not differ much from their counterparts in Iberia or, perhaps, in Appleby.

PUSHKAR FAIR
Horse lines at the Pushkar Fair in Rajasthan where trade, tourism, and thousands of pilgrims to the holy waters exist side by side.

COB

A COB IS A BIG-BODIED, compact utility horse, standing four-square on short, powerful legs. In terms of conformation, it is much closer to the strength structure of the heavy horse than to the structure of light horses, such as the long-limbed Thoroughbred, which are designed for speed. Welsh Cobs and Norman Cobs are recognized as breeds, but the English or Irish cob is a type of horse, without any set pattern to its breeding. Even so, it is entirely distinctive, and in the UK and Ireland is regarded with great affection, not only on account of its appearance and ability, but also because of its intelligence and character.

BREEDING AND HISTORY

Cob breeding is rarely deliberate and may even be accidental. Some of the best cobs are Irish Draught crosses, and more than one champion cob has been a pure Irish Draught (see pp.396–97). Sometimes, good cobs are bred from or by Shires, Clevelands, or Welsh Cobs (see pp.288–89, pp.306-7, and pp.184–85), although the latter, in their pure form, are very different in outline and action from the established cob type.

Before the invention of the motor car, every country house in England kept a smart cob which was used in harness for shopping trips and other errands, could be ridden round the farm, and would carry the heavier members of the family for a day's hunting. It used to be said that the cob was usually the fittest and soundest horse in the stable, because of the amount of work it was given. Like modern cobs, particularly those of Irish origin, it was easy and economical to keep, and a "good doer" on moderate rations. (The Irish Draught and the Draught crosses do not, in fact, do well on over-generous rations, and will work satisfactorily on far less food than would be needed by a Thoroughbred, for example.)

BUILT FOR WEIGHT

The cob is a cheerful all-rounder that is capable of carrying heavyweight riders in a variety of circumstances. The height, at just over 1.52 m (15 hh), makes mounting and dismounting an easier operation for the older rider, and the "stuffy", compact build often gives a comforting sense of security. However, there is nothing dull about a good cob. It is expected to give a steady, calm

LIGHT IN HAND

A good cob is never heavy in its ride. Instead, it should be light, comfortable, well-mannered, and very well-balanced.

NECK
The thick, muscular neck is fairly short but is in proportion to the head and shoulders.

HEIGHT
1.52 m
(15 hh)

SHOULDERS
The slope and length of the shoulders are not exaggerated and give some lift to the action.

HEAD
This is a good, workmanlike head of quality, with a "knowing" expression.

CHEST
The chest is broad and the forelegs are set well apart.

LEGS
Short, strong legs "set at each corner", with open feet and very good bone measurement, are an essential requirement in a riding cob.

ride and to have the very best of manners. Most cobs are also excellent hunters that jump willingly and carefully. One term that is often applied to the cob is "confidential", which means that it is safe and dependable, or, endearingly, the horse may be referred to as "a gentleman's gentleman". Cobs are almost always very intelligent animals of great character, and are usually entirely good-natured.

CHARACTERISTICS

The stocky appearance is unmistakeable, but it is important that the outline should present a picture of complete symmetry. Because of its build, a cob cannot afford to have conformational faults such as a long back, a badly set-on head and neck, or small, mean quarters. Such faults would have a

ATTRIBUTES
A heavyweight cob will carry any weight, and is well able to gallop and jump. By nature, cobs are noted as being knowing and full of character.

totally disproportionate effect upon the action and balance, and would make the animal most uncomfortable to ride.

The ideal cob is traditionally said to have "the head of a lady's maid and the bottom of a cook", and that is no bad description. There should be no suspicion of coarseness about the head. The ears should be alert and mobile, and the widely spaced eyes generous. The quarters should be exceptionally muscled, broad, and very strong. They may not be conducive to great speed as a result, but they will carry weight and are usually associated with jumping ability. The neck, in accordance with the overall "strength structure", is short and powerful, but is nonetheless arched and not without elegance. The horse's shoulders should never be too upright, lest they produce an exaggerated lift of the knee and a correspondingly jarring action. Instead, the shoulders should be adequately sloped, to give a lower, more economical, and comfortable movement. The trot is the pace usually associated with the cob, but the horse should also be able to stretch out into a respectable gallop.

Until the Docking and Nicking Act of 1948, which made these practices illegal in the UK, it was traditional to dock the tail of cobs, as well as hogging the mane. Docking gave them a jaunty, sporting appearance, but it was a cruel and unnecessary custom. Today cobs are still hogged, which suits the neck shape, but the tail is now left full.

In the show ring, the classes are divided into lightweight, heavyweight, and working cobs. Working cobs are required to jump, and no cob must exceed 1.55 m (15.1 hh).

QUARTERS
The quarters are broad and often massively muscled. They are built for strength rather than speed.

SECOND THIGHS
The muscles of the second thighs are pronounced and well-developed.

BODY
The body is deep, solid, compact, and stocky, with a fairly short back and broad, strong loins.

ORIGINS

COBS ARE NOT BRED DELIBERATELY, but they occur frequently in the UK and Ireland. They have maintained their popularity through showing classes at the major shows in these countries. Some of the best cobs come from Ireland; these are usually of Irish Draught extraction, while others may even be pure-bred Irish Draughts. Otherwise, good riding cobs are to be found in parts of south-west England, and some are also bred in Wales and on the Welsh borders. In all instances, good horse-raising country is a vital requirement for producing cobs that have substance, size, and good bone.

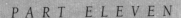

PART ELEVEN

HORSE MANAGEMENT

MANAGEMENT OF THE HORSE, to ensure optimum health, condition, and therefore maximum working efficiency for the purpose required, has exercised the mind of the horsemaster ever since the first known manual of horse-care was written by Kikkuli the Mittanian for the Hittite chariot corps in 1360 BC. Then as now, the basis of good management lay in a working knowledge of the body systems (*anatomy*) and the functions they perform (*physiology*). An appreciation of the horse's nature and mental processes is also important if the animal is to remain temperamentally stable in the domestic environment.

A detail from *In the Forge*
by Edward Robert Smythe (1810–99)

STRUCTURE IN MOTION

THE BASIC HORSE

S TUDYING THE STRUCTURE of the horse's body, and the functions of the principal components, provides the most reliable guide to the content, planning, and implementation of training programmes. Furthermore, it can indicate how well a horse is likely to perform. A horse with the correct proportions will have the greatest potential, as this governs the effectiveness of the movement and reduces immeasurably the risk of disease and/or strain imposed on joints, sinews, ligaments, and muscles caused by the work routines. Similarly, a rudimentary knowledge of the digestive process is vital to the management of the horse and the overall efficiency of the horse's body (it is no less important than a proper understanding of the function of the various feed constituents).

THE BASIS FOR MOVEMENT

The framework of the body is the skeleton made up of connected bones. Their movement, activated by joints and muscles, produces motion. The joint surfaces are separated by a layer of gristle (cartilage), and the whole is encased within a two-layer capsule. The outer layer provides support, while the inner one secretes an oily fluid (synovia or joint oil). In this way, the joint works within a vessel of oil and is in a state of constant lubrication.

The structure is held firmly together by connecting ligaments – tough, flexible tissues attached to each bone. While permitting free movement, ligaments also serve to prevent over-extension of the joint, which would result in its being damaged. The structure is covered by muscle, with fat rounding off the corners and providing a reserve of food if required.

Muscle, by being attached to bones, compels movement in the joints and, in consequence, to the body mass. Movement is produced by the contraction of the muscle drawing together the two points of attachment and thereby initiating action in the joint.

Muscles are elastic but would be torn without the support of tendons – tough, inelastic substances running like a rope through the length of the muscle, one end being attached firmly to the bone and the other plaited into the body of the muscle.

A peculiar property of muscle, very relevant to the schooling and conditioning of the horse, is that the degree to which it can contract is matched equally by its ability to extend, or be stretched.

A principal object of training is to encourage the initial stretching of the muscles so as to increase their ability to contract and thus to improve the flexion of the joints they control. Muscles are of two types: flexors and extensors. The former act to contract the joint and the latter extend to allow the opposite effect. They are, therefore, acting in pairs but they also oppose, or compensate.

For example, the rounded top-line of the back is brought about by the big back muscles acting as extensors, while three muscles over the abdomen and three running from the fifth and ninth ribs to the pubis act as flexors, raising the abdomen and bringing the hind legs under the body. (Involuntary muscles occur within the internal organs, like those controlling the bowels and the independent cardiac muscle of the heart.)

Lack of muscle development, or incorrect development due to faults in the training methods, makes it impossible to achieve the carriage and movement that

THE SKELETON

The framework of the body is composed of bones forming the skeleton on which the subsequent locomotion of the body mass depends.

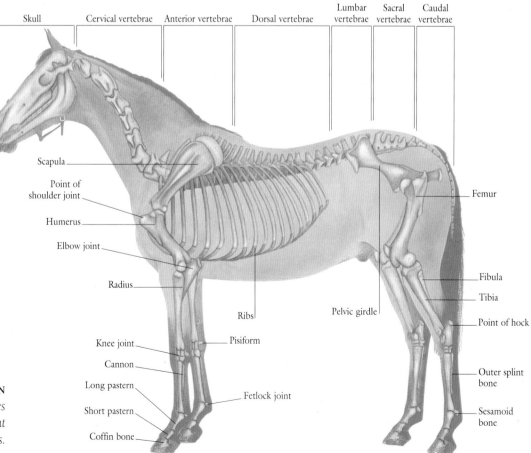

Skull | Cervical vertebrae | Anterior vertebrae | Dorsal vertebrae | Lumbar vertebrae | Sacral vertebrae | Caudal vertebrae

Scapula
Point of shoulder joint
Humerus
Elbow joint
Radius
Knee joint
Cannon
Long pastern
Short pastern
Coffin bone
Pisiform
Ribs
Fetlock joint
Pelvic girdle
Femur
Fibula
Tibia
Point of hock
Outer splint bone
Sesamoid bone

results in a mechanically efficient structure. Damage to a ligament affects the movement of the joint in the same way as disease and injury. Tendon damage will also impair the action of the joint more or less seriously. Unfit or physically immature animals are more likely to suffer ligament or tendon damage when worked injudiciously. Bad shoeing or neglect of the feet (allowing the foot to grow too long) will also contribute to tendon problems in the lower leg.

The basis for movement lies within the brain and its continuation – the spinal cord. The nervous system is often compared with a telephone exchange with the brain as the control box: it takes orders and relays messages to and from the body. (Nerves are either those giving rise to feeling, *sensor*, or those concerned with movement, *motor*.) While it is not proven beyond doubt, it seems likely that the more refined, better-bred horse is more receptive and responsive than its common-bred plebeian cousins because of a more efficient nervous system.

CONFORMATION AND PROPORTION

The word conformation relates to the shape of the framework and its overlying tissues, and the symmetrical proportion of the individual parts comprising the whole. It is the conformation of the animal that governs the quality of balance and movement. Early vets made exhaustive studies of conformation, observing and measuring hundreds of horses.

Today, there might well be differences in detail between the proportions most suited to an event horse, for example, and those appropriate to the dressage horse and, perhaps, the showjumper. In all instances, however, there are three significant proportions to be observed. They are, first, that the measurement from the top of the wither to the deepest part of the body behind and below the elbow should equal the distance from that point to the ground. This will allow for the unrestricted expansion of the lungs. Second – particularly if speed is, within reason, a requirement and also in the interest of balance – the length of neck should be 1.5 times the measurement taken from the

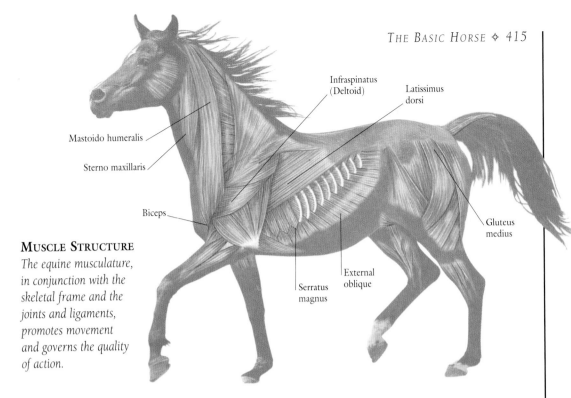

MUSCLE STRUCTURE
The equine musculature, in conjunction with the skeletal frame and the joints and ligaments, promotes movement and governs the quality of action.

Mastoido humeralis

Sterno maxillaris

Biceps

Infraspinatus (Deltoid)

Latissimus dorsi

Gluteus medius

External oblique

Serratus magnus

poll, down the front of the face, to the lower lip. Finally, for the sake of the structure's strength and overall efficiency, the measurement from the point of shoulder to the last of the "false" ribs (asternal ribs) must be about twice that from the rear of the wither to the highest part of the croup.

THE DIGESTIVE SYSTEM

The method and principles of feeding are dependent on the digestive system and the position of the relatively small stomach.

The stomach lies behind the diaphragm, separating it from the chest cavity. It is in contact with the lungs in front, and lies between the liver and the spleen. Following a feed, stomach and bowels (the latter still digesting the previous food intake)

Small colon

Small intestine

Stomach

Liver

Rectum

Spleen

Position of caecum

Large colon

DIGESTIVE TRACT
Digestion begins in the mouth and continues via the stomach to the small and large bowel before waste is excreted.

become distended and the stomach presses against the diaphragm. Should the horse be ridden immediately, the exertion would cause the lungs to expand as the animal breathed more deeply. The lungs would then press on the elastic diaphragm, which, in turn, would be pushed against the distended stomach, impairing both the breathing and the digestive process. It is likely that the outcome would be indigestion, which might develop into a severe colic. If the work was at speed, the lungs could choke with blood and the stomach might be ruptured. The first rule, therefore, is *do not work after feeding*, at least not for an hour or so. The bowel structure (small and large bowel) is capacious but, even so, the system is designed for the absorption of food consumed slowly and almost continuously.

Ideally, the feeding of the stabled horse should conform to that requirement, the animal being given small feeds every ten minutes. Since that is clearly impractical, the total needs to be divided into as many as four small feeds, none being more than 1.8 kg (4 lb) in weight, in consideration for the size of the stomach. The second rule, therefore, is *feed little and often*.

VETERINARY MEDICINE

19TH-CENTURY HORSE SLING

VETERINARY MEDICINE in the 21st century is certainly keeping abreast of the advances made in the human equivalent and may even, in some areas, be in advance of them. Equine veterinary practice expanded enormously in the post-war years as a result of increased participation in equine sports and recreational pursuits and a corresponding rise in the value of competition horses and those bred in the racing industry. A further factor providing extra encouragement to research is the now-commonplace transportation of valuable Thoroughbreds and racehorses by air, increasing the need to control the spread of viral and other infections.

THE ROLE OF THE VET

Today, the veterinary surgeon has an essential role to play in every sort of horse-keeping activity. The equine practitioner, who is increasingly a specialist in his or her field, provides three principal services. First, there is clinical veterinary medicine, which includes and emphasizes preventive medicine, such as immunization from tetanus – a killer disease in the past – and vaccination against equine influenza. Second, there is surgical diagnosis and the subsequent treatment, including operative procedures. Third, and probably the most frequent requirement, is the diagnosis and treatment of lameness, which may include the use of X-rays.

Largely because of the high value of competition horses and the risks of injury involved in sports, even at a local level, insurance is a necessary item in the budget of many horse-owners. Examination for soundness by a veterinary surgeon in relation to the issue of insurance policies, as well as to the purchase of an animal, has therefore become a matter of prime importance. When premiums are high – as in the instance of Thoroughbred stallions and racehorses valued at six figures and beyond, or in the case of competition horses and even hunters, which are all exposed to special risks – dependence upon efficient veterinary support is especially great.

MODERN ADVANCES

Advances made in anaesthetics and the use of antibiotics, along with the increasing incidence of well-equipped operating theatres, have all contributed to the success of modern equine surgery. The use of X-ray equipment is now commonplace, and medical treatment has benefited from the availability of new drugs and antibiotics. Also, far more use is made of laboratory testing, which is both quick and accurate.

The old diseases, known as "scheduled disease" and requiring notification to the appropriate authority, have been largely eradicated. Glanders,

VETS IN TRAINING

By the end of the 19th century, students, as seen in this picture, were able to obtain practical training in London under the aegis of the Royal College of Veterinary Surgeons.

parasitic mange, and epizootic lymphangitis have all gone. It is possible that laminitis, the disabling disease of the foot, may be more prevalent in certain areas, but new and effective treatments continue to become available as intensive research into the disease is carried out.

The operation of "firing" the legs in the treatment of particular forms of lameness, including tendon strains and ruptures, has, to the satisfaction of numerous owners and the veterinary profession itself, been replaced in many countries by less draconian treatments, such as electrotherapy and short-wave therapy. In Britain, "firing" has been banned by the Royal College of Veterinary Surgeons. "Firing" and "blistering" are both forms of counter-irritant treatment used to stimulate repair of

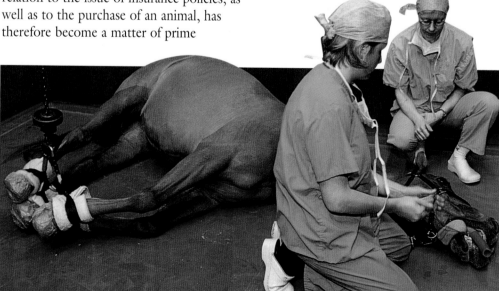

VETERINARY HOSPITAL

Administering the anaesthetic prior to surgery in a modern veterinary clinic, where operating theatres are as well equipped as those in the medical field.

chronic injuries. "Blistering", the milder of the two, involves the use of a chemical irritant, while "firing", producing acute inflammation, depends upon the application of a heated firing iron with the object, as in both cases, of causing an influx of fluid and cells to the area. "Firing" is an ancient practice. It is still an accepted treatment in Tibet, Mongolia, and Central Asia generally, while "blistering", whether under veterinary instigation or not, is a fairly common practice in the US.

ANCIENT PRACTITIONERS

Veterinary medicine has been practised almost since the beginning of man's association with the horse. In ancient India there were animal hospitals treating sick horses, elephants, and cattle, and there are numerous texts devoted to the treatment of animal disease, notably the Hindu *Asva Sastram*. A scale of fees for the treatment of asses and oxen was laid down in about 1800 BC by King Hammurabi of Mesopotamia, and a century earlier the Egyptians had a manual of treatment recorded on papyrus for ailments of dogs.

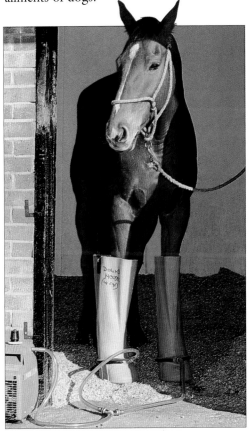

WATER THERAPY
The use of water in the treatment of leg injuries is a long-established practice. The modern method employs these special whirlpool boots.

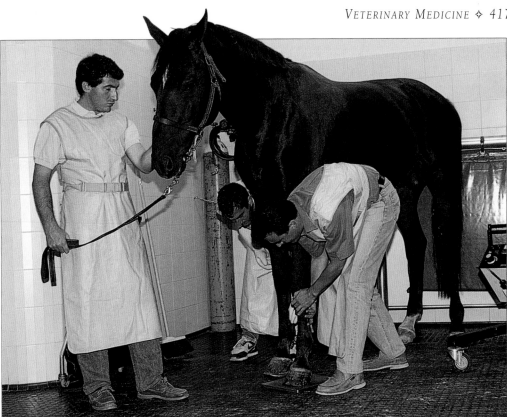

PREPARING FOR X-RAY
The use of investigative X-rays is an essential in modern veterinary practice, particularly in the diagnosis and treatment of lameness.

The pioneers of veterinary practice, as for human medicine, were the Greeks. Their horse doctors were called *hippiatori,* and the first physicians, foremost of whom was Hippocrates, were versed in the treatment of animals. Such was the pre-eminence of Greek medicine, both human and animal, that the Romans employed Greek practitioners almost to the exclusion of all others. The term *veterinarius* came into use for those practising animal medicine and the word *veterinarium* referred to a horse surgery or hospital.

The most famous of the Greek veterinarians were Aspyrtus, whose texts, written in about AD 330, were republished in the 10th century as *Hippiatrika,* and Vegetius, who published, in about AD 450, *The Veterinary Art,* the book that was to be regarded as the standard work for almost the next thousand years. It is clear that Vegetius was well acquainted with numerous viral infections as prevalent, it would seem, at that time as in the present day. In Rome, there were certainly severe epidemics of what would now be recognizable as equine flu and African horse sickness.

During the Middle Ages and, indeed, into the 20th century the treatment of animal disease – in horses particularly and in some cases humans – was within the province of the farrier, who enjoyed the sort of prestige and respect accorded to the ancient Shaman.

VETERINARY SCHOOLS EMERGE

While little progress was made in veterinary science up to the early 18th century, it gathered pace as the nations of Europe went to war and became dependent on the maintenance of a powerful mounted arm, backed by extensive horse-breeding programmes. It was for this reason that the first school of veterinary medicine, the Royal Veterinary School, was founded at Lyons, France, in 1762, with Claude Bourgelat (1712–79) as its principal.

In 1791, a school was founded in London, and in 1844 a Royal Charter was granted and the Royal College of Veterinary Surgeons became the governing body of the profession in Britain. The chief veterinary schools in Britain are the Royal Veterinary College, University of London, and those at the universities of Cambridge, Liverpool, Edinburgh, Glasgow, and Bristol, while the Irish veterinary school is at Dublin. At all, the course of study covers five or six years.

The US has numerous schools dating from the foundation at Iowa State College in 1879, and there are many prestigious establishments throughout Europe.

ALTERNATIVE MEDICINE

DANDELION

THE LAST 50 YEARS of the 20th century were characterized by an ever-increasing awareness of environmental issues. In such a climate of concern, genetically modified products became a matter for contention and, side by side with the support for organic foodstuffs, there was growing public interest in alternative, natural medicine to complement conventional medical treatment based on carefully screened synthetic drugs. A similar movement towards natural therapies was just as evident in the field of equine veterinary practice and, by the end of the century, complementary therapies were forming an increasingly significant dimension in the care and management of horses.

MASSAGE AND MANIPULATION

The physiotherapist, under whatever name, along with the skilled herbalist, has influenced healing techniques almost from the beginning of recorded history; within groups of the tribal peoples of India, for instance, deeply rooted traditions of instinctive massage and manipulative therapy survive and are handed down from one generation to the next. These practices, now a major part of modern complementary therapies, preceded conventional medicine by many hundreds of years.

The early physiotherapist had to rely upon his hands to relieve pain, whereas his modern counterpart has the advantage of a number of therapeutic machines appropriate for the treatment of differing conditions, ranging from bone damage to deep bruising and muscle strains.

The modern physiotherapist is highly qualified with an in-depth knowledge of anatomy and physiology. Physiotherapists work in conjunction with the veterinary surgeon, relying largely on his accurate diagnosis of the condition. However, in unskilled, unqualified hands treatment with machines could be dangerous, and it is for this reason that in the UK, for instance, the Veterinary Act restricts treatment of an animal to the owner, a veterinary surgeon, or another qualified person approved by a veterinary surgeon. Similar constraints are also in force elsewhere in Europe.

Chiropractic is similarly controlled and is an invaluable therapy in misalignments of the spinal column, for instance, that may arise from falls, from injuries sustained in the stable or when travelling, or, just as frequently, from inexpert initial handling of the horse, or from plain bad riding.

HEALING WATERS
The specially constructed equine swimming pool is used increasingly in convalescence. It allows full use of the muscular structure without the limbs carrying weight or being subjected to the inhibitive effects of concussion caused by conventional exercise routines on firm ground.

EXPERT CHIROPRACTOR
The expert, qualified chiropractor is able to correct skeletal misalignment arising from injuries or falls. Such structural damage can cause lameness and restriction of the natural movement.

Misplacement of any part of the skeletal structure, resulting in damage to the nerve supply, can cause lameness, restricted movement, and behavioural problems as a result of the pain experienced. Swimming therapy, with all four limbs engaged, is often recommended following physiotherapy or the attentions of a chiropractor, but it needs to be carried out under expert supervision.

LIKE CURES LIKE

As large as any area of alternative medicine is the established practice of homeopathy, a fundamentally difficult subject in which full qualifications are not obtained without four-to-five years' intensive study.

The principles of homeopathy, "the rational art of healing", were first developed by the German doctor Christian Samuel Hahnemann in 1796, although an incomplete and consequently flawed understanding existed with the early herbalists long before then.

TOOLS OF PHYSIOTHERAPY
The basic tool of the physiotherapist is the hand, but today use is also made of a variety of therapeutic instruments to treat deep bruising, bone damage, and other specific injuries.

Hahnemann was a physician of note, as well as a chemist. As a fundamental principle of the science of homeopathy he adopted the phrase, *Similia similibus curentur* – "Let like be treated by like".

In simple terms, homeopathy is about stimulating the body to heal itself – rather like the principle of vaccination, when a small dose of a harmful organism is given to build up the natural resistance in the body. Possibly the greatest and most versatile of the homeopathic remedies is Arnica, produced by the flowers of the mountain plant *Arnica montana*. It is used to counter the effects of extreme exertion, severe bruising, physical and mental shock, and stress-related conditions. Strains and sprains are treated with *Rhus toxicadendrum* and *Ruta*, the latter being especially suited to bone damage. There are few conditions, either equine or human, that cannot be treated by homeopathy, other than those requiring surgical interference, and even in those instances homeopathy can be used in a supportive role.

HERBS AND PLANTS

Allied to homeopathy are the less complex and sophisticated herbal remedies now packaged in large numbers. Comfrey (the medieval "knit bone"), devil's claw, dandelion, and nettle can all be used to counter inflammatory arthritic conditions and problems of reduced circulation. Sulphur-rich herbs, like calendula, garlic, seaweed, and thyme, are effective in cases of mud fever, rain scald, and associated

complaints, and there are many, many more. Even aromatherapy, an art in which essential oils and essences extracted from plants are inhaled or massaged into the skin, is now used to treat some equine disorders, particularly skin problems. Tea tree, eucalyptus, lime, and almond oils are the most widely used essential oils.

As old as any medical therapy is the science of acupuncture, records of which show its use in China over 3,000 years ago. Banned in China in the 19th century in favour of Western medicine, it was later reinstated under Mao Tse-Tung, and it is increasingly popular in the West.

Through the strategic placing of fine needles at specific points in the body's energy channels, the body is stimulated to increase its own healing process. Each Chinese country commune has two vets, one practising Western medicine, the other practising acupuncture. Equine acupuncture using 20-cm (8-in) needles is strengthened by a mild cautery of herbs, either set alight at acupuncture points on the skin, or inserted beneath it by the needles. Acupuncture, again a science only to be practised by the qualified practitioner, is claimed to be effective in all sorts of conditions, particularly in the case of arthritis, rheumatism, stress-related illness, muscle and joint problems, skin disorders, and bladder and bowel complaints.

While some of the alternative therapies are not scientifically proven and have yet to become mainstream, they are, nonetheless, claimed to produce amazing results, free from side-effects, for a variety of ailments.

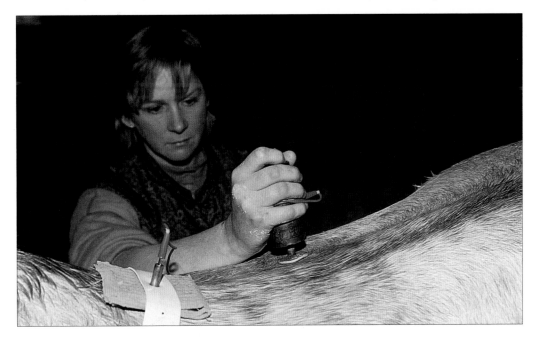

THE FARRIER'S ART

THE FARRIER AT WORK

THE OLD ADAGE "No foot – no 'oss" remains as much a truism as ever it was. For centuries the art of farriery has complemented veterinary medicine in the treatment of diseases of the foot, and at the start of the new Millennium the practice of horse-shoeing is properly recognized as being an art based on scientific fact, with the farrier being recognized increasingly as a skilled craftsman and integral to the horse's welfare. The modern horse-owner is, indeed, as much reliant on the services of the farrier as on those of the veterinary surgeon, and the importance of these services being delivered only by properly qualified practitioners is highlighted by the fact that farriery is now regulated by law in many parts of the world.

AS IT WAS
A welcome break at the village smithy. This remarkable photograph by Fred Marsh was taken in 1896, when the smithy was at the centre of rural life, horses being brought there from neighbouring farms throughout the day.

development of farriery lay principally with France and Italy.

Claude Bourgelat, first principal of the veterinary school at Lyons (see pp.416–17), made notable contributions to the study of the foot's anatomy. He designed a shoe to maintain the foot as nearly as possible in the natural state, and this remained in general use in France well into the 20th century. In the interim period, however, experimentation produced some appalling patterns.

The modern, far more enlightened, farrier will know exactly what shoe to fit, whatever the horse. He is, too, capable of correcting faulty conformation and action, and the very experienced are adept at shoeing to combat surgical conditions.

THE ANATOMY OF THE FOOT

The anatomy of the foot is complex. In simple terms it is a sensitive, vascular structure containing three bones, the "coffin" or pedal bone, the navicular bone, and the lower parts of the coronet bone. Together they form the foot, or pedal joint.

The whole is contained in an enveloping outer protective case, called the wall, a horny substance that grows down from the coronet and can be likened to the human toe- or finger-nails. The underside of the foot comprises the sole and the frog – a triangular, rubbery substance lying between the angles of the heels, which protects the

THE ORIGINS OF FARRIERY

In Britain, the Farriers Acts of 1975 and 1977 make it unlawful for persons not listed on the Register of Farriers, maintained by the Worshipful Company of Farriers, to shoe horses. The Worshipful Company is one of London's ancient Livery Companies, dating from the 14th century. The Company received its Charter from King Charles II of England in 1674 and is active in encouraging and organizing the craft through a system of examinations.

The word "farrier" comes from the old French *ferrier,* which, in turn, comes from the Latin *ferrum* (iron). From 1356 the name farrier was applied by the Worshipful Company to a man who attended a sick horse, and before the advent of the veterinary schools (see pp.416–17) the farriers were the horse doctors of the day.

Both Greeks and Romans devised means of protection for horses going lame on the march. These were a form of sandal, made initially from woven grass, *soleae sparteae,* then from leather, and finally from metal, *soleae ferreae.* Like the Roman *hipposandal,* they were attached to the foot by thongs. The horn of the hoof of horses operating in hot, dry climates is so hard that to a great extent they can work unshod. In wet climates, as in Roman Britain, the horn becomes soft, and on hard, rough surfaces, would have worn away before the natural growth could make up the loss.

Celtic burial sites in Europe provide the first evidence of nailed-on metal shoes and it is accepted that the Celts, noted ironworkers and horsemen, were making horseshoes before and during the Roman occupation of Britain following its invasion by Julius Caesar in AD 54–55. Thereafter, the

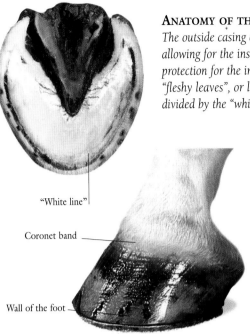

ANATOMY OF THE FOOT

The outside casing of the foot is insensitive, allowing for the insertion of nails, and is a protection for the inner highly sensitive "fleshy leaves", or laminae, the two being divided by the "white line".

"White line"

Coronet band

Wall of the foot

HOT-
SHOEING

HOT AND COLD

(Inset) The preferred hot-shoe method. (Main picture) Farriers shoeing by the "cold" method, which is considered the less satisfactory.

sensitive area above. The frog helps to bear the animal's weight, the burden of which is carried on the outer edge of the wall and the bearing surface to which the shoe is fitted. The frog is a perfect shock-absorber and anti-slip device.

The outside of the protective casing is insensitive and is separated from the sensitive inside by the "white line" running round the inside of the hard wall. The "white line" is clearly visible on the sole of a scrubbed, unshod foot. The nails securing the shoe to the foot have to be placed outside the line in the insensitive wall, which allows little room for error on the part of the farrier, who must also ensure that the frog functions as it was intended.

In the regularly shod foot, the horn growth varies between 6–10 mm (¼–⅜ in) per month, necessitating removal of the shoes at intervals of not more than four to five weeks to rasp away, from the underside, the excessive growth.

Feet that turn in or out can often be corrected by rasping the overgrowth, which is usually the source of the problem. Toes turning in are corrected by rasping the overgrowth on the inside of the wall. Conversely, toes turn out because of an overgrowth on the outside wall.

The farrier strives to maintain the correct Foot Pastern Axis (FPA). The ideal is for the FPA, involving angles produced at fetlock, toe, and heel, to correspond to the slope of the shoulder, which in the well-conformed horse will be between 43–45° from the highest point of the wither to the point of shoulder. A correct FPA ensures the

most economical and smoothest flight path for the foot.

Most farriers prefer hot-shoeing, where the heated shoe is placed on the foot, burning a brown rim where it touches. The object is to check the fit and ensure the whole is in perfect contact. Cold-shoeing is sometimes necessary but is less satisfactory.

The well-made shoe follows the rim of the wall. It is neither too long, too short, nor too wide. In short, it *fits the foot* rather

SHAME THE DEVIL

The cottager nails a lucky horseshoe over the door as a protection against evil. Clearly, it has frustrated the intentions of the Devil and his "familiar", the black cat on the roof.

than the foot being rasped to fit the shape and size of the shoe. The worst failing in this respect is the practice of "dumping" the foot, when the toe is rasped to shorten it so as to correspond with the size of the shoe.

The number of nails securing the shoe should be as few as possible. Four nails on the outside and three on the inside should be sufficient. A nail driven too close to the sensitive laminae is said to "press" and will cause painful bruising. One that enters the sensitive wall is said to "prick" and causes immediate lameness. When the nails are driven home the protruding points are wrung off, the shanks being turned up to form the securing "clenches". These are hammered down and rasped briefly. No further rasping is necessary.

MAGICAL POWERS

For centuries, horseshoes have been nailed above doors to ward off evil and bring good luck, perhaps because the shoe is crescent-shaped, the symbol of the moon goddess and of fertility. One story is that St Dunstan, a patron saint of farriers, was asked by the Devil to shoe his feet. The saint, recognizing his visitor, inflicted such pain on him that the Devil promised never again to enter a building displaying a horseshoe.

The carrying of horseshoes by brides is said to have originated with Lars Persena, King of Tuscany, whose wife's horses were shod with silver on their wedding day.

Keeping & Usage

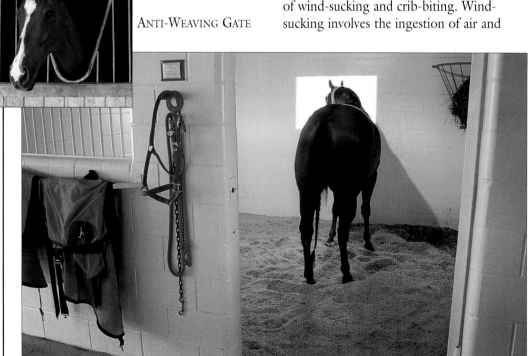

PAPER BEDDING

THE METHODS of keeping horses in the domestic or semi-domestic state relate directly to the purpose required of the animals, to the climate, to the environment, and to the facilities available. The variation between horse husbandry in the Northern and Southern hemispheres is very great. The spectrum ranges from the semi-feral herds raised to provide meat, milk, and associated products like hides, fats, and even dung for fires, to the carefully cosseted racehorse, housed in purpose-built stables and attended by a personal groom. Even then, methods differ from country to country, the common factor being the observance of common-sense principles to achieve an end result.

FIT TO HUNT

For many people in Britain, Eire, and in certain parts of the US, the very *raison d'être* for horse-keeping was to hunt during the winter months, a situation that was particularly pronounced before and, especially, between the two World Wars. The method of horse-keeping and management was therefore directed at producing fit horses for the hunting season and then maintaining their condition during that period. Hunters spent the summer months turned out at grass. They were "brought up" to be put in work in early September so as to be ready, after the preliminaries of cub-hunting, for the opening meet on 1 November. Between September and April the hunters were usually kept stabled.

ANTI-WEAVING GATE

Nowadays, in Europe and the US, horses are generally kept for pleasure and recreation. Increasingly, this involves competitive sports at a number of levels. It has become the practice to turn the stabled horse out for some period of the day wearing a waterproof New Zealand rug as a protection against the elements. An hour or two at liberty, possibly in the company of companions, gives the horse an opportunity to relax, both mentally and physically, and goes a long way to preventing what are termed "stable vices", which should more properly be seen as expressions of boredom and frustration arising from the imposition of a wholly unnatural lifestyle. They may also indicate unsympathetic management.

STABLE BEHAVIOUR

Aberrant behaviour is typified by the habits of wind-sucking and crib-biting. Wind-sucking involves the ingestion of air and subsequent digestive problems. The crib-biter grasps any available object with its teeth, grinding them together while flexing the neck on its underside. This can cause serious damage to the teeth, as well as to property, and causes difficulties in the mastication of feed. Since the habit is practised continually, the horse is rarely at rest. It then becomes difficult to maintain condition and performance.

Stable vices also include the nervous habit of weaving, when the horse incessantly shifts its weight from one foreleg to another while continually waving its head. This habit can be extremely contagious and is likely to be detrimental to the horse's physical condition, as well as indicating a poor mental state.

Box-walking is not listed as a vice, but the constant circling of the box – noticeable, like weaving, in caged animals – is a worrying indication of hypertension. It results in loss of condition and wears out the shoes. Incessant pawing is another symptom of tension and stress.

The horse in serious competition, usually on a high-energy diet of artificial foods, is even more prey to tension since it may be stabled almost throughout the year. It is, therefore, more than ever necessary to ensure that it is allowed regular periods of relaxation away from the stable.

The type of stabling provided is crucial to the horse's wellbeing. The best kind is probably the American barn method, where animals are housed in one building and are

THE STABLED HORSE
(Inset) A door is fitted with an anti-weaving gate to discourage the weaving habit. (Main picture) This box in an American barn is the ultimate in equine accommodation. It is light, airy, and spacious.

COMMUNAL LIVING

Mares and foals live together in a well-arranged barn at the world-famous Hungarian state stud of Bábolna, the home of the renowned Shagya Arabian horse. The deep bedding and capacious feed troughs are a feature of the barn.

able to see each other, a very important factor contributing to a settled outlook.

The stabling of horses in stalls, where the animals, although next door to each other, have to be tied up is less satisfactory, although many horses live happily enough in these conditions and it is common practice in army barracks, where horse management is usually of the very highest order.

The horses are secured by a rope passing from the headcollar, through a ring or hole in the manger in front of them, and then through a manger "log", a sphere of lignum vitae, resting on the bedding. The rope is sufficiently long to allow restricted movement and also to enable the animal to lie down. In case of emergency, the rope, having been passed through the "log", is secured using a quick-release knot.

A loose box ("loose" because the horse is at liberty within the space provided) is ideally about 3.7 x 4.3 m (12 x 14 ft) in size, and the door must open outwards in case the horse should block the entrance, as it might if it were to become "cast", that is, unable to get up after lying down.

Whatever the type of stabling, the three essential factors that need to be observed are ventilation, insulation, and drainage. Ventilation has to be ample and without draughts. Top doors are best left open at all times. Insulation and drainage are a matter of construction and maintenance.

The traditional bedding for horses was long, wheat straw, but today, wood shavings

FURIOSO HERD

A herd of Hungarian Furioso mares and youngsters graze at pasture near the famous stud of Mezőhegyes. Hungary's horse culture goes back to antiquity and horses are reared communally in natural conditions.

are often used. Shredded paper, which has the advantage of being dust-free, is also used. The latest development in bedding is the custom-made rubber floor, which is easily cleaned and less labour-intensive.

CLOSER TO NATURE

In complete contrast is the system of horse husbandry employed in Central Asia by traditional horse-people of predominantly Mongolian origin, who use the Asian version of the lariat, a long slender bamboo with a loop at the end to catch horses as and when necessary. Among the steppe people, the keeping of horses is entirely utilitarian in purpose, any recreational use, whether racing or the playing of wild games on horseback, being no more than an enjoyable subsidiary to the main purpose.

Huge herds are kept commercially all year round on the steppe lands, many being grazed on highland pastures during the

summer months and driven down to the foothills in the winter. They provide meat, hides, and milk to support a sizeable industry and are employed as pack animals and in draught as the principal means of transport. Mares are milked routinely and the Bashkir mares, of the southern foothills of the Urals, will yield on average 1,500 litres (330 gallons) of milk, with the best giving as much as 2,700 litres (550 gallons) during the seven- to eight-month lactation period. These animals, kept without subsidiary feeding, can survive temperatures well below freezing point, with the ground covered in deep snow, while a pair harnessed to a sleigh can cover 120–140 km (75–85 miles) inside 24 hours.

Outer Mongolia has the largest number of horses per head of human population in the world, and nowhere is the traditional drink of the steppes, *kumiss,* more appreciated. *Kumiss* is an alcoholic liquid produced from fermented mares' milk and is now produced commercially at co-operative equine dairy farms. Yoghurt, which is so fashionable in the West, was probably first made from mares' milk in Mongolia.

It is a far cry from the horse management of Europe, but it is closer to nature, and steppe horses are unlikely to suffer the psychological problems of their European cousins.

CONDITIONING & MANAGEMENT

PREPARING FEEDS

To BRING A HORSE to the physical condition required to perform effectively at a given level, and to do so without risk of strain or injury, it is usual and more convenient to keep the animal stabled, allowing for daily periods of relaxation in a paddock or turn-out area. Additionally, peak condition and a willing, obedient frame of mind will be achieved only by a proper balance of the three constituent elements: feeding, exercise and work, and grooming. While the quantity and, where appropriate, the duration of these elements are of obvious importance, the quality of all three is equally and especially significant.

A BALANCED DIET

Domestication has imposed on the horse a mode of life that is in contradiction to its basic nature. In the natural state, a diet of grass, herbs, and the like is sufficient to maintain the life requirements, and, indeed, animals kept entirely at grass will be capable of working at slow paces. In general, however, grass, particularly at times of maximum growth, produces fat horses in soft condition, although that is not so much the case with alfalfa grass, which grows extensively in the US, and on areas of the steppe lands, and is a highly nutritious food with a good protein content.

In domestication, however, where the competition horse, in any discipline and at a variety of levels, is expected to carry weight (in many instances at speed and over obstacles), the natural foodstuffs are insufficient to meet the demands made on the body. To correspond with its unnatural state the horse must be fed unnatural, or artificial, foodstuffs that, when fed in the correct balance, will provide strength and energy for the activities required.

The constituents comprising a balanced diet are six: protein; fats, starches, and sugar; water; fibrous roughage; minerals; and vitamins – all more or less interdependent.

A balanced feed intake for an average horse in work can be divided into three categories: food providing bulk; food providing energy; and auxiliaries that supplement or emphasize particular needs. These auxiliary foodstuffs include glucose, molasses, various vitamin and mineral supplements, as well as the more commonplace "green food" like grass, and roots, such as carrots, mangolds, and turnips.

Bulk feed is provided by hay, made from grasses peculiar to different parts of the world. Grass is, of course, a bulk feed and in

'DR GREEN'
Good grass is an important constituent of the conditioning programme, and so is the time spent at liberty in the paddock.

India, for example, workers harvest up to 18 kg (40 lb) per day. Chaff, a mixture of cut hay and straw, also provides bulk, as does silage, which must be fed with care.

Energy and body-building foods are based on grains of various types – such as oats, barley, and maize – but increasingly the practice is to feed one or other of the carefully balanced proprietary mixes, nuts, or pellets, which are formulated to meet the needs of animals at every level. They range from low-energy, non-heating mixes to high-performance compounds. Fibrous roughage is essential to the diet, since it assists in breaking up the concentrate energy foods and absorbing them into the system. The proportion of bulk food to concentrates

THE NOSE BAG
An essential piece of equipment for the cab horse and the milk cob, the nose bag allowed the animal frequent, small meals. Here, a pair of Indian troop horses get their noses into the bag.

HORSE WALKER
A "horse walker" at a stable in Florida, US. This useful piece of machinery can be used to exercise horses in a busy yard or to cool them off after work.

is accepted as being two-thirds bulk to one-third concentrate ("short") feed for horses in light work. The proportion alters to 50–50 for animals in moderate work. The bulk content may be reduced to one-third (but never less) of the total feed intake when horses are in hard, fast work.

ATTAINING CORRECT BODYWEIGHT

The total food requirement per day is estimated as between 2–2½ per cent of the bodyweight in mature horses and 3 per cent in the case of youngstock. Much, of course, depends upon the horse being neither grossly over or underweight at the beginning of the conditioning programme. Once the desirable weight is established, many trainers will continue to check the weight on a regular basis.

Without access to a weighing machine, a horse's weight is easily calculated by using a tape measure put round the girth at its deepest point. Weight can be fairly accurately assessed by the following formula:

$$\frac{\text{Girth (cm)}^2 \times \text{length}}{8700} = \text{weight in kg}$$

$$\frac{\text{Girth (in)}^2 \times \text{length}}{300} = \text{weight in lb}$$

Girth is measured round the largest part of the barrel; the square of the girth (girth^2) is found by multiplying the figure by itself (e.g. 1.8 m x 1.8 m [78 in x 78 in]). Length is measured from the point of the shoulder upwards to the point of the buttock.

As a general guide, the total daily feed intake appropriate to a horse of 1.63 m (16 hh) and over is between 10.8–11.7 kg (24–26 lb), whereas that for a pony of between 1.32–1.42 m (13–14 hh) is about 8.1–9 kg (18–20 lb). Youngstock, on the basis of height, should be fed according to its estimated height at maturity.

TROUBLESHOOTING

In any feeding programme it would be impossible to ignore the need for worm control. Worm infestation is an almost direct result of domestication, and regular worming is integral to any conditioning programme and to the general care of the horse. The most common and dangerous worm affecting horses is the Red Worm (strongyle), which, in both the large and small varieties, attacks the intestines and the gut wall. Heavy infestations result in grave debility and, if neglected, in death.

Regular inspection of the teeth is also a necessity. Uneven wear and similar problems can cause such discomfort as to discourage mastication and will therefore affect the proper digestion of food.

The feed-intake, increased to the appropriate level in gradual stages, builds up the body, supplies the materials for making muscle, and produces the necessary energy. Exercise and work develop, strengthen, and tone the muscles; remove the burden of excess fat; harden legs, sinews, and tendons; and accustom the horse to carrying weight. Ideally, the intake of energy food should equal the output of energy expended by exercise and work, if a consistent level of condition is to be maintained.

The difference between exercise and work should be appreciated. Exercise has a longer duration and is not necessarily strenuous; work takes place over short periods, is concentrated, and is interspersed with frequent periods of rest. Both are increased little by little as the conditioning programme progresses, and both need to be combined intelligently. In the course of six weeks or so, it should be possible to devote at least two-and-a-half hours a day to the exercise/work period.

The exercise, or hacking, periods should be as varied as possible and take in whatever sort of terrain is available, as well as including roadwork. In general, exercise is relaxation for the horse. The animal should be allowed to enjoy periods of rest on a long rein, but must, nonetheless, carry itself within the frame imposed by hand and leg and be active in its paces. The introduction of a steady canter and the occasional burst at speed ("pipe-opener") is beneficial to the conditioning of the lungs and respiration.

Work periods will involve schooling on the flat, jumping exercises, and the occasional practice session over cross-country fences. Horses should never be brought home sweating in case they catch a chill. It is better to walk the last mile home to give them a chance to cool off.

HACKING OUT
Hacking is part of every conditioning programme. It exercises the horse while providing a change of scene and a period of relaxation.

GROOMING

ELECTRIC GROOMER

THE THIRD FACTOR in conditioning a horse is grooming, which is far from being a cosmetic process. It is, indeed, entirely necessary for the maintenance of health in the stabled horse kept under artificial conditions and consuming large quantities of artificial food. Because of the latter, the body produces an increased quantity of waste matter. Much is disposed of by normal excretion and through an increased rate of breathing as a result of exercise, but just as much is dispersed through the skin. To fulfil that function the skin has, therefore, to be kept clean. Grooming, however, is not solely concerned with cleaning the horse. It also helps to stimulate circulation and promote growth and tone of muscle.

THE CORRECT EQUIPMENT

A full grooming kit comprises: a dandy brush (a stiff-bristled brush used to remove mud from the legs, that is too harsh to be used on the body and would pull out hair if used on mane or tail); a body brush (a soft-bristled brush for the body, mane, and tail); a water brush (a soft, boat-shaped brush used dampened to lay the mane and tail); a curry comb (a flat metal comb with a handle or hand strap used to clean the brushes, not the horse); sponges (one sponge is kept for cleaning eyes and nose and another for the dock and possibly the sheath of geldings); a stable rubber (a linen cloth used to give a final polish to the coat); a mane comb (a small metal trimming comb – there are also special combs for shortening the mane without pulling out the hairs and various other rubber and plastic combs for use on the body); a hoof-pick (a strong, curved hook for picking out the feet); and a chamois leather, to put a finish on the coat.

Grooming is best carried out after morning exercise when the horse is warm and the pores open. It begins with a body brush, starting high up the neck behind the ears. The brush is worked from front to rear, with the full weight of the groom's body behind each stroke. After three or four strokes, the brush is cleaned on the curry comb held in the opposite hand.

In an age of technology designed to save labour there are, of course, a number of electrically operated grooming machines based on the domestic vacuum cleaner, as well as heavy-duty machines operating a flexible shaft and a rotating brush. Both are highly efficient coat cleaners and very useful when a horse is losing a winter coat.

Wisping and massage are usually reserved for the end of the day to stimulate the horse's circulation, which naturally slows down during the night.

A traditional wisp is made from a 2.4-m (8-ft) length of woven hay, twisted in itself to make a pad. Otherwise, ready-made wisping pads of soft leather, stuffed with hay and sewn up in a bag shape, can be bought. After being dampened, the wisp is applied vigorously, following the lay of the coat. Its use is confined to the quarters, shoulders, and neck; it should never be used on the loins, belly, head, and legs.

The purpose of wisping is to develop and harden muscle while stimulating the skin and circulation. As a bonus, it creates a bloom on the coat caused by the release of oil from the glands surrounding each hair follicle. Ideally, about 45 minutes per day should be set aside to groom a horse thoroughly, with a similar period for wisping and hand massaging.

Massage of the body is certainly beneficial and will help to relax tensed

BATHTIME
After exertion, as well as when the coat is shampooed, horses can be washed to remove sweat and make them comfortable. However, it is necessary to make sure that they are well dried.

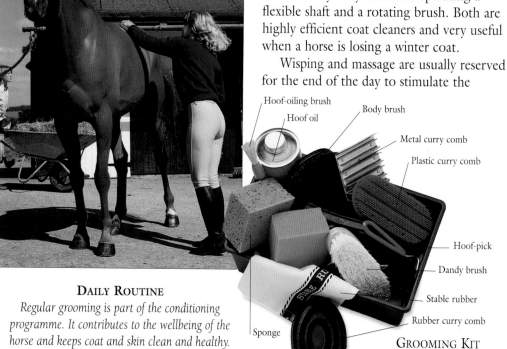

DAILY ROUTINE
Regular grooming is part of the conditioning programme. It contributes to the wellbeing of the horse and keeps coat and skin clean and healthy.

Hoof-oiling brush
Hoof oil
Body brush
Metal curry comb
Plastic curry comb
Hoof-pick
Dandy brush
Stable rubber
Rubber curry comb
Sponge

GROOMING KIT

HAIRCUT

When horses are in work the winter coat needs to be removed by clipping to save excessive sweating and loss of condition.

Usual clip for driving horses

TRACE CLIP

Hair left unclipped over back

BLANKET CLIP

Saddle patch left unclipped

HUNTER CLIP

c20TH CLIPPERS

FOOT POWERED
This 19th-century clipping machine was driven by human leg-power. Others were powered by a hand-turned driving wheel, which was far harder work.

muscles. However, unlike wisping, the action (while being firm) must be gentle.

THE BENEFITS OF CLIPPING

In the Northern hemisphere it is necessary to remove heavy winter coats by clipping. The origins of the practice are obscure, but in the 19th century coats were frequently removed by a barber wielding either a pair of scissors or a razor. Cold and wet conditions encourage the growth of a thick protective coat and an accumulation of grease on the skin that acts with the coat as an effective water repellant. The heavy coat is no hindrance to horses living in natural conditions, but it is a positive drawback to the stable horse in work who would quickly lose condition by excessive sweating.

Removing the coat allows the horse to work and gallop without distress, and makes it much easier to keep the animal clean. Also, a clipped horse can be dried more quickly than one with a heavy coat.

In Europe, the winter coat begins to grow in September and needs to be "set", that is fully grown and established, before being removed. Most horses are clipped in early October and need to be clipped again before or just after Christmas. The type of clip depends, in theory, upon the sort of work being done. In reality, it is usually a matter of personal preference as well as the skill of the operator.

The two main clips are the *full* and *hunter* clip. The former removes the entire coat, the latter leaves a saddle patch and the four legs unclipped. The arguments in favour of the hunter clip are that a) the saddle patch will prevent galls or scalding,

and b) the unclipped legs are protected against thorns, cuts, cracked heels, and so on. Whether that is so is likely to be a matter of opinion. Variations are the *blanket* clip, leaving, literally, a blanket of hair and not clipping the legs, and the *trace* clip used for harness horses, which removes hair from head, neck, trace area, and belly.

Modern electric clippers are light, easy to handle, and efficient. They are also quiet – an important consideration. Heavy-duty machines, with the clipping head on a flexible shaft and employing a powerful engine, are necessary in larger yards where numbers of horses are to be clipped. Early commercial machines involved a stable-lad turning a wheel to drive the cutting head.

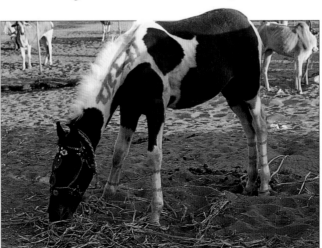

TRADITIONAL DECORATION
This Marwari foal in Rajasthan, India, has been painted with dye in celebration of a special occasion. The markings often have a religious significance and are frequently more elaborate than this.

PLAITING THE MANE

Horse-owners since the beginning of time have taken a certain pride in their horses' appearance, with the exception, perhaps, of the Mongol hordes. Certainly, the Assyrian cavalry and charioteers of the pre-Christian era were expert in creating the most elaborate coiffeurs for their always well-conditioned animals.

Modern horse-owners and keepers, while not attempting anything so extravagant, thin the tail and mane and trim surplus hair from the heels. Polo ponies, troop horses, and thick-necked cobs, all have the mane removed entirely by clipping, a practice known as hogging or roaching in the US, where there are some very individual and often rigid ideas about braiding (plaiting) the mane. On special occasions manes are plaited and sewn up with smart linen thread. The number of plaits is specified in a dozen manuals, ignoring the real reason for the practice. The number used depends on the length of neck and, to a degree, on its conformation. A long neck looks better with fewer plaits than a short one, a weak neck is improved by plaiting loosely to give a false line, a strong neck benefits from having the plaits sewn up tightly. On a well-proportioned neck six plaits and one on the forelock is probably the most satisfactory. On a short neck eight plus one at the forelock is better.

Tails, too, can be plaited, if the groom is sufficiently expert.

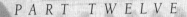

PART TWELVE

TRAINING & EQUIPMENT

FROM THE SYSTEMATIC EQUESTRIAN training developed
by Xenophon and then refined by Pluvinel, the first of
the French classical Masters, and afterwards expanded
into a rational science by Guérinière, there has evolved a
progression of schooling systems based on the
development of the physical and mental powers of the
horse that is accepted to all intents throughout the world.
There are, of course, different methods, reflecting different
philosophies and cultures – those of Mongolia, South
America, and the American West being prime examples.
Necessarily, each school of thought has devised its own
equipment, with the modern classicism tending increasingly
to the more simplistic training aids.

A detail from *Morning Exercise in the Hofreitschule, Josephsplatz 1890*
by Julius von Blaas

EQUINE EDUCATION – STAGE 1

SUCKLING FOAL

THE EDUCATION of the horse begins as a young foal and follows in relatively undemanding terms up to the age of three years. In a sense, this stage of a horse's education can be compared to the human nursery school or kindergarten, and, like those institutions, it lays the foundations for the young animal's future in respect of both physical and mental development. One of the greatest of French horsemen, General Alexis L'Hotte (1825–1904), defined equitation as "the art of managing the powers of the horse". It follows, therefore, that the first requirement of equine education is to *develop* those powers and then to *direct* them towards the purpose to which the horse is to be put in later life.

WEANING THE FOAL

Underlying the process of training the horse is the need to continually strengthen the animal's trust in its human trainer.

Although this introductory stage is, like human playschool, undemanding, it includes an event directly contradicting the trusting relationship that is a primary objective. This is the practice of weaning, when the foal is arbitrarily separated from its dam. This traumatic experience ends the elemental foal–mother relationship and may, in consequence, put a strain on the second relationship, that between horse and human.

Foals are usually weaned at around 4½–6 months, when the foal has become accustomed to feeding on its own account. Usually, colt foals are gelded while they are "on the mare" and before weaning takes place, but a good case can be made for delaying castration until the animal is a yearling on the grounds that the retention of the male hormone testosterone encourages the foal's development. Yearling colts can, however, become impossibly boisterous and will stretch the patience and management skills of the trainer to the full.

The generally accepted practice, after the foal has been weaned, is to separate mare and foal for short periods at a time, the foal being left in the box with a companion – ideally another foal – and a feed while the mare is ridden or otherwise exercised.

SEPARATION FROM THE MARE

The final break is made when the mare is moved away out of sight and earshot and preferably off the property altogether. The foal and its companion are then confined to the box for a few days until they settle and

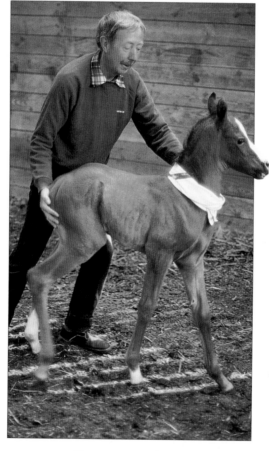

TEACHING TO LEAD
The first lesson is taught with a soft stable rubber round the little animal's neck, the trainer's right hand behind the rump encouraging it to move forward.

can be released into a paddock. Distress is inevitable, and while a companion for the foal is essential, the human keepers must also try to mitigate the stress.

It is, however, quite possible, in circumstances in which there is no other alternative, to keep the foal with the mare until her milk dries up at around 9–12 months. In some countries the mare is even ridden and the foal allowed to run alongside, which has the advantage of letting the youngster learn from its dam, the best of teachers if she is a sensible sort.

In parts of the world in which the upbringing of young horses could be charitably described as rough and ready, natural weaning is the usual practice.

The weaning apart, there are objectives to be achieved in Stage 1. Between birth and becoming a yearling the foal should:

1. Become accustomed to the presence of humans and allow itself to be handled and have its feet picked up.
2. Be fitted with a halter and be taught to lead in-hand – the first introduction to discipline and obedience.
3. Be taught a simple vocabulary. In time, a young animal will understand and respond to commands like "come here", "stand still", "lift" (for the feet), and a number more.
4. Be taken occasionally with its dam to a show, for instance, which will involve entering and leaving a box or trailer and provide experience of exciting situations.

During the early months natural growth is encouraged by good feeding and management. As well as good and ample grazing, a healthy foal needs to be fed approximately 450 g (1 lb) of concentrate feed a day for every month of its age up to 5–6 months. Feeds can be supplemented with such items as powdered milk and cod-liver oil to promote bone growth, and soft hay can be given ad lib. (This should be soft, meadow hay on account of the immature dentition.)

While it is tempting to make a pet of the foal, titbits should never be given. The practice only encourages it to become cheeky, demanding, and often a bully, too.

FOAL SLIP

Introducing the foal to the headcollar, or "foal slip", is made with great care. The soft leather slip must be "slipped" on very gently so as not to startle the foal. It is an important lesson.

Within days, the foal should be handled and allow itself to be held firmly by an arm round its front and another round its rear. This is best done in the familiar confines of the stable, where the first lessons in leading can also be taught.

Leading alongside the mare is best done initially from a soft stable rubber round the foal's neck, the right arm cradling the rump and urging it forward, gently. While this is another early lesson in submission, it is also the beginning of an important first principle – that of going forward. Quite soon it is possible, again in the stable, to introduce a halter and to carry the leading education a stage further, eventually using a lead rein.

THE YEARLING/TWO-YEAR-OLD

As the foal grows into a yearling and a big two-year-old, there is a temptation to do more with the animal, and it has to be resisted. Thoroughbred horses are bred to mature early and, for financial reasons, are prepared to race at two years, but the bone structure is still immature and the wastage rate from unsoundness can be considerable.

It is sufficient in the yearling and two-year-old to increase the food rations commensurately, introduce a headcollar and bit, and teach them to walk out confidently

in-hand, being encouraged from behind by a helper. The horse has also to submit to being tied up for short periods. This basic lesson can be taught while the animal is being groomed, the attendant passing the headcollar rope through the tie-ring and keeping hold of it while brushing the horse with the free hand. Every time the horse takes a step backwards it is brought back into position. It is a simple lesson, quickly learnt, and far less traumatic than tying the horse to a telegraph pole and allowing it to fight the rope until exhausted!

As the youngster gets older the vocabulary can be extended to include stable manners, being required to "move over" on command, for instance.

At the end of this stage, the horse should lead freely in hand, at walk and trot, and should have been taught, combining the voice with the rein, to halt squarely.

RISK OF DAMAGE

In Europe, Warmblood horses are lunged and loose jumped at two years, but there are dangers to the practice. Lungeing on a circle is difficult for a young horse, still at this age lacking co-ordination, and there is a risk of damaging the limbs. In fact, while many of the Warmbloods are big and well-grown at two, they take longer to reach maturity than the Thoroughbred. The Lipizzaner, for instance, may not be fully mature until six but then enjoys a long working life.

Indeed, the growth plates (epiphyses) on the long bones of the legs do not close entirely until after the second year. Up to that time the limb cannot sustain the effects of constant work without the risk of becoming misshapen. The epiphysis at the end of the cannon bone, above the fetlock joint, usually closes at around 9–12 months. That at the end of the radius, immediately above the knee joint, closes at some time between 2 and 2½ years.

MARE AND FOAL

Quietly, gently, but positively, mare and foal are led together; the mare follows the youngster calmly, and the foal is relaxed but interested.

EQUINE EDUCATION – STAGE 2

THE FIRST STAGE in a horse's training is likened to nursery school or kindergarten. The second stage, beginning in the animal's third year, is concerned with primary education and is more work-intensive, bringing the horse into the physical condition that will allow it to carry weight upon its back. In the Northern hemisphere this period begins in April and extends over about four months up to August. The horse is then turned out to live at grass until April of the following year and allowed to grow naturally, while being given generous supplementary feeding. The practice of lungeing forms the larger part of the young horse's primary education. It constitutes the preparation of the horse, both physically and mentally, for the later work under saddle.

CALM, FORWARD, STRAIGHT

As with Stage 1, there are specific objectives to be achieved in this phase of training:

1. The horse's acceptance of discipline and of handling should be extended and consolidated. The horse will be shod and the boxing drill confirmed.
2. The animal should be progressively conditioned so as to be physically able to carry weight.
3. It must then to be taught to accept weight on its back.
4. The horse is taught, under the rider, to carry weight on its back, which involves making adjustments to its balance.
5. It learns the rudiments of the system of aids – the language of communication.

The broad objective throughout is to work towards the first principles as laid down by General L'Hotte: "Calm, Forward, Straight". A state of calm is a prerequisite for training, even in potentially exciting situations. No progress can be made until

the horse is calm and, therefore, receptive. Until the horse is calm it cannot be taught to go forward. Going forward is certainly a willing and immediate response to the action of the rider's leg, but it is also a physical manifestation of a mental quality – a positive attitude that results in an urge to advance vigorously.

Straightness is something else and at this stage cannot be expected to become confirmed, although the training lays the foundations for the straight horse. To be perfectly straight the hind feet always directly follow in the track of the forefeet. This is particularly difficult on the circle, the tendency being to carry them outside the track of the forefeet.

The education begins when the horse is brought up (stabled) and a routine is established, although a period of liberty in the paddock must be allowed each day.

LONG-REINS

Long-reins are introduced quite early in the training and are valuable in teaching the horse obedience to the bit and for improving the horse's overall carriage, while confirming the essential forward movement.

Lunge line — Cavesson — Side-reins — Body-roller

LUNGEING

Lungeing is a gymnastic exercise that develops the musculature, supples the body, and improves the balance. It prepares the horse to carry weight and is also an exercise in concentration and obedience.

THE LUNGEING EXERCISE

Within a week of being brought up the horse needs to be shod. After being led about in-hand for a few days, to become acquainted with its surroundings, work on the lunge can begin. Lungeing is an exercise central to training, but there can be dangers if the trainer is less than skilful.

The equipment needed for lungeing is:

1. A lightweight cavesson, carefully fitted.
2. A lunge line made of soft, tubular web with the fastening (hook or strap and buckle) set on a swivel to prevent it twisting. It should be 6.5–11 m (21–36 ft) long and 2.5 cm (1 in) wide.
3. A lunge whip of fibreglass, which should be light and well-balanced.
4. A body-roller and crupper. Ideally, the roller should be adjustable on both sides

BACKING

The backing of the young horse, i.e. the introduction of a rider on its back, is a watershed in the training. Initially, however, the horse is prepared by the rider lying quietly over the back.

so that it can be fitted precisely, and be made with three dee-rings on each side to allow a choice of positions for the side-reins. A breast girth helps to keep the roller in place without the roller having to be fastened too tightly. Although the crupper is unlikely to be needed to stop the roller sliding forward, it serves the purpose of "bringing the horse together" and accustoms the horse to being fitted with equipment.

5. Side-reins are an essential aid in "suggesting" the horse's carriage but are never adjusted tightly. The classical side-rein is a plain leather one with ample adjustment. Some trainers use reins inset with rubber or elastic, thinking to produce a give-and-take effect, but there is a danger of the horse evading contact.
6. A set of boots that give protection from the coronet up to the knee or hock joint.
7. Finally, a pair of gloves for the trainer will prevent the hand getting burned by a rein being pulled through it.

A simple definition of the lungeing exercise is that which states: "The horse describing a circle around the trainer – the two being connected by a line from the horse's head to the trainer's hand". The objects and benefits of the exercise are more complex.

For the young horse, lungeing is a basic gymnastic exercise designed to improve balance and prepare it to carry weight. Furthermore, it develops the powers of concentration. It is, indeed, an exercise aimed at both physical objectives and mental

development, both of which are of equal importance. The physical objectives are:

1. The promotion of equal muscular development on both sides of the body, without it being formed in opposition to the rider's weight.
2. The lateral suppling of the horse by the equal stretching and contraction of the concerned muscles on each side.
3. To induce a degree of light tension in the spinal complex (not stiffness) as a result of encouraging lowering of head and neck and engagement of the quarters.
4. The increase of flexion in the joints as a result of larger and more supple muscles.
5. To correct any natural curvature that encourages the hind legs to be carried away from the track of the fore legs.
6. The improvement of balance through the engagement of the hocks and the refinement of the paces.

The mental benefits are:
1. The inculcation of calm.
2. The acceptance and development of habitual discipline and, in particular, obedience to the voice.
3. The development of instinctive forward movement.

Lungeing is continued regularly throughout the second stage, which also incorporates the bench mark represented by the backing of the horse – that is, the introduction of a rider on its back. If the preparation has been logical and thorough, with the horse first made accustomed to carrying a saddle, this need present no difficulties. As soon as the horse accepts the weight of the rider, simple aids, combined with the voice, can be taught – the horse still being on the lunge and under the control of the trainer.

When it is possible to dispose of the lunge line and ride the young horse from the bit, it will be necessary for a time to work in the confines of the school. As soon as possible, however, the youngster should be ridden together with a steady, older companion. (Initially, it is advisable to retain the cavesson, fitted over the bridle, and to fasten an extra pair of reins to it, transferring the control little by little to the bit rein.)

At the end of Stage 2, it should be possible to work in the arena for 30–40 minutes a day, allowing frequent rests, and to hack out for 1–2 hours.

HASTEN SLOWLY
With the rider in the saddle, the horse is made accustomed to the weight while the trainer leads it quietly round the arena.

EQUINE EDUCATION – STAGE 3

SCHOOLING

The THIRD STAGE represents the "secondary education" of the horse in the fourth year of its life. The overall objectives, based on the increase in suppleness, strength, and stamina, are to produce within a period of some eight months an obedient, mentally well-balanced horse, which is comfortable and a pleasure to ride in all its paces and in a variety of circumstances. That implies an animal safe to ride in traffic and able to jump a range of obstacles – both natural fences and coloured ones. At the end of this stage of training the horse will be capable of a full season's hunting, for example, and be able to compete creditably at local level and possibly beyond.

THE FIRST FEW WEEKS

The effect of a logical training progression and cumulative good feeding over a period of years should be a big, strong, well-grown young horse, physically and mentally prepared for more exacting training.

Nonetheless, the first few weeks in this stage are given over to a recapitulation of the work done in the previous year. In fact, at every point in the training, work done in the previous lesson is consolidated before the trainer attempts to teach anything new. The overall objective is clear but, as always, is composed of a number of subsidiaries. They can be defined as:

1. Continuation of the physical conditioning.
2. Furtherance of the horse's mental development.
3. Work that places the horse "on the bit". That is, acceptance of the bit without resistance, with the face held slightly in advance of the vertical, the head flexed at the poll and the lower jaw, with, in accord with the classical principle, the quarters advancing to the head, not the head retreating to the quarters.
4. Increase of lateral and longitudinal suppling, that is, the ability to shorten and extend the outline, through gymnastic exercises.
5. Refining the aids up to a good secondary standard.
6. Inducing a greater degree of straightness in the horse using the simple school figures.
7. Continuing and extending the jumping training.
8. Exposing the horse to traffic conditions.
9. The introduction to a double bridle.

JUMPING TRAINING

Lungeing remains an important element, often providing the basis for ridden work, particularly in the jumping training. The

HACKING OUT
Riding the young horse in company on quiet roads and over whatever countryside is available is an essential part of training. Hacking provides welcome relaxation from the schooling work.

horse learns to use its own initiative, without the control and distraction of a rider, by being lunged over a variety of schooling fences that will include uprights, staircases, parallels (spreads), and pyramids. It is also possible to introduce combination fences. Fences are "related" when they are placed 12–24 m (39 ft 4 in – 80 ft) apart; they become "combinations" when placed less than 11.9 m (39 ft) apart.

Given that the average canter stride is around 3.3–3.6 m (11–12 ft), becoming longer as the speed increases, a distance of 5.4 m (18 ft) between fences will allow the horse one non-jumping canter stride from the point of landing over the first to the take-off for the second. In general, the optimum take-off point for a 1.2 m (4 ft) fence is one-and-a-third times its height. Fences placed 10 m (33 ft) apart allow two non-jumping strides between the elements.

Bounce combinations, allowing no stride between the elements, are made when the fences are sited 3.6 m (12 ft) apart, causing the horse to take-off immediately after landing. Bounce fences, along with jumping grids of up to six fixed fences placed 3.6 m (12 ft) apart at a height of about 45 cm (18 in), increase gymnastic ability and suppleness and are also regarded as a strengthening exercise. To help the horse judge the take-off it is usual to make use of "distance" poles placed at an appropriate distance in front of the fence. (For instance, for a simple parallel fence 0.9 m [3 ft] high and with a spread of 1.2 m [4 ft] a distance pole, providing a ground line to the fence, needs to be placed 3 m [10 ft] in front of the fence.) Loose jumping is good exercise for the horse and a great confidence-builder.

Successful jumping training depends upon setting exactly correct distances

between fences. Very much later, problems can be introduced when half non-jumping strides exist between elements, but this is beyond the scope of the young horse.

In fact, the constitution of the combination, such as upright to parallel, governs the distances set and takes into account differences in the angle of descent and the effect upon the length of the get-away stride. In the case of an upright to a spread fence, the distance is shortened around 15–30 cm (6–12 in). When a spread element follows a vertical, up to 30 cm (12 in) is added between the two.

OBEDIENCE TO THE BIT

Long-reining is frequently carried out as a part of the primary schooling and can be continued into the more advanced stage. It involves the use of two lunge reins, one from the bit or cavesson through a ring on the roller, and one passed from the bit, through the ring and behind the animal's quarters, both returning to the trainer's hands. The trainer, positioned three-quarters on to the horse's rear, drives the horse forward. It is a valuable exercise in teaching obedience to the bit, changes of

JUMP TRAINING
Young horses are taught over small, inviting fences that will give confidence and will establish a sound technique. It is a prerequisite for fences to be jumped calmly out of a state of balance.

WORKING ON THE CIRCLE
All school figures have their basis in the circle. Here, the horse is moving forward energetically and with impulsion. The outline is good and the horse is in commendable overall balance.

direction, and so on, and in skilful hands can produce more advanced movements in preparation for the work under the rider.

The schooling on the flat is on the base of the circle and the accepted school figures. It is directed at improving the outline and the quality of the paces and at suppling, strengthening, and straightening the horse.

The movements contributing to these objectives are leg-yielding, shoulder-in, and half-pass. In leg-yielding the horse is moved sideways by means of lateral aids; for example, in leg yield to the left, the right hand acts in conjunction with the right leg to push the horse over. Shoulder-in is the more productive exercise, with the horse being "bent" round the inside leg – the quarters being held square in relation to the wall and moving parallel to it. Head and neck are inclined slightly away from the movement, which is led by the outside shoulder. In half-pass the horse moves forward obliquely, "bent"

slightly round the inside leg with the head held in the direction of the movement.

Almost as important are the turns made on the forehand and quarters. The former serves to supple the quarters, ensuring their mobility, while the latter supples the forehand. Both improve balance and confirm obedience to the legs.

THE FINAL STAGES

Not until the horse is on the bit is the much misunderstood rein-back taught. It is, in fact, a two-time movement, not a walk backwards in four-time, the pace to the rear being made by the diagonal pair of legs moving in unison.

Cross-country rides in company with an older horse accustom the horse to moving over undulating terrain and provide an introduction to natural hazards like water and ditches. Small fences on the flat, uphill, and downhill will also be incorporated.

A steady companion is very necessary to give the young horse confidence and help it become used to traffic. Road hacking should not be neglected.

Towards the end of the training, the horse will be sufficiently advanced to take a double bridle. This sophisticated bitting arrangement has to be carefully fitted, however, and the horse first made accustomed to the action of bradoon and curb from the ground.

The neck rounds over the fence

The rider carries the weight forward

THE NATURE OF THE HORSE

THE SECURITY OF THE STABLE

THE INSTINCTIVE behavioural pattern of the horse, involving the highly tuned defence mechanism, developed during the process of evolution and was influenced by the environmental changes that took place over the millions of years preceding its domestication.

Those deeply rooted instincts, contributing to the horse character, remain unaltered by the passage of time; although such is the horse's ability to adapt to human requirements that it is possible for some of those instincts to be subdued and, in certain situations, largely overcome by intelligent training, which instils obedience while recognizing the limitations imposed by the nature of the animal.

THE SECURITY OF THE HERD

Central to any study of the horse is the herd instinct. Membership of the herd provides essential security and also means acceptance of an established pecking order, which is as evident in present-day animals belonging to a small domestic group as it is in those living in the feral state. However, there is usually no single dominant stallion, other than in the mating season. A wild herd is composed of a number of family groups, usually controlled by strong-minded old matriarchs who are more than able to cope with the boisterous behaviour of young colts. Indeed, while

HERD INSTINCT

Horses in the wild are members of a herd, which provides security. Herds are composed of family groups, recognizing each other by a corporate smell. In semi-feral herds the leader is often an old, experienced mare. She wears a bell collar to indicate her whereabouts and is known as the "bell-mare".

THE BELL– MARE'S COLLAR

stallions are almost always dominant in character, mares are not necessarily submissive and can be just as dominant and forceful. In large semi-feral herds, like those in Argentina, parts of Asia, and eastern Europe, the herd leader is more often than not an old, experienced mare with a bell fastened round her neck to indicate her whereabouts. She is known as the "bell-mare". Sex, of course, has its effect upon

PLAYTIME

Young horses fight in play but rarely come to any harm as a result. Horses will rear to display dominant qualities when seeking to establish a pecking order within the group. Rearing also occurs when horses are startled.

behaviour. Mares in season can suffer a temporary change of character, often becoming tetchy and moody. The presence of in-season mares will, naturally, induce a powerful sexual response from stallions. Although geldings are not much affected, they may still retain dominant traits. However, most are more or less submissive.

DOMINANT OR RECESSIVE?

Fundamental to the training of the horse is the recognition of the dominant/recessive factor. In general terms, the majority of horses lie between the extremes, inclining by varying degrees to one side or the other. All horses, however, whether dominant or otherwise, will at some time test the authority of their trainer (the equivalent of the equine group leader) just as naturally as they do within their own species. The solution lies in quick, calm but unmistakably firm action. If that is not forthcoming then it is likely that "behavioural problems" will snowball to an unacceptable level.

Strongly dominant horses are, nonetheless, encountered from time to time (they are sometimes described as "difficult" or more euphemistically as "characters"). In fact, these usually highly courageous individuals often prove to be outstanding performers if they are fortunate enough to fall into the right hands.

To come to terms with the dominant animal calls for sympathy and skill of a high order and not a little practical psychology. Above all, the temptation to react in similarly aggressive terms has to be avoided. Experienced horsemen and women will appear to meet the horse halfway without ever relinquishing their position as the senior member of the partnership.

The recessive horse, possibly unsure of himself and lacking in confidence, presents a different problem but is just as demanding of understanding and positive management. He needs, and looks for, strong, dominant leadership that leaves him in no doubt as to what is required of him. A bold horseman makes a bold horse, and the opposite may also have an element of truth.

Security is as much a basic need for horses as for humans, and for the domestic horse it is provided by the stable, the animal's familiar surroundings, and, ideally, a companion. It is these factors that produce the gravitational pull of the herd syndrome, and it is important that they should be

associated with pleasurable experiences: comfort, shelter, relaxation, safety, and, very importantly, food and water.

Such is the importance of the familiar stable that horses will often display a greater enthusiasm when turned for home than when leaving the yard for exercise.

HORSE SENSE

Essentially, a nervous, highly strung horse shows signs of the defence mechanism developed as a means of survival in the wild. Horses are herbivores and in the wild were the natural prey of aggressive, predatory carnivores. The horse's defence lies in the ability to take swift, instant flight from the threat of danger, whether real or imagined. A sudden rustle in the hedgerow will activate the defence system and provoke a quick shying away.

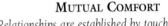

MUTUAL COMFORT
Relationships are established by touch and smell. The practice of mutual grooming serves as a means of communication and reassurance.

Even more important than the physical capacity for flight are the horse's highly developed senses, all far more acute than the human equivalents. Tactile communication and an established body language is very evident between horses, who commonly indulge in mutual grooming, while the sense of smell is similarly acute, with smell messages (pheromones) being constantly produced by the skin glands to identify individuals and groups. Horses are also able to detect nervousness or fear in human body scent and will react accordingly, becoming tense and nervous themselves.

The range of equine hearing is great. The remarkably mobile ears have the ability to turn almost through 360° and can be directed like a radar dish. Horses are exceptionally responsive to the human voice, or, more particularly, to the tone employed.

Equine sight is unusual and quite different from human vision, the large eye increasing the acuity as well as the field of sight. Dependent upon the placement of the eyes and the position of the head, the horse has virtually all-round vision. Finally, the horse possesses a heightened perception amounting to what could be called a sixth sense, which is far less evident in humans.

READY TO RUN
Foals are on their feet within 30 minutes of birth, and in a short space of time they are able to run with the dam – a necessary accomplishment in the wild.

THE OTHER PHILOSOPHY

GALVAYNE

WHILE THERE ARE NATIONAL differences in emphasis in the structured training programmes of Europe and countries following that school, there is an unmistakable division between these methods and those employed elsewhere in the world, as well, of course, as in the philosophies inherent to them. On one hand there is the European pattern, directed at the recreational sports horse kept for pleasure and/or profit; on the other, there are the ways used to produce working animals on which an entire economy may depend. The latter are typified by the horse-management techniques of the nomadic people of the Central Asian steppes and demonstrated in the practice of large-scale ranching enterprises like those of South America and the American West.

ELEMENTAL CONTEST

On the whole, the alternative techniques are directed at the quick result and are rough and ready to the point of being an elemental contest between man and horse, exemplified in modern times by the rodeo bronc-riding competitions staged throughout the American West. Such competitions, were they to be staged in Europe, would provoke immediate protests from animal welfare groups.

American breaking methods are possibly more robust than those practised in Europe but at their best, as they are demonstrated by the Californian reinsmen, for instance (see p.382), the system of schooling, directed to a different end product, is as progressive as that of its European counterpart.

ONE MAN'S MEAT...

These pictures show the methods of Eastern Europe, the Asian steppes, and areas of the American West and Australia. However, they are demonstrated with an obviously older, quiet horse. A young horse, experiencing the treatment for the first time, could be expected to offer violent resistance and the whole process would become more elemental in character. The conventional European horseman would not dispute the efficacy of the system, but would question its relevance to modern progressive training.

Paradoxically, American horsemen, with backgrounds unrelated to the academic and sporting traditions of European equitation, have, nonetheless, had a passing influence in Europe from the mid-19th century up to the present day.

The first and one of the most skilful in a line of evangelical "horse-tamers-whisperers" to appreciate the potential of the European market was John Solomon Rarey, who arrived in Britain in 1857 describing himself as "a missionary of civilization and mercy".

Rarey, as accomplished a showman and publicist as he was a skilled horseman, toured the country demonstrating his methods somewhat in the manner of his present-day successor, Monty Roberts, and appeared before Queen Victoria.

THE "PROFESSORS"

Of equal stature among the motley of 19th century American tamers exploiting the European market was "Professor" Sydney Galvayne ("Professor" was the self-assumed title adopted by many of them), who came to Britain in 1884. Galvayne was, in fact, an Australian whose real name was Osborne and was an associate of another American, the less attractive "Professor" Sample.

Despite his dubious antecedents, Galvayne achieved widespread recognition in the British horse-world and acceptance in the highest veterinary circles, in which he was as much respected for his literary output as for his well-promoted demonstrations with unruly horses.

1. SNUBBING

2. CASTING

3. APPLYING HOBBLES

4. JOIN-UP

5. LEANING OVER HORSE

The methods of the tamers all involved some form of mild physical restraint. Rarey tied up a leg with a strap and Galvayne perfected a range of simple harnesses to create a psychological force applied by a mechanical one. Galvayne also "gentled" by means of the "Third Hand", a wooden stick with an egg-shaped blob at the end, which was passed over the body while the horse was immobilized by one means or another, even to the point of being hobbled and thrown. The system is attributed to a German horse trainer named Lichtwark who settled in Australia in 1865. He may have been the inspiration for Galvayne's work and may, unknowingly, be the influence in that of Monty Roberts, certainly in respect of the "Join-Up" technique and the restricted space of the "Pen."

MONTY ROBERTS

Monty Roberts, another in the horse-whisperer succession, has also enjoyed the distinction of appearing before royalty, HM Queen Elizabeth II.

Like his predecessors Roberts is a shrewd showman and consummate self-publicist but that should not detract from the essential value of his performance.

A feature of Roberts's act is the saddling, bridling and mounting of a young horse in 30 minutes. Conventional, but nonetheless sympathetic and highly experienced horse-people, question whether Roberts's act is relevant to modern horsemanship, while acknowledging his considerable skills.

NATURAL HORSEMANSHIP

Roberts has, nonetheless, been the inspiration for other performers aspiring to his pre-eminence in the field, and he is seen as a central figure in the movement that has become known as Natural Horsemanship. The title was assumed by the organization developed by Pat Parelli, an ex-rodeo rider, to become the Parelli Method of Natural Horsemanship. The Parelli organization has a centre of Natural Horsemanship in Britain and claims to have achieved huge changes to the structure of the French Equestrian Federation by causing Equine Ethology, *Equitation ethologique methode Parelli*, to be required study for all new French instructors.

Parelli's highly effective marketing has attracted a certain following for Natural Horsemanship and it has, undoubtedly, something to offer in logical, horse-friendly training advice. But many established practical horse-people, competitive and otherwise, are uncomfortable with the display of evangelical zeal overlaid with commercial considerations. Moreover,

JOIN UP
Roberts demonstrating his "Join Up" technique in the confines of the "Pen" which is an important feature of his work.

advocates of more traditional methods resent being regarded by devotees of the movement as barbarians in their own use and treatment of horses.

Conversely, competition riders and trainers following established training progressions may consider followers of Natural Horsemanship as natural non-achievers who try to make pets of horses to the detriment of the animals.

Whatever the answer, Natural Horsemanship or "equine ethology" adds another dimension to the horse-world that it reflects with a fair degree of accuracy.

6. CASTING THE EXPERIENCED HORSE

7. SUBMISSION

8. BROKEN HORSE

THE LANGUAGE OF RIDING

IN THE ULTIMATE rapport between horse and rider, communication is made through the medium of the mind. On the physical plane, it is achieved by a system of signals known as the "aids" (the "helps" of the Renaissance horsemen and the "cues" of the US), through which the rider makes requests of the horse and influences its posture and movement. The natural aids are defined as being the voice, the hands, the legs, the back and seat, and the disposition of the bodyweight. "Artificial" aids are provided by the whip and spur, which may act to support, reinforce, or refine the physical actions. In order to respond correctly to the rider's aids, the horse has to be taught this language of signals. It must also be physically capable of compliance.

LEARNING THE LANGUAGE

The aids are in every sense interdependent, acting in concert and not in isolation, but their effectiveness is reliant, first, upon the rider's seat being secure, independent of the reins, and in balance with the movement (see pp.442–43) and, second, on the horse itself. Before the horse can respond to the rider's signals it has to be taught their meaning and the reactions that are expected of it. In brief, communication calls for both partners to be fluent in the language.

The aids operate in what is a virtually inviolable sequence: they prepare, act, and yield, and on occasions they may be used to resist unwanted movement. A preparatory aid secures the horse's attention and corrects the balance before the request for a specific movement made by the acting aid.

For instance, when moving from halt to walk, the horse is warned of an impending request by the legs closing in a light, momentary, inward squeeze, followed almost simultaneously by the closing of the fingers on the rein. The legs then act in a smooth, inward squeeze that brushes slightly forward against the lie of the coat, while the fingers yield by opening to allow the movement forward (the little forward squeeze of the legs is entirely logical, whereas the frequently delivered backward kick is not, since there is little sense in pushing backwards to go forwards).

The yielding of the hand not only allows the horse to respond to the leg driving it forward but also conveys that it has done

Knuckles upright and facing out

Thumb secures rein

HAND AND REINS
The arm lies naturally, the hand, following the line of the forearm, is slightly curved with thumb held uppermost over the index finger. The rein is held between the little and first fingers.

what was wanted, the easing of the slight rein pressure being in the way of a thank-you for its co-operation.

Finally, the aids may resist, to combat an unwanted or evasive action on the part of the horse. The hands may close to resist and frustrate an impetuous forward plunge, or one leg closed firmly inward to the rear of the girth can discourage an unwanted shift of the quarters to one side or the other. The utmost care has to be taken that aids are not applied unintentionally, thereby causing confusion in the horse's mind. For example, if a rider wearing a spur should inadvertently give the horse a dig in the flank, the horse will not understand why its swift leap forward in response is punished by a contradictory pull on the bit caused by the rider's momentary loss of balance. The prime requirement of the riding horse, and

CORRECTLY FITTED SPUR

ARTIFICIAL AIDS
The properly fitted spur and the whip are called "artificial" aids and are used in support of the "natural", physical aids. To be effective, the schooling whip is held to lie across the thigh.

of equitation itself, is forward movement. Without it nothing is achieved either on the flat or over fences. It is in this respect that the artificial aids of spur and whip are a valuable and legitimate support when used to encourage, not punish.

A horse may be persuaded to go forward more energetically by a tap with the whip immediately following the squeeze of the leg, until the lightest application of the leg produces a response so immediate as to amount to a conditioned reflex. Similarly, the mere presence of the spur is usually enough to induce a more vigorous reaction.

Integral to the aid system is the ability to think ahead and organize the horse for the required movement before applying the aid.

The voice helps to calm the nervous horse or to encourage the hesitant and fearful, and sometimes it is useful in reprimanding the recalcitrant. However, it is neither sufficiently sophisticated nor subtle to have more than a limited effect.

Paramount in the aid combination is the leg, the principal driving aid. Legs control the quarters and hindlegs and by acting cause the latter to be engaged under the body to provide the propulsive thrust that produces movement. They also position the quarters, preventing their deviation to one side or the other. Additionally, each leg governs the movement of the corresponding hindleg. On the circle, the inside leg is applied to increase the engagement of the horse's inside hindleg, its partner supporting to prevent any evasion caused by the quarters being carried outwards.

However, legs must be held still – if they swing about they transmit unintelligible messages to the horse. Still, however, does not imply stiffness – the leg moves in the sense that it responds to the movement of the horse's flank and has therefore to be supple throughout its length.

THE CONTROL PANEL

To obtain the best results, the rider uses what amounts to a "control panel" centred on the lower part of the girth. It has four "buttons", A–D (see far right). The most important is A, the impulsion button situated on the rear edge of the girth. Both legs act simultaneously on this point to produce movement to the front. Button B is behind the girth and behind A, and it is used by the single leg to move the quarters

Driving inside leg

Outside leg in support

or hold them and also in lateral work. Both legs act at B when asking for the rein-back. In the secondary education the legs must make a clear distinction between the two optimum points if the horse is not to misinterpret the aid. Button D lies behind button B and is necessary in advanced movements – flying change, *piaffe*, and *passage*. Button C is only for use by the expert, who can apply a gentle dig there to encourage the horse to greater extension.

Hands are the principal restraining aids and, in conjunction with legs and seat, contribute to the overall outline. They receive the impulsion produced by the legs, regulating the created energy by containing it or releasing it as required. Closing the fingers to contain the energy shortens the outline and the base. The opposite, in judicious measure, results in extension.

An educated hand is able to re-channel the created energy, as when one rein is

THE AIDS APPLIED

The horse prepared to turn right. The inside leg drives forward, weighting inside iron and seat bone. The outside leg controls quarters and is held in support. The position is exemplary.

LEG POSITION

The seat is broad, the trunk rests on the seat bones, allowing the leg to hang naturally, in light contact throughout its length, without gripping at the knee. The toe is slightly raised without the heel being pushed down.

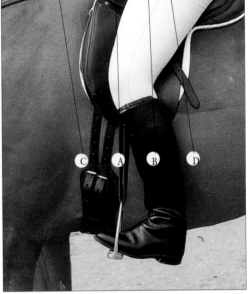

A is impulsion button

B controls quarters, acts as support button

C is extension button

D is button for advanced movements

applied to block the forward surge and redirect it to one side or the other. The ultimate objective is reached when the reins, regulating the balance, control the direction of the movement, including that of lateral work, while the legs supply the impulsion. The hands may move upwards, downwards, and sideways but never back. A backward pull immediately interrupts the pace and balance and shortens the stride.

Seat, back, and weight distribution are just as potent a force within the aid combination. The stretching of the back and the push forward of the seat bones (upwards, towards the horse's ears) produce powerful driving aids, which should be used with discretion if they are not to hamper the movement. In lateral work and change of direction the horse is assisted positively by the rider weighting the inside seat bone so as to remain in balance with the lateral shift of the horse's centre of gravity.

THE RIDER'S SEAT

IN PERFECT BALANCE

MIGUEL DE CERVANTES (1547–1616), creator of the immortal Don Quixote, famously wrote: "The seat on a horse makes gentlemen of some and grooms of others". In the 21st century that has to be extended, in the interests of political correctness and veracity, to include ladies, also. The seat adopted should certainly be a picture of elegance, but it also has to be practical and effective. Indeed, de Cervantes' epigram could be paraphrased with some advantage to read, "The seat on a horse makes riders of some and *passengers* of others". The "seat" is a convenient description of the posture adopted on the horse by the rider, and it is fundamental to successful riding. Its acquisition is a matter of application.

SITTING IN BALANCE

In its essentials, the modern seat differs little from that developed by the classical Masters. It is upon the seat that the balance and free, unrestricted movement of the horse depends, and that may be seen as a measure of its importance. If the rider is out of balance, so is the horse. It follows, therefore, that to sit in balance there has to be an understanding of the horse's balance and what is meant by being "with the movement".

The centre of gravity in the horse, or the centre of balance, is in the middle of the horse's body at the point of intersection of two imaginary lines. The first is drawn vertically to the ground from a point just behind the withers when the horse is standing squarely with the head and neck held naturally. The second is taken horizontally from the point of the shoulder to the rear. When the horse is moving at speed with the head and neck extended, or at the point of take-off over a fence, the point moves forward.

Conversely, in the state of collection – when the croup is lowered, the hind legs engaged strongly under the horse so as to shorten the base line, and when the neck is arched and carried high with the head in the vertical plane – then the point of balance shifts perceptibly to the rear. When the horse turns or moves sideways the centre of gravity is shifted to the side in the direction of the movement.

The head and neck, likened to a weighted pendulum, are, in fact, the balancing agent for the body weight. When, for instance, the horse is crossing broken ground, the constant adjustments necessary to maintain the balance are made by the pendulum being either raised or lowered.

The rider is in balance with the horse when his or her bodyweight is carried lightly over the centre of the horse's balance where it will cause minimal interference to the free movement. The rider is out of balance when the weight is carried in front or behind the centre of balance. In the first instance, the forehand of the horse is overburdened; in the second, the quarters (the source of the power) are forced to operate while carrying a proportion of the rider's weight. The result, in both cases, is to restrict the free action of the horse.

In the turns and lateral work, the bodyweight must similarly accord with the

RELAXATION
This modern hunting man relaxes in a less than classical position, but in action he would be a hard man to follow!

shift of the balance to the inside. This is accomplished by the rider weighting the inside seat bone by pressing down on the corresponding stirrup iron. In making changes of direction, the shoulders and hips must correspond by being in alignment with those of the horse. In turning to the right or left, the rider's head will incline in the same direction. As a result, the outside shoulder (and, in consequence, the outside hand) as well as the outside hip, will be slightly in advance, both hips conforming to the movement by being held in parallel to those of the horse.

Claude Bourgelat, the eminent French veterinarian (see pp.416–17) and his colleague Duhousset made a comprehensive study of the horse's balance, concluding incontrovertibly that the horse becomes lighter in front (and on the hand) as the

THE NATURAL SEAT
Lorenzo de Medici (1449–92) exemplifies the medieval seat which, disregarding the leg position, accords entirely with that of the 21st century. The body is held centrally and is commendably upright.

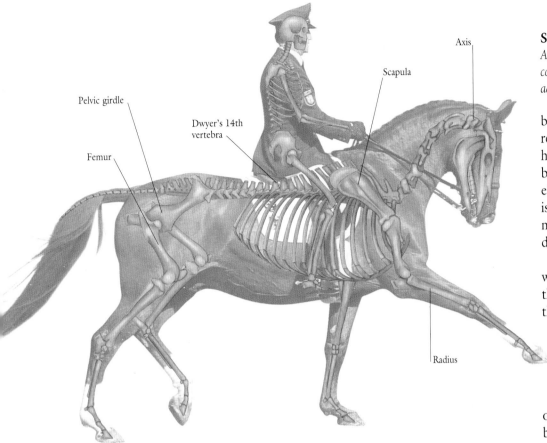

Pelvic girdle

Femur

Dwyer's 14th vertebra

Scapula

Axis

Radius

SKELETAL COMPARISON

An interesting study of the human skeleton conforming to that of the horse. The rider is admirably balanced with the movement.

weight shifts to the quarters, but there is also the rider to consider.

A rider weighing 58 kg (128 lb) sitting over the centre of balance places 37 kg (82 lb) on the forehand and 21 kg (46 lb) over the quarters. If the rider inclines or shifts the weight to the rear, 46 kg (101 lb) of the total bodyweight is carried by the hind legs, and the same applies when the weight is tipped forward to overburden the forehand.

A definition of the effective, balanced seat is that in which the bodyweight, by virtue of an erect trunk, flexible hips, and supple back, conforms softly to the movement and remains in balance with it in all circumstances. It is independent of the reins for security and allows freedom of movement to the limbs (i.e. in the application of the aids) in "managing and directing the powers of the horse".

THE PERFECT SEAT

Two thousand years ago, Xenophon (see p.38) described the seat of a man on a horse as "not as though he were sitting in a chair but rather as though he were standing upright with his feet apart", to which might be added, "and with the knees bent".

Much later in time, the doyen of the cavalry gurus of the 19th century, Francis Dwyer, an Anglo-Irishman employed in the

Austrian cavalry, analysed the seat comprehensively. He argued that the rider should be positioned over the 14th dorsal vertebra, which he termed "the keystone to the arch", because it is the only upright vertebra. The first 13 from the point of the neck's attachment incline backwards, while vertebra 15–18 and the six lumbar vertebrae slope forwards. He argued, rightly, that the 14th vertebra represented "the centre of movement" and, since his concern was very much with a suitable cavalry saddle, he promulgated the ruling, pretty well accepted ever since: "The saddle in the centre of the horse's back, the girths, stirrups and rider in the centre of the saddle".

The late Colonel Hans Handler, Director of the Spanish Riding School, went one stage further in his definition of the seat: "The torso is in a natural position, the hips pressed slightly forwards. The resultant position of the spine ensures that the pelvis is tipped so that the weight of the body rests on the seat bones where there is almost no covering of muscle. The seat is broad, the buttocks open". The broader the base the

THE SEAT
The rider sits centrally, the weight on the seat bones, with the leg stretched down and in light contact with the barrel of the horse throughout its length. No tension is apparent.

better the balance. To comply with those requirements, the rider's shoulder, hip, and heel should form one straight line – that being balanced by another connecting elbow, hand, and horse's mouth. The back is then held in its natural curve and, after much application, is able to exert a strong driving influence on the horse.

As an equal simplification: the head, the weight of which is out of all proportion to the body, is held upright, but not stiffly, on the top of the shoulders. If it tips forwards (a common failing) the trunk is thrown out of balance in all its components and a locking effect occurs right down to the ankle joint.

The chest is open but not thrown outwards, which would involve the back being hollowed. When that happens the hips cease to lead the movement, the weight is put on the front of the seat bones, and the bottom is pushed out inelegantly behind.

The leg is extended downwards and, to all intents, wrapped for its whole length round the barrel of the horse. No inward, gripping pressure at the knee is necessary and would in any event immobilize the lower leg. A relaxed lower leg embraces the barrel lightly. The aim is to feel the horse breathe through the leg.

Straight line from shoulder to heel

Straight line from elbow to bit

THE SADDLE

PARADE
SADDLE –
TIBET

WHETHER FOR GENERAL use or for one of the sporting disciplines, the modern saddle retains in its shape a lingering memory of those that carried both the medieval knights and the horse-archers of the Asian steppes. Like those early models, modern saddles are, for the most part, a reflection of current equestrian thinking and practice. With each new technological breakthrough saddles have become increasingly specialized as manufacturers seek to effect the perfect compromise between the needs of horse and rider. The design of the saddle tree develops continually to accommodate new theories and the latest available materials.

SPORTING DISCIPLINES

In broad terms, modern saddles equate to the principal sporting disciplines. The easily recognizable dressage saddle, the modern version of the 18th-century *selle royale* (see p.99), is cut straight in the flap and supporting panel and has the stirrup bar fitted further to the rear to assist the correct placement of the seat and the necessarily lengthened leg position. Cross-country and jumping saddles are built to allow the use of the shortened stirrup necessary for those activities.

Increasingly, as the sport grows in popularity, there are a variety of saddles designed for the endurance rider.

The best-known saddle is the "general purpose", which lies between the extremes of the jumping and dressage saddles and is the most suitable for the recreational rider.

SADDLE TREES

The modern saddle tree, the foundation on which the saddle is built, is a far cry from its prototype – the roughly shaped wooden

SPORTS SADDLE
The 18th-century version of the modern general purpose saddle. The fit appears to conform to basic principles and the characteristic dip to the seat is evident enough.

frame that was employed by the Sarmation heavy horsemen at the beginning of the Christian era (see p.93). Today's saddle trees are still made of wood, usually beech wood, but consist of several (usually 11 or more) thin layers that are moulded together with urea-formaldehyde resin and then reinforced with lightweight steel or Duralumin.

A significant innovation in the latter half of the 20th century was the introduction of the injection-moulded polymer saddle tree, which is now preferred by a number of European manufacturers. It has the advantage of absolute, fatigue-free consistency in shape and, importantly, can be mass-produced.

Its dimensions apart, the wooden saddle tree is available in spring or rigid form, the majority of saddles employing the former.

A spring tree is so called on account of the two strips of sprung steel laid on the underside of the frame from head to cantle.

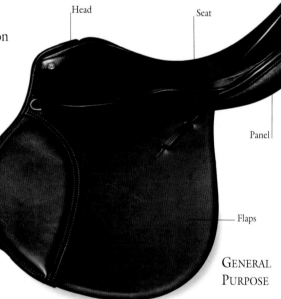

Head   Seat

Panel

Flaps

GENERAL
PURPOSE

SADDLE FOR ALL SEASONS
The general-purpose saddle, above, is the middle-of-the-road choice for the majority of riders. It lies between the dressage and jumping patterns and is the most suitable for the recreational rider.

JUMPING AND DRESSAGE
Left: The forward cut of the jumping saddle allows for the shorter stirrup employed in the jumping position and the need to place the weight further forward. Far left: The dressage saddle is cut straight in front to allow for the longer leg position.

Seat   Cut-back head

Flap

DRESSAGE
SADDLE

Cantle
Waist or Twist

Flap

JUMPING
SADDLE

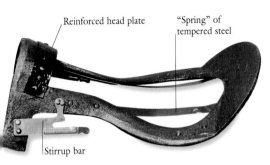

Reinforced head plate
"Spring" of
tempered steel

Stirrup bar

SPRING TREE

The modern spring tree is made of strips of laminated wood, reinforced with either steel or Duralumin; the "springs" are laid along the frame from head to cantle to give the characteristic resilience to the saddle seat.

These give the seat a notable resilience that is missing in the rigid tree.

SADDLE FITTING

The potential of the saddle as a precision instrument able to contribute to or detract from the performance of both horse and rider is now recognized increasingly in both competitive and recreational riding. Its correct fitting is therefore a matter of the utmost importance.

Appreciating that the conformation of the back alters significantly as the training progresses (and the horse becomes fitter and more muscular) saddle manufacturers, led by the British industry, have, increasingly, employed space-age technology to produce an adjustable saddle that will meet the changing demands.

One leading UK manufacturer has solved the problem by involving saddle-makers, computer programmers, aeronautic engineers and one or two selected riders to produce a tri-form tree with interchangeable heads in five fittings, and three seat sizes. Such is the quality of the precision engineering that it is possible to assemble any combination in a matter of minutes and at any time in the life of the saddle.

In the field of moulded polymer trees Britain's leading manufacturers of synthetic saddles in quantity has expanded its range of fittings to cover five back formations between narrow and XX wide with longitudinal wither profiles to match. The fitting can then be fine-tuned by slim inserts

THE OLD PATTERN

The Portuguese campino rides in a very deep-seated saddle that has altered little in design over the centuries and uses the traditional "slipper" stirrup.

that are easily slipped into the panel to accommodate weight fluctuations.

Patent registrations in the last half of the 19th century included a few registering the replacement of "the usual padding" with pads "filled with compressed air."

However, it was not until the opening years of the 21st century that the principle and the product was perfected by an innovative British company. The system involves the building of air-bags into the existing panel of any saddle, the air content being controlled by valves inset under the saddle skirt.

A properly fitted saddle is said to be one that (with the rider in position):

a) conforms completely to the shape of the horse's back,
b) avoids the possibility of damage to any part of the horse's back with which it comes into contact,
c) affords absolute comfort in respect of the equal distribution of the rider's weight over the available weight-bearing surfaces,
d) does not at any time restrict the potential for the horse's natural movement.

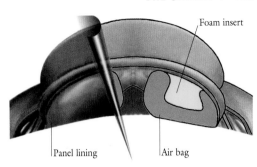

Foam insert

Panel lining   Air bag

RIDING ON AIR

The diagram shows a cross-section of the air-bags incorporated into the saddle's panel around a foam insert. The system involves four air-bags that can be adjusted using valves under the front skirts.

These are basic requirements. More particularly:

1. There must be clearance of the spine along its length and across its width.
2. There must be no impingement of the scapula's free movement.
3. The panel must be in longitudinal and lateral balance, bear evenly on the back, and cover as large an area as possible.
4. The panel must be smooth and free from any irregularity.
5. The seat should assist in positioning the rider centrally and in balance.

BITS & BITTING

ESSENTIALLY, THE BIT IS AN extension of the hand aid, an interdependent component of the combination of natural aids. Western riding tends to rely on the hackamore system leading to a single curb bit, whereas the "academic" riding of Europe is based on the progression from snaffle to double bridle, but can also involve other bitting groups, some of which may be supported by auxiliaries, such as nosebands and martingales, to emphasize a particular aspect. In recent years, however, use of the double bridle has declined and the emphasis has shifted to the snaffle and noseband combination, usually of the Flash pattern.

A CHANGING EMPHASIS

Up to the closing years of the 20th century it was generally accepted that every type of bridle could be classified as belonging to one or other of five groupings: snaffle, double bridle (either with a fixed or sliding curb cheek), Pelham, gag, and nose (or "bitless") bridle.

However, the increasingly global character of the industry; the emphasis on the snaffle, supported by a noseband that effectively prevents the mouth being opened to evade the bit action; and the influence of the American bit patterns now evident in the European market has altered that simplistic view and possibly confused the average rider's understanding of the role of the bit.

The most numerous of the American-inspired patterns is the three-ring bit with a snaffle mouthpiece of one design or another that is frequently made from polyurethane.

Indeed, the three-ring bit is now in such general use that under the heading "multi-ring" it comes close to qualifying as an independent, additional bit grouping.

The multi-ring construction allows for three rein positions and exerts, depending on the rein fitting, a commensurate downward pressure on the poll, one of the characteristics of the conventional curb bit. When the multi-ring cheek is extended into a full shank the downward pressure on the poll is naturally intensified.

A variety of American "combination" bridles are also available in Europe. They act on the nose and through a sharp snaffle mouthpiece, and may also have an upward gag action.

One reputable American company with a strong distributive network in the UK markets a wide range of bits, many of them incorporating curb cheeks. The snaffle bits, more relevant to Europe, are notably well-made with a variety of ingenious features. Much attention is given to the mouth conformation and the comfort zone afforded, and the bits are classified in three

SNAFFLE

The earliest and the most straightforward bitting system is represented by the snaffle group, which is the largest of the traditional five main bit families.

sections according to the horse's level of training (and perhaps that of the rider also).

PRINCIPLES

The conventional five bitting groups, together with the additional sixth group formed by the "multi-ring" bits act on one or more of seven parts of the horse's head:

1. The corners of the lips.
2. The bars of the mouth.
3. The tongue and, to a degree, the tongue channel.
4. The curb groove.
5. The poll.
6. The roof of the mouth (rare, occurring only with a very high port).
7. The nose, when a bitless bridle is used or some particular auxiliary.

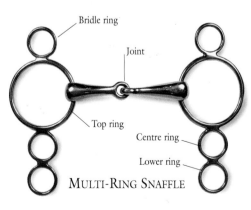

Bridle ring · Joint · Top ring · Centre ring · Lower ring

MULTI-RING SNAFFLE

POPULAR BITS

The variety of bits available is confusingly large. The simple snaffle bit is the most popular, but the multi-ring snaffle and the Pelham are also widely used.

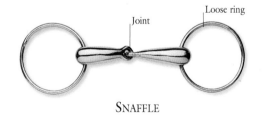

Joint · Loose ring

SNAFFLE

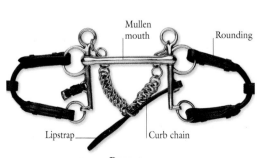

Mullen mouth · Rounding · Lipstrap · Curb chain

PELHAM

ADVANCED RIDING
The schooled horse and the educated rider obtain the advanced outline in a double bridle, which allows so much more finesse to the rider's hands.

DOUBLE BRIDLE

In brief, the pressures applied through the agency of the bit vary in intensity and character according to four factors: the construction of the bit; the conformation of the mouth; the angle at which the mouth is carried in relation to the hand; and the type and fitting of any accessory. Ultimately, the action of the bit (whatever its construction) and the subsequent result become more or less effective in relation to the rider's ability to use the supporting aids.

PRINCIPAL GROUPS

The snaffle group employs a primary lifting action against the corners of the lips but is otherwise governed by the position of the head and its relationship to the hand. As the horse approaches a working outline, with the face carried nearer the vertical plane, the bit acts less on the corners of the mouth and more across the lower jaw.

The double bridle comprises snaffle bit (bradoon) and curb bit with curb chain. It is the most complex system in its action and the most productive in obtaining and maintaining an advanced head carriage.

Simplistically, the bradoon, in the hands of an educated horseman, raises the head while the curb bit – acting on the poll, the bars, to one degree or another on the tongue, and on the curb groove via the curb chain – lowers the nose and (through relaxation in the lower jaw) causes it to be retracted. The bit becomes more or less definitive in its action according to the leverage made possible by the length of the cheek, the adjustment of the curb chain, and the shape of the ported mouthpiece, which governs the degree of pressure that can be placed on either the tongue or the bars of the mouth.

A Pelham bit, employing two reins but only one mouthpiece, is the compromise between the snaffle and the double bridle. It suits horses with a short jaw formation.

By definition, a gag bridle, using a pulley effect, acts upwards against the corners of the lips to raise the head.

However, since its construction allows for a contradictory, downward pressure on the poll in a sort of both-ends-against-the-middle exercise, it is also a powerful control bit and popular in the fields of polo and eventing. (In recent years, the word "gag" has been used to describe what is no more than a curb bit without a chain, i.e. American gag, Dutch gag, and so on.)

There are numerous patterns of bitless bridles acting on the nose that are legitimate enough. Increasingly, however, they have become wrongly included in the generic term hackamore.

THE HACKAMORE SYSTEM

The hackamore is in reality a system of bitting based on the initial use of the nose and a series of increasingly light nosebands, *bosal*, leading to a long-cheek curb.

In its true Western context, the hackamore comprises a heavy, braided rawhide noseband (*bosal* or *bosalillo*) made with a large heel knot at the rear that lies between the jawbones. To this is attached a heavy, plaited rope rein (*mecate*) and a throatlatch (*fiador*), which to a degree fixes the position of the *bosal*. By a system of carefully adjusted "wraps" on the heel knot neither nosepiece nor knot is other than in the lightest contact.

― Nosepiece

― Cheek

BITLESS BRIDLE
This is a simple pattern of bitless bridle, with the short cheekpiece tightening the curb strap and putting pressure on the padded nosepiece.

ONE EAR THROUGH THE BRIDLE
The one-ear bridle is common in Western tack. It is simple, quick and easy to fit, but has no practical application beyond that.

DRIVING HARNESS

OX-DRAWN CART

THE CHARIOT HARNESS used in the pre-Christian era was derived from the yoke used successfully with ox-drawn carts from about 3500 BC, and the practice of hitching a pair of horses to a central pole is of the same origin. However, it fell to the Chinese, always somewhat reluctant horsemen and far from being in the mould of chariot people like the Hittite-related tribes, to make improvements in driving harness that were subsequently adopted all over the world. The innovative Chinese had been making use of sophisticated wheeled vehicles from as early as 1300 BC and by 250 BC had invented a breast harness almost identical to that in use today.

YOKE-BASED SYSTEM

The adapted yoke harness persisted for over 1,000 years. To allow for the conformation of the horse, the yoke was bowed and made lighter than the much heavier ox-yoke, which in its essentials has not changed much over the past 5–6,000 years. It was then fitted with pads to save galling. It lay over the withers, a little in advance of where the pommel of a riding saddle would rest, and was secured to the central pole, being kept in place by a girth and a broad strap passing round the horse's neck. The horses pulled the load from that point and held the vehicle by leaning back on the yoke.

In movement the neck strap would have risen up to press on the windpipe, an action that would have been intensified when the horses were travelling at speed. It is probably for this reason that early chariot horses developed pronounced muscles on the underside of the neck.

To correct this obvious disadvantage a "harness martingale" was devised that was fitted to the centre of the neck strap and then passed through the forelegs to be secured to the girth. The martingale prevented the neck strap from rising too far upwards and improved the efficiency by lowering the point of traction. It was still unsatisfactory in terms of ratio of effort to load, but that could be overcome by the addition of two extra horses hitched as outriggers, one each side of the pole pair, a system followed in the harnessing of a team of four to the Roman *quadriga*.

Chariot teams were controlled by jointed bits, often fitted with spikes to increase their severity. Frequently, the rein was passed downward from the bit through rings set low on the harness pad before coming to the hand, an arrangement that increased the possible leverage very considerably.

The greatest improvements were made by the ingenious Chinese whose roadways were carefully constructed to match the width of vehicles of surprisingly advanced design. They invented the single-horse vehicle drawn by lateral shafts and were the first people to drive horses in tandem, that is, one behind the other, an arrangement made necessary by the width of the road.

The breast girth, also introduced by the Chinese, was a most important advance in driving harness and towards more efficient traction. Of equal importance was the breeching strap, passing round the quarters

ROAD AND FIELD

The road coach goes by, its style contrasting sharply with the pair of plough horses in simple agricultural harness with chain traces.

and allowing the horse to hold, or brake, the load in a manner previously impossible.

Finally, there was the horse-collar, acclaimed as one of the world's most significant inventions. It allowed maximum tractive force to be applied and although, like so much else (the stirrup, for example), it did not reach Europe until around the 8th century, it ensured the use of heavy horses in agriculture, a function previously carried out by teams of oxen.

HARNESS COMPONENTS

A driving harness comprises a bridle; a collar, with traces, fastened to the vehicle; a driving pad or saddle, supporting the shafts or traces; and the breeching.

The driving bridle is brass-mounted with rosettes at the browband and is fitted with blinkers (also known as winkers, blinds, or blinders). The blinkers save the horse from being frightened by the sight of the wheels moving round behind it. On the other hand, army horses are always driven in open bridles (i.e. without blinkers) and some "whips" (drivers of horse-drawn vehicles)

SUNDAY BEST

In this fanciful show turnout, the horse is wearing elaborately embellished driving harness that, though eye-catching, is not entirely appropriate to the vehicle.

DRIVING TRIALS

DRIVING TRIALS
The Duke of Edinburgh's team of Fell ponies are seen here competing at Windsor in workmanlike sets of breast harness.

claim that horses that are able to see around them are less likely to have accidents. Bearing reins, to govern the head position, may also be attached.

Reins, 4 m (13 ft) long in single harness, are made from russet leather, and it is normal to have brown reins with both a black and a brown harness, since the black dye might mark the whip's clothing.

While collars vary greatly in pattern and shape, there are two general types: the neck collar and the Dutch collar, more commonly known as a breast girth or breast collar. The latter is extensively used in mainland Europe and always with army horses, although the army collar differs in its design and is stouter than that used in civilian driving.

Saddles are worn in single harness when the horse takes most of the weight on the back. Pads, which need only support the traces, are lighter and are used with pair-and-team harness. Both have ring terrets on the top panels to take the reins and a hook to which the bearing rein can be attached. They are held in place by a crupper, a padded leather loop under the horse's tail, connected by the back strap.

The breeching passes round the quarters, between the dock and the point of the hock. It allows the vehicle to be braked when slowing down or descending hills.

Pair-and-team harness involves the use of coupling reins. The offside horse's coupling rein is attached to the nearside horse and vice-versa. The exact adjustment of the coupling reins is very important. The aim, in a pair, for instance, is to have both horses moving with their heads held straight to the front. Too long a rein turns the heads outwards, too short bends them inwards.

In a tandem, the lead horse's rein passes through rings on the shaft horse's bridle and thence to the whip's hand via the terrets.

In the English method the reins for single harness, pair, tandem, unicorn (three horses harnessed as two wheelers and one leader), or for a team are held in the left hand. The American Stage Driver, however, drives a team of four or six with the reins divided between both hands.

THREE BASIC BITS

At the turn of the 19th century the variety of driving bits was enormous. Today, reliance is placed almost entirely on three basic patterns: the Wilson (Four-ring snaffle), the Liverpool, and the Buxton, the last two varying in construction. All three, however, offer alternatives in the way the rein is attached that will make the action stronger or milder as required.

The Wilson is attached to the bridle head by the loose inside ring, the reins being fastened round both rings to give a mild action. The action becomes more severe if the rein is fastened to the outside ring and so emphasizes the nutcracker action of the jointed mouthpiece.

The Liverpool bit offers up to five positions for the rein if the cheek is made with three rein slots. It is the bit favoured for sporting vehicles (the break or chaise) but needs a connecting bar between the bottom of the cheeks to prevent the cheek being caught up in the coupling reins or the bridle of the pair horse.

The Buxton, a more ornate bit, is used for formal occasions. Like the Liverpool, it offers a number of rein positions and is also made in a variety of mouthpieces.

PAIR HARNESS
An elegant illustration from a 19th-century trade catalogue shows a very smart pair harness for formal driving. Catalogues of this period were often of considerable artistic merit.

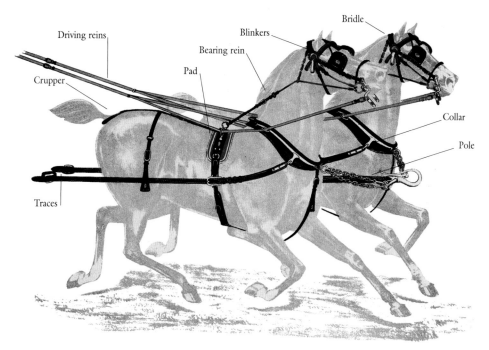

Driving reins

Bearing rein

Blinkers

Bridle

Pad

Crupper

Collar

Pole

Traces

GLOSSARY

Words in **bold** within an entry have their own entry in the glossary.

A

ACTION The movement of the skeletal frame in respect of locomotion.

ABOVE THE BIT When the horse carries the mouth above the level of the rider's hand. This practice reduces the rider's control.

AIDS Signals made by the rider or driver to communicate their wishes to the horse. The "natural" riding aids are the legs, hands, body-weight, and voice. The "artificial" aids are the whip and the spurs.

AIRS ABOVE THE GROUND **High School** movements performed with either the forelegs or all four feet off the ground.

AGED A horse of seven years old or more.

AGEING The process of estimating a horse's age by the appearance of the teeth.

AMBLE The slower form of the lateral pacing gait. See **Pacer.**

ARTICULATION Where two or more bones meet to form a joint.

B

BACK AT THE KNEE A conformational fault in which the forelegs are curved back below the knee. Also called calf-knee or buck-knee.

BACK-BREEDING The practice of breeding back to a particular individual to preserve distinctive character. Thereafter, **in-breeding** can be used to fix a **type.**

BAR The area between the lower-jaw molars and incisors on which the bit rests.

BARREL The body between the **forearms** and the **loins.**

BLEMISH A permanent mark left by either an injury or a disease.

BLOOD HORSE A **Thoroughbred** horse.

BLOODSTOCK **Thoroughbred** horses bred for racing.

BLOOD WEED A lightly-built **Thoroughbred** of poor quality lacking **bone** and **substance.**

BLUE FEET Dense, blue-black colouring of the horn.

BONE The measurement around the leg just below the knee or hock. The bone measurement determines the horse's ability to carry weight.

BOOK, THE Colloquial term for the *General Stud Book for Thoroughbred Horses.* **Thoroughbreds** are said to be "in the book".

BOSAL A plaited nosepiece used in Western equitation.

BOW-HOCKS Outward turned hock joints. (The opposite of **cow-hocks.**)

BOXY FEET A narrow, upright foot with small **frog** and a closed heel. Also known as club, donkey, or mule feet.

BREAKING The early schooling or education of a horse for the various purposes for which it may be required.

BREED An equine group bred selectively for consistent characteristics over a long period, whose **pedigrees** are entered in a **stud book.**

BROKEN COLOURED The term applied to a coat of two colours, i.e. **skewbald** or **piebald.** Generally refers to donkeys.

BROOD MARE A **mare** used for breeding.

BUCK A leap in the air with the back arched, the horse coming down on stiff forelegs with its head lowered.

BUNG-TAIL **Docked** tail.

BY Word used in conjunction with the sire, i.e. so-and-so. A horse is said to be "out of" a **mare.**

C

CANNON BONE The bone of the foreleg between the knee and the fetlock. Also called the "shin bone". The corresponding bone in the hind leg is the **shank.**

CAPPED HOCKS Swelling on the point of the hocks caused by a blow.

CAPRIOLE Classical **air above the ground**. The horse leaps from all four feet, striking out with the hind legs while the body is in mid-air. Literally translated as "the leap of the goat" from the italian word *capra.*

CARRIAGE HORSE A relatively light, elegant horse for private or hackney carriage use.

CART HORSE A **coldblood draught** horse.

CAVALRY REMOUNT A horse used for service in an army unit. Also called a "trooper".

CHARABANC (char-a'-banc) A high, open vehicle, sometimes equipped with a canopy, with forward-facing seats for several passengers. The name came from the translation "car with benches".

CHARGER The mount of military officers.

CHESTNUTS (i) Small, horny excrescences on the inside of all four legs. Also called castors. (ii) A rich brown coat colour.

CHIN GROOVE The declivity above the lower lip in which the curb chain of the bit lies. Also called the curb groove.

CLEAN-BRED An animal of any **breed** of pure **pedigree** blood.

CLEAN-LEGGED Without **feather** on the lower limbs as in the case of the Cleveland Bay and Suffolk.

CLOSE-COUPLED Short connections between component parts, with no slackness in the **loins.**

COACH HORSE A powerful, strongly built horse capable of drawing a heavy coach.

COLDBLOOD The generic name for the heavy European **breeds** descended from the prehistoric Forest Horse.

COLLECTION The concentration of the horses's forces towards the centre as a result of a shortened base line accompanied by a lowered croup, a raised carriage of the neck, and the head held on the vertical plane.

COLT An uncastrated male horse up to four years old. Male foals are called "colt foals".

COMMON A horse of coarse appearance, usually the progeny of **coldblood** or non-**pedigree** parents.

COMMON BONE Bone of inferior quality: coarse-grained, lacking density, and with a large, central core.

COMMON-BRED Horse bred from mixed, non-**pedigree** parents.

CONFORMATION The manner in which the horse is "put together" with particular regard to its proportions.

COURBETTE Classical **air above the ground.** From the **levade,** the horse bounds forwards on bent hind legs.

COW-HOCKS Hocks turned in at the **points** like those of a cow.

CRACKED HEELS Inflammation of the heels resulting in a discharge of pus.

CROSS-BREEDING The mating of individuals of different **breeds** or **types.**

CURB Thickening of the tendon or ligament below the point of the hock as a result of a strain. "Curby hocks" are those affected by curb or those shaped as to be predisposed to the formation of curbs.

CURB BIT Mouthpiece fitted with cheeks and a chain lying in the **chin groove,** operating on the principle of levers on the lower jaw. Usually used with a snaffle.

D

DAM A horse's female parent.

DEEP GOING Wet or soft ground made heavy by rain into which the feet sink.

DEPTH OF GIRTH The measurement from the wither to the elbow. "Good depth of girth" describes generous measurements between the two **points**.

DESERT HORSE The term used to describe horses bred in desert conditions or horses bred from such desert stock. They are resistant to heat and able to cope with a minimal water intake. See also **Dry**.

DIPPED BACK An unusually hollow back between the withers and the croup. Often occurs in old age.

DISHED FACE The concave head profile as exemplified by the Arab horse.

DISHING The action of the foreleg when the toe is thrown outward in a circular movement. Considered to be faulty action.

DOCK The part of the tail on which the hair grows. Also the hairless underside.

DOCKING Amputation of the tail for the sake of appearance. Illegal in the UK.

DONKEY FEET See **Boxy Feet**.

DORSAL STRIPE A continuous strip of black, brown, or dun hair extending from the neck to the tail. It is a feature of stock with a **primitive** connection and is most usually found in dun-coloured animals.

DOUBLE MUSCLING Pronounced muscling at the croup, especially in heavy **breeds**.

DRAUGHT A term applied to a horse drawing any vehicle but more usually associated with the heavy **breeds**.

DROOPING QUARTERS **Quarters** that fall away pronouncedly behind the croup.

DRY Used to describe the lean appearance of the head of desert-bred stock. There is an absence of fatty tissue and the veins stand out clearly on the skin.

E

EEL STRIP See **Dorsal Stripe**.

ENGAGEMENT The hind legs are engaged when they are brought well under the body.

ENTIRE A term used to describe an uncastrated male horse (**stallion**).

ERGOT The horny growth on the back of the fetlock joint.

EWE NECK A neck concave along its upper edge with a consequent protrusion of muscle on the underside.

EXTENSION The extension of the paces is the lengthening of the stride and outline. The opposite of **collection.**

EXTRAVAGANT ACTION High knee and hock action like that of the Hackney Horse and Pony, and the Saddlebred Horse.

F

FALSE RIBS The 10 asternal ribs to the rear of the eight "true" (sternal) ribs.

FEATHER Long hair on the lower legs and fetlocks. Abundant on heavy horse breeds.

FILLY A female horse under four years old.

FIVE-GAITED American term for the Saddlebred Horse, shown at walk, trot, and canter, as well as at the "slow gait" (a four-beat prancing movement) and the **rack**.

FLEXION The horse shows flexion when it yields the lower jaw to the bit with the head bent at the poll. The term also describes the full bending of the hock joints.

FLOATING The action associated with the trotting gait of the Arab horse.

FOAL **Colt**, **gelding**, or **filly** up to a year old.

FOREARM The upper part of the foreleg, above the knee.

FOREHAND The horse's head, neck, shoulder, withers, and forelegs.

FORELOCK The mane between the ears, which hangs over the forehead.

FOUR IN HAND A team of four harness horses.

FROG The rubbery pad of horn in the sole of the foot, which acts as a shock absorber.

FRUGAL See **Thrifty**.

FULL MOUTH A horse at six years with permanent teeth has a "full mouth".

G

G.S.B. The *General Stud Book* in which all **Thoroughbred mares** and their progeny foaled in the UK and Ireland are entered. It was founded in 1791 by James Weatherby.

GAITED HORSE American term for horses schooled to artificial as well as natural gaits.

GASKIN The "second thigh" extending from above the hock upwards to the stifle.

GELDING A castrated male horse.

GIRTH The circumference of the body measured from behind the withers round the **barrel**.

G (cont.)

GOING A term indicating the nature of the ground, i.e. good, deep, rough, etc.

GOOD FRONT A horse that carries its saddle behind a long, sloped shoulder and a generous length of neck has a "good front".

GOOSE-RUMPED A pronounced muscular development at the croup from whence the **quarters** run down to the tail. Sometimes called the "jumper's bump".

H

HACK (i) A recognized **type** of light riding horse. (ii) "To hack", i.e. to go for a ride.

HALF-BRED A cross between a **Thoroughbred** and any other **breed**.

HAMES Metal arms fitting into the **harness** collar and linked to the traces.

HAND A unit of measurement of medieval origin, which describes a horse's height. One hand equals 10.16 cm (4 in).

HARD HORSE A tough, enduring horse not susceptible to unsoundness or injury. See **Sound Horse**.

HARNESS The collective term for the equipment of a driven horse. Not applicable to the **riding horse**.

HARNESS HORSE A horse used in **harness** with "harness" type **conformation** in respect of straight shoulders etc, and in consequence having elevated "harness action".

HAUTE ÉCOLE The classical art of advanced riding. See also **Airs Above the Ground.**

HEAVY CAVALRY See **Light Horseman**.

HEAVY HORSE Any large **draught horse**, i.e. Shire, Percheron, Ardennais, etc.

HEAVY TOP A heavy body carried on disproportionately light legs.

HEAVYWEIGHT A horse that, by virtue of its bone and substance, is judged capable of carrying weights of over 89 kg (14 st.).

HIGH SCHOOL See **Haute École**.

HIND QUARTERS The body from the rear of the flank to the top of the tail down to the top of the **gaskin** (second thigh).

HOCKS WELL-LET-DOWN The term indicates the horse has short **cannon bones** (**shanks**), which is considered a structure of great strength. Long cannons, the opposite, are viewed as a conformational weakness.

HOGGED MANE A mane that has been removed by clipping.

HOLLOW BACK See **Dipped Back**.

HOT A horse becoming unduly excited is said to be "hot" or to "hot up".

HOTBLOOD The term describing Arabs, Barbs, and **Thoroughbreds**.

HYBRID A cross between a horse on one side and an ass, zebra, etc. on the other.

I

IN-BREEDING Literally "incest" breeding. The mating of sire/daughter, son/dam, or brother/sister to fix or accentuate a particular characteristic.

IN FRONT OF THE BIT A term used to describe a horse pulling or hanging heavily on the hand.

IN HAND When a horse is controlled from the ground rather than ridden.

J

JIBBAH The peculiar bulged formation of the forehead of the Arab horse.

JOG-TROT A short-paced trot.

L

LEADER Either of the two leading horses in a team of four, or a single horse harnessed in front of one or more horses. The "near" leader is the left-hand horse, and the "off" leader is the right-hand one.

LEAN HEAD A fine head with muscles, veins, and bony protuberances showing clearly. Very fine-skinned Arabs are often said to have a "dry" head.

LEVADE A classical **air above the ground** in which the **forehand** is lifted with bent forelegs on deeply bent hind legs – a controlled half-rear.

LIGHT HORSE A horse, other than a **heavy horse** or a pony, that is suitable for riding or carriage work.

LIGHT HORSEMAN Light cavalry capable of swift movement as opposed to heavily armed cavalry (heavy cavalry) relying principally upon the shock tactic of the charge.

LIGHT OF BONE Insufficient bone below the knee to support the horse and rider's body weight without strain. A serious fault.

LIGHTWEIGHT A horse that, by virtue of its **bone** and **substance**, is judged capable of carrying weights up to 79 kg (12 st. 7 lb)

LINE-BREEDING The mating of individuals with a common ancestor some generations removed to accentuate particular features.

LOADED SHOULDER Excessive muscle formation lying over and inhibiting the shoulder region.

LOINS The area on either side of the spinal vertebrae lying just behind the saddle.

LOPE Slow western canter performed with natural head carriage.

M

MANÈGE An enclosure used for teaching and schooling horses.

MARE A female horse aged four or over.

MEALY NOSE Oatmeal-coloured muzzle, like that of the Exmoor Pony.

MIDDLEWEIGHT A horse that, by virtue of its **bone** and **substance**, is judged capable of carrying weights of up to 89 kg (14 st.)

MITBAH The term describing the angle at which the neck of the Arab Horse enters the head. This gives the arched set to the neck and gives it almost all-round movement.

N

NARROW BEHIND When a deficiency in the musculature of the croup and thigh gives a narrow appearance from behind.

NATIVE PONIES Another name for the British Mountain and Moorland **breeds**.

NICK (i) The division and re-setting of the muscles under the tail to give an artificially high carriage. (ii) A term used to describe a mating likely to produce the desired offspring, i.e. "a good nick".

NISEAN A superior **breed** of antiquity raised in north-west Iran. The Nisean Horse formed the mainstay of the Persian armies.

O

ON THE BIT A horse is "on the bit" when he carries the head in a near-vertical plane, the mouth a little below the rider's hand.

ON THE LEG Used to describe a horse disproportionately long in the leg. Usually associated with inadequate depth in the body.

ORIENTAL HORSES A loosely applied term referring to horses of eastern origin, either Arab or Barb, in use during the formative years of the English **Thoroughbred**.

OUTCROSS The mating of unrelated horses; introduction of outside blood to the breed.

OVERBENT The mouth held close to the chest to evade control. The horse is "behind the bit".

OVER-TOPPED A body over-developed (heavy) in respect of the **substance** of the supporting legs.

OXER Obstacle of parallel poles with a brush fence set between the two to increase the difficulty.

P

PACER A horse employing a lateral action at trot rather than the conventional diagonal movement, i.e. near fore and near hind together followed by the offside pair.

PACK HORSE A horse used to transport goods in packs carried on either side of its back.

PALFREY A medieval light **saddle horse** that could **amble**.

PARIETAL BONES The bones on the top of the skull.

PART-BRED Progeny of a **Thoroughbred** and another **breed**, e.g. Welsh part-bred.

PEDIGREE Details of ancestry recorded in a **stud book**.

PIEBALD English term for body colour of black and white patches.

PIGEON TOES A conformational fault in which the feet are turned inwards. Sometimes called pin-toes.

PLAITING A faulty and dangerous **action** in which the feet cross over each other.

POINTS (i) External features of the horse comprising its **conformation**. (ii) Relating to colour, e.g. bay with black points, meaning bay with black lower legs, mane, and tail.

POSTILLION A rider driving a **harness horse**, usually one of a pair or team, from the saddle.

PREPOTENCY The ability consistently to pass on character and type to the progeny.

PRIMITIVE A term used generally for the early subspecies of *Equus caballus*: the Asiatic Wild horse, the Tarpan, the Forest Horse, and the Tundra Horse.

PRIMITIVE VIGOUR Highly dominant character and **prepotency** associated with early wild horses.

PURE-BRED Horse of unmixed breeding.

Q

QUALITY The element of refinement in **breeds** and **types**, usually due to Arab or **Thoroughbred** influence.

QUARTERS See **Hind Quarters**.

R

RACEHORSE A horse bred for racing, usually a **Thoroughbred** but also other **breeds**.

RACK The fifth gait of the American Saddlebred. "A flashy, fast, four-beat gait", unrelated to pacing.

RAGGED HIPS Prominent hip-bones lacking flesh and muscle.

RAM-HEAD A convex profile like that of the Barb. Similar to **Roman nose**.

RANGY Description of a horse having size and **scope** of movement.

REMOUNT See **Cavalry Remount**.

RIDING HORSE A horse suitable for riding with the **conformation** associated with comfortable riding action (as opposed to **draught** or carriage).

RISING A horse approaching five years old is said to be "rising five".

ROACH BACK A convex curvature of the spine between the withers and the **loins**. The opposite of **hollow back**.

ROACHED MANE American term for **hogged mane**.

ROADSTER (i) The famous Norfolk Roadster, a trotting saddle horse, ancestor of the modern Hackney. (ii) In the US, a light **harness horse**, usually a Standardbred.

ROMAN NOSE The convex profile as found in the Shire and other heavy **breeds**.

ROSIN-BACK A broad-backed horse used in the circus for trick-riding acts. Rosin is used on shoes, etc., to increase the grip.

RUNNING HORSE The English racing stock, also called Running Stock, which provided the base for the **Thoroughbred** when crossed with imported eastern sires.

S

SADDLE HORSE (i) A riding horse. (ii) A wooden trestle to support saddles.

SADDLE MARKS White hair in the saddle area probably caused by galls.

SCHOOL MOVEMENTS The gymnastic exercises carried on within a school. Also "school figures" involving movement patterns. See also **Airs Above the Ground** and **Manège**.

SCOPE Capability for freedom of movement to a special degree.

SECOND THIGH See **Gaskin**.

SET TAIL A tail broken or nicked and set to give artificially high carriage.

SHANK BONE Hind cannon bone.

SHORT-COUPLED See **Close-Coupled**.

SHORT OF A RIB A conformational fault arising from slack **loins**. There is a marked space between the last rib and the hip. It occurs in horses with overly long backs.

SICKLE-HOCKS Weak, bent hocks resembling a sickle shape.

SKEWBALD English term for body colour of irregular white and coloured patches other than black.

SLAB-SIDED Flat ribbed.

SLACK IN THE LOINS Weak **loins**. The last rib is short and there is a noticeable space between it and the hip.

SLIP HEAD Head strap and cheekpiece supporting the bradoon of a double bridle.

SOUND HORSE A sound horse is one that "should possess a perfect state of both frame and bodily health, without exception or ambiguity, the total absence of blemishes as well as defects, a freedom from every imperfection and from all impediments to sight and action".

SPLIT-UP BEHIND Conformational faults caused by weakness of the **second thighs**. Seen from behind, the thighs divide too high, just beneath the **dock**.

STALLION An uncastrated male horse of four years old or more.

STAMP A prepotent **stallion** is said to stamp his stock with his own character and physical attributes. See **Prepotency.**

STAMP OF HORSE A recognizable **type**, or pattern, of horse.

STUD (i) A breeding establishment – a stud farm. (ii) A **stallion**.

STUD BOOK A book kept by a **breed** society in which the **pedigrees** of stock eligible for entry are recorded.

SUBSTANCE The physical quality of the body in terms of its build and general musculature.

T

TACK A stable word for saddlery. An abbreviation of "tackle".

TAIL MALE LINE Descent through the male parent line.

TEASER A substitute **stallion** used to test whether a **mare** is ready to mate with the regular **stud** stallion.

THRIFTY To describe a horse that is economical to keep, maintaining condition on small feed rations. Also called **frugal**.

THROAT LATCH A strap on the headpiece, which passes around the horse's throat.

TIED-IN BELOW THE KNEE Where the measurement below the knee is substantially less than that above the fetlock. This is a conformational fault in which the horse is necessarily short, or **light of bone**.

TOP LINE The line of the back from the withers to the end of the croup.

TRAVOIS An American Indian horse sled.

TURNOUT Standard of dress and accoutrements of a horse and rider, or of a driven vehicle.

TYPE A horse fulfilling a particular purpose (such as a cob, a hunter, and a hack) but which does not necessarily belong to a specific **breed**.

U

UNDERSHOT A deformity in which the lower jaw projects beyond the upper.

UP TO WEIGHT A term describing a horse that, on account of its **substance, bone**, size, and overall **conformation,** is capable of carrying a substantial weight.

W

WARMBLOOD In general terms, a **half-** or **part-bred** horse, the result of an Arab or **Thoroughbred** cross with other blood or bloods.

WEED A horse of poor, mean **conformation**, carrying little flesh, and often long-legged. Generally of **Thoroughbred** type.

WEIGHT CARRIER A horse capable of carrying 95.2 kg (15 st.). Also called a **heavyweight** horse.

WELL RIBBED-UP A short, deep, rounded body with **well-sprung ribs**.

WELL-SPRUNG RIBS Long, rounded ribs giving ample room for lung expansion, which are well-suited to carrying a saddle.

WHEELER The team horse harnessed nearest to the vehicle behind the **leaders**.

WHIP The driver of a carriage.

WHIPPER-IN The assistant to the huntsman of a pack of hounds.

Z

ZEBRA BARS Dark, striped markings on the **forearms** and occasionally on the hind legs as well. A **primitive** feature.

INDEX

Entries in *italic* indicate
featured breeds

ACKNOWLEDGMENTS

FOR MUCH OF THE EASTERN CONTENT of this book I have to express my gratitude to: Dr. Digvijay Sinh of the Royal House of Wankaner, an expert on the Indian indigenous breeds; Mukundan S. Chettiyappa, who has a deep knowledge of Rajasthan and its horses; Lt. Col. U.P.S. Godara, 61st Cavalry, for his help with the polo pictures; Major B.P. Singh, owner of the Guru Hari Stud, Delhi; Col. O.P. Tehlan, formerly Secretary General, Equestrian Federation of India; and to my very dear friends Col. Girdhari Singh AVSM (retd.) and Shri Jimmy Bharucha for their inestimable help at all times and over many years. Finally, I have to thank my friend Gurcharan Singh, taxi-driver no.2600, for conveying me safely in every circumstance and with unfailing cheerfulness. I also owe a debt of gratitude to the unflappable Mrs. Julie Thomas, who typed and filed my manuscripts with unfailing accuracy. ELWYN HARTLEY EDWARDS

REVISED EDITION (2001): Renewed thanks are due to Julie Thomas, whose mastery of the new technology allows my copy and much more to be processed without my further involvement. Sharon Lucas and Derek Coombes of DK have been especially helpful and, of course, I have to acknowledge with gratitude the contribution made by the Studio Cactus team, whose expertise is very apparent in this New Encyclopedia. Finally, I have to thank my long-suffering literary agent, and my friend of 30 years, John Pawsey – always a tower of strength and common sense. ELWYN HARTLEY EDWARDS

STUDIO CACTUS would like to thank Kate Grant (project management), Sharon Rudd (Project Art Editor), and Donna Wood (Project Editor). Thanks also to Jenni Close for her editorial assistance and Rob Walker for his picture-research assistance for the 2007 revision.

DORLING KINDERSLEY would like to thank The Royal Mews, Buckingham Palace, for permission to photograph horses and tack; The Household Cavalry Mounted Regiment, for permission to photograph a Household Cavalryman and a Household Cavalry Black; The King's Troop, Royal Horse Artillery, for permission to photograph an artilleryman and gun-horse; the Avon and Somerset Constabulary Mounted Branch, for permission to photograph a police horse and police woman; the Musée Vivant du Cheval, Chantilly, France, for permission to photograph their horses; the Château de Saumur – Musée de Cheval, France, for permission to photograph saddlery and clothing; Radhika Singh of Fotomedia, India, for her help in organizing the Indian photography; Alan Proud and Manu Pal Godara, for modelling in India; Jo Weeks, Susie Behar, Laura Harper, Nick Turpin, and Miranda Tidman for editorial help; Alison Donovan and Dingus Hussey and Colin Walton for design help; Juliet Duff for picture research; Janos Marffy for maps and the artwork on p.12 (bl); Sean Milne for artworks on pp.10–15 and pp.22–23; Samantha Elmhurst pp.414–15, pp.443, pp.446; Deborah Myatt for line drawings on pp.10–15; Susan Sturrock and Lesley Riley for proofreading; and Hilary Bird for the index.

BOB LANGRISH would like to thank Dr. Mikhail Alexeev for his help in Russia; Peggy Sue Carroll and all the staff at the Kentucky Horse Park; and Jan Gyllensten for his assistance in Scandinavia.

KIT HOUGHTON would like to thank Steve Kobza, Agoston Sarlos, and Beata Plesko (Hungary), Dr. Gebhardt and Klaus zum Borge (Germany), and the Instituto Ippico di Crema (Italy).

PICTURE CREDITS

Key: t top, b bottom, l left, r right, c centre

p.1 Tersk (see pp.88–89)

pp.2–3 B. Langrish p.3 c **Shagya Arab** (see pp.76–77)

p.4 br K. Houghton; p.5 tr K. Houghton

THE GRANDES ÉCURIES AT CHANTILLY
The Grandes Écuries (big stables) attached to the Château at Chantilly were commissioned in 1719 by Louis-Henri de Bourbon, the 7th Prince of Condé, from the architect Jean Aubert. According to legend, Louis-Henri believed in metempsychosis, the migration of the soul from one body to another, and thought he would be reincarnated as a horse after his death. As a result, he built himself suitably sumptuous quarters for his next life. The stables are deemed to be the most beautiful in the world and in the 18th century housed 240 horses and up to 500 dogs. They now house a teaching museum, the Musée Vivant du Cheval (Living Horse Museum).

p.6 b Tate Gallery/The Bridgeman Art Library; p.7 see pp.334-335; 342-343; 346-347

pp.8–9 Ronald Sheridan/Ancient Art & Architecture Collection

p.10 tl by permission of the Syndics of Cambridge University Library; br Imitor; p.11 tl Imitor

p.14 tr K. Houghton; bl Hutchison Library; p.15 tc Jean-Paul Ferrero/Ardea London; br V. Nikiforov/Animal Photography

p.16 tl G.D. Plage/Bruce Coleman Limited; cr Peter Stephenson/Planet Earth Pictures; bl Jerry Young; p.17 tr John Bracegirdle/Planet Earth Pictures; c Anup Shah/Planet Earth Pictures; br Karl Shone

pp18–19 **Asiatic Wild Horse** – Marwell Zoological Park/ Jerry Young; p.18 tr P. Morris/Ardea London; p.19 tc Terry Whittaker/Frank Lane Picture Agency; cr Kenneth W. Fink/Ardea London

p.20 tl A. Harrington/Planet Earth Pictures; cr Mary Evans Picture Library; p.21 tl **Huçul** (see pp.194–95); tr **Konik** (see pp.194–95); bc Jean-Paul Ferrero/Ardea London

p.22 br Sally Anne Thompson/Animal Photography; bl K. Houghton; p.23 bl B Langrish; br B. Langrish

p.24 tl Science Photo Library; bl **Ardennais** (see pp.264–65); bc **Thoroughbred** (see pp.120–21); br **Welsh Section A** (see pp.182–83); p.25 tr **Trakehner** (see pp.140–41)

pp.26–27 Chicago Press, USA/The Bridgeman Art Library, London

p.28 tl Dover Books; bl Mary Evans Picture Library; br Robert Harding Picture Library; p.29 t Dr. Eckart Pott/Bruce Coleman Limited; bl Paul Harris/Select; br Hermitage Museum, St. Petersburg/C.M. Dixon

p.30 cl Hermitage Museum, St. Petersburg; cr Schimmel Collection, New York/Werner Forman Archive; p.31 tr Ancient Art & Architecture; b British Museum/E.T. Archive; cl Hermitage Museum, St. Petersburg/C.M. Dixon

p.32 tl C.M. Dixon; cl British Museum, London/Michael Holford; cr Château de Saumur – Musée de Cheval, France/ K. Houghton; br British Museum, London/Michael Holford; p.33 tc Hassia/Sonia Halliday Photographs; cl Werner Forman Archive/British Museum, London; br British Museum, London/Michael Holford

p.34 tl Ancient Art & Architecture; cr British Museum/C.M. Dixon; bc British Museum, London/The Bridgeman Art Library; p.35 c British Museum, London/Robert Harding Picture Library; br Hermitage Museum, St. Petersburg/C.M. Dixon

pp.36–37 **Caspian** – *Hopstone Jamshyd*, Mrs. J. Quinny, Easton Hill, Redditch, Worcs., UK/B. Langrish; p.36 tr British Museum, London/The Bridgeman Art Library; bl B. Langrish; p.37 br Sally Anne Thompson/Animal Photography

p.38 tl Mary Evans Picture Library; bl Ronald Sheridan/ Ancient Art & Architecture Collection; bc Louvre Paris: Giraudon/The Bridgeman Art Library; p.39 tr Ronald Sheridan/Ancient Art & Architecture Collection; c National Archaeological Museum, Athens/C.M. Dixon; bl British Museum, London/ Michael Holford

p.40 tl British Museum, London/Michael Holford; b National Archaeological Museum, Naples/E.T. Archive; p.41 tr Ronald Sheridan/Ancient Art & Architecture Collection; c Ronald Sheridan/Ancient Art & Architecture Collection

pp.42–43 **Pindos** – *Marco*; **Skyrian** – *Pearl*, both owned by Penny Turner, Greece/B. Langrish; p.42 bl K. Houghton; tr B. Langrish; p.43 br R. Willbie/Animal Photography

pp.44–45 British Museum, London; p.44 tl Ronald Sheridan/Ancient Art & Architecture Collection; bl British Museum, London/The Bridgeman Art Library; p.45 tl National Archaeological Museum, Rome/C.M. Dixon; tr National Archaeological Museum, Rome/C.M. Dixon; br Gloucester City Museum, England/C.M. Dixon

pp.46–47 **Ariègeois** – *Vizir d'Olmes*, Haras National de Tarbes, France/B. Langrish; p.46 bl B. Langrish; p.47 tl Agence Nature/NHPA

pp.48–49 **Friesian** – *Peter*, Kelli Murphey, Sanger, Texas, USA/B. Langrish; p.48 bl Sally Anne Thompson/Animal Photography; p.49 tc K. Houghton

pp.50–51 **Noriker** – *Dinolino*, Josef Waldherr, Wackersberg, Germany/B. Langrish; p.50 bl Sally Anne Thompson/ Animal Photography; p.51 tl Sally Anne Thompson/Animal Photography; br **Black Forest Horse** – *Riejel*, Marbach Stud, Germany/K. Houghton

pp.52–53 **Haflinger** – *Moritz*, Heiner Eppinger, Germany/K. Houghton; **Avelignese** – *Refe*, Centro Regionale Incremento Ippico, Crema, Italy/K. Houghton; p.52 tr R. Willbie/Animal Photography

p.54 tl Werner Forman Archive; b Edimedia; p.55 tl E.T. Archive; r Werner Forman Archive/Idemitsu Museum of Arts, Tokyo

p.56 tl B. Langrish; c Ronald Sheridan/Ancient Art & Architecture Collection; bl Chicago Press, USA/The Bridgeman Art Library; br Freer Gallery, Smithsonian Institute, Washington dc, USA/The Bridgeman Art Library; p.57 tr British Museum,

London/Michael Holford; cl Mary Evans Picture Library; br Christie's, London/The Bridgeman Art Library

pp.58–59 Private Collection/The Bridgeman Art Library

p.60 tl Mary Evans Picture Library; b M.P.L. Fogden/Bruce Coleman Limited; p.61 tl Prado, Madrid/The Bridgeman Art Library; cr Christie's Images; bc Christie's, London/The Bridgeman Art Library

p.62 tl Biblioteca Nacional, Madrid/Werner Forman Archive; tr Biblioteca Nacional, Madrid/Werner Forman Archive; cl Topkapi Museum, Istanbul/E.T. Archive; br Private Collection/The Bridgeman Art Library; p.63 tl Christie's Images; br Mary Evans Picture Library

pp.64–65 **Arab** – *Cavu The Prophet*, Don and Jo Ann Holson, Cavu Arabians, Sanger, Texas, USA/B. Langrish; p.64 tr Sally Anne Thompson/Animal Photography; cl B. Langrish; p.65 tc E.H. Edwards

pp.66–67 **Barb** – *Ouassal*, Haras National de Compiègne, France/B. Langrish; p.66 bl P. Hagdorn/ZEFA; tl Robert Harding Picture Library; p.67 br Michael Fogden/Bruce Coleman Limited

p.68 tl Explorer; bl E.T. Archive; br Château de Saumur – Musée de Cheval, France/K. Houghton; p.69 tl Bibliothèque Nationale, Paris/E.T. Archive; tr Edimedia; bc Bibliothèque de la Sorbonne, Paris/The Bridgeman Art Library

p.70 tl Ronald Sheridan/Ancient Art & Architecture Collection; c Ronald Sheridan/Ancient Art & Architecture Collection; p.71 c Ronald Sheridan/Ancient Art & Architecture Collection; tr Mary Evans Picture Library

p.72 tl By courtesy of the Board of Trustees of the Victoria & Albert Museum, London/The Bridgeman Art Library; c Peter Newark's Military Pictures; bl Ancient Art & Architecture Collection; p.73 The Mansell Collection

pp.74–75 **Akhal-Teke** – *Sopoly*, Pearl of Switzerland Trade Association, Moscow, Russia/B. Langrish; p.74 c Sally Anne Thompson/Animal Photography; p.75 tc V.M. Nikiforov/Animal Photography; br B. Langrish

pp.76–77 **Shagya Arab** – *Kemir V*, Bábolna State Stud, Hungary/K. Houghton; **Gidran Arab** – *Frèdi*, Sagar Uttjelep, Hungary/K. Houghton; p.76 tr Konrad Wothe/Oxford Scientific Films p.77 cl K. Houghton

pp.78–79 **Anglo-Arab** – *Mimosa du Maury*, Haras National de Tarbes, France/B. Langrish; p.78 tr K. Houghton; p.79 br K. Houghton

pp.80–81 **Don** – *Bakhchevod*, Pyatigorsk Hippodrome, Russian Federation/B. Langrish; p.80 bl **Ukrainian Riding Horse** – *Park*, Bronnitsy Riding School, Russian Federation/B. Langrish; p.81 tc Sally Anne Thompson/Animal Photography

pp.82–83 **Kabardin** – *Dagmar*, Karachay Stud Farm, Cherkessk, Russian Federation; **Karabakh** – Moscow Hippodrome, Russia; p.82 tr B. Langrish; p.83 br The Hutchison Library

pp.84–85 **Karabair** – *Klad*, Bronnitsy Riding School, Russian Federation/B. Langrish; p.84 bl Sally Anne Thompson/Animal Photography; tr Sally Anne Thompson/Animal Photography

pp.86–87 **Budenny** – *Reactive*, Pearl of Switzerland Trade Association, Moscow, Russia/B. Langrish; p.86 bl B. Langrish; p.87 tr B. Langrish

pp.88–89 **Lokai** – *Volna*, Moscow Agricultural Academy, Russia/B. Langrish; **Tersk** – *Bastion*, Stavropol Stud Farm, Russian Federation/B. Langrish; p.88 bc Sally Anne Thompson/Animal Photography

p.92 tl Château de Saumur – Musée de Cheval, France/

MURAKÖZI

K. Houghton; bl Musée de Bayeux, France/Michael Holford; cr University Library, Heidelberg/E.T. Archive; p.93 t Galleria degli Uffizi, Florence/The Bridgeman Art Library; bl Château de Saumur – Musée de Cheval, France/K. Houghton; bc Château de Saumur – Musée de Cheval, France/K. Houghton; cr Château de Saumur – Musée de Cheval, France/K. Houghton

pp.94–95 **Percheron** – *Aimable*, Haras National du Lion d'Angers, France/K. Houghton; p.94 bl K. Houghton; p.95 tl **Black Percheron** – *Charlie*, Kentucky Horse Park, USA/B. Langrish; br K. Houghton

p.96 tl Peter Newark's Historical Pictures; c British Museum, London/Michael Holford; bl Mary Evans Picture Library; br Château de Saumur – Musée de Cheval, France/K. Houghton; p.97 r Palazzo Ducale, Mantua/The Bridgeman Art Library

p.98 tl Mary Evans Picture Library; c Stapleton Collection/The Bridgeman Art Library; br The Mansell Collection; p.99 tl Château de Saumur – Musée de Cheval, France/K. Houghton; tc Château de Saumur – Musée de Cheval, France/K. Houghton; br Jean-Luc Petit/Frank Spooner Pictures

p.100 tl Dover Book of Animals; bc Mary Evans Picture Library; p.101 l, r Theatre Museum, London/E.T. Archive; c Theatre Museum, London/E.T. Archive

p. 102 tl Mary Evans Picture Library; bl Elisabeth Weiland; p.103 tl Robert Harding Picture Library; br Erich Lessing/Magnum Photos

pp.104 tl K.Houghton; bc K. Houghton; p.105 tl K.Houghton; br K. Houghton

pp.106–7 **Sorraia** – *Giro*, Portuguese National Stud, Alter do Chão, Portugal/B. Langrish; p.106 tr K. Houghton; p.107 tc K. Houghton; br Magnum Photos/Burt Glinn

108–9 **Andalucian** – *Morito*, Kelli Murphey, Sanger, Texas, USA/B. Langrish; **Lusitano** – *Glorioso*, Y. Bienaimé, Musée Vivant du Cheval, Chantilly, France/K. Houghton; p.108 tr K. Houghton; p.109 br K. Houghton

pp.110–11 **Alter-Real** – *Casto*, Portuguese National Stud, Portugal/B. Langrish; p.110 bl B. Langrish; p.111 br **Hispano-Arab** – *Ultima*, Mr. & Mrs. Davies, Alphington, UK/B. Langrish

pp.112–13 **Lipizzaner** – *Siglavy Szella*, John Goddard Fenwick & Lyn Morgan, Ausdan Stud, Dyfed, UK/B. Langrish; p.112 tr R. Willbie/Animal Photography; p.113 br Elisabeth Weiland

pp.114–15 **Frederiksborg** – *Lotus Glerup*, Lone & May Zielinski, Solrød, Denmark/B. Langrish; **Knabstrup** – *Føniks*, Poul Elmerkjaer, Jyderup, Denmark/B. Langrish; p.114 cl Sally Anne Thompson/Animal Photography; tr R. Willbie/Animal Photography; p.115 tr Sally Anne Thompson/

Animal Photography

pp.116–17 E.T. Archive

p.118 tl K. Houghton; b K. Houghton; p.119 tr Hiroji Kubota/Magnum Photos; cl K. Houghton; br Steenmanns/ZEFA

pp.120–21 **Thoroughbred** – *Ardent Lodger*, Mr. & Mrs. P. Duffy, Pencefn Stud, Clwyd, UK/B. Langrish; p.120 cl B. Langrish; tr B. Langrish; p.121 tr K. Houghton

pp.122–23 **Shales Horse** – *Finmere Grey Shales*, Elizabeth Colquhoun, Little Tingewick House, Buckingham, Bucks., UK/B. Langrish; p.122 tr from *The Horses of the British Empire*, Walter Southwood & Co. Ltd., 1907; p.123 br Christie's Images

p.124 tl **Danish Warmblood** (see pp.150–51); c Popperfoto; bl **Friesian** (see pp.48–49); br **Groningen** (see pp.126–27); p.125 tc K. Houghton; bl **Gelderlander** (see pp.126–27); br **Thoroughbred** (see pp.120–21)

pp.126–27 **Gelderlander** – *Fantast*, Vaux Breweries, UK/B. Langrish; **Groningen** – *Loeks*, Jacob Melissen, Pesse, Netherlands/B. Langrish; p.126 bl K. Houghton; p.127 br B. Langrish

pp.128–29 **Dutch Warmblood** – *Tokyo Joe*, Lorna Tew, Cirencester, Glos., UK/B. Langrish; p.128 bl K. Houghton; p.129 tc B. Langrish

p.130 tl K.Houghton; br B. Langrish; p.131 tc Jean-Paul Ferrero/Ardea London; bc Sally Anne Thompson/Animal Photography; br B. Langrish

pp.132–33 **Selle Français** – *Soir d'Avril*, Haras National du Lion d'Angers, France/K. Houghton; p.132 tr K. Houghton; p.133 **Selle Français racing type** – *Useful*, Haras National du Lion d'Angers, France/K. Houghton

pp.134–35 **French Trotter** – *Haut de Bellouet*, Mr. Moïse Monthéan, France/K. Houghton; p.134 tr Sunset (G. Lacz)/NHPA; p.135 br K. Houghton

pp.136–37 **Einsiedler** – *Monte Carlo*, Swiss National Stud, Avenches, Switzerland/B. Langrish; **Freiberger** – *Judäea*, Swiss National Stud, Avenches, Switzerland/B. Langrish; p.136 c K. Houghton; p.137 tc B. Langrish; cr B.Langrish

p.138 tl B. Langrish; cr K. Houghton; b Sally Anne Thompson/Animal Photography; p.139 tl K. Houghton; tr K. Houghton; bc B. Langrish

pp.140–41 **Trakehner** – *Suchard*, Dr. U. Mittermayer, Aachen, Germany/K. Houghton; p.140 bl B. Langrish; p.141 tc B. Langrish

pp.142–43 **Holsteiner** – *Cosima*, Heiner Eppinger, Münsingen, Germany/K. Houghton; p.142 tr K. Houghton; p.143 br K. Houghton

pp.144–45 **Hanoverian** – *Demonstrator*, Broadstone Stud, Oxon., UK/B. Langrish; p.145 br **Westphalian** – Sian Thomas BHSI, Snowdonia Equestrian Centre, UK/B. Langrish

pp.146–47 **Belgian Warmblood** – *Trudo Darco*, Paesen Martinus, Peer, Belgium/B. Langrish; **Bavarian Warmblood** – *Samurai*, Heiner Eppinger, Münsingen, Germany/K. Houghton; p.146 tr B. Langrish

pp.148–49 **Rhinelander** – *Hasdrubal*, Marlis Decker, Aachen, Germany/K. Houghton; **Württemberger** – *Andlus*, Heiner Eppinger, Germany/K. Houghton; p.148 cl K. Houghton; p.149 tc B. Langrish

pp.150–51 **Danish Warmblood** – *Broadstone Landmark*, Broadstone Stud, Oxon, UK/B. Langrish; **Swedish Warmblood**

– *Asterix 694*, Interbreed AB, Flyinge, Sweden/B. Langrish; p.150 c K. Houghton; p.151 tc B. Langrish

p.152 tl, cl, br, K. Houghton; p.153 tr Sally Anne Thompson/Animal Photography; b Sally Anne Thompson/Animal Photography

pp.154–55 **Wielkopolski** – *Mikado*, Manor Park Stud, Surrey, UK/B. Langrish; p.154 tr B. Langrish; p.155 cr Elisabeth Weiland

pp.156–57 **Nonius** – *Nónius IX-165*, Mezohegyes State Stud, Hungary/K. Houghton; **Furioso** – *Furioso IX-3 (Rinaldo)*, Mezohegyes State Stud, Hungary/K. Houghton; p.156 bc B. Langrish; p.157 tr K. Houghton

pp.158–59 **Czechoslovakian Warmblood** – *Mikeš*, Mrs. J. Wolfenden, Pen-y-Bont, Gwynedd, UK/B. Langrish; p.158 bl K. Houghton; p.159 tc B. Langrish

p.160 tl, cr E.H. Edwards; b J. Collier; p.161 tl E.H. Edwards; bl J.H.C. Wilson/Robert Harding Picture Library; bl Akhil Bakhshi

pp.162–63 **Kathiawari** – K. Houghton; tr Mounted Branch, New Delhi Police, India/Akhil Bakhshi; p.162 tr J.M. Labat, Y. Arthus Bertrand/Ardea London

pp.164–65 **Marwari** – K. Houghton; p.164 tr Fotomedia; bl M. Ranjit/FLPA

pp.166–67 **Indian Half-Bred** – Col. Girdhari Singh AVSM, New Delhi, India/Akhil Bakhshi; p.166 tr Akhil Bakhshi; p.167 tr, bc, Akhil Bakhshi

pp.168–69 Sir Alfred Munnings Art Museum/Christie's Images

p.170 tl **Highland** (see pp.176–77); c K. Houghton; bl Only Horses Picture Agency; br Jean-Paul Ferrero/Ardea London; p.171 tl B. Langrish; cr B. Langrish; br Christie's Images

pp.172–73 **Fell** – *Heltondale Daisy III*, K.A. & S.B.M. Feakins, Llancloudy, Hereford, UK/B. Langrish ; **Dales** – *Whitworth Prince*, B. & C. Gobey, Swayfield, Lincs., UK/B. Langrish; p.172 tr K. Houghton; bl B. Langrish

pp.174–75 **Dartmoor** – *Blythe Jessica*, Miss M. Houlden, Munstone, Herefordshire, UK/B. Langrish; **Exmoor** – *Blackthorn Piccottee*, Mrs. Carter, Wilton, Wilts., UK/B. Langrish; p. 174 tr B. Langrish; p.175 cr K. Houghton

pp.176–77 **New Forest** – *Knightwood Dragonfly*, Mrs. P.A. Harvey Richards, Bromshaw, Hants., UK/B. Langrish; p.176 tr Only Horses Picture Agency; bl Jean-Paul Ferrero/Ardea London; p.177 tc Richard Coomber/Planet Earth Pictures

pp.178–79 **Shetland** – *Hose Element*, J.A. & J.R. Stevenson, Hose Shetland Pony Stud, Melton Mowbray, Leics., UK/B. Langrish; **Highland** – *Monarch of Dykes*, Countess of Swinton, Dykes Hill House, Ripon, Yorks., UK/B. Langrish; p.178 cl K. Houghton; p.179 tl Michael Jenner/Robert Harding Picture Library

pp.180–81 **Connemara** – *Garryhack Tooreen*, Mrs. Beckett, Shipton Connemara Pony Stud, Cheltenham, Glos., UK/B. Langrish; p.180 tr B. Langrish; p.181 br K. Houghton

pp.182–83 **Welsh Section A** – *Blackhill Sparkle*, D. & R. Powell, Craswall, Hereford, UK/B. Langrish; **Welsh Section B** – *Elmead Lockets*, Mr. & Mrs. L. Bigley, Escley, Hereford, UK/B. Langrish; p.182 cl. tr B. Langrish

pp.184–85 **Welsh Section C** – *Wernderris*, Mrs. S. Crump, Kentchurch, Hereford, UK/B. Langrish; **Welsh Section D** – *Llanarth Sally*, Mr. & Mrs. L. Bigley, Escley, Hereford, UK/B. Langrish; p.185 tr **Welsh Part-Bred** – *Carolina's Pussycat*, Mr. & Mrs. L. Bigley, Escley, Hereford, UK/B. Langrish

p.186 tl **Pottok** (see pp.188–89); b Only Horses Picture Agency;

A MOUNTED POLICEMAN, KENTUCKY HORSE PARK

p.187 tl R. Willbie/Animal Photography; tr Hans Reinhard (Okapia)/Oxford Scientific Films; bl B. Langrish

pp.188–89 **Landais** – *Tresor des Pins*, Haras de Pau, France/B. Langrish; **Pottok** – *Ortzi*, Y. Bienaimé, Musée Vivant du Cheval, Chantilly, France/K. Houghton; p.188 tr B. Langrish; p.189 br Jean-Paul Ferrero/Ardea London

p.190–91 **Bardigiano** – *Orchidea*, S. Adamo Tombini, Perego, Italy/K. Houghton; p.190 bl S. Savoli/K&B News Foto; tr B. Langrish; p.191 tr S. Savoli/K&B News Foto

pp.192–93 **Gotland** – *Ripadals Benni 398*, Carina Andersson, Anderslöv, Sweden/B. Langrish; **Fjord** – *Windy Poplar Andrea*, Ted & Yvette Swendson, Calgary, Alberta, Canada/B. Langrish; p.192 tr Elisabeth Weiland; p.193 tc Paolo Koch/Robert Harding Picture Library; br Elisabeth Weiland

pp.194–95 **Huçul** – *Lubas*, Janusz Utrata, Warsaw, Poland/B. Langrish; **Konik** – *Hewal*, CWKS "Legia", Warsaw, Poland/B. Langrish; p.194 bl Sally Anne Thompson/Animal Photography; p.195 br Hans D. Dossenbach/Ardea London

pp.196–97 **Icelandic** – *Little Elska*, Glenn & Heather Greenfield, Blackie, Alberta, Canada/B. Langrish; p.196 tr R. Willbie/Animal Photography; p.197 tc Only Horses Picture Agency

p.198 tl Sanjay K. Saxena/Fotomedia; cr Paul Harris/ Select; bl Brian Moser/Hutchison Library; p.199 tc Sarah Errington/Hutchison Library; b Elisabeth Weiland; br B. Langrish

pp.200–1 **Bashkir** – *Mel's Lucky Boy*, Mr. D. Stewart, Lexington, Kentucky, USA/B. Langrish; p.200 bl V. Nikiforov/Animal Photography; tr B. Langrish; p.201 br Sarah Errington/Hutchison Library

pp.202–3 **Indian Country-Bred** – Sainik Riding School, Rohtak, Haryana, India/Akhil Bakhshi; p.202 tr Joanna van Gruisen/Fotomedia; bl Akhil Bakhshi; p.203 bc Aditya Aria/Fotomedia

pp.204–5 **Sumba** – *Mitzi*, Tung Kurniawan, Sumatra, Indonesia/B. Langrish; **Timor** – *Meriam Bellina*, Pelita Jaya Stable, Jakarta, Indonesia/B. Langrish; p.204 tr B. Langrish; bl Michael Mackintyre/Hutchison Library; 205 tc B. Langrish

pp.206–7 **Sandalwood** – *Arthur*, Oetari Soehardjono, Pamulang Equestrian Centre, Indonesia/B. Langrish; **Batak** – *Dora*, Tung Kurniawan, Sumatra, Indonesia/B. Langrish; p.206 tr B. Langrish; p.207 c, cl B. Langrish

pp.208–9 **Java** – *Dewi Mar*, Oetari Soehardjono, Pamulang

Equestrian Centre, Indonesia/B. Langrish; **Padang** – *Semangat*, Tung Kurniawan, Sumatra, Indonesia/B. Langrish; p.208 tr B. Langrish; p.209 tc B. Langrish; br Spectrum Colour Library

pp.210–11 **Australian Pony** – *Malibu Park Command Performance*, K. & L. Sinclair, Tynony North, Victoria, Australia/B. Langrish; p.210 Sally Anne Thompson/Animal Photography; bl B. Langrish; p.211 br B. Langrish

pp.212–13 **Hokkaido** – *Ayme*, Japanese Racing Association, Tokyo, Japan/B. Langrish; **Kiso** – *Syuzan*, Japanese Racing Association, Tokyo, Japan/B. Langrish; **Kagoshima** – *Tokara*, Japanese Racing Association, Tokyo, Japan/B. Langrish; p.212 tr Orion Press; p.213 tc Orion Press; br Orion Press

pp.214–15 Michael Holford

p.216 tl Mary Evans Picture Library; c E.T. Archive; bl Biblioteca Nacional, Madrid/The Bridgeman Art Library; p.217 tr Private Collection/E.T. Archive; cl Peter Newark's American Pictures; bl Peter Newark's Western Americana

pp.218–19 **Mustang** – *Mestava*, Rowland H. Cheney, Stockton, California, USA/B. Langrish; **Galiceno** – *Java Gold*, Billy Jack Giles, Godley, Texas, USA/B. Langrish; p.218 tr B. Langrish; bl David E. Rowley/Planet Earth Pictures; p.219 c K. Houghton

pp.220–21 **Criollo** – *Azuleca*, Claire Tomlinson, Westonbirt, Glos., UK/B. Langrish; **Paso** – *Gavulan de Campanero*, Snr. Juan E. Villanueva, Association of Horses and Paso Finos, Puerto Rico 00709/B. Langrish; p.220 tr B. Langrish; p.221 br B. Langrish

p.222 tl Peter Newark's Western Americana; tr The Mansell Collection; bl Peter Newark's Western Americana; p.223 tr Peter Newark's Western Americana; bc Peter Newark's Western Americana; br Peter Newark's Western Americana

pp.224–25 **Palomino** – *Golden Wildfire*, Monica Comm, Calgary, Alberta, Canada/B. Langrish; **Pinto (Paint)** – *Ruffit*, Annette Gadberry, Z-Arabians, Argyle, Texas, USA/B. Langrish; p.224 bl B. Langrish; p.225 tr B. Langrish

pp.226–27 **Appaloosa** – *Shines Sunburst*, Terri L. Crabtree, Bowling Green, Kentucky, USA/B. Langrish; p.226 tr B. Langrish; bl Jean-Paul Ferrero/Ardea London; p.227 bc **Cayuse Indian Pony** – *Teton*, Wild Horse Research, Porterville, California, USA/B. Langrish

p.228 tl Peter Newark's Western Americana; bl Adam Woolfitt/Robert Harding Picture Library; cr Peter Newark's Western Americana; p.229 cl Geoff Brightling; tr Peter Newark's Western Americana; br Peter Newark's Western Americana

pp.230–31 **Quarter Horse** – *Royal Zippe*, Riding for the Handicapped, Lexington, Kentucky, USA/B. Langrish; p.230 tr Sally Anne Thompson/Animal Photography; c Geoff Brightling; p.231 br B. Langrish

pp.232–33 **Morgan** – *Shaker's Supreme*, Fred & Bonnie Neuville, Georgetown, Kentucky, USA/B. Langrish; p.232 bl B. Langrish; p233 tr B. Langrish

pp.234–35 **American Saddlebred** – *Forever Simbara*, Steve White, Grandeur Arabians, Citra, Florida, USA/B. Langrish; p.234 bl K. Houghton; p.235 tc B. Langrish

pp.236–237 **Missouri Fox Trotter** – *Velvet*, Paul Fornaciari, San Pasqual, Pasadena, Texas, USA/B. Langrish; p.236 tr B. Langrish; p.237 tr B. Langrish

pp.238–39 **Tennessee Walking Horse** – *Generator's Volunteer*, TWHBEA, Lewisburg, Tennessee, USA/B. Langrish; p.238 tr B. Langrish; p.239 br K. Houghton

p.240 tl "Supreme Sultan" sculpture by Patricia Crane/B. Langrish; bl B. Langrish; p.241 tl, c B. Langrish;

pp.242–43 **Colorado Ranger Horse** – *Magic McCue*, Barbara Bradford, Quincy, Florida, USA/B. Langrish; **Pony of the Americas** – *Chiefton*, Kentucky Horse Park, USA/ B. Langrish; p.242 tr J. Collier; p.243 c B. Langrish

pp.244–45 **Falabella** – *Barley Sugar*, Lady Fisher, Heathfield, East Sussex, UK/B. Langrish; **American Shetland** – *M.A.M. Snooty's Mr. Spats*, McCabe, Greenville, Ohio, USA/ B. Langrish; p.244 bl B. Langrish; p.245 tc B. Langrish

pp.246–247 **Chincoteague** – *Chi Chi*, Steve White, Grandeur Arabians, Citra, Florida, USA/B. Langrish; p.246 tr John E. Swedberg/Ardea London; p.247 tl, br B. Langrish

pp.248–49 Christie's Images

p.250 tl Mary Evans Picture Library; c The Hulton-Deutsch Collection; br Private Collection/The Bridgeman Art Library; p.251 tr Mary Evans Picture Library; bl Mary Evans Picture Library; Akhil Bakhshi

p.252 c Jerry Young; bl Peter Newark's Historical Pictures; p.253 tl Peter Newark's Western Americana; tr Photo: AKG Berlin; b By courtesy of the Board of Trustees of the Victoria & Albert Museum, London/The Bridgeman Art Library

p.254 c The Hulton-Deutsch Collection; bl The Mansell Collection; p.255 t The Royal Academy of Art, London/The Bridgeman Art Library; br Robert Francis/ Robert Harding Picture Library

p.256 c The Mansell Collection; bl Christie's Images; p.257 tl Sally Anne Thompson/Animal Photography; cl The Bettmann Archive Inc./The Hulton-Deutsch Collecton; br Richard Coomber/Planet Earth Pictures

pp.258–59 **Maremmana** – *Trottola*, Barbara Suter, Spirano, Italy/K. Houghton ; **Murgese** – *Urialo*, Centro Regionale Incremento Ippico, Crema, Italy/K. Houghton; p.258 K. Houghton

pp.260–261 **Italian Heavy Draught** – *Nobile*, Centro Regionale Incremento Ippico, Crema, Italy/K. Houghton; p.260 bl A. Sigismondi/K&B News Foto; p.261 tc S. Cellai/ K&B News Foto

pp.262–63 **Camargue** – *Vent Terau*, M. Contreras, Les Saintes Maries de la Mer, France/K. Houghton; p.262 bl Sally Anne Thompson/Animal Photography; tr Silvestri/ FLPA; p.263 tc Château de Saumur – Musée de Cheval/K. Houghton

pp.264–265 **Ardennais** – *Trojan*, Charlie Pinney, Honiton, Devon, UK/K. Houghton; p.265 tl K. Houghton; br **Comtois** – *Attila*, Haras de Pau, France/B. Langrish

pp.266–67 **Boulonnais** – *Bienvenu*, Y. Bienaimé, Musée Vivant du Cheval, Chantilly, France/K. Houghton; p.266 tr K. Houghton; p.267 br K. Houghton

pp.268–69 **Breton** – *Saturnin*, Haras National de Tarbes, France/B. Langrish; p.268 tr K. Houghton; p.269 br B. Langrish

pp.270–71 **Norman Cob** – *Atilmo*, Haras National du Lion d'Angers, France/K. Houghton; p.270 bl K. Houghton

pp.272–73 **Poitevin** – *Vitrisse*, Haras National de La Roche sur Yon, France/K. Houghton; **Baudet de Poitou** – *Ceylan*, Y. Bienaimé, Musée Vivant du Cheval, Chantilly, France/ K. Houghton; p.272 bc K. Houghton; p.273 tc K. Houghton

pp.274–75 **Brabant (Belgian Draught)** – *Roy*, Kentucky Horse Park, USA/B. Langrish; p.274 tr Elisabeth Weiland; p.275 **Dutch Draught** – *Marquis van der Lindenhoeve*, Albert ter Wal, Dwingeloo, Netherlands/B. Langrish

pp.276–77 **Jutland** – *Ditte*, Jørgen Neilsen, Mørkøv, Denmark/B. Langrish; **Schleswig** – *Nora*, Klaus zum Berge,

Fallingbostel, Germany/K. Houghton; p.276 tr Sally Anne Thompson/Animal Photography

pp.278–79 **Vladimir** – *Vostorg*, Central Moscow Hippodrome, Russia/B. Langrish; **Russian Heavy Draught** – *Bespechny*, Moscow Agricultural Academy, Russia/ B. Langrish; p.278 bl **Latvian Riding Horse** – *Volts*, Kaliningrad Stud, Russian Federation/B. Langrish

pp.280–81 **Muraközi** – *Baba*, Kobza István, Lajosmizse, Hungary/K. Houghton; p.280 cl K. Houghton; p.281 tc K. Houghton

pp.282–83 **Døle Gudbrandsdal** – *Vollaugblesen*, National Team for Dølehest, Norway/B. Langrish; **Døle Trotter** – *Teighlands Teira*, Karl Gerhardsen Mysen, Norway/ B. Langrish; p.282 B. Langrish; p.283 br B. Langrish

pp.284–85 **North Swedish Horse** – *Ysterman*, Ingvar Andersson, Lövestad, Sweden/B. Langrish; **Finnish Horse**– *Oikka*, Equine Research Station, Ypäjä, Finland/B. Langrish; p.284 bl K. Houghton; p.285 Sally Anne Thompson/Animal Photography

pp.286–87 **Clydesdale** – *Blue Print*, Mervyn & Pauline Ramage, Mount Farm Clydesdale Horses, Tyne & Wear, UK/B. Langrish; p.286 tr John Daniels/Ardea London; l B. Langrish

pp.288–89 **Shire** – *Duke*, Jim Lockwood, Courage Shire Horse Centre, Berks., UK/B. Langrish; p.288 cl Robert Harding Picture Library; p.289 tc Only Horses Picture Agency

pp.290–91 **Suffolk Punch** – *Laurel Keepsake II*, P. Adams and Sons, UK/B. Langrish; p.290 tr K. Houghton; p.291 br K. Houghton

pp.292–93 **Australian Stock Horse** – *Howes Boomer*, Michael Howes, Yarragon, Victoria, Australia/B. Langrish; **Brumby** – *Pone*, Ron & Anna Baker, Tonimbuk, Victoria, Australia/B. Langrish; p.292 tl Jean-Paul Ferrero/Ardea London; bl B. Langrish

p.294 tl Jason Wood Photographs; c Mary Evans Picture Library; cr Château de Saumur – Musée de Cheval/K. Houghton; bl Mary Evans Picture Library; p.295 tl The Mansell Collection; br Mary Evans Picture Library

p.296 tl Jerry Young; cr E.T. Archive; bl The Mansell Collection; p.297 tl Guildhall Library, London/E.T. Archive; bl The Hulton-Deutsch Collection; br Peter Newark's Western Americana

p.298 tl Jerry Young; tc Mary Evans Picture Library; b E.T. Archive; p.299 tr Peter Newark's Historical Pictures; bc Jerry Young; p.300 tl Christie's Images; b Jerry Young; p.301 tl Spectrum Colour Library; br K. Houghton

pp.302–03 K. Houghton; p.302 tl Dover Books; bl K. Houghton; b. K. Houghton; p.303 tl, tr K. Houghton

pp.304–5 **Royal Carriage Horse (Windsor Grey)** – *St. Patrick*, HM The Queen/K. Houghton; p.304 bl **Cleveland Bay/Thoroughbred cross** – *Luke*, HM The Queen/ K. Houghton; br K. Houghton; p.305 tr K. Houghton

pp.306–7 **Cleveland Bay** – *Clarence*, HM The Queen/ B. Langrish; p.306 tr B. Langrish; p.307 br K. Houghton

pp.308–9 **Oldenburger** – *Vivaldi*, Dr. U. Mittermayer, Aachen, Germany/K. Houghton; p.308 bl B. Langrish; p.309 K. Houghton

p.310 tl K. Houghton; cr K. Houghton; bl Nisha Erwitt/Maghum Photos; p. 311 tl J.M. Labat/Ardea London; bl K. Houghton; br Corbis

pp.312–13 **Police horse** – Avon and Somerset Constabulary, Mounted Branch, Bristol/B. Langrish; p.310 tr, bl B. Langrish; p.311 tr Only Horses Picture Agency

pp.314–315 Peter Newark's Military Pictures

p.316 tl British Library, London/The Bridgeman Art Library; br Dover Books; p.317 tl Ancient Art & Architecture Collection; tr Pushkin Museum, Moscow/Giraudon; c Cheltenham Art Gallery & Museums, Glos./The Bridgeman Art Library

p.318 tl Bonhams, London/The Bridgeman Art Library; cr The Hulton-Deutsch Collection; br Cavalry Museum, Pinerolo/E.T. Archive; p.319 tc Peter Newark's Military Pictures; br Peter Newark's Military Pictures

pp.320–21 Château de Versailles, France/Giraudon/The Bridgeman Art Library; p.320 tl Ronald Sheridan/Ancient Art & Architecture Collection; tc Château de Versailles, France/ Giraudon/The Bridgeman Art Library

p.322 tl Mary Evans Picture Library; b Christie's, London/ The Bridgeman Art Library; p.323 c C.M. Dixon; tr Jeremy Whitaker

p.324 tl Peter Newark's Military Pictures; cr E.T. Archive; bl Peter Newark's Military Pictures; p.325 tr Peter Newark's Military Pictures; bl E.T. Archive; cr Peter Newark's Military Pictures

p.326 tl Popperfoto; cr Julian Gearing/Camera Press, London; bl Laurent Sazy/Frank Spooner Pictures; p.327 tr Amit Pasricha/PBG/Fotomedia; cl Raymond Piat, Gamma/ Frank Spooner Pictures; br Gamma/Frank Spooner Pictures

pp.328–29 **Blues & Royals Trooper** – *Ormond*, with Paul Goldsmith, The Household Cavalry Mounted Regiment, Hyde Park Barracks, London/K. Houghton; p.328 tr **Blues & Royals Trooper** – *Lancer*, The Household Cavalry Mounted Regiment, Hyde Park Barracks, London/ K. Houghton; p.328 bl Only Horses Picture Agency; p.329 **Gun-Horse (Trooper) of the King's Troop, Royal Horse Artillery** – *Nibble*, with Gunner Atkinson, St. John's Wood, London/K. Houghton

pp.330–31 **Mammoth Mule**, Kentucky Horse Park, USA/ B. Langrish; p.330 tr Robert Harding Picture Library; c Karl Shone; p.331 tr R. Willbie/Animal Photography

pp.332–33 Fine Art Photographic Library

p.334 c Jockey Club, Newmarket/E.T. Archive; b Oscar & Peter Johnson Ltd./The Bridgeman Art Library; p.335 tl B. Langrish; c B. Langrish; br Colorsport

COPY OF PERSIAN SILVER PLATE, 6TH CENTURY AD

p.336 cr K. Houghton; bl Paul Fusco/Magnum; p.337 tl Bob Martin/Allsport; bl B. Langrish

p.338 c B. Langrish; br Peter Newark's American Pictures; p.339 t B. Langrish; bc K. Houghton

pp.340–41 **American Standardbred** – *Castleton Seek*, Kentucky Equine Institute, Kentucky Horse Park, USA/ B. Langrish; p.340 tr B. Langrish; p.341 tr B. Langrish

pp.342–43 **Orlov Trotter** – *Kopeysk*, Central Moscow Hippodrome, Russia/B. Langrish; p.342 bl B. Langrish; p.343 tc Elisabeth Weiland

pp.344–45 **Russian Trotter** – *Meridian*, Cubansky Stud, Russian Federation/B. Langrish; p. 344 bl B. Langrish; p.345 tc B. Langrish

pp.346–47 B. Langrish; p.346 tl Elisabeth Weiland; bl Frick Collection, New York/The Bridgeman Art Library; p.347 t Stapleton Collection/The Bridgeman Art Library

p.348 tl Mary Evans Picture Library; bl Mary Evans Picture Library; br Gray Mortimore/Allsports; p349 tr Allsort/Hulton Getty; bl K. Houghton

p.350 tl E. H. Edwards; cr E. H. Edwards; bl E. H. Edwards; p.351 tr E. H. Edwards; c E. H. Edwards; bl E. H. Edwards

p.352 tl K. Houghton; cr K. Houghton; bl K. Houghton; p.353 tr K. Houghton; br K. Houghton

pp.354–55 **Salerno** – *Jeraz*, Sig. Giorgio Caponitti, Grosseto, Italy/ K. Houghton; **Sardinian** – *Nemo II*, Centro Regionale Incremento Ippico, Crema, Italy/K. Houghton; p.354 bl K. Houghton

p.356 tl David Miller; cr K. Houghton; b K. Houghton; p.357 tl K. Houghton; br K. Houghton

p.358 tl K. Houghton; b K. Houghton; p.359 tl K. Houghton; cr K. Houghton; bl B. Langrish.

p.360 tl K. Houghton; bl K. Houghton; br K. Houghton; p.361 tl K. Houghton; br K. Houghton

p.362 c Adam Woolfitt/Robert Harding Picture Library; bc B. Langrish; p.363 tr B. Langrish; bl David Miller; br E.H. Edwards

p.364 tl K. Houghton; bl K. Houghton; p.365 tc David Miller; b David Miller

pp.366–67 **Rocky Mountain Horse** – *Kentucky Horse Park/Studio Cactus*, p.366 tr B. Langrish; p.367 br Michael K. Nichols/Magnum Photos

p.368 tl B. Manu/Fotomedia; bl Robert Cundy/Robert Harding Picture Library; cr Werner Forman Archive; p.369 tl Aditya Aria/Fotomedia; bl The Hulton-Deutsch Collection p.370 tl K. Houghton; bl Only Horses Picture Library; p.371 tl Only Horses Picture Library; br David Miller

pp.372–73 **Polo Pony** – *Ballarina*, William Lucas, London; p.372 tr Akhil Bakhshi/Fotomedia; bl Akhil Bakhshi; p.373 tr Akhil Bakhshi

p.374 b Victoria & Albert Museum, London/C.M. Dixon; p.375 l, tr Akhil Bakhshi

p.376 tl B.Langrish; cr K.Houghton; bl Studio Cactus; p.377 tr K. Houghton; bl K. Houghton

p.378 bl Sarah Errington/Hutchison Library; br Jyoti Bannerjee/Fotomedia; p.379 tl Only Horses Picture Agency; tr Mike Roberts/Only Horses Picture Agency; br Elisabeth Weiland/Robert Harding Picture Library

pp.380–81 J.P. Lenfant, Agence Vandystadt/Allsport; bc

A JOCKEY, DELHI RACECOURSE

H. Armstrong/ZEFA; p.381 tl D. Corner/B & C Alexander; tr Mike Powell/Allsport; b Brylak-Liaison, Gamma/Frank Spooner Pictures

p.382 bl K. Houghton; p.383 tl K. Houghton; br K. Houghton

p.384 tl Jane Burnand; cr Jane Burnand; bl Melony Jackson; p.385 tc Jane Burnand; bl Jane Burnand

p.386 tl K. Houghton; bl FLPA; p.387 tl K. Houghton; b Only Horses Picture Library

p.388 tl Powerstock Zefa-Kitchin; bc Kryn Taconis/ Magnum; p.389 Corbis

p.390 tl Peter Newark's Historical Pictures; cr K. Houghton; bl Mary Evans Picture Library; p.391 tr Studio Cactus; cr B. Langrish; bl K. Houghton

p.392 tl K. Houghton; bc K. Houghton; p.393 tr K. Houghton; cl K. Houghton; bl K. Houghton

pp.394–95 **Hunter** – Robert Oliver, Upleadon, Newent, Glos., UK/B. Langrish; p.394 tr B. Langrish; p.395 cl B. Langrish

pp.396–97 **Irish Draught** – *Miss Mill*, Mr. R.J. Lampard, Bilstone, Warks., UK/B. Langrish; p.396 bl K. Houghton; p.397 tc K. Houghton

p.398 tl B. Langrish; c K. Houghton; br K. Houghton; p.399 bl K. Houghton; tr K. Houghton

p.400 tl Only Horses Picture Agency; cr Ardea; bl K. Houghton; p.401 tl Only Horses Picture Agency; br Only Horses Picture Agency

pp.402–03 **Hackney** – *Hurstwood Consort*, Mr. & Mrs. Hayden, Hurstwood Stud, UK/B. Langrish; **Hackney Pony** – Mr. & Mrs. C. Hayden/B. Langrish; p.402 tr K. Houghton; p.403 cr R. Willbie/Animal Photography

pp.404–05 **Hack** – *Radiant Hills*, Robert Oliver, Upleadon, Newent, Glos., UK/B. Langrish; p.404 bl K. Houghton; p.405 tr B. Langrish

pp.406–07 **Riding Pony** – *Blue Mink II*, owned by Mr. & Mrs. D. Curtis, produced by Mrs. Dorian Williams, Winslow, Bucks., UK/B. Langrish; **Poney Français de Selle** – *Ramses Desanghoues*, Haras National du Lion d'Angers, France/K. Houghton; p.406 tr B. Langrish

p.408 tl Robert Harding Picture Library; cr K. Houghton; bl K. Houghton; p.409 tc Robert Harding Picture Library; br Elwyn Hartley Edwards

pp.410–11 **Cob** – *Portman*, Robert Oliver, Upleadon, Newent, Glos., UK/B. Langrish; p.410 bl B. Langrish; p.411 tc B. Langrish

pp.412-13 Ackermann and Johnson Ltd London/The Bridgeman Art Library

p.414 tl Only Horses

p. 416 tl and cr Mary Evans Picture Library; b K.Houghton p.417 t & b K.Houghton

p.418 cl & b K.Houghton; p.419 t Jim Stratford/Black Star /Colorific; b K.Houghton

p.420 cl Mary Evans Picture Library; tr K.Houghton; bc Mary Evans Picture Library

p.422 tl K.Houghton; bl K.Houghton; 423 t K.Houghton.

p.424 tl, K.Houghton; p. 425 t K.Houghton; b B.Langrish

p.426 all K.Houghton; p. 427 b K.Houghton

pp.428-9 Kunsthistorisches Museum, Vienna / The Bridgeman Art Library

p.430 tl Only Horses; c K.Houghton; p.431 both K.Houghton

pp.432 all B.Langrish; p. 433 B.Langrish

p.434 t K.Houghton; b B.Langrish; p.435 t K.Houghton; b B.Langrish

p. 436 all K.Houghton; 437 t K.Houghton

p. 438 all K.Houghton; p.439 all K.Houghton

p. 440 all B.Langrish; p.441 all B.Langrish

p.442 cr K.Houghton; b Palazzo Medici-Riccardi, Florence / The Bridgeman Art Library; p.443 b B.Langrish

p.445 tr First Thought Equine Ltd (www.wowsaddles.com) for use of the Flair/WOW saddle with air image; b K.Houghton

p.446 bl Studio Cactus; cb Studio Cactus; bc Studio Cactus; p.447 bl K.Houghton

p.449 t K.Houghton

p.460 bl Musée Vivant du Cheval, Chantilly, France/ K. Houghton; p.461 tc **Muraközi** (see pp.280–281)

p.462 tc B. Langrish; p.463 bc Château de Saumur – Musée de Cheval/K. Houghton

p.464 tc Akhil Bakhshi